Jewish Piety in Islamic Jerusalem

AMERICAN ACADEMY OF RELIGION

RELIGION IN TRANSLATION

SERIES EDITOR
John Nemec, University of Virginia
A Publication Series of
The American Academy of Religion
and
Oxford University Press

DAMASCIUS' *PROBLEMS & SOLUTIONS CONCERNING FIRST PRINCIPLES*
Translated with Introduction and Notes by Sara Ahbel-Rappe

THE SECRET GARLAND
Āṇṭāḷ's Tiruppāvai *and* Nācciyār *Tirumoḻi*
Translated with Introduction and Commentary by Archana Venkatesan

PRELUDE TO THE MODERNIST CRISIS
The "Firmin" Articles of Alfred Loisy
Edited, with an Introduction by C. J. T. Talar
Translated by Christine Thirlway

DEBATING THE DASAM GRANTH
Robin Rinehart

THE FADING LIGHT OF ADVAITA ĀCĀRYA
Three Hagiographies
Rebecca J. Manring
The Ubiquitous Śiva
Somānanda's Śivadṛṣṭi and His Tantric Interlocutors
John Nemec

PLACE AND DIALECTIC
Two Essays by Nishida Kitarō
Translated by John W.M. Krummel and Shigenori Nagatomo

THE PRISON NARRATIVES OF JEANNE GUYON
Ronney Mourad and Dianne Guenin-Lelle

DISORIENTING DHARMA
Ethics and the Aesthetics of Suffering in the Mahābhārata
Emily T. Hudson

THE TRANSMISSION OF SIN
Augustine and the Pre-Augustinian Sources
Pier Franco Beatrice
Translated by Adam Kamesar

FROM MOTHER TO SON
The Selected letter of Marie de l'Incarnation to Claude Martin
Translated and with Introduction and Notes by Mary Dunn

DRINKING FROM LOVE'S CUP
Surrender and Sacrifice in the Vārs *of Bhai Gurdas*
Selections and Translations with Introduction and Commentary by Rahuldeep Singh Gill

THE AMERICA'S FIRST THEOLOGIES
Early Sources of Post-Contact Indigenous Religion
Edited and translated by Garry Sparks, with Sergio Romero and Frauke Sachse

GODS, HEROES, AND ANCESTORS
An Interreligious Encounter in Eighteenth-Century Veitnam
Anh Q. Tran

POETRY AS PRAYER IN THE SANSKRIT HYMNS OF KASHMIR
Hamsa Stainton

THE UBIQUITOUS ŚIVA VOLUME II
Somānanda's Śivadṛṣṭi and His Tantric Interlocutors
John Nemec

FIRST WORDS, LAST WORDS
New Theories for Reading Old Texts in Sixteenth-Century India
Yigal Bronner and Lawrence McCrea

THE LUMINOUS WAY TO THE EAST
Texts and History of the First Encounter of Christianity with China
Matteo Nicolini-Zani

RELIGIOUS READING AND EVERYDAY LIVES IN DEVOTIONAL HINDUISM
Emilia Bachrach

JEWISH PIETY IN ISLAMIC JERUSALEM
The Lamentations Commentary of Salmon ben Yerūḥīm
Jessica Andruss

AMERICAN ACADEMY OF RELIGION

Jewish Piety in Islamic Jerusalem

The Lamentations Commentary of Salmon ben Yerūḥīm

JESSICA ANDRUSS

OXFORD
UNIVERSITY PRESS

OXFORD
UNIVERSITY PRESS

Oxford University Press is a department of the University of Oxford. It furthers the University's objective of excellence in research, scholarship, and education by publishing worldwide. Oxford is a registered trade mark of Oxford University Press in the UK and certain other countries.

Published in the United States of America by Oxford University Press
198 Madison Avenue, New York, NY 10016, United States of America.

Library of Congress Control Number: 2022900149

ISBN 978–0–19–763955–9

DOI: 10.1093/oso/9780197639559.001.0001

Printed by Integrated Books International, United States of America

For Professoressa
Patricia Lyn Richards

Ognuno riconosce i suoi
—Eugenio Montale

Contents

Acknowledgments xi
Abbreviations xiii
Preface xvii
Notes on the Translation xxiii

PART 1: STUDIES

1. Lamentations and the Mourners for Zion 3
The Mourners for Zion: The Karaite "Return" to Jerusalem 7
Biblical Scholarship in the Threefold Mandate to Return 9
Scholars of the Karaite Community in Jerusalem 14

2. The Lamentations Commentary of Salmon ben Yerūḥīm 18
Salmon b. Yerūḥīm and His Commentary on Lamentations 18
Structure of the Commentary 22
Programmatic Introduction (*Ṣadr* or *Muqaddima*) 23
The Translation of Lamentations 29
Translation and Figurative Imagery 30
Linguistic Principles to Justify a Translation Choice 31
The Verse Comments 34
Biblical Citations from Outside Lamentations 35
Citations from Other Scholars 42
Actualizing Interpretations 44
The Refrain 48
Consolations (*Neḥamot*) 52

3. Salmon's Engagement with Rabbinic Sources 56
Rabbinic Knowledge Among Salmon and the Jerusalem Karaites 57
Explicit Citation of Rabbinic Sources, Including the Targum 61
Using Midrash in Contextual Exegesis: The Transfer of the Divine Glory in Lamentations 1:6 63
Rabbinic Hermeneutics: The Ten Commandments and Requital in Kind in Lamentations 1:8 66
Rabbinic Mourning Practices and the Jerusalem Karaites in Lamentations 1:8 70

4. Salmon's Approach to Figurative Language 74
Salmon's Arabic Terminology for Figurative Language 78
Figurative Language (*Majāz*) and Metaphor (*Istiʿāra*) 79
The True Sense (*Ḥaqīqa*) 88
Likening, Analogy, or Extended Metaphor (*Tamthīl*) 91
Mathal and *Mashal*: Interpreting a Biblical Parable (The Pot of Ezekiel 11 and 24) 97
Conclusions 100

5. The Art of the Homily 102
Salmon's Homiletical-Exegetical Project 103
The Homiletical Voice in Jewish Literature 107
Oratory (*Khuṭba*) and Pious Counsel (*Waʿẓ*) in Arabic-Islamic Contexts 112
The Edifying Narrative (*Qiṣṣa*) 115
Admonition and Emotional Response: Fear and Grief 117
Orality and the Karaite Homily 123
Exhortation as a Religious Obligation 126

6. The Hermeneutics of Historical Reflection 130
Salmon's Historical Thought in the Context of Lamentations 131
The Historical-Contextual Method 136
The Historical-Theological Reading 138
Salmon's Historical-Homiletical Method: *Iʿtibār* 142
Oholah and Oholibah: A Parable of Historical Reflection 145
The Tabernacle at Shiloh: Analogy with the Past 148
The Sins of the Fathers: *Iʿtibār* and the Purpose of Scripture 151
Mourning for Zion: *Iʿtibār* and the Foundations of Karaite Ritual 155
Conclusions 160

Conclusion 163

PART 2: SELECTED TRANSLATIONS FROM THE COMMENTARY

Invocation 169

Introduction to the Lamentations Commentary 171
Mourning as a Religious Obligation 175
The Sufferings of Israel and the Sufferings of Job 177
Jeremiah as the Prophet of Lamentations 181
Seven Meanings of Lamentations 183
The Structure of Lamentations and Its Significance 185

Lamentations 1 187
Lamentations 1:1 187
Lamentations 1:2 194

Lamentations 1:6 199
Lamentations 1:8 203
Lamentations 1:12 213
Lamentations 1:16 216
Lamentations 1:18 219

Lamentations 2 221
Lamentations 2:1 221
Lamentations 2:4 229
Lamentations 2:6 244
Lamentations 2:18 248
Lamentations 2:20 249

Lamentations 3 253
Lamentations 3:1–66 253

Lamentations 4 314
Lamentations 4:1 314
Lamentations 4:6 322
Lamentations 4:11 323
Lamentations 4:15 324
Lamentations 4:17 327
Lamentations 4:20 330
Lamentations 4:22 332

Lamentations 5 335
Lamentations 5:1 335
Lamentations 5:2 337
Lamentations 5:7 338
Lamentations 5:15 342
Lamentations 5:16 342
Lamentations 5:17 343
Lamentations 5:18 344
Lamentations 5:19 344
Lamentations 5:20 345
Lamentations 5:21 346
Lamentations 5:22 346

Glossary of Salmon's Arabic Terms 347
Bibliography 351
Index 367
Biblical Verses 367
Rabbinic Sources 383
Qurʾānic Verses 385
General Index 387

Acknowledgments

I would like to express my appreciation for the individuals and institutions that have supported me in the completion of this work. I am deeply grateful to Daniel Frank, Meira Polliack, and James T. Robinson for their erudition and exceptional mentorship over many years. They have read drafts of the manuscript and offered countless suggestions that improved my translation and expanded my sensitivity to the implications of this study for our knowledge of Jewish life and thought in the Islamic world. Daniel Frank and James T. Robinson generously provided me with their transcriptions or preliminary editions of unpublished manuscripts.

Many other scholars supported my efforts with their time and expertise. I thank Michael Fishbane and Tahera Qutbuddin for their constructive advice on the project in its early stages; Camilla Adang, Miriam Goldstein, and Michael Rand for their guidance during my research at the Institute for Microfilmed Hebrew Manuscripts at the National Library of Israel in 2012–13; Sabahat Adil, Shatha Almutawa, and Uri Shachar for their intellectual camaraderie; and W. Randall Garr for his incisive counsel throughout my scholarly endeavors.

My current academic home is the department of Religious Studies at the University of Virginia, where colleagues have encouraged me in the final stages of this work. The department chairs—first Kurtis Schaeffer, then Willis Jenkins—assisted me in securing time and funding for research and writing. Elizabeth Alexander, Martien Halvorson-Taylor, Sonam Kachru, Jane Mikkelson, and Janet Spittler each helped to move the project forward.

I thank the following institutions for their generous support: the Chicago Center for Jewish Studies, the Martin Marty Center for the Advanced Study of Religion, and the Fuerstenberg Fellowship, all at the University of Chicago; Fulbright (Israel); and the Memorial Foundation for Jewish Culture. At the University of Virginia, I benefitted from two course releases from the Institute for Humanities and Global Cultures, as well as summer research funding and a Sesquicentennial Leave in fall 2020 from the College and Graduate School of Arts and Sciences.

It has been a pleasure to work with the staff of Oxford University Press. John Nemec has been an exemplary editor from start to finish. Cynthia Read, Steve A. Wiggins, and Brent Matheny at OUP-New York guided the book through the stages of production with professionalism and care. Jubilee James and Maria Cusano gave meticulous attention to a complex text. I thank the two anonymous reviewers for their valuable comments on the initial draft. I am especially indebted to the second reviewer, whose lucid observations led me to reframe parts of chapters 5 and 6. I thank Samuel Stafford for proofreading the Arabic and Hebrew portions of the book, and Jess Klaassen-Wright for preparing the index. I am grateful that this book appears in the "Religion in Translation" series alongside the book of my dear friend Rahuldeep Singh Gill, of blessed memory.

Most of the writing and revision of this volume took place during the COVID-19 pandemic. My family supported my work with love, kindness, and genuine curiosity. My husband, Brian Campbell, has been a constant source of good sense and good humor. My children, Leila and Marina, brought joy to my efforts just by being themselves. I offer my heartfelt thanks to them all.

Jessica Andruss
February 2022

Abbreviations

For full references, see the Bibliography. Standard abbreviations for scholarly journals are not included in this list.

MANUSCRIPT COLLECTIONS

BL	London, British Library
BN	Paris, Bibliothèque National
JTSA	New York, Jewish Theological Seminary of America
RNL	St. Petersburg, Russian National Library

TEXTS AND REFERENCE WORKS

Abdul-Karim	Mohammed Abdul-Latif Abdul-Karim, ed., *Commentary of Salmon Ben Yeruham on Lamentations*
Al-Fāsī	Solomon Skoss, ed., *Kitāb Jāmiʿ al-Alfāẓ (Agron) of David ben Abraham al-Fāsī*
BDB	Brown, Driver, and Briggs, eds., *Hebrew and English Lexicon of the Old Testament*
Blau, *Dictionary*	Joshua Blau, *A Dictionary of Medieval Judaeo-Arabic Texts*
BT	Babylonian Talmud
EALL	*Encyclopedia of Arabic Language and Linguistics*
EI2	*The Encyclopedia of Islam*, 2nd ed.
EJIW	*Encyclopedia of Jews in the Islamic World*
EJM	Études sur le Judaïsme Médiéval
EQ	*Encyclopedia of the Qurʾān*
Gil, *History*	Moshe Gil, *A History of Palestine, 634–1099*
Hava	J. G. Hava, *Arabic English Dictionary*
HB/OT	*Hebrew Bible/Old Testament: The History of Its Interpretation*
Ibn Nūḥ, *Diqduq*	Geoffrey Khan, *The Early Tradition of Hebrew Grammatical Thought: Including a Critical Edition, Translation, and Analysis of the* Diqduq *of Abū Yaʿqūb Yūsuf ibn Nūḥ on the Hagiography*
Jastrow	Marcus Jastrow, *A Dictionary of the Targumim, Talmud Bavli, Talmud Yerushalmi and Midrashic Literature*
JSAI	*Jerusalem Studies in Arabic and Islam*

KA	Leon Nemoy, ed., *Karaite Anthology: Excerpts from the Early Literature*
Karaite Judaism	Meira Polliack, ed., *Karaite Judaism: A Guide to Its History and Literary Sources*
KTS	Karaite Texts and Studies
Lam R	*Midrash Lamentations Rabbah*
Lane	Edward W. Lane, *An Arabic-English Lexicon*
LK	Simha Pinsker, ed., *Liqqute qadmoniyyot*
PdRK	*Pesikta de Rav Kahana*
Qirqisāni Studies	Hartwig Hirschfeld, *Qirqisāni Studies*
Qūmisī, Sermon	Leon Nemoy, trans., "The Pseudo-Qūmisīan Sermon to the Karaites"
Robinson, *Asceticism*	James T. Robinson, *Asceticism, Eschatology, Opposition to Philosophy: The Arabic Translation and Commentary of Salmon ben Yeroham on Qohelet (Ecclesiastes)*
Saadia, Dan	Joseph Alobaidi, *The Book of Daniel: The Commentary of R. Saadia Gaon, Edition and Translation*
Saadia, Esth	Michael Wechsler, *The Book of Conviviality in Exile* (Kitāb al-īnās bi-'l-jalwa): *The Judaeo-Arabic Translation and Commentary of Saadia Gaon on the Book of Esther*
Saadia, Job	Joseph Derenbourg et al., eds. *Version Arabe du Livre de Job de R. Saadia ben Iosef al-Fayyoûmî*
Saadia, Lam	Yehuda Ratzaby, "Targum of Rabbenu Saadia Gaon on Lamentations"
Salmon, Pss 1–10	Joseph Alobaidi, ed. *Le commentaire des Psaumes par le Qaraïte Salmon ben Yeruham: Psaumes 1–10*
Salmon, Pss 11–41	Salmon b. Yerūḥīm, Commentary on Psalms, RNL Evr. Arab. I 1345
Salmon, Pss 42–72	Lawrence Marwick, ed., *The Arabic Commentary of Salmon ben Yeruham on the Book of Psalms, Chapters 42–72*
Salmon, Pss 73–89	Salmon b. Yerūḥīm, Commentary on Psalms, RNL Evr. I 557
Salmon, Pss 90–106	Salmon b. Yerūḥīm, Commentary on Psalms, RNL Evr. I 558
Salmon, Pss 107–150	Salmon b. Yerūḥīm, Commentary on Psalms, RNL Evr. I 556
Tg. Lam	Targum on Lamentations
Yefet, Esth	Michael G. Wechsler, *The Arabic Translation and Commentary of Yefet ben ʿEli the Karaite on the Book of Esther*
Yefet, Gen	Marzena Zawanowska, *The Arabic Translation and Commentary of Yefet ben ʿEli the Karaite on the Abraham Narratives (Genesis 11:10–25:18)*
Yefet, Isa	Yefet ben ʿEli, Commentary on Isaiah, BL Or. 2502 (Marg. 281)

Yefet, Jer	Joshua A. Sabih, *Japheth ben Ali's Book of Jeremiah: A Critical Edition and Linguistic Analysis*
Yefet, Lam	Yefet ben ʿEli, Commentary on Lamentations; preliminary edition by Daniel Frank, based on RNL Evr.-Arab. I 213 and RNL Evr.-Arab. I 3806
Yefet, Prov	Ilana Sasson, *The Arabic Translation and Commentary of Yefet ben ʿEli on the Book of Proverbs, vol. 1: Edition and Introduction*

Preface

The tenth century marks a turning point in Jewish intellectual history: the transition from ancient rabbinic culture to the Arabized Judaism of the medieval period. Medieval Jews inherited an expansive tradition of biblical interpretation from their rabbinic predecessors, yet the formal commentary genre, with its programmatic introductions, discussions of grammar, and interests in the historical context and literary construction of the Bible, was their own innovation. Jewish scholars of the Islamic world shifted away from the languages, genres, and hermeneutical frameworks of the rabbinic academies, and created in their place an exegetical corpus shaped by the Arabic language and its intellectual resources. By translating the Bible into Arabic and interpreting it with insights gleaned from the nascent fields of linguistic and literary theory, religious philosophy, and the natural sciences, Jewish thinkers simultaneously contributed to the scholarly discourse of the Arabic-Islamic world and transformed their own religious culture.

This book traces the cross-pollinations of Jewish and Muslim modes of exegesis, homiletics, and historiography through one of the oldest Jewish Bible commentaries, the tenth-century Arabic translation and interpretation of Lamentations by Salmon ben Yerūḥim. Salmon was a prominent figure among the "Mourners for Zion," the Karaites of Jerusalem whose dedication to biblical scholarship was central to their comprehensive spiritual program of piety, penitence, and preparation for the redemption of the Jewish people. As the earliest Karaite exegete with an extant corpus in Arabic, Salmon demonstrates a nuanced negotiation between rabbinic hermeneutics and the intellectual offerings of the Islamic world. His writings on Lamentations in particular display his genius for redefining Jewish piety through the work of biblical translation and commentary.

For Salmon, the biblical book of Lamentations was God's "instruction for Israel"—spiritual guidance for the Jewish people in exile. While he subscribes to the normative view of Lamentations as the prophet Jeremiah's response to the historical destruction of Jerusalem by the Babylonians in the sixth century BCE, he directs the book's moral message to the Jews of his own time. Thus, the historical suffering of the ancient Israelites becomes an admonition for medieval Jews, who continue to endure the humiliations of exile because they continue to sin. Within this pious interpretive frame, Salmon embeds de facto sermons that draw on his hermeneutic of biblical history and his Karaite sensibilities. This homiletical approach to exegesis positions Salmon at the center of a dynamic cultural reorientation, as he both borrows rabbinic explanations and contradicts them outright, and he interprets Lamentations with the tools of Arabic homily, historiography, and literary theory at the same time that he purports to dismiss Islamic-Arabic learning as an impediment to true knowledge.

Salmon stands at the dawn of Karaite commentary writing, yet scholars tend to define Karaite exegesis by the magisterial corpus of Yefet ben ʿElī, the biblical translator-interpreter who followed a generation afterward. However, while Yefet's commentaries represent a high point of Jewish exegetical practice in Arabic, they would not be possible apart from the foundational efforts of Salmon, which occurred when the purpose and conventions of the commentary genre were still undefined. Salmon's commentaries on the Psalms and the Five Scrolls (Song of Songs, Ruth, Lamentations, Ecclesiastes, and Esther) constitute the first commentary series of the Jerusalem Karaites, and reveal the experimental beginnings of the Jewish commentary form. In their wide scope, they also preserve significant elements of the liturgy, homily, polemic, historical thought, and pious practice of the emerging Karaite community in Jerusalem. This book resists the characterization of Salmon's thought as not properly exegetical, and instead posits Salmon's writings as formative in establishing a genre whose contours were just coming into focus. The homiletical excursuses of Salmon's commentary are not digressions from his exegesis, but the very substance of it: if Lamentations is God's "instruction for Israel," as Salmon insists, then the only authentic approach to exegesis must be homiletical. Thus, Salmon's commentary on Lamentations is also a manual for Jewish piety in Islamic Jerusalem, designed to educate and inspire the tenth-century Jewish community in the practices and perspectives that will lead to their redemption.

Jewish Piety in Islamic Jerusalem explores Salmon's construction of Karaite Judaism through his commentary on Lamentations. It examines the intra-Judaic context of Salmon's writings as well as the emerging Arabic scholarly discourse through which he formulates his exegetical and pietistic approach to the Scriptures. By considering Salmon's intellectual world, informed not only by the Bible but also by rabbinic tradition and Karaite, Rabbanite, and Muslim scholarship of the ninth and tenth centuries, this study explores the methods and sources that Salmon relied on to reshape Jewish piety in an Arabic environment, consolidating and communicating a distinctively Karaite spiritual program.

The book begins by introducing Salmon's own community, the "Mourners for Zion," and identifying the themes of Lamentations that resonate with their communal aspirations and affirm the biblical foundations of their penitential rituals and attitudes (chapter 1). As one of the earliest examples of Arabic biblical exegesis, Salmon's commentary provided a model for the genre that defined the Karaite community and influenced Jewish biblical study ever afterward. The book includes a systematic treatment of Salmon's Lamentations commentary, presenting its unique features and describing the elements that became standard in later commentaries (chapter 2). This chapter also functions as a guide to the abridged translation of Salmon's Lamentations commentary that appears in Part 2 of this volume.

The next chapter explores Salmon's engagement with texts and ideas from the broader Jewish tradition, including rabbinic hermeneutical methods and Midrashic traditions, which he reformulates for his own purposes. Salmon's familiarity with rabbinic precedents proves that even though Karaites rejected the authority of the rabbis and their Rabbanite successors, they were not ignorant of their teachings. Salmon creatively reinterprets rabbinic traditions to attack his Rabbanite rivals and advocate for Jewish piety on strictly Karaite terms (chapter 3).

Having established the Jewish background for Salmon's project, the book also explores its Arabic-Islamic dimensions by focusing on three interwoven aspects of the commentary: Salmon's analysis of figurative language (chapter 4), his penchant for admonition and exhortation in a homiletical style (chapter 5), and his hermeneutic of reflection on history to determine its ethical teaching (chapter 6). In each case, we find evidence of Salmon drawing on rabbinic and Arabic-Islamic resources as he constructs and frames his religious message for a medieval Jewish audience. These elements of Salmon's approach illustrate the depth of his engagement with, and active participation in, an intercommunal Arabic cultural and intellectual sphere.[1]

[1] The fields of Arabic scholarship that I explore in this book—literary theory, homiletics, and historiography—are not the only areas of intersection between Salmon's commentary and the broad spectrum of Jewish and Muslim culture. Elements of the commentary suggest possible lines of connection to Sufi pietism, Isma'īlī missionizing, and early strains of Mu'tazilite theology, for example, as well as the Jewish tradition of *Piyyuṭ* (synagogue poetry). I have indicated some of the more enticing resonances in the footnotes, and I hope to return to them in future studies.

Figurative language was a shared challenge for Jews and Muslims, especially in the context of Scripture, where metaphors or analogies risk obscuring the meaning of sacred writ. Salmon relies on terminology from the Arabic literary tradition to explain the figurative imagery of Lamentations. In chapter 4, I show that Salmon's fluid use of this technical vocabulary places him alongside Muslim exegetes, who also implemented such terminology experimentally as its meaning evolved over the course of the tenth century. For Salmon, linguistic and rhetorical analysis was not an end unto itself, but rather a technique for understanding biblical language, establishing the spiritual meaning of Lamentations, and conveying it persuasively to a Jewish audience.

In chapter 5, I explore the homiletical dimensions of Salmon's project by examining the words of pious exhortation embedded within his excursuses and comparing them to rabbinic homiletical Midrash, literary exhortation in Karaite and Rabbanite texts, and Islamic sermon culture. Salmon reworks rabbinic homilies and adapts the structural and rhetorical features of Arabic-Islamic oratory to support the Karaite program of mourning and penitence. His homilies aim to rouse Jews to weeping and other expressions of grief. In this way, he both subverts Muslim concerns that excessive mourning belies faith in God, and undermines Rabbanite efforts to moderate Jewish mourning over the ruined Temple.

In chapter 6, I examine the hermeneutical work that Salmon performs in order to read the Bible along Karaite lines. The most extensive analysis concerns Salmon's hermeneutic of reflection on history. In this project, as well, Salmon positions himself between the rabbinic tradition and the currents of Arabic thought. Like the rabbis of antiquity, Salmon is attuned to the moral message of the biblical past. However, where the rabbis constructed a Midrashic homiletical meaning by reading biblical details atomistically and paradigmatically, Salmon evinces genuine historical thinking. He evaluates and corroborates biblical and post-biblical accounts, determining a timeline of events and interpreting biblical passages with respect to their historical context. He discovers the homiletical meaning of history through a hermeneutical process of reflection, which he draws from the emerging field of Arabic historiography but develops in a distinctively Karaite vein. He refers to this hermeneutic as *iʿtibār*—reflecting on history in order to take warning from the sins of the wicked and emulate the deeds of the righteous. By reflecting on the destruction of the Temple and the sins that caused it, Salmon determines that the end of exile will come only when the Jews of his own day cease to sin, and return to Jerusalem in a spirit of penitence. This formulation censures the Rabbanites as those who extend the exile by failing to reflect on history and realize the errors of their Oral Law. Thus, Salmon applies a concept from Arabic historiography to long-standing Jewish debates over religious authority and the path toward redemption, in order to locate within Lamentations an affirmation of the Karaite program of repentance and mourning in Jerusalem.

Notes on the Translation

Readers will find selected translations from Salmon's Lamentations commentary in Part 2 of this book. There, I translate the passages in which Salmon articulates his religious message most explicitly and extensively, and which most clearly demonstrate his distinctive homiletical approach to exegesis. These passages include Salmon's introduction to the commentary, his excursuses and embedded homilies, and his comments on the first verse of each chapter (which function as a preface to that chapter and a presentation of its major themes). Also included are Salmon's running commentary on the entire third chapter of Lamentations—which he treats as a coherent pietistic composition—and the full translation of the passages from which I draw textual evidence within the analytical chapters. My aim has been to provide a broadly representative sample of the commentary, enabling readers to experience for themselves the erudition and variety of Salmon's remarks.

I have treated the verse comment—that is to say, Salmon's Arabic translation of and comment on a single biblical verse—as the basic textual unit of the commentary. Therefore, each verse comment that appears in Part 2 is presented in its entirety, without elisions. While elements of Salmon's writings may suggest affinities with prayer books, grammatical manuals, or theological treatises, it is through the framework of biblical exegesis that Salmon discovers, substantiates, and communicates his ideas. The inclusion of complete verse comments thus preserves the structure of the commentary and offers an array of linguistic, theological, historical, and pietistic content for scholars of Jewish and Islamic intellectual history. This organization should also prove useful for biblical scholars who may be curious about how Salmon handles a certain exegetical conundrum or the translation of a difficult verse.

My English translation is based on the edition of Mohammed Abdul-Latif Abdul-Karim (Ph.D. dissertation, St Andrews, 1976).[1] Abdul-Karim's work is effectively a diplomatic edition of BL Or. 2516, a complete manuscript that was copied in the mid-eighteenth century. Abdul-Karim consulted

[1] Now accessible online through the St Andrews Research Repository: https://research-repository.st-andrews.ac.uk/handle/10023/11285.

three additional manuscripts (from the British Library [BL] in London, the Bibliothèque Nationale [BN] in Paris, and the Jewish Theological Seminary of America [JTSA] in New York) as well as nine short fragments from the British Museum, and he notes the variants, which are generally minor and overwhelmingly orthographic in nature.[2] I consulted additional, older manuscripts from the Firkovitch Collections of the Russian National Library [RNL] in St. Petersburg on microfilm at the Institute for Microfilmed Hebrew Manuscripts in the National Library of Israel in 2012–13, before they were readily available online. I observed remarkable consistency across the catalogued manuscripts. The unusual degree of standardization suggests that Karaite communities were quick to adopt the commentary and that it enjoyed heavy rotation in their scholarly circles and liturgical sessions. Older manuscripts were replaced with newer copies after they were worn out from repeated use. This explanation would account for the prevalence of late manuscript witnesses to Salmon's Lamentations commentary as well as their remarkable uniformity.

Abdul-Karim's edition of the commentary went uncited and apparently unknown for over three decades. To my knowledge, it surfaced in the scholarly record only when Barry Dov Walfish and Mikhail Kizilov listed it in their exhaustive *Bibliographica Karaitica*.[3] The few studies that addressed Salmon's Lamentations commentary prior to the publication of the *Bibliographica Karaitica* drew independently on manuscripts, without recourse to Abdul-Karim's dissertation.[4] In the years since Abdul-Karim completed his project, Karaite manuscript holdings have become increasingly accessible, initially in microfilm and now in digital formats, thus facilitating and expanding manuscript research. The National Library of Israel lists over one hundred separately indexed manuscript fragments of Salmon's Lamentations commentary. These resources make it possible, in some cases, to propose emendations and resolve textual difficulties by consulting other manuscript witnesses, although frequently the most stymieing textual corruptions recur across the

[2] The four principal MSS of Abdul-Karim's edition are: BL Or. 2516 (= A); BL Or. 2515 (= B); BN Heb. 295 (= P); JTSA Ms. Mic. 3362 (Adler 114) (= J). For descriptions of these MSS and the fragments from the British Museum, see Abdul-Karim, 43–55.

[3] Barry Dov Walfish and Mikhail Kizilov, *Bibliographica Karaitica: An Annotated Bibliography of Karaites and Karaism*, EJM 43; KTS 2 (Leiden: Brill, 2011).

[4] See e.g., Haggai Ben-Shammai, "Poetic Works and Lamentations of Qaraite 'Mourners of Zion'—Structure and Contents" [Hebrew], in *Kenesset Ezra: Literature and Life in the Synagogue; Studies Presented to Ezra Fleischer*, ed. S. Elizur et al. (Jerusalem: Ben Zvi, 1994); Daniel Frank, *Search Scripture Well: Karaite Exegetes and the Origins of the Jewish Bible Commentary in the Islamic East*, EJM 39 (Leiden: Brill, 2004).

known manuscripts. It may be impossible to reconstruct an original text in spite of the numerous manuscript witnesses, simply because the scribal errors that were fossilized early in the transmission of the text were preserved in later copies. Manuscript evidence did make it possible, however, to restore the Arabic invocation that opens the commentary, which is missing from Abdul-Karim's edition. This passage, drawn primarily from a seventeenth-century manuscript, is included in my English translation.[5] I have relied on manuscript sources and parallel texts from Salmon's corpus to support my translation of Abdul-Karim's edition, which remains valuable for its astute scholarly notes in addition to the text of the commentary that it provides.

Salmon's commentary, of course, is also an Arabic translation of the Hebrew Bible, which means that my English translation must represent Salmon's Arabic translation of biblical Hebrew. There are many challenges in translating a translation, and no solutions are entirely satisfactory. My goal has been to represent Salmon's understanding of the biblical Hebrew text—which he conveys through Arabic translation, Arabic paraphrase, reference to biblical prooftexts, and direct explanation—and to note the occasions on which his reading departs from the Hebrew source text. To this end, I have cited biblical verses from the Revised Standard Version (RSV) of the Bible, freely modifying them to accord with Salmon's usage and noting the divergences in the footnotes when necessary.[6] References to these differences are intended to highlight the ingenuity or angle of Salmon's reading, not to promote the RSV as uniformly preferable to Salmon's translation. It is a truism that all translation is interpretation, and the RSV has no greater or lesser claim to veracity than Salmon does.

In the commentary, I begin each verse comment with the fully pointed Masoretic Hebrew verse and Salmon's Arabic translation of it, followed by my English rendering of Salmon's verse translation and then his Arabic comment. When Salmon enlarges his Arabic verse translation with material that does not originate in the Masoretic Text of the Hebrew Bible, I underline these additions.

In my translation of the verse comments, I have included significant Hebrew and Arabic terms parenthetically. Vocabulary that Salmon uses

[5] I thank Daniel Frank for sharing his collation of manuscript evidence for this section from JTSA Ms. Mic. 3362 (Adler 14) and RNL Evr. I.561.

[6] In addition, I routinely adjust the RSV to match contemporary style, e.g., replacing archaisms such as "thou" and "thine" with "you" and "your." I also capitalize pronouns referring to God, which reflects Salmon's practice of referring to God with pious epithets throughout the commentary. These deviations are standard and thus not noted in individual footnotes.

repeatedly is listed in the glossary at the end of the volume, along with my standard English translations of those terms. Arabic transliteration follows the system of the *Encyclopedia of Islam 3*. Hebrew transliteration follows the General Purpose Style of the Society for Biblical Literature, with the exceptions of *ṣ* for *ts* (צ) and *ś* for *s* (שׂ). Since Salmon—or the scribes—often omit the vowels of Hebrew words, a fully reversible transliteration style would be inappropriate and potentially misleading. However, when Salmon makes a morphological point that requires detailed knowledge of Hebrew or Aramaic, I employ the Society for Biblical Literature's Academic Style with its more precise system of notation. My intention has been to produce a translation that is at once accessible to nonspecialists and informative for those with knowledge of Hebrew and Arabic.

All Hebrew words and phrases, whether or not they are biblical, are italicized in the English translation, with further comment often provided in the footnotes. Proper nouns (e.g., the names of prophets, biblical place names, or the Tetragrammaton) are exempted from this italicization practice. Arabic *allāh* and Hebrew *ʾel* and *ʾelohim* are translated "God," Arabic *rabb* is translated "Lord," and the Hebrew Tetragrammaton appears as LORD. Certain words appear predominantly in Hebrew but intermittently in Arabic (e.g., covenant, exile, commandment, the nations, Temple), and the italicization mirrors these shifts.[7] Hebrew and Arabic words that are common in English (e.g., Israel, Qurʾān) are spelled in the familiar ways.

When Salmon gives a Hebrew verse followed by an Arabic comment, I translate everything into English. However, when Salmon provides a Hebrew incipit that he then translates in full into Arabic, I leave the incipit in Hebrew and mark the Arabic translation with quotation marks rather than offer a double translation. This strategy replicates Salmon's practice in the original composition, for it is his Arabic translation that instructs the reader in how to understand the Hebrew incipit.[8]

When the lacunae of Salmon's Arabic prose lead me to expand the English translation for the sake of clarity, I enclose my expansions in square brackets [].

[7] Israel (Hebr. *yiśraʾel*) appears only twice in its Arab. form (*isrāʾīl*), and only according to some MSS; see notes to the Invocation and Lam 4:22. Jerusalem (Hebr. *yerushalayim*) appears in its Arab. form (*al-quds*) very rarely; see notes to Lam 3:1. Typically, *al-quds* refers to the Temple in Salmon's writings.

[8] On this approach to Hebrew incipits, see Robinson, *Asceticism*, 160.

I also use square brackets to extend biblical citations beyond the abbreviated citations that appear in Salmon's text, when such extensions are necessary to understand his points. Clauses from the Lamentations verse that is under discussion are set off in bold type in order to provide a visual touchstone for the exegetical structure that is obscured occasionally by Salmon's many competing interests. I have removed the pious epithets that Salmon uses reflexively (e.g., "peace be upon him" after the name of a prophet; "the mighty and sublime," "may He be praised," or "most high" after the name of God), except when they stand in for the proper name itself. I have retained the pagination that corresponds to manuscript BL Or. 2516 (and therefore also to Abdul-Karim's edition) in angle brackets < >. The formatting, headings, and punctuation are of my own design and do not appear in the manuscripts.

The annotations are intended to elucidate Salmon's meaning; provide bibliography on relevant parallels in Salmon's corpus and the broader Karaite, Rabbanite, and Muslim intellectual and cultural background; and invite readers into the analytical process. The footnotes contain cross-references to Salmon's other commentaries and the works of his contemporaries as well as the rabbinic tradition. These translations are my own, unless otherwise noted.

I have been inspired in my task by Laura Lieber's words on the purpose of scholarly translation:

> The act of translation has intellectual merit beyond the important task of making these works accessible to a wider readership. Precisely because translation demands interpretation of the idiomatic and evocative language of the original texts, the exercise offers the translator the opportunity to highlight and clarify elements of the original that might otherwise be glossed over and erased.[9]

If my footnotes climb high on a given page or my annotations linger over a relatively minor point, it is only out of appreciation for Salmon's text and the scholarly questions that it allows us to ask about a formative moment in the Jewish intellectual culture of the medieval Islamic world.

[9] Laura Suzanne Lieber, *Jewish Aramaic Poetry from Late Antiquity: Translations and Commentaries*, EJM 75; Cambridge Genizah Studies 8 (Leiden: Brill, 2018), 13.

Judeo-Arabic Alphabet

ى/ء/ا	א
ب	ב
ت	ת
ث	ת'
ج	ג'
ح	ח
خ	כ'
د	ד
ذ	ד'
ر	ר
ز	ז
س	ס
ش	ש
ص	צ
ض	צ'
ط	ט
ظ	ט'
ع	ע
غ	ג
ف	פ
ق	ק
ك	כ
ل	ל
م	מ
ن	נ
ه	ה
و	ו
ي	י
ة	ה̈

PART 1
STUDIES

1

Lamentations and the Mourners for Zion

> *Neither are the people of the exile [cut off] from His beneficence. Jeremiah prophesied that a book would be established for them with lamentation within it, which would be authorized for them as long as they were in the land of exile, lamenting for themselves with it and regretting what had left them: power, statehood, Temple, prophecy, signs, proofs, kingship, the priesthood, wisdom, learning, and service in God's house with song and melody.*
>
> —Salmon b. Yerūḥīm
> Introduction to the Lamentations Commentary

The biblical book of Lamentations is a literary response to the trauma of Jerusalem's destruction at the hands of the Babylonians in 586 BCE. For the ancient Israelites, Jerusalem was the city of David and the capital of the kingdom of Judah, the site of the Temple with its priestly hierarchy and sacrificial rites, and God's chosen dwelling place on earth. The psalms praise its beauty and rejoice in the divine protection bestowed upon Zion. Biblical passages record the popular sentiment that God would never abandon this holy city. The fact that it was spared even when the northern kingdom of Israel fell to the Assyrians in the eighth century BCE was widely perceived as a sign of God's unconditional devotion to the city and its sacred precincts—in spite of the prophets' warnings that Jerusalem too would be destroyed if the people persisted in their sins. When the city indeed fell to Nebuchadnezzar of Babylon, the destruction was violent, comprehensive, and devastating. The walls of Jerusalem were torn down, and Babylonian soldiers raided the treasures of the Temple before burning it down along with the palace of the king and the homes of Jerusalem's elites. King Zedekiah himself was captured, blinded, and carried off to Babylon in chains after witnessing the murder of his sons. Priests, military commanders, and government officers were put to death, while thousands of others were forced into exile, weak and

Jewish Piety in Islamic Jerusalem. Jessica Andruss, Oxford University Press. © Oxford University Press 2023.
DOI: 10.1093/oso/9780197639559.003.0001

miserable from famine and the other hardships of a yearlong siege. Only a remnant remained on the land. Years of Babylonian subjugation and peril culminated with the devastating loss of life, territory, state authority, and religious institutions.[1]

The five chapters of Lamentations are a collection of laments over this cataclysmic destruction. These poems express, with shattering immediacy, the grief and anger caused by the enemies' destruction of Jerusalem and their unbridled brutality against its people. They voice the profoundly disorienting sense that God had betrayed the people by permitting such bloodshed and devastation to occur, and thus they reveal the spiritual depths of the crisis. They search for words to communicate the pain of those who endured these harrowing catastrophes, and they demand acknowledgment of their collective suffering.

In historical terms, the Babylonian exile was short-lived. By the end of the sixth century, many of the exiles and their descendants had been repatriated, the Temple and cult were restored, and the walls and city of Jerusalem were rebuilt—albeit under the administration of the Persian Empire. Yet the experience of destruction and displacement cast a long shadow in Jewish memory, due in part to the vivid imagery and searing expressions of pain recorded in the book of Lamentations. The Babylonian exile became the paradigmatic catastrophe against which all later afflictions were measured.[2] The fall of Jerusalem to the Babylonians continued to define the depths of communal anguish even after the Second Temple was destroyed by the Romans toward the end of the first century CE, and Jews were barred from the holy city and subjected to the humiliations of prolonged exile for centuries afterward.

The rabbinic sages whose words are preserved in the Talmud and Midrashic compilations expanded upon the imagery of Lamentations in order to make spiritual sense of their own suffering. The rabbis left scant record of their own historical circumstances in the wake of the second destruction, but instead appropriated the details of the first destruction, which they embraced as timeless paradigms through which to formulate their religious perspectives and practices. The rabbis so thoroughly knitted the second destruction to the first that they commemorated both tragedies on the same

[1] For the biblical historical account, see 2 Kgs 25 and 2 Chr 36.

[2] On the legacy of the Babylonian exile, see Martien Halvorson-Taylor, *Enduring Exile: The Metaphorization of Exile in the Hebrew Bible* (Leiden: Brill, 2010).

day—the ninth of Av—and developed a liturgy of mourning, drawn heavily from the scroll of Lamentations, to commemorate both losses.

As Jewish life continued under conditions of exile, rabbinic theology reflected a quietist acceptance of the Diaspora and a belief that only God could initiate the ingathering of the exiles in Jerusalem.[3] Yet this ideology, along with other rabbinic sensibilities and modes of learning that developed during the exile, was fundamentally challenged in the context of the Islamic expansion, which began in the seventh century and eventually brought most of the world's Jews into contact with the Arabic and Islamic cultural spheres. As Jews adopted and contributed to the development of new Arabic literary models, they broke long-standing continuities with the rabbinic tradition. The biblical commentaries that emerged in the ninth and tenth centuries, then, reflect the dynamic reorientation of Jewish scholarship and religious practice that define this period of intellectual history. The vanguard of this shift were the Karaites—a Jewish movement that rejected the authority of rabbinic law and elevated, in its place, a return to the Bible as the sole legal and spiritual authority, and the role of independent reason in interpreting Scripture. The Karaite movement was also characterized by a spirit of messianic expectation. By the end of the ninth century, Karaites had established a penitential community in Jerusalem where those who called themselves "Mourners for Zion" engaged in prayer, lamentation, and ascetic behaviors intended to hasten the End Times.[4]

The existence of a Karaite community in Jerusalem fundamentally altered the exilic context for reading and interpreting Lamentations. No longer was exile universally accepted as an interminable reality over which the Jewish people had no control. Instead, prominent Karaites interpreted the political shifts that made immigration to Jerusalem possible as proof that it was time to quit the Diaspora and return to the holy city in order play their part

[3] The theological implications of the rabbis' response to the destruction of Jerusalem can be discerned through their literature, e.g., the Targum (an expansive Aramaic translation of Lamentations); *Midrash Lamentations Rabbah* (an exegetical compilation of narratives on Lamentations); and *Pesikta de Rav Kahana* (a homiletical compilation organized according to the liturgical calendar, and including seven chapters related to the commemoration of the ninth of Av). On rabbinic liturgy for the Ninth of Av, see Elsie R. Stern, *From Rebuke to Consolation: Exegesis and Theology in the Liturgical Anthology of the Ninth of Av Season* (Providence, R.I.: Brown Judaic Studies, Brown University, 2020); for Aramaic liturgical poetry (*piyyuṭim*) for the Ninth of Av, see Lieber, *Jewish Aramaic Poetry*, ch. 3.

[4] On the history of the term "Mourners for Zion," see Daniel Frank, "Mourners of Zion," in *Encyclopedia of the Bible and Its Reception*, vol. 19 (Boston/Berlin: Walter de Gruyter, 2021), 1303–7.

in the eschatological drama of repentance and redemption. Verses from Lamentations were part of the Jerusalem Karaites' daily liturgy and rituals of mourning, rather than an annual rite to memorialize the ancient destruction of Jerusalem. In this way, the Karaites transformed Lamentations from a text about the archetypal sins of the past, as it had been understood in rabbinic circles, to a text about the need for piety in the present, and the promise of redemption in the immediate future.

The purpose of this chapter is to situate Lamentations within the complex spiritual and intellectual projects of the emerging Karaite community. In the book of Lamentations, the Karaites found a vocabulary of mourning and lament that resonated with their own worldview and ritual praxis, and through which they substantiated their claims that mourning behaviors were obligatory for Jews during the exile. They discovered in Lamentations a framework for theological discourse about matters of sin and retribution, repentance and redemption, as well as a spiritual anchor for their own presence in Jerusalem. Yet Lamentations, like any biblical book, was not ready-made for this purpose. Rather, Lamentations achieved its status as a resource for Karaite piety and spiritual practice through the ongoing efforts of Karaite scholars—grammarians and linguists, homilists and propagandists, translators and exegetes—who translated its ancient words into urgent instruction for the medieval Jewish community.

The earliest Karaite commentary on Lamentations was written by Salmon ben Yerūḥīm, a Karaite "Mourner for Zion" in mid-tenth-century Jerusalem. As the seminal comprehensive treatment of this biblical book, Salmon's commentary reveals a Karaite perspective on Lamentations and its religious purpose, as well as the intertwining of exegesis and constructive theology. Salmon considers Lamentations to be "instruction for Israel" (*taʿlīm le-yiśraʾel*)—a book filled with divine directives, recorded by the prophet Jeremiah, about the acts of mourning and repentance that God requires Jews to perform in order to end the punishments of exile. Thus, Salmon's explication of Lamentations engages the same concerns that brought the Karaite pious to Jerusalem, structured their daily lives there, and inspired their hopes for redemption. This book explores the ways that Salmon articulates and advances a Karaite theology through his study of Lamentations, as he draws from rabbinic and Arabic-Islamic intellectual resources in order to craft an exegetical work with pious concerns at its core. In the next chapter, I will describe the commentary and its contents in order to provide a textual foundation for the analytical studies that follow. In the present chapter, however,

I wish to introduce the Karaites of Jerusalem—the "Mourners for Zion"—and their program of biblical scholarship and practical piety, with particular attention to the resonances between their communal project and the themes of the biblical book of Lamentations. This discussion will show how early Karaites construed Lamentations as relevant and instructive for their communal identity and eschatological aims.

The Mourners for Zion: The Karaite "Return" to Jerusalem

The Karaite movement arose in Iraq and Persia where, by the late ninth century, several Jewish sectarian communities coalesced around overlapping principles of opposition to rabbinic leadership, respect for localized traditions of biblical interpretation, return to Jerusalem, and an apocalyptic worldview.[5] While Jews had been free to settle in Jerusalem since the Islamic conquest of the city in the seventh century, few had chosen to do so prior to the formation of an elite Karaite community there. Life in the holy city was strenuous, with limited economic opportunities. The Jews who did come to the city were mainly pilgrims or travelers from the Jewish communities of the East, or residents of Palestinian cities such as Ramla and Tiberias, where the rite of the Palestinian Yeshiva was followed.[6] Political shifts in the late ninth century opened Jerusalem up to new patterns of Jewish settlement. With the conquest of Palestine by Aḥmed ibn Ṭulūn in 878, the region experienced renewed visibility: trade relations expanded following improvements to the ports, and changing geopolitics transformed Palestine into a strategic location for staging military operations between Byzantine, Abbasid, and Ṭulūnid armies.[7] The advent of Ṭulūnid authority meant that Jerusalem was

[5] On the Karaite movement, from its origins to the settlement in Jerusalem, see Yoram Erder, "The Mourners of Zion: The Karaites in Jerusalem of the Tenth and Eleventh Centuries," in *Karaite Judaism*, 213–36; Moshe Gil, "The Origins of the Karaites," in *Karaite Judaism*, 73–88; Gil, *History*, chapters 8–9; Jacob Mann, *Texts and Studies in Jewish History and Literature*, vol. 2 (Philadelphia: Jewish Publication Society, 1935); and Barry Walfish, "The Mourners of Zion (*'avelei ṣiyyon*): A Karaite *'Aliyah* Movement of the Early Arab Period," in *Eretz Israel, Israel, and the Jewish Diaspora: Mutual Relations*, ed. Menachem Mor (New York: University Press of America, 1991), 42–51.

[6] Evidence for Jewish immigration patterns to Palestinian cities during the Arab period comes largely from Geniza documents. See Gil, *History*, 609 ff., and Gil, "Aliya and Pilgrimage in the Early Arab Period (634–1009)," *The Jerusalem Cathedra* 3 (1983): 162–73. Cf. Avraham Grossman, who speaks of earlier waves of migration to Jerusalem and depicts a stronger presence of Babylonian Jews in Palestine: "Aliya in the Seventh and Eighth Centuries," *The Jerusalem Cathedra* 3 (1983): 174–87.

[7] Gil, *History*, 306–7.

no longer under the direct control of the centralized Abbasid government, making the city an attractive haven for the Karaites, as a sectarian community eager to distance itself from the rabbinic institutions of Baghdad and the Abbasid authorities that supported them. Messianic-minded Karaites actively campaigned for the Jewish communities of the Diaspora to immigrate to Jerusalem, and they crafted a religious program with immigration at its core.[8] In their language, this settlement constituted a return to the sacred place that God had chosen for the Jewish people. Only in Jerusalem, they contended, would it be possible to carry out the penitential practices that were necessary to bring about the redemption.[9]

The practical, pietistic theology of immigration, repentance, and redemption is articulated as early as the last quarter of the ninth century, in a lengthy exhortation—often referred to as a sermon—that circulated among the Karaite communities of the Islamic East. This Arabic text is attributed to Daniel al-Qūmisī, a native of northern Persia near the Caspian Sea, whose biblical commentaries in Hebrew are still partly preserved.[10] With strong language and brazen rhetoric, al-Qūmisī calls upon the Karaites to fulfill their religious responsibilities through immigration, repentance, and ascetic withdrawal. In this way, he stakes an unequivocal Karaite position in long-standing Jewish debates about whether or not redemption was dependent on repentance.[11] For al-Qūmisī, repentance is a necessary precondition of redemption, and true repentance is possible only in Jerusalem. He argues that the obligation to return to Jerusalem in a spirit of penitence could be discerned through logical deduction even if it had not been commanded already by God:

> For had the Lord not decreed a precept upon us to go from the lands (of the Dispersion) to Jerusalem, (to pray) in mourning and bitterness, would we

[8] Note, however, Haggai Ben-Shammai's reminder that the theme of immigration to Jerusalem was not consistent in all periods of Karaite thought; see "Rabbanite and Karaite Attitudes Toward Aliya," *The Jerusalem Cathedra* 3 (1983): 190–91. The emphasis on immigration was a hallmark of the Mourners for Zion specifically, rather than the Karaite community in general.

[9] On the Mourners' ideology, see Yoram Erder, "The Negation of the Exile in the Messianic Doctrine of the Karaite Mourners of Zion," *HUCA* 68 (1997): 109–40.

[10] On al-Qūmisī, see *KA*, 30–41, and Gil, *History*, 617–22 and 784–87, and extensive bibliography there.

[11] Such debates are recorded in rabbinic literature and placed in the immediate aftermath of the destruction of the Second Temple. In one Midrash, Rabbi Eli'ezer declares that "If Israel repents, it will be redeemed, if it does not repent, it will not be redeemed," while Rabbi Yehoshua contradicts him with the statement that all will be redeemed at the end of days, regardless of whether or not they repent (ctd. in Erder, "The Mourners of Zion," 214). The respective positions on immigration to Jerusalem cannot be neatly divided along Rabbanite–Karaite lines in the early medieval period; see Grossman, "Aliya," esp. 180–84.

not have known with our own intelligence that it is for all objects of wrath to come to the gate of him who is wroth, in order to entreat him, as I have written above? How much more so when the Lord has (in fact) commanded the people of the Dispersion to come to Jerusalem and to stand constantly within it before Him, lamenting, fasting, weeping, mourning, (clad) in sackcloth and bitterness, day and night?[12]

Al-Qūmisī uses persuasive, Bible-based rhetoric to emphasize that returning to Jerusalem and embracing ascetic practices there are prerequisites for redemption. Determined to practice what he preached, al-Qūmisī settled in Jerusalem around 880 with a small group of immigrants, and waves of Karaites followed thereafter.[13] His statements about the necessity of mourning and lamentation are echoed throughout the literary tradition of the Jerusalem Karaites, who continuously assert that rituals and liturgies of mourning are a religious obligation, mandated in Scripture and required by God. By the time of Salmon, the Karaite community of Jerusalem was flourishing and articulating their spiritual commitments with ever greater acumen, sophistication, and creativity of form. Salmon and his circle expressed and expounded upon the same religious concerns that animated al-Qūmisī, and they promoted this ideology in the context of biblical scholarship. Alongside their pious practices and their efforts to draw Rabbanite Jews into the Karaite fold through sermons and polemics, the Mourners devoted themselves to the study of the Bible. Further, they used the language of "return" to promote the new centrality of biblical study within their spiritual platform.

Biblical Scholarship in the Threefold Mandate to Return

The notion of return pervades Karaite writings. As just described, "return to Jerusalem" was a major rallying cry for the Mourners for Zion, who made their way to Palestine beginning in the late ninth century. The Karaite emphasis on repentance was similarly coded as a "return to God," since in both Hebrew and Arabic, "return" and "repentance" are conveyed with a single word, building on long-standing associations between a physical

12 Qūmisī, Sermon, 73–74.

13 Daniel al-Qūmisī left his birthplace after 874 CE and was active in Jerusalem after 900 CE; see Haggai Ben-Shammai, "Fragments of Daniel al-Qūmisī's Commentary on the Book of Daniel as a Historical Source," *Henoch* 13 (1991): 260.

change in direction and a spiritual reorientation.[14] Finally, Karaites located their biblical scholarship within a far-reaching program of "return to the Bible." As Haggai Ben-Shammai has demonstrated, the ideology of returning to a Scripture that has been abandoned or corrupted by the normative practitioners of a religious community was common in sectarian Islamic and Jewish discourse.[15] For the Mourners for Zion, the doctrine of returning to the Bible—and thereby returning to a correct and faithful performance of the divine commandments—was not merely a polemical trope. The Jerusalem Karaites advanced biblical scholarship on several fronts, studying the language of the Hebrew Bible with great seriousness and producing seminal works in the interrelated disciplines of grammar, translation, and exegesis.[16]

That the Karaites understood their commitment to Scripture as the defining feature of their communal identity is apparent from their primary name—Karaites (Hebr. *qara'*; pl. *qara'im*)—and the related terms, *ba'alei miqra'* and *benei miqra'*, which may be rendered as "masters of the Bible" or "biblicists."[17] In Daniel Frank's formulation, the Karaites "derive their name from the Hebrew word for Scripture and their identity from its interpretation."[18] While the commitment to biblical scholarship is without doubt a hallmark of medieval Karaism, the term *qara'* is far more layered than it first appears. Recognizing additional historical and etymological possibilities for the term allows us to see Karaite biblical scholarship

[14] Hebr. *teshuvah* and Arab. *tawba*. On biblical usage of the term, see David A. Lambert, *How Repentance Became Biblical: Judaism, Christianity, and the Interpretation of Scripture* (Oxford: Oxford University Press, 2016), esp. 73–75. Lambert demonstrates that the moral connotations of this term are largely post-biblical.

[15] Haggai Ben-Shammai, "Return to the Scriptures in Ancient and Medieval Jewish Sectarianism and in Early Islam," in *Les Retours aux Écritures Fondamentalismes Présents et Passés*, ed. Évelyne Patlagean and Alain Le Bouilluec (Louvain-Paris: Peeters, 1993), 319–42.

[16] See, e.g., Frank, *Search Scripture Well*; Frank, "Karaite Exegesis," in *HB/OT*, vol. 1, bk. 2, ed. Magne Saebø (Göttingen: Vandenhoeck & Ruprecht, 2000), 110–28; Geoffrey Khan, "The Contributions of the Karaites to the Study of the Hebrew Language," in *Karaite Judaism*, 291–318; and Meira Polliack, "Major Trends in Karaite Biblical Exegesis in the Tenth and Eleventh Centuries," in *Karaite Judaism*, 363–416.

[17] These names may also suggest Karaite associations with Masoretic circles; see Meira Polliack, "Rethinking Karaism: Between Judaism and Islam," *AJS Review* 30, no. 1 (2006): 92. The Masoretes (*ba'alei masorah*) were scribes and scholars, active in Palestine through the tenth century, who successfully developed a system of diacritics and cantillation marks to standardize biblical pronunciation and verse divisions.

[18] Frank, *Search Scripture Well*, 1. The Karaites identified themselves with "biblical code-names" such as: *maśkil* ("Teacher"), *temimei derekh* ("The Perfect of Way"), *shavei pesha'* ("The Penitent"), *she'erit yiśra'el* ("Remnant of Israel"), *shoshanim* ("Lilies"), and of course *'avelei ṣiyyon* ("Mourners for Zion"). Such appellations enabled Karaites to interpret biblical passages prognostically, as allusions to the Karaites' role in salvation history (ibid., 17–18; 160–61).

as one feature—albeit a pivotal one—in a complex social and spiritual program.

Moshe Gil observes that the Hebrew word *qara'* is a calque on the Arabic word *dāʿī*—a missionary or propagandist who "calls" others to the truth. Such figures were common in the Ismaʿīlī Muslim circles that were active in the same lands and circumstances in which the Karaite movement emerged.[19] Leon Nemoy likely has the Ismaʿīlī *dāʿī* in mind when he suggests the presence of "itinerant Karaite missionaries all over the Near East, in market places and on street corners."[20] Although there is no documentary evidence for Karaite preachers in the public square doing the same work as their Ismaʿīlī peers, Karaite literature, with its persuasive tone and ideological intensity, provides a plausible literary corollary to the public mission of the Ismaʿīlī movement. The Karaite movement had a strong missionary element, and Karaite writers urgently called upon the Jews of the Diaspora to join their cause by returning to Jerusalem and practicing Karaite penitential rites.

Recently Yoram Erder has affirmed a connection between the Karaites and the Ismaʿīlī *dāʿī*, while also revisiting the claim for internal Jewish roots for the term. Erder argues that the earliest Karaites took their name from the post-biblical phrase *qeri'ei ha-shem*—"those who call upon the name [of God]"—which they discovered in the Damascus Covenant, an ancient sectarian text from Qumran that was discovered and copied by medieval Jews at the turn of the ninth century.[21] The authors of the Damascus Covenant described themselves as a righteous remnant who would "call upon the name of God" and spread true religious instruction in order to bring about redemption. Erder contends that early Karaites were inspired by this mission and called themselves *qara'im* in reference to the ancient *qeri'ei ha-shem*, whose vision they shared. Thus, for the Mourners for Zion, the messianic conception of the word *qara'* was primary, while "the meaning of *qara'* in the sense of scripturalist is secondary."[22] According to this explanation, the alternative names for the Karaites—*baʿalei miqra'* and *benei miqra'*—initially designated

[19] Gil, *History*, 784. For further discussion of Muslim influences on Karaite origins, see ibid., 779 ff; *KA*, xvii; Daniel J. Lasker, "Islamic Influences on Karaite Origins," in *Studies in Islamic and Judaic Traditions*, vol. 2, Brown Judaic Studies, ed. William M. Brinner and Stephen D. Ricks (Atlanta, Ga.: Scholars Press, 1989), 23–48; and Meira Polliack, "Rethinking Karaism."

[20] *KA*, 111.

[21] Erder, *The Karaite Mourners of Zion and the Qumran Scrolls: On the History of an Alternative to Rabbinic Judaism* (Turnhout, Belgium: Brepols, 2017), 384–407.

[22] Erder, *Karaite Mourners*, 406.

scripturalist movements that were outside the Karaite fold. It was only after several anti-traditionalist movements in Iraq and Persia united under the Karaite umbrella in the late ninth century that all three terms became synonymous, with scripturalism as their primary definition.[23] Although not all scholars accept the premise that the medieval Karaites were influenced directly by the ancient sectarians of Qumran, Erder's analysis has the merits of highlighting the messianic goals and missionizing elements of Karaism while simultaneously acknowledging the increasingly prominent role of biblical scholarship within the evolving Karaite project.[24] He brings these themes together by stating that

> The *qara'* is the one who imparts Torah to the people of Israel and who shall, in the future, impart it to the whole of mankind, so that everyone will call upon the name of God. In this sense, the *qara'* resembles the Shīʿite propagandist of his period, the *dāʿī*, the caller.[25]

These discussions provide a social and historical context for Karaite biblical studies, in which we may inquire about Karaite motivations for undertaking the study of the Bible and the pietistic, homiletical, or eschatological significance of their exegetical methods. In emphasizing the biblical core of Karaite intellectual activity, by contrast, Geoffrey Khan argues that the label *qara'im* functioned exclusively to indicate the biblicist orientation and scholarly focus of Karaism. For Khan, the proposed connection between the Karaites and the Ismaʿīlī missionary culture rests on "too great an emphasis on [the Karaites'] supposed religio-political division from mainstream Judaism."[26] Yet it is possible to emphasize the high value that Karaites placed on biblical scholarship without rejecting the missionary aspects of the Karaite

[23] Erder, *Karaite Mourners*, 407. Further, Erder posits that Rabbanite attacks against the Karaites motivated them to distance themselves from Qumran literature and obfuscate the true origins of their name.

[24] Seminal research on Karaite connections to the Dead Sea Scrolls was conducted by Naphtali Wieder; see, e.g., his reprinted articles in *The Judean Scrolls and Karaism* (Jerusalem: Ben Zvi, 2005). For an overview of this research and its reception, see Fred Astren, "The Dead Sea Scrolls and Medieval Jewish Studies: Methods and Problems," *DSD* 8:2 (2001): 105–23; and Daniel J. Lasker, "The Dead Sea Scrolls in the Historiography and Self-Image of Contemporary Karaites," *DSD* 9:3 (2002): 281–94. Daniel Lasker evaluates Erder's claims in a book review; see *European Journal of Jewish Studies* 15 (2020): 1–8.

[25] Erder, *Karaite Mourners*, 406.

[26] Geoffrey Khan, *The Early Karaite Tradition of Hebrew Grammatical Thought: Including a Critical Edition, Translation and Analysis of the* Diqduq *of ʿAbū Yaʿqūb Yūsuf ibn Nūḥ on the Hagiographa*, SSLL 32 (Leiden: Brill, 2000), 3 n. 13.

name and spiritual project, and to recognize parallels between Karaites and contemporary Muslim sectarian communities without downplaying Karaite participation in the broader culture of medieval Judaism. Karaism is a thoroughly Jewish movement, led by Jewish thinkers who drew upon Jewish texts and traditions in order to contribute their perspectives on matters of shared concern within the Jewish community—and yet Karaites, like Rabbanites, were also shaped by the resources and challenges of the Islamic environment in which they lived and carried out their work. Biblical scholarship and missionary zeal were no strangers to one another in the Karaite movement, from its origins to its heyday in late tenth- and eleventh-century Jerusalem. As the Karaites were sensitive to aspects of shared meaning between Hebrew and Arabic, it is likely that multiple dimensions of the word *qaraʾim* resonated with them, and that evolving circumstances could bring one dimension or another to the foreground.

All of these associations with the word "Karaite"—biblical scholarship, missionizing, summoning others to the truth—represent vital strains of Karaite thought and activity, in the movement as a whole and in the corpus of Salmon b. Yerūḥīm specifically. Salmon produced works of biblical scholarship, from Arabic translations and commentaries on biblical books to a linguistic treatise on Hebrew letters.[27] Yet he also composed a Hebrew polemical poem, *The Wars of the Lord* (*Sefer Milḥamot Adonai*), which proclaims the superiority of Karaite thought and practice, and antagonizes Saadia Gaon and his Rabbanite followers.[28] Within Salmon's Bible commentaries themselves we find passages of homily, liturgical poetry, and polemic interspersed with lexical and grammatical analysis, and careful Arabic translation. Salmon's practice of centering biblical scholarship within a broad spiritual and social platform was hardly unique among the Karaites of medieval Jerusalem. In the tenth and eleventh centuries, prominent Karaite intellectuals rarely limited themselves to a single discipline of biblical studies. Instead, they vigorously applied their biblical learning to solve practical questions and promote the goals of their community. By acknowledging the full range of Karaite activities—and the full scope of the term "Karaite"—it becomes clear that biblical scholarship was never independent of the larger

[27] *Aḥruf al-ibdāl*. The text is lost, but its existence is known from internal references within Salmon's corpus (e.g., comments to Lam 3:16, 26, and 33).

[28] Israel Davidson, *The Wars of the Lord: The Complete Arguments of the Karaite Salmon ben Yeruhim Against Rav Saʿadyah Gaʾon* (New York: Bet Midrash ha-Rabanim de-ʾAmerikah, 1934); *KA*, 71–82; Samuel Poznanski, "Karaite Miscellanies," *JQR* 8 (1896): 684–91.

religious and political goals of the Karaite movement. For Salmon, as for his contemporaries, biblical scholarship was the framework in which overlapping communal and spiritual projects coalesced.

Scholars of the Karaite Community in Jerusalem

The Karaite settlement in Jerusalem dates to the final decades of the ninth century, and already by the tenth and eleventh centuries the community had gained a reputation as the center of Karaite scholarship. In that relatively short span of time, Karaites made tremendous advances in biblical studies. They researched the Hebrew language, often from the vantage point of comparative Semitics, and they adapted their techniques of biblical translation to produce both literal and free models of Arabic translation. The art of commentary writing evolved to keep pace with the progressive states of scholarship, the religious perspectives of the exegetes, and the spiritual and political needs of the growing community. Thus, the writings of other Mourners for Zion who were active in carrying out the scholarly aims of the community provide a context that is essential for understanding Salmon's commentary, as well as the role of Lamentations within Karaite religious development.

While Salmon may have been the first Karaite to compose a systematic commentary on Lamentations, he was certainly not the first or only Karaite to use Lamentations in literary, liturgical, and linguistic contexts, or to leave a written record of this engagement. Therefore, throughout this book I will consider parallels and points of connection between Salmon's commentaries and the works of other Jerusalem Karaites, such as David b. Abraham al-Fāsī, Yūsuf b. Nūḥ, Yefet b. ʿEli, and Sahl b. Maṣliaḥ—all of whom came after Salmon—as well as Daniel al-Qūmisī, the missionary-exegete and prominent immigrant to Jerusalem who preceded him. The writings of Yaʿqūb al-Qirqisānī also provide an instructive framework for evaluating Salmon's contributions to Karaite exegesis. Even though al-Qirqisānī remained in Iraq rather than joining his coreligionists in Palestine, his early tenth-century writings on religious history and the legal and narrative portions of the Bible were influential among the Jerusalem Karaites.[29] Together these scholars

[29] On al-Qirqisānī see, e.g., Bruno Chiesa and Wilfrid Lockwood, eds., *Yaʿqūb al-Qirqisānī on Jewish Sects and Christianity: A Translation of "Kitāb al-anwār," Book I, with Two Introductory Essays* (Frankfurt am Main: Lang, 1984); Frank, *Search Scripture Well*, esp. 8–12; Hartwig Hirschfeld, *Qirqisānī Studies*, Jews College 6 (London: University of California Libraries, 1918); *KA*, 42–68;

represent the breadth of Karaite scholarship in its golden age. I will also refer to the Arabic translation of Lamentations produced by Saadia—the Gaon Saadia ben Joseph al-Fayyūmī (882–942), the renowned tenth-century Rabbanite thinker and leader of the rabbinic academy in Sura. Saadia attracted polemical fire from Karaites, including Salmon, because of his leadership in the Rabbanite establishment and his espousal of rabbinic positions inimical to Karaite values.[30] While certain Rabbanite commitments place Saadia at odds with the Karaite scholars, it is without question that he participates in the broader Judeo-Arabic culture alongside, and in response to, the Karaite community. Salmon seems to be familiar with Saadia's Arabic translation and commentary on Lamentations, and these works provide a point of comparison to the Karaite approaches.[31]

Salmon and, in the next generation, Yefet composed commentaries on Lamentations that are still extant.[32] The reference works by Ibn Nūḥ and al-Fāsī include ample references to Lamentations, with a focus on the difficult words and other linguistic issues (*masāʾil*) that the scholars attempt to understand in their biblical context. Although there are no extant Lamentations commentaries from Sahl or al-Qūmisī, the surviving corpus of each Karaite includes frequent references to Lamentations. Both figures produced homiletical works saturated with Karaite ideology, and the invocation of verses from Lamentations within them indicates the centrality of Lamentations to the religious thought and praxis of the Jerusalem Karaites and to their emerging communal identity.

Geoffrey Khan, "The Opinions of al-Qirqisānī Concerning the Text of the Bible and Parallel Attitudes Towards the Text of the Qur'ān," *JQR* 81 (1990): 59–73; and Leon Nemoy, *Yaʿqūb al-Qirqisānī's Kitāb al-Anwār wa-l Marāqib—Code of Karaite Law*, 5 vols. (New York: Alexander Kohut Memorial Foundation, 1939–43). Walfish notes the absence, in al-Qirqisānī's writings, of any discussion of immigration to Jerusalem, suggesting that this principle was not shared among all Karaites ("The Mourners of Zion," 48).

30 On Saadia, with attention to his contributions to biblical scholarship and his engagement with Karaism, see, e.g., Robert Brody, *The Geonim of Babylonia and the Shaping of Medieval Jewish Culture* (New Haven, Conn.: Yale University Press, 1998), esp. chapters 6, 15, 19; Richard C. Steiner, *A Biblical Translation in the Making: The Evolution and Impact of Saadia Gaon's* Tafsīr (Cambridge, Mass.: Harvard University Center for Jewish Studies, 2010); as well as Samuel Poznanski's works on "The Anti-Karaite Writings of Saadiah Gaon," *JQR* 10 (1897–98): 238–76; and "The Karaite Literary Opponents of Saadiah Gaon in the Tenth Century," *JQR* 18 (1906): 209–50 (with reference to Salmon on 220–22).

31 Yehudah Ratzaby has published Saadia's translation of Lamentations in "Targum of Rabbenu Saadia Gaon on Lamentations," *Tarbiz* 13 (1942): 92–106. Only fragments of Saddia's commentary are extant; see Ratzaby, "Selections from Rav Saʿadia's Commentary on Lamentations," *Bar Ilan Annual* 20–21 (1983): 349–80; and Ratzaby, "New Passages from R. Saadia's Commentary on Lamentations," *Sinai* 95 (1985): 1–23.

32 See chapter 2 for discussion of Yefet's commentary on Lamentations.

David b. Abraham al-Fāsī was a lexicographer and exegete in Jerusalem in the middle of the tenth century. His major contribution to Arabic linguistics and exegesis was the *Kitāb Jāmiʿ al-Alfāẓ*, an Arabic lexicon of biblical Hebrew, arranged alphabetically in two-letter combinations.[33] The lexicon includes over fifty references to words and verses from Lamentations, many of which correspond to the readings presented in Salmon's commentary. James T. Robinson has observed a similarly high degree of correspondence between al-Fāsī's dictionary and Salmon's Ecclesiastes commentary, and he notes the impossibility of determining definitively whether one Karaite drew from the work of the other, or whether they drew independently from a common source.[34]

In the generation after Salmon and al-Fāsī, the preeminent Jerusalem Karaite scholars Yefet b. ʾEli, Sahl b. Maṣliaḥ, and Yūsuf b. Nūḥ flourished in the last third of the tenth century. Ibn Nūḥ founded a college (*dār lil-ʿilm*) in Jerusalem that included a library and served as an important institution for the development and dissemination of Karaite knowledge for some time after Ibn Nūḥ's own disciples, including Abū al-Faraj Hārūn and Yūsuf al-Baṣīr, had made their own contributions to Judeo-Arabic scholarship. In Ibn Nūḥ's grammar-based commentary, the *Diqduq* ("Grammar"), he elucidates difficult or ambiguous Hebrew words by rendering them in grammatically analogous Arabic. The section on Lamentations includes Ibn Nūḥ's concise remarks on over fifty separate linguistic issues from the biblical book.[35]

Sahl b. Maṣliaḥ composed legal codes and select biblical commentaries, although he is remembered principally as a propagandist among the Jerusalem Karaites.[36] He traveled throughout the Islamic East, missionizing in speech and in writing, in both Hebrew and Arabic, with the stated intent of converting Rabbanites to Karaism. While Sahl cites verses from Lamentations in his epistle to the Rabbanite leader Jacob b. Samuel,

[33] *The Hebrew-Arabic Dictionary of the Bible, Known as Kitāb Jāmiʿ al-Alfāẓ* (Agrōn) *of David ben Abraham al-Fāsī*, 2 vols., ed. Solomon L. Skoss (New Haven, Conn.: Yale University Press, 1936). See Aaron Maman, *Comparative Semitic Philology in the Middle Ages*, trans. David Lyons, SSLL 40 (Leiden: Brill, 2004), esp. 182–275; Meira Polliack, "David ben Abraham al-Fāsī," in *EJIW*.

[34] Robinson, *Asceticism*, 29.

[35] On Ibn Nūḥ, see Miriam Goldstein, *Karaite Exegesis in Medieval Jerusalem: The Judeo-Arabic Pentateuch Commentary of Yūsuf ibn Nūḥ and Abū al-Faraj Hārūn* (Tübingen: Mohr Siebeck, 2011), esp. 12–14; Khan, *The Early Karaite Tradition*; Khan, "Ibn Nūḥ, Joseph (Abū Yaʿqūb Yūsuf)," in vol. 2 of *EJIW*; and Khan, "Biblical Exegesis and Grammatical Theory in the Karaite Tradition," in *Exegesis and Grammar in Medieval Karaite Texts*, JSSSupp 13, ed. Geoffrey Khan (Oxford: Oxford University Press, 2001).

[36] Portions of his works on the Pentateuch, Hosea, and Isaiah are still extant. There is no evidence that he composed a commentary on Lamentations.

his principal relevance to our study lies in his articulation of Karaite principles and religious themes, and in his homiletical style, both of which also characterize Salmon's Lamentations commentary. Verses from Lamentations appear in key passages of Sahl's compelling sermons on Karaite spirituality, suggesting a common Karaite practice of drawing spiritual instruction from Lamentations.[37]

In the final decades of the tenth century, Yefet b. ʿEli (fl. ca. 960–1005) completed a comprehensive verse-by-verse Arabic translation and commentary of the entire Bible, including the book of Lamentations. Yefet's exegetical corpus, which followed Salmon's by one generation, is celebrated for its attention to the historical and cultural context of biblical books as well as their editorial development.[38] His commentary on Lamentations provides a counterpoint to the more successful and widely disseminated commentary of Salmon on the same biblical book. Yefet's Lamentations commentary—and its relationship to Salmon's—will be addressed further in the following chapter.

Together these texts provide a context for understanding the character and purpose of Salmon's Lamentations commentary, as well as the impact of Salmon's distinctive homiletical outlook. In the next chapter, I outline Salmon's Lamentations commentary and illustrate its most salient features with excerpts from the annotated English translation that appears in Part 2 of this volume. In this way, I position Salmon and his commentary in the traditions of Jewish discourse as well as the flourishing Arabic-Islamic intellectual milieu in which he and his contemporaries carried out the projects that came to shape the Jewish exegetical tradition.

[37] On Sahl b. Maṣliaḥ, see Miriam Goldstein, "Sahl (Abū'l-Sarrī) ben Maṣliaḥ," *EJIW*; *KA*, 109–22; *LK* 25–43; Leon Nemoy, "The Epistle of Sahl ben Maṣliaḥ," *PAAJR* 38/39 (1970–71): 145–47.

[38] On Yefet b. ʿEli, see Wechsler, "Japheth (Abū ʿAlī Ḥasan) ben ʿEli," in *EJIW*; Meira Polliack and Eliezer Schlossberg, "Historical-Literary, Rhetorical and Redactional Methods of Interpretation in Yefet ben ʿEli's Introduction to the Minor Prophets," in *Exegesis and Grammar in Medieval Karaite Texts*, JSSSupp 13, ed. Geoffrey Khan (Oxford: Oxford University Press, 2001); *KA*, 83–108. As Wechsler explains, Salmon is commonly held to be older than Yefet because his scholarly career preceded that of Yefet. However, Salmon's birth is dated to 910–915 and Yefet's to 910–920, which would make them close peers in age. See *The Arabic Translation and Commentary of Yefet ben ʿEli the Karaite on the Book of Esther*, EJM 36; KTS 1 (Leiden: Brill, 2008), 125 n. 10.

2
The Lamentations Commentary of Salmon ben Yerūḥīm

This, too, is instruction for Israel, on how to lament for themselves.
—Salmon b. Yerūḥīm
Comment to Lamentations 4:1

For Salmon, the book of Lamentations was God's "instruction for Israel"—religious mandates for the Jewish community in exile, as conveyed through the prophet Jeremiah. He perceived no friction between his pietistic sensibility and his exegetical labors. To the contrary, his study of biblical history and Hebrew grammar, etymology, and syntax was the foundation of his mission to apprehend the spiritual meaning of Lamentations and convey it to his community.

The commentary offers a systematic framework for building homiletical insights on top of scholarly foundations, and for incorporating liturgical materials alongside the intellectual evidence used to justify them. The purpose of this chapter is to introduce Salmon's commentary, highlighting its distinctive or seminal features, and positioning it within the Arabic-Islamic cultural sphere of medieval Jewish scholarship—all with an eye toward demonstrating Salmon's skill for weaving pious instruction and exegesis together. Readers unfamiliar with Jewish biblical exegesis in Arabic will find an introduction to the genre in addition to the discussion of Salmon's innovations and idiosyncrasies. This chapter also functions as an overview of the commentary and my English translation of it.

Salmon b. Yerūḥīm and His Commentary on Lamentations

Salmon ben Yerūḥīm (known in Arabic as Sulaym or Sulaymān ibn Ruḥaym)[1] is the earliest Karaite writer with an extant, identifiable exegetical corpus in

[1] On the varied forms of Salmon's name, see Michael Wechsler, *The Arabic Translation and Commentary of Yefet ben ʿEli the Karaite on the Book of Esther: Edition, Translation, and Introduction*, EJM 36, KTS 1 (Leiden: Brill, 2006), 125 n. 9.

Jewish Piety in Islamic Jerusalem. Jessica Andruss, Oxford University Press. © Oxford University Press 2023.
DOI: 10.1093/oso/9780197639559.003.0002

Arabic.[2] In addition to his commentary on Lamentations,[3] Salmon's commentaries on Psalms,[4] Song of Songs,[5] Ecclesiastes,[6] and Esther[7] are also extant. The works on Psalms, Song of Songs, and Lamentations were written in quick succession, beginning with the commentary on Psalms in 953 and ending with the commentary on Lamentations in 954.[8] Other exegetical compositions fared less well in the historical record: only fragments remain from Salmon's commentaries on Genesis, Proverbs, Daniel[9] and Ruth,[10] while his commentary on Job is completely lost.[11]

[2] The only earlier Karaite exegetes were al-Qirqisānī, whose Pentateuch commentary only exists in a small portion, and Daniel al-Qūmisī, whose Hebrew commentary on the Minor Prophets contains Arab. glosses (Michael Wechsler, "Salmon ben Jeroham," in *EJIW*).

[3] The complete text, and the basis of my own translation, is the edition of Mohammed Abdul-Latif Abdul-Karim, "Commentary of Salmon ben Yeruham on Lamentations" (Ph.D. diss., The University of St Andrews, 1976). An edition of chapter 1was published by Salomon Feuerstein, *Der Commentar des Karaërs Salmon ben Jerucham zu den Klaglierdern* (Krakau, 1898). The commentary is the focus of Ben-Shammai, "Poetic Works and Lamentations"; Lawrence Marwick, "Studies in Salmon ben Yeruham," *JQR* 34:3 (1944): 313–20; and Lawrence Marwick, "Studies in Salmon ben Yeruham," *JQR* 34:4 (1944): 475–80.

[4] Portions of the Psalms commentary have been edited. See Lawrence Marwick, *The Arabic Commentary of Salmon ben Yeruham on the Book of Psalms, Chapters 42–72, Edited from the Unique Manuscript in the State Public Library in Leningrad* (Philadelphia: Dropsie College, 1956); Jonathan Shunary, "Salmon ben Yeruham's Commentary on the Book of Psalms," *JQR* 73 (1982); and Joseph Alobaidi, *Le commentaire des Psaumes par le Qaraïte Salmon ben Yeruham: Psaumes 1–10* (New York: Peter Lang, 1996). Uriel Simon treats the commentary in *Four Approaches to the Book of Psalms from Saadia Gaon to Abraham Ibn Ezra* (Albany: State University of New York Press, 1991), 59–71.

[5] See Daniel Frank, *Search Scripture Well*, chapter 4.

[6] For discussion as well as the complete edition and translation, see Robinson, *Asceticism*.

[7] Michael Wechsler has described Salmon's commentary on Esther, particularly in relation to Yefet ben ʿEli's commentary on the same book, inYefet, Esth, 78–83.

[8] These dates are based on internal references; see my calculations in the note to Lam 3:6. Others have proposed that the commentaries were written between 955–956 (Poznanski, "Karaite Miscellanies," 688 nn. 2–4) or 950–51 (Gil, *History*, 798–99).

[9] Salmon refers to his Daniel commentary in his comments to Lam 2:4, 4:22, and 3:20.

[10] See Michael Wechsler, "Salmon ben Jeroham (Sulaym ibn Ruḥaym)," in *EJIW*. Wechsler has identified the only witness to Salmon's commentary on Ruth, which includes the introduction along with the translation and commentary on most of the first two verses. Previously the existence of a commentary on Ruth by Salmon was the subject of debate. See Leon Nemoy, "Did Salmon ben Jeroham Compose a Commentary on Ruth?" *JQR* 39 (1948): 215–16. Note that I. D. Markon mistakenly attributed Yefet ben ʿEli's commentary on Ruth to Salmon in "The Commentary on the Scroll of Ruth by the Karaite Salomon ben Yerōḥam," in *Livre d'Hommage à la mémoire du Dr Samuel Poznański (1864–1921) offert par les amis et les compagnons du travail scientifique* (Hebrew) (Leipzig: Warsaw Committee of the Great Synagogue 1927), 78–96. In addition, a liturgical poem has been attributed tentatively to Salmon; see Simḥah Assaf, "Prayer by Salman ben Yerūḥam [?] the Karaite" [Hebrew], *Zion* 3 (1928–29): 88–94.

[11] Note Marwick's suggestion that Salmon also authored commentaries on the books of the prophets, which are now lost. Marwick reasons that Salmon cites extensively from the Psalms in his commentary on Lamentations, and we know that he wrote a commentary on that book; since he also cites extensively from the prophetic books, he must have also written commentaries on those books ("Studies in Salmon ben Yeruham," 316–19). This hypothesis seems unlikely in the absence of any references to such commentaries within Salmon's extant corpus or outside of it.

Salmon's choice of biblical books is eclectic—particularly in contrast to the later comprehensive project of Yefet ben ʿEli, who seems to have composed his series of commentaries according to the order of the biblical books within the canonical Jewish Bible.[12] Yet Salmon's more curated corpus points to the communal needs that motivated his exegetical endeavors: his research agenda concentrated on biblical books with foundational religious instruction for the Karaite community. Daniel Frank has perceptively observed that Salmon chose to explicate the biblical books that held special significance within the religious outlook of the Mourners for Zion. Their liturgy was drawn from Psalms and Lamentations, prognostic interpretations of history were based in the Song of Songs and Daniel, and ethical instruction was sought from Ecclesiastes and Proverbs.[13] While each of Salmon's commentaries offers a Karaite perspective on core biblical texts, his commentary on Lamentations must have provided unparalleled spiritual and intellectual resources, since it was copied and disseminated especially widely. Over one hundred separately indexed manuscripts of Salmon's Lamentations commentary are extant—over three times as many as his commentaries on Psalms or Ecclesiastes—and several manuscripts are dated as late as the seventeenth or eighteenth century.[14]

In evaluating the remarkable durability of Salmon's Lamentations commentary, it is again useful to compare Salmon's work with that of Yefet ben ʿEli, the Karaite exegete who followed on his heels and composed a complete Arabic translation and commentary on the Hebrew Bible in the final decades of the tenth century (ca. 960–1005). Yefet was an innovative exegete, and in recent scholarship he is often treated as the paragon of Karaite exegesis.[15] In the course of his continuous translation and interpretation of the entire Hebrew Bible, he necessarily attends to the same books that Salmon addressed shortly before him. When Yefet interprets one of the biblical books that Salmon has already commented upon, however, he rarely reproduces Salmon's results. Yefet and Salmon have their own translation techniques, which yield distinctive Arabic renderings of the biblical verses. In grammatical representation

[12] Lawrence Marwick, "The Order of the Books in Yefet's Bible Codex," *JQR* 33 (1942–43): 445–60.

[13] Frank, *Search Scripture Well*, 12–13.

[14] For the count, see Wechsler, "Salmon ben Jeroham (Sulaym ibn Ruḥaym)," in *EJIW*.

[15] On the trajectory of scholarship on Yefet, see Marzena Zawanowska, "Review of Scholarly Research on Yefet ben ʿEli and His Works," *REJ* 173 (2014): 97–138. Scholars of the late nineteenth and early twentieth centuries tended to underestimate Yefet's originality and describe him as merely a compiler of others' interpretive work.

as well as in word choice, Yefet charts a different course than his predecessor, perhaps deliberately avoiding the words that Salmon used in order to produce a unique Arabic version of the biblical text. The content of the exegetes' verse comments also differs, as though Yefet justifies the duplication in subject matter by formulating an interpretive line that is unexplored by Salmon.[16] There is no doubt that Yefet overshadows Salmon in the history of Jewish exegesis, not only in terms of his own productivity, but also in the proclivity of later exegetes to weave his explanations into their own, and in the volume of manuscripts of his writings that remain extant today. This imbalance in the text reception history of the two exegetes suggests that Yefet's commentaries largely supplanted Salmon's commentaries on the same biblical books. In the case of Lamentations, however, we find an exception to the rule: Salmon's commentary was extensively copied, transmitted, and preserved, while Yefet's commentary nearly faded away and, for much of the twentieth century, was presumed lost. The absence of clearly cataloged manuscript evidence for Yefet's commentary on Lamentations prompted scholars to hedge their bets when describing his otherwise complete oeuvre by stating that he had written commentaries on every book of the Hebrew Bible with the possible exception of Lamentations, or noting that manuscript evidence for such a work had yet to be found or identified.[17] While Yefet's commentary has now been recovered and restored to the scholarly record by Daniel Frank, who identified manuscripts and compiled a preliminary edition in 2012, the fact remains that it was neglected almost to the point of disappearance while Salmon's commentary on the same biblical book was continually copied and transmitted.[18]

The unexpected primacy of Salmon's Lamentations commentary over that of his more-celebrated successor calls us to consider the commentary

[16] A full comparative study of Salmon and Yefet, on the basis of commentaries that they have written on the same biblical book, is a research desideratum. My remarks here are based on localized differences that I have observed between the two translator-exegetes in their respective writings on Lamentations, which I have flagged in the notes to my translation. Robinson observes similar differences between the two scholars in their commentaries on Ecclesiastes (see *Asceticism*), as does Wechsler in his studies of Judeo-Arabic commentaries on Esther (see Saadia, Esth, and Yefet, Esth).

[17] See Marzena Zawanowska, "Review of Scholarly Reseach," 99 n. 3; Ben-Shammai, "Japheth ben 'Eli ha-Levi," in *EJ*, 2nd ed., vol. 11, 86–87; Frank, *Search Scripture Well*, 250 n. 10.

[18] I thank Daniel Frank for sharing with me his preliminary edition of Yefet's Lamentations commentary, based on MSS RNL Evr-Arab. I.213 and RNL Evr-Arab. I.3806. My comparative observations about Yefet's approach to Lamentations are based on that as-yet-unpublished edition, and supplemented with notes from Frank's paper, "Recovering Japheth Ben 'Eli's 'Lost' Commentary on Lamentations," from the 17th Annual Conference of the Society for Judaeo-Arabic Studies, Vanderbilt University, August 15–18, 2016.

especially closely, in an effort to understand why this work held special value for the communities that received it and transmitted it forward. Why was Salmon's vision of Lamentations and its message so compelling for the Mourners for Zion and their intellectual heirs? What exegetical methods and interpretive techniques does Salmon demonstrate in this work, and what resources did they provide to other Jewish scholars of the Bible? How does Salmon represent and respond to the themes of Lamentations and parlay them into a spiritual discourse that resonates with pious readers? Throughout this book I argue that Salmon develops the Jewish and Arabic-Islamic models of his age in order to craft an exegetical document with a pietistic message at its core. In this chapter, I wish to introduce the commentary itself. I will describe its structure and principal components, with particular attention to the innovative or idiosyncratic elements of the work and their points of connection to the nascent frameworks of Jewish biblical commentaries in the Islamic world.

Structure of the Commentary

The basic structure of Salmon's commentary on Lamentations follows that of his other extant commentaries and became normative within the later tradition of Judeo-Arabic biblical commentaries. I will outline the format of Salmon's commentary in this paragraph and discuss each component in turn in greater detail below. The commentary opens with a programmatic introduction (*muqaddima* or *ṣadr*) in which Salmon presents the biblical book, indicates its major themes and questions, and notes his exegetical rubric. In the commentary itself, he addresses each verse of Lamentations in order, first providing the Hebrew incipit, followed by his translation of the verse into Arabic and an Arabic comment. The length and content of each comment vary and include some combination of: lexical and grammatical information, an Arabic paraphrase of the verse (which is distinct from the verse translation), Salmon's remarks on the meaning of the verse in the context of the passage and the Bible more broadly, a response to another scholar's interpretation, the insertion of a homily or verses of liturgical poetry (*piyyuṭim*), comments on a related biblical passage, and perhaps an excursus on historical or homiletical themes. While these features are standard for biblical commentaries even at this early stage, there are two elements of Salmon's

Lamentations commentary that stand out as distinctive. First, Salmon concludes his comment on almost every verse of Lamentations with a refrain consisting of two parts: a pious exhortation in Arabic joined to a Hebrew biblical verse that he repeats consistently within each chapter of Lamentations. I refer to this feature as a "refrain" because it regularly recurs at expected intervals and because its presence suggests a liturgical context for the commentary. Second, at the end of the verse-by-verse commentary, Salmon appends a litany of consolation verses drawn from the prophetic literature of Scripture. As Salmon explains, the purpose of this concluding section is to reassure the community that God has promised, through the prophets, a reversal of each punishment that is described in Lamentations, so that ultimately every injury will be healed and every loss will be restored. Salmon does not provide a separate title for this lengthy section of the commentary, although he refers to it as the "consolations" (Hebr. *neḥamot*) that were revealed to Jeremiah and other prophets even before the destruction of Jerusalem was decreed. Thus, I follow Haggai Ben-Shammai in informally titling this section *Neḥamot*. Like the refrains, this litany of consolations may suggest a liturgical purpose for the commentary, as will be discussed below. At this point I will discuss each of these features in greater depth and illustrate them with passages from the commentary. The full translation of passages that are excerpted here will be found in Part 2 of this volume.

Programmatic Introduction (*Ṣadr* or *Muqaddima*)

Programmatic introductions became a regular feature of biblical commentaries, both Karaite and Rabbanite, starting in the tenth-century Islamic milieu, and the examples from Salmon's texts provide some of our earliest evidence for Jewish implementation of this genre.[19] These introductions amounted to highly organized treatises in which exegetes considered issues such as the authorship, editorial composition, and historical context of the biblical book; enumerated its notable features; discussed its themes and religious purpose; and detailed the method and techniques of their own exegetical process. Introductions also offered an opportunity to mount sophisticated theological arguments, or to rebut an opponent's view directly

[19] See Frank, *Search Scripture Well*, 252–54.

or indirectly.[20] As was the convention with prose compositions in the Arabic tradition, these introductions open with a formal *taḥmīd*, or dedicatory statement in praise of God.

Salmon's Lamentations commentary likewise begins with a *taḥmīd*: "*In the name of the true Judge, blessed be His name. He judges with justice and truth.*[. . .] *The LORD is just in all His ways* (Ps 145:17). *Just are You, O LORD* (Ps 119:137). *The LORD is just, for I have rebelled against His word* (Lam 1:18)."[21] The entire statement is in Hebrew and incorporates biblical verses from the Psalms and Lamentations. Through his choice of biblical prooftexts, Salmon emphasizes the teachings that, in his view, lie at the heart of Lamentations: that God is absolutely just, and that the destruction and punishment recorded in Lamentations and extended through years of exile are a just and fair divine response to unabated human sin.

Salmon's introduction builds on this foundation of divine justice from the *taḥmīd* while also invoking evidence of divine mercy. Salmon intertwines these concepts by teaching his readers that God "requites His servants with nothing other than what they deserve" and also reminding them of God's promise at Sinai that Israel would never be completely annihilated, even if their sins became great.[22] For Salmon, the Bible provides ample proof of divine mercy, not in its contents alone but also in its very existence: "In His beneficence and favor, the Mighty and Sublime promised Israel His holy books in the time of exile so that they would be fortified by them."[23]

The conviction that the Bible as a whole—and Lamentations in particular—manifests God's kindness to the Jewish community in times of exile profoundly influences Salmon's approach to Lamentations. He considers the book to be a repository of instruction for the generations in exile. Thus, while he appreciates its historical and contextual details, he emphasizes the book's prophetic nature and its relevance to his own community. This dual focus on historical context and contemporary application appears already in Salmon's introduction to the commentary when, for example, he offers parallel interpretations of Jeremiah 51:5, *For Israel and Judah have been forsaken by their God*. Salmon first states that the verse means "that Israel and Judah will not

[20] E.g., the introduction to Salmon's Psalms commentary, in which he argues *contra* Saadia that psalms are prophetic prayers and the community is obliged to recite them in exile. See Shunary, "Salmon ben Yeruham's Commentary on the Book of Psalms," and Simon, *Four Approaches*, 59–71.

[21] The opening lines of Salmon's introduction.

[22] Salmon's invocation; building on Lev 26:44.

[23] Salmon's introduction (opening section).

be widowed from their God. That is to say, God did not cut them off from His mercy and His beneficence." Then he continues, "Neither are the people of the exile [cut off] from His beneficence." Thus, Jeremiah's words simultaneously convey historical information about God's care for ancient Israel and Judah, and a prophetic promise about the continuation of God's care for the Jewish community during the exile. Salmon grants that the prophets' words had a contextual meaning during the biblical period, and he avers that they are also relevant for his own generation. Within the introduction, then, Salmon offers a succinct presentation of the instruction that he believes Lamentations offers to his community.

For Salmon, the essential instruction that Lamentations imparts to the Jewish community in exile concerns the obligation to mourn. According to him, the book's imagery of punishment, destruction, and loss affects readers with an overwhelming urge to mourn; its details offer practical guidance about when, where, and how to mourn; and its underlying theology indicates the efficacy of mourning and penitence to prompt divine forgiveness and usher in the age of redemption. Salmon reminds readers of their obligation to mourn throughout his Lamentations commentary, but he presents his thoughts most systematically in a section of the introduction that is dedicated to this issue. Notably, the section of Salmon's introduction that deals with mourning draws heavily on verses from the biblical prophets but does not include verses from Lamentations. Salmon uses the prophetic verses to emphasize all that Israel has lost since the destruction of Jerusalem, and he urges reflection (*iʿtibār*) on the narratives from Israel's past in order to persuade readers of the necessity of mourning while in exile. The absence of citations from Lamentations here suggests that Salmon uses the introduction to present an overarching hermeneutical framework for readers to bear in mind when studying this biblical book. By bringing together biblical verses and pietistic phrases, Salmon crafts a pietistic approach to Lamentations that is based in a Karaite ideology and practice of mourning.

This hermeneutic of mourning, constructed from external biblical verses and brought to bear on Lamentations, provides an overall framework for understanding Lamentations. In a later section of the introduction, Salmon draws exclusively on verses from the book of Lamentations in order to identify the seven "meanings" or "purposes" of the book. There he demonstrates each meaning by linking it to a pertinent verse from Lamentations, thus weaving his pietistic interpretation into the biblical book itself. Salmon presents this list of meanings somewhat telegraphically, with limited explication of each one, and yet he reiterates these themes frequently throughout the commentary. The seven purposes of Lamentations, according to Salmon, are to: (1) present the community's regret over all that they have lost, (2) enumerate the calamities that have befallen the community, (3) disclose information that is not recorded in other prophetic books, (4) petition God about the severity of the enemies' deeds, (5) instruct the community to summon one another to repentance, (6) urge the confession of sins, and (7) announce that exile will have a permanent end. These themes are integral to the text of Lamentations itself, and Salmon reflects upon each point further in his comments on the verses from Lamentations to which it is linked.[24] These seven meanings do not constitute an approach to interpretation, but rather, they represent the major purposes of the book in Salmon's view. This organized enumeration of themes is well suited to a programmatic introduction, and Salmon shares this practice with other exegetes in the Judeo-Arabic tradition.

Within the introduction, Salmon's inquiry into the homiletical meaning of Lamentations and its purpose for his community overshadows his attention to the book's text-critical issues. This emphasis reflects Salmon's priorities; for him, exegesis is a tool for determining the spiritual instruction contained within biblical books. Still, Salmon's introduction gives some attention to basic textual questions. In addressing the authorship of Lamentations, he cites the community consensus that the book is a prophecy of Jeremiah.[25] He explains the division of the book into five chapters on liturgical grounds: each chapter of Lamentations should be said following the corresponding "book" of Psalms, which is also divided into five sections. He notes that chapters 1, 2, and 4 of Lamentations take the form of an alphabetic acrostic and states that the verses were arranged in this way in order for the educated to recall them more easily.

Salmon's homiletical and liturgical emphasis—to the virtual exclusion of serious inquiry into certain textual features—stands in contrast to the introduction to the Lamentations commentary of Yefet ben ʿEli. The core of Yefet's introduction is formed by his enumeration of fourteen questions or issues, and their answers. Like Salmon, Yefet is concerned with the religious significance of Lamentations, but he also gives sustained attention to literary

[24] (1) Lam 1:1, 7; (2) Lam 1:4, 5, 6, 10, 13; (3) Lam 1:10; (4) Lam 5:11, 12; (5) Lam 3:40; (6) Lam 1:18; 3:42; (7) Lam 4:22.

[25] Salmon's introduction, section on "Jeremiah as the Prophet of Lamentations." On the tradition of naming Jeremiah as the author of Lamentations, see Jason Kalman, "Authorship, Attribution, and Authority: Jeremiah, Baruch, and the Rabbinic Interpretation of Lamentations," *HUCA* 90 (2019): 27–87.

and textual issues that Salmon notes in passing or not at all. Yefet may pose a series of questions on a topic that Salmon addressed perfunctorily in his own introduction. For example, Yefet not only notes the alphabetic structure of Lamentations 1–4, as Salmon does, but he also asks why Lamentations 5 is not alphabetical even though it has the appropriate number of verses, and he queries why the standard order of the letters *peh* and *ʿayin* is reversed in Lamentations 2, 3, and 4.[26] Surely Salmon did not overlook such details, and yet they do not draw his sustained consideration.

It is in the introduction that Salmon indicates, often obliquely, the exegetical methods and goals that underlie the commentary. Salmon's comments incorporate a large number of prooftexts from other biblical books, so that often the meaning of his comment is not spelled out but must be deduced from the biblical verses that he has drawn together. He hints at the rationale behind this practice by stating that "many of the prophets had lamented over us, and their lamentation was set down for us so that we would add them to this separate book in order to lament for ourselves." Put another way, Salmon claims that expressions of lamentation that are similar to those of Lamentations, but found elsewhere in the biblical corpus, should be included in communal rituals of lament. Such verses are of the same kind and inspire the same spiritual practices, regardless of whether they are sourced from Lamentations or from the prophetic books; for this reason Salmon incorporates the lament verses from other biblical books into his commentary.

Salmon's project of designating and assembling lament verses follows a common exegetical practice among Jews and Muslims of using scripture to interpret scripture.[27] There is sound exegetical reasoning behind such a technique: if the words and phrases of scripture came from the same source or were revealed to communities with shared historical and social experiences, then clear linguistic usage in one passage may shed light on ambiguities in another. That said, this exegetical practice also carries religious and liturgical weight, and Salmon concerns himself primarily with these applications. By bringing far-flung verses of lament together, Salmon not only uses them to interpret the meaning of Lamentations itself but also constructs a rich composite text that effectively expands the book of Lamentations and enlarges

[26] David Noel Freedman calls Lam 5 a "nonalphabetic acrostic" to emphasize its similarity to alphabetic acrostics; see "Acrostic Poems in the Hebrew Bible: Alphabetic and Otherwise," *CBQ* 48 (1986), 415.

[27] Represented, e.g., by the maxim attributed to Ben Bag-Bag in Pirke Avot 5:22, "Turn it [Torah] and turn it again, for everything is in it," or by the Islamic principle of using one part of the Qurʾān to interpret another (*tafsīr al-qurʾān bi-l-qurʾān*).

its connections to the whole of Scripture. Just as the Karaites compiled florilegia in order to construct a tradition of liturgical poetry drawn fully from the Bible, so Salmon collects an array of biblical lament verses in order to construct a "biblical" liturgy of mourning.[28]

Salmon neglects to identify the remarkable, possibly liturgical, aspects of his commentary in his introduction. He does not explain the function of the refrains with which he concludes each verse comment, nor does he comment upon the extensive consolations (*neḥamot*) with which he concludes the commentary. While his silence on these two features may signal that they were familiar to his immediate audience and required no explanation, it is worth noting that neither feature is common among the extant commentaries of the Judeo-Arabic tradition. A litany of consolations concludes Yefet's Lamentations commentary—most likely as an echo of the *neḥamot* in Salmon's work—while refrains of the sort that Salmon appends to each verse comment may be altogether unique. The purpose of these most distinctive features remains mysterious, without explicit exposition from Salmon.[29]

Salmon presents the religious message of the book in his introduction, but he declines to explain the mechanics of his hermeneutical techniques. His lone description of the commentary's format and his exegetical approach appears straightforward but does not reveal much. At the end of the introduction, he states:

> Now I will begin the explication of the language (*alfāẓ*) of this book, then [proceed to] a summation of its meanings (*maʿānī*) and the uncovering of its intentions (*aghrāḍ*). I will mention what I have comprehended from it, based on the words of the scholars (*ʿulamāʾ*), and I will add to that what occurs to me, if there is a benefit for students in setting it down.[30]

While this statement leaves much unsaid, it does accurately describe the underlying structure of individual comments within the commentary.[31]

[28] On Karaite liturgy and biblical florilegia, see Frank, *Search Scripture Well*, 166.

[29] Salmon prefaces the *Neḥamot* section with a few sentences but does not outline a specific ritual or liturgical application. See discussion below and in chapter 5.

[30] See notes in the translation; Salmon's introduction, section on "The Structure of Lamentations and Its Significance."

[31] Yefet makes a similar statement in the introduction to his commentary on Genesis: "Our intention has been (to provide) a translation (*tarjamah*) of the words (*ʾalfāẓ*) of this Book (i.e., Genesis) and an explanation (*takhlīṣ*) of its meanings (*maʿānīhi*) according to what its words require"; see Meira Polliack, *The Karaite Tradition of Arabic Bible Translation: A Linguistic and Exegetical Study of Karaite Translations of the Pentateuch from the Tenth and Eleventh Centuries C.E.*, EJM 17 (Leiden: Brill, 1997), 41.

Salmon generally begins by explicating the language of the verse, focusing on lexicology, morphology, syntax, or grammar. He often defends an aspect of his translation by referring to biblical prooftexts or the Aramaic Targum, or by invoking a linguistic principle. Having established the linguistic level of interpretation, Salmon next considers the contextual meaning of the words and then addresses the purpose behind the verse as a whole. The distinction between the literal rendering of the language (*lafẓ*)—which Salmon represents with his Arabic translation (*tafsīr*)—and an interpretive level of meaning (*maʿnā*) is familiar from the broader tradition of Jerusalem Karaite linguistics, as represented by Salmon's younger contemporary, Yūsuf ibn Nūḥ.[32] While this tidy distinction may accurately represent the principle behind Salmon's translation and interpretation, there are many instances in which he blurs the line between the literal linguistic rendering of the biblical words and his interpretation of their meaning, as we will explore below. Salmon's programmatic statement about references to "the words of the scholars" also requires further discussion. While it is not certain exactly which scholars Salmon designates with the term *ʿulamāʾ*,[33] he routinely invokes the interpretations of others, often anonymously, either to add his voice to theirs or to point out the ways in which the scholars err. Salmon often traces such scholarly misapprehensions back to mistakes in the interpretation of biblical grammar, syntax, and vocabulary, or the failure to recognize and properly interpret figurative language in Scripture. The danger of such errors, according to Salmon, is that they may yield incorrect theological conclusions, lead to faulty religious behavior, and result in ongoing suffering and exile. In offering a correct interpretation of the language of Lamentations, Salmon endeavors also to purify the "people of the exile" and bring about their redemption.

The Translation of Lamentations

Salmon's translation of Lamentations is integral to the exegetical work of his commentary. While he aims for a literal translation of the biblical Hebrew text, following its word order and representing its syntax with parallel Arabic forms, he also takes liberties with the translation so that it better reflects and supports the way he has interpreted a given verse. This approach to

[32] Khan, *The Early Karaite Tradition*, 133–35.
[33] See note at the end of Salmon's introduction.

translation appears consistently across Salmon's exegetical corpus. In his study of Salmon's commentary on Ecclesiastes, Robinson observes that Salmon's translation style is both literal and readable and that it "works closely with the commentary, supporting and representing, really mirroring the interpretive work of the commentator."[34] Salmon's technique of using translation and commentary to reinforce one another appears in his work on Lamentations as well. The following examples illustrate Salmon's translation techniques and describe the exegetical or theological circumstances that occasion them.[35]

Translation and Figurative Imagery

The biblical text of Lamentations abounds with poetic imagery, even in its depictions of divine action.[36] Salmon generally translates figurative language into Arabic literally, even when the figure of speech compromises God's absolute incorporeality, and he expounds upon the significance of the image within his comment.[37] Occasionally, however, he decodes the imagery within the translation itself, as in his Arabic rendering of Lamentations 3:3. The biblical verse reads: *Surely against me He turns His hand again and again the whole day long.* Apparently wary of the theological untenability of attributing

[34] Robinson, *Asceticism*, 38. Robinson places Salmon's translation style in an "intermediate position" between those of Saadia and Yefet. Saadia adapted the Hebrew text in order to produce a fluid and idiomatic Arabic version, while Yefet prioritized fidelity to the Hebrew source above the creation of a readable Arabic version. A full systematic comparison between the Arabic Lamentations translations of Saadia, Salmon, and Yefet is beyond the scope of the present project. However, I have compared the three translations on certain verses of Lamentations and noted their respective features in the notes to the English translation. In the cases that I have examined, Salmon indeed represents a more flexible approach to translation, and a willingness to compromise on exact linguistic representation of the biblical text when his exegetical goals require it. From time to time Salmon adds Arabic words and phrases that are not occasioned by the biblical Hebrew source text. He may justify such additions in his comment, or let them pass without explanation. For a comparison of Saadia, Salmon and Yefet's translation of Esther, see Yefet, Esth, 191ff. On the difficulty of creating historical paradigms to account for shifts in translation style, see Dmitri Gutas, *Greek Thought, Arabic Culture: The Graeco-Arabic Translation Movement in Baghdad and Early ʿAbbasid Society*, Arabic Thought and Culture (London: Routledge, 1998), 143.

[35] On Karaite techniques of biblical translation, see Meira Polliack, *The Karaite Tradition of Arabic Bible Translation*. As Polliack's study draws from Arabic translations of the Pentateuch, Salmon's translations of the prophets and writings are not included. However, Salmon used many of the translation strategies that Polliack discusses in the book. I have noted certain examples in the notes to my translation of Salmon's Lamentations commentary.

[36] For full discussion, see chapter 4.

[37] Likewise, in his commentary on the Song of Songs, Salmon provides a literal rendering (*peshaṭ* or *ẓāhir*, i.e., the exoteric sense) in the verse translation and decodes its significance in the comment (see Frank, *Search Scripture Well*, 153).

a hand to God, Salmon renders the Hebrew word "hand" with the Arabic word *ḍarba*, meaning a "blow" or "strike."[38] Notably, Salmon does not justify his translation in his comment. Since the translation already incorporates Salmon's understanding—that God's "hand" means a divine punishment—there is no need to explain the figure of speech within the comment.

Salmon's departures from literal translation are frequently motivated by his desire to represent the contextual meaning (*maʿnā*) of the verse within the translation. In the case of Lamentations 3:32, Salmon expands his Arabic translation in order to spell out details that he says are only alluded to within the Hebrew verse. The biblical text, as translated in the RSV, reads: *But, though He cause grief* (*hogah*), *He will have compassion according to the abundance of His steadfast love.* However, for Salmon—and also for Saadia and Yefet—the meaning of the Hebrew word *hogah* was not, in this verse, "to cause grief," but rather, "to drive out," which they rendered with the Arabic root n/ḥ/w. As Salmon explains in his comment, "When [Jeremiah] says, *even though He drove out*, he alludes to the expulsion of Israel from this holy land."

In spite of his awareness that this interpretation is an allusion rather than the literal meaning of the verse, Salmon incorporates this sense into his verse translation: "Even though He drove Israel <u>out of this country and this Temple</u>, He will be merciful according to the abundance of His grace." This expansion brings Salmon's interpretation into the level of translation and happens to destroy the neat parallelism of the Hebrew verse in the process.

Linguistic Principles to Justify a Translation Choice

Salmon occasionally justifies his translation on the basis of a linguistic or exegetical principle. One linguistic principle that licenses Salmon's translations of individual words is that of interchangeable letters (*ḥurūf al-ibdāl* or *aḥruf al-ibdāl*). Salmon was personally invested in the promulgation of this linguistic rule, as he notes within the commentary that he has authored a treatise on the subject.[39] The contents of the treatise may only be guessed at, since the work is no longer extant. According to the way that Salmon

[38] In this case, Saadia translates "hand" literally into Arabic, while Yefet, like Salmon, opts for "blow." Aramaic translators made a similar move, translating "hand" to *maḥaʾ* ("stroke"); see Sasson on Yefet, Prov, 88.

[39] In his comment to Lam 1:14, he notes that he has completed a separate book on the topic of interchangeable letters: *wa-qad kuntu ʿamiltu li-hādhā l-aḥruf kitāb mufrad.*

invokes the principle in his Lamentations commentary, it seems to be based not in historical or comparative linguistics, but rather, in the observation that some Hebrew letters seem to be interchangeable, so that one letter may be substituted for its pair in order to make sense of a word whose meaning would otherwise be unclear. The pairings that Salmon suggests and supports with prooftexts in the Lamentations commentary include *zayin* and *ṣād* (Lam 1:14), *bāʾ* and *fāʾ* (Lam 3:16), *hāʾ* and *mem* (Lam 3:26), and the Hebrew letters *kaf* and *gimmel* (Lam 3:33).[40] The principle is particularly serviceable in the case of interpreting hapax legomena.[41] Salmon seems to apply this principle in the Lamentations commentary not to justify a unique or unusual translation, but rather to attach a scientific explanation to the prevailing understanding of the biblical word.

Salmon also identifies an exegetical principle that has a noticeable impact on his Arabic translations: "a term that governs itself and governs others" (*menaheg ʿaṣmo u-menaheg aḥerim*). This exegetical rule has been considered a rabbinic principle because of its Hebrew formulation and its application by later grammarians and exegetes of Rabbanite background. However, Karaite scholars also used Hebrew grammatical terminology, and Salmon provides one of the earliest attested mentions of this syntactical principle.[42] In his Lamentations commentary, Salmon uses the rule to extend the force of the Hebrew expression *ki loʾ ʿinnah millibo* (*He does not willingly*; Lam 3:33a) to the following two clauses (Lam 3:33b–34). Following the Hebrew, the RSV translates these verses as *For He does not willingly afflict or grieve the sons of men / to crush underfoot all the prisoners of the earth* (Lam 3:33–34). Yet Salmon wishes to clarify and emphasize that God does not inflict *either* of these punishments willingly. He states that the Hebrew expression governs its action—to afflict—as well as the two following actions—to grieve and to crush underfoot. He explains this interpretation in his comment to Lamentations 3:34, where he mentions the linguistic principle as well as the theological meaning that it reveals:

> *For He does not of His own accord afflict* (Lam 3:33) governs itself and others (*menaheg ʿaṣmo u-menaheg aḥerim*). This means that crushing Israel

[40] Note that Salmon uses both Arabic and Hebrew words for the Hebrew letters, except for the last pair, in which he does not name the letters, but rather demonstrates their interchangeability by citing relevant word pairs.

[41] See, e.g., *va-yagares* in Lam 3:16.

[42] See Robinson, *Asceticism*, 53–55 and bibliography there.

> beneath His blows and making them prisoners in the earth, among the nations, is not by the Lord's desire, but rather because of their offenses and their crimes.

Following this explanation, Salmon renders the "missing" component in the verse translation itself: "And it is not at all His desire to crush underfoot all the prisoners of the earth."[43]

Our final example also demonstrates Salmon's application of linguistic reasoning to biblical translation. The passage that culminates with Lamentations 3:56–60 has long troubled exegetes. The Hebrew verbs are in the past tense, but the episode to which they refer is not explicitly identified. Further, the surrounding text suggests that the actions would be better understood as future indicatives, imperatives, or precatives.[44] With a mixture of Hebrew and Arabic linguistic terminology, Salmon explains:

> Know that the articulation of all of these words (*alfāẓ*) is an articulation of the *past* (*ʿavar*) [. . .] but their meaning (*maʿnā*) is in the *future* (*ʿatid*). In the Hebrew language, there are many such as these. [. . .] All of this language (*lafẓ*) [is expressed] in the *past* (*ʿavar*), but at the time when it was said, nothing of the sort had happened. The meaning (*maʿnā*) of all of them is *future* (*ʿatid*).[45]

Here Salmon invokes principles of linguistic analysis that are also found in Karaite exegetical manuals of his near contemporaries, al-Qirqisānī and Ibn Nūḥ.[46] In Ibn Nūḥ's remarks on Proverbs 30:9 in the *Diqduq*, for example, he uses an identical mixture of Hebrew and Arabic terminology to state authoritatively that "there are words that have a *past* form but a *future* meaning (*ʾalfāẓuhā ʿavar wa-maʿnāhā ʿatid*)." With this formulation, Ibn Nūḥ similarly differentiates between the language (*lafẓ*) and the meaning (*maʿnā*) in matters of Hebrew tense.

From this point onward, Salmon translates both the language and its meaning in his Arabic rendering of Lamentations 3:57–60. The doubling of

[43] Underlined passages indicate Arab. words that Salmon has added to his translation, which are not present in the Masoretic Hebrew text.

[44] See Iain W. Provan, "Past, Present, and Future in Lamentations 3:52–66: The Case for a Precative Perfect Re-Examined," *VT* 41 (1991): 164–75.

[45] See Salmon's comment to Lam 3:56 and notes there.

[46] See Hirschfeld, Qirqisāni Studies, 35–36 (eighteenth premise), and Khan, *The Early Karaite Tradition*, 134–35.

language and meaning in each verse results in a clumsy, cacophonous Arabic prose. Salmon translates Lamentations 3:57, for example, as follows: "You came near—that is to say, 'You will come near'—when I call on You. You said—that is to say, 'You will say'—'Do not fear!' " It sounds as though Salmon speaks two voices with a single breath. But his intention is to demonstrate that language and meaning both inhere in the biblical text.

In this case, the linguistic principle behind Salmon's translation is further supported by his concept of prophecy. Salmon follows the traditional view that these verses from Lamentations were spoken by the prophet Jeremiah. Like similar prophetic locutions and imagery from the psalms, the words of Lamentations had meaning during their own historical time, and they also communicate instruction to later generations, during the exile.[47] Salmon considers these verses to be Jeremiah's instruction for Jews in exile. The verse teaches that "Whenever we cried out to Him and returned to Him, He would accept us and transfer us out of this exile," and it thereby instructs the Jews of the exile to call out to God and repent.[48] As with his use of *menaheg ʿaṣmo u-menaheg aḥerim* described above, Salmon first explains the grammatical principle in his comment, and thereafter he applies it to his translation without comment.

The Verse Comments

Salmon further articulates his exegetical and doctrinal agenda within the verse comments. The comments are governed by an overall structure that is shared with other Arabic biblical commentaries: for each individual verse there is a Hebrew incipit, an Arabic translation of the verse, and an Arabic comment.[49] To this pattern Salmon adds a refrain at the conclusion of nearly every comment, consisting of a pious exhortation and a biblical verse. Yet within this fixed structure there is tremendous variety in the content, literary style, and length of each comment. Some are mere Arabic paraphrases of the verse while others constitute extended essays including lexical points,

47 Salmon gestures toward the prophetic underpinnings of his distinction between past and future by citing Ps 79:1–2 in his linguistic explanation of past language and future meaning in his comment to Lam 3:55. See Salmon's comment to Lam 3:1 for the full reference.

48 Salmon's comment to Lam 3:55.

49 Note that Salmon does not cluster verses together in order to treat them as a unit, as does Yefet ben ʿEli. Even in the case of Lam 3, where three biblical verses represent each letter of the alphabet and often form a syntactic unit, Salmon maintains his pattern of presenting each verse separately.

citations of another scholar's interpretation, references to rabbinic literature, applications of the verse to Salmon's own time, polemics, homilies, and phrases of Hebrew religious poetry (*piyyuṭ*). Salmon draws heavily on biblical literature outside of Lamentations—primarily the Psalms and prophetic corpus, and even the historical books when background information is required—and in some cases his sustained attention to these passages amounts to a second commentary embedded within the Lamentations commentary. The comment on the first verse of each chapter generally yields an introduction to the specific themes of that chapter, and homiletical excursuses on related themes pop up throughout the commentary. The richness and variety of Salmon's responses to the verses of Lamentations suggest a supple hermeneutic, in which the biblical book provides an open framework for religious instruction and reflection. While Salmon operates within the basic pattern of the commentary, he freely explores whatever linguistic, historical, or ideological matter seems to him worthy of discussion. In one moment a pedagogue, in another moment a preacher or a poet, Salmon speaks in the voice that best carries his message in explicating that particular verse and conveying its instruction to the community.

Biblical Citations from Outside Lamentations

If the Bible speaks in human language, as the saying goes, then Salmon speaks in the language of the Bible.[50] His commentary is written in Arabic, and yet it is thoroughly infused with Hebrew, from Hebrew words to biblical or rabbinic phrases, to long Hebrew passages—whether of his own design or directly imported from the Hebrew Scriptures. Of course, the use of prooftexts and parallel passages to explicate Scripture is not unique to Salmon, to Karaite exegesis, or to the tradition of Jewish biblical scholarship. Yet the way that Salmon consistently and deftly weaves biblical language into his own illustrates the degree to which Karaite scholars actively absorbed biblical parlance. There is little distinction, especially in certain homilies,

[50] Karaites were not shy about using this originally rabbinic phrase (BT Berakhot 31b: דברה התורה בלשון בני אדם) in their own exegetical contexts. Al-Qirqisānī lists it among his exegetical principles (Hirschfeld, *Qirqisāni Studies*, 25–26; fourth premise). Salmon repeats it in Hebrew in his commentary on Song of Songs (see Frank, *Search Scripture Well*, 152) and paraphrases it in his Arab. commentary on Lamentations (*taqrīb ʿalā ifhām banī ādam*; see Salmon's comments on Lam 1:22 and 2:6 and the discussion in chapter 4).

between Salmon's citation of a biblical verse and his own creative voice, as he uses the language of the Bible to communicate medieval piety. The mission of Karaism was to draw all religious and social practices from the well of Scripture, and to reject any practices, be they legal or liturgical, that were borne of human innovation rather than divine instruction. The ability to speak the language of the Bible, then, plays a crucial role in the Karaite project of aligning Jewish spirituality with God's command, and ensuring that Karaite principles match biblical teachings in form as well as substance.

The most frequent, and perhaps the most scholarly, attention to biblical language arises in Salmon's project of clarifying biblical grammar, syntax, or vocabulary on the basis of biblical prooftexts. Salmon seems always to have a prooftext at the ready, which suggests his personal mastery of the Bible as well as his familiarity with the interpretive connections that circulated within his scholarly community. Often the prooftext consists of only a single word or brief phrase, set up to demonstrate the linguistic similarities between a problematic case in Lamentations and a more straightforward one elsewhere, in terse formulations that Ibn Nūḥ would also employ.

These prooftexts generally provide justification for an interpretive choice that Salmon has also woven into his Arabic translation or paraphrase. At Lamentations 1:12, for example, Salmon notes that the absence of an interrogative *heh* notwithstanding, the ostensible statement ought to be understood as a question: "Is it nothing to you?" To support this reading, he lines up two other cases in which a simple negative particle is understood, through context, to indicate a negative interrogative. He exercises some restraint in comparison with al-Qirqisānī who, less than half a century beforehand, offered no fewer than twenty-two prooftexts to illustrate the same syntactic principle. Al-Qirqisānī indicates that there is some controversy over the matter, but Salmon says no such thing; perhaps this exegetical issue was less contested by his own time.[51] In his comment to Lamentations 1:16, Salmon marshals five single-word prooftexts to support his translation of the word *bokhiyyah* as a feminine active participle. Salmon does not explain the morphology behind this irregular verbal pattern but relies on the amassing of analogous cases to make his point. By contrast, Ibn Nūḥ makes the same point without any prooftexts, simply by noting that the letter *yod* was added to the original, regular pattern.[52]

[51] Hirschfeld, *Qirqisāni Studies*, 35.
[52] Ibn Nūḥ, *Diqduq*, 476.

The quick, language-based prooftexts typically appear in the first lines of Salmon's comments, where he sorts out linguistic obscurities before delving into more complicated matters. In addition to those short biblical citations, Salmon also reproduces long narrative passages from the Bible in his excursuses. These longer passages may provide biblical-historical context for a verse from Lamentations or lend concrete meaning to the book's poetic imagery. Salmon's sources for such biblical passages include the books of Kings and Chronicles, each of which he identifies as a "copy" (*nuskha*) of the other, as well as relevant historical narratives from the prophets Jeremiah and Ezekiel. As often as not, Salmon's historical-contextual applications of such biblical passages open the door to the homiletical or theological points that are never far from his mind.

Salmon cites 2 Kings 17:7–23 in just such a capacity in his excursus to Lamentations 1:8, which opens with the statement that *Jerusalem sinned grievously*. Not satisfied to read such a theologically provocative statement vaguely, Salmon crafts an extended excursus to indicate the precise sins that the Israelites committed in the biblical period and continue to commit during the exile. He begins this barrage of biblical evidence by rehearsing the sins committed during the reign of Hoshea ben Elah, which resulted in the exile of the ten tribes. Salmon accomplishes this task by citing 2 Kings 17 in extenso.

In other cases, Salmon cuts and pastes biblical narratives in order to craft his own argument out of the raw materials of biblical history. In his comment to Lamentations 4:1, Salmon enumerates the grave sins committed during the reigns of Jehoiakim and Zedekiah by bringing together various pieces of the narrative from Jeremiah. Rather than adhering to the order of Jeremiah's account as recorded in the Bible, Salmon constructs his own narrative arrangement, linking each sin to the preceding one with phrases such as *wa-min dhālika* ("and [included] among [the vile deeds] is"); *fa-ʿind dhālika* ("so at that point"); and *thumma* ("then" or "next"), crafting a coherent narrative with great rhetorical impact, in which the persecution of Jeremiah himself provides the climax. In Salmon's reconstructed biblical chronicle, the king burns Jeremiah's scroll rather than heeding the prophet's warning (Jer 36:22–23); he strategizes about murdering the Lord's prophets (Jer 26:20–23, 38:4) only because they brought the threatening word of God (Jer 26:11, 11:21), and finally, Jeremiah is attacked (Jer 37:15, 38:6; 37:15–16). Salmon structures the prophet's narrative as a litany of the grave sins committed by the Israelites, as sanctioned and even commanded by the kings of the time.

Just as Salmon uses biblical verses to craft a homiletical reading of history, so he uses biblical language to articulate his theological principles. A case in point is the premise that God may cause the death of a righteous person not as punishment, but in order to rescue that individual from imminent suffering. Salmon expounds upon this principle with reference to passages from Kings, Chronicles, and Isaiah in the course of his discussion of Lamentations 4:20. The verse, according to Salmon's translation, reads as follows: "The breath of our nostrils, the LORD's anointed, was ensnared by their corruption, of whom we said, 'Under his shadow we shall live among the nations.' "

Salmon's verse comment follows traditional Jewish exegesis in identifying King Josiah as the figure obliquely referred to with phrases such as "breath of our nostrils," "the LORD's anointed," and "his shadow." These references to the praiseworthy Josiah direct Salmon's attention to a long-standing conundrum in religious history. Josiah is uniformly recognized as a good and pious leader, who took it upon himself to bring the Israelites back to the Torah and to proper worship of the one God. Salmon confirms Josiah's excellence by citing 2 Chronicles 34:2–3 and 2 Kings 23:25 and neatly summarizing both passages in Arabic: "The entire account explicates his virtues and his seemly deeds." Given Josiah's unsullied reputation as a heroically pious leader in an age of religious disobedience, it is difficult to account for his death in battle at the peak of his kingship and in the midst of his program of religious reform.

Salmon considers this historical moment in theologically charged terms. He notes that the Israelites "did not deserve for someone like Josiah to remain among them." He justifies this reading with a purposeful translation of the verse. The Hebrew phrase *nilkad beshḥiytotam*, which literally means, "he was taken in their pits," means, for Salmon, that Josiah was "ensnared by their corruption." In other words, because the pious Josiah was surrounded by evil and sin, he would suffer unfairly under whatever communal punishment his community brought upon themselves—in this case, the exile—unless God intervened. Thus, in an act of divine mercy and fairness, God arranged for the early death of this righteous leader and spared him from undeserved retribution:

> Since God willed that Josiah would not see the exile, He made him pass away as a trial (*mumtaḥin*) in order to compensate him (*li-yaʿūḍahu*) in the Abode of the Hereafter (*dār al-ākhira*), as it is said, *For the righteous man is taken away from calamity* (Isa 57:1). This was elucidated by the prophecy of Hulda the prophetess, when she said, *because your heart was penitent*

> *and you humbled yourself before God when you heard His words* (2 Kgs 22:19 = 2 Chr 34:27); but, *Behold, I will gather you to your fathers, and you shall be gathered to your grave in peace* [*and your eyes shall not see all the evil which I will bring upon this place and its inhabitants*] (2 Kgs 22:20 = 2 Chr 34:28). *In peace* means that he would not see the exile, just as it was said to Abraham, *As for yourself, you shall go to your fathers in peace* (Gen 15:15)—in other words, "you will not see servitude and affliction."

Salmon locates the foundational biblical evidence for this theological principle in Isaiah 57:1: *The righteous man perishes, and no one lays it to heart; devout men are taken away, while no one understands. For the righteous man is taken away from calamity.* The righteous die prematurely not because they have sinned but because God wishes to exempt them from the suffering that is due to their generation. Salmon expounds upon this biblical teaching with theological vocabulary and concepts that also drive Muʿtazilite discussions of God's just role in human suffering. He hastens to assert, for example, that God compensated King Josiah for the trial of his premature departure. Salmon advances this interpretation of Josiah's death not with explicitly theological arguments, but rather with supporting examples from Scripture.

The verse from Isaiah is explicated in this fashion also by Yefet ben ʿEli. Although Yefet does not mention an allusion to King Josiah in his own comment to Lamentations 4:20, he shares with Salmon the conviction that God removed the righteous Josiah as an act of kindness. Yefet also explains the confusion that this act may cause for those who witness it—and, presumably, for those who interpret the biblical account of it:

> *And no man lays it to heart* shows that they do not consider (*yafkurū*) when they do not see (*yabṣirū*) the righteous one among them, and similarly, they do not think discriminately (*yumayyizūna*) about their conditions when they see that the righteous one has died. They say, "Woe is upon us, because the death of the pious ones (*al-ṣāliḥīn*) indicates great wrath, as it is said, *that the righteous man is gathered from calamity*." Indeed, God made him die before the affliction that you will see, because his death was better (*aṣlaḥ*) for him than his being in the midst of the trouble, just as it was said to Josiah, *Therefore, behold, I will gather you to your fathers* (2 Kgs 22:20).[53]

[53] Yefet, Isa 57:1–2.

Like Salmon, Yefet draws upon the passages from Kings, Chronicles, and Isaiah in order to produce compelling theological explanations of historical events. These exegetical passages are rich with Muʿtazilite concepts, from the compensation (*ʿiwaḍ*) awarded for trials endured, to God's kindness in doing what is best (*aṣlaḥ*) for the individual human being. Even the exegetes' confidence in divine justice in the face of apparently contrary evidence suggests the influence of Muʿtazilite thought. The biblical context of such discussions enables Karaite exegetes to affirm and explore Arabic theological concepts by rooting them in Jewish Scripture.

In the examples above, Salmon pulls biblical passages from outside Lamentations into the commentary in order to explain difficult language, provide historical context, or substantiate a theological reading. Our next and final example of biblical citations from outside Lamentations concerns Salmon's practice of embedding sustained commentaries on pericopes from other biblical books within his excursuses. In these cases, Salmon temporarily shifts his attention away from the Lamentations verse at hand and produces a methodical, organized comment on another biblical passage, complete with Hebrew lemmata, Arabic translations, and Arabic comment.[54]

These mini-commentaries on passages from other biblical books follow the same exegetical patterns that structure Salmon's main commentary. Thus, Lawrence Marwick remarked that "these passages reveal all the features of independent commentaries" and hypothesized that Salmon had compiled full commentaries on biblical books such as Jeremiah and Ezekiel, which he excerpted in the Lamentations commentary.[55] On its face, this suggestion is not unreasonable. The embedded commentaries of Psalms 42 and 79 (in the excursuses at Lam 3:20 and 2:4, respectively) are verbatim citations from Salmon's Psalms commentary, which shows that Salmon was not averse to importing lengthy citations from his own previously written commentaries into the commentary on Lamentations. Salmon's ability to produce major commentaries on Psalms, Song of Songs, and Lamentations in less than two years suggests that additional exegetical compositions would not have exceeded his intellectual reach. Still, it is improbable that Salmon would have authored commentaries on Kings, Isaiah, Jeremiah, Ezekiel, and the Minor

[54] The following embedded commentaries are included in my translation (Part 2): Salmon's excursuses to Lam 1:2 (Ezek 23); Lam 2:4 (Ps 79); Lam 3:1 (Isa 22); Lam 3:20 (Ps 42); and Lam 4:1 (Jer 8; Ezek 11 and 24).

[55] Marwick, "Studies in Salmon," 315–19.

Prophets, all of which were entirely lost and never mentioned, either by Salmon himself or by later authors.

The presence of well-developed miniature commentaries within Salmon's excursuses may reflect a compilatory aspect of Salmon's exegetical project and indicate that he drew on his considerable experience studying these biblical texts prior to composing the commentaries. Further, the insertion of such comments from biblical books on which Salmon is not known to have written commentaries indicates that he did not draw so heavily on his Psalms commentary simply out of convenience. A more likely explanation for the prevalence of material from Psalms in the Lamentations commentary is that Salmon detected an affinity between the two books, especially in their liturgical capacities and suitability for prayer, but in additional senses as well, and that, on those grounds, he considered the verses from Psalms to be particularly relevant to those of Lamentations.[56] Indeed, verses from Psalms are heavily represented in Salmon's excursuses and throughout the Lamentations commentary.

In his excursus at Lamentations 3:20, Salmon introduces Psalm 42:7/6 as a parallel passage. The verse from Lamentations reads: *My soul continually calls it to mind, and is bowed down within me.* Salmon glosses this verse and immediately connects it to its twin from Psalms: "'She remembers what has passed and departed from her, and she is bowed down and is broken since she has no consolation and no comforter.' Likewise, the [sage of the] Koraḥites said, *My God, my soul is cast down within me,* [*therefore I remember You from the land of Jordan and of Hermon, from Mount Mizar*] (Ps 42:7/6)." From this point onward, Salmon focuses his exegetical attention on the passage from Psalms with no explicit discussion about what it offers his interpretation of Lamentations 3:20. He cites his interpretation almost verbatim from the commentary on Psalms that he completed the previous year, which would have been fresh in his mind, quick to hand, or simply part of his acquired hermeneutical reserve. This embedded commentary leads Salmon into exegetical territory that the Lamentations verse itself does not immediately suggest. Salmon presents an actualized interpretation of the Psalms imagery in which he discusses the instability of Jewish life in exile—and specifically under Islamic rule[57]—and insists that pilgrimage, sacrifice, gratitude to God, and

[56] On Psalms and Lamentations in the Jerusalem Karaite liturgy, see Frank, *Search Scripture Well*, chapter 5. Salmon himself notes in his introduction that Lamentations, like the Psalms, is divided into five sections so that a section of Lamentations could be recited following a section of Psalms.

[57] This interpretation will be discussed in the next section, "Citations from Other Scholars."

patience are obligatory for Jews during this distressing time. It is only after concluding this lengthy comment on Psalm 42:7/6–43:4 that Salmon returns to Lamentations 3:20, and even then, he makes no attempt to apply the message of Psalms to this verse. Rather, he closes the frame in the same terms that he used to introduce the embedded commentary: simply by noting that one verse is like the other. This rubric suggests a Karaite hermeneutic of parallel biblical passages that, to my knowledge, has not been fully explored.

Citations from Other Scholars

Salmon routinely cites the opinions of other scholars in the commentary. He identifies his sources not by name but occasionally by their affiliation, as when he attributes a perspective to the rabbinic sages, whom he refers to as "the first ones" (*al-awāʾil*).[58] Rarely he uses a dysphemistic epithet, such as "one of those who does not understand," to refer to a source with whom he disagrees.[59] For the most part Salmon accepts the interpretations that he flags as coming from an external source, tacitly approving them by drawing them into the flow of his own comment. If not for introductory formulae such as "it is said" (*qīla*), "they said" (*qālū*), or "one of the scholars said" (*qāla baʿḍ al-ʿulamāʾ*), the comment's external origin would go unnoticed. In accord with Karaite principles of scripturalism, Salmon condones the opinions of other scholars not on the basis of their personal authority but on the basis of their relevance to the discussion.[60]

Salmon incorporates a preexisting interpretation into his own in his excursus to Lamentations 3:20. At this point in the excursus, Salmon uses a verse from the Psalms to refer to the miserable conditions of exile that motivate the pious to call upon God for salvation.[61] Salmon notes that "some of the scholars—may God have mercy on them—said that in this verse he means the four kingdoms" because the biblical imagery alludes to the empires of Babylon, Persia, Greece, and Islam (= "the son of Hagar"). Salmon does not explicitly evaluate the admissibility of this interpretive tradition,

[58] See Salmon's comments to Lam 1:8 and 3:1. On Salmon's engagement with rabbinic sources, see chapter 3.

[59] See Salmon's comment to Lam 3:53.

[60] On Karaite scripturalism, see Daniel Frank, "The Limits of Karaite Scripturalism: Problems in Narrative Exegesis," in *"A Word Fitly Spoken": Studies in Qurʾān and Bible Exegesis, Presented to Haggai Ben-Shammai*, ed. M. Bar-Asher et al. (Jerusalem: Ben-Zvi Institute, 2007), 41–82.

[61] Ps 42:7/6.

but his discussion continues to build on it, showing that he accepts it as a legitimate interpretation. Further proof of Salmon's approval appears in his Psalms commentary, where he weaves the same explanation into his comment without attributing it to other scholars.

Since Salmon implicitly offers this explanation in his own name in the Psalms commentary, we may wonder why he accredits it to others in the Lamentations commentary. This particular interpretation reads the words of Psalm 42:7/6 prognostically, as direct references to the world empires that arose in the post-biblical era.[62] More to the point, it carries great apocalyptic weight in the Karaite construction of history. The Jerusalem Karaites believed their community and its spiritual program to be a vital step in the march toward redemption and the End of Days.[63] This apocalyptic sensibility pervades the Karaite commentaries on Daniel and the Song of Songs, and it remains operative even in the Karaite works for which it is not a central theme. While Salmon repeatedly insists that Lamentations offers "instruction for Israel" (*taʿlīm le-yiśraʾel*), his Lamentations commentary contains relatively few examples of actualizing interpretations, in which a biblical verse alludes to specific events in Karaite salvation history. In other words, Salmon strives to elucidate the message and purpose of Lamentations for his community through homiletical excursuses and passages of liturgical poetry. Only rarely in the Lamentations commentary does Salmon communicate these messages at the level of biblical interpretation per se. The actualizing interpretation of Psalm 42:7/6 fits Salmon's religious ideology, but not his generally contextual approach to biblical interpretation. Thus, presenting it as the opinion of other scholars may be Salmon's way of suggesting this reading without burdening himself with having to prove its biblical bona fides in this passage of the commentary.

In other cases, Salmon is more explicit about his judgment of the opinion that he cites. In his comment to Lamentations 3:4, he conveys two different interpretations and notes that the first is more likely. In his comment to Lamentations 4:6, he cites three separate interpretations and affirms one of them by incorporating it into his own translation of the verse.

Salmon does not condone all of the opinions that he elects to cite. In at least two cases he cites the opinion of another scholar so as to refute and correct it. These pedagogical comments have significant theological and eschatological

[62] On prognostic exegesis in Karaism, see Polliack, "Major Trends," 379–88.
[63] See Erder, "The Negation of Exile"; and Frank, *Search Scripture Well*, chapter 4.

implications. In one excursus, Salmon argues that the scholars' erroneous interpretations of Numbers 14:33 lead them to misconstrue the nature of retribution, continue to sin, fail to repent, and thereby prolong the exile.[64] In his discussion of Lamentations 3:55, Salmon shows how a scholar's misinterpretation of the biblical verses leads him to ignore valuable prophetic instruction and, again, to prolong the days of exile. The first case is discussed in some detail in chapter 6, which addresses the role of historical reflection in Salmon's hermeneutic. The second case merits further attention here, especially since, in addition to showing Salmon's refutation of an established scholarly opinion, it offers some insight into Salmon's negotiation between historical-contextual and actualizing forms of interpretation. I shall turn to that case now.

Actualizing Interpretations

The Karaite reputation for historical-contextual modes of interpretation is well earned. Yet Karaite exegetes did not practice this form of exegesis to the absolute exclusion of the nonliteral interpretive strategies that are typically associated with the rabbinic tradition. To the contrary, they purposefully read certain biblical passages as references to their own movement or their role in salvation history. Meira Polliack describes this hermeneutic as the Karaite tendency to "actualize" Scripture and notes that it is especially prominent in connection with prophetic works, since "the prophets were conceived as imparting an eternally divine message, whose relevance is a-temporal, in that it may be realized beyond the specific limitations of historical time and place."[65] Salmon's Lamentations commentary certainly fits this description. The commentary is shaped as much by his homiletical, spiritual, and didactic styles of interpretation as it is by his skill for grammatical, philological, and contextual scholarship. Indeed, Salmon's ability to weave the contextual and actualizing modes together is the greater part of his genius. He embraces the actualizing potential of Lamentations, using historical and literary analysis to determine the prophet Jeremiah's original message and then projecting it forward to the "people of the exile."

[64] See comment to Lam 5:7 and my discussion in chapter 6.
[65] Polliack, "Major Trends," 380, 367.

Salmon's commentary on Lamentations 3:52–55 presents a fine example of his actualizing tendencies, because he advances this interpretation *contra* the contextual interpretation of another exegete. In the biblical passage, a first-person voice describes his suffering at the hands of his enemies. The enemies hunt him down without cause and then fling him into a pit and cast stones at him. As the water threatens to drown him, he calls on the divine name "from the depths of the pit." Salmon explicates the passage as follows:

> He means that they call upon You, O Lord, from this *exile*, which resembles *the depths of the pit*, as it is said, *You have put me in the depths of the pit* (Ps 88:7/6). One of those who does not understand has supposed that the verse *They smothered my life in the pit* (Lam 3:53) and the rest of what is mentioned were Jeremiah's words to himself when he was thrown into the pit, but this errs in [several] respects. The first of them is the statement *and cast stones upon me* (Lam 3:53), for neither stones nor anything else was thrown at him. The second is that he said, *water flowed over my head* (Lam 3:54), but the pit into which Jeremiah was thrown had no water in it, as he said, *and there was no water in the cistern, but only mire* (Jer 38:6). Indeed, it is correct in all respects that this [passage] is not said about Jeremiah, but it must be that all of these verses were said about Israel, as instruction (*taʿlīm*) for them, as we have explained above. [. . .] "I called on Your name, O LORD, from the depths of the pit." He means that when he compared this *exile* to the *depths of the pit*, he said, *I called on Your name, O LORD.* [. . .] The Mighty and Sublime had promised that whenever we cried out to Him and returned to Him, He would accept us and transfer us out of this *exile*.

Salmon begins with an Arabic paraphrase in which "the pit" of the biblical text is rendered prognostically as a reference to the exile. Taking a step back, Salmon explains that another scholar—to whom he refers dismissively with the epithet "he who does not understand"—has tried to interpret the verses according to their historical-contextual meaning. In this interpretation, the verses seem to be Jeremiah's own expressions of fear and frustration during the time when he was thrown into a cistern by his enemies, as recorded in Jeremiah 38. But this interpretation is not supported by the facts. The report of Jeremiah's abuse at the hands of his enemies does not corroborate the details of the imagery from Lamentations since, in that account, no stones were hurled at the prophet and no water covered his head. Having discredited this other scholar's interpretation on textual grounds, Salmon proceeds to support his own, actualizing reading. The image of the pit alludes to the exile, and the prophet's words about crying out to God inform the community in exile that they too must call out to God for salvation. As soon as the community cries out to God in penitence, Salmon explains, God will accept the community and bring the exile to an immediate end. When redemption is the reward of correct interpretation, the penalties of misinterpretation are severe.

The other scholar's interpretation, which Salmon cites and rejects, is historical-contextual. It relates the verses to the prophet's time and indeed to the prophet's lived experience, while Salmon extends the verses to speak to his own time, and to resonate with the political difficulties and messianic aspirations of the medieval Jewish community. Polliack has noted that such actualizing readings of Scripture "tend to appear when the text yields itself to such possibilities, for instance, when it uses metaphors or other forms of symbolic language."[66] Yet determinations of symbolic language are often subjective. Here the contradictions between the two biblical accounts involving Jeremiah and a pit are sufficient to suggest that a literal reading of the pit is untenable. More to the point, Salmon's actualizing reading is rooted in, and mandated by, his overarching approach to the book of Lamentations, and to its third chapter in particular. In his opening excursus at Lamentations 3, Salmon identifies the chapter as prophetic speech designated as instruction for Israel. He draws extensively on Psalm 79 in order to argue that the prophet's words do not refer to his own past experience but carry a message for the future people of the exile. The offending interpretation of Lamentations 3:52–55 thus threatens to undermine the actualizing foundations of Salmon's approach to the book of Lamentations. Salmon rejects this interpretation in no uncertain terms in order to uphold the liturgical purpose and homiletical value that he has assigned to Lamentations as a whole.

Salmon's definitive rejection of the literal-contextual interpretation of these verses recalls the ongoing Karaite–Rabbanite debate about the purpose of the psalms.[67] In that debate, Salmon argues *contra* Saadia that the psalms are prophetic utterances, which Jews are required to use as their own prayers while in exile. Thus, his interpretation of Lamentations 3:55 as

66 Polliack, "Major Trends," 386.
67 See Simon, *Four Approaches*, esp. chapters 1–3.

further prophetic instruction for exilic prayer coheres with his position in the Karaite–Rabbanite debate about prayer.

The actualizing sensibility within Salmon's commentary is grounded in his approach to Lamentations as a source of ethical instruction for the community in exile. Certain verses or images allude to the exile in order to alert the pious that they must apply the prophet's words to their own situation. The focus here is not on the predictive value of such imagery, but on its applicability to the religious life of medieval Jewry. This focus on piety as the ultimate purpose of an actualizing reading is apparent in Salmon's comment to Lamentations 3:48. The weeping imagery of the verse elicits this explanation:

> By this he means the abundant crying and mourning over what has befallen us during this long, lingering, difficult, afflicted exile. The first thing a person is obliged to do is cry over his sins because they are the cause of our tarrying in this exile, as it is said, *My eyes shed streams of tears* (Ps 119:136). Next [he is obliged to cry over] the weakness and rupture, decline, humiliation, and disgrace that we experience in [exile].

The connection between this imagery and the exile is not the end goal of Salmon's interpretation, but only its preliminary foundation. Having established that this verse alludes to the exile, Salmon directs the community in exile to follow through on its instruction, fulfilling their religious obligation by weeping over their sins and shedding tears over the lowly state of the community.

Salmon's actualizing tendencies run alongside his commitments to contextual reading and support his efforts to draw religious instruction from the biblical text. He teaches a practical piety in which repentance, enacted through mourning and rituals of lamentation, brings redemption and the end of exile. While the focus of this instruction concerns ritual and religious praxis, these actions fit into a broader Karaite theological perspective. Salmon foregrounds the pietistic elements of this theology in his homiletical excursuses, where he discourses at length on the sins of Israel and their eschatological consequences. Elsewhere, however, he communicates and confirms the same religious teachings in more precise formulations. Perhaps the most succinct expression of Salmon's theological framework appears in the refrains that conclude his comment on each verse of Lamentations.

The Refrain

Salmon caps each verse comment with a formula consisting of two parts: a pious statement in Arabic, which leads into a Hebrew biblical verse. This refrain changes from chapter to chapter but remains largely consistent within each individual chapter of Lamentations.[68] The refrain following Salmon's comment to each verse of Lamentations 1, for example, combines an explanatory confession along with a verse from Jeremiah: "All these calamities befell us because of the magnitude of our offenses, as it is said, *And the LORD says: 'Because they have forsaken My law which I set before them, and have not obeyed My voice, or walked in accord with it'* (Jer 9:12)." The refrain in Lamentations 4 echoes the same teaching: "And all these calamities overtook us because of the magnitude of our offenses, as it is said, *Your iniquities have turned these away, and your sins have kept good from you* (Jer 5:25)." The other chapters include biblical refrain verses from Jeremiah 22:21 (Lam 2); 2 Kings 18:12 (Lam 3); and Lamentations 5:16 (Lam 5).

In each instance, the Arabic portion of the refrain is a confession of communal sin, either explicitly or implicitly presented as the cause of exile and punishment. This confession is largely expressed in the first-person plural, except in Lamentations 3, where it is in the third-person plural. The Hebrew verse then confirms the Arabic expression of guilt, providing specific biblical proof of Israelite sin. Taken cumulatively, the refrains convey a dogmatic narrative of sin and its requital. The Israelites have forsaken the divine law (Lam 1), refused to listen to God in their time of prosperity (Lam 2), transgressed the covenant that God commanded through Moses (Lam 3), and committed iniquities (Lam 4). For all these reasons they say, *Woe to us, for we have sinned!* (Lam 5:16; the biblical verse used in the refrain throughout Lam 5). Thus, both individually and collectively, the refrains recapitulate the central doctrine of Lamentations according to Salmon's perspective. Further, they carry out the obligation of confessing sins that Salmon has listed among the seven principal themes of Lamentations.[69]

Curiously, Salmon does not announce this feature or explain its purpose in the introduction to the commentary. He does not indicate whether the refrains are his own contribution or whether he has inherited them, whether he is advocating for their inclusion or whether they are already part

[68] The Arab. element may be phrased differently between comments, but the biblical verse remains the same. The refrain is missing from Lam 3:25–33, 38–41, 50, 55–66.

[69] See Salmon's introduction, section on "Seven Meanings of Lamentations."

of normative Karaite practice. He does not inform the reader of a function that these verses may have had among the Mourners for Zion, in their worship or ritual service. They do not seem to have an exegetical value—for example, in summarizing the specific religious themes of a given chapter of Lamentations—yet they appear as though they are part of the verse comment. Even the manuscripts make no effort to set these formulas apart from the surrounding exegetical text. The scribes may incorporate distinct scripts to differentiate between Hebrew incipits and Arabic comments, for example, but when it comes to the refrains, they faithfully transmit them without paleographic differentiation. Scribes generally copy the Arabic statement in full even when they abbreviate the biblical verse component of the refrain.

Haggai Ben-Shammai has proposed that Salmon's Lamentations commentary was a liturgical model for the Jerusalem Karaites, and that the refrain formula provided a frame for their liturgical practice.[70] According to this theory, the community of Mourners would publicly recite the verses of Lamentations and the refrain, and the leader would insert into this frame *piyyuṭim*, pious exhortations, homilies, and even commentary. The exegetical aspects of the commentary, then, are secondary to these liturgical components. In Lamentations 3, especially, Ben-Shammai argues, each of Salmon's brief comments is mere preamble for the liturgical refrain.

Such a liturgical context reflects the religious priorities that Salmon advocates throughout the Lamentations commentary, and that are familiar from other Karaite sources. The communal recitation of these verses would fulfill the obligation to confess sins, mourn, and repent, which Salmon enumerates in his introduction and reiterates countless times thereafter. The biblical source of these prayers is appropriate to the Karaite program of drawing exclusively on Scripture for religious instruction.

However, the presence of a refrain does not necessarily mean that this text was intended for, or derived from, public recitation in an oral life-setting. Barbara Johnstone has questioned the once-dominant scholarly notion that repetitive discourse, such as the refrain, is the mark of orality or poetry.[71] In her study of modern Arabic written discourse, Johnstone explores the persuasive potential of repetition in written documents. In religious arguments especially, she notes, "argumentation by presentation"—that is

70 Ben-Shammai, "Poetic Works and Lamentations."

71 Barbara Johnstone, *Repetition in Arabic Discourse: Paradigms, Syntagms, and the Ecology of Language* (Philadelphia: J. Benjamins, 1991), 113–14.

to say, the repeated presentation of a truth, elegantly expressed, as opposed to arguments based in evidence and proof—may prove the most effective means of argumentation.

Johnstone notes that examples of "argumentation by presentation" are found in the Hebrew Bible as well as the Qur'ān and classical Arabic oratory.[72] These sources straddle the divide between the oral and the written, as all three existed, at least in part, in oral settings before gradually achieving the written formulations that were known in Salmon's time. The oral roots of such literature, however, do not negate Johnstone's point that repetition carries persuasive force in written language as well. The fact that repetition has persuasive potential in both oral and written contexts explains why Salmon's refrains would have been compelling in the Karaite liturgical rites where they may have been performed, as well as the scholarly venues where they may have been studied, and were certainly copied, throughout the Middle Ages.

In other words, even if Salmon's refrain was a component of Karaite liturgical performance, its persuasive function was not limited to an oral-ritual setting. In the written commentary as well, repeated doctrinal statements appended to biblical verses work to persuade pious readers of the truth of Salmon's dogma. Repetition exists purposefully in both oral and literate contexts. Moreover, the line between oral and written forms is a blurry one, indeed, where homily and liturgy are concerned.[73] These genres are inherently dynamic; they may be oral or written in their original formulations, then developed into literary forms or real-life practices, and continue to evolve in written and oral settings, both before and after having been set down in writing.

Salmon's refrains in the Lamentations commentary may be rare in an exegetical context, but formal analogues are found in other Jewish homiletical traditions. One instructive point of comparison is the *Pesikta de Rav Kahana*, a collection of rabbinic traditions organized according to the Jewish liturgical calendar. Each chapter (*piska*) in the *Pesikta de Rav Kahana* contains a series of homilies relating to the themes of the respective holiday and concluding with a biblical verse drawn from the synagogue lectionary reading assigned to that day. These traditions were collected and redacted into their current literary form in an early stage, no later than the fifth

[72] Johnstone, *Repetition*, 115–18.
[73] See chapter 5 for discussion.

century, and it has long been supposed that the text preserves strata of the sermons that were once delivered orally in ancient Palestinian synagogues by the rabbinic sages.[74]

The chapters commonly begin with a series of introductory Midrashim, called proems (*petiḥta*; pl. *petiḥta'ot*). Each proem begins with a biblical "verse from afar" that gradually leads to the target verse from that holiday's lectionary reading. The target verse is then introduced by a formula such as "therefore it is said [in Scripture]" or "therefore Scripture is required to say." To illustrate this pattern, I present below the perorations from the first six proems of Piska 13. This Piska relates to the first of the three Sabbaths preceding the Ninth of Av, the traditional date of the destruction of the Temple. The rabbis designated Jeremiah 1:1–2:3 as the lectionary reading of rebuke for this sad occasion, since the prophet Jeremiah warned the ancient Israelites to repent when he foretold the fall of Jerusalem. The proems all begin by establishing the sins of Israel on the basis of biblical prooftexts; these sins then explain why Jeremiah was sent with prophecies of destruction and punishment. Thus, the respective narratives of sin conclude as follows:

1. But because Israel disregarded Isaiah's warning, it became necessary for Scripture to set down *The words of Jeremiah the son of Hilkiah* (Jer 1:1).
2. But because Israel disregarded wisdom's warning, Scripture deemed it necessary to set down *The words of Jeremiah the son of Hilkiah* (Jer 1:1).
3. And because Israel disregarded Zechariah's admonition [to hearken unto the Lord], Scripture deemed it necessary to set down *The words of Jeremiah the son of Hilkiah* (Jer 1:1).
4. Therefore Scripture deems it necessary for the Book to begin with *The words of Jeremiah* (Jer 1:1).
5. Hence Scripture deems it necessary for the Book to begin with *The words of Jeremiah* (Jer 1:1).
6. Therefore the Book begins *The words of Jeremiah* (Jer 1:1).[75]

[74] Recently Burton Visotzky has argued that "there was no homiletic midrash in the classical period of rabbinic literature." His research calls into question both the existence of homily in the ancient synagogue and the accuracy of homily as a classification for literary Midrash. See "The Misnomers '*Petihah*' and 'Homiletic Midrash' as Descriptions for Leviticus Rabbah and Pesikta De-Rav Kahana," *JSQ* 18 (2011): 19–31. For descriptions of the structure of "homiletic Midrashim," see Norman J. Cohen, "Structure and Editing in the Homiletic Midrashim," *AJS Review* 6 (1981): 1–20, and bibliography on pp. 1–2. See further discussion in chapter 5.

[75] *PdRK* 13.

In their literary context, this series of proems with their concluding formulas strongly resembles Salmon's refrains. To be sure, this perceived repetition is entirely a result of the redactional construction of the proems. If they had been delivered in the synagogue or the study house one by one over the course of multiple generations, auditors would have discerned no repetition, and rightly so. The ostensible refrain is a byproduct, an accident of the complicated editorial history of the collection known as the *Pesikta de Rav Kahana*. Yet by the mid-tenth century, when Salmon composed his own commentary on Lamentations, it is in this literary formulation that the proems would have been encountered and experienced. In this context, therefore, they represent a homiletical literary genre, and they incorporate literary features that resonate with the refrains of Salmon's homiletical commentary.

The point here is not that Salmon modeled his refrains on those of the *Pesikta de Rav Kahana*—although it is likely that he was familiar with the work—or that this Midrashic anthology is the only source of such refrains.[76] I am noting, however, that the features of the refrain from Salmon's Lamentations commentary were not unprecedented or unknown to medieval Jewish scholars. Refrains are present in biblical texts, for example, and they have a long history in *piyyuṭ* compositions. They also appear, thanks to the process of editorial redaction, in early medieval rabbinic anthologies such as the *Pesikta de Rav Kahana*.

Consolations (*Neḥamot*)

Following his remarks to Lamentations 5:22 (the final verse in the biblical book), Salmon offers biblical words of consolation (Hebr. *neḥamot*) to the Jewish community. This part of the commentary was no mere afterthought. It takes up roughly ten percent of Salmon's complete text and reflects his deep biblical knowledge as well as his ideological efforts as a Mourner for Zion.[77] For each clause of each verse from Lamentations that describes punishment and suffering, Salmon adduces prophetic words that foretell the reversal of these conditions. This final excursus reads like exegesis in reverse. In the

[76] On Salmon's engagement with the traditions preserved in *PdRK*, see chapter 3.

[77] I treat *Neḥamot* as a separate unit with a special standing within the commentary. Cf. Marwick, who considers this passage to be an extensive comment on Lam 5:22 ("Studies in Salmon ben Yeruḥam," 316).

commentary, Salmon repeatedly emphasizes reversal as the hermeneutical key for understanding Lamentations: every blessing that God once bestowed upon Israel was overturned and replaced by its opposite when the people sinned.[78] Now he reverses that reversal by refuting every worrisome image of Lamentations and replacing it with the promise of redemption and healing. He defines his project as follows:

> I have surely explained in this book [i.e., the commentary] that graces and excellences belong to God, [who bestowed them on] this community even though they sinned. It is because of these [i.e., His graces and excellences] that He did not exact [complete punishment] against them, as we have explained.[79] And because of this, He did not threaten to do so with this community *for the sake of His great name*, as He says, *For My name's sake I defer my anger* (Isa 48:9); and *For My own sake, for My own sake, I do it, for how should* [*My name*] *be profaned?* (Isa 48:11). It is among His excellences, also, that the Mighty and Sublime promised to change everything that befell this community in this exile. Dispersion, scattering, and exile; humiliation, degradation, and scorn; distress and contemptible things; the confiscation of money and the sacred precinct; damage and the destruction of the Temple; the cessation of the state and the cessation of sacrifices, leaders, and reverence—all this will be overturned, to the opposite of what is upon the community [now].

For Salmon, the book of Lamentations bears evidence of divine mercy and grace. The survival of the community testifies to God's restraint in not annihilating a people whose sins would have justified total punishment. Such restraint is only one of God's many excellences. God further promised to reverse all the miserable conditions of exile and ignominy, and God communicated these promises through the prophets. In this excursus, Salmon turns his focus to the promise of redemption, reminding the community that their experience of suffering is not God's final word in human affairs. To make this soteriological point, Salmon undertakes the exegetical task of correlating the verses of Lamentations with their opposites from elsewhere in the prophetic

[78] See esp. the excursuses at Lam 2:4 and 4:15.

[79] See Salmon's comments to Lam 1:12 and 3:22. In both cases Salmon discusses the verse, *For thus says the LORD, "The whole land shall be a desolation; yet I will not make a full end"* (Jer 4:27) to remind his audience that the continued existence of Israel is proof of divine mercy.

corpus, as well as the homiletical task of preaching this message of hope to the community.[80]

Salmon painstakingly matches each individual image of suffering in Lamentations with its opposite. One excerpt will demonstrate the exegetical precision required to construct this homiletical excursus. The passage below presents Salmon's consolation in response to the verse *She weeps bitterly in the night, tears on her cheeks; among all her lovers she has none to comfort her; all her friends have dealt treacherously with her, they have become her enemies* (Lam 1:2).

> Before Jeremiah said, ***She weeps bitterly in the night*** (Lam 1:2), Isaiah said, *You shall weep no more. He will surely be gracious to you* (Isa 30:19). Before Jeremiah said, ***tears on her cheeks*** (Lam 1:2), Isaiah said, *the Lord GOD will wipe away tears from all faces* (Isa 25:8). Before Jeremiah said, ***among all her lovers she has none to comfort her*** (Lam 1:2), Isaiah said, *Comfort, comfort My people, says your God* (Isa 40:1). Before Jeremiah said, ***all her friends have dealt treacherously with her*** (Lam 1:2), Isaiah said, *the sons of those who oppressed you shall come bending low to you* (Isa 60:14).

Salmon addresses each verse in turn, countering its images of destruction with parallel promises of healing. He scarcely repeats a verse of consolation and he asserts in nearly every case that the consolation was prophesied even before the destruction that it overturns. This chronology underscores the full extent of divine mercy: God assured the people of their ultimate salvation even before issuing the punishments.[81] Via this process of interpreting Scripture through Scripture, Salmon constructs a Karaite manifesto that confirms divine justice, praises divine grace, and holds fast to the promise of redemption.

[80] See chapter 5 for further discussion of the homiletical elements. Note also that these verse correlations were not entirely of Salmon's invention. The operative principle behind such correlations was expressed already in rabbinic texts. See, e.g., the teaching attributed to R. Levi in *PdRK* that "Whenever Scripture says that something is not, it is implying that the converse will be. Thus Scripture says *Sarai was barren; she had not a child* (Gen 11:30); afterwards she did have a child: *Sarah gave children suck* (Gen 21:7)," etc. (*PdRK* 18:3, 20:3). More specifically, in a Midrash on Lam 1:22 from *Lam R*, there is a list of biblical verses that illustrate the following principle: "You find that with the thing through which Israel sinned they were punished, and with the same thing they were comforted."

[81] Salmon makes this ordering explicit in his preface to the *Neḥamot*: "You will also learn that before Jeremiah was commissioned to establish these *lamentations* (*qinot*), *consolations* (*neḥamot*) were revealed through him and the rest of the prophets, with sublime meanings that are contrary to every word and every meaning in Lamentations."

This litany of consolations, like the refrains discussed above, may represent an element of the Jerusalem Karaites' liturgical practice. Ben-Shammai has proposed that the *Neḥamot* were part of the Karaites' compulsory mourning liturgy, and that the public recitation of these consolations was as central to Karaite religious service as the public recitation of the lamentation verses themselves.[82] Regardless of their liturgical role, these consolations impressively demonstrate the hermeneutical art of expressing religious doctrine through the inventive juxtaposition of biblical verses. The *Neḥamot*, like Salmon's Lamentations commentary as a whole, demonstrates Karaite patterns of constructing and articulating religious attitudes and actions through the language of the Bible.

Many of the passages presented here to illustrate the style and contents of Salmon's commentary also suggest points of connection between Salmon's writings and rabbinic liturgical and literary traditions. Indeed, some of Salmon's homilies are directly in conversation with rabbinic discourses on sin and punishment, rebuke and consolation. The following chapter, on Salmon's engagement with rabbinic sources, maps these connections more extensively, exploring the rabbinic background—and the profoundly Judaic context—of Salmon's project.

[82] Ben-Shammai, "Poetic Works and Lamentations," 217–18. Comparison with Yefet's version of *Neḥamot* is also instructive for addressing the use of Lamentations in Karaite liturgy. Yefet is less thorough than Salmon in his assemblage, and he rarely duplicates the prophetic verses that Salmon cites to reverse the clauses from Lamentations. His apparently deliberate avoidance of Salmon's pairings raises the possibility that he produced a new *Neḥamot* for exegetical reasons—namely, the challenge of assembling a fresh collection of aptly paired consolations—rather than liturgical ones. The idiosyncratic nature of the two collections complicates the theory that Salmon's *Neḥamot* records an authoritative communal liturgy.

3
Salmon's Engagement with Rabbinic Sources

Karaite Judaism is associated chiefly with its rejection of rabbinic law and, by extension, all things rabbinic, from the traditions of the ancient rabbis to the institutions, doctrines, and leadership of their intellectual heirs, the medieval Geʾonim of Babylonia. For this reason, there has been a tendency in the history of scholarship on Karaism to stress the sectarian elements of the movement and its isolation from the rest of the Jewish community. Studies in this vein have drawn primarily from literary and intellectual sources, which are rich in anti-Rabbanite polemics and separatist declarations, often in response to equally vitriolic literary attacks from Rabbanite leaders. The Karaites' reputation for sectarianism is rooted in such texts, and indeed their movement posed a credible, fundamental challenge to Rabbanite culture. Yet a primary focus on literary polemic has led some scholars to overemphasize Karaite estrangement from the Jewish fold and underestimate the complexity of Karaite involvement in Jewish religious and intellectual life.

The Karaites' rejection of rabbinic Oral Law in favor of biblical scholarship and independent interpretation did not lead them to abandon discussion with Rabbanites, or to promote ignorance of Rabbanite texts and traditions. Recent research has affirmed the wide-ranging connections between Karaites and Rabbanities, not only in social, political, and economic contexts, but also in religious and literary ones.[1] This growing body of scholarship has demonstrated with copious and compelling evidence that Karaite savants maintained and cultivated their knowledge of rabbinic hermeneutical

[1] Social history provides a more integrated picture of the Jewish community than intellectual history alone. See Marina Rustow on the "tripartite Jewish community," which includes Babylonian and Palestinian Rabbanites, and Karaites, in *Heresy and the Politics of Community: The Jews of the Fatimid Caliphate* (Ithaca, N.Y.: Cornell University Press, 2008), chapter 1. Rustow characterizes each group as a "school" (*madhhab*) of Judaism, coexisting alongside one another. Meira Polliack appreciates that Rustow's formulation recognizes Karaism's centrality to medieval Judaism, but she cautions against obscuring "the Karaites' self-conception of their intellectual and religious distinctiveness" ("The Karaite Inversion of 'Written' and 'Oral' Torah in Relation to the Islamic Arch-Models of Qurʾan and Hadith," *JJSQ* 22 no. 3 (2015): 283–84).

Jewish Piety in Islamic Jerusalem. Jessica Andruss, Oxford University Press. © Oxford University Press 2023.
DOI: 10.1093/oso/9780197639559.003.0003

principles, exegetical methods, translation techniques, and even Midrashic expansions on the biblical text. In their study of rabbinic thought, Karaites were not motivated exclusively, or even primarily, by a sectarian drive to learn rabbinic traditions in order to dispute or discredit them. To the contrary, countless examples from Karaite literature prove not only that Karaite scholars were conversant in rabbinic Hebrew and well informed in rabbinic matters, but also that they were receptive to rabbinic insights and willing to consider them on their merits. This chapter examines the dynamics of rabbinic citation, allusion, and appropriation in the Lamentations commentary of Salmon ben Yerūḥīm. Salmon provides a model of active Karaite engagement in rabbinic discourse, demonstrating the possibilities for strategically, selectively granting authority to rabbinic knowledge, and using it to construct a distinctively Karaite Judaism.

Rabbinic Knowledge Among Salmon and the Jerusalem Karaites

At first glance, Salmon's career fits the image of the sectarian, polemically minded Karaite. He was a vigorous advocate of the Karaite religious program and a harsh polemicist against Rabbanite Judaism. Throughout his corpus, he forcefully rejects Rabbanite models of religious practice, belief, and interpretation and blames the ongoing exile on Rabbanite sins. Yet a careful consideration of Salmon's commentary on Lamentations shows that his rejection of Rabbanite teachings was not borne out of ignorance, but out of deep familiarity with—and measured consideration of—rabbinic sources, and that he is as likely to incorporate a rabbinic explanation as he is to refute it. Salmon was well acquainted with rabbinic culture, from the oral traditions of the ancient sages to the religious discourse of the Babylonian Ge'onim in his own generation. Salmon cites rabbinic approaches to Lamentations, often explicitly, throughout the commentary, but his engagement with rabbinic thought far surpasses superficial acquaintance with the Midrash on a given verse from Lamentations. Rather, Salmon draws on the full breadth of rabbinic literature, from the Aramaic Targum to the Babylonian Talmud, and including material from Midrashic compilations such as *Pesikta de Rav Kahana*, *Mekhilta de Rabbi Ishmael*, and *Lamentations Rabbah*. He reads traditional rabbinic sources creatively and then uses them to advance his own Karaite agenda. He weaves rabbinic locutions and post-biblical Hebrew expressions into his Arabic prose with fluency.[2] He justifies elements of his Arabic translation of Lamentations on the basis of the Aramaic Targum, demonstrating his competency in using comparative Semitics as an exegetical tool. Even when Salmon's debts to rabbinic literature cannot be traced to a specific rabbinic text, his hermeneutical framework silently draws on the interpretive principles and reading practices that held sway in the rabbinic academies of Iraq.

Salmon's awareness of rabbinic traditions—and his willingness to invoke rabbinic explanations—is not entirely surprising. Salmon acknowledges his study of rabbinic literature even in his most acerbic critique of Rabbanite thought and practice, the Hebrew polemical poem *The Wars of the Lord* (*Sefer Milḥamot Adonai*), which he composed as a literary rebuke of Saadia Gaon.[3] In the second canto of the poem, where Salmon argues against the validity of the Oral Torah and the Mishnah in particular, he claims, "I have looked again into the six divisions of the Mishnah," and "I have set the six divisions of the Mishnah before me, and I looked at them carefully with mine eyes."[4] There is no doubt that such statements serve a rhetorical function in Salmon's polemic. His claims to rabbinic learning allow Salmon to position himself as a qualified judge of the deficiencies of rabbinic thought. Salmon claims, in this case, that his study of the Mishnah's form and content prove that it is a document of human invention rather than a repository of divine law, as the Rabbanites claim. However, Salmon's engagement with rabbinic sources in his Lamentations commentary indicates that such pronouncements about his awareness of rabbinic texts were not merely the posturing of a skilled polemicist. Perhaps the real fiction of these lines from *The Wars of the Lord* is that Salmon boned up on the Mishnah quickly and reached his conclusions about its fraudulence in one sitting. To the contrary, Salmon's references to rabbinic teachings, texts, and terminology throughout the Lamentations commentary suggest real familiarity with rabbinic thought and literature.

Salmon's stated interest in rabbinic thought was not unique among the Jerusalem Karaites. His younger contemporary, Sahl ben Maṣliaḥ, proudly describes a Karaite practice of consulting rabbinic texts in his epistle to the

[2] For examples of rabbinic Hebrew in Salmon's corpus beyond the Lamentations commentary, see Aharon Maman, "Karaites and Mishnaic Hebrew: Quotations and Usage," *Scripta Hierosymitana* 37 (1998), esp. 271–72.

[3] Israel Davidson, ed., *The Book of the Wars of the Lord* (New York: 1934). For an English translation of the first three cantos, see *KA*, 71–82. See also Samuel Poznanski, "The Karaite Literary Opponents of Saadiah Gaon in the Tenth Century," *JQR* 18 (1906): 209–50.

[4] *KA*, 75 (l. 2), 76 (l. 7).

Rabbanite Jacob ben Samuel.[5] There Sahl states that "the Karaites search and investigate in the Law of Moses and in the books of the Prophets, and they even look into the words of the Rabbanite forerunners (*ri'shonim*)."[6] This investigative process seems to have been methodical and serious. In the same epistle, Sahl describes a Karaite practice of comparing inherited traditions against biblical law and continuing to practice traditional teachings as long as they match divine precepts.[7]

The polemical agenda of both Sahl's and Salmon's epistles may compromise the absolute accuracy of their claims, but their descriptions still indicate that there was a place for rabbinic learning in Karaite society. First, Sahl and Salmon both announce their scholarship of Rabbanite texts without compunction or apology. The unabashed quality of their statements suggests that it was acceptable, and perhaps even laudatory, for Karaite elites to examine Rabbanite texts seriously. Of course, Salmon and Sahl may not be representative of the majority of Jerusalem Karaites.[8] As polemicists, they were obliged to be conversant with rabbinic thought. As exegetes with demonstrated mastery of biblical material and commitment to the Karaite cause, their exposure to Rabbanite texts may not have aroused the communal concerns that would have met less experienced or committed members of the community. Yet the proud professions of rabbinic knowledge that both Karaites make in these epistles challenge any presumption that early Karaites were ashamed to include rabbinic materials in their commentaries, or that they drew on rabbinic texts without full awareness of their debt to extra-biblical discourse. We must consider other explanations for the apparent Karaite reticence to name specific rabbinic sources in their biblical commentaries. In addition, having determined that Karaites knew rabbinic sources and willingly drew upon them, we must focus not on *whether* the Karaites consulted rabbinic explanation, but instead on *how* and *when* they did so, and on what this borrowing suggests about a medieval Jewish intellectual culture that spread across Karaite–Rabbanite boundaries.

Second, the statements above indicate that Karaites had access to rabbinic learning in a range of formats. Salmon's description of reading the

[5] *LK* II: 25–43. See also Leon Nemoy, "The Epistle of Sahl Ben Maṣlīaḥ," *PAAJR* 38/39 (1970–71): 145–77.

[6] *LK*, 34 = *KA*, 119.

[7] *LK*, 34 = *KA*, 118.

[8] Moshe Gil hypothesizes that the title "Mourner for Zion" may have been reserved for the Karaite elites rather than the community as a whole; see "Aliya and Pilgrimage in the Early Arab Period (634–1009)," *The Jerusalem Cathedra* 3 (1983): 163.

six tractates of the Mishnah with his own eyes suggests that this material was not only written down, but that it was in circulation and available for textual study. Sahl's comments do not preclude his exposure to rabbinic teachings in textual form, but they also gesture toward oral and observational modes of learning. He describes scrutinizing the "ways" (*derakhim*) and "deeds" (*ma'aśim*) of the fathers in addition to the "words" (*debarim*) of the early sages. This description invites speculation about the kinds of direct experiences that Sahl may have had with Rabbanites and their communities, which offered him the opportunity to study their words and observe their ways firsthand.[9] This posturing certainly functions as a snub against Rabbanite skills and educational models, since Salmon and Sahl claim that they have thoroughly digested and discredited the entire body of rabbinic knowledge, even without proper rabbinic training. Nevertheless, the fact that Salmon and Sahl present themselves as readers or observers of rabbinic traditions in their epistles to prominent Rabbanites implies that such intercommunal exposure was common enough for the rabbis—or for Karaite readers—to find such depictions credible and rhetorically effective.

The use of rabbinic sources in Karaite literature has been studied in great detail by Ofra Tirosh-Becker.[10] After analyzing copious manuscript sources of works written in the tenth and eleventh centuries, Tirosh-Becker has identified three primary ways that Karaites embed Rabbanite material in their own compositions: through explicit citation, paraphrase, and translation into Arabic.[11] She mentions Salmon in connection with the broad range of rabbinic sources from which he cites and notes that the many references and paraphrases found in his work—as well as the corpus of his predecessor al-Qirqisānī—indicate "their extensive familiarity with this [i.e., rabbinic] literature."[12] Tirosh-Becker pays special attention to Salmon's *Wars of the Lord*, in which he modifies rabbinic citations in order to fit the rhyme scheme or

[9] On the range of social, political, and economic contexts in which Karaites and Rabbanites interacted, see Rustow, *Heresy*. On the changing modes of oral and textual communication within these communities, see 36–41 of Rustow's book and also Rina Drory, *Models and Contacts: Arabic Literature and Its Impact on Medieval Jewish Culture* (Leiden: Brill, 2000), chapters 5 and 6, which include linguistic shifts as well.

[10] See Ofra Tirosh-Becker, "The Use of Rabbinic Sources in Karaite Writings," *Karaite Judaism*, 319–37; Tirosh-Becker, *Rabbinic Excerpts in Medieval Karaite Literature*, 2 vol. (Jerusalem: Bialik Institute, 2011); and Tirosh-Becker, "Linguistic Study of a Rabbinic Quotation Embedded in a Karaite Commentary on Exodus," *Scripta Hierosolymitana* 37 (1998): 380–407.

[11] Tirosh-Becker, "The Use of Rabbinic Sources," 324–29. Tirosh-Becker further subdivides the category of quotations according to language and script of the quotation (Hebr. or Arab.) in "Rabbinic Quotation," 382.

[12] Tirosh-Becker, "The Use of Rabbinic Sources," 323.

acrostic structure of his poetic form. The commentary on Lamentations is also replete with evidence of Salmon's creative engagement with rabbinic tradition. There, he makes extensive use of the first two modes that Tirosh-Becker lists, explicit citation and paraphrase.

Explicit Citation of Rabbinic Sources, Including the Targum

Salmon often cites rabbinic materials, although he rarely names a specific source text. Instead, he indicates such citations with introductory formulas such as *qālū* ("they said") or *qawluhum* ("their saying"), followed by a given translation or interpretation. He acknowledges the rabbinic provenance of his sources with labels such as *al-awāʾil* ("the first ones"), *al-riʾshonim* ("the sages"), and *rabbāniyyūn* ("rabbis/Rabbanites").[13]

Salmon frequently cites the Targum, the ancient Aramaic translations of the Bible.[14] These translations date back to the Palestinian communities of the first through seventh centuries, their transmission history runs parallel to those of other rabbinic compilations, and they were a standard component of the rabbinic curriculum.[15] Salmon associates the Targum with the rabbis, and he refers to Aramaic interchangeably as "the language of the Targum" and "the language of the Rabbis."[16] He consults the Targum freely and justifies his Arabic translation on the basis of the Targum's Aramaic translation. He accepts the reading suggested by the Targum without explanation, presuming its authority as a source for biblical translation and interpretation. By recognizing the linguistic authority of the Targum, if not its ideological authority as well, Salmon applies the principles of comparative Semitics to his exegetical work.

[13] For *al-awāʾil*, see comments to Lam 1:8 and 3:1.. For *al-riʾshonim*, see comments to Lam 2:4, 5, and *Neḥamot*. For *rabbāniyyūn*, see comments to Lam 1:10, 4:2, and 4:19. It is not clear whether Salmon uses the term *al-ʿulamāʾ* ("the religious scholars") to indicate Rabbanites or Karaites. See Salmon's use of the term in his introduction, and at Lam 3:20, and my notes there.

[14] On the Targum to Lamentations, see Philip S. Alexander, *The Targum of Lamentations*, The Aramaic Bible 17b (Collegeville, Minn.: Liturgical Press, 2007); Christian Brady, *The Rabbinic Targum of Lamentations: Vindicating God* (Leiden: Brill, 2003), and Brady, "Targum Lamentations," in *Great Is Thy Faithfulness? Reading Lamentations as Sacred Scripture*, ed. Robin A. Parry and Heath A. Thomas (Eugene, Ore.: Pickwick, 2011), 70–76.

[15] For an overview of the Targums, see Étan Levine, "The Targums: Their Interpretive Character and Their Place in Jewish Text Tradition," 323–31 in *HB/OT* I/1.

[16] See, e.g., Salmon's comment to Lam 4:2.

A typically straightforward reference to the Targum appears in Salmon's comment to Lam 3:11. There he explains his Arabic translation as follows: "I translated *va-yefashḥeni* as 'he tore me to pieces' [in accord with] the language of the Targum, for the Targum of *And Samuel hewed Agag in pieces [va-yeshassef] before the LORD in Gilgal* (1 Sam 15:33) is, in the Targum, *u-fashaḥ yat ʾagag*." Salmon opens his comment to Lam 3:18 in a similar way, by explaining his translation on the basis of Targum: "They say *niṣḥi* is 'my victory,' *niṣaḥon* in the language of the Targum; they say that *niṣḥi* is from *neṣaḥ* and means my extent, which is to say, my perseverance." In each case, the reference to Targum seals the matter. Salmon adds no further comment but allows the Targum's linguistic reasoning to stand in for his own.

Perhaps Salmon's comfort with the Targum stems from his awareness that its language, Aramaic, exists also within biblical literature. In a remark at Lamenations 3:28, Salmon notes that the word *naṭal* has a certain meaning in "the language of Targum" and then cites a verse from Daniel 7:4 to prove his point. This identification shows that Salmon recognizes Aramaic as both the language of the rabbis and the language of the biblical book of Daniel. Here as well, Salmon's own interpretation follows the meaning that he identifies as the Aramaic one.

Salmon's primary references to the Targum are linguistic and lexical, and he is attuned particularly to issues of vocabulary and meaning. It seems that Salmon values this Aramaic tradition for its linguistic insights but ignores its theological content. The Targum on Lamentations is particularly expansive, far exceeding the limits of translation as Salmon understands and applies them. In some cases, the targumist renders a Hebrew verse with many lines of Aramaic paraphrase, including Midrashic explanations so thick that they threaten to overwhelm the translation itself.[17] These methods of

[17] The best way to illustrate the dense interpretive content of Tg. Lam is to compare a biblical verse to its Aram. translation. For example, in the biblical text, Lam 1:1 reads: "How lonely sits the city that was full of people! How like a widow she has become, she that was great among the nations! She that was a princess among the cities has become a vassal." The Targum to Lam 1:1 expands upon the biblical verse with considerable Midrashic content, which is here italicized: "*Jeremiah the Prophet and High Priest told* how *it was decreed that Jerusalem and her people should be punished with banishment and that they should be mourned with ʾekhah. Just as when Adam and Eve were punished and expelled from the Garden of Eden and the Master of the Universe mourned them with ʾekhah. The Attribute of Justice spoke and said, 'Because of the greatness of her rebellious sin that was within her, thus she will* dwell alone *as a man plagued with leprosy upon his skin who sits alone.' And* the city which was full *of crowds and many* peoples *has been emptied of them and* she has become like a widow. She who was great among the nations and a ruler over the provinces *which* had *brought her* tribute *has become lowly again and gives head tax to them from thereafter*" (Brady, *The Rabbinic Targum*, 155). Note that not every verse in the Targum is rendered so expansively.

the targumist could not be further from Salmon's distinctions between the exact translation of the biblical verse into Arabic and the lengthy interpretive comment in which he includes paraphrase, digression, and homily.[18] Yet, in some of Salmon's comments, he accepts the theological force of the interpretation embedded within the Targum's Aramaic translation. For example, he reads *the LORD's anointed* (Lam 4:20) as a reference to King Josiah and understands the biblical locution *daughter of Zion* as a reference to the congregation or community, just as the Targum does.[19] I note these examples when they arise within the commentary. For now I wish to leave open the possibility that Salmon may have absorbed certain theological sensibilities from the Targum at the same time that he mined its linguistic insights.

Using Midrash in Contextual Exegesis: The Transfer of the Divine Glory in Lamentations 1:6

In consulting the Targum, Salmon applies the linguistic reasoning of an ancient biblical translation to his own translation project. Another avenue by which rabbinic sources travel into Salmon's Lamentations commentary is that of Midrash, the narrative traditions of the rabbinic sages that, in Salmon's time, existed as written compilations of originally oral material.[20]

In his interpretation of Lamentations 1:6—*from the daughter of Zion has departed all her majesty*—Salmon draws on a Midrashic treatment that appears in two such compilations, *Lamentations Rabbah* (proem 25) and *Pesikta de Rav Kahana* (13:11). The former compilation was likely a source for the latter. These rabbinic texts narrate the gradual withdrawal of the divine presence—represented in *Lamentations Rabbah* as the Shekhina, the rabbinic concept of the manifestation of God's presence in the world—from her dwelling place in the Temple. In each case, the Midrash begins with the claim that the divine presence departed the Temple in ten stages. In the

[18] Note, however, that Salmon himself may blur these boundaries on occasion. See the discussion of Salmon's approach to translation in chapter 2.

[19] On the references to King Josiah in Tg. Lam, see Brady, *The Rabbinic Targum*, 39–44; on the understanding of *daughter of Zion* as "the congregation of Zion," see ibid., 83–88. I discuss the former in chapter 2, in the section on "Biblical Citations from Outside Lamentations."

[20] In most cases it is impossible to give a terminus a quo for the date when oral texts began to circulate in writing. Moshe Bar-Asher discusses the transition of orally transmitted traditions into writing in "From Oral Transmission to Written Transmission: Concerning the Meaning of Some Orthographic Forms in the Manuscripts of the Mishnah and Rabbinic Literature," *Hebrew Studies* 52 (2011): 201–12.

Pesikta de Rav Kahana, the specification of ten as the number of journeys is also presented in an alphanumeric Midrash: the letters of the name Jeremiah [ירמיהו] are broken apart and read as an indication that the divine presence [יה] made ten [י] upward [רם] journeys.[21] Next, each Midrash charts the movements of the divine presence, from the innermost parts of the Temple outward, then to the city wall and eventually beyond Jerusalem entirely, eastward to the Mount of Olives. These movements are established by an assortment of prooftexts, primarily from the book of Ezekiel but including verses from Proverbs, Amos, and Micah as well. In marshaling the prooftexts necessary to represent ten distinct journeys, the Midrashim run into a sticky problem: as they have arranged the verses, the divine presence seems to leave the Temple, then return to it before departing again. In order to explain this frenetic back-and-forth movement, both Midrashim include a parable comparing the divine presence to a king who leaves his palace and then, overcome with emotion, returns to kiss its walls and pillars before resuming his journey. Both Midrashim conclude with the divine presence proclaiming, "I will return again to My place" (Hos 5:15), which they take to refer to a place beyond the Temple, where the divine presence will remain until the Israelites repent.

Although neither version of the Midrash links this narrative to Lamentations 1:6, Salmon interprets the "majesty" (*hadar*) of this verse as a reference to the "glory" (*kavod*), or divine presence, which is the central figure of the Midrash. Thus, for Salmon, the image from Lamentations in which the "majesty" departs from Zion recalls this Midrashic tradition. Yet Salmon modifies the fanciful narrative in several ways, bringing it into alignment with his stated principles of contextual exegesis. This excerpt from Salmon's commentary appears below, followed by a discussion of the techniques that Salmon uses to neutralize the Midrashic elements in order to apply this tradition as a contextual interpretation of Lamentations 1:6:

> In this account, the *glory* ascended from upon *the dome*, from between the two *cherubim*, and came to be upon the single *cherub*. Then it ascended from upon the *cherub* to the threshold of the Temple, as it is said, *Now the glory of the God of Israel had gone up from the cherubim on which it rested to the threshold of the house* (Ezek 9:3). Then it ascended from the platform of the house until it came to be upon the firmament

[21] *PdRK*, 13:11.

> which was upon the head of the living creatures. Then it stopped at the eastern gate of the house of the LORD, as it is said, *Then the glory of the LORD went forth from the threshold of the house, and stood over the cherubim. And the cherubim lifted their wings and mounted up from the earth in my sight as they went forth, with the wheels beside them; and they stood at the door of the east gate of the house of the LORD; and the glory of the God of Israel was over them* (Ezek 10:18–19). Then it was transferred away from the eastern gate to the center of the town, as it is said, *Then the cherubim lifted up their wings, with the wheels beside them; and the glory of the God of Israel was over them* (Ezek 11:22). We learn that this transfer [of the *glory*] to the center of the town was from two directions. One of them is [learned from] the statement, *and the cherubim lifted their wings*, but it does not say from where, or to where [the *cherubim* went]. However, since the last one arrived at the eastern gate, you learn that the transfer was from the eastern gate to *the midst of the city*. The second direction is [learned from] the statement, *and the glory of the LORD went up from the midst of the city, and stood upon the mountain which is on the east side of the city* (Ezek 11:23). This is what indicates that the transfer from the eastern gate was to the center of the city, and from the center of the city it was transferred to the Mount of Olives—which is Jerusalem from the eastern direction—and from the Mount of Olives it was transferred to the gate of the Garden of Eden, as it is said, *I will return again to My place* (Hos 5:15). The dwelling place of the *glory* since ancient times was there, as it is said, *And at the east of the Garden of Eden He placed the cherubim* (Gen 3:24). The verse *and at the east of the garden of Eden He placed* serves to indicate that the gate of the Garden of Eden faces toward the east. When the *glory* was transferred, all the majesty was transferred with it, including the majesty of kingship, the majesty of the elders, and the majesty of the name of Israel, about which it is said, *And your renown went forth among the nations because of your beauty, for it was perfect through the splendor which I had bestowed upon you* (Ezek 16:14).

In his Lamentations commentary, Salmon strips this rabbinic tradition of its heightened mythological content and presents it instead as an instance of Scripture interpreting itself—that is to say, by using the pericope from Ezekiel to interpret Lamentations 1:6. After stating that *hadar* (Lam 1:6) refers to *kavod* (Ezek 8–11), Salmon interprets the verses from Ezekiel in which the *kavod* moves ever outward from the innermost parts of the Temple. He addresses the verses from Ezekiel in their biblical order and thereby charts the departure of the divine glory in precise spatial terms.

The numerological detail of ten journeys, which appears in *Pesikta de Rav Kahana*, is not part of the Ezekiel narrative, so Salmon has no reason to include it. Without the task of finding additional journeys recorded in the biblical text, Salmon has no need to include biblical prooftexts from beyond Ezekiel, as the Midrashic versions do. In this way, his sustained reading of Ezekiel 8–11 resembles the framed sub-commentaries found elsewhere within Salmon's Lamentations commentary.[22] With no complicating movement out of the Temple and back again, Salmon omits the distinctively noncontextual parable comparing the divine presence to the king who returns to kiss his palace walls.

Salmon's modified version of the Midrash is notable not just for what it omits, but also for what it adds. Salmon brings a geographic sophistication to his exegesis of the verses from Ezekiel, noting that the divine glory entered the midst of the city from two directions, and clarifying that the Mount of Olives lies to the east of Jerusalem. Further, while all three versions conclude the journey narrative with the verse in which God declares that he will return to his place (Hos 5:15), only Salmon makes the effort to determine the geographic location of the "place" to which God refers. On the basis of Genesis 3:24 he determines that it must be the Garden of Eden, which lies in the east and which was the ancient dwelling place of the divine glory. These insights fit into Salmon's Karaite approach, combining his skills of close reading with his personal, lived experience of the topography of Jerusalem. While Salmon paraphrases portions of the Midrash and likely takes it as his starting point, he has transformed this rabbinic tradition into an acceptably Karaite exegetical passage, in full accord with scripturalist principles.

Rabbinic Hermeneutics: The Ten Commandments and Requital in Kind in Lamentations 1:8

Salmon's engagement with rabbinic sources emerges especially strongly in the homiletical passages of the commentary. There, he is less constrained by exegetical concerns and he addresses his audience directly about the

[22] For discussion of Salmon's embedded commentaries see "Biblical Citations from Outside Lamentations" in chapter 2.

social and religious issues that seem to him most urgent. In his excursus at Lamentations 1:8, Salmon demonstrates his familiarity with the rabbinic corpus, his knowledge of rabbinic hermeneutics, and his ability to use both in the service of articulating distinctively Karaite doctrines.

Lamentations 1:8 begins with the declaration that, according to Salmon's translation, "Jerusalem sinned grievously, therefore she came to wander." For Salmon, this verse presents cause and effect with great clarity, and preserves it for the edification of future generations. The people of Jerusalem are punished because they have sinned. Behind this statement lies a principle of requital—*bāb al-muqābala*—to which Salmon often refers throughout the commentary. In his comment to this verse from Lamentations, Salmon notes that Scripture has recorded this religious principle in a single passage (2 Kgs 17:7–23), and in an array of prophetic books. Salmon further demonstrates this principle with an excursus on the Ten Commandments that is both homiletically compelling and exegetically rigorous. He methodically introduces each commandment in turn, then marshals biblical prooftexts to prove that the Israelites transgressed it, and then lists a second set of prooftexts to show how they were punished in kind, measure for measure, as a result of their transgression. In addition, Salmon includes a discussion of how the Jews of his own day continue to violate four of the commandments in particular.[23]

In its most basic structure, this excursus resembles a teaching from *Pesikta de Rav Kahana* 13:8, one of the rabbinic sermons connected to the Sabbaths preceding the Ninth of Av.[24] There, the homily begins by invoking the first verse of the Haftarah reading for that day, Jeremiah 1:1: *The words of Jeremiah*. The rabbinic homilist suggests that the "words" (*dibrei*) mentioned in the verse could be understood as "My words" (*debaray*), in reference to the Ten Commandments, spoken by God. In this brief homily, each commandment is paired with a single prooftext to indicate that it was violated in biblical times. For example:

> My word to them was *Honor your father and your mother* (Exod 20:12), which they did not heed: *Father and mother are treated with contempt* (Ezek 22:7).

[23] Specifically: the Sabbath (Exod 20:8) and the prohibitions against killing (Exod 20:13), adultery (Exod 20:14), and stealing (Exod 20:15).

[24] The date on which the destruction of the Temple(s) is commemorated in rabbinic Judaism.

It is possible that Salmon was familiar with this rabbinic homily, and that he considered it relevant to his exegetical project because of its connection to mourning over the Temple. The fact that Salmon's prooftexts match those of *Pesikta de Rav Kahana* in six of ten cases suggests that Salmon was building on the same tradition that is presented in the rabbinic work.[25] Yet Salmon's homily far surpasses the rabbinic version in its assembly of biblical material, its construction of a theological argument, and its powerful voice of pious exhortation.

Where the *Pesikta de Rav Kahana* presents only proof of the commandment's transgression, Salmon provides proof as well of the punishment. For example:

> God said on Mount Sinai: *Honor your father and your mother* (Exod 20:12). Israel transgressed this commandment, as it is said, *Father and mother are treated with contempt* (Ezek 22:7); and *For the son treats the father with contempt, the daughter rises up against her mother* (Mic 7:6). Therefore, we deserve to lament for ourselves and say, *We have become orphans, fatherless* (Lam 5:3).

The homily consists of three elements—the commandment from Sinai, the violation, and the punishment—and the choice of prooftexts emphasizes the hermeneutical and religious principle of requital in kind. This principle of reciprocal punishment is often invoked in Rabbanite contexts and appears throughout the rabbinic tradition. An early formulation of the principle appears in *Mekhilta de Rabbi Ishmael*, where it is used to make sense of the drowning of the Pharaoh and his armies in the Red Sea, as fitting recompense for the Pharaoh's decree that Israelite male children be drowned. There the phrase is *be-middah she-ʾadam moded bah moded loʾ* ("with what measure a man metes it is measured unto him").[26] In later articulations, this explanation is codified as the principle of *middah keneged middah*, or "measure for measure."[27]

[25] The commandments in which Salmon and *PdRK* use the same prooftexts concern not taking the Lord's name in vain (Exod 20:7; Jer 5:2); remembering the Sabbath (Exod 20:8; Ezek 22:8); honoring father and mother (Exod 20:12; Ezek 22:7); and the prohibitions against stealing (Exod 20:15; Jer 7:9), bearing false witness (Exod 20:16; Jer 9:2/3), and coveting (Exod 20:17; Mic 2:2).

[26] *Mekhilta de Rabbi Ishmael* II:35.

[27] On the rabbinic background of *middah keneged middah*, see, *m. Soṭah* 1:7–9; Ephraim Urbach, *The Sages*, trans. Abraham Israels (Jerusalem: Magnes, 1975), 438–40; Jonathan Wyn Schofer, "Protest or Pedagogy: Trivial Sin and Divine Justice in Rabbinic Narrative," *HUCA* 74 (2003): 7 n. 14; Ishay Rosen-Zvi, "Measure for Measure as a Hermeneutical Tool in Early Rabbinic Literature: The Case of Tosefta Sotah," *JJS* 57, no. 2 (2006): 269–86; and Ishay Rosen-Zvi, *The Mishnaic Sotah Ritual: Temple,*

Salmon does not use this Hebrew phrase, but he seems to have the reciprocal principle in mind when he invokes the phrase *bāb al-muqābala* in cases where the punishment fits the crime. This principle has great interpretive capacity, and Salmon uses it to justify not only the punishments recorded in Scripture, but those sustained by his own generation as well. Further, it reveals an underlying religious principle about God's relationship to the world and the pedagogical value of suffering. There is a message in pain, when the sufferer examines the precise features of his or her suffering, just as a reader would interpret a text to determine its meaning. Since the punishment fits the crime, it informs the sinner of the specific sins that caused it. For Salmon, the punishment not only points back to the sins that caused it, but also points forward to the repentance that will end it.

By turning his attention to the sins of his own time, Salmon appropriates the flexible structure of the *Pesikta de Rav Kahana* to fit his own Karaite agenda. The sectarian elements of Salmon's revised homily are most pronounced in his treatment of the violations of the Sabbath commandment. The Sabbath was a notoriously well-trod topic in Karaite doctrinal disputes with other Jews, since Karaites adhered to different norms of observing the occasion each week. Salmon rehearses the biblical evidence that this commandment has been transgressed in ancient times: *You have despised My holy things, and profaned My Sabbaths* (Ezek 22:8) and *In those days I saw in Judah men treading wine presses on the Sabbath day* [. . .] *"What is this evil thing which you are doing, profaning the Sabbath day?"* The past tense and the biblical phrase "*In those days*" firmly establish the ancient time period of these infractions. Immediately thereafter, however, Salmon initiates a list of how the Sabbath is defiled "in Israel today." The list includes activities that were acknowledged as forbidden throughout the Jewish community, but it focuses specifically on the activities that were acceptable in Rabbanite contexts but not in Karaite ones. Salmon's attention to the sins of his own day reflects two of his ideological commitments. First, it supports his teaching that the conditions of the exile continue because the Jews of his own day continue to sin, not because they are punished for their forefathers' sins.[28] Second, it enables him to advance a sectarian agenda, interpreting the Sabbath

Gender and Midrash, trans. Orr Scharf (Leiden: Brill, 2012). Thanks to Liz Alexander for introducing me to the work of Rosen-Zvi.

[28] On this doctrine, see Salmon's excursus to Lam 5:7 and the discussion in chapter 6.

commandment in distinctly Karaite ways and then blaming non-Karaite Jews for the harsh conditions to which the entire community is subjected.

Salmon transforms the short Midrash from *Pesikta de Rav Kahana* into a full Karaite homily. Just as he modified the rabbinic narratives about the departure of the divine presence from the Temple, so here Salmon excises the portions of the homily that do not complement his contextual approach to biblical interpretation. He does not include the Midrashic play on words, in which the *dibrei* ("words") of Jeremiah are transformed into the *debaray* ("My words") of God's commandments. He uses the pairs of commandment and transgression from the *Pesikta* as a jumping-off point for a more elaborate homily, so that the biblical sins become a mere prologue to the sins that most concern Salmon: the sins of his own day, the sins of the Rabbanites, with their power to prolong suffering and delay redemption.

Rabbinic Mourning Practices and the Jerusalem Karaites in Lamentations 1:8

The climax of Salmon's homily at Lamentations 1:8 comes when he taps into rabbinic literature to call upon the Karaites to mourn for Jerusalem. This invocation of a passage from the Talmud to praise Karaite commitments to mourning constitutes a brazen act of ventriloquism. Salmon uses the rabbis' words against them, constructing a doctrinal statement that would have inspired a Karaite audience and infuriated a Rabbanite one.

After methodically discussing each of the Ten Commandments and its historical and continuing violations, Salmon turns to the sins of his own generation. At this point, Salmon no longer correlates the contemporary sins with the commandments in a one-to-one format. Instead, he rebukes the Jews of his own day for their general lack of commitment to the Torah, their easy distractibility by the affairs of this world, and their failure to cultivate an overarching attitude of penitence and mourning. For Salmon, the failure to mourn is tantamount to the rejection of Jerusalem, and ultimately of God. He proclaims,

> Surely, He clarified for us, through the righteous prophet, that whoever forgets Jerusalem "forsakes the LORD," as it is said, *but you who forsake the LORD, who forget My holy mountain* (Isa 65:11); and *if I forget you, O Jerusalem* (Ps 137:5). This oath [to] God compelled the nation itself not

> to forget the destruction of Jerusalem, and therefore He goes so far as to command that the nation itself is compelled to remember the destruction of Jerusalem in every respect, even including diet, and in every prayer and in every Sabbath and festival, so that when one builds a dwelling or dons a garment or rejoices, he does nothing perfectly and completely; rather, he leaves something missing from everything that he produces so that he remembers thereby the destruction of the LORD's house, as it is said, *if I do not set Jerusalem above my highest joy!* (Ps 137:6). Whoever grieves for Jerusalem deserves to see her joy, as it is said, *Rejoice with her in joy, all you who mourn over her* (Isa 66:10). The only one who mourns over her is the one who loves her structures, as it is said, *Be glad for her, all you who love her* (Isa 66:10).

Salmon's homily, framed by Psalm 137:5 and Isaiah 66:10, closely resembles a rabbinic tradition recorded in the Babylonian Talmud. In the rabbinic text, the passage is framed by a historical narrative situated in the aftermath of the destruction of the Second Temple. Following the destruction, the Talmud explains, there were many ascetics who consumed neither meat nor wine, on the grounds that these ingredients could no longer be offered at the Temple as they had been when the Temple was standing. Rabbi Joshua encounters some of these ascetics and inquires about the rationale behind their mourning behaviors. In a spirit of *reductio ad absurdum*, Rabbi Joshua suggests that in order to be consistent, the ascetics should also remove from their diets everything that once was used sacrificially in the Temple, from bread to fruit to water itself. Once Rabbi Joshua has pressed the ascetics to the point that they can no longer reply, he discloses his own, more moderate, approach to mourning. He tells them:

> My sons, come and listen to me. [...] To mourn excessively is impossible, because we do not impose on the community a hardship which the majority cannot endure, as it is written, *Ye are cursed with a curse, yet ye rob me [of the tithe], even in this whole nation* (Mal 3:9). The Sages therefore have ordained thus. A man may plaster his house, but he should leave a little bare. (How much should this be? R. Joseph says, A cubit square; to which R. Ḥisda adds that it must be by the door.) A man can prepare a full-course banquet, but he should leave out an item or two. (What should this be? R. Papa says: The hors d'oeuvre of salted fish.) A woman can put on all her ornaments, but leave off one or two. (What should this be? Rab

> said: [Not to remove] the hair on the temple.) For so it says, *If I forget thee, O Jerusalem, let my right hand forget, let my tongue cleave to the roof of my mouth if I remember thee not, if I prepare not Jerusalem above my chief joy.* [. . .] Whoever mourns for Zion will be privileged to see her joy, as it says, *Rejoice ye with Jerusalem etc.*[29]

Salmon does not translate this Talmudic passage exactly or even paraphrase it. Yet the parallels between it and Salmon's homily are highly suggestive. Both present a treatise on mourning for Jerusalem framed by Psalm 137:5 and Isaiah 66:10. Just as the Sages ordain that home repairs go unfinished, banquets proceed with certain dishes missing, and a woman dress without completing her coiffure, so Salmon speaks telegraphically of remembering Jerusalem "in diet" and "when one builds a dwelling or dons a garment or rejoices." The mourning behaviors may be identical in both texts, but the presentations could not be more different. Rabbi Joshua advocates these behaviors as a circumscribed program of mourning and steers the ancient ascetics toward life-sustaining accommodation and away from the hazards of supererogation. By contrast, Salmon urges the medieval Jewish community to practice these behaviors as a greater—but still obligatory—form of piety and penitence. Most remarkably, the mourning practices that the Talmud explicitly identifies as the teaching of the Sages are, in Salmon's rendition, attributed to the psalmist (or perhaps even to God). Salmon teaches that the commandment to mourn in this way—in the way described by the rabbis in BT Baba Batra 60b—is the clear meaning of Psalm 137:5–6.

With his closing citations from Isaiah 66:10, Salmon extends the Talmudic passage into territory that is overtly polemical, and distinctively Karaite. The true lovers of Jerusalem, who deserve to experience her redemption, are those who have fulfilled the duty of mourning appropriately for her, within the city herself. For Salmon, only the Mourners for Zion, the Karaites of Jerusalem, truly uphold the commandment to mourn that this rabbinic source describes. They have settled in Jerusalem, and there they perform their pious mourning rituals and prayers; their reverence for the ruins of the Temple demonstrate that they are the true lovers of Jerusalem and that they, unlike the Rabbanites who remain in the Diaspora, are actively working toward redemption. Salmon's ability to mount this Karaite message on the

[29] BT Baba Batra 60b.

back of a rabbinic tradition is testament to his fluency with rabbinic texts and ideas, and to his ability to manipulate such traditions to suit the homiletical and exegetical program of the Karaite community.

In this chapter we have explored Salmon's knowledge of rabbinic literature and his citation and imaginative appropriation of rabbinic traditions for exegetical, homiletical, and polemical purposes. That Salmon's theology of sin, punishment, and consolation also aligns with rabbinic readings of Lamentations in notable ways is yet another, perhaps more profound, matter of engagement, which will be discussed in later chapters. The next chapter addresses Salmon's approach to figurative language in Lamentations. In his interpretation of biblical metaphor and parable, Salmon continues to draw on the parts of rabbinic thought that accord with his hermeneutical program. The rabbinic principle that "Scripture speaks in human language," found in the Talmud but repeated across medieval Jewish literature, is foundational to Salmon's reading of figurative language, even when he uses the terminology of Arabic literary theory to identify poetic expressions. Regardless of whether Salmon draws from rabbinic Midrash or Arabic theory, he always justifies his interpretation with the words of Scripture.

4

Salmon's Approach to Figurative Language

Modern scholars of the Bible routinely classify Lamentations as a work of poetry. Even while they debate the book's theological message, its historical referents, the circumstances of its composition, and its possible liturgical life-setting, they concur that Lamentations has a poetic form. This consensus is especially noteworthy in light of the vexed attempts of biblical scholars to define biblical Hebrew poetry in the first place, as well as their conflicting perspectives about whether Lamentations constitutes an immediate, oral response to the destruction of Jerusalem, or a later literary or liturgical composition.[1] Scholars have analyzed the syntax and meter of Lamentations[2] in addition to its literary devices such as personification,[3] repetition, synonymy, alliteration, parallelism, and imagery.[4]

[1] Note also that examples from Lamentations are rarely considered in critical studies of biblical poetry. Among the helpful studies on biblical Hebrew poetry that nevertheless give slight or no attention to Lamentations, see Robert Alter, *The Art of Biblical Poetry* (New York: Basic Books, 1985); J. P. Fokkelman, *Reading Biblical Poetry: An Introductory Guide*, trans. Ineke Smit (Louisville, Ky.: Westminster John Knox, 2001); James L. Kugel, *The Idea of Biblical Poetry: Parallelism and Its History* (New Haven, Conn.: Yale University Press, 1981); David E. Orton, comp., *Poetry in the Hebrew Bible: Selected Studies from* Vetus Testamentum (Leiden: Brill, 2000). Cf. two studies of biblical poetry in which Lamentations makes a stronger appearance: Adele Berlin, *The Dynamics of Biblical Parallelism* (Bloomington, Ind.: Indiana University Press, 1985); and Luis Alonso Schökel, *A Manual of Hebrew Poetics*, Studia Biblica 11 (Rome: Editrice Pontifico Instituto Biblico, 1988).

[2] On meter, see Raymond de Hoop, "Lamentations: The Qinah-Metre Questioned," in *Delimitation Criticism: A New Tool in Biblical Scholarship*, ed. Marjo Korpel and Josef Oesch (Assen, The Netherlands: Van Gorcum, 2000), 80–104; and Delbert Hillers, "Observations on Syntax and Meter in Lamentations," in *A Light unto My Path: Old Testament Studies in Honor of Jacob M. Myers*, ed. Howard N. Bream, Gettysburg Theological Studies 4 (Philadelphia: Temple University Press, 1974), 265–70. W. Randall Garr's study of the Qinah genre is also instructive even though he does not consider examples from the book of Lamentations; see "The Qinah: A Study of Poetic Meter, Syntax and Style," in *Zeitschrift für die alttestamentliche Wissenschaft* 95 (1983): 54–75.

[3] Personification in Lamentations has received extensive treatment. For a small sample, see, e.g., David A. Bosworth, "Daughter Zion and Weeping in Lamentations 1–2," *JSOT* 38:2 (2013): 217–37; Knut M. Heim, "The Personification of Jerusalem and the Drama of Her Bereavement in Lamentations," in *Zion, City of Our God*, ed. Richard S. Hess and Gordon J. Wenham (Grand Rapids, Mich.: Eerdmans, 1999), 129–69; and Charles William Miller, "Reading Voices: Personification, Dialogism, and the Reader of Lamentations 1," *Biblical Interpretation* 9 (2001): 393–408.

[4] Discussion of these literary features is routine in works on Lamentations. For studies that give particular attention to its poetic features, see, e.g., Adele Berlin, *Lamentations: A Commentary*, Old Testament Library (Louisville, Ky.: John Knox, 2002); Heath A. Thomas, *Poetry and Theology in the Book of Lamentations: The Aesthetics of an Open Text* (Sheffield, U.K.: Sheffield Phoenix, 2013).

Jewish Piety in Islamic Jerusalem. Jessica Andruss, Oxford University Press. © Oxford University Press 2023.
DOI: 10.1093/oso/9780197639559.003.0004

While the literary features of Lamentations are extensive, it is the book's metaphors that have proven most compelling for biblical scholars. Thus, Adele Berlin remarked that, in her own commentary on Lamentations, she was "especially concerned to understand metaphors, the vehicle through which poetry expressed its view of the world."[5] Berlin locates the message and experience of Lamentations within its tropes and figurative content, which she analyzes from a literary perspective. While Berlin's approach is informed by current models of literary analysis, her focus on metaphor as the locus of textual meaning is not unique to modern biblical exegesis.

Metaphors drew sustained attention also from medieval exegetes and grammarians, who were particularly sensitive to the challenges that figurative expressions posed in the context of Scripture. The authoritative status of the Bible and the Qurʾān, and the human expectation for truth and clarity in divine communication, led interpreters to scrutinize figurative language with great acuity, as much in Karaite circles as in Rabbanite and Muslim ones. The ostensibly literary qualities of biblical or Qurʾānic language generated sophisticated philosophical questions about the modes of divine speech, prophetic transmission, and human understanding, as well as the connections between language and imagination, and the potential for art to convey a message free of artifice. This chapter will focus on Salmon ben Yerūḥīm's own approach to the figurative language of Lamentations, and its place in the broader context of tenth-century Arabic literary theory.[6]

In his translation technique and in the substance of his exegetical comments, Salmon reveals his concept of figurative language, his classification of nonliteral linguistic forms, and his methods for analyzing imagery, metaphor, and parable. Lamentations is saturated with metaphors and Salmon, like all interpreters of this biblical book, must account for the presence of figurative language. While Salmon shies away from technical theoretical discourse about the purpose and function of figurative language, certain comments and terminology reveal an underlying hermeneutic that is informed by a combination of biblical context, Jewish exegetical principles, and emerging Arabic theory.

[5] Adele Berlin, "On Writing a Commentary on Lamentations," in *Lamentations in Ancient and Contemporary Cultural Contexts*, SBL Symposium Series 43, ed. Nancy C. Lee and Carleen Mandolfo (Atlanta, Ga.: Society of Biblical Literature, 2008), 9.

[6] For an examination of medieval Jewish approaches to biblical metaphor that differ from Salmon's, see Sivan Nir and Meira Polliack, "'Many Beautiful Meanings Can Be Drawn from Such a Comparison': On the Medieval Interaction View of Biblical Metaphor," in *Exegesis and Poetry in Medieval Karaite and Rabbanite Texts*, 40–79 (EJM 68; KTS 9; Leiden: Brill, 2017).

It is worth noting at the outset that Salmon's concern with the imagery, metaphors, and parables of Lamentations was primarily exegetical, and he engages in literary analysis only to the extent that it supports his interpretive work and homiletical goals. The rich poetic qualities of Lamentations were not lost on Salmon, of course, but they were not his priority as an interpreter whose fundamental project was to parlay the prophet Jeremiah's ethical instruction to the Jews of the exile. Salmon is inattentive to the categories of poetic device that he does not consider important to the exegetical process or the homiletical purpose of his work. For example, the verses of Lamentations are replete with Hebrew alliteration, yet Salmon makes no consistent effort to represent this distinctive aural feature in his Arabic translation. At times the alliteration appears incidentally, as when Salmon renders the Hebrew alliteration *paḥad wa-faḥat* (Lam 3:47) with the Arabic *al-fazaʿ wa-l-fakhta*, but he does not draw attention to the alliteration in either language. The few instances in which Salmon happens to replicate a literary feature in his translation are vastly outweighed by countless others in which he makes no such effort. It seems that Salmon did not consider the imitation of sound—as in assonance, consonance, or alliteration, all of which recur frequently in Lamentations—to be a significant component of translation. He may produce a poetic translation when the linguistic possibilities of Arabic invite it, but the representation of poetic sounds is not required by his hermeneutical program. This casual attention to the aural quality of biblical poetry suggests that Salmon did not consider this kind of poetic device to be essential for conveying religious meaning, which was the focus of his project.

Salmon's literary interest centers almost exclusively on biblical figurative language, a subject to which he was keenly attentive. The metaphors of Lamentations arise in the very first verse. Unlike the Song of Songs, for example, in which the initial attribution to Solomon was interpreted as a frame to introduce the allegory to follow, the book of Lamentations immediately begins with a central metaphor, in which the formerly populous city of Jerusalem is compared to a lonely widow and a one-time princess who has now fallen into slavery. These feminized metaphors of humiliation, deprivation, and suffering continue in succeeding verses and provide a recurring trope within the biblical chapters of Lamentations. Other metaphors may appear only once in the text, expressed circumstantially in the service of a larger motif. Whether addressing a recurring metaphor that runs throughout the text or the many clauses with smaller, supporting metaphors, Salmon focuses on the literal and spiritual meaning of such biblical imagery.

In his interpretation of figurative language—as with his interpretation writ large—Salmon relies heavily on parallels from other biblical passages. He draws on biblical prooftexts to elucidate metaphors and discover their significance in establishing the religious message of Lamentations. Because he finds interpretive direction and verification within the ancient Hebraic linguistic context, he privileges biblical source material over theoretical analysis. In addition, Salmon reads some metaphors intuitively, following cognitive rather than lexical clues to reach the allegorical signification.[7] These intuitive methods lead Salmon to decode a metaphor in accordance with his observations of the natural world or human society. For example, Salmon explains the deer imagery of Lamentations 1:6 in zoological terms, as I will discuss below, and he explains the tears of the widow in Lamentations 1:2 in sociological terms, describing the difficulties that widows face after the death of their spouses. When Salmon discusses a metaphor, he typically emphasizes its "meaning" (*maʿnā*)—that is to say, its applied meaning, or spiritual message—without explaining the literary mechanisms by which the metaphor communicates that meaning. Often he calls no explicit attention to the fact that this meaning is conveyed through figurative language.[8]

Occasionally, however, Salmon indicates an underlying theoretical approach with words that are now familiar from the Arabic theoretical tradition of literary exegesis, such as *majāz* (figurative language), *istiʿāra* (metaphor), *tamthīl* (analogy), or *mathal* (parable). These occasions reveal Salmon's basic sensitivity to questions about how Scripture establishes meaning through language, as well as his awareness of a broader Arabic discourse of literary theory. The classic theories of Arabic literature were articulated by the first half of the tenth century, just before Salmon began his career as a biblical exegete. Disciplinary boundaries were particularly permeable in the Islamic world, so scholars of grammar and lexicography, theology, jurisprudence, logic, ethics, and mysticism all grappled with the problems and opportunities of figurative language alongside exegetes of the Torah or the Qurʾān. This robust and interconnected discussion of figurative speech and how to understand it provided Salmon with the exegetical tools for interpreting biblical imagery and explaining its function in Scripture.

[7] On lexical vs. cognitive clues for interpreting figurative language, see Hussein Abdul-Raof, *Arabic Rhetoric: A Pragmatic Analysis* (New York: Routledge, 2006), 211.

[8] Note that Salmon also marks figurative speech obliquely. He may use the common verb *faṣaḥa* ("to be eloquent") to indicate figurative speech; see comments to Lam 1:2, 2:1, 2:4, and 5:7.

In many cases Salmon uses this literary terminology according to its common meaning, rather than in a specialized technical sense. His somewhat inchoate and flexible application of literary terminology points toward three related conclusions. First, it confirms the research from historians of Arabic rhetoric that the concepts behind such terminology continued to develop during the early centuries of Islam, which created some confusion and inconsistency in the application of terms even after their meaning was largely established in the tenth century. Second, it indicates that Salmon was both attuned to the literary and exegetical thought of the Islamic world, and autonomous in his application of such concepts to the unique biblical conundrums that faced his interpretive community. This appropriation and adaptation of literary terminology occurred through the medium of Arabic language and culture, of which Salmon was both a recipient and an active contributor. Third, it shows that Salmon was not superficially applying this terminology to biblical literature but was conscientiously responding to the precise context and obscurities of the biblical passage under consideration. If this Arabic terminology informed Salmon's biblical inquiry, then it is equally true that Salmon's understanding of the Bible and his hermeneutical approach to it, drawn from rabbinic sources and his own scholarly training, also informed his use of the Arabic concepts. In the following sections I analyze the passages in which Salmon presents biblical metaphor through the categories of Arabic linguistic and literary theory.

Salmon's Arabic Terminology for Figurative Language

Salmon interprets figurative language whenever it arises; the format of his verse-by-verse translation and commentary compels him to respond to each image and metaphor. Even when he does not explicitly identify and label literary phenomena as such, Salmon's treatment of figurative language proves that he recognizes it when he encounters it in biblical texts.[9] In some cases, Salmon does explicitly invoke a technical framework for his interpretation of figurative language by using specific Arabic terminology. He may aver that a

[9] Although most Muslim exegetes also accepted the existence of figurative language, some denied it altogether, or denied that it appeared in the Qur'ān. On these "deniers of *majāz*," see Wolfhart Heinrichs, "On the Figurative Language (*majāz*) in Muslim Interpretation and Legal Hermeneutics," in *Interpreting Scriptures in Judaism, Christianity, and Islam: Overlapping Inquiries*, ed. Mordechai Z. Cohen and Adele Berlin (Cambridge: Cambridge University Press, 2016), 260–65.

given expression should be understood figuratively (*ʿalā sabīl al-majāz*), or he may designate a short passage as a metaphor (*istiʿara*), analogy (*tamthīl*), or parable (*mathal*).[10] These terms constitute the technical vocabulary of Arabic literary theory and Qurʾānic exegesis in the tenth century and beyond, and they increasingly appear in Karaite and other Jewish exegesis in Arabic in the generations after Salmon. Yet we cannot presume that Salmon, or his Muslim contemporaries, used these words in exactly the same sense that they acquire in later Arabic thought. Rather, we must analyze them in the context of Salmon's commentaries and exegetical practice, in order to appreciate Salmon's precise use and adaptation of this emerging technical vocabulary.[11] In this way, Salmon's oeuvre provides evidence for how such terms were conceptualized and applied in a formative period of biblical exegesis. The following discussion offers a close examination of the specific instances in which Salmon applies one of these terms to a given biblical expression. These cases provide preliminary evidence for Salmon's approach to figurative language in Scripture, and for his adaptations to the literary and exegetical resources that were available to him.

Figurative Language (*Majāz*) and Metaphor (*Istiʿāra*)

In his discussion of figurative language, Salmon incorporates the terms *majāz* and *istiʿāra*. Although these terms have come to be identified with figurative language, on the one hand, and metaphor or trope, on the other, both words have a long history in Arabic hermeneutical discourse prior to the tenth century. In its earliest attestations, *majāz* indicated the explanation or interpretation of any linguistic ambiguities whatsoever, including a range of literary devices, but by Salmon's time it came to denote the idioms and

[10] Cf. the near-absence of such terminology in Salmon's Ecclesiastes commentary, where Salmon takes pains to assert that there are no parables or allegories (*amthāl*) within the book (Robinson, *Asceticism*, 83). This difference suggests that (1) Salmon's approach to Lamentations was borne out of his sensitivity to its specific poetic and literary structure and (2) the aim of Salmon's exegetical work as a whole was to impart pious instruction. In the case of Ecclesiastes, such religious guidance was located in the literal meaning of the text; in the case of Lamentations, the poetic imagery must be decoded in order to yield such a message.

[11] Note also the Arab. terms for figurative language that Salmon does not use. The Lamentations commentary does not include *muḥkam* and *mutashābih* ("clear" and "ambiguous"). He uses the terms *ẓāhir* and *bāṭin* not in reference to the "external, apparent" and "internal, hidden" meanings of Scripture, but instead in reference to the external and internal demonstrations of pious commitment. See Salmon's comments to Lam 2:11 and 2:19.

figures of speech themselves, and focused most specifically on metaphor.[12] The term *isti'āra* also evolved between its earliest attestations and the mid-tenth century. Initially denoting a metaphor based in analogy, it came to refer to a metaphor based in comparison, as will be discussed below.[13] By Salmon's time the type of metaphor referred to as *isti'āra* was recognized as a subcategory—perhaps even the primary subcategory—of *majāz*.

Salmon uses the term *majāz* four times in his commentary on Lamentations, in his treatment of three different verses (1:22, 2:6, and 2:18). In these comments, *majāz* does not have an overtly technical function but seems to designate, generally, a category of language in which words mean something apart from their primary veridical sense. In the first two cases that I discuss here (Lam 2:6 and 1:22), Salmon's nonliteral interpretation of biblical imagery serves to uphold a theological principle of divine incorporeality. Like his Muslim contemporaries, Salmon finds *majāz* a useful hermeneutical tool for protecting God from any suspicion of corporeality.[14]

The threat of divine anthropomorphism is acute in the first pericope of Lamentations 2. This passage assembles a series of metaphors that represent divine anger.[15] For Salmon, the ascription of human emotion to God violates the principle of divine incorporeality. Thus, Salmon's main concern is not with the images themselves, in which, for example, God is depicted as an enemy firing arrows at Israel or laying waste to its strongholds (Lam 2:4–5), since the figurative aspect of this imagery is obvious. Rather, his most urgent concern is with a deeper level of comparison, namely, the attribution of a human emotion, such as violent rage, to God. This pious concern motivates Salmon's interpretation of Lamentations 2:6 as an example of *majāz*.

[12] On the development of *majāz* in early Islamic thought, see Wolfhart Heinrichs, "On the Genesis of the Ḥaqîqa-Majâz Dichotomy," *Studia Islamica* 59 (1984): 111–40, and Heinrichs, "Contacts Between Scriptural Hermeneutics and Literary Theory in Islam: The Case of Majāz," *Zeitschrift für Geschichte der Arabisch-islamischen Wissenschaften* 7 (1991): 253–84. In Heinrich's studies, the early period is represented by the philologist Abū 'Ubayda (d. 209/824–25); the intermediate stage by the theologian al-Jāḥiẓ (d. 255/868), both of Basra; and the later stage by Ibn Qutayba (d. 276/889). See "Contacts," 255–58. General overviews of *majāz* include Peter Heath, "Metaphor," in *EQ*; B. Reinert, "Ma<u>dj</u>āz; in Arabic Literature," in *EI2*; and Udo Simon, "*Majāz*," in *EALL*.

[13] Wolfhart Heinrichs, *The Hand of the Northwind: Opinions on Metaphor and the Early Meaning of Isti'āra in Arabic Poetics* (Wiesbaden: Deutsche Morgenländische Gesellschaft, 1977).

[14] See Heinrichs, "Contacts," 258–66. The neutralization of anthropomorphism is a significant factor in Salmon's use of the term *majāz* in his Psalms commentary as well. There the term appears in connection with Pss 5:2, 11:4, 91:4 (5×), 114:3 (2×), and 119:78. His remarks at Ps 91:4 constitute a minor excursus on the topic. The imagery of the biblical verse represents God as having pinions and wings; for Salmon all these images are "in the way of *majāz*."

[15] See Antje Labahn, "Fire from Above: Metaphors and Images of God's Actions in Lamentations 2:1–9," *JSOT* 31, no. 2 (2006): 239–56.

In the central imagery of Lamentations 2:6, God erupts in anger, wrathfully destroying "His booth" like a garden and demolishing the cultic and royal institutions of Zion: *He has scattered* [*va-yaḥmos*] *His bower like a garden, laid in ruins His Temple; the LORD has brought to an end in Zion festival and Sabbath, and in His fierce anger has spurned king and priest.* Salmon interprets the figures of speech methodically, one image at a time. First, he compares the imagery of agricultural destruction to parallel imagery in the book of Job:

> They say that *va-yaḥmos* is from [the root] *ḥamas* as in the verse, *He will shake off his unripe grape, like the vine* (Job 15:33). In other words, He is angry like the grapevine that is angered by its unripe grapes, which do not ripen and become grapes [so] he throws them off [while] they are still unripe. These meanings [i.e., "shaking off" and "uncovering"] are similar to each other. Their purpose is to provide a parable (*mathal*) for the disgrace and the cessation of [divine] support that have overtaken this nation, so that everyone who contemplates them will apprehend their intended meaning.

The verse from Lamentations, like the verse from Job, forges a comparison between the destruction of a garden and the destruction of the community, deprived of divine support. For Salmon, the basis of this comparison is clear, so that anyone who considers the imagery will reach the meaning that it conveys. He then proceeds to another level of figurative expression in the verse:

> They say also that the meaning (*maʿnā*) of *va-yaḥmos* is that God became angry with His shelter, in the sense (*maʿnā*) of seizing His Temple and all that was within it, including *the ark and the glory and the altars and the musical instruments and the sacrifices and the temple instruments*, just as every good thing that was in the garden was taken from it and it was left empty and vacant, as it is said, *And I will make it a waste; it shall not be pruned or hoed* (Isa 5:6). One who translates *va-yaḥmos* as "He became angry" is justified. However, if someone should say, "How can this relate back to the anger of the Creator?" we would say, "The sterility of the seeds relates back to the Creator and He changes them from one state to [another] state, and the meaning (*maʿnā*) of sterility is like the meaning (*maʿnā*) of anger." All these statements conform to the standards of figurative language (*majāz*) and accessibility to human understanding (*taqrīb ʿalā ifhām banī ādam*).

In this comment, Salmon presents divine anger as an instance of figurative speech. The focus of the comparison in Lamentations 2:6 is the destruction, and the analogy between the destruction of an agricultural plot and the destruction of Jerusalem. In order to cast God as the agent of this destruction, however, the verse extends the metaphor, comparing God to an angry gardener. To those who would object that the Creator cannot be angry, Salmon simultaneously affirms their theological correctness and refutes their exegetical criticism. The suggestion of divine anger must not be taken literally, but rather must be accepted as a figurative expression (*majāz*), crafted in order to accommodate the limits of human comprehension (*taqrīb ʿalā ifhām banī ādam*). With this doubled explanation, Salmon pinpoints his notion of the purpose of *majāz* within Scripture. Figurative imagery expresses theological truth in terms that humans may understand, so that all who consider the image will understand its meaning.

This accommodating function of biblical language was not an innovation of medieval Jewish thought.[16] It was already noted by the ancient rabbis that "Scripture speaks in human language," and later Jewish thinkers continued to reflect on the interpretive freedoms and responsibilities implied by such an approach.[17] Salmon's older Karaite contemporary, Yaʿqūb al-Qirqisānī, included this principle among his thirty-seven exegetical premises, which he enumerates in the introduction to his *Book of Gardens and Parks* (*Kitāb al-Riyāḍ wa-l-Ḥadāʾiq*), a commentary on the non-legal portions of the Pentateuch, which he completed in 938.[18] There al-Qirqisānī affirms traditional observations about the accommodating function of biblical locutions: "Scripture addresses mankind in a manner accessible to their own understanding and about matters familiar to them from their own experience; this is what the Rabbanites mean when they say, 'The Law speaks with the tongue of men.'"[19] The examples that al-Qirqisānī produces fit into two categories. He first addresses biblical descriptions of God as having eyes or

[16] The general principle that Scripture contains figurative speech because it was revealed in human language is a commonplace in Islamic discourse as well. There scholars note that the Arabic language includes *majāz* and the Qurʾān is in Arabic; therefore, the Qurʾān contains *majāz*. See Heinrichs, "Muslim Interpretation," 262 and notes there.

[17] BT Berakhot 31b: דברה התורה בלשון בני אדם. Nevertheless, Zawanowska notes that Karaites may have been the first to apply this rabbinic statement to the problem of biblical imagery that suggests divine anthropomorphism; see "The Bible Read Through the Prism of Theology: The Medieval Karaite Tradition of Translating Explicit Anthropomorphisms into Arabic," *Journal of Jewish Thought and Philosophy* 24 (2016), 197 n. 104.

[18] *KA* 53–68. Qirqisānī's text breaks off in the middle of the twenty-fourth premise.

[19] *KA* 63; *Qirqisāni Studies*, 25–26.

ears, which he explains as locutions that convey divine awareness of all sights and sounds. Next, he considers divine speech. Granting that God's speech is entirely distinct from human speech, al-Qirqisānī must nevertheless affirm that the revealed commandments were in fact communicated by God. He compares the difference between divine speech and human language to the way that humans communicate with animals through "signs, hints, and noises" rather than proper language.

It is precisely this accommodating function of *majāz* that Salmon highlights in his comment to Lamentations 1:22. As with al-Qirqisānī's examples, this biblical verse has bearing on the doctrine of divine incorporeality. The speaker exhorts God to consider the evildoing of Israel's enemies, and to punish them just as the crimes of Israel have been punished: *Let all their evil-doing come before You; and deal with them as You have dealt with me.* Salmon explains this exhortation by way of an Arabic paraphrase—"Let our petition be raised to You, and let befall our adversary whatever he deserves"—followed by his conclusion that "This speech is in the way of accommodation and figurative language (*hādha-l-qawl ʿalā l-taqrīb wa-l-majāz*)." Salmon's paraphrase mirrors the biblical text so closely that his recourse to *majāz* is initially puzzling. Typically, the meaning (*maʿnā*) that Salmon assigns to a *majāz* expression transforms at least one of the figurative elements into a homiletical teaching, but in this case, the transformation is subtle indeed.

Salmon's concern would seem to be the anthropomorphism inherent in the biblical expression *before You.* Taken literally, this wording presumes to locate God in physical space. Such spatial references are so intrinsic to the Hebrew language that their metaphorical origins are easily overlooked.[20] Without drawing attention to the theological difficulty, Salmon asserts that this biblical locution accords with the principles of *majāz* and that it functions to make meaning accessible to human comprehension. The point here, so it would seem, is to alert students of the Bible to the metaphorical constructions that underlie all speech, in Hebrew as in Arabic, in Scripture as in common parlance. An awareness of the spatial metaphors that inhere in all

[20] On such "dead metaphors" in later medieval Jewish exegesis, see Mordechai Z. Cohen, *Three Approaches to Biblical Metaphor from Abraham Ibn Ezra to Maimonides and Kimhi*, EJM 26 (Leiden: Brill, 2008), 24–25. Salmon's concept is not exclusively motivated by theological propriety; he also points out the metaphorical underpinnings of common language when it does not apply to God. For example, in his comment to Lam 2:21—*In the dust of the streets lie the young and the old*—Salmon explains that "by *lie down* he does not mean sleep; rather, he alludes to death." In biblical Hebr., "lying down" is such a common idiom for death that it may be considered a dead metaphor.

linguistic expression is particularly serviceable for correctly interpreting the verses that concern God.

In both of these examples, Salmon presents *majāz* alongside *taqrīb ʿalā ifhām banī ādam*. This possible hendiadys suggests that the purpose or defining feature of *majāz* is that it renders complicated ideas through language, enabling human beings to comprehend them. This notion of *majāz* resembles the earlier concept of the term, in which "any imaginable violation of the mirror character of language" could be identified as *majāz*, including ellipsis, lack of grammatical agreement, and any other ambiguity.[21] As Salmon offers no theory or explanation of *majāz*, his sense of the term must be determined by examining his interpretation of the precious few passages that he designates as such. However, the biblical statements that he so identifies have little in common with one another when parsed on a linguistic level. Their shared feature exists, rather, on a conceptual and hermeneutic plane. Taken literally, both verses conflict with Salmon's theological stance: Lamentations 2:6 attributes the emotion of anger to God, and Lamentations 1:22 suggests that God has a physical presence. It is these theological issues that lead Salmon to interpret the verses figuratively or, as he puts it, "according to the *majāz*."[22] Thus, Salmon's concept of *majāz* may be informed more by ideological considerations than linguistic ones, and justified more by cognitive clues than by lexical ones.

In the third example, Salmon pairs *majāz* not with *taqrīb* but with *istiʿāra*. Here Salmon considers the imagery of Lamentations 2:18: *Let tears stream down like a wadi day and night!* This poetic imagery does not concern God, and the impetus behind Salmon's comment is literary. What does it mean for tears to stream down "like a wadi" (Hebr. *ka-naḥal*; Arab. *mithl-al-wādi*)?[23] Salmon explains:

> *Like a wadi* is an example of figurative language (*majāz*), just as it is said, *let the pupil of your eye not rest*, even though rest does not fall upon the

[21] Heinrichs, "On the Genesis," 122–23. John Wansbrough provides the complete list of thirty-nine kinds of *majāz* from the same source, Abū ʿŪbayda's mid-ninth century *Majāz al-Qurʾān*, in "*Majāz al-Qurʾān*: Periphrastic Exegesis," *BSOAS* 33 (1970): 247–66, esp. 248–54.

[22] The use of emergent literary theory in solving theological problems is well attested. See, e.g., Heinrichs, "Contacts," 258–66; and, in the Karaite sphere, Meira Polliack and Eliezer Schlossberg, "Historical-Literary, Rhetorical, and Redactional Methods of Interpretation in Yefet ben ʿEli's Introduction to the Minor Prophets," in *Exegesis and Grammar in Medieval Karaite Texts*, *JSSS* 13, ed. Geoffrey Khan (Oxford: Oxford University Press, 2001), 1–40.

[23] Note that this biblical expression includes the comparative particle *ka*, which makes the simile explicit.

> pupil. Rather, this is said by way of figurative language (*majāz*) and metaphor (*istiʿāra*).

Salmon observes that the literal reading of this verse does not correspond to reality. In order to clarify the figurative aspect, he compares this phenomenon to another figurative expression from the same biblical verse: *let the pupil of your eye not rest.* In this expression Salmon finds a cognitive clue that the verse cannot be interpreted literally: the eye is not capable of rest because rest belongs only to those creatures that are capable of sleeping. Thus, the poet has borrowed the concept of rest from those creatures and lent it to the eye. Salmon has appropriately labeled this biblical image as a case of *istiʿāra* (lit., "borrowing"). Still, Salmon has failed to provide an analysis of the initial image, *let tears stream down like a wadi.* He has asserted that this image adheres to the same literary patterns of *istiʿāra* that characterize the second example, *let the pupil of your eye not rest*, and that his explication of the latter expression applies equally well to the former. In this way he glosses over the fact that the former expression is quite different.

When we compare these two expressions, we find that the foundations of the comparison are not the same. *Let tears stream down like a wadi* is based on a simple comparison, while *let the pupil of your eye not rest* is based on an analogy. This distinction corresponds to the distinction that Heinrichs has identified between "old" and "new" concepts of metaphor in the tradition of Arabic poetic theory.[24] In his study of *istiʿāra* between the eighth and eleventh centuries, Heinrichs finds that the earlier literary scholars identified a certain kind of metaphor, based on analogy (*tamthīl*), as *istiʿāra*. He illustrates this "old" idea of *istiʿāra* with the following line of pre-Islamic poetry: "When Death sinks its claws in, you find all amulets of no avail." The opening image cannot be understood literally, since death, in reality, has no claws. This type of metaphor is the result of two ideas linked by an analogy, which Heinrichs spells out as follows: "When death comes to somebody, it is inevitable, just as a beast of prey, when it clings to its victim, does not let go."[25] It is for this reason that the metaphor was originally called *istiʿāra*, or "borrowing": "It means borrowing an object from an owner who possesses it in our real world"—in this case, the claws of the

[24] Heinrichs, *The Hand of the Northwind.*
[25] Ibid., 6.

beast of prey—"and giving it on loan to one who does not"—in this case, death. Heinrichs identifies this kind of expression as a metaphor of "imaginary ascription."[26]

Salmon's interpretation of *let the pupil of your eye not rest* adheres to this "old" definition of *istiʿāra*. The underlying analogy may be expressed as, "When the pupil of the eye produces tears, it does not stop, just as a creature, when overcome with emotion, does not rest." Indeed, Salmon's exegetical remarks follow the standard formula for indicating metaphors of imaginary ascription in Arabic-Islamic contexts. The biblical imagery ascribes to the eye an attribute that it only possesses in the imagination: the capacity for rest.[27] In effect, it borrows the physiological capability for sleep and rest from the creatures that possess it in our own world, and transfers it to the eye, which does not naturally have this capacity. Salmon draws our attention to the imaginary aspect of this borrowing by stating that "rest does not fall upon the pupil." His Muslim near-contemporaries pointed out cases of *istiʿāra* with a similar formula. In response to the metaphor of death sinking its claws in, for example, Thaʿlab (d. 291/904) notes only that "death has no claw," and he repeats this formula ("A has no a") as an explanation for five additional cases of *istiʿāra*.[28] In the context of the Lamentations commentary, Salmon's parallel observation that "rest does not fall upon the pupil" seems so obvious that it hardly bears mentioning. But this formula is precisely the kind used to designate metaphors of imaginary ascription. Further, the prevalence of such statements in the texts that Heinrichs examines suggests that this formulation may have been shorthand for identifying instances of *istiʿāra* in the broader Arabic tradition of literary analysis.

Returning to Salmon's comment on Lamentations 2:18, we find that *let tears stream down like a wadi* does not involve an analogy like the one found in *let the pupil of your eye not rest*. Rather, this image is established by the similarity (*tashbīh*) between floods of tears and the floods of a wadi. This image corresponds to what Heinrichs considers the "new" metaphor, which became prominent especially in the Abbasid poetry of Salmon's era. Heinrichs notes that the shifting definition of *istiʿāra* continued to perplex medieval

[26] Ibid., 9.
[27] On metaphor as imaginary ascription in later Jewish contexts, see Cohen, *Three Approaches*, 57–62.
[28] Heinrichs, *The Hand of the Northwind*, 9.

literary scholars, particularly when the less precise application of these literary terms in Qurʾānic exegesis influenced later literary theory.[29] Salmon's comment suggests that even as he equates the expressions *let tears stream down like a wadi* and *let the pupil of your eye not rest*, he also distinguishes between them. He identifies the first phrase as *majāz* and the second phrase as *majāz* and *istiʿāra*. It is possible that Salmon understands *majāz* as the overarching rhetorical category, with *istiʿāra* as a particular subset.[30] Moreover, Salmon seems to consider *let the pupil of your eye not rest* as the *locus classicus* of *istiʿāra* within Lamentations. He uses the term *istiʿāra* only twice in the commentary, and in both cases it refers to this image.[31]

As always, Salmon's interest in literary imagery serves his exegetical and homiletical mission. For him, it is crucial to recognize instances of *majāz* and *istiʿāra* because interpreting them literally would yield false religious conclusions. However, the theoretical minutiae and the distinctions between analogy-based metaphors and comparison-based metaphors are tangential to Salmon's project. As a Karaite exegete, and not a poet or literary scholar, Salmon is concerned principally with the spiritual meaning of such imagery. Thus, he frames his discussion of this imagery by clarifying the meanings to which each phrase alludes. The expression *let tears stream down like a wadi* "alludes to the amount of crying over what happened to this nation and her sanctuary." As for *let the pupil of your eye not rest*, "its meaning is that you will be overwhelmed with crying in these times of prayer and these times of lament over our rebellions and over what happened to us in the way of affliction and exile and abandonment." In introducing the applied meaning of figurative language, Salmon almost always uses the term *maʿnā* ("meaning") or, secondarily, the term *ishāra* ("allusion"), which he uses interchangeably with *maʿnā*. Only once does he use the term *ḥaqīqa*, which became prevalent in the Arabic discourse of the tenth century as the veridical counterpart to, and opposite of, *majāz*.

[29] Ibid., 14.

[30] The relationship between *majāz* and *istiʿāra* is still subject to imprecision in Salmon's time. For example, Heinrichs refers to two rhetorical manuals, one from the first half of the tenth century and the other from the second half, in which *majāz* and *istiʿāra* appear roughly as synonyms ("Contacts," 271, 273–74). It is impossible to determine Salmon's theoretical concept of these terms, either on their own or in relation to one another, on the basis of so few attestations in the Lamentations commentary.

[31] See also Salmon's comment to Lam 3:49.

The True Sense (*Ḥaqīqa*)

Majāz was articulated in contradistinction to *ḥaqīqa* even before this pairing fully crystallized in the tenth century. While *ḥaqīqa* designates the accurate lexical definition of a given term, *majāz* represents the figurative expansion of that word beyond its standard lexical meaning. In works of Arabic grammar, poetics, and theology, the terms often appear together, with one word analyzed in relation to the other. In Salmon's Lamentations commentary, the opposite holds: while he uses the term *majāz* repeatedly, the word *ḥaqīqa* appears only once in a linguistic or literary capacity. While the single attestation of this term does not provide sufficient evidence for a full analysis of Salmon's approach to *ḥaqīqa*, it is worth noting that his use of the term reflects the same conflation between the literal meaning and the spiritual significance that we find throughout his exegetical project. The interpretation that Salmon presents as the *ḥaqīqa* derives from his examination of biblical prooftexts with similar imagery, rather than any analysis of the lexical, real-world meaning of the biblical word.

Salmon's single reference to *ḥaqīqa* appears in his treatment of "God's footstool" in Lamentations 2:1. This verse presents the themes of divine wrath and punishing destruction that frequent the second chapter of Lamentations: *How the Lord in His anger has set the daughter of Zion under a cloud! He has cast down from heaven to earth the splendor of Israel; He has not remembered His footstool in the day of His anger.* In this formulation, Zion—which is identified with God's footstool through synonymous parallelism—sits in the crosshairs of God's wrath.[32] Salmon's comment is lengthy—as we would expect for the opening verse of a biblical chapter, in which the comments provide a thematic overview of the chapter as a whole—and he discusses the footstool image almost as an afterthought, in the final sentences of his comment.

God's footstool appears in five other passages of the Hebrew Bible.[33] It is always closely linked with the institutions of Zion, such as the Temple and the Davidic dynasty, and it is based in ancient Near Eastern traditions of a

[32] The identification of the Temple and the footstool is long-standing, and already woven into the Aram. Targum: "He did not remember *the Temple which was* His footstool." See Christian M. M. Brady, *The Rabbinic Targum of Lamentations: Vindicating God*, Studies in the Aramaic Interpretation of Scripture 3 (Leiden: Brill, 2003), 158. I have cited the RSV here, to emphasize Salmon's interpretation of the verse's Hebr. imagery.

[33] Pss 99:5, 110:1, 132:7; Isa 66:1; and 1 Chr 28:2.

warrior deity who rests his feet in times of peace and rises to trample his enemies in times of war. Salmon is not concerned with the ancient religious logic behind the biblical imagery, but he is always alert to the homiletical possibilities contained in the Bible itself. Here he invokes prooftexts from the historical books of the Bible in order to determine the *ḥaqīqa* of the footstool in Lamentations 2:1:

> *He has not remembered His footstool in the day of His anger.* [Jeremiah] eloquently alludes to the Temple and the *ark* and the *glory* that are within it, as it is said, *I had it in my heart to build a house of rest for the ark of the covenant of the LORD, and for the footstool of our God* (1 Chr 28:2). The real sense (*ḥaqīqa*) of *He has not remembered His footstool* is, He did not have compassion on this holy place in the time of Nebuchadnezzar, as He did in ancient times, when it was said, *because He had compassion on His people and on His dwelling place* (2 Chr 26:15).

Just as Salmon so often uses *maʿnā* to refer to the homiletical meaning of an image, here he uses *ḥaqīqa* to signal the religious significance of the image rather than the real-world, dictionary definition of this word. Put another way, Salmon has conflated the *ḥaqīqa* and the *maʿnā*, so that the "real sense" of the footstool is not an actual footstool, as we would expect, but rather the Jerusalem sanctuary to which it alludes, and the pious interpretation of God's abandonment of that sanctuary in the historical narrative. Essentially Salmon has interpreted the footstool not as *majāz*, but as a word to be explained in light of biblical verses that incorporate the same terminology. Even at the first level of interpretation, Salmon does not approach the footstool as a real-world object—that is to say, as a cushion for resting one's feet—but rather as a religious symbol whose spiritual meaning may be ascertained by cross references to other biblical attestations of the same image. Unlike the Muslim theorists who use *ḥaqīqa* for the nonfigurative, veridical meaning of language, Salmon uses the term to indicate the homiletical message. Thus, in this case, the *maʿnā* and the *ḥaqīqa* are synonymous.[34]

[34] Nevertheless, Salmon uses the term *maʿnā* constantly and the term *ḥaqīqa* only once in the Lamentations commentary, suggesting that the two terms were not equally apt. Note that *maʿnā* was "an extremely rare term" in the earliest (i.e., eighth century) Qurʾān commentaries, although Muslim exegetes of the period frequently used the verb *yaʿnī* ("it means"); see C. H. M. Versteegh, *Arabic Grammar and Qurʾānic Exegesis in Early Islam*, SSLL 19 (Leiden: Brill, 1993), 97.

Still, Salmon's application of the term *ḥaqīqa* suggests analogues in the Islamic intellectual tradition. In his monograph on the history of the term *maʿnā*, Alexander Key argues that Muslim scholars used *ḥaqīqa* to mean "accuracy," whether in reference to the correct meaning of a word or the truth of divine revelation. Scholars in all fields recognized the need to achieve an accurate understanding of reality, making the concept of *ḥaqīqa* broadly applicable (beyond strictly lexical or literary contexts) as the literal counterpart to figurative speech. Key explains that "*ḥaqīqa* was the theologians' goal: to accurately align their mental contents (and their vocal forms) with the truth of the divine creation."[35] Key coins the phrases "mental contents" and "vocal forms" to render the Arabic words *maʿnā* and *lafẓ*, respectively. He argues that theologians and other thinkers aspired to accuracy when they articulated their ideas through language, and for this reason *ḥaqīqa* could refer both to the accuracy of the concept itself (*maʿnā*) and to the accuracy of its representation through language (*lafẓ*). The work of theology was to understand the world and God's role within it, and also to give reliable verbal expression to that truth. Therefore, *ḥaqīqa* can refer to the truth, the concept of that truth, and the linguistic expression of that truth. In this way, Muslim theologians in the decades after Salmon treated *ḥaqīqa* as the true and accurate reality, even when this reality was ascertained through *majāz*, suggesting that, like Salmon, they did not conceive a strictly binary relationship between the two terms.

Salmon's comment to Lamentations 2:1 suggests lines of inquiry to be considered in future studies of Arabic literary theory and its development in this period. Salmon uses the word *ḥaqīqa* as a pointer to the true spiritual import of the footstool image. While *majāz* and *ḥaqīqa* are two separate concepts in his work, they are not antithetical to one another. For Salmon, the correct homiletical interpretation of figurative language must always discover and disclose true and accurate divine instruction. Thus, Salmon's initially perplexing application of the term *ḥaqīqa* to his highly symbolic interpretation of God's footstool affirms his commitment to homiletical interpretation as the most accurate and true understanding of biblical content, regardless of whether or not that content is expressed figuratively.

[35] Alexander Key, *Language Between God and the Poets:* Maʿnā *in the Eleventh Century* (Oakland: University of California Press, 2018), 241.

Likening, Analogy, or Extended Metaphor (*Tamthīl*)

Figurative language is rooted in comparison, and comparative reasoning is central to Salmon's hermeneutic in the Lamentations commentary. In fact, Salmon identifies the command to compare within the biblical book itself, and he justifies his extensive comparative inquiry on the basis of verses such as *Look and see if there is any sorrow like my sorrow* (Lam 1:12) and *What can I say for you, to what compare you, O daughter of Jerusalem?* (Lam 2:13). For Salmon these verses constitute divinely authorized commands to engage in comparative thinking, and to find pious instruction within such comparisons. Thus, Salmon thinks comparatively whenever he finds an opportunity to do so, and he grounds his pietistic conclusions in the practice of comparison.

The comparisons that Salmon recognizes in the biblical text, and the comparisons that he generates through exegesis, are wide-ranging. At this point I will focus on the comparisons that Salmon explicitly designates as instances of *mathal* (pl. *amthāl*) or *tamthīl* (pl. *tamāthil*). In Salmon's usage, this pair indicates a parable (*mathal*) and the process of likening one thing to another analogically (*tamthīl*); this sort of comparison may stand on its own or may lay the groundwork for an extended metaphor or parable.[36] The study and collection of Arabic *amthāl* flourished in Salmon's time, and yet the concept of *amthāl* that drives Salmon's discussion is derived not from Arabic culture but from biblical literature and traditional Jewish interpretation of it.[37] The Arabic term *mathal* is cognate to the Hebrew term *mashal* (pl. *meshalim*), which appears throughout the Bible, although the specific criteria for this rhetorical category are ambiguous. It may be that Salmon uses the Arabic term *mathal* primarily to refer to a parable when it has been designated as a *mashal* in the Bible, whereas he uses *tamthīl* to refer more generally to the act of likening one thing to another. This act of comparison often suggests or even produces parables, but Salmon prefers to designate such analogies with the term *tamthīl* rather than *mathal*. In the passages from Lamentations that

[36] In more technical contexts, *tamthīl* would signify an extended metaphor (vs. *tashbīh*, simile). For Salmon, however, the term has a wider and more general application to different kinds of comparisons, although it nonetheless includes extended metaphors. Note also that Salmon rarely uses the term *tashbīh* (never in the commentaries on Lamentations or Ecclesiastes [see Robinson, *Asceticism*, 83]; twice in the commentary on Psalms).

[37] Note, however, that much of the content of medieval Arab. *amthāl* collections would more accurately be called "proverbs" than "parables." For a catalog of *amthāl* collections from the eighth century onward, see Riyad Aziz Kassis, *The Book of Proverbs and Arabic Proverbial Works*, VTSupp 74 (Leiden: Brill, 1999), 14–22.

Salmon identifies as *tamthīl*, a narrative does not necessarily accompany the comparison, although Salmon himself may develop a narrative expansion in the course of his comment. As with his use of *majāz* and *istiʿāra*, Salmon's primary guide in the figurative interpretation of instances of *tamthīl* and *mathal* is the biblical text itself.

One example of Salmon's use of *tamthīl* appears in his comment to Lamentations 1:6b–c. This verse presents a metaphor in which the "princes" of Zion are compared to harts: *Her princes have become like harts that find no pasture; they fled without strength before the pursuer*. Salmon explains the verse as follows:

> *Her princes have become like harts*. This is because Israel has been likened to harts on the basis of the intensity of their thirst, as it is said, *As a hart longs for flowing streams* [*so longs my soul for You, O God*] (Ps 42:2/1). The reason for likening (*tamthīl*) Israel to harts is that it is in the nature of harts to eat vipers, which are extremely poisonous. When harts consume them, they become hot and urgently seek out water. Yet when they come to streams of water, they do not drink immediately, for God has instilled it in their nature not to drink immediately. When they do drink immediately, they suffer diarrhea and die. So now, seeing water, they remain thirsty for a while, unable to drink; all the same, they cry out and make a clamor. Thus, Israel during this exile is likened to them. The LORD's Torah and the words of the prophets are likened to water, and now they are thirsting for wisdom, when there is among them much conflict and discord, just as it is said, *"Behold, the days are coming," says the Lord GOD, "when I will send a famine on the land; not a famine of bread, nor a thirst for water, but of hearing the words of the LORD"* (Amos 8:11).

Salmon does not pause to explain why "princes" represent Israel, but he immediately begins explaining the grounds for the comparison between Israel and harts. He presents this relationship as one of comparison or likening, using the formula that he repeats throughout the commentary: *tamthīl* X *bi*-Y. In this case, the phrase is *tamthīl yiśraʾel bi-ʾayyalim*, which we might translate as "Israel is likened to harts" or perhaps even "an extended metaphor of Israel as harts."

Salmon's first line of justification comes through corroboration with a verse from Psalms that espouses the same imagery. This verse also presents an analogy, in which the harts' thirst for water is likened to the soul's longing for God. This prooftext enables Salmon to circumscribe the analogy of Lamentations 1:6, protecting it from freewheeling interpretations by restricting the comparison to the intense thirst experienced by harts and, analogically, by Israel.[38] It is only after this biblical foundation that Salmon supplies a naturalistic explanation for the harts' thirst. This naturalistic excursus explains why harts are associated with thirst and, therefore, why Israel is compared to them. However, Salmon's description of the harts' urge to eat vipers, the extreme thirst that results, their refusal to drink, and the agony that they endure even when water is available to ease their misery is not only a scientific justification for the accuracy of the extended metaphor. Rather, Salmon chooses which details to provide, and how to present them, in anticipation of the allegorical message that he intends to assert within his comment.

The analogy that undergirds Salmon's metaphor might be expressed as "As a hart thirsts for water after swallowing a viper, so Israel thirsts for Torah in a time of discord." Israel is compared to the hart, the divine words of Scripture are compared to water, and the conflict and discord are compared to the scalding poison of the viper.[39] Salmon hardly need spell out the full implications of this allegory: just as the hart suffers from his refusal to drink the water, so the Jews endure continued exile because of their refusal to return to the Torah even when its precepts are accessible to them. In this way Salmon embeds an anti-Rabbanite polemic—blaming the exile on the Rabbanites' neglect of Torah—within his interpretation of the central metaphor of Lamentations 1:6.

Still, a metaphorical expression remains, for how can Israel "thirst" for Torah? Rather than describing the features of thirst that make it an appropriate metaphor for Israel's desire for Torah, or drawing once more on Psalm 42:2/1, which equates the harts' thirst with the soul's longing, Salmon supports this figurative application of "thirst" with another biblical prooftext. In one of Amos's prophecies of doom, God threatens that famine and thirst will befall Israel. However, the people will not thirst for water, as Amos explains, but rather, for the words of God (Amos 8:11). A biblical locution in which one may hunger and thirst for divine speech rather than food and water offers Salmon an avenue for presenting the expression in Lamentations 1:6 not as

[38] In Arabic rhetoric the thirst would be designated as the *wajh al-shabah*, "the feature of similitude," but Salmon does not use this term. See Abdul-Raof, *Arabic Rhetoric*, 211.

[39] In his comment to Ps 42:2/1, Salmon reports a range of opinions that justify comparisons between the word of God and water.

figurative language, but as part of the literal semantic range of thirst in the biblical Hebrew language.

This exegetical move may signal Salmon's preference for literal interpretation, whenever possible, over figurative interpretation. Such a preference accords with known principles of exegesis in both Karaite and Rabbanite schools. Salmon's older contemporaries, the Karaite al-Qirqisānī and the Rabbanite Saadia Gaon, both make normative pronouncements about this exegetical priority in their respective tomes, the *Book of Gardens and Parks* and the *Book of Beliefs and Opinions*. Al-Qirqisānī's second principle of exegesis is that "Scripture as a whole is to be interpreted literally, except where literal interpretation may involve something objectionable or imply a contradiction."[40] Saadia addresses the topic in his treatise on resurrection, where he builds an argument for the absolute truth of this religious principle on the basis of correct interpretation of key biblical verses. In establishing the foundations of his argument, he declares that "it is a well-known fact that every statement found in the Bible is to be understood in its literal sense except for those that cannot be so construed for one of the following four reasons."[41] For Saadia, verses that contradict sense perception, reason, another biblical verse, or rabbinic tradition must be interpreted nonliterally.[42] While neither Salmon nor al-Qirqisānī would include rabbinic tradition among the sources that overturn literal readings of biblical verses, they all agree that nonliteral interpretation should be limited only to those circumstances in which literal interpretation is impossible. By reading Lamentations 1:6 in light of Psalm 42:2/1 and Amos 8:11, Salmon manages to produce a surprisingly literal and contextual interpretation of figurative language.

Salmon hears the call to comparative reasoning most clearly in Lamentations 1:12. In Salmon's interpretation, the verse demands precisely the kind of comparative thought that dominates his own approach to Lamentations. The speaker of the verse calls out, *Look and see if there is any sorrow like my sorrow*. Salmon accepts this exegetical challenge with a range of comparisons that run throughout the commentary. In the introduction, this verse initiates Salmon's extensive comparison between the sufferings of Israel and the sufferings of Job, and here Salmon reminds readers of that

[40] *KA*, 60.

[41] *Book of Beliefs and Opinions*, Treatise VII, 265.

[42] On Saadia's hermeneutic in practice, see Haggai Ben-Shammai, "The Tension Between Literal Interpretation and Exegetical Freedom: Comparative Observations on Saadia's Method," in *With Reverence for the Word: Medieval Scriptural Exegesis in Judaism, Christianity, and Islam*, ed. Jane Dammen McAuliffe, et al. (Oxford: Oxford University Press, 2003), 33–50.

project and its conclusion: that indeed the calamities of Israel are greater. He reinforces the results of the comparison with prooftexts from Daniel and Ezekiel that confirm the uniqueness of Israel's punishment.

At this point in the excursus, however, Salmon's comparative work takes a turn: he compares the destruction of Israel to the destruction of the Pharaoh and Canaan, as recorded in the Bible. Whereas the previous comparisons emphasized the severity of Israel's suffering, this line of comparison allows for the exceptional quality of God's mercy toward Israel. For while these other peoples were completely annihilated, the Israelites were merely sent into exile. In the words of Jeremiah, God did not "make a full end" of Israel, as God did with the other nations. Salmon explains this distinction with an exquisite example of figurative reasoning:

> In what follows, He also says, *I will make a full end of all the nations* (Jer 30:11). Then it is said, *By measure* (*besa'sse'ah*), *by expulsion* (*beshalḥah*), *You did contend with them* (Isa 27:8). This means their destruction only resembled the destruction of their enemies to a certain extent because the word *besa'sse'ah* means "by the measure," as in *for every measure* (*se'on*) (Isa 9:4/5) and *a measure* (*se'ah*) *of fine meal* (2 Kgs 7:18). The meaning of "by the measure" is, in other words, "to a certain extent." [. . .] *By expulsion You did contend with them* (Isa 27:8) is a statement about its branches; he means to liken (*tamthīl*) Israel to a tree. He says that the destruction that happened to them was in their branches and not in their root, because *expulsion* (*shalḥah*) is like *its shoots* (*sheluḥoteha*) *spread abroad* (Isa 16:8).

Salmon may juxtapose Jeremiah 30:11 with Isaiah 27:8 in order to make a homiletical point, but his initial reading of both verses is straightforward and literal: God punished the Israelites "to a certain extent," namely, in this case, by exile. To this literal explanation he appends a striking figurative interpretation inspired by paronomasia, a typically Midrashic technique for generating non-contextual readings. Salmon presents the exile (*shalḥah*) as an allusion to the branches (*sheluḥot*) of a tree. With this wordplay in mind, Salmon declares that Isaiah compares Israel to a tree, thereby laying down the components of an extended metaphor. Salmon himself explains the meaning of such a parable: "The destruction that happened to them [i.e., Israel] was in their branches and not in their root." Just as the destruction of a tree's branches is far less severe than the destruction of a tree's roots, so the divine punishment of exile, which Israel endured, is far less severe than the punishment of complete annihilation, which Pharaoh and his armies, and the people of Canaan, endured. The exile then provides the remnant of Israel with proof of divine care.

Our final example of *tamthīl* occurs in Salmon's figurative interpretation of the phrase *under the rod of His wrath* (Lam 3:1) and stands apart from the examples considered above. Here Salmon applies the word *tamthīl* to a metaphor of the kind that Heinrichs has dubbed a metaphor of "name transfer" rather than one of "imaginary ascription."[43] Salmon decodes the "rod of His wrath" as a reference to the enemy of Israel, dispatched by God to execute punishment. As with all his interpretations of figurative language, Salmon looks first to the biblical text to support his interpretation:

> *Under the rod of His wrath* alludes to the likening (*tamthīl*) of the enemy to the rod, as it is said first regarding the king of Assyria, *Ah, Assyria, the rod of My anger, the staff of My fury* (Isa 10:5) and as it is said of Nebuchadnezzar, *The rod has blossomed, pride has budded* (Ezek 7:10). The "four kingdoms" are likened to "two staffs," as we have explained in the commentary on the Song of Songs. Indeed, they were *the generation of His wrath*, as it is said, [*for the LORD has rejected and*] *forsaken the generation of His wrath* (Jer 7:29).

The image of the rod points to a parable, encountered elsewhere in Scripture, in which the enemies of Israel are depicted according to their function in sacred history. For just as one uses a rod to strike another down in punishment, so God uses the Assyrians or the Babylonians to bring calamity upon Israel. While such a parable underlies these figures, here Salmon invokes this reading not on the comparative basis of the parable, but rather on the prooftexts that directly and unequivocally identify Assyria or Nebuchadnezzar as the "rod" and Israel as the "generation of His wrath." Salmon prefers to marshal biblical verses instead of explaining the mechanisms of analogical thinking that underlie such biblical metaphors. This example indicates that even when Salmon uses Arabic terminology, his concepts are formed by and articulated through his knowledge of the Bible. In the next and final example, we will see that Salmon follows biblical reasoning and Hebrew literary categories even

[43] I.e., a "new metaphor"; cf. an "old metaphor." See Heinrichs, *The Hand of the Northwind*. Salmon presents such "name transfer" style metaphors throughout his commentary. See, e.g., his reading of "the vultures" (Lam 4:19) as an allusion to Nebuchadnezzar or his reading of "the breath of our nostrils" (Lam 4:20) as an allusion to King Josiah.

when applying Arabic terminology to his explanations, and that his Arabic concepts of figurative language reflect his understanding of biblical language and literary forms.

Mathal and *Mashal*: Interpreting a Biblical Parable (The Pot of Ezekiel 11 and 24)

Salmon considers biblical parables in his excursus to Lamentations 4:1. There, he identifies Ezekiel's prophecy of the foul-smelling pot as a parable (*mathal*) and interprets it accordingly. For Salmon, a *mathal* is a similitude—based on *tamthīl*, the likening of one thing to another, as discussed above—that is intended "to represent something other than what it literally depicts."[44] Salmon treats Ezekiel's prophecy as an extended narrative in which each individual image relates to a specific aspect of historical reality. Even while he approaches this passage as a parable and identifies it as such throughout his excursus, his understanding of its allegorical quality comes not from Arabic literary theory, or from his own observations about its literary construction, but rather from the authority of Scripture itself: God refers to Ezekiel's prophecy as a *mashal* in the Hebrew text, and it is this biblical concept of a parable that dictates and defines Salmon's treatment of the prophecy as a *mathal*. Further, while Salmon relies on techniques of allegorical interpretation, his explanation of Ezekiel's pot is not itself allegorical. Already the interpretation of the parable is woven into the biblical parable itself. Thus, Salmon is able to expound a literal reading of the Bible's own figurative interpretation of a prophetic allegory.

The excursus at Lamentations 4:1 focuses on the Israelites' historical refusal to heed the warnings of their prophets. Salmon recounts the abuses that the prophets Jeremiah and Uriah suffered when they dared to communicate God's threats about the destruction of Jerusalem. The book of Jeremiah records that the people of Jerusalem, from the king to the common people, resented the prophets and even sought to kill them. Moreover, they developed their own figurative language to convey their stubborn disbelief in the prophets' warnings. They contradicted the prophetic threats with their own

[44] This description of a *mathal* comes from Alfred L. Ivry, "The Utilization of Allegory in Islamic Philosophy," in *Interpretation and Allegory: Antiquity to the Modern Period*, Studies in Intellectual History 101, ed. Jon Whitman, 153–80 (Leiden: Brill, 2000), 156.

metaphor: *This city is the caldron, and we are the meat!* (Ezek 11:3).[45] With this image, the people liken Jerusalem to a pot, and themselves to the meat, safe and protected within the confines of the pot. God uses the peoples' own metaphor to correct their misapprehensions: *This city shall not be your caldron, nor shall you be flesh in the midst of it; I will judge you at the border of Israel* (Ezek 11:11). Through this metaphor, God communicates that Jerusalem will no longer shelter its residents.

Salmon explains, in Arabic, that God commanded Ezekiel "to coin a parable (*mathal*) of the [same] kind that they were saying, as it is said, *and utter a parable* (mashal) *to the rebellious house and say to them, Thus says the Lord GOD: set on the pot, set it on, pour in water also* (Ezek 24:3)." The Israelites have spoken figuratively, and God responds in kind. The ensuing parable describes, in step-by-step detail, the preparation of stock, which comes to a sudden halt when the cooking pot is found to be filthy. First the water is drawn, the choice pieces of meat are laid in, and a fire is kindled to boil the meat and seethe the bones (Ezek 24:3–5). When the foul odor of the pot is detected, the pieces of meat are flung out, the broth is dumped out, and the bones are burned directly in the fire. The pot is returned to the smoking coals so that the heat will burn out the stench. But the odor is too great for such a measure to be effective. Only divine fury will cleanse the pot of its terrible odor (Ezek 24:6–14).

This parable is interlaced with its own interpretation. God identifies *the pot whose odor is in it* (Ezek 24:6) as the city and continues to decode the imagery throughout the passage. For example, God announces that the odor of the pot *is your filthy lewdness* (Ezek 24:14). Salmon picks up on this biblical technique of interpretation, explaining that God "interpreted the meaning" (*fassara al-maʿnā*) of the prophecy. God's own interpretation then provides the model for Salmon's interpretation of Ezekiel's parable. When he decodes the meaning of each element within the allegory, Salmon is filling in the details of an interpretive framework that is already established in Scripture.

Since Salmon follows the Bible's own interpretation of this parable, it is not surprising that he offers a historical, rather than an actualizing, reading of Ezekiel's prophetic imagery. The fire beneath the cooking pot alludes to Nebuchadnezzar, the Babylonian king through whom God's threats of destruction would be fulfilled. The overturned pot communicates both that

[45] In his excursus to Lam 3:1, Salmon also refers to the expressions that the people uttered in defiance of prophetic warnings, e.g., *The days grow long and every vision comes to nought* (Ezek 12:22), which is labeled as a *mashal*; and *Let Him make haste, let him speed His work that we may see it; let the purpose of the Holy One of Israel draw near, and let it come, that we may know it!* (Isa 5:19).

Jerusalem would be emptied of all treasures after Nebuchadnezzar's conquest and that Jerusalem would be emptied of its sinners after they had been sent into exile. The pot's odor represents the sins of Israel, which would only be purified through the punishing fires of divine vengeance. Salmon's reading of Ezekiel's parable strongly implies that these meanings were inherent in the prophetic message at the time of its delivery, intelligible to anyone who chose to take the prophets' warnings seriously. This historical-contextual meaning is all the more apparent from Salmon's post-biblical vantage point.[46]

Salmon's discussion of Ezekiel's parable illustrates his nuanced concept of biblical figurative language. For Salmon and the other Jerusalem Karaites, enigma and ambiguity have no place in the holy book.[47] God does not use parables in order to complicate Scripture. To the contrary, God issues figurative language through the prophets because figurative speech is part of human conventional language, familiar and accessible to human understanding. Salmon makes this point when designating certain expressions from Lamentations as figurative (*majāz*) and therefore constructed in such a way that they approach human understanding (*taqrīb ʿalā ifhām banī ādam*). The point is asserted once more in Salmon's link between the two pot parables in Ezekiel 11 and 24. In the Bible, the second parable begins with no reference to the first. God abruptly commands Ezekiel to *utter a parable* (mashal) *to the rebellious house* (Ezek 24:3) and begins describing the pot, without any nod to the peoples' similar metaphor from Ezekiel 11. Salmon treats this gap as an ellipsis within the biblical text, and he supplies the missing words that connect the two passages:

> When he [i.e., Ezekiel] described the magnitude of their offenses—to which they said, *This city is the caldron, and we are the flesh* (Ezek 11:3)—God

[46] The historicizing approach identified here is further developed by Yefet ben ʿEli, who articulates theoretical justifications for historical-contextual exegesis of prophetic literature at the beginning of his commentary on the minor prophets. See Meira Polliack, "Historicizing Prophetic Literature: Yefet ben ʿEli's Commentary on Hosea and Its Relationship to al-Qūmisī's *Pitron*," in *Pesher Naḥum: Texts and Studies in Jewish History and Literature from Antiquity Through the Middle Ages Presented to Norman (Naḥum) Golb*, ed. Joel Kraemer et al. (Chicago: Oriental Institute of the University of Chicago, 2012), 149–86.

[47] Marzena Zawanowska has persuasively attributed such a view to Yefet ben ʿEli in "Islamic Exegetical Terms in Yefet ben ʿEli's Commentaries on the Holy Scriptures," *JJS* 64 (2013): 306–25. Her argument is grounded in the fact that Yefet regularly uses terms borrowed from Qurʾānic hermeneutics to designate clear and apparent meaning (sc., *muḥkam* and *ẓahir*) while avoiding or limiting the terms that designate unclear or secret meaning (sc., *mutashābih* and *bāṭin*). Salmon's straightforward approach to the figurative expressions of the Bible is similar and likely emerges from a shared Karaite sense that the meaning of Scripture is clear and accessible, even when expressed figuratively.

> commanded Ezekiel to coin a parable (*mathal*) of the [same] kind that they were saying, as it is said, *And utter a parable* (mashal) *to the rebellious house* (Ezek 24:3).

Salmon's connective expansion does not merely supply a temporal link between the two passages. Its more important function is to demonstrate that God chose to communicate figuratively in order to respond in kind to human beings, speaking with the same figurative expressions that were already in use within human society. Salmon has applied and affirmed a common exegetical principle: Muslim texts routinely note that in the Qurʾān God speaks in the language of the Arabs, and Jewish texts routinely invoke the rabbinic maxim that the Torah speaks in human language. In linking the pot parables from Ezekiel 11 and 24, Salmon provides inner-biblical proof for this mechanism of divine–human communication.

Conclusions

This inquiry shows that Salmon had circumstantial familiarity with Arabic rhetorical terminology, and that he used this terminology when he found it beneficial to do so. He draws on it to designate the linguistic features on which his homiletical readings are based, and to justify his hermeneutical approach. Even so, his references to the technical vocabulary of Arabic linguistics are brief and often imprecise, suggesting that Salmon's principal guide in the interpretation of figurative language was not Arabic theory, but biblical text. His primary method, so appropriate to the values of Karaite biblical scholarship, is to compare the figures of speech in one passage to similar examples from elsewhere in Scripture. He approaches Lamentations as a biblical book whose meaning can be grasped through reason and the craft of careful reading, along with an awareness of historical context and linguistic convention. Figures of speech do not obscure biblical meaning, in Salmon's estimation, but only convey it in more familiar and accessible forms. Although Lamentations has no shortage of metaphors and other poetic devices, Salmon does not approach the text as a storehouse of examples to be collected and analyzed with the tools of Arabic rhetoric. He interprets most figurative language without calling attention to the fact that it is figurative at all, focusing his attention on its contextual or religious significance (*maʿnā*) without pinpointing the literary techniques through which this meaning is achieved. The fact that Salmon carries out his homiletical-exegetical task without referring to Arabic technical discourse through most of the commentary invites the question of why he invokes these Arabic terms at all, and why he uses them when he does. For each example cited above, in which Salmon designates a certain expression as *majāz*, *istiʿāra*, *ḥaqīqa*, *tamthīl*, or *mathal*, there are countless other examples of the same feature that he scarcely acknowledges as figurative language at all.

Salmon may express his interpretations through an Arabic literary vocabulary, but the Arabic terms that he employs are shaped by his own sense of biblical language and its meaning. Thus, Salmon is an active contributor, within his community, to the fields of literary and linguistic analysis that were developing at this time, and that became expansive intellectual resources for later Jewish interpreters in the Islamic world. The Karaite exegetes who follow Salmon use such terms with increasing sophistication, in part because Salmon and other tenth-century thinkers made the vocabulary relevant and useful for biblical studies. As later exegetes work to justify their interpretations through rational argument over homiletical instinct, they rely on the terms that Salmon implicitly defined in light of biblical evidence. Salmon brought this vocabulary into alignment with the Bible and Jewish intellectual culture, even when he used it sparingly. In this way, he helped to create a Jewish interpretive context for understanding the Arabic terms and their range of meaning.

Another dimension of Salmon's creative engagement with Jewish tradition through Arabic culture is manifested in his homiletical art. The Lamentations commentary has a strong homiletical bent, articulated through its pietistic themes and its persuasive rhetorical forms, as well as the insertion of self-contained homilies into key excursuses, all of which suggest an oral layer or the literary representation of oral features. In the next chapter, we consider Salmon's homiletical passages in the context of other Arabic sermons from the medieval Islamic East, in order to examine the interplay of Jewish spirituality and Arabic rhetoric from another angle.

5
The Art of the Homily

> *O Israel, repent and return to the Merciful One! Pity your souls for the Day of Judgment, for a day of rebuke (Hos 5:9), for a day of vengeance (Jer 46:10), for a day of burning like an oven, as it is said, "For behold, the day comes, burning like an oven" (Mal 3:19/4:1).*
>
> —Salmon b. Yerūḥīm
> Comment to Lamentations 5:7

For Salmon, Lamentations is a book of pious instruction. Over the course of his commentary, he necessarily attends to questions of grammar and syntax, literary expression, and historical context, but his deepest attention is directed to the book's meaning—the moral lessons found within its verses and the piety that its words inspire. He exhorts his readers to lament over their sins and repent, warning them of God's wrath and reminding them of God's promises. Salmon traces these homiletical elements back to Lamentations itself: since the biblical book is God's "instruction for Israel," revealed through the prophet Jeremiah, then clarifying and communicating that instruction is the only responsible approach to exegesis. In the same way that medieval Jewish philosophers considered biblical sages to be the earliest philosophers, thus creating a circular hermeneutic that justified their philosophical reading of the Bible, Salmon considers Jeremiah to be a homilist, and crafts his commentary to deliver the prophet's ancient exhortations to his own medieval audience.

Although Salmon roots his homiletical discourse in the verses of Lamentations, the character of his persuasive rhetoric suggests closer analogues in contemporary Karaite writings and the vibrant sermon culture of the Islamic world. Salmon's homiletical voice particularly resembles the Arabic genres of pious counsel (*waʿẓ*) and homily (*mawʿiẓa*), in content as well as form. The purpose of this chapter is to interrogate the distinctive interplay of homily and exegesis in Salmon's commentary, and to explain why the Arabic homiletical tradition provided Salmon with the most compelling

Jewish Piety in Islamic Jerusalem. Jessica Andruss, Oxford University Press. © Oxford University Press 2023.
DOI: 10.1093/oso/9780197639559.003.0005

means of amplifying Jeremiah's pious message for the Karaite readers of his own day.

Salmon's Homiletical-Exegetical Project

For Salmon ben Yerūḥīm, the biblical book of Lamentations is replete with calls for repentance and words of pious counsel. The invocations of suffering that appear in one verse after the next are not merely records of ancient misery but also proof that punishment awaits those who reject divine law in any generation. The biblical catastrophes are astounding in their range and severity, but they all convey the same lesson: sin brings pain and suffering, and only sincere repentance will bring alleviation and redemption. God destroyed Jerusalem and sent the people into exile in order to chastise the community, and Jeremiah recorded these calamities in order to convey their moral implications and inspire Israel to repent. The commentary on Lamentations, then, is Salmon's attempt to relay this prophetic call to the medieval Jewish community, translating Jeremiah's message into language intended to motivate his own generation to repent.[1]

In calling his community to repent, Salmon presents himself as fulfilling one of the principal obligations enjoined by the book of Lamentations. He states in the commentary's introduction that Lamentations instructs "the nation to summon (*istidʿā*) one another to repentance, as it is said, *Let us test and examine our ways, and return to the LORD* (Lam 3:40)."[2] In Salmon's reading of Lamentations 3:40, the prophet directs the community to collectively evaluate their sins and shortcomings, in order to purify themselves in preparation for repentance. But Jeremiah does not only educate the community about the actions and attitudes that are required for true repentance; he also models the role of the communal leader in summoning the people to these spiritual practices. Thus, Salmon's focus here is not on repentance alone—although, of course, the need to repent is paramount for him—but also on the obligation *to call others* to repent. Salmon fulfills that obligation through his commentary on Lamentations, which brings his homiletical inclination into an exegetical framework.

[1] Later Jewish sermons share Salmon's contention that Jewish homilies are a continuation of biblical prophetic discourse. See Marc Saperstein, *Jewish Preaching 1200–1800* (New Haven, Conn.: Yale, 1989), 26.

[2] Salmon's introduction, section on "Seven Meanings of Lamentations."

While Salmon finds the mandate to exhort his community to greater devotion within the book of Lamentations itself, the vocabulary, rhetoric, and themes of his exhortations diverge from those of the biblical text. Salmon's explication of *Let us test and examine our ways* (Lam 3:40), for example, seems more attuned to Sufi models of piety than to the conceptual world of biblical prophecy. According to Salmon's interpretation of the verse, Jeremiah calls upon the people of the exile to purify their intention (*ikhlāṣ al-niyya*) and improve their innermost thoughts (*aṣlāḥ al-ṭawīya*); then, he warns them that their external (*ẓāhir*) deeds will be accepted by God only insofar as their belief (*iʿtiqād*) is correct.[3] Salmon's interpretation recasts the biblical call to examine one's deeds in a medieval register of interior piety and self-purification. While passages like this one challenge scholarly divisions between exegesis and eisegesis, they also reveal the complexity of Salmon's homiletical-exegetical project. His objective was not only to translate the Hebrew words accurately into Arabic, but also to communicate the deepest spiritual meaning of Lamentations in a register that would resonate with his own community and transform them. Thus, homily is the intended aim of Salmon's exegetical practice, and the content of his exegesis is often homiletical.

The homiletical nature of Salmon's commentary is manifest not only in its content—frequent ethical instruction and pious exhortations—but also in its rhetoric, which bears affinities with the breadth of Arabic oratory as it is recorded and described in written texts. Throughout this book, I use the words homily and homiletical to refer to an ethical message, substantiated and illustrated through scriptural verses, presented as an exhortation, either in the form of actual oration or in writing that bears the features of oral discourse. A fine example of Salmon's homiletical rhetoric—and the epigraph for this chapter—appears in his excursus to Lamentations 5:7. The biblical verse reads: *Our fathers have sinned, and are no more; and we bear their offenses*. Salmon begins his discourse with a straightforward explication of the verse's words, then he informs readers of the obligation not to return to one's sins after confessing them in prayer. After methodically laying out this religious instruction, he proclaims, "O Israel, repent (*tūbū*) and return (*irjiʿū*) to the Merciful One! Pity your souls for the Day of Judgment, for *a day of rebuke* (Hos 5:9), for *a day of vengeance* (Jer 46:10), for a day of *burning like an oven*, as it is said, '*For behold, the day comes, burning like an oven*' (Mal 3:19/4:1)."

[3] Salmon's comment to Lam 3:40.

The urgency and intensity of this summons distinguishes it from the scholarly tone of the surrounding text. Here Salmon addresses his readers directly, targeting them with the vocative form and imperative verbs. He demands that they repent, and he recites a series of apocalyptic phrases from the biblical prophets to warn them about the imminence of judgment and the pain of hellfire. The homiletical techniques of this call stand in sharp relief when we compare it with Salmon's exegetically oriented remarks immediately beforehand. There, he explains the contents of the verse in detached, scholarly terms: it teaches that "our fathers sinned and were punished for their deeds by [...] all of the calamities that befell them" and that "it was obligatory for their children, the people of the exile, to reflect (*yaʿtabirū*) and to return (*yarjiʿū*) to God, great is His memory, and to repent (*yatūbū*)."[4] This passage presents the same themes and vocabulary of repentance that Salmon articulates with much greater force in his exhortation. Yet it shares none of the rhetorical features of the exhortation—direct address, the vocative, imperative verbs, a simple register of language with short sentences and clipped biblical citations. It states, somewhat impersonally, that repentance is an obligation for "the people of the exile," while the homiletical call leaves no doubt about who those people are. Here, Salmon calls directly upon his audience—"O my brethren" and "O Israel"—and draws on emotional power as much as biblical authority in order to persuade them to repent.[5] The eschatological phrases build to an affective climax. Salmon commands his audience to have pity for their souls, he frightens them with the Arabic concept of a "Day of Judgment," then he elevates and expands upon his discourse with biblical Hebrew images of a *day of rebuke*, a *day of vengeance*, and *a day of burning like an oven*, and finally concludes with the complete prophetic pronouncement of inescapable divine judgment: *"For behold, the day comes, burning like an oven."* Salmon may expound upon repentance as a biblical teaching throughout the commentary, but here, in the voice of a homilist, he demands that each person repent, and he warns them of the punishments that await those who fail to heed his call.

The rhetorical shift between these twin presentations of repentance in Salmon's comment to Lamentations 5:7 elucidates the function of Salmon's

[4] Salmon's comment to Lam 5:7.

[5] The technique of calling directly on the people is shared with the biblical prophets. Salmon includes such verses in the Lamentations commentary, e.g., Hos 9:1, 11:8, and 14:2/1. Salmon conveys his awareness that this is a standard prophetic locution when he uses it to paraphrase Jeremiah in his introduction: "If you do not accept this prophecy, then I know that the LORD will be angry and I will cry over you, O my children, O Israel."

homilies, as well as the relationship between homily and exegesis throughout the commentary. In the contexts of both exegesis and homily, Salmon seeks to persuade his readers of a theological point. To persuade readers of the exegetical accuracy of a given interpretation, Salmon draws on lexical and grammatical reasoning, often substantiated through reference to biblical prooftexts.[6] To persuade readers of the urgency and necessity of a homiletical point, by contrast, Salmon crafts sermons of pious counsel that draw on an array of rhetorical and affective techniques. Through the rhetorical techniques mentioned above, as well as others to be discussed below, Salmon creates a context of immediacy and shared concern that enables him to connect with his audience. Within this context of direct connection, Salmon invokes the terrifying images of death and judgment that will motivate his audience to greater piety and more committed religious observance. Such imagery is drawn predominantly from biblical sources, and the authority of Scripture lends emotional force to such alarming images. This homiletical treatment, however, is rooted in and reinforced by the exegetical context of the commentary; it is the initial scholarly interpretation of Lamentations 5:7 that introduces and authorizes Salmon's homily.

Although most verses do not occasion admonitions of this kind, it is not unusual for Salmon to follow his scholarly explication of a given verse with a longer excursus that includes homiletical elements. At times, he embeds lengthy, self-contained homilies within his verse comments, as though he intends his commentary to serve as a Karaite lectionary. These self-contained homilies suggest the preservation of actual or proposed homilies within the commentary.[7] At other times Salmon's homiletical impulse emerges in the ethical implications that he assigns to a given verse. While the presence of homily may be unexpected within the historical-contextual program of Karaite exegesis, the pious themes and oratorical techniques of Salmon's Lamentations commentary are familiar throughout medieval Arabic culture, including its Karaite manifestations.

[6] On Salmon's use of biblical prooftexts, see chapter 2.

[7] Such homilies appear to be set pieces. They are not tightly connected to the exegesis of the biblical verse where they are placed, and they are repeated between Salmon's compositions. For example, the homily at Lam 4:15 appears also at Ps 42:4/3; a story from the introduction to Salmon's Lamentations commentary appears also at Ps 77:3; the Hebr. dirge at Lam 3:1 appears also in Song 1:13 (on the latter, see Frank, *Search Scripture Well*, 153–54). Ben-Shammai argues that Salmon inserts bits of liturgical poetry and sermon into the commentary in order to demonstrate how to include post-biblical reflection in the Karaite mourning liturgy. It is unclear whether Salmon composed these passages or borrowed them from another source ("Poetic Works and Lamentations," 216).

The Homiletical Voice in Jewish Literature

The Karaite enthusiasm for admonishing and exhorting one's coreligionists, especially through the written word, not only predates Salmon but in fact stands at the foundations of the Jerusalem Karaite community. The success of the Karaite settlement in Jerusalem has been attributed in part to the persuasive sermon of Daniel al-Qūmisī, which circulated among the eastern Karaite communities and urged them to immigrate to the Holy Land where they could fulfill their obligations of mourning and repentance.[8] This written Hebrew document from the late ninth century employs the techniques of direct address—al-Qūmisī addresses his missive to "my brethren" and fills his prose with direct commands and rhetorical questions—as well as copious biblical citations and an emphasis on pious themes in a distinctively Karaite vein. This seminal Karaite composition has been characterized as disorganized, rambling, and awkward, especially in comparison to the polished texts attributed to the skilled Karaite preachers that followed al-Qūmisī by a generation or two.[9] Nevertheless, al-Qūmisī plied the same homiletical techniques that we find in Salmon's commentary. Regardless of whether al-Qūmisī chose this rhetorical register by his own instinct or by convention, it proved effective: Karaites settled in Palestine in significant numbers, perhaps motivated by his sermon along with his leadership and messianic vision. Roughly a century later, the Jerusalem Karaite Sahl b. Maṣliaḥ continued the tradition of exhortation, albeit in a more sophisticated homiletical style, as is recorded in his epistles.[10]

Sahl's Hebrew epistle to the Rabbanite Jacob ben Samuel dates to the second half of the tenth century.[11] It is saturated with the features of direct address that we have pinpointed in Salmon's commentary and al-Qūmisī's circular, showing that he, too, appreciated the art of oratory. But Sahl offers something

[8] Leon Nemoy, "The Pseudo-Qūmisīan Sermon to the Karaites," *PAAJR* 43 (1976): 49–105. See my discussion in chapter 1.

[9] See Nemoy's description in "The Pseudo-Qumisīan Sermon," 50.

[10] Gil gathers choice phrases from Karaite texts that urged settlement in Jerusalem, including those of al-Qūmisī, Salmon, and Sahl. Gil finds Geniza documents attesting to the success of the Karaite immigration program between the ninth and eleventh centuries. See *History*, 617–22.

[11] Originally published in *LK* vol. 2, 25–43; abridged Eng. translation by Nemoy in *KA* 109–22. For detailed discussion, see Nemoy, "The Epistle of Sahl Ben Maṣlīaḥ," *PAAJR* 38/39 (1970–71): 145–77. Note that Sahl's linguistic formation was Arab.; he composed the epistle in Hebr. because his Rabbanite opponent requested he do so, and he planned to translate it into Arab. thereafter. Nemoy presents evidence of frequent arabisms within Sahl's text ("Sahl's Epistle," 49).

else as well: clear statements about the purpose of hortatory preaching within the Karaite community. Early in the epistle, Sahl distinguishes the Karaites from the Rabbanites by virtue of his community's respect for preachers and preaching. He states,

> It is not enough for you Rabbanites that you neither admonish (*tokiḥu*) others nor oblige yourselves and others to repent; you even look with hostile eyes upon the preaching of an admonisher (*mokiaḥ*) like me, yet it is written: *He that rebukes* (mokiaḥ) *a wise man shall in the end find more favor than he that flatters with the tongue* (Prov 28:23).[12]

This accusation offers some insight into the role of preaching in Karaite society. To be sure, its placement in a polemical epistle means that it represents the aspirations and self-image of the Karaite community as much as an objective historical reality. Still, it is noteworthy that Sahl presents hortatory sermons as a distinctive element of the Karaite religious program, rejected by Rabbanites in spite of its incontrovertible biblical bona fides. From Sahl we learn that summoning one's fellows to repentance—which Salmon elevates as a key teaching of Lamentations—was a central project in Karaite Judaism writ large. Sahl presents his missionary activities with a range of Hebrew vocabulary related to preaching—for example, "reminding" (*le-hazkir*) and "warning" (*le-hazhir*)—but his epistle contains little description of what this activity looked like on the ground in tenth-century Jerusalem. There is no indication of specific locations and life-settings in which sermons were delivered, nor is there any discussion of who was qualified to admonish one's fellows, on what occasions, and whether or how audiences were assembled. Rather, the image of preaching that emerges from Sahl's epistle is a literary one. Sahl's epistle and other writings were collected and anthologized in a text entitled *Sefer Tokaḥah*, "The Book of Admonition," which confirms that admonitions could be conveyed through texts. In this regard, exhortation and admonition were comparable to other genres that gradually shifted from oral to textual modes of transmission in the Islamic world of the ninth and tenth centuries.[13]

[12] *KA* 112 = *LK* 30. Nemoy's translation adds words— "you Rabbanites" and "like me"— thus making explicit reference to figures that Sahl gestures to more obliquely: לא די לכם שלא תוכיחו וגם לא תשובו שיקשה בעיניכם דבר מוכיח וכתוב מוכיח חן ימצא ממחליק לשון

[13] On this transition, see Gregor Schoeler, *The Genesis of Literature in Islam: From the Aural to the Read*, rev. ed., trans. Shawkat M. Toorawa (Edinburgh: Edinburgh University Press, 2009).

Homiletical themes and oratorical techniques also exist within Rabbanite culture, notwithstanding Sahl's polemical statements to the contrary. The broader Jewish tradition offers homiletical models of its own, from classical rabbinic Midrash to the Rabbanite culture of the tenth century. The rabbinic tradition preserves vast collections of homiletical Midrashim, which provided a conceptual resource for Karaites and Rabbanites alike. Moreover, since both ancient rabbinic and medieval Karaite homilies are represented overwhelmingly in textual forms, they occasion similar debates among scholars about the degree to which literary homilies may preserve actual sermons that were delivered orally. Further, there is evidence for Rabbanite practices of exhortation in both written and public oral forms, in the tenth-century Islamic East. These examples demonstrate that the Arabic-Islamic environment was as essential for Rabbanites as it was for Karaites, since both communities translated long-standing Jewish homiletical sensibilities into the kinds of homiletical language, messages, and occasions that are represented throughout Salmon's commentary on Lamentations.

Homiletical Midrash (*derashah*; pl. *derashot*) are devotional pieces relating to the main theme of the weekly Torah portion or the cycle of synagogue readings for holy days.[14] They may draw upon homilies that once were delivered orally in the synagogue or the study house, and they emphasize the moral content of biblical passages. Their most distinctive element is the proem (*petiḥta*), which introduces the homily with a chain of biblical verses that leads artfully into the theme verse for that Sabbath or festival day. These written proems contain features of orality, which have led scholars to posit original, oral sermons, embedded within the textual form.

In a pioneering form-critical study of proems, Joseph Heinemann argues that editors compiled Midrashic homilies by drawing from "a variety of actual sermons, fully or in part, and combin[ing] them into a new entity, which we may perhaps call the 'literary homily.' "[15] Heinemann admits that this literary construction offers very little information about actual sermons as they may have been delivered in the rabbinic period. Indeed, recent scholarship has disputed that literary homilies are based on actual sermons at all, citing

[14] On the classification of Midrash and description of homiletical Midrash, see H. L. Strack and Günter Stemberger, *Introduction to the Talmud and Midrash*, 2nd ed., ed. and trans. Markus Bockmuehl (Minneapolis, Minn.: Fortress Press, 1996), 240–46, 288–314.

[15] Heinemann, "The Proem in the Aggadic Midrashim," *Scripta Hierosolymitana* 22 (1971), 100. For an expansion on Heinemann's study of homiletical Midrashim, with particular focus on their literary qualities, see Norman J. Cohen, "Structure and Editing in the Homiletic Midrashim," *AJS Review* 6 (1981): 1–20.

a lack of evidence for the public delivery of sermons in the rabbinic period.[16] Nevertheless, Heinemann's concept of a literary homily, in which elements of oral exhortation are represented in a textual form, is instructive for our analysis of Salmon's homiletical passages. Salmon's commentary incorporates liturgical formulas and refrains, repetition, direct address, imperative verbs, and other features that imply a link with oral discourse, although it is impossible to know whether Salmon or other Karaites ever preached these words before an assembly. The concept of a literary homily enables us to recognize elements of orality and communal exhortation when they appear in written contexts.[17]

One of the earliest collections of rabbinic homiletical Midrash is the *Pesikta de Rav Kahana*, a cycle of discourses structured according to the calendar of festival Sabbaths.[18] The chapters dedicated to the "Three Sabbaths of Judgment" and "Seven Sabbaths of Consolation" that surround the Ninth of Av draw upon the verses of Lamentations and other biblical books to produce a liturgical commemoration for the destruction of the Temple. Salmon reworks some of these Midrashic traditions in his Lamentations commentary, building on their themes and adapting their imagery.[19] However, even when these literary homilies from the rabbinic tradition appear, *mutatis mutandis*, in Salmon's homiletical excursuses, they do not display the rhetorical, formal, and stylistic elements that Salmon and other Karaites share with contemporary Arabic-Islamic homilies—and with fellow Jews of the Arabic-Islamic milieu.

The distinctive genre of the Arabic-Islamic homily, which provided a resource for Karaite pious exhortations, also served as a model for the Rabbanite community. Rabbanite literature incorporates the same forms of oral admonition that we find in the writings of al-Qūmisī, Sahl, and Salmon.

[16] E.g., Günther Stemberger, "The Derashah in Rabbinic Times," in *Preaching in Judaism and Christianity: Encounters and Developments from Biblical Times to Modernity*, SJ 41, ed. A. Deeg et al. (Berlin: W. de Gruyter, 2008), 7–21; and Burton L. Visotzky, "The Misnomers '*Petihah*' and 'Homiletical Midrash' as Descriptions for Leviticus Rabbah and Pesikta de-Rav Kahana," *JSQ* 18 (2011): 19–31.

[17] Another way of mediating the connections between orality and textuality in the case of homilies is through the idea of written homilies as "sourcebooks" for preachers. For discussion and bibliography of homiletical Midrash as sourcebooks, see Stern, *Rebuke to Consolation*, 82. Ben-Shammai has suggested a similar explanation for the homiletical materials in Salmon's commentary ("Poetic Works and Lamentations," 225).

[18] *Pesikta de Rav Kahana* is of Palestinian origin; its date of redaction is difficult to determine. Leopold Zunz dates it to ca. 700 CE, while later scholars follow Lewis Barth in dating its central chapters to the period 451–527 CE. See Strack and Stemberger, *Introduction*, 295–96. It shares contents with other Midrashic collections such as *Pesikta Rabbati*.

[19] See chapter 3 for discussion.

In a series of letters written in the third decade of the tenth century, Saadia exhorts his readers with formulas of direct address such as "O my brethren" or "O Israelites," which he uses as a refrain to structure a litany of moral instruction. He employs the techniques of public oratory to good effect without losing sight of his textual framework. In a missive to the Jewish community of Egypt, for example, Saadia writes, "We command warnings and admonitions *to be written* to you in order to awaken your hearts and to keep your minds vigilant towards the commandments of our Lord."[20] With written assertions such as "We are bound to warn you,"[21] Saadia implies both that exhortation is a religious obligation and that it may be accomplished through the written word. This interplay of orality and textuality reappears in a letter from Saadia to several rabbis. There he instructs the recipients that a copy of his letter "should always be with you and before your eyes, you should read it continually. [. . .] Learn it by heart; let one teach it the other and copy it for him, so that each of you shall read [. . .] to the other, until you are all of one mind."[22] These directions demonstrate the interlacing of oral and written modes of learning—a hallmark of tenth-century book culture, as will be discussed below. Saadia instructs the rabbis to keep the written document in their possession, copy it, and read it—all underscoring its textuality—in order to support a communal project of memorization, discussion, and in-person instruction. In this way, he centers new modes of textual transmission within a deep-rooted but dynamic system of live, oral, communal discourse. Saadia, like his Karaite contemporaries, understands the capacity for texts to foster the oral dissemination of pious guidance.[23]

There is also evidence that Rabbanites delivered public sermons, as we know Muslims did and as we have reason to expect Karaites did as well. One eyewitness to Rabbanite sermon practice is Nathan ha-Bavlī, whose Arabic "Chronicle of Baghdad" (*Akhbār Baghdād*) reports the tenth-century investiture ceremony of the Exilarch, the political leader of the Jewish community in exile.[24] The Exilarch was based in Baghdad and derived his authority not

[20] Franz Kobler, *Letters of Jews Through the Ages* (Philadelphia: Jewish Publication Society, 1978), I: 83–84, emphasis mine.

[21] Ibid., 85–86.

[22] Ibid., 82.

[23] It is possible that Karaite homiletical writings inspired Saadia's written exhortations. Rina Drory considers Saadia to be a "mediator" who introduced Karaite literary models into Rabbanite culture (*Models and Contacts*, 142–43, 152).

[24] The chronicle is preserved in an undated Hebrew manuscript published by Adolf Neubauer, *Medieval Jewish Chronicles and Chronological Notes*, vol. 2 (Oxford: Clarendon Press, 1887–95), 78–88. Fragments of the Judeo-Arabic original were found in the Geniza and published by Israel Friedlander, "The Arabic Original of the Report of R. Nathan Hababli," *JQR* o.s. 17 (1905): 747–61.

only from his Davidic lineage, but also from the support of the Ge'onim—the heads of the rabbinic academies of Sura and Pumbeditha—and the ruling Muslim caliph. According to Nathan's account of the ceremony, the Exilarch gave a sermon expounding on the Torah or—more likely—delegated permission for the Ge'onim to do so on his behalf. Nathan describes a solemn environment in which the Ga'on of Sura delivered the sermon "in an awe-inspiring manner with his eyes closed" before a rapt congregation. An "interpreter" was on hand, either to translate the sermon into Aramaic or Arabic, or to amplify the speaker's words to the vast congregation, as was also common practice in mosques.[25] Nathan does not record the contents of the sermon, although he glosses the word "sermon" as "expounding upon the Torah portion for that Sabbath," highlighting the connection between biblical interpretation and Jewish homiletical practice.

The existence of Rabbanite preaching assemblies underscores the importance of exhortation and ethical instruction across tenth-century Jewish society. Further, it suggests that Karaites, too, may have gathered to hear the kinds of exhortations that appear so frequently in the pages of their writings. The written works of al-Qūmisī, Salmon, and Sahl show that prominent Karaites plied their homiletical skills as an extension of their entwined commitments to biblical scholarship and communal exhortation. The admonitory passages of their literature demonstrate that Karaites adapted emerging homiletical models from the Arabic-Islamic sphere at the same time that they continued to engage with the themes and teachings of rabbinic homiletical Midrash. Karaite homilies—in Arabic or in Hebrew—were an expression of their Jewish identity and concerns.

Oratory (*Khuṭba*) and Pious Counsel (*Waʿẓ*) in Arabic-Islamic Contexts

The homiletical style of Salmon's Lamentations commentary—and of tenth-century Jewish writings more broadly—reflects Arabic-Islamic practices of oratory and public exhortation. Salmon's homiletical excursuses incorporate

The Eng. translation cited here is from Norman A. Stillman, *The Jews of Arab Lands: A History and Sourcebook* (New York: Jewish Publication Society, 1979), 171–75. See also Robert Brody, *Geonim of Babylonia*, 26–30, and Eve Krakowski, "Nathan ha-Bavlī," in *EJIW*.

25 Stillman, *Jews of Arab Lands*, 173.

the themes, imagery, language, rhetoric, and formal elements that characterize the traditions of oratory (*khuṭba*) in general, and the subgenre of *waʿẓ*—"admonitions" or "sermons of pious counsel"—in particular. Thus, it is useful to consider Salmon's hortatory writing in the context of his Muslim contemporaries and their precursors. Jews and Muslims shared a language and literary structure for expressing their homiletical insights and calling their coreligionists to confess their sins and repent. However, whereas the social context for Muslim preaching is well-defined—we have countless examples of sermons that were actually delivered, by trained religious professionals, in formal liturgical contexts and public spaces, incorporating mandatory elements of dress, speech, and behavior, and conforming to established ritual order—in the Jewish context, by contrast, our evidence is almost exclusively literary. As much as Salmon' exhortations and fully developed homilies—to say nothing of Sahl's lofty remarks about the Karaite commitment to admonishing wrongdoers, al-Qūmisī's summons to the Karaites of the Diaspora, or real affinities between the missions of Karaites and Ismāʿīlī preachers—justify our image of an active culture of Karaite public preaching, we have no concrete historical evidence for such a practice. Nevertheless, the parallels between Jewish and Muslim homiletical writing coupled with evidence of actual Muslim preaching invite speculation about the broader cultural background of Karaite homiletical thought. Let us now outline the features of classical Arabic oratory, a genre that also moves between oral and textual forms, focusing on the ways that it shapes medieval Muslim and Karaite homiletical expression.

Classical Arabic oratory (*khuṭba*) dates back to the pre-Islamic era, and particularly eloquent or persuasive examples of this prose genre were memorized, transmitted, and eventually recorded in writing.[26] While the genre developed over many centuries, *khuṭba*s are typically characterized by features such as direct address (often expressed with the vocative), imperative verbs, real and rhetorical questions, rhyme, and simple language. They routinely address pious themes such as repentance and obedience to God, as well as the imminence of death and the suffering that awaits sinners. They employ vivid imagery and draw their authority from citations—from poetry in the oldest examples, but increasingly from the Qurʾān thereafter. By the

[26] This discussion of classical Arabic oratory is informed by Tahera Qutbuddin, "*Khuṭba*: The Evolution of Early Arabic Oration," in *Classical Arabic Humanities in Their Own Terms: Festschrift for Wolfhart Heinrichs*, ed. Beatrice Gruendler and Michael Cooperson (Leiden: Brill, 2008).

mid-eighth century *khuṭbas* began to be written down. The development of written oratory fostered the memorization of exemplary sermons that initially had been delivered spontaneously and orally, and it also encouraged speakers to draft oratories in order to revise and study them before delivering them publicly. Thus, by Salmon's time, Arabic oratory was closely connected with the written word, and there was a tradition of expository writing that incorporated the persuasive features—and thereby imported the persuasive force—of oral discourse. Over time, the term *khuṭba* came to denote only the ritualized sermon delivered in the mosque on Fridays and religious festivals. In turn, a particular type of *khuṭba*—the *waʿẓ* or *mawʿiẓa*, the "sermon of pious counsel" or "homily"—emerged as a genre in its own right, mostly associated with popular or paraliturgical contexts.[27] The *waʿẓ* was a type of homiletical exhortation that used standard oratorical features in the service of inducing listeners to repent by warning them of the dire eschatological consequences of continued sin and disobedience. Unlike other genres of oratory, however, the *waʿẓ* was most often delivered by scholars or educated laypeople rather than religious or political leaders. Further, although the *waʿẓ* was often delivered orally to an assembled audience, some were transmitted exclusively in writing.[28]

Much of our knowledge of the *waʿẓ* is derived from the corpus of Ibn al-Jawzī, a twelfth-century Sunnī scholar who penned over one hundred works on the art of the homily.[29] A respected hortatory preacher (*wāʿiẓ*) himself, Ibn al-Jawzī composed manuals for preachers that included instruction in the art of preaching as well as collections of exemplary sermons, admonitions, and stories for preachers to work into their sermons. Merlin Swartz has examined several of these texts and analyzed both the theoretical foundations and the literary structure of the homily (*mawʿiẓa*) as presented by Ibn al-Jawzī.[30] In these homilies, Swartz identifies "four quite distinct

[27] Linda G. Jones, *The Power of Oratory in the Medieval Muslim World* (Cambridge: Cambridge University Press, 2012), 158–63.

[28] Qutbuddin, *Arabic Oration*, 265–66.

[29] On the fascinating biography and accomplishments of Ibn al-Jawzī, see H. Laoust, "Ibn al-Djawzī," in *EI2*; Jane Dammen McAuliffe, "Ibn al-Jawzī's Exegetical Propaedeutic: Introduction and Translation," *Alif: Journal of Comparative Poetics* 8 (1988), esp. 101–4; and Merlin Swartz, "Ibn al-Jawzi: A Biographical Sketch," in *A Medieval Critique of Anthropomorphism: Ibn al-Jawzī's* Kitāb Akhbār Aṣ-Ṣifāt: *A Critical Edition of the Arabic Text with Translation, Introduction and Notes*, Islamic Philosophy, Theology and Science, Texts and Studies 46 (Leiden: Brill, 2002), 3–32. Ibn al-Jawzī's homiletical works are counted to be 114 by Merlin Swartz in "Arabic Rhetoric and the Art of the Homily in Medieval Islam," in *Religion and Culture in Medieval Islam*, ed. Richard G. Hovannisian and Georges Sabagh (Cambridge: Cambridge University Press, 1999), 38.

[30] Swartz, "Arabic Rhetoric and the Art of the Homily in Medieval Islam."

forms (or sub-genres), each of which had its own specific content and served a particular purpose within the context of the homily as a whole."[31] There is an introductory portion of highly stylized poetry in praise of God (*khuṭba*), a story (*qiṣṣa*), the admonition itself (*waʿẓ*), and finally a conclusion with poetic verses (*maqāṭiʿ*, *khawātīm*).[32] Salmon incorporates all of these elements into his own homiletical-exegetical project. He opens the commentary with the *khuṭba* or *taḥmīd*—which, of course, is a standard convention of Arabic literature beyond oration as well—and the refrains that conclude each verse comment bear superficial similarities to the form of the *maqāṭiʿ*, although not its amorous poetic themes.[33] The most important homiletical components—for Salmon and for the Muslim preachers whom Ibn al-Jawzī anthologizes—are the prose elements, the *qiṣṣa* and the *waʿẓ*. These two pieces form the centerpiece of the homily.

The Edifying Narrative (*Qiṣṣa*)

As Swartz describes, the *qiṣṣa* "is composed in a relatively straightforward prose style" (although it may be interspersed with lines of poetry) and "the importance of these stories taken collectively resides in the fact that they set forth, often in dramatic detail, the Islamic conception of history."[34] Linda G. Jones affirms the importance of edifying narratives in hortatory preaching, while noting that the preachers themselves generally avoid using the term *qiṣṣa* on account of its associations with storytellers, whose tales were viewed as prone to embellishment or faulty theology.[35] The *qiṣṣa* is vital for Salmon, who relies on biblical narratives both as evidence for his homiletical teachings and as an emotional touchstone for his readers. He deploys the *qiṣṣa*, for example, to provide a biblical foundation for the obligation to mourn. Salmon argues repeatedly that Jews must mourn over the

[31] Ibid. 41. Note that Qutbuddin advances a different typology, in which the *qiṣṣa* ("homiletic lecture") and the *waʿẓ* ("homiletic discourse") are separate but frequently blurred categories of non-oratorical genres of pious counsel (*Arabic Oration*, 266).

[32] It is not clear whether every Jawzīan homily must contain all four subgenres. Swartz notes that Ibn al-Jawzī's respective compilations may contain more examples of one subgenre than others. He does not explain whether this imbalance is the result of Ibn al-Jawzī's focus on a certain component or whether it indicates that all four subgenres need not be represented in a single homily.

[33] Note, however, that there is little to no rhyme in Salmon's commentary; cf. Islamic oratory both before and after Ibn al-Jawzī.

[34] Swartz, "Arabic Rhetoric and the Art of the Homily in Medieval Islam," 43.

[35] Jones, *Power of Oratory*, 172.

destruction of the Temple. Yet the destruction occurred relatively late in biblical history, and biblical law provides no explicit command to mourn. So, Salmon legitimizes the obligation of mourning through the narrative of two early Israelite heroes, the patriarch Jacob and King David:

> It is obligatory to reflect upon Jacob our forefather. He had twelve sons, and he was full of abundant grace and strength and wealth, and intimate with his Lord. So when he was deprived of one of his children, his soul cleaved to its mourning over him until the day of his death. [. . .] We also reflect upon the report about David, King of Israel, and all his companions when news reached them of the killing of Saul and his children. Some of the people of Israel mourned and wept and fasted and lamented.[36]

In this passage, Salmon tells the narratives of Jacob and David so as to emphasize the piety and rightness of their mourning behaviors. The narrative is woven through with biblical citations, but it is not, strictly speaking, exegetical—that is to say, Salmon does not provide a straightforward explanation of the biblical words themselves. Rather, he constructs a homiletical narrative about the biblical foundations for the rituals and attitudes that define the Jerusalem Karaite community. This *qiṣṣa* sets Jacob and David more firmly into the arc of Jewish history as understood from a Karaite perspective. The fact that this narrative turns up, in nearly the exact same formulation, in Salmon's commentary on the Psalms gives further evidence that it was a homiletical set piece rather than an exegetical remark.[37] While the version of the narrative that Salmon includes in his commentaries is a mere outline, formulated in bare, terse prose, one can imagine an artful preacher—perhaps Salmon himself—filling in this sketch with rich details before an assembled audience. Such a hypothesis recalls Gregor Schoeler's concept of "hypomnēma," written notes that scholars kept as aides-mémoires in preparation for lectures or other oral discourse, which took on more systematic textual forms afterward.[38] If, as Haggai Ben-Shammai

[36] Introduction to Salmon's Lamentations commentary, in the section on "Mourning as a Religious Obligation."

[37] In the Psalms commentary it appears as a verse comment (Ps 77:3) whereas in the Lamentations commentary it appears in the introduction.

[38] Schoeler uses this Greek term to distinguish private notes or outlines intended for oral delivery from "syngramma," or systematic compositions. See Schoeler, *Genesis*, 8–9. Schoeler includes Christian homiletical literature and the exegetical and historical writings of al-Ṭabarī in the category of "hypomnēma"; see "The Transmission of the Sciences in Early Islam Revisited," in *The Oral*

has argued, Salmon's Lamentations commentary provided a sparse framework for the Karaite liturgy of mourning, to which additional material could be added, then it is quite possible that Salmon's *qiṣṣa* about Jacob and David was intended as a homiletical sketch or outline to be expanded upon by Karaite preachers.[39]

Admonition and Emotional Response: Fear and Grief

In Ibn al-Jawzī's four-part schema of the homily (*maw'iẓa*), it is the third component, the *wa'ẓ*, that conveys "the moral or ethical content of revelation." At this stage, the hortatory preacher (*wā'iẓ*) addresses the audience, recites verses of ascetic poetry (*zuhdiyyāt*), and presents eschatological imagery, exhorting listeners to comply with the law (*sharī'a*) and warning them of the suffering that awaits those who disobey divine precepts.[40] This essential element of the Arabic homily, which appears throughout the Muslim corpus on which Ibn al-Jawzī bases his typology, appears also in Salmon's writings.

The exhortation with which we opened this chapter provides an ideal illustration of the *wa'ẓ*:

> O Israel, repent and return to the Merciful One! Pity your souls for the Day of Judgment, for *a day of rebuke* (Hos 5:9), for *a day of vengeance* (Jer 46:10), for a day of *burning like an oven*, as it is said, "*For behold, the day comes, burning like an oven*" (Mal 3:19/4:1).

Although these words appear in an exegetical framework, they stand out from the surrounding exposition by calling directly on the reader, warning, frightening, and demanding immediate spiritual reorientation. The brevity of this admonition is one of its virtues. Often, the exhortations that are reported in Islamic sources are extremely short, little more than maxims

and the Written in Early Islam, Routledge Studies in Middle Eastern Literatures 13., ed. James E. Montgomery, trans. Uwe Vagelpohl (London: Routledge, 2006), 45–46.

[39] Ben-Shammai, "Poetic Works and Lamentations," 225.

[40] Swartz, "Arabic Rhetoric and the Art of the Homily in Medieval Islam," 44–45. On ascetic poetry, see A. Hamori, "Ascetic Poetry (*zuhdiyyāt*)," in *Abbasid Belles Lettres*, ed. Julia Ashtiany et al. (Cambridge: Cambridge University Press, 1990), 265–74.

consisting of two or three phrases from the Qurʾān or ḥadīth.[41] While it is possible that short admonitions are excerpts from longer sermons, there is also evidence that speedy, straight-shooting admonitions were highly valued, as in the curt command of caliph Harūn al-Rashīd (ca. 766–809) to the hortatory preacher in his court: "Admonish me (*ʿiẓnī*), and make it quick."[42] Salmon incorporates watchwords from the biblical prophets where Muslim homilists would rely on phrases from the Qurʾān or ḥadīth, but in both communities the purpose of citation is the same: eschatological threats, spoken in the authoritative voices of the prophets, to generate an emotional response that spurs the audience to repentance and renewed piety. Sincere emotional responses are essential to the success of the homiletical project. For this reason, homilists in both traditions select the verses with the most viscerally terrifying imagery, which have the greatest potential to rouse the audience to a transformative state of fear and grief.

The emotional states of fear and grief intersect to considerable extent. However, Salmon tends to emphasize grief in his commentary on Lamentations, while Islamic homilies often emphasize fear—particularly fear of death and fear of punishment—to motivate repentance. Ibn al-Jawzī defines *waʿẓ* as "instilling the fear that softens the heart," and he instructs preachers to "make use of [stories and exhortations] that arouse fear in people (*mukhawwifāt*)."[43] Frightening reminders about the imminence of death remind listeners that they must account for their wrongdoings, for they cannot escape judgment and punishment.[44] Genuine grief was appreciated by Muslim homilists as well, although the efficacy of real grief was tempered by a suspicion that open displays of weeping and lamentation could be fraudulent, as will be discussed below.

Fear figures prominently in Salmon's pious vocabulary—as illustrated in our epigraph—and yet the primary emotional valence in the Lamentations homilies is not one of fear, but rather one of regret, grief, and mourning. Since mourning is obligatory within Salmon's religious program, his homilies position mourning not as punishment but as an act of penitential

41 Jones, *Power of Oratory*, 166. For a list of citations from the Qurʾān that often appear in sermons of pious counsel, see Qutbuddin, *Arabic Oration*, 259.

42 Jones, *Power of Oratory*, 166.

43 Merlin L. Swartz, ed. and trans., Ibn al-Jawzī's *Kitāb al-Quṣṣāṣ wa'l-Mudhakkirīn*. Pensée Arabe et Musulman 47. Beirut: Dar el-Machreq Éditeurs, 1971, paragraphs 5 and 324.

44 Qutbuddin, *Arabic Oration*, chapter 5. Note that fear of death or punishment is fundamentally different from *taqwā*, which is often rendered imprecisely as "fear of God." Qutbuddin more accurately glosses this Arab. term as "piety in consciousness of God" (229–30).

piety. This thematic emphasis on mourning is especially evident in the litany from Salmon's comment to Lamentations 4:15. There, Salmon declares that God made it obligatory to weep over the destruction of the Second Temple and then presents a homily in which he confronts the reader with a grief-inducing list of all the blessings that Israel has forfeited. This homily on weeping is a set piece; it also appears, with minor variations, in Salmon's commentary on Psalms, and it is only indirectly related to the theme verse from Lamentations.[45] It is structured around a repeated rhetorical question—"how could we not weep?"—and biblical prooftexts that emphasize weeping as a natural response to the communal suffering and loss caused by sin:[46]

> **How could he not weep for himself**—for the dispossession of His grace, and being handed over to His enemies? *From this inheritance of the beautiful* [*land*], *then Zion, the royal city, then Jerusalem, the holy city, then our holy Temple and our splendor*, as it is said, *And I will give it into the hands of foreigners for a prey* (Ezek 7:21)? **And how could he not weep** over the transfer of the LORD's glory from among Israel, as it is said, *And the Spirit lifted me up and brought me in the vision* (Ezek 11:24), and it is said, *From the daughter of Zion has departed all her majesty* (Lam 1:6)? **And how could he not weep** over the lack of prophecy and prophets, as it is said, *I will also command the clouds* [*that they rain no rain upon it*] (Isa 5:6)? **And how could we not weep** over the cessation of kingship, as it is said, *Without king or prince* (Hos 3:4)? **And how could we not weep** over the cancellation of offerings, as it is said, *Because cereal offering and drink offering are withheld from the house of your God* (Joel 1:13)? **And how could we not weep** over the idleness of the priests from their steps, as it is said, *Gird on sackcloth and lament, O priests* (Joel 1:13)? **And how could we not weep** over the idleness of the Levites from their melodies, and the elders from sitting in wisdom, as it is said, *The elders have ceased from the gate* (Lam 5:14)? **And how could we not weep** over the falling of our crown and our glory, as it is said, *The crown has fallen from our head* (Lam 5:16)? **And how could we not weep** over the magnitude of our sins, as it is said, *Woe to us, that we have sinned!* (Lam 5:16)? **And how could we not weep**

[45] Comment to Ps 42:4/3. See the note at Lam 4:15.

[46] The refrain is marked in bold for ease of reference. Refrains on the theme of grief also appear in liturgical poetry (*piyyuṭim*) recited on the Ninth of Av; see Lieber, *Jewish Aramaic Poetry*, chapter 3, esp. poems 18–21.

> over the blackening of our faces, as it is said, *Now their visage is blacker than soot* (Lam 4:8)? **And how could we not weep** over our lowliness, as it is said, *You foolish and senseless people* (Deut 32:6)? **And how could we not weep** over the blindness of our vision, as it is said, *We grope for the wall like the blind* (Isa 59:10). **And how could we not weep** over our ignorance, as it is said, *Some were fools through their sinful ways* (Ps 107:17). **And how could we not weep** over the impudence of our faces, as it is said, *Yet you have a harlot's brow, [you refuse to be ashamed]* (Jer 3:3), and over descriptions like these? It is said, *Awake, you drunkards, and weep* (Joel 1:5) and *My tears have been my food* (Ps 42:4/3); *O that my head were waters* (Jer 8:23/9:1).

In this passage, Salmon poses a series of rhetorical questions—a common homiletical device—to persuade Jews that they are obliged to mourn. The biblical prooftexts may function in a similar way to the lines of ascetic poetry that are woven into Islamic examples of *waʿẓ*.[47] Together with the repeated rhetorical questions, these biblical verses create a rhythm that runs through the passage.[48] The repeated examples of Israelite sin and loss build to a powerful affective climax, as the implied answer to the rhetorical question becomes ever clearer: it is neither natural nor possible for anyone who has experienced these afflictions to refrain from lamentation. Indeed, the first-person plural forms of the questions and many of the biblical verses insist that the trials of Israel are not only historical and biblical, but also present, persistent, and part of the lived experience of Salmon's own community. The homily draws its audience to a full recognition of their own suffering and pulls them to an emotional state in which neglecting to mourn is impossible. They weep not for the sins of the ancient Israelites and their bygone punishment, but for their own sins, and the conditions of exile in which they continue to suffer. Salmon uses exegetical or polemical arguments to advocate mourning practices elsewhere in the commentary, but in this homily, he draws on the affective power of the *waʿẓ* to bring his audience to a state of intense, active grief.

[47] See Hamori, "Ascetic Poetry (*zuhdiyyāt*)," 269.

[48] Repetition, as found in this homiletical excursus, has been discussed both as a marker of orality and as an indication of careful written composition. On the former, see Walter Ong, *Orality and Literacy: The Technologizing of the Word* (New York: Routledge, 1991); on the latter, see Barbara Johnstone, *Repetition in Arabic Discourse: Paradigms, Syntagms, and the Ecology of Language* (Philadelphia: J. Benjamins, 1991), esp. 110–18.

This homily illustrates Salmon's recourse to intense emotion within the commentary. Scholars and preachers of the medieval Islamic world were perfectly aware of the heightened emotional response that well-crafted sermons could generate. Jonathan P. Berkey presents an array of richly suggestive evidence for the connections between mourning and homily in the medieval Islamic Near East.[49] One of Ibn al-Jawzī's manuals for preachers, *al-Yāqūta fī l-waʿẓ*, opens with a chapter that "extols weeping and crying for one's sins" and includes stories in which Noah and David are depicted primarily as mourners.[50] Less scholarly homiletical texts reflect even more strongly an appreciation for the spiritual value of lamentation and the recognition that skilled preachers could rouse their audience to open displays of sincere grief. Tales of the pre-Islamic prophets weeping over their sins were a favorite theme of Muslim popular preachers and storytellers, who promoted weeping as expiation from sin. In the late medieval period, and perhaps earlier as well, cemeteries became popular venues for Muslim preaching in spite of orthodox denunciations of the practice. References to death within sermons of pious counsel were as frequent and visceral as ever.[51]

In light of these associations between homily and mourning in medieval Arab culture, it is not surprising to find homiletical themes as well as formal homilies within a Lamentations commentary written for the Mourners for Zion. Sermons of pious counsel may have provided an emotionally resonant source for the Jerusalem Karaite community precisely because the structures and themes of such homilies were closely associated with mourning and lamentation in the broader culture. Notably, Salmon does not share his Muslim contemporaries' concern that urging one's community to experience grief may cause spiritual harm by creating an environment in which affectation and exaggeration are rewarded, distracting one's audience from true penitence and atonement.[52] Muslim skepticism about the purity of weepers' motives is recorded, for example, in an early report in which Ḥasan

[49] Jonathan P. Berkey, *Popular Preaching and Religious Authority in the Medieval Islamic Near East* (Seattle: University of Washington Press, 2001), chapter 2.

[50] Ibid., 48. However, Berkey also notes that Ibn al-Jawzī considered excessive weeping to be a distortion of the true purpose of preaching.

[51] Ibid., 49.

[52] For a discussion of weeping in Muslim preaching assemblies, see *Kitāb al-Quṣṣāṣ*, paragraphs 106, 118, 131, 277, 297; Jones, *Power of Oratory*, 244–47; and Jones, "'He Cried and Made Others Cry': Crying as a Sign of Pietistic Authenticity or Deception in Medieval Islamic Preaching," in *Crying in the Middle Ages: Tears of History*, ed. Elina Gertsman (New York: Routledge, 2012).

al-Baṣrī (ca. 642–728) accosts a man who is weeping during a sermon and warns him, "God will most assuredly call upon you to explain your motive for doing this!"[53] Whereas Islamic sources reveal an ambivalence, at best, about weeping in response to hortatory preaching, Salmon's commentary indicates confidence in the capacity of a sound homily to prompt authentic, spiritually transformative grief. This confidence rests squarely in the quality of the homily itself, rather than any inherent spiritual capacity of the community, since elsewhere Salmon cautions his readers against insincere outward displays that are unmatched by true internal piety.[54]

Salmon's absolute confidence—not only in the power of homilies to instill grief, but in the power of grief itself to redeem the community—marks the Karaite articulation of grief as doubly subversive. Salmon undermines Muslim concerns about excessive grief by inciting Jews to lament and pinning all hope of redemption on the intensity of their grief. While Muslim pietists claim that grief belies faith in God, Salmon endorses grief as the essential expression of piety. Weeping does not contradict hope in God; it substantiates it. Salmon's radical insistence on grief defies Muslim socio-religious expectations at the same time that it contests Rabbanite Jewish norms of religious behavior. His call to grieve as a daily spiritual practice destabilizes long-standing rabbinic measures designed to limit mourning over the destruction of the Temple and to console Jews as they passively await the redemption. Rabbinic liturgy surrounding the Ninth of Av restricts Jewish mourning to a cycle of three Sabbaths of judgment followed by seven Sabbaths of consolation, thereby constraining and controlling the potentially overwhelming outpouring of grief, and redirecting Jewish energy to socially constructive projects.[55] Salmon's program of continual lament rouses Jews to the emotional fervor that the rabbis worked to avoid. Thus, his homiletical performance of grief forcefully demarcates Karaite Judaism both from Rabbinic Judaism and from Islam.[56]

[53] *Kitāb al-Quṣṣāṣ*, paragraph 325.

[54] E.g., Salmon's comments to Lam 3:40–41.

[55] On rabbinic construction of the Ninth of Av liturgy, see Philip Alexander, "The Mourners for Zion and the Suffering Messiah: *Pesikta rabbati* 34—Structure, Theology, Context," in *Midrash Unbound*, ed. Michael Fishbane and Joanna Weinberg (Oxford: Littman, 2013), 156–57; and Lewis M. Barth, "The 'Three of Rebuke and Seven of Consolation': Sermons in the 'Pesikta de Rav Kahana,'" *JJS* 33 (1982): 503–16.

[56] Meira Polliack masterfully explains the mechanics of Karaite differentiation from both Rabbanite Judaism and Islam. See "Inversion," 275, where she describes a dual process of "inter-religious inversion and inner-religious subversion."

Orality and the Karaite Homily

Since we have identified several excursuses from Salmon's commentary as homiletical on literary and textual grounds, it is worth considering whether Karaites may have delivered sermons in settings and circumstances similar to those in which Muslims delivered their admonitions. There are no tenth-century eyewitness reports with descriptions of an active sermon culture among the Jerusalem Karaites. Yet to dismiss the possibility that such activities occurred would be to presume—based on an argument from silence—that a Jewish community so thoroughly situated within the Arabic milieu did not participate in one of its defining cultural practices or adapt it to their own purpose. Such a stance would also imply that the Karaites managed to endow their exegetical and other writings with a robust homiletical discourse and striking features of orality, all while lacking any actual experience of delivering pious instruction to an assembly. The existence of homiletical passages in the rabbinic tradition, which could provide a textual source for Salmon's homiletical style, does not preclude the possibility that Karaites also convened and preached to pious assemblies in real-life settings. To the contrary, Jewish literary analogues to Islamic preaching would have supplied further encouragement for Karaites to take up a practice that was familiar in Jewish tradition and resonated with their own spiritual goals. Thus, it is reasonable to look to medieval Muslim contexts of preaching and oral learning as likely parallels to real-life Karaite homilies. I will begin with socio-historical observations from the sermon culture of the Islamic West and then illustrate the interplay of oral and textual forms of knowledge in Salmon's own environment, the cities of the Islamic East in the ninth and tenth centuries.

The social and performative dimensions of Muslim preaching have been profitably explored by Jonathan P. Berkey and Linda G. Jones on the basis of historical and literary evidence. Their studies focus on preachers and audiences two or more centuries after Salmon, and often in the context of the Islamic West. Still, their research suggests the possibility of an oral background for the kind of written homiletical discourse that is represented in Salmon's commentary and in the texts of his fellow Karaites.

The medieval sources that Berkey consults refer to the setting in which scholars "transmitted religious knowledge to and exhorted the common people" as the *mīʿād* ("appointment"). The term is inherently flexible. It could refer to a range of actual venues from the madrasa, where teachers occupied a formal position, to more casual sites where an impromptu audience could assemble.[57] Notably, Berkey has identified a close connection between the activity of the *mīʿād* and Qurʾānic exegesis (*tafsīr*). Not only would sermons be filled with citations from the Qurʾān, as discussed above, but the Qurʾān could also provide the impetus for such homilies. The biographer of one fourteenth-century scholar notes that "in his *mīʿād* sessions, he completed his reading of the Qurʾān, infusing it with preaching (*waʿẓ*)."[58] Ibn al-Jawzī, too, instructs preachers to first complete their interpretation of the Qurʾān and then "deliver a discourse on a subject relevant to the verses along with profitable exhortations and severe warnings," reminding listeners of God's promises and threats, urging them to adhere to the law and live a virtuous life.[59]

This combination of exegesis and homily, which characterizes the *mīʿād* sessions, also defines Salmon's Lamentations commentary. It may reflect a similar Karaite practice of publicly teaching the Bible with occasional departures into homiletical territory to impress upon audiences the pious message of Scripture. The centrality of mourning within the Karaites' scripturalist program suggests that affective homilies may have fit into liturgically oriented contexts of Karaite biblical study, even while Karaite scholars after Salmon differentiated more sharply than he between homily and historical-contextual biblical scholarship.[60] The difference between Salmon's pietistic commentaries and the more academically oriented works of the later Karaite tradition may also reflect the changing contours of the commentary form as the community matured. The liturgical elements that Salmon embeds in his commentary may have become routinized within Karaite prayer and ritual thereafter, leaving little need for recording homilies in commentaries, and thereby opening the commentary form to other domains of intellectual inquiry, such as law, religious philosophy, and a more robust treatment of philology.

The fact that Salmon's medium was definitively textual does not necessarily mean that it was exclusively so. Rather, Salmon and his circle flourished in an environment where even written texts were taught and disseminated orally. The Islamic cities of the ninth and tenth centuries were transformed by the introduction of paper and the resulting surge in Arabic literary production,

57 Berkey, *Popular Preaching*, 38–39.
58 Ibid., 39.
59 *Kitāb al-Quṣṣāṣ*, paragraph 323.
60 On the connections between Salmon's Lamentations commentary and the Karaite mourning liturgy, see Ben-Shammai, "Poetic Works and Lamentations."

to be sure, but this burgeoning textual culture only expanded public and aural opportunities for intellectual engagement. Educated readers encountered books in scholastic contexts, where texts were dictated and recited,[61] and also in the symposium (*majlis*), the soirée (*samar*), the study circle (*ḥalqa*), and the booksellers' market (*sūq al-warrāqīn*), where texts were memorized, debated, and discussed.[62] This "Arabic writerly culture"—to use Shawkat M. Toorawa's apt phrase—promoted literacy and textuality through the work of writing, editing, and copying, at the same time that it encouraged orality through the work of teaching, telling, reciting, and memorizing. In short, "one of the curious effects of writing is that it does not reduce orality but, rather, enhances it."[63] Salmon created a textual corpus during a time when the boundaries between orality and textuality were permeable.

This permeability explains why Jewish and Muslim homilies turn up in a range of genres, both oral and textual. Written texts were recited or performed in public, just as live oratory could be outlined ahead of time, recorded, and recirculated in textual forms, then dusted off for presentation in a new study session or before a different audience. Homiletical texts could be encountered in shifting contexts as well, from liturgical to political to academic settings.[64]

Even though orality and written forms of learning were mutually reinforcing, some feared the emerging textual culture and its potential to displace or transform traditional modes of oral transmission. In Muslim and Jewish communities alike, there were tensions between scholars with competing religious and intellectual commitments, who debated the respective merits of orality and literacy with great seriousness. The Karaite insistence on the authority of written knowledge, for example, was a provocative challenge to Rabbanite allegiances to oral transmission and the Oral Torah.[65]

[61] Schoeler, *Genesis*, chapter 8.

[62] Beatrice Gruendler, *Book Culture Before Print: The Early History of Arabic Media* (Beirut: American University of Beirut, 2011), 25; Beatrice Gruendler, "Aspects of Craft in the Arabic Book Revolution," in *Knowledge in the Post-Antique Mediterranean, 700–1500*, ed. Sonja Brentjes and Jürgen Renn (London: Routledge, 2016), 40–44; Shawkat M. Toorawa, *Ibn Abī Ṭāhir Ṭayfūr and Arabic Writerly Culture: A Ninth-Century Bookman in Baghdad*, Routledge Studies in Arabic and Middle Eastern Literatures 7 (New York: Routledge, 2005), 25. On the *majlis* in particular, see Samer M. Ali, *Arabic Literary Salons in the Islamic Middle Ages: Poetry, Public Performance, and the Presentation of the Past*, Poetics of Orality and Literacy (Notre Dame, Ind.: University of Notre Dame Press, 2010), chapter 1.

[63] Toorawa, *Arabic Writerly Culture*, 11.

[64] Oratorical prose influenced later Arabic literary developments such as epistolary writing, and written epistles were often delivered orally; see Tahera Qutbuddin, "*Khuṭba*: The Evolution of Early Arabic Oration,", 209.

[65] Drory, *Models and Contacts*, 130–38, 153–54; Polliack, "Inversion," esp. 268–85.

Ultimately, the turn to textuality was undeniable and unavoidable, and in practical terms the Rabbanites came to embrace textual transmission and literary expression no less than the Karaites. Moreover, the Karaites did not dismiss oral forms of learning entirely, but rather maintained a certain ambivalence about the entanglements between oral and written forms of knowledge. Meira Polliack has perceptively observed that Karaites "still retained methods of live oral teaching and learning and that in some ways the prestige of this kind of learning persisted, despite or alongside the book culture that informed so much of their new identity."[66] Karaite and Rabbanite practices of oral and written learning were nuanced, complicated, and dynamic. Even so, the perceived alignments between Karaism and text, on the one hand, and Rabbanism and orality on the other, persisted—in the context of the Written and Oral Torah, of course, but also in connection with mundane forms of learning and literature. The Karaite celebration of textuality and its authority may supply some explanation for the predominantly textual locus of Karaite homily and exhortation, as evidenced by Salmon's commentaries as well as the writings of Sahl and al-Qūmisī. Throughout the commentary on Lamentations, Salmon codes his pious homiletical endeavors as a textual practice.

Exhortation as a Religious Obligation

Salmon's homilies reflect the pious themes and generic conventions familiar in Arabic homiletical oratory and yet, speculation aside, we lack direct evidence that the Jerusalem Karaites engaged in the kind of oral, public preaching that flourished among their Muslim neighbors. Moreover, we do not know whether Salmon personally composed the homilies that he embeds within the commentary, or whether they represent the common liturgy of his community. Nor do we know whether these homilies were ever delivered—and to whom, and in what circumstances—or whether, like some Islamic words of pious counsel, they were inherently textual. For now, these questions about the intersections of orality and textuality in Salmon's corpus, as well as a possible life-setting for Karaite homilies, must remain unresolved. And yet Salmon leaves no doubt about the centrality of exhortation and admonition in Karaite religion. In addition to the deep imprint of pious

[66] Ibid., 279.

instruction and independent homilies within the commentary, Salmon declares that admonishing and exhorting the community is among the sacred duties of religious elites. The way that he carries out this duty highlights the intertwining of exegesis and homily—and textuality and orality—within his project.

Salmon's most direct statements about the obligation to exhort appear in *Neḥamot*, the litany of consolations that follows the verse-by-verse exegesis of the book of Lamentations. In this pious appendix, Salmon pairs each verse from Lamentations, in which pain and punishment are described, with a verse that prophesies healing and restoration in parallel terms. Salmon's homiletical and hermeneutical skills blend as he counters each individual image of affliction with a biblical image of its reversal. First, he establishes an exegetical foundation for these consolations:

> When you examine the book of God, you will see in His promises and in the good news that He sent us through His prophets, the opposite of everything that is in the book of Lamentations, and you will also learn that before Jeremiah was commissioned to establish these *lamentations* (*qinot*), *consolations* (*neḥamot*) were revealed through him and the rest of the prophets, with sublime meanings that are contrary to every word and every meaning in Lamentations—except for whatever contains gratitude or the confession of offenses.[67]

Having determined that the Bible includes a priori consolations for every suffering that Israel will endure, Salmon then organizes these prophetic consolations into a homiletical-exegetical masterpiece. He justifies this homily by explaining that

> God obliges the scholars (*ʿulamāʾ*) of the nation to exhort (*yaʿiẓū*) her constantly, and to fortify her and strengthen her and ask her to patiently endure the severity of [the circumstances that] she is in, and to remind (*yudhakkir*) her of what the Mighty and Sublime promised her. *Strengthen the weak hands, and make firm the feeble knees. Say to those who are of a fearful heart, "Be strong, fear not!"* (Isa 35:3–4).[68]

[67] Salmon's commentary, *Neḥamot*; Abdul-Karim, 185.
[68] Ibid.

These words serve as the preamble for Salmon's methodical reinterpretation of every clause of Lamentations. While the commentary itself stresses the justice of Israel's suffering after centuries of sin, *Neḥamot* emphasizes the promise of redemption. The warnings that Salmon repeats throughout the commentary are thoroughly reversed in the reminders that he presents in *Neḥamot*.

A salient point in Salmon's explanation is that he considers exhortation to be one of his responsibilities as a religious scholar. Yet the vision of hortatory preaching that Salmon presents here, as the commentary draws to a close, is distinct from the obligation of summoning one's fellows to repentance that he declares in the commentary's introduction. There the emphasis was on warning the community of God's threats and punishments in order to motivate their piety. Here Salmon's task, like the threats themselves, is reversed: he must comfort the community and reassure them that an end to their collective suffering will come. The familiar vocabulary of warning and admonition has been upended in the context of this statement as well. By the term *yaʿiẓū* Salmon designates the act of preaching solace rather than admonition; by the term *yudhakkir* he indicates the reminder of God's mercies and promises, rather than God's threats. These passages of consolation do not cancel, or even balance, the long pages of admonition that dominate the commentary, but they do suggest another side to the message of Lamentations, and another dimension to Salmon's duty as a homilist. Just as Arabic pious counsel may include a warning and a reminder, in order to both push and pull the errant to penitence, so does Salmon's commentary include both the warnings of Lamentations and the reminders of the prophets who temper that message with verses of consolation.

To some extent, Salmon's textual practice of exhortation sidelines our questions about whether his homilies were delivered orally, and when, where, to whom, and by whom. It is likely that there was an oral life-setting for some or all of this material, whether before or after Salmon compiled the commentary. Yet Salmon seems to designate the Lamentations commentary itself, complete with the consolations, as the fulfillment of his obligation to exhort and admonish. The acceptance of written homily as a viable form of Karaite "preaching" is implied also in the title given to Sahl's collection of written epistles, "The Book of Admonition," and in the contents of al-Qūmisī's literary circulars rebuking the Jews of the Diaspora for their reluctance to immigrate to Jerusalem. Islamic sources likewise include sermons of pious counsel that follow all the conventions of public oratory in spite of credible evidence that they were never uttered aloud. In the same way, it is within the pages of the Lamentations commentary that Salmon discharges his obligation to exhort—and to console—his community.

6
The Hermeneutics of Historical Reflection

We are obliged to reflect.

—Salmon b. Yerūḥīm

Jewish interpreters have traditionally ascribed Lamentations to the prophet Jeremiah and understood its verses in relation to the fall of Jerusalem. Salmon, too, places the book within an ancient historical context of siege and suffering, the fall of the Temple, and the loss of all the blessings that once God bestowed upon the Israelites. Yet for Salmon, this historical context is not merely a backdrop against which Jeremiah uttered his words of rebuke and lamentation. Rather, the historical episodes that are recorded, mostly obliquely, in the verses of Lamentations and throughout the Bible have their own lessons to teach. For this reason, Salmon devotes sustained attention to the real historical events that lie behind Lamentations, first to determine the book's historical context, and then to reflect upon this past in order to find the "instruction for Israel" encoded within it.

Salmon's strategies for thinking historically about Scripture suggest a multilayered historical consciousness. There are two levels to his historical thought: one that entails the methodical research of past events through texts, and one that amounts to a homiletical reflection on the past and its meaning. At times, Salmon evinces genuine historical thinking, recognizable as historical even in our own terms: he charts chronological developments, considering factors of geography and economy, and he corroborates biblical sources in order to produce an ordered, coherent account of a specific historical situation. These cases point to Salmon's historical outlook and his commitments to determining the historical realities of the biblical period. At other times, Salmon's interest in the past takes a more pietistic hermeneutical turn, as he considers the meaning and purpose of biblical history for his own time, its instructions for pious practice, and its guidance in matters of salvation history. This homiletical approach to the biblical past is connected to, and informed by the results of,

Jewish Piety in Islamic Jerusalem. Jessica Andruss, Oxford University Press. © Oxford University Press 2023.
DOI: 10.1093/oso/9780197639559.003.0006

the more systematic historical inquiries that Salmon conducts. Thus, Salmon's historical research, like his use of Arabic literary terminology or homiletical forms, exists as a framework for his pietism.

Salmon's hermeneutic of historical reflection is rooted in the Arabic concept of *iʿtibār*—reflection on edifying narratives of past events in order to find instruction or admonition within them—which he develops in distinctively Jewish modes. His historical analysis supports the broader homiletical program of his commentary. Like his tenth-century Muslim contemporaries working in the emerging Arabic genres of commentary (*tafsīr*) and historiography (*taʾrīkh*), Salmon comes to interpret the past with the same techniques that he uses to interpret Scripture. The past, as it is known from biblical and post-biblical sources, contains religious instruction for the Jews in exile. By reflecting on past accounts of sin and punishment as well as righteousness and reward, Salmon argues, the Jews of his own age will learn that they are obliged to repent, and they will find practical instruction in how to do so sincerely and effectively.

For Salmon, then, *iʿtibār* is a religious obligation with pietistic significance and eschatological consequences: sincere contemplation of the past leads to righteous behavior in the present, and redemption in the future. This approach to biblical history also opens a hermeneutical line of attack in the internal Jewish polemics between Salmon's community—the Jerusalem Karaites—and the Rabbanite establishment based in Iraq. Salmon identifies the Rabbanites as those who fail to fulfill the commandment of reflecting on Scripture, thereby perpetuating the sins that caused the destruction of the Temple and keeping the Jewish people in exile. The aim of this chapter is to consider the varied role that history, and reflection upon the past, play in Salmon's exegetical and hermeneutical work.

Salmon's Historical Thought in the Context of Lamentations

The biblical book of Lamentations is commonly interpreted in a certain historical context—namely, the destruction of the city and Temple of Jerusalem by Babylonian armies in the sixth century BCE. However, within the five chapters of Lamentations there is no attempt to report concrete historical occurrences, let alone to produce a systematic or chronological record of military, political, or social events as they unfolded in ancient Judea. Lamentations 1–2 and 4–5 hint at historical context with vague references to "Judah," "Zion," "Jerusalem," and "her enemies," as well as nebulous allusions to downfall, loss, and degradation. The third chapter of Lamentations lies far afield from anything recognizably historical. It lacks all references to concrete places, persons, and happenings. It shares with the chapters that surround it a plaintive tone, a fixation on the themes of suffering and divine abandonment, and an alphabet-based organization, and yet its verses are so focused on the speaker's individual, personal experience of grief that they entirely ignore any communal concerns or broader sociopolitical realities. If a reader encountered this chapter independently of the other poems of Lamentations, there would be no reason to understand it as a response to the fall of Jerusalem, or to any other historical episode in particular. The book of Lamentations, taken as a whole, is concerned not with recording historical circumstances, but with responding to them in emotional or religious terms. Together, the five poems represent with poetic immediacy the suffering, outrage, and anguish that the people of Jerusalem experienced in the midst of a cataclysmic historical moment.[1]

Just as the authors of Lamentations forego the conventions of ancient historical writing—their poems bear no resemblance to the annalistic style found in the biblical books of Kings or Chronicles—so they also turn from any systematic theological speculation, even while sharp accusations of unbridled divine wrath slice through the poems. The voices of Lamentations express grievances against God, accuse God of cruelty and injustice, and demand God's action, but they do not appear to represent a consistent theological perspective.[2] Thus, while verses of Lamentations may relate obliquely to historical events or issue theological challenges, the book as a whole has little to offer in the way of explicit historical references or a unified theological perspective.

[1] Modern commentaries on Lamentations generally dispense with the book's historical references quickly, although the question of when the poems were written—in the immediate aftermath of the destruction, or several generations later—has been the subject of debate. See, e.g., Berlin, "Psalms and the Literature of Exile: Psalms 137, 44, 69, and 78," in *The Book of Psalms: Composition and Reception*, VTSupp 99, ed. Peter W. Flint and Patrick D. Miller (Leiden: Brill, 2005), 65–86; F. W. Dobbs-Allsopp, *Weep, O Daughter of Zion: A Study of the City-Lament Genre in the Hebrew Bible* (Rome: Pontifico Biblico, 1993); and Edward L. Greenstein, "The Book of Lamentations: Responses to Destruction or Ritual of Rebuilding?," in *Religious Responses to Political Crisis*, ed. Henning Graf Reventlow and Yair Hoffman (London: T&T Clark, 2008), 52–71.

[2] Modern biblical scholars have attempted to reconstruct the book's theological perspective. See, e.g., Bertil Albrektson, *Studies in the Text and Theology of the Book of Lamentations*, STL 21 (Lund, Sweden: Gleerup, 1963); F. W. Dobbs-Allsopp, "Tragedy, Tradition, and Theology in the Book of Lamentations," *Biblical Interpretation* 7 (1999): 235–71; Norman K. Gottwald, *Studies in the Book of Lamentations*, SBT 14 (Chicago: Allenson, 1954); and Patrick D. Miller, *They Cried to the Lord: The Form and Theology of Biblical Prayer* (Minneapolis, Minn.: Fortress, 1994). Cf. Alan Cooper, who concludes that Lamentations "has no *univocal* theological message. It is in its very essence a book that speaks with many voices, and conveys many messages"; see "The Message of Lamentations," *JANES* 28 (2001): 18.

One of Salmon's central projects in the Lamentations commentary, however, is to uncover the real historical events behind the book and to proclaim their religious significance. Salmon's interest in the past plays out on two levels: a scholarly project of determining the process of Jerusalem's destruction and exile as it unfolded in history, and a hermeneutical project of discovering the religious meaning and message of these historical events. The passages of legitimate historical analysis within the commentary must be understood in service of the larger homiletical thrust of the work and the ideological perspectives of its author. It is in the historical developments of the biblical past that Salmon finds religious instruction for the medieval Jewish community.

Salmon's concern with the historical dimensions of biblical literature takes three principal forms. I will identify the forms briefly in this section and examine each one more extensively in the remainder of the chapter. The first form, the "historical-contextual," is most recognizable as history since it shares the aims and methods of later historical scholarship. On this level of historical thought Salmon considers sources from outside of Lamentations, weaving accounts together in order to construct a detailed chronological timeline of events. The second and third dimensions of Salmon's historical perspective are more clearly attached to his religious commitments. The second form, the "historical-theological," entails the application of historical evidence to theological arguments, ultimately producing a theological reading of history. The third form—which is the central focus of this chapter, and a major hermeneutical method throughout Salmon's corpus—is Salmon's practice of reflecting upon narratives about the past in order to locate a pious homiletical teaching for his community. I shall refer to this form as the "historical-hermeneutical."[3]

In his historical-contextual task, Salmon attempts to pinpoint the real historical background of the events to which Lamentations alludes. To this end, he consults parallel accounts of the Babylonian conquest of Judah, as found in the biblical books of Kings and the prophetic texts of Ezekiel and Jeremiah.[4] At other points, he decodes a poetic metaphor in order to place it within a specific historical context of reference. This approach is

[3] Following Robinson, who identifies a "historical/homiletical" method in Salmon's commentary on Ecclesiastes (*Asceticism*, 101–5).

[4] Salmon's method of filling in the gaps of Lamentations by looking at other biblical books accords with the Karaite exegetical principle that all twenty-four books of the Hebrew Bible provide complementary data and are subject to equal interpretive scrutiny. Karaite exegetes posited that the Hebrew Bible had an editor (Arab.: *mudawwin*) who repeated the same information in different genres, so that exegetes could supply missing information by consulting a parallel report in another book. On the *mudawwin*, see Haggai Ben-Shammai, "Major Trends in Karaite Philosophy and Polemics in the

predicated on Salmon's concept of the Bible as a historical document that was produced in the past and that reflects certain realities and conditions that are no longer familiar in his own time. In order to recover these past events and fully appreciate their meaning, one must first engage in the real historical work of determining the chronological sequence of events, figuring out where certain episodes occurred and who was involved in them, and deciding what factors contributed to them. Conflicting sources must be evaluated and reconciled in order to produce a coherent narrative of past events. There is an interpretive dimension to this work, since Salmon must resolve the ambiguities and obscurities in his biblical sources. However, the project itself, and the questions Salmon asks of the texts, are properly historical.

The second manifestation of Salmon's interest in history—the historical-theological—brings the text of Lamentations into alignment with Salmon's theological concerns. In these cases, Salmon collects biblical evidence about the sins that the Israelites committed in order to assert that the destruction of Jerusalem in no way impinges on the justice of God. Salmon marshals biblical verses to show that the Israelites continued to sin in defiance of repeated prophetic calls for repentance, and he uses these prooftexts as historical evidence that God gave the people ample opportunity for reform. By continually violating the covenant and commandments, the Israelites came to deserve God's chastising punishment. The radical crisis that befell the Israelites when Jerusalem was destroyed constitutes nothing more than the stern correction of a just and merciful deity. Salmon makes this point with litigious precision, giving evidence of specific sins and citing the exact historical circumstances in which they were committed, as a means of exonerating God and placing blame instead on the sinful populace.[5]

The third dimension of Salmon's attention to history is bound up with the pietistic dimensions of his hermeneutical program. In this

Tenth and Eleventh Centuries," in *Karaite Judaism*, 350–51; Meira Polliack and Eliezer Schlossberg, "Historical-Literary, Rhetorical and Redactional Methods of Interpretation in Yefet ben Eli's Introduction to the Minor Prophets," in *Exegesis and Grammar in Medieval Karaite Texts*, JSSSupp 13, ed. Geoffrey Khan (Oxford: Oxford University Press, 2001), 25–36; and Uriel Simon, *Four Approaches to the Book of Psalms from Saadia Gaon to Abraham Ibn Ezra* (Albany: State University of New York Press, 1991), 88–93.

5 The most systematic example is Salmon's excursus at Lam 1:8; see discussion below. Mintz notes that "One of the great problems of Lamentations as a whole is its elusiveness on the score of the precise nature of the sin for which Israel has been made the subject of such massive retribution" (*Ḥurban*, 25). Salmon uses a historical-theological process to fill this biblical gap, confirming nebulous accusations of sin with historical evidence.

historical-hermeneutical project, Salmon urges reflection [*iʿtibār*] on the historical figures and events that Scripture narrates, so that these accounts of the past may provide moral exempla for the present. In this way, the biblical-historical record serves to instruct future generations, lending a pedagogical or applicative force to Scripture. When biblical narratives are understood as a series of *iʿtibārāt* (objects of contemplation) that provide the pious reader with *ʿibrāt* (admonitions or lessons),[6] then history itself becomes both a warning and a model: one must not repeat the sins of the past, lest one incur the same punishments, and one must emulate the deeds of the righteous, in order to reap their rewards. The homiletical excursuses that Salmon includes in his Lamentations commentary often approach Scripture as a compendium of moral exempla from history. This exegetical stance encourages the homiletical or didactic interpretation of Scripture and cultivates a sense that the past unfolds in order to convey instruction to future generations.

In each manifestation of Salmon's attention to history, Scripture is the principal source for information about the past. This focus may reflect Salmon's sense that biblical history, as reported by the prophets and the pious and vouchsafed by God, exists for the edification and eventual salvation of the Jewish people during their time in exile. This attitude follows the Karaite insistence that only the Bible—and not the post-biblical, rabbinic traditions of interpreting it—provides an authentic source of information about Jewish history. Salmon places great stock in the unparalleled power of the Bible, even stating, "If [the holy books] had not been among [the people], they would have been destroyed."[7] Yet Salmon was also realistic about the historical value of post-biblical sources, so long as they were properly contextualized and their authority was acknowledged to be secondary to that of Scripture.[8] Therefore, he occasionally consults post-biblical, oral traditions as acceptable secondary sources for historical analysis. In his catalogue of the ten exiles that Israel has endured, for example, Salmon distinguishes between the eight exiles that are recorded in Scripture and the two that are transmitted orally.[9] Salmon also draws on his own experience and observations in Jerusalem, both to clarify the meaning of biblical passages and to voice

[6] Salmon uses the form *ʿibrāt* (sg. *ʿibra*) rather than the more typical Arab. plural, *ʿibar*.
[7] See the introduction to Salmon's Lamentations commentary.
[8] For example, Salmon's measured use of rabbinic materials; see chapter 3.
[9] See comment to Lam 2:4 and discussion below. The last two exiles occur in the Second Temple period.

his opinions, often polemical, about the humiliations of his own time.[10] Still, it is the history that is preserved within Scripture that carries the most ethical and theological weight for Salmon. It is this biblical history that Salmon has in mind for his hermeneutical program of reflection on the past, as we will see later in the chapter. First, however, we will explore Salmon's drive to bring historical specificity to the imagery of Lamentations, his methods for determining historical context and development, and his theological pronouncements of divine justice, which are based on historical evidence of Israelite sin.

The Historical-Contextual Method

Salmon often directs his impulse for historical specificity to the poetic language of Lamentations.[11] The dense figurative imagery of Lamentations may reflect and arouse intense emotional responses, but it also threatens to obscure historical realities. Thus, even while Salmon appreciates the emotive qualities of the poetry and incorporates the images into his own prose, he is also concerned with uncovering the historical-contextual meaning of these images and drawing moral instruction from their concrete details. When discussing the image of the widow who weeps in the night (Lam 1:2), for example, Salmon reads each element of this poetic figure as a pointer to a given historical circumstance: the widow represents the people of Jerusalem, and the night refers to the exile. Salmon's verse comment decodes the figurative image by applying it to the people in the time of exile.

Salmon conducts a more sophisticated historical-exegetical operation when he attempts to understand verses from Lamentations in their historical context. In his comment on Lamentations 4:4—*the children beg for food, but no one gives it to them*—Salmon is not satisfied with describing this verse as a generic depiction of siege conditions, which tend to include food

[10] For Salmon's remarks about Muslims on the Temple Mount, see his comment to Lam 1:7 (Abdul-Karim, 34–38); Haggai Ben-Shammai, "The Attitude of Some Early Karaites Toward Islam," in *Studies in Medieval Jewish History and Literature*, vol. 2, ed. Isadore Twersky (Cambridge, Mass.: Harvard University Press, 1984), 9.

[11] Likewise, Mary Louise Mitchell considers the poetry of Lamentations to be a form of historiography. See "Reflecting on Catastrophe: Lamentations 4 as Historiography," in *The Function of Ancient Historiography*, LHBOTS 489, ed. Patricia Kirkpatrick and Timothy D. Goltz (London: T&T Clark, 2008), 78–90. Mitchell reads Lam 4 as the attempt, made by the survivors of the fall of Jerusalem, to understand their situation through the process of narrating the historical events that they had experienced; thus Lam 4 is a work of historiography that is expressed lyrically.

shortages and starvation. Instead, he fleshes out the historical context of the verse by drawing on accounts from parallel biblical narratives. He begins by asserting that "This is the history of King Zedekiah [*wa-hādhā al-tāʾrīkh li-melekh zedkiyahu*]," and then he correlates historical data from 2 Kings 25 and Jeremiah 52 in order to establish the timeline of the siege and locate the periods in which the children would have been deprived of bread. Salmon thus compares and attempts to integrate historical accounts in order to arrive at an accurate understanding of on-the-ground conditions. This example indicates the foundation of a genuinely historical method of biblical interpretation in Salmon's time.

Salmon's sense of the Bible as a lasting source of truth for future generations does not diminish his awareness of the historical-contextual meaning of biblical verses. Indeed, it is only through attention to the historical context of a given verse that a correct spiritual interpretation of it is possible. Salmon confronts this issue directly when addressing apparently contradictory biblical passages. In discussing the verse *The chastisement of the daughter of my people has been greater than the punishment of Sodom* (Lam 4:6), Salmon recognizes an ostensible contradiction with a verse from Jeremiah in which the sins of Jerusalem are equal to, rather than worse than, the sins of Sodom. He resolves the apparent conflict by reminding his readers that biblical texts reflect changing historical circumstances. As he explains,

> We say that God described their conditions in every time as they were at that time. When they were equal in sin to Sodom, He said, *All of them have become like Sodom unto Me* (Jer 23:14), and when they surpassed the deeds of Sodom, it is said, *As I live, says the Lord God, your sister Sodom and her daughters have not done as you and your daughters have done* (Ezek 16:48).[12]

This comment demonstrates Salmon's approach to the Bible as a historical artifact. Scripture records pronouncements as they were issued, without corruption or modification. By stating that "God described their conditions in every time as they were at that time," Salmon affirms an exegetical practice of interpreting biblical verses in light of the varied historical situations in which they emerged.

[12] Comment to Lam 4:6.

The Historical-Theological Reading

In the second level of Salmon's historical study—what I have labeled his historical-theological reading—Salmon uses biblical history as a foundation for his theological assertions about divine justice. At times the book of Lamentations threatens to undermine Salmon's convictions about God's justice, both implicitly (by rehearsing the extreme suffering of the Israelites) and explicitly (by calling God to account for this suffering). In the face of such biblical verses, Salmon takes pains to vindicate God by demonstrating both that the sins of Israel justified such a punishment and that the punishment itself is designed to chastise the sinful people, thereby leading them to repent. It is particularly in service of the first point—that the sins of Israel were heinous and repeated to the point that such a severe chastising punishment was necessary—that Salmon mines the narratives of biblical history.

Salmon's commitment to the precept of divine justice is in keeping with the theological positions that were ascendant in the medieval Islamic world. Already by the mid-tenth century, when Salmon flourished as an exegete, the tenets of Muʿtazilite theology were clearly articulated. The principal tenets—affirmation of God's unity and justice—were established as the defining theological framework of Muʿtazilite thought, and Muʿtazilite-inflected treatises written by Jews, Christians, and Muslims in Arabic were widespread.[13]

Salmon establishes divine justice as a special theme of his commentary already in the opening *taḥmīd*, the dedicatory preface that begins Arabic prose texts in the medieval Islamic milieu.[14] As a rule, such prefaces open the text with words of praise for the deity, yet the precise terms in which God is exalted differ from treatise to treatise. This flexibility invites authors to exercise literary creativity by inventing new rhymes and images. It also enables them to establish the key themes of their texts through the words that they select

[13] Perhaps the most renowned Jewish Muʿtazilite treatise is *Kitāb al-Amānāt wa-l-Iʿtiqadāt* (*The Book of Beliefs and Opinions*) by Salmon's older contemporary, Saadia Gaon. On the Muʿtazilite background of medieval Jewish thought, see Haggai Ben-Shammai, "Kalām in Medieval Jewish Philosophy," in *History of Jewish Philosophy*, ed. Daniel H. Frank and Oliver Leaman (New York: Routledge, 2003); Joel Kraemer, "The Islamic Context of Medieval Jewish Philosophy," in *History of Jewish Philosophy*, ed. Daniel H. Frank and Oliver Leaman (New York: Routledge, 2003), 38–68; Daniel Lasker, "Islamic Influences on Karaite Origins," in *Studies in Islamic and Jewish Traditions II*, ed. William M. Brinner and Stephen D. Ricks (Atlanta, Ga.: Scholars Press, 1989), 23–47; and Colette Sirat, "The Mutakallimūn and Other Jewish Thinkers Inspired by Muslim Theological Movements," in *A History of Jewish Philosophy in the Middle Ages* (Cambridge: Cambridge University Press, 1996), 15–56. For an overview of Muʿtazilite influences on Karaite Bible commentaries, see Wechsler on Yefet, Esth, 40–58, and Sasson on Yefet, Prov, chapter 4.

[14] See Salmon's Invocation and chapter 2, section on "Programmatic Introduction."

and the scriptural citations that they embed within the *taḥmīd*. Salmon—or an early editor of his work—crafts a *taḥmīd* that emphasizes divine justice, prefacing the Lamentations commentary as follows: "*In the name of the true Judge, blessed be His name. He judges with justice and truth* [. . .] *The LORD is just in all His ways* (Ps 145:17). *Just are You, O LORD* (Ps 119:137). *The LORD is just, for I have rebelled against His word* (Lam 1:18)." By opening the commentary with a pastiche of biblical verses that emphasize God's justice, Salmon primes readers to expect a thorough treatment of God's righteous judgment in the commentary itself.

The last of these three biblical prooftexts on the theme of divine justice reappears later in the introduction to the commentary, when Salmon identifies the seven themes of the book of Lamentations. One of the book's purposes, according to Salmon, is to urge "the confession of offenses, as the nation says, *The LORD is just, for I have rebelled against His word; but hear, all you peoples* (Lam 1:18) and *We have transgressed and rebelled* (Lam 3:42)." Both of these prooftexts from Lamentations link the assertion of divine justice to the confession of human sin. In Salmon's framework, the epic punishment that befell the Israelites is inherently just. Therefore, the people must confess their sins and affirm God's righteousness in punishing them, as these verses dictate.

While Salmon uses such biblical citations to affirm his belief in divine justice, it is within his historically oriented excursuses in the body of the commentary that he articulates this theological position most clearly and argues for it most forcefully. In these historical excursuses, Salmon exposes and charts the sins of the biblical Israelites with legal acuity, demonstrating the severity of the sins and the stubborn persistence of the sinners throughout biblical history. Moreover, Salmon argues that a significant purpose behind the composition of the Bible is to justify God's punishment on the basis of Israelite sin. In his comment to the verse, *Jerusalem has sinned grievously* (Lam 1:8), he states,

> [This verse exists] in order to teach that God did not cause whatever befell Israel—in this case, the magnitude of these calamities—to befall them. Rather, it was because their sins increased. [. . .] Know that God explained in His holy books, through His prophets, the magnitude of the sins of the house of Israel and Judah in order to instruct *the generations to come* that everything that God did to Israel with respect to *this exile* was proper, equitable, and just, because they had transgressed all the *commandments*.[15]

[15] See Salmon's comment to Lam 1:8.

In other words, the historical details of the Bible, which record the community's sins, have a dual function. They both confirm the justice of God's past actions and serve the pedagogical purpose of guiding future generations in their religious obligations. The destruction of Jerusalem and the exile of her people—which the book of Lamentations presents most vividly—were not God's crimes, even though the poet of Lamentations may accuse the deity of inflicting unbearable punishment on God's chosen people. Rather, the sinners themselves were responsible for the punishment, which they brought upon themselves and certainly deserved. Furthermore, it is the punishments themselves that constitute proof of God's mercies, since they notify the people of the need to repent, and repentance will bring redemption.

In order to make his case stick, Salmon must describe the sins endured by the Israelites in as much painful detail as the poet of Lamentations describes the punishments inflicted by God. Salmon emphasizes the sins of Israel through refrains such as, "All these calamities befell us because of the magnitude of our offenses" or *Woe to us, for we have sinned!* (Lam 5:16), but these recurring lament formulas lack the concrete proof of historical evidence.[16] It is Salmon's systematic, historical inquiries that provide the most damning indictments of Israelite misbehavior and thereby exonerate the punishing deity most fully. In a lengthy excursus at Lamentations 1:8, Salmon presents each of the Ten Commandments followed by biblical evidence of how the Israelites violated it, and the commensurate punishment that ensued. For example,

> God said on Mount Sinai: *Honor your father and your mother* (Exod 20:12). Israel transgressed this commandment, as it is said, *Father and mother are treated with contempt* (Ezek 22:7); and *For the son treats the father with contempt, the daughter rises up against her mother* (Mic 7:6). Therefore, we deserve to lament for ourselves and say, *We have become orphans, fatherless* (Lam 5:3). God said on Mount Sinai, *You shall not kill* (Exod 20:13). We transgressed this commandment, as it is said, *Also on your skirts is found the lifeblood of guiltless poor* (Jer 2:34). We killed the prophets and among us today there are those who kill many people by slander. *Woe to us, for we have sinned!* (Lam 5:16). Therefore we were met with those who spilled our blood: *They have poured out their blood like water* (Ps 79:3). How many

[16] I.e., refrains for Lam 1 and Lam 5, respectively.

> of Israel were killed in every age among the nations, and we are in great strife![17]

By pairing each commandment with the evidence that the Israelites violated it in the past, Salmon proves that Israel sinned repeatedly, violating each commandment in turn. In each case, the punishment matches the crime. Thus, the failure to honor one's parents is requited when children are made to be orphans, while murder is requited with murder.[18] Salmon's catalogue of transgressions, which is based on the biblical record, adds historical specificity to his theological argument. Rather than insisting in generic terms that sin is repaid by punishment, Salmon treats each sin in precise detail and shows how it was repaid, measure for measure, in accord with the principles of theodicy.

In this excursus on the violations of the Ten Commandments, Salmon demonstrates an impressive grasp of Scripture, bringing prooftexts from the entire canon to prove each point. Here, as elsewhere in the commentary, he draws historical evidence from the prophetic books of the Bible more than from those that are considered properly historical, such as the annalistic books of Kings or Chronicles. Salmon himself addresses this question of historical source material in the context of his excursus on the Ten Commandments. He introduces his argument by stating that the sins of Israel and Judah brought about the exile of Hoshea ben Elah and the ten tribes. Then he cites the narrative of 2 Kings 7:17–23, in which the aforementioned sins are spelled out. Afterward he states that "this is established in other parts of the prophetic books" and cites similar evidence of Israelite transgressions from the pages of Ezekiel, Jeremiah, and Amos. While Salmon presents passages from the historical and prophetic books together, as mutually reinforcing, he seems to prefer the prophets' vision of the past over the accounts offered by the historical books of the Bible. Salmon's affinity for prophetic depictions of the past may be owed, in part, to the ethical perspective on history that is especially pronounced in the words of the prophets. Salmon conducts his exegetical tasks in the context of a broader homiletical project: the purpose of his commentary is to discover the ethical message within the biblical passages, and to convey that instruction to his own

[17] See Salmon's excursus at Lam 1:8.

[18] Salmon builds on the rabbinic concept of *middah keneged middah*, or "measure for measure," in which God's punishment corresponds in some detail to the crime. See discussion in chapter 3, section on "Rabbinic Hermeneutics: The Ten Commandments and Requital in Kind in Lamentations 1:8."

community. It is the prophets—and particularly Jeremiah, the purported author of Lamentations—who model for Salmon the techniques of translating historical happenings into a powerful rhetoric of spiritual reorientation.

Salmon's Historical-Homiletical Method: *Iʿtibār*

Finally, in the third level of his historical project, Salmon draws on biblical history to craft homiletical statements intended to inspire his community to undertake their religious commitments with renewed energy and intentionality. This form of historical thought is the culmination of the previous two: it builds on Salmon's historical-contextual method by using real historical research as the basis of its claims, and it incorporates Salmon's historical-theological conclusions as the foundation of its homiletical interpretation. Moreover, this application of historical scholarship draws on the exegetical and homiletical dimensions of Salmon's project. The Lamentations commentary is inherently exegetical—it proceeds methodically though the biblical verses, explicating grammar and semantics, unpacking obscure references, striving for accurate interpretations—and yet Salmon never loses sight of the homiletical purpose that inspires his exegetical labor. For Salmon, the payoff of exegesis is a homily so rich and compelling, so meticulously researched, that it rouses the Jews of the exile to religious devotion so radical that it brings about redemption.

Salmon's primary tool for finding the spiritual message of a given historical narrative is *iʿtibār*, a process of reflection or contemplation in order to discern spiritual instruction. Biblical verses and historical accounts are not the only appropriate objects of reflection; *iʿtibār* also encompasses contemplation of the works of the Creator or the operations of the cosmos, and Salmon uses the term in this way in his commentary on Psalms.[19] However, in his commentaries on Lamentations and Ecclesiastes, Salmon focuses on the historical narratives of Scripture as the principal objects of reflection.[20] By considering biblical records of the wicked and the righteous, and their

[19] See Salmon's comment on Ps 19:2/1, in which one learns to feel humility toward the Creator by reflecting on the cosmos. *Iʿtibār* in the context of contemplating the works of creation is also the way that Baḥya ibn Paqūda uses the term a century after Salmon in *Bāb al-Iʿtibār*, the second chapter of his Jewish pietistic work, *Kitāb al-Hidāya ilā Farāʾiḍ al-Qulūb* (*Book of Direction to the Duties of the Heart*); for discussion, see Diana Lobel, *A Sufi-Jewish Dialogue: Philosophy and Mysticism in Bahya ibn Paquda's* Duties of the Heart (Philadelphia: University of Pennsylvania Press, 2007), chapter 6.

[20] On *iʿtibār* in Salmon's Ecclesiastes commentary, see Robinson, *Asceticism*, 101–5.

respective punishments and rewards, the pious reader will uncover the deep meaning of biblical exempla and thereby learn to avoid the sins of the wicked and emulate the good deeds of the righteous. In this way, Salmon posits a practical application to biblical study: the aim of exegesis is spiritual instruction and pious response.

This practice of reflecting on historical exempla in order to draw out their spiritual meaning informs much of Salmon's exegesis throughout the commentary on Lamentations. He presents the method of *iʿtibār* most systematically in an excursus within his commentary on Ecclesiastes.[21] There, Salmon presents this prooftext from Deuteronomy as the biblical foundation of his method: "Remember the days of old, consider the years of many generations" (32:7). Working chronologically through the first narratives from the book of Genesis, Salmon identifies Adam, Cain, the generation of the flood, and the cities of the plains as examples of those who committed sins and received this-worldly punishment. These figures, spread through the narrative of early human history, demonstrate the following principle: "In each and every generation there exist different reflections [*iʿtibārāt*] on the nature of retribution." Scripture also reports the deeds of the righteous, to provide a complementary object of reflection. The stories of primordial righteous men and the Israelite forefathers provide examples of true belief and proper behavior, proving that "in each generation, moreover, He [= God] singles out a community of obedient ones and reveals to them a celestial good. All of this points to reward in the Hereafter." The reports of the wicked and the reports of the righteous are two sides of the same coin; the pious student of the Bible recognizes that God "established these two states by way of exemplum [*ʿalā sabīl al-iʿtibār*]." Thus, the past events themselves, as well as the written or oral record of their occurrence, exist for the edification of those who reflect upon them. This historical-homiletical method enables Salmon to interpret biblical verses in light of historical narratives, and to draw out the spiritual import of the past.[22]

Salmon was not alone in attributing a spiritual purpose to past events and the historiography that preserves them. Indeed, the religious interpretation of historical figures and events through the lens of *iʿtibār* was a feature of intellectual discourse throughout the medieval Islamic world. The Arabic root ʿ/b/r appears at least as early as the Qurʾān, where listeners are enjoined to

21 See Salmon's comment to Eccl 9:1 in Robinson, *Asceticism*, 482–88.
22 Ibid., 101–5.

reflect on narratives about ancient peoples—often the biblical Israelites—and derive a lesson (*ʿibra*) thereby.[23] The Muslim exegetes of Salmon's day emphasized the possibility of taking warning from the Qur'ān's historical examples of sin and punishment while gaining spiritual counsel from the examples of righteous behavior.[24] Notably, the terms *iʿtibār* and *ʿibra* appear throughout early Islamic historiographical texts and even within their titles, further solidifying the links between historical thought and moral instruction.[25] As the Arabic tradition of historical writing emerged in the early tenth century—only a generation or so before Salmon—the homiletical project of using examples from the past in order to teach or inspire was thoroughly intertwined with the broader historical project.[26] For Salmon, who explicates the term *iʿtibār* through biblical narratives, the homiletical approach to history has deep roots in the Hebraic tradition and a redemptive potential for medieval Jewry.

In the following sections, I explore Salmon's extensive and multifaceted hermeneutic of *iʿtibār* through the excursuses of his commentaries. Salmon methodically interprets Ezekiel's parable of Oholah and Oholibah in order to demonstrate that reflection on history is a religious obligation (excursus to Lam 1:2). He recalls God's destruction of the Tabernacle at Shilo (the precursor to the Jerusalem Temple) in order to teach the importance of recognizing similarities between one's own time and the past, which will lead one to renounce the sins of a previous generation and escape the punishments that they bore (excursus to Lam 4:1). Salmon revisits the wilderness narratives of the Torah to show that Scripture preserves edifying events of the past specifically so that readers will reflect upon them (excursus to Lam 5:7). He retells the stories of David and Jacob, mourning over their dead loved ones, in order to promote *iʿtibār* as the hermeneutical tool for discerning reliable instruction in ritual and religious law (introduction to the commentary). These passages are among the most engaging and impassioned homiletical selections of Salmon's Lamentations commentary. Read together, they form Salmon's philosophy of reflection on history, and the process that will lead not only to the correct homiletical interpretation of the Bible, but also to piety, penitence, and, ultimately, redemption.

[23] E.g., Q3:14, 12:111, and 59:2–3.
[24] See, e.g., Tabari's comment on Q12:111.
[25] Chase Robinson, *Islamic Historiography* (Cambridge: Cambridge University Press, 2003), 130–31.
[26] Ibid., 12.

Oholah and Oholibah: A Parable of Historical Reflection

As much as Salmon advocates for the practice of *iʿtibār* among his contemporaries, he also laments the missed opportunities for *iʿtibār* within the biblical past. This dimension of *iʿtibār* is particularly strong in Salmon's commentary on Lamentations, given the long tradition of interpreting the biblical book in relation to the historical destruction of Jerusalem. Salmon is convinced not only that Jerusalem fell as a direct result of Israelite sin, but also that this loss could have been avoided, had the people of Jerusalem reflected upon, and taken warning from, the examples from their own past. In this respect, Salmon's enthusiasm for the Karaite program—above all, its emphasis on penitential return to the land as a means of rectifying the current Jewish state of exile—colors his interpretation of the biblical past. Salmon wrote his commentaries in an exceptionally messianic period of Karaite activity, and his understanding of biblical history is informed by his conviction that the Karaite interpretation of the biblical past has the power to transform the Jewish present.

This distinctive notion of *iʿtibār* emerges in Salmon's reading of the parable of Oholah and Oholibah (Ezek 23), which he explicates at length in his comment on Lamentations 1:2. Ezekiel tells of two sisters: the elder, Oholah, represents Samaria, a metonym for the northern kingdom of Israel, while the younger, Oholibah, represents the southern kingdom of Judah, including Jerusalem. In the historical record, the northern kingdom was destroyed and taken into exile by the Assyrians, while the southern kingdom suffered a similar fate at the hands of the Babylonians two centuries later. Within the parable, Oholah lusted after the Assyrians, defiling herself so egregiously with their idol worship that God punished her by turning her over to the Assyrian armies, who then slew her. Oholibah witnesses the entire ordeal, from her older sister's lust and adultery to her murder at the hands of her former lovers. Yet Oholibah is undeterred by her sister's fate, as she not only repeats her sister's sins but actually increases them by whoring after the Assyrians as well as the Babylonians. In the words of Ezekiel, *Her sister Oholibah saw this, yet she was more corrupt than she in her doting and in her harlotry, which was worse than that of her sister* (Ezek 23:11).

In its biblical context, the ethical-political message of the prophet's parable is blunt: the southern kingdom of Judah will suffer a greater punishment than the northern kingdom of Israel because its sins were greater. Salmon takes the verse in a different direction, seizing on the first part—*Her sister Oholibah saw this*—as an indication of the obligation to reflect. He interprets this clause to mean that "Oholibah was obliged to reflect (*yajib ʿalā ʾoholibah ʾan taʿtabir*) upon what happened to Oholah, and to fear God, may He be elevated. However, she did not do so; rather, she perverted herself even more than Oholah." Having witnessed her sister's sins, Oholibah was obligated to reflect upon them and change her own course. Her failure to do so consigns her to a harsher punishment than that of her sister, who may not have had the benefit of prior examples to consider.

For Salmon, this parable offers a clear explanation for the destruction of Jerusalem. He invokes it throughout his corpus, when discussing the catastrophes that befell the community. In his commentary on the Psalms, for example, he returns to the tale of Oholibah and her failure to reflect on her elder sister's punishment. He explicates Psalm 79:1—*O God, the nations have come into Your inheritance; they have defiled Your holy Temple; they have laid Jerusalem in ruins*—by noting that, just like Oholibah, "the kingdom of Judah was obligated to reflect (*yajib taʿtabir*), but they did not do so."[27] He blends the techniques of historical thinking with the hermeneutics of historical reflection again in his long excursus at Lamentations 2:4. There Salmon embeds a chronological survey of the ten exiles that Israel experienced. For each exile, he names the Israelite king who reigned at the time, the foreign king who caused the exile, and the successive tribes that were exiled from their territories. Salmon introduces this historical chart with a summary of the ten exiles, and a reference to the parable of Oholah and Oholibah:

> When [Israel] disobeyed excessively, He first gave the kings of Assyria dominion over the ten tribes, as it is said, *Therefore I delivered her into the hands of her lovers, into the hands of the Assyrians, upon whom she doted. These uncovered her nakedness; they seized her sons and daughters; and her they slew with the sword* (Ezek 23:9–10). [The Assyrians] uprooted them three times, which means they exiled them on three occasions. Then, when Judah and Benjamin and the residents of Jerusalem did not reflect (*lam yaʿtabirū*) [and learn their lesson], He gave Nebuchadnezzar dominion over them, and He exiled them four

[27] Salmon's comment to Ps 79:1 (Salmon, Pss 73–89).

> times after Pharaoh Necho had exiled Jehoahaz, making a total of eight exiles. Then, when they returned from Babylon and built the Second Temple and resumed their disobedience, they were exiled twice. This makes ten times [in all]—eight of them are scriptural and two have been transmitted orally.

Salmon does not articulate the precise factors behind the rebellions of the northern kingdom, Israel. He is more concerned with the failure of the southern kingdom, Judah, to reflect upon these acts and their punishment, which he identifies as their sin. In this framework, the failure to reflect on the sins of others constitutes a sin in and of itself. The destruction of Jerusalem and the exile of the people by the Babylonians are described at least in part as the result of this lack of reflection.

This application of *iʿtibār* explains in historical terms, and justifies in religious terms, the destruction of Jerusalem in the sixth century BCE. More to the point, it offers pious guidance to Salmon's own generation. For just as the ancient Israelites perished when they failed to reflect on the examples of their predecessors, so will medieval Jews continue to suffer if they fail to reflect on the examples recorded in Scripture. This interpretation also intervenes in the Karaite–Rabbanite polemic of Salmon's day by asserting that the Rabbanites cause the entire Jewish community to suffer by failing to reflect on their sins and misinterpretations, while only the Karaites fulfill this religious obligation. Further, by insisting that reflection is an obligation, Salmon implies that it is on par with the commandments, thereby besting the rabbis in their own game of enumerating and expounding upon the commandments.[28] Just as Oholah saw but did not reflect, implies Salmon, so do the Rabbanites read the Torah but fail to reflect upon its religious instruction. Not only do they fail to reflect; they fail even to recognize that they are commanded to do so! In Salmon's interpretation, Ezekiel's parable of Oholah and Oholibah establishes the divine mandate that humans must reflect on narratives about the past, and it teaches the pious reader how to read history. The parable of Oholah and Oholibah, then, is a parable that teaches the obligation to interpret the past.

[28] The rabbis generally derived laws from the Torah alone, while Karaites validated the entire Bible as a source of legal authority (Lasker, "Islamic Influences," 24).

The Tabernacle at Shiloh: Analogy with the Past

Once Salmon has articulated the obligation to take warning from historical narratives, the Bible becomes rich with further examples of Israel's failure to interpret its own past. The book of Lamentations is especially concerned with the destruction of the Temple in Jerusalem and the debilitation of priest and prophet. Salmon notes that the Jerusalem establishment would not have been shocked by this loss—and more importantly, they could have avoided it altogether—if they had recognized their similarity to Shiloh. In many ways, Shiloh was the forerunner to Jerusalem: a prominent site of cultic and prophetic activity where the Ark of the Covenant was housed during the era of the Judges.[29] The fact that God abandoned this site, where the divine presence once dwelled, would have signaled to the receptive historical thinker that God was capable of abandoning Jerusalem as well, if the sins of the Israelites again exceeded all bounds.

Salmon's discussion of Shiloh builds on the methods of historical reflection that he outlines in his interpretation of Oholah and Oholibah. Yet in that parable, the sins of Oholah are regrettable in their own right; the prophet laments the sins of both sisters, even while the sins of Oholibah are compounded by her failure to learn from her sister's example and correct herself. In Salmon's description of Shiloh and Jerusalem, however, Shiloh is reduced to an instrument of divine instruction, as though the site and its religious activities existed merely to provide a lesson for later Jerusalem. Likewise, the ignominious Saul, who ruled Israel when the Ark of the Covenant resided at Shiloh, exists purely as a warning to the kings of the house of David. Salmon explains:

> [The Israelites] used to presume that God would not destroy this Temple. [. . .] He did not leave them to their presumption, but rather He informed them that if they persisted in their rebellions, He would destroy the Temple just as He had destroyed Shiloh, and that this presumption of theirs was a false presumption, as it is said, *Do not trust in these deceptive words* (Jer 7:4) and *Therefore I will do to the house which is called by My name, and in which you trust,* [*and to the place which I gave to you and to your fathers, as I did to Shiloh*] (Jer 7:14). Indeed, the Mighty and Sublime made Shiloh an object of

[29] On Shiloh, see Donald Schley, *Shiloh: A Biblical City in Tradition and History*, JSOTSupp 63 (Sheffield, U.K.: JSOT Press, 1989).

> reflection (*i'tibār*) for Israel. In other words: whenever they disobeyed, He would destroy the Temple, just as He had destroyed Shiloh, as He said: *Go now to My place that was in Shiloh, where I made My name dwell at first, and see what I did to it for the wickedness of My people Israel* (Jer 7:12). Likewise, He made King Saul an object of reflection (*i'tibār*) for the kings of the house of David. Since they chose rebellions and sins, they deserved the destruction of this Temple, as it is said in the *covenant*: *And I will lay your cities waste, and will make your sanctuaries desolate* (Lev 26:31).[30]

The assertion that "God made an object of reflection" (*ja'ala i'tibār*) out of Shiloh or King Saul brings a theological question to the fore. Did God cause destruction and suffering in a certain historical moment in order to provide an example for future generations to reflect upon? Salmon's sense of divine justice would not necessarily preclude such a reading, for Salmon notes elsewhere that in certain circumstances God inflicts undeserved suffering, and in such cases God compensates the sufferer, either in this world or in the world to come.[31] Even so, Salmon's discussion of *i'tibār* raises questions about the distinction between history and historiography. Is it Shiloh itself, and God's abandonment of this early sanctuary, that teaches the lesson, or is it rather the biblical recounting of that event that imparts ethical instruction? Does God make Shiloh a warning by abandoning the site, or by ensuring that the tale of Shiloh is recorded in Scripture? To what degree does God work through human history, according to Salmon, and to what degree does God teach through biblical historiography? Further, as much as Salmon's formulation places God in an authoritative role—to render places and people as objects of reflection for future generations—it also frees God from responsibility for punishing the Israelites: "Since *they* chose rebellions and sins, *they* deserved the destruction of this Temple."[32] Suffering and punishment occur not because God so desires it, but because the sins of Israel mandate such an outcome.[33]

[30] Comment to Lam 4:1.

[31] Salmon explicates this principle in his comment to Lam 4:20: God caused the righteous king Josiah to die prematurely so that he would not suffer the punishments that were about to befall his community, and He compensated him for this trial. On the Mu'tazilite conceptions that resonate with this approach, see Margaretha T. Heemskerk, *Suffering in the Mutazilite Theology: 'Abd al-Jabbār's Teaching on Pain and Divine Justice*, Islamic Philosophy, Theology, and Science 41 (Leiden: Brill, 2000), esp. chapters 4–5; and J. R. T. M. Peters, *God's Created Speech: A Speculative Theology of the Mu'tazilî Qâḍî l-quḍāt Abûl-Ḥasan 'Abd al-Jabbâr bn Aḥmad al-Ḥamadânî* (Leiden: Brill, 1976).

[32] Salmon's comment to Lam 4:1; emphasis mine.

[33] Salmon expounds upon this theology in his comment to Lam 3:33–34.

Salmon's concept of *iʿtibār* also emphasizes a past-oriented direction to prophetic activity. The prophets of the Bible often have predictive abilities, and seers may prophesy future events as a tool for inspiring their listeners to repent. In some cases, it is precisely this prophetic vision of impending doom that motivates the community to change their ways in hopes of averting such an outcome. By contrast, Salmon locates ethical impulses in the process of reflecting upon the past—the historical narratives of the Bible—and he endows prophets with the ability to correctly interpret the events that have already occurred. Salmon emphasizes this wide temporal horizon of prophetic understanding in his excursus to Lamentations 2:4, in which he remarks that Asaph—whom he considers a prophet—recognized the possibility of Jerusalem's destruction, and communicated that through an analogy with Shiloh:

> When he saw with his prophetic eye the acts of disobedience Israel would commit, he informed [us] that the enemy would triumph over the Temple and destroy it. He juxtaposed [Ps 78 with] *O God, the nations have come into Your inheritance* (Ps 79:1) in order to inform [us] that just as Shiloh had been destroyed because of Israel's acts of rebellion, so would Jerusalem be destroyed. Therefore, he mentioned Shiloh before this psalm, as it is said, *He forsook His dwelling at Shiloh* (Ps 78:60).

The regrettable fates of Shiloh and Samaria offer transhistorical significance for Salmon. In the biblical periods that followed the destruction of Shiloh and Samaria, the narratives about their prominence and the circumstances that led to their downfall were intended as instruction, teaching the later community to avoid the sins of Shiloh and Samaria, lest similar catastrophes befall Jerusalem as well. Salmon transfers this insight to the Karaite–Rabbanite context of medieval Jewish discourse and implores his coreligionists to reflect on the historical examples of Jerusalem and Judah, who were punished with exile because they failed to reflect upon the warnings embedded in the examples of Shiloh and Samaria. While Salmon's generation is not responsible for the sins that initiated the exile, they—specifically, the Rabbanites—are responsible for their own sins, which have extended it. By contemplating the historical narratives that appear in the Bible, the Jews of Salmon's own day have the opportunity to repent and bring the exile to an end. Yet only the Karaite

Jews, infused with messianic fervor and a fierce commitment to repentance, have accepted this responsibility.[34]

The Sins of the Fathers: *I'tibār* and the Purpose of Scripture

For Salmon, one of the major purposes of Scripture is to deter future generations from repeating the sins that were committed by the Israelites in the biblical era. By reflecting upon these sins and taking admonition from the punishments that followed them, the pious will forestall a similar fate. Salmon articulates this view of Scripture most straightforwardly in his treatment of Psalm 78. This psalm reviews the key moments of Israelite history, including the establishment of the covenant, slavery in Egypt, the sojourn in the wilderness, the fall of Shiloh, and the rise of the Davidic monarchy. In Salmon's view, "All these narratives (*kull hādhihī l-qiṣaṣ*) are in the Bible so that they will reflect (*ya'tabirū*) and not become like their fathers."[35]

The sins of the ancestors are a significant concern to Salmon, as they caused the destruction of Jerusalem, the loss of sovereignty, prophecy, and priesthood, and the exile itself. But the sins of the current generation are no less severe, as they cause the indefinite extension of these misfortunes. Salmon presents his attitudes about the relationship between the sins of the past and the sins of the present at length in his homily on Lamentations 5:7. The biblical verse reads, *Our fathers have sinned, and are no more; and we bear their offenses*. Salmon responds with one of the most cohesive, exegetically precise, and rhetorically effective homilies in the Lamentations commentary. He begins his remarks with a straightforward formulation of the theological message of the verse, which he systematically defends thereafter:

> *Our fathers have sinned, and are no more* means that our fathers sinned and were punished for their deeds by violent death, plague, hunger, captivity,

[34] Salmon is not consistently clear as to whether all Jews, including Rabbanites, must embrace the Karaite program before redemption is possible, or whether Karaite mourning is sufficient to bring about the redemption even with some number of Rabbanite holdouts. A comparison to the ancient "Mourners for Zion" (who may or may not have been forerunners to the tenth-century Karaites) is stimulating in this regard. According to their theology of redemptive suffering, the Mourners would elicit God's pity in part by enduring the mockery of righteous, Torah-observant Jews who derided them and their ascetic practices. This pity would inspire God to bring salvation through the messiah. Thus, the existence of Torah-observant but misguided Jews—whose humiliations the Mourners must suffer—is necessary for bringing about the redemption. See Alexander, "The Mourners for Zion and the Suffering Messiah," 147–57.

[35] Comment to Ps 78:8 (Salmon, Pss 73–89).

> exile, and all of the calamities that befell them. It was obligatory for their children, the people of the exile, to reflect (*ya'tabirū*) and to return to God, great is His memory, and to repent and not to do as it is said, *we bear their offenses*, which means that we persist in the offenses of our fathers and thereby extend our tarrying in this *exile.*[36]

Salmon tells his generation that their sins are no less egregious than the sins of the past. Even though they did not cause the exile directly, their sins extend it—a charge no less damning. For Salmon, the "fathers" whose sins must be rejected are not exclusively—or even primarily—those ancient forefathers from the biblical era, who practiced child sacrifice or idol worship, but rather the elders from their own time, who adhere to the faulty religious laws of rabbinic Judaism. He reminds his own generation that they must not continue to practice the inherited traditions that are antithetical to the correct meaning of the Bible. In essence, the exile continues because Israel will not break away from the sins of the Rabbanites. This comment also carries insights into Salmon's religious perspective. One generation is not responsible for the sins of the generation that came before, but they are responsible for deciding to perpetuate their sins or break away from them. The fact that rabbinic law is ancient and established does not mean that it is correct. Salmon urges the Jews of his own day to denounce and discontinue Rabbanite practices, which are derived from long-standing erroneous interpretations of the Bible.

The second clause of the biblical verse—*we bear their offenses*—points to a theological problem: can one generation suffer punishment for sins committed by its predecessors? Salmon addresses this conundrum first by airing his dissatisfaction with the theological explanations offered by other scholars, and then by turning to his own reflections on biblical history. The narrative of the Israelites who must wander forty years in the wilderness before entering the Promised Land may appear to support the argument that collective punishment falls equally on the guilty as well as the innocent. Yet Salmon offers a counter-reading of the Torah wilderness narrative, based on close attention to the historical record. According to Salmon, the narrative itself distinguishes sharply between the fathers—the wicked generation that was punished—and the children—the righteous generation that merely endured the punishment before receiving full compensation in

[36] Comment to Lam 5:7.

this world, in the form of access to the Holy Land. Salmon then moves from a historical argument about these two generations to homiletical remarks about his own "generation of the exile" and the sins that forestall their redemption:

> One scholar has said that the meaning of *and we bear their offenses* is that we are imprisoned in this *exile* because of the deeds of our fathers who came before, and that this is like what happened to the *generation of the wilderness*, since it is said, *And your children shall be shepherds in the wilderness forty years, and shall suffer for your faithlessness* (Num 14:33). This statement errs in two respects. The first respect is that God does not requite the children for the offenses of their fathers and does not requite the fathers for the offenses of their children, just as He does not reward the children for the obedience of their fathers and He does not reward the fathers for the obedience of their sons. Indeed, this holy book stipulates that *the soul that sins shall die* (Ezek 18:20). [. . .] The other respect [in which the scholar errs] concerns the forty-year delay for the *generation of the wilderness*. Rather, it was to destroy the fathers—the judgment of destruction was upon them—as it is said, *In this wilderness they shall come to a full end, and there they shall die* (Num 14:35). Thus [God] said, *shall suffer for your faithlessness* (Num 14:33), so that the children would grow up and enter into the land with knowledge and they would be strong and they would fight. The meaning of *shall suffer for your faithlessness* alludes to them [i.e., the children] being detained because you [i.e., the fathers] exceeded all bounds of iniquity. In other words, "So that you will perish just as they perished," as it is said, *after all the men of war had perished* (Deut 2:16). At that point [i.e., after the older generation had perished], [the children] were commanded to enter the land. There is also a distinction between the people of the *exile* and the children of the people of the wilderness, which is that the children of the *generation of the wilderness* were *righteous*, as it is said, *But you who held fast to the LORD your God are all alive this day* (Deut 4:4). Regarding the people of the exile, however, it is said, *their iniquities and their fathers' iniquities together, says the LORD* (Isa 65:7). It is said about [the people of the exile], *They have all gone astray, they are all alike corrupt; there is none that does good* (Ps 14:3). He eloquently expressed [this] in the *covenant*, with the meaning that we mentioned: *And those of you that are left shall pine away in your enemies' lands because of their iniquity; and also because of the iniquities of their fathers they shall pine away like them* (Lev 26:39).

> *Those of you that are left shall pine away in your enemies' lands because of their iniquity* indicates that the people of the exile will be requited for their [own] offenses. *And also because of the iniquities of their fathers they shall pine away like them* (Lev 26:39) means from what is in their hand as well as the offense of their fathers, as it is said, *and we bear their offenses.*[37]

In Salmon's comment, it is history itself, as recorded in the books of Numbers and Deuteronomy, that provides the keys to correct theology and correct exegesis. The Bible's own historical narrative indicates the religious significance of the present exile. Salmon's generation continues to experience the conditions of exile not because they have inherited the punishment that was due their ancestors, but rather because they have continued to sin, carrying on the misdeeds of the previous generations. These sins, according to Karaites, are spelled out in the Oral Torah, the false tradition of law and interpretation that was crafted by—but not revealed to—the ancient sages. Therefore, exile is not an inevitability of Jewish history, as rabbinic thought would have it, but rather a state that can be reversed and rectified by the Jews' reflection upon their current sins. Salmon's sense of history endows his own generation, in which Karaism has emerged, with the awesome eschatological power to repent and bring the centuries of exile to an end.

Salmon's method of contemplating narratives from biblical history in order to avoid the sins of the fathers unapologetically advances the Karaite religious program. It places the project of redemption from exile within the grasp of his contemporaries, lending a messianic quality to biblical history.[38] In Salmon's formulation of *iʿtibār*, proper reflection on examples from the biblical past necessarily leads to enacting the ethical lessons that one learns through this process of reflection. This active model of religious philosophy envisions redemption as its ultimate and immediate aim, and this aim is intrinsic to the Karaite ethos. Thus, Salmon's insistence that members of his own generation are continuing the sins that they have inherited from their fathers accentuates his anti-Rabbanite polemic. Those who undertake the required contemplation are the Karaite Jews, who will redeem the Jewish people. Meanwhile, in Salmon's polarized reading, Rabbanite notions of inherited tradition, oral transmission, and obedience become indicative of a lack of reflection: these inherited precedents were invented by the rabbis

[37] Ibid.
[38] On Karaite messianism, see Yoram Erder, "The Negation of Exile in the Messianic Doctrine of the Karaite Mourners of Zion," *HUCA* 68 (1997): 109–40.

in the post-biblical period and have since been upheld, blindly, without examination or true contemplation. In his comment on Lamentations 5:7, Salmon reminds his readers that each person is responsible for whatever sins he commits, even if his forefathers mistakenly validated these sins as proper religious behavior. In this way, Salmon's articulation of *iʿtibār* promulgates elements of a distinctively Karaite religious philosophy.

Mourning for Zion: *Iʿtibār* and the Foundations of Karaite Ritual

Salmon connects *iʿtibār* with the Karaite religious program most directly in his presentation of the obligation to mourn for Zion. The Jerusalem Karaites were known—in their own writings and by their Rabbanite opponents—by the biblical epithet from Isaiah 61:3, "Mourners for Zion" (*ʾavelei ṣiyyon*). The obligation to mourn through ritual and liturgy was a central and foundational activity of the Karaite community in Jerusalem. One of the earliest articulations of this religious tenet appears in the ninth-century sermon attributed to the early Karaite, al-Qūmisī.[39] There al-Qūmisī urges the Karaites of Iraq and Persia to immigrate to Jerusalem, where they will hasten the redemption by undertaking a rigorous program of mourning and penitence. He justifies this appeal on several grounds, beginning with an analogy about mourning behavior within human society. When a king becomes angry with an official in his court and sends him to prison, al-Qūmisī explains, the official is obliged "to mourn, to don different clothing, and to forego the (customary) pleasures of high officials, until such time as the king may hear of it and be mollified by him, and restore him to his former [place of] honor." Al-Qūmisī argues that the same protocols of compunction that are proper in human settings are also proper in the exilic Jewish context of responding to divine punishments. He continues, "How much less, then, if the Creator, God of [all] the world, waxes wroth with a creature, is it fitting for the latter to eat and drink until he has returned [in repentance] to Him."[40] In this line of argumentation, a penitent ought to approach God with the same attitudes and behaviors of mourning that he adopts when requesting pardon from a human superior. Al-Qūmisī insists, therefore, that the Jewish community

39 See discussion of al-Qūmisī's sermon in chapters 1 and 5.
40 Qūmisī, Sermon, 24.

must return to Jerusalem and take up the mourning rituals that befit a penitent in order to merit divine forgiveness and hasten the redemption.[41]

After encouraging mourning through this analogy to human society, al-Qūmisī moves on to a scripturalist tactic and assembles biblical verses on the theme of mourning:

> He [i.e., God] has burned His Sanctuary, He has forsaken His place and His Temple, the dwelling of His Holy of Holies, to be trampled under the feet of the unclean ones, the uncircumcised ones, men and women soiled with suppuration, menstruation, and leprosy. He has abolished priests and sacrifices, [as well as Levites] who sang over the sacrifices to the accompaniment of lutes and harps. Our festivals have turned into mourning, all our songs into lament, and our appointed seasons into sorrow and sighing [. . .] *And I will turn your feasts into mourning* (Amos 8:9–10); *For this will I wail* (Mic 1:8); *The ways of Zion do mourn* (Lam 1:4); *For these things I weep* (Lam 1:16). [. . .] And now, our brethren in Israel, in all your cities, *For this gird you with sackcloth, lament and wail, for the fierce anger of the Lord is not turned back from us* (Jer 4:8).[42]

The biblical verses that al-Qūmisī lists here reappear in later Karaite homilies about the duty of mourning, and all are attested at key points of Salmon's commentary on Lamentations. As an advocate for the rituals of communal penitence and mourning in Jerusalem, Salmon repeats the same prooftexts from Lamentations and the prophetic books that al-Qūmisī drew upon a century beforehand. Yet Salmon takes these verses one step further because he is committed to establishing the analogy between the historical context of the biblical verses and the conditions of exile in his own day. With full awareness of the Karaite religious program, he states that

> [Certain verses] indicate the duty of mourning over the affliction that befell this nation. In the era of statehood, Israel was rebuked for their display of joy, delights, and amusement, for they were not pained over the afflictions that He planned to befall them. As it is said, *who drink wine in bowls, and anoint themselves with the finest oils, but are not grieved over the ruin of*

[41] This example operates along familiar polemical lines: al-Qūmisī and other Karaites denounce the excesses and luxuries of Rabbanite life in the Diaspora, thus promoting asceticism as an expression of their alternative ideology.

[42] Qūmisī, Sermon, 25.

> *Joseph!* (Amos 6:6). If they were thus reproached in the time of statehood for neglecting to mourn, then all the more [would they be reproached] afterward, in the time of exile.[43]

Salmon's exegetical stance is one of analogy between past and present. Verses from the prophet Amos, for example, do not command the Jewish people of Salmon's time to undertake a rigorous schedule of mourning. Rather, they record that mourning behaviors were necessary at the moment in history in which Amos prophesied. For Salmon, the contemplative reader of the Bible notices the similarities between past historical conditions and present ones, and reasons analogically that he must undertake the same mourning behaviors that were commanded in the time of the prophets. This approach to religious instruction is predicated on historical awareness.

Salmon also presents mourning as a natural human response to suffering and loss, although he does not express this argument through the rhetorical fiction of a king and his official, as al-Qūmisī does. Salmon focuses his readers' emotional attention instead on the historical moment in which Israel fell from grace. This homiletical arrangement does not merely tell the audience that communal suffering should elicit a mournful response; it draws them into an emotional context that induces their own grief and mourning. This affective element is found in Salmon's homiletical excursus to Lamentations 4:15. In this passage Salmon includes a homily structured around the repeated rhetorical question, "How could we not weep over . . . " followed by invocations of the many losses that continue to afflict the Jewish people. For example:

> How could we not weep over the cessation of kingship [. . .] and how could we not weep over the idleness of the *priests* from their steps [. . .] and how could we not weep over the falling of our crown and our glory [. . .] and how could we not weep over the magnitude of our sins

and so forth.[44] This litany of loss makes ancient suffering present and personal for Salmon's audience. Such a homily persuades the audience that mourning is the only appropriate response to such unmitigated loss not by

[43] Introduction to Salmon's Lamentations commentary, in the section on "Mourning as a Religious Obligation."
[44] See Salmon's comment to Lam 4:15 and discussion in chapter 5.

arguing the case, but by creating an atmosphere of immediacy that motivates readers or listeners to mourn.

After presenting the obligation to mourn first through the exegesis of biblical verses and second through a homily on the inevitability of mourning, Salmon adds a third justification for Karaite mourning rites. Specifically, he invokes *iʿtibār* to forge a hermeneutical foundation for the Karaite religious practice of mourning. By reflecting upon the biblical examples of the patriarch Jacob and King David as each responds to news of death, Salmon argues, one realizes the duty of mourning in the period of exile:

> It is obligatory to reflect (*yajib al-iʿtibār*) upon Jacob our forefather. He had twelve sons, and he was full of abundant grace and strength and wealth, and intimate with his Lord. So when he was deprived of one of his children, his soul cleaved to its mourning over him until the day of his death, as it is said, *Then Jacob rent his garments, and put sackcloth on his loins, and mourned for his son many days. All his sons and all his daughters rose up to comfort him; but he refused to be comforted; and said, "No, I shall go down to Sheol to my son, mourning"* (Gen 37:34–35). How would it be, then, for someone who has been deprived of the celestial commandments, prophecy, signs, proofs, *fire from heaven, the glory of the God of Israel, sovereignty, priesthood, sacrificial offerings, prophets, seers, teachers, wise men, those who mend breaches in the wall, sages of good intellect, Temple singers and melody carriers, judges, administrative officials, porters, teachers, high priests, the joy of the three festivals, the inheritance of the glorious land and the worship service of the day of atonement?! It is all the more incumbent upon such a person to mourn and chant laments for his soul with great bitterness.*
>
> [. . .] We also reflect (*naʿtabir*) upon the report about David, King of Israel, and all his companions when news reached them of the killing of Saul and his children. Some of the people of Israel mourned and wept and fasted and lamented, as it is said, *And David lamented with this lamentation over Saul and Jonathan his son* (2 Sam 1:17). [. . .] Then how [could it be otherwise] for us, to whom it was said in the way of a command that we [must] lament for ourselves?[45]

[45] Introduction to Salmon's Lamentations commentary, in the section on "Mourning as a Religious Obligation."

In the biblical cases of both Jacob and David, a prominent individual mourns over the death of another human being. By reflecting upon these exempla, Salmon concludes that the same behaviors that a person undertakes in response to the death of a loved one are also obligatory for a community in response to a national catastrophe.[46] In this way Salmon supports distinctively Karaite practices through reflection on biblical narratives about the past.

The presentation of Jacob as an exemplar of mourning—and the extension of his example to a post-exilic context of communal mourning—also appears in Salmon's comment on Psalm 77:3.[47] There he explains that reflection on the story of Jacob teaches us how to mourn for ourselves. The doubling of this prooftext—even while it was absent from al-Qūmisī's earlier statements about the necessity of mourning—suggests that the Jerusalem Karaites may have turned to the narrative of Jacob for supplementary justification of the distinctive orientation toward mourning that already defined their community. It is unlikely that Jacob's response to the death of his son would have provided the initial impetus for Karaite ritualized mourning over the catastrophes surrounding the destruction of Jerusalem. Rather, Jacob could be invoked as additional biblical background and support for this medieval practice. As Fred Astren explains in his book on historical understanding in Karaite literature, "Once facts of identity are constructed—having to do with community, practice, ritual, or belief—then the logic of sacred history demands the connection of those facts with the authoritative and more esteemed past."[48] In this case, the ascetic practices of the Karaite community in Jerusalem required a connection with, and justification through, sacred Scripture. Yet the Karaite commitment to historical-contextual reading precludes an interpretation in which Jacob mourns preemptively or anachronistically for the future destruction of the Temple. So, it is the hermeneutic of *iʿtibār*—reflection upon past events, in order to be guided or admonished by them—that brings the biblical passage into alignment with the Karaite religious program. Jacob does not mourn for the fate of his descendants, but his

[46] In the Bible, too, mourning over the death of an individual provides the paradigm for mourning in other circumstances, such as petitioning the deity or responding to natural or national catastrophes. See Gary Anderson, *A Time to Mourn, a Time to Dance: The Expression of Grief and Joy in Israelite Religion* (University Park: Pennsylvania State University Press, 1991); and Saul Olyan, *Biblical Mourning: Ritual and Social Dimensions* (Oxford: Oxford University Press, 2004). Salmon, however, uses the technique of reflection (*iʿtibār*) to determine that the biblical-historical examples of mourning must be re-enacted during the exile.

[47] Salmon, Pss 73–89.

[48] Fred Astren, *Karaite Judaism and Historical Understanding* (Columbia: University of South Carolina Press, 2004), 12.

response to his son's death, as recorded in Scripture, teaches the generations of the exile that they must remain in perpetual mourning for the catastrophes that continue in their time.

Salmon's deployment of *iʿtibār* to promote Karaite mourning practices underscores the Jewish context of his project. The word *iʿtibār* has limited resonances in medieval Islamic thought, in spite of its Qurʾānic pedigree and its function in Islamic historiography, so Salmon's presentation of *iʿtibār* is rooted less in Islamic intellectual culture than in the needs of his own religious community to locate redemptive spiritual guidance in the words of the Bible. For him, the Bible itself teaches that reflection is a religious duty, commanded by God. Salmon defines the concept of *iʿtibār* and demonstrates its utility through biblical examples rather than Arabic exposition, and he uses it as a polemical attack against his Rabbanite rivals: the Karaites are the true Jews because they alone practice the commandment of reflection, and they alone lead the way to repentance and redemption. *Iʿtibār* thus constitutes an intervention in Jewish hermeneutics, ritual, and law, and shows the intra-Judaic core of Salmon's project. The Karaites, like the Rabbanites, were immersed in the Arabic-Islamic context of their time, and they used its vocabulary as a common ground on which to formulate and advance their respective agendas. But it is the Jewish tradition, and the debates between Jewish religious leaders, that motivate Salmon's application and adaptation of *iʿtibār*.

Conclusions

Historical thought is a cornerstone of Salmon's commentary on Lamentations. His study of the biblical past is sophisticated and purposeful, even though his pious application of history stands apart from the critical standards of the modern historian. Salmon's search for a coherent historical narrative, assembled from disparate biblical accounts, and his inquiry into the social and political settings of past events are the foundation, rather than the endpoint, of his project. Through methods of historical-contextual analysis, Salmon creates a historical framework for theological assertions and homiletical instructions. He uses the historical record to support theological claims, finding proof of divine justice in biblical accounts of human sin and divine punishment, prophetic warnings and divine fulfillment. Both of these threads—the historical-contextual and the historical-theological—underpin the greater historical-homiletical aims of Salmon's commentary. Through the mechanism of *iʿtibār*, Salmon reflects upon the historical data that he has collated and interpreted in order to promote a homiletical message of Jewish repentance, return, and redemption.

Salmon's practice of mining the past for pious instruction may run counter to our own expectations that historical scholarship should be an objective, critical exercise conducted outside of ideological agendas or sectarian politics—in theory if not always in practice. But Salmon's historical perspective is, in fact, representative of historical writing in the medieval Islamic world. Early Islamic historiography was valued for its capacity to educate and inspire readers. In this sense, the historically oriented excursuses of Salmon's commentary reflect the Arabic aphorism "The fortunate is he who takes warning [*iʿtabara*] by others, and the unfortunate is he by whom others take warning [*iʿtabara bihi*].[49] For Salmon, it seems, there are two kinds of people in the world: those who reflect upon history and those who fail to reflect upon it, suffer punishment, and serve as a warning to future generations. In the biblical accounts of the destruction of Jerusalem, Salmon reads an appeal for future generations to reflect upon the sins that caused the exile and repent. In his own day, Salmon positions his Karaite community as the properly reflective people who serve a corrective function for their antithesis, the unreflective Rabbanites. He urges the entire Jewish community to follow the Karaite model: to accept the Karaite reading of biblical history and its implications, and to adopt Karaite religious practices, which will end the exile and restore divine favor to the Jewish people.

Salmon's contention that *iʿtibār* is a compulsory element of biblical interpretation may represent a characteristically Karaite approach to Jewish biblical exegesis. Further, his exposition of *iʿtibār* reminds us of now-familiar scholarly observations about the tensions between individual insight and communal tradition in Karaism. Specifically, the practice of *iʿtibār* fits into a long-standing Karaite paradox, in which inherited tradition is rejected in favor of individual interpretation, yet a profoundly compelling interpretation may itself become tradition, surpassing and suppressing new interpretive efforts in later generations. The lines between individual and community, and innovation and tradition, are especially blurry in Salmon's use of *iʿtibār*. He gives the impression that *iʿtibār* is a hermeneutical operation required of each reader of the Bible, an individual commitment to

[49] *Al-saʿīd man iʿtabara bi-ghayrihi wa-l-shaqī man iʿtabara bihi ghayruhu* (Lane, vol. 5, 1937).

reflect on biblical narratives in order to ascertain the moral or religious instruction encoded within them. There is no space for inherited traditions of interpretation, as each exegete must consider the biblical passage afresh and contemplate its spiritual message for himself, embracing *iʿtibār* as a spiritual practice. Yet the results of such reflection have communal ramifications. After all, Salmon enjoins his community to mourn and repent in precisely the way that he has determined through his own practice of *iʿtibār*. It would seem that Salmon is justifying Karaite institutional norms of penitence and mourning on the basis of his own private reflection. Although he states that the entire community is obliged to reflect, he provides no techniques or practical instruction to guide the reader in this task, and he presumes that all who reflect will reach the same pietistic conclusions that he does. The only assurance of reproducibility—that all practitioners of *iʿtibār* will deduce the same religious instruction from their reading of the Bible—lies in the shared starting point provided by the Karaite religious framework, and in the transmission of Salmon's teachings as a predetermined endpoint. Thus, *iʿtibār* is as much a spiritual practice and affirmation of Karaite identity as it is an exegetical strategy.

Since reflection on narratives about the past leads to ethical-theological insight and, ultimately, to repentance and redemption, the historical passages of Scripture become gateways to the most profound truths of the Bible. Reflection upon historical examples teaches the proper implementation of the commandments and inspires the piety that will reverse the conditions of exile and lead to Jewish redemption. Salmon's concept of *iʿtibār*, then, elevates the historical narratives of the Bible and places the interpretation of history at the core of his homiletical and exegetical project.

Conclusion

This project emerged out of my studies of the Arabic-Islamic context of medieval Jewish culture, and my interest in Salmon's work on Lamentations as an early, experimental form of the Jewish Bible commentary. My research focused on the Arabic modes of exegesis, literary theory, homily, and historiography that inform Salmon's writings on Lamentations, and the chapters of this book demonstrate the breadth of Salmon's participation in Arabic culture. However, my research also reveals the deep Hebraic-Judaic context that motivates Salmon's scholarship and gives it meaning. Arabic culture provides Salmon with a vocabulary and a scholarly apparatus for addressing Jewish concerns to a Jewish audience. It is precisely when we focus on Salmon's adaptation of Arabic-Islamic learning that we see most clearly the Jewish core of his project.

The Jewish world of Salmon's era was divided between Karaites and Rabbanites, each of them striving to attract and retain adherents by convincing them that their version of Judaism was the true one. Salmon's Lamentations commentary is not only an example of translation and exegesis in the medieval Islamic world, but also a witness to early Karaite identity, ideology, and religious practices. Salmon reacts against attempts to concretize rabbinic oral tradition as the principal expression of divine authority in Jewish affairs. He rejects rabbinic passivity in favor of active repentance and striving for redemption. He resists forms of biblical interpretation that threaten to obscure the penitential message of Scripture. Salmon's Arabic Lamentations commentary differs from his Hebrew polemical poem, the *Wars of the Lord*, in its form, but it has the same purpose: to support the redemption of the Jewish community by countering Rabbanite teachings with a compelling vision of Karaite Judaism.

Karaites and Rabbanites both translated the Bible into Arabic and composed commentaries in that language. Salmon's implementation of Arabic is not an appeal to Islam, but rather an attempt to advance Karaite perspectives through a shared idiom of reason and discursive analysis. He establishes his cultural allegiances through the Bible, the common inheritance of Rabbanites

Jewish Piety in Islamic Jerusalem. Jessica Andruss, Oxford University Press. © Oxford University Press 2023.
DOI: 10.1093/oso/9780197639559.003.0007

and Karaites, which he reads in distinctively Karaite ways. It is the message of his biblical interpretation, not its form or its language, that conveys his argument against Rabbanite practices of Judaism.

Salmon may include literary homilies in the mode of Islamic preaching assemblies or employ terminology familiar from Qurʾānic exegesis, but his imagined readership is not Muslim. Arabic oratory suits his purposes because it builds also upon a tradition of Jewish homiletics—in literature if not in practice—and takes up Jewish themes such as the covenant, Israelite history, and mourning over the destruction of the Temple and the loss of statehood and prophecy. Arabic literary and linguistic terminology serves Salmon not because it aligns his project with Qurʾān commentaries or puts him in conversation with Muslim literary theorists, but because it enables him to justify his pietistic reading of Scripture according to a shared rationalist framework. Salmon is no Muʿtazilite, but he knows how to avail himself of common—and thus, to some extent, secular—grounds of proof for his spiritual agenda.

The form of Salmon's commentary exemplifies the conventions of Arabic expository texts, with its thematic introduction and excursuses, explication of grammar and historical context, and strong authorial voice. Yet the building blocks of Salmon's argument are biblical. Moreover, there is an almost Midrashic quality to Salmon's exegetical prose: he juxtaposes biblical verses against one another to fashion a theology of piety and redemption constructed from biblical teachings. His use of Arabic distinguishes his project from the Aramaic models esteemed by the ancient rabbis, and places it squarely in competition with the Arabic works of his Rabbanite contemporaries, most notably Saadia Gaon.

Salmon's Jewish formation means that comparisons between his commentary and Arabic-Islamic culture must be explained within Jewish interpretive and historical contexts. The Arabic term *iʿtibār*—which Salmon uses to describe a process of reflecting on biblical history to find its ethical message—is decisive in the Lamentations commentary but has limited resonance in Islamic circles. For Salmon it is a Jewish term that represents a Jewish way of reading Scripture. He anchors this pious hermeneutical practice in the Jewish tradition by presenting it as a religious obligation commanded by God in Torah and reinforced throughout the Scriptures—a *miṣvah* in all but name.

Salmon's forays into Arabic and Islamic learning serve his purpose of intra-Judaic argumentation. He is wary of Arabic on its own terms. He expresses concerns about the ubiquity of the language—the lengths that some Jews go to learn it, its potential to distract from biblical study—and warns against the perils of reading foreign books. Karaite scholars embraced Arabic, albeit with some reservations, not for its own sake, but because it provided them with vocabulary and literary models for proving the truth of their religious vision against that of their rivals. Thus, Salmon's application of Arabic poetics, homiletics, and historiography are ancillary to his Karaite mission. The Lamentations commentary is not ultimately an intellectual exercise, but a spiritual one.

The form and function of the commentary genre were still undefined when Salmon composed his works in the middle years of the tenth century. He used the commentary form, with its introduction and excursuses, as scaffolding to organize and make accessible a library of Karaite sermons, prayers, liturgical poetry, and polemics. His commentary provides a hermeneutical model, but it also conveys ritual instruction and pietistic historical sensibilities. The presence of liturgical elements and embedded homilies shows the elasticity and expansiveness of Salmon's concept of exegesis, to be sure, but there is no doubt that his work on Lamentations qualifies as a commentary. It uses the conventions that later became standard for the genre, from the programmatic introduction to the verse-by-verse structure based on the tripartite formula of Hebrew lemma, Arabic translation, and Arabic comment. His comments include grammatical remarks, biblical parallels, and historical context designed to explain the biblical verse. Even his excursuses fit into the framework of the commentary: they attach to specific verses, and often enough they entail systematic treatment of other biblical passages, appearing as miniature commentaries embedded within the main text. Salmon's pietistic readings may at times depart from the contextual meaning of a given verse, but they are presented consistently in an exegetical structure. In the Lamentations commentary, exegesis is the form, and pious instruction is the content.

The purpose of Salmon's commentaries is to support the spiritual and practical needs of the Karaite community in Jerusalem. These Karaites faced the monumental task of transforming scattered local traditions and general antipathy to rabbinic institutions into a coherent religious system capable of contesting the dominance of Rabbanite authority across the Jewish world. Beyond the lines of the Karaite–Rabbanite schism, Jews also faced opposition from Muslim and Christian polemicists who claimed that God's loyalties had shifted irreversibly from the Jewish people to their own communities. Even among Karaites who were confident in the righteousness of their cause, practical questions abounded about exactly how to implement biblical instructions for the rituals, prayers, and penitential practices enjoined upon the community in times of exile. These pressing challenges shape the themes and contents of Salmon's Lamentations commentary and mark his composition with a sense of urgency.

Throughout the commentary, Salmon promotes Karaism as the only authentic expression of Judaism. In his view, it is the Karaite community of Jerusalem, with their ascetic practices and spiritual devotion, that represents the path to redemption. His arguments validate piety as the decisive act for ending exile and reclaiming the covenantal relationship between God and Israel. But Salmon must go further in order to articulate exactly what piety is and how it should be done. In his verse comments, particularly for the third chapter of Lamentations, Salmon shows how to find concrete religious instruction in Scripture. Long excursuses demonstrate techniques for inferring pious practices and attitudes by reflecting on the historical past. The insertion of homilies and liturgical refrains supplies the substance of prayer, a biblical script for communal and individual worship.

Salmon is not the original author of every component of the commentary. From the duplication of set pieces within in his own corpus to the recurrence of excursuses found also in the works of others, Salmon's work on Lamentations is to some extent a compilation. To consider the commentary merely as a collation of preexisting materials, however, would be to disregard Salmon's creativity in arranging, adapting, and developing these traditions in order to instruct his readership in why and how to embrace a distinctive form of Jewish piety. The commentary is more than the sum of its parts precisely because Salmon uses it to construct and confirm a pietistic program for the Karaite community. The Lamentations commentary functions as a bridge, connecting the Bible to the religious life of tenth-century Jews.

Salmon found the most efficient and effective means of delivering his message to the Jewish community in the new form of the Arabic Bible commentary—flexible and expansive, a repository for biblical instruction in a Karaite mold. Thus, my inquiry into Salmon's Arabic Lamentations commentary reveals not only the technical possibilities of the commentary genre, but also the creation of a Jewish piety rooted in the Bible, supported and substantiated through exegesis in and about Jerusalem. The Karaites embraced biblical scholarship as the central expression of their communal identity and their defining intellectual project. It is no surprise, then, that Salmon ben Yerūḥīm formed and transmitted Karaite pietistic ideals through the pages of a biblical commentary.

PART 2

SELECTED TRANSLATIONS FROM THE COMMENTARY

Invocation

In the name of the true Judge, blessed be His name.
He judges with justice and truth.[1]

And take not the word of truth utterly out of my mouth (Ps 119:43). *Hear, O heavens, and give ear, O earth;* [*for the LORD has spoken: "I have reared children and brought up, but they have rebelled against Me"*] (Isa 1:2). *Hear the word of the LORD, O house of Jacob* (Jer 2:4). *Hear, you mountains, the accusation of the LORD* (Mic 6:2). *The LORD within her is just* (*ṣaddiq*; Zeph 3:5). *The LORD our God is just* (*ṣaddiq*) [*in all His works which He has done, but we have not obeyed His voice*] (Dan 9:14). *You have been just* (*ṣaddiq*) *in all that has come upon us* [*for You have dealt faithfully and we have acted wickedly*] (Neh 9:33). *The LORD is just* (*ṣaddiq*) *in all His ways* (Ps 145:17). *Just* (*ṣaddiq*) *are you, O LORD* (Ps 119:137). *The LORD is just* (*ṣaddiq*), *for I have rebelled against His word* (Lam 1:18).[2]

[1] The opening *taḥmīd*, or words in praise of God. On the features of the Arabic *taḥmīd*, see Tahera Qutbuddin, "*Khuṭba*: The Evolution of Early Arabic Oration," in *Classical Arabic Humanities in Their Own Terms: Festschrift for Wolfhart Heinrichs*, ed. Beatrice Gruendler and Michael Cooperson (Ledein: Brill, 2008), 182. The initial phrase, "in the name of the true Judge," appears to be an alternative version of the *basmala*, the invocation of the divine name in order to consecrate the following action, which typically appears at the beginning of Arabic texts. In Islamic texts the *basmala* is commonly formulated as *bismi-llāhi-l-raḥmān al-raḥīm* ("in the name of God, the Merciful, the Compassionate"), while medieval Jewish texts often use Gen 21:33 as a *basmala*: *In the name of the LORD, the Everlasting God* (Robinson, *Asceticism* 166 n. 1). Salmon's near-contemporary Yaʿqūb al-Qirqisānī claims that the biblical King David used the *basmala* upon beginning any work; see Miriam Goldstein, "'Arabic Composition 101' and the Early Development of Judaeo-Arabic Bible Exegesis," *JSS* 55 (2010), 467.

[2] These verses incorporate Hebr. *ṣaddiq* ("just"), which Salmon translates variously in his Pss commentary: e.g., *munṣif* ("equitable") in Ps 145:17; *ʿādil* ("just") in Ps 119:137. His translation of the latter verse emphasizes the divine origins of justice: not *right are <u>Your judgments</u>*, as in Hebr., but rather, "<u>You</u> are upright (*mustaqīm*) in Your judgments." He interprets that verse as follows: "This is the acknowledgment [made by] the righteous ones, of the justice of God concerning the occasions of trials, and especially the trials of exile, as it is said, *The LORD is in the right, for I have rebelled against His word* (Lam 1:18); and *yet You have been just in all that has come upon us* (Neh 9:33). In this sense, our master Moses, peace be upon him, prefaced [the section] *Ha'azinu* with, *The Rock, His work is perfect; for all His ways are justice. A God of faithfulness and without iniquity, just and right is He* (Deut 32:4). This describes His justice (*ʿadl*) and His equity (*inṣāf*), and that He calls upon us to witness, and He obliges us to give testimonies (Salmon, Pss 107–150)."

Jewish Piety in Islamic Jerusalem. Jessica Andruss, Oxford University Press. © Oxford University Press 2023.
DOI: 10.1093/oso/9780197639559.003.0008

Blessed be God, the god of Israel,[3] the True God, Unique, Pre-existent, whose Existence is without beginning, He who endures without end, the Living One, the Knowing One [who has knowledge of] all the other creatures, which He has created. He who guides His creatures, in their abundance and their breadth, and confers benefit upon them until the end of time, as the psalmist (*musabbiḥ*) says: *O LORD, how manifold are Your works!* (Ps 104:24). Another psalmist (*musabbiḥ*) says, *How great are Your works, O LORD!* (Ps 92:6/5).

He is the Eternal One, the Enduring One, whom His speaking, rational creatures know, since [His creation contains] evidence indicating that it is created and not pre-existent, [and] governed, possessing a Creator who brought it into being *ex nihilo*.[4] He established proof that its Maker was none other than the One, and that it is impossible for Him to be described with the attributes of the created beings. On the contrary, He whose mention must be exalted is distinguished by His essential attributes (*ṣifāt al-dhātīyya*), which are coeternal with Him. Human beings[5] know that an All-Wise Being created them, since His creatures are made with wisdom,[6] as it is said, *In wisdom You have made them all* (Ps 104:24). *The LORD by wisdom founded the earth* (Prov 3:19).[7] He impressed every single species with a permanent mark, as it is said, *By Your marks they stand this day* (Ps 119:91). *The Rock, His work is perfect* (Deut 32:4). We shall seek assistance from the Merciful One for success, through His goodwill, His goodness, and His beneficence.[8]

[3] Arab. *isra'īl*
[4] Lit.: "after it had not existed."
[5] Lit.: "rational creatures" (*al-nāṭiqīn*).
[6] Emending the text to read *muḥakama* instead of מתקנם.
[7] This representation of God is familiar in Judaism and Islam. On its resonances with Muʿtazilite theology, see Wechsler on Yefet, Esth, 44–47; Sasson on Yefet, Prov, 82–88; and Robinson, *Asceticism*, 166–67.
[8] Thus concludes the *khuṭba* or *dībāja*, the opening invocation and praise of God. It is almost entirely missing from the Abdul-Karim edition, which begins abruptly with a copyist's note: "This volume (*muṣḥaf*) is the explication of Lamentations (*sharḥ al-qinot*)." The missing text was supplied to me by Daniel Frank, who collated MSS JTSA Ms. Mic. 3362 (Adler 14) and RNL Evr. I.561.

Introduction to the Lamentations Commentary

The interpreter,[1] may God most high be pleased with him, says:

Since the revealed books[2] have made it clear to us that the Creator is just, and that fairness and true judgment are part of His [very] nature, it follows that you [must] also know that beneficence and kindness are His as well, and that He requites His servants with only what they deserve, as it is said, *The LORD is just in all His ways* (Ps 145:17), which is concluded with the words, *kind in all His doings* (Ps 145:17). On account of these attributes, the Mighty and Sublime is called "the One who Bestows Kindness"[3] as it is said, *For I am merciful, says the LORD; I will not be angry forever* (Jer 3:12).

When He made the covenant with our fathers on Mount Sinai, <2a> He guaranteed in it that even if we sinned and our offenses became great, He would remain with us and He would not destroy us unless we deserved destruction and we deserved to perish, as it is said, *Yet for all that, when they are in the land of their enemies, I will not spurn them, neither will I abhor them so as to destroy them* (Lev 26:44). In the same manner, Isaiah said that Israel deserved to be requited with what the people of Sodom and Gomorrah had been requited, as it is said: *If the LORD of hosts had not left us a few survivors, we should have been like Sodom, and become like Gomorrah* (Isa 1:9). Another prophet spoke [the words of] God: *How can I give you up, Ephraim? How can I hand you over, O Israel?* (Hos 11:8). Because they transgressed the bounds of obedience to God and committed acts of disobedience more heinous than

[1] Arab. *al-mufassir*—"translator" or "interpreter." The Arab. term encompasses both functions, just as Salmon's text contains both a translation of the biblical text and his interpretation of it. Insofar as the work of translation includes interpretation, I have rendered *al-mufassir* here as "the interpreter." Salmon follows the convention of opening in the third person; in the body of the commentary, he refers to himself in the first person.

[2] Arab. *al-kutub al-munzala*, i.e., the prophetic books of the Bible (see Robinson, *Asceticism*, 49).

[3] Following Evr. I.561: *al-muḥsin bi-l-afḍāl*.

Jewish Piety in Islamic Jerusalem. Jessica Andruss, Oxford University Press. © Oxford University Press 2023.
DOI: 10.1093/oso/9780197639559.003.0009

the deeds of Sodom, as it is said, *For the chastisement of the daughter of my people has been greater than the punishment of Sodom* (Lam 4:6) and *As I live, says the Lord GOD, your sister Sodom and her daughters have not done as you and your daughters have done* (Ezek 16:48).[4]

All these and similar verses indicate that God had compassion upon His nation, [even though] they sinned and rebelled. <2b> Indeed, He made them suffer under the *four kingdoms*[5] and banished them during the *exile* in order for Him to discipline them and make them good,[6] as it is said, *I will chastise them for their wicked deeds* (Hos 7:12). This means He chastised them in accordance with the message of the covenant that was made between them.[7]

There are two kinds of chastisements: a punishing chastisement of destruction and annihilation, and a bettering chastisement,[8] as it is said, *As a man disciplines his son, the LORD your God disciplines you* (Deut 8:5).

[4] See Salmon's comment to Lam 4:6 for further discussion.

[5] Hebr. *'arba' malkuyot*—the "four kingdoms," as mentioned in Dan 8:22—are identified with various historical empires in post-biblical Jewish literature, although there was great variation in the specific identifications. Most problematic was the role of the Islamic empires in this framework. On Karaite and other medieval Jewish interpretations of the four kingdoms, see Daniel Frank, *Search Scripture Well: Karaite Exegesis and the Origins of the Jewish Bible Commentary in the Islamic East*, EJM 29 (Leiden: Brill, 2004), 129–34, 179, n. 58 and bibliography there; and also Haggai Ben-Shammai, "The Attitude of Some Early Karaites Towards Islam," in *Studies in Medieval Jewish History and Literature*, vol. 2, ed. Isadore Twersky (Cambridge, Mass.: Harvard University Press, 1984), 8–12. In the commentary on Daniel, Yefet ben 'Eli identifies the kingdoms as the Chaldeans, Persia, Greece, and Rome. He places the Arabs outside of this framework, since they have scorned and humiliated Israel but stopped short of exiling and destroying them, as the previous kingdoms did. Sahl ben Maṣliaḥ identifies each kingdom with a pair of nations: Babylonia and the Chaldeans, Media and the Persians, Greece and Macedon, and Edom and Ishmael (see Leon Nemoy, "The Epistle of Sahl ben Maṣliaḥ," *PAAJR* 38/39 (1970–71): 145–77). Salmon takes his own approach: the kingdoms are Babylon, Persia and Media, Greece, and "the son of Hagar," namely, the Arab-Islamic empires. He develops this trope in his excursuses to Lam 3:1 and 3:20, which are based on a similar approach to Pss 42:7/6 and 43:1 in his commentary on the Psalms.

[6] Yefet also uses this language in the introduction to his commentary on Lamentations: "Know that this was by way of discipline (*'alā sabīl al-ta'dīb*), so they would become good."

[7] The intent here is that God justly disciplines Israel because the covenant stipulates it, and not out of a desire for vindication or revenge. Throughout the commentary, Salmon depicts punishments as the mechanical result of Israelite violations of covenant and commandment, sometimes de-emphasizing divine agency in orchestrating the punishments.

[8] Arab. *adab 'āqabata* and *adab istiṣlāḥ*. Cf. Saadia Gaon, who divides human suffering into three categories in the introduction to his commentary on Job: instructive discipline, punishment and purgation of sin, and trial. Saadia justifies the second category—suffering as punishment for sin—with the prooftext from Deut 8:5 and extends the metaphor of divine punishment and the chastisements of a human father; see Lenn Goodman, *The Book of Theodicy: Translation and Commentary on the Book of Job by Saadiah ben Joseph al-Fayyūmī*, YJS 25 (New Haven, Conn.: Yale University Press, 1988), 125. Although Salmon does not use rabbinic terminology, he seems to build on the notion that "suffering is precious," and he incorporates common rabbinic prooftexts on the theme. See, e.g., Ephraim Urbach, *The Sages: Their Concepts and Beliefs*, vol. 1, trans. Abraham Israels (Jerusalem: Magnes, 1975), 444–48.

This makes clear to us that in His beneficence and favor, the Mighty and Sublime promised Israel His holy books in the time of exile so that they would be fortified by them.[9] If [the holy books] had not been among [the people], they would have been destroyed, as it is said, *If Your law had not been my delight, I should have perished in my affliction* (Ps 119:92).[10] In addition, were it not for the mercy of the Most High, we would have been destroyed, as it is said, *If it had not been the LORD who was on our side, when men rose up against us, then they would have swallowed us up alive, when their anger was kindled against us* (Ps 124:2–3).[11] As the sons of Koraḥ said, *By day the LORD commands His steadfast love; and at night His song is with me* (Ps 42:9/8).[12]

It is also said, *And I said to her, "You must dwell as mine for many days; you shall not play the harlot, or belong to another man* (Hos 3:2/3). We learn <3a> that the Mighty and Sublime instructs us in worshiping Him and being obedient to Him and repenting to Him in this exile, so that He may be merciful with us, as He said through Moses, our master: *When you are in tribulation, and all these things come upon you in the latter days, you will return to the LORD your God and obey His voice, for the LORD your God is a merciful God; He will not fail you or destroy you or forget the covenant with your fathers which He swore to them* (Deut 4:30–31).

[9] For Salmon, as for many of his Jewish and Muslim contemporaries, the divine provision of holy books constitutes a *luṭf*, a kindness that God bestows on humankind, in order to aid them in carrying out divine commands. In the Islamic tradition, see, e.g., Abd al-Jabbār's chapter on *luṭf* in the *Mughnī*, a comprehensive work on Muʿtazilite doctrine, which he began dictating in 970 (Heemskerk, "ʿAbd al-Jabbār").

[10] Salmon explains Ps 119:92 in his Pss commentary: "Just as You established this world, so You established this law (*al-torah*). In this vein, he opened by mentioning heaven and earth (Ps 119:89–90), then he said, 'If it were not for Your law (*sharīʿa*), then my joy in the exile would surely have been destroyed.' The meaning of *in my affliction* is 'in the land of exile,' as Joseph, peace be upon him, says, *for God has made me fruitful in the land of my affliction* (Gen 41:52)." Note the shift from "my joy" in the Pss commentary to the people Israel in the Lam commentary.

[11] Salmon specifies that these verses refer to two historical moments: "the Babylonian exile, and after the destruction of the Second Temple, when the three kingdoms rose up." He explains that the psalmist "compares the enemies to wild beasts that chomp, and in this vein he says, *rebuke the beasts that dwell among the reeds* (Ps 68:31/30) and *four great beasts* (Dan 7:3). Therefore, he says [here], *then they would have swallowed us alive*." (Salmon, Pss 124:2–3).

[12] In his comment to Ps 42:9/8, Salmon contextualizes this verse as a call to God while suffering under the great empires. In these circumstances, the psalmist recalls God's covenantal promise, *Yet for all that, when they are in the land of their enemies, I will not spurn them, neither will I abhor them so as to destroy them utterly and break my covenant with them; for I am the LORD their God* (Lev 26:44): "And I, throughout the night, in thanksgiving and praise—as it is said, *at night His song is with me, a prayer to the God of my life*—I pray a prayer to the Enduring One, for my salvation and for safeguarding my soul from destruction.'" (Salmon, Pss 42–72).

His promises, which point to His favor and His beneficence, became numerous through His faithful prophets. Even though offenses and sins preceded us and those who came before our fathers, still the Mighty and Sublime would not let us despair[13] of His favor and His beneficence, as He said through Jeremiah, *For Israel and Judah have not been forsaken by their God, the LORD of hosts; but their land is full of guilt against the Holy One of Israel* (Jer 51:5). The interpretive sense (*ʿibāra*) of this [verse] is that Israel and Judah will not be widowed from their God.[14] That is to say, God did not cut them off from His mercy and His beneficence. Even if their land had been made barren because of [their] guilt, still they would not be widowed from the Holy One of Israel. As it is said, *But their land is full of guilt before the Holy One of Israel* (Jer 51:5). It is also said, in what follows, *And in that day, says the LORD, you will call Me "my husband," and no longer will you call Me, "my Baʿal"* (Hos 2:16/18); <3b> and *For as a young man marries a virgin, so shall your sons marry you* (Isa 62:5); and *For your maker is your husband, the LORD of hosts is His name* (Isa 54:5). All of these [verses] mean that *Israel and Judah have not been forsaken* (Jer 51:5).

Neither are the people of the exile [cut off] from His beneficence.[15] Jeremiah prophesied that a book would be established for them with lamentation within it, which would be authorized for them as long as they were in the land of *exile*, lamenting for themselves with it and regretting what left them: power, statehood, Temple,[16] prophecy, signs, proofs, kingship, the priesthood,[17] wisdom, learning, and service in God's house with *song and melody*.[18] All these and similar things are explained in this book, which I intend to interpret: *the scroll of Lamentations*. In it there are references to the disasters that overtook this nation, which cannot be enumerated quickly.

[13] See Abdul-Karim, 56, for the colloquialism.

[14] Salmon takes pains to show that Israel has not been widowed by God, in defense against such a reading of Lam 1:2, *how like a widow she has become*, where he restates this point.

[15] Arab. *ahl al-jāliya* ("people of the exile") is Salmon's standard Arab. designation for the Jewish people; only rarely does he use the Arab. collective noun *al-yahūd* or the Hebr. *yehudim*. In Salmon's writings as in the Karaite corpus more broadly, *ahl al-jāliya* designates all Jews who experienced exile, from the time of the Greek conquest of Palestine through their continued exile in the medieval period; see Meira Polliack and Eliezer Schlosssberg, "Historical-Literary, Rhetorical and Redactional Methods of Interpretation in Yefet b. Eli's Introduction to the Minor Prophets," in *Exegesis and Grammar in Medieval Karaite Texts*, JSSSupp. 13, ed. Geoffrey Khan (Oxford: Oxford University Press, 2001), 11 n. 31.

[16] Arab. *al-quds*. On the identification of this term with the Temple in Salmon's writings, see Haggai Ben-Shammai, "Jerusalem in Early Medieval Bible Exegesis," in *Jerusalem: Its Sanctity and Centrality to Judaism, Christianity, and Islam*, ed. Lee I. Levine (New York: Continuum, 1999), 450–59.

[17] Arab. *al-imāma*; cf. Hebr. *kehunnah* in note 22.

[18] Referring to the Temple service in ancient Jerusalem.

Mourning as a Religious Obligation

It is said, *O daughter of My people, gird on sackcloth, and roll in ashes; make mourning as for an only son* (Jer 6:26), and *For this gird you with sackcloth, lament and wail* (Jer 4:8), and *For this I will lament and wail* (Mic 1:8). All these verses indicate the duty of mourning over the affliction that befell <4a> this nation. In the era of statehood, Israel was rebuked for their display of joy, delights, and amusement, for they were not pained over the afflictions that He planned to befall them. As it is said, *who drink wine in bowls, and anoint themselves with the finest oils, but are not grieved over the ruin of Joseph!* (Amos 6:6). If they were thus reproached in the time of statehood for neglecting to mourn, then all the more so [would they be reproached] afterward, in the time of exile.[19]

It is obligatory to reflect (*yajib al-iʿtibār*)[20] upon Jacob our forefather. He had twelve sons, and he was full of abundant grace and strength and wealth, and intimate with his Lord. So when he was deprived of one of his children, his soul cleaved to its mourning over him until the day of his death, as it is said, *Then Jacob rent his garments, and put sackcloth on his loins, and mourned for his son many days. All his sons and all his daughters rose up to comfort him; but he refused to be comforted, and said, "No, I shall go down to She'ol to my son, mourning"* (Gen 37:34–35).[21]

How would it be, then, for someone who has been deprived of the celestial commandments, prophecy, signs, proofs, *fire from heaven, the glory of the God of Israel, sovereignty, priesthood,*[22] *sacrificial offerings, prophets, seers, teachers,* <4b> *wise men, those who mend breaches in the wall* (Amos 9:11), *sages of good intellect, Temple singers and melody-carriers, judges, administrative officials, porters, teachers,*[23] *high priests, the joy of the three festivals,*[24]

[19] The logic here derives from rabbinic hermeneutics, specifically *kal va-ḥomer*, or reasoning by analogy from a minor point to a major one. Since the people were rebuked for their failure to mourn local tragedies during the time of statehood, then certainly they would be rebuked for their failure to mourn in the wake of total destruction and ongoing exile. Further, this statement represents a polemical attack against the Rabbanites, who refused to accept the Karaite program of returning to Jerusalem to perform rituals of asceticism and mourning.

[20] On the religious obligation to contemplate narratives about the biblical past in order to find admonition or moral instruction (*iʿtibār*), see chapter 6.

[21] See the parallel discussion in Salmon's comment to Ps 77:3.

[22] Hebr. *kehunnah*; cf. Arab. *imāma*, in note 17.

[23] E.g., the Levites in 2 Chr 35:3.

[24] Hebr. *shalosh ḥaggim:* the three pilgrimage festivals (Passover, Shavuot, and Sukkot) when Israelite males would come to the Temple in Jerusalem, as commanded in the Bible (Exod 23:14–17; 34:23; Deut 16:16). The destruction of the Temple and the closure of the city to Jews prevented the observance of this commandment.

the inheritance of the glorious land,[25] *and the worship service of the day of atonement?! It is all the more incumbent upon such a person to mourn (lehit'avel) and chant laments (leqonen) for his soul with great bitterness.* Therefore it is said, *For this I will lament and wail* (Mic 1:8) and *For this gird you with sackcloth, lament and wail; for the fierce anger of the LORD has not turned back from us*" (Jer 4:8). This verse makes it clear that when they did not repent, the anger of the LORD of hosts was not removed from us.[26] Thus, it is obligatory for us to direct ourselves to mourning and the pain of our hearts, as it is said, *Lament like a virgin girded with sackcloth for the bridegroom of her youth* (Joel 1:8).

We also reflect (*na'tabir*) upon the report about David, King of Israel, and all his companions when news reached them of the killing of Saul and his children. Some of the people of Israel mourned and wept and fasted and lamented, as it is said, *And David lamented with this lamentation over Saul and Jonathan his son* (2 Sam 1:17), even though prophecy, *signs, the glory of the LORD God of Israel, His sacrificial offerings and Temple singers*, and the state were still in existence. If anyone <5a> other than the likes of David and the mighty ones who were with him, who had strength within them, had been among them, they would have done nothing other than recount the illustrious circumstances [of their lives]. Yet even with all of this, it is said, *Then David took hold of his clothes, and rent them; and so did all the men who were with him; and they mourned and wept and fasted until evening for Saul* (2 Sam 1:11–12).

So it was when Josiah was killed, as it is said, *Jeremiah also uttered a lament for Josiah* (2 Chr 35:25). Then how [could it be otherwise] for us, to whom it was said in the way of a command that we [must] lament for ourselves, as it is said, *Thus says the LORD of hosts: Consider, and call for the mourning women to come* (Jer 9:16/17). God surely turned all of our joys into mourning and the delights of our festivals into mourning and lamentation, as it is said, *I will turn your feasts into mourning and all your songs into lamentation* (Amos 8:10).

25 Hebr. *ereṣ ṣvi*—a standard cognomen for the land of Judea, drawn from Dan 11:16.

26 Salmon affirms a central Karaite religious principle—that penitence is the proper salve to divine anger—on the basis of these prooftexts. See also Qūmisī, Sermon, esp. 24–25, and note the same biblical prooftexts there.

The Sufferings of Israel and the Sufferings of Job

There is no calamity that is greater than our calamity, and no pain that is greater than our pain, as it is said in this book: [*Look and see*] *if there is any sorrow like my sorrow* (Lam 1:12) and *For vast as the sea is your ruin; who can restore you?* (Lam 2:13). When we call to mind an enumeration of trials in this world, we find that the trial of Job surpasses all trials. If we compare his trial with the trial of Israel, <5b> we find that the trial of Israel is equal to it in its parts, yet [the trial of Israel] surpasses it in the meanings of its significance. Here follows an explication of the calamities of Job which are equal to the calamities of Israel, in order to make evident thereby the magnitude of the calamities of Israel.[27]

As for the calamities of Job, the Chaldeans raided him, as it is said: *The Chaldeans formed three companies* (Job 1:17). It is said about Israel: *He brought up against them the king of the Chaldeans, who slew their young men* (2 Chr 36:17).[28] It is said about Job: *The fire of God fell from heaven* (Job 1:16). It is said about Israel: *From on high He sent fire; into my bones He made it descend* (Lam 1:13). It is said about the children of Job: *And it fell on the young people, and they are dead* (Job 1:19). It is said about Israel: *Even though they bring forth, I will slay their beloved children* (Hos 9:16). It is said about Job: *Then Job arose, rent his robe* (Job 1:20). It is said about Israel: *Cut off your hair and cast it away* (Jer 7:29). It is said about Job: *and inflicted Job with loathsome sores* (Job 2:7). It is said about Israel: *From the sole of the foot even to the head, there is no soundness in it, but bruises and sores and bleeding wounds* (Isa 1:6) and *every sickness also, and every affliction* (Deut 28:61), and it is said also: *The LORD will smite you on the knees and on the legs with grievous boils* (Deut 28:35).

[27] See *PdRK* 16.6 for an earlier, and much shorter, comparison between the sufferings of Israel and Job. The homily that appears there is connected to Isa 40:1–26, the *haftarah* passage that is read on the first of the seven "Sabbaths of Consolation," i.e., the Sabbaths following the Ninth of Av, on which the destruction of the Temple is commemorated. In *PdRK*, the purpose of the comparison is one of consolation: "The words that Jeremiah uses of Israel and her suffering are much the same as those used of Job and his suffering; hence what is intended by the parallels that follow is reassurance of Israel that as the outcome for Job was comfort for his suffering, so the outcome for Israel will be comfort for her suffering." Cf. the purpose that Salmon designates for the comparison, below. Saadia Gaon does not systematically compare the sufferings of Israel with those of Job in his commentary on Job. The Byzantine Karaite Aaron b. Elijah of Nicomedia notes in passing that the story of Job "is a valid symbol for Israel: for if Israel perverts their spiritual existence, they are punished in their physical existence" (*'Eṣ ḥayyim*, ch. 90; see Daniel Frank, "The Religious Philosophy of the Karaite Aaron ben Elijah: The Problem of Divine Justice," [Ph.D. diss., Harvard, 1991], 178–79 and n. 188).

[28] See *Lam R*, proem 12, for a historical-Midrashic use of the same prooftext.

As it is said about the sufferings of Job: *For the arrows of the Almighty are in me* (Job 6:4), so it is said also about the sufferings of Israel: *For Your arrows have sunk into me* (Ps 38:3/2).[29] It is said about Job: *Men have gaped at me with their mouth* (Job 16:10). <6a> It is said about Israel: *They open wide their mouths at me* (Ps 22:14/13).[30] It is said about Job: *They have struck me insolently upon the cheek* (Job 16:10). It is said about Israel: *You shall be a reproach and a taunt, a warning and a horror, to the nations round about you, when I execute judgments on you in anger and fury, and with furious chastisements* (Ezek 5:15).[31] It is said about Job: *He has made me a byword of the peoples* (Job 17:6). It is said about Israel: *You have made us a byword among the nations* (Ps 44:15/14).[32] It is said about Job: *He broke me asunder* (Job 16:12). It is said about Israel: *He bent his bow and set me as a mark for His arrow* (Lam 3:12). It is said about Job: *He has kindled His wrath against me* (Job 19:11). It is said about Israel: *Therefore the anger of the LORD was kindled against His people* (Isa 5:25). It is said about Job: [He has] *closed his net about me* (Job 19:6). It is said about Israel: *And I will spread My net over him* (Ezek 12:13, 17:20) and *As they* [Ephraim] *go* [to Assyria], *I will spread over them My net* (Hos 7:12). It is said about Job: *He has walled up my way; so that I cannot pass* (Job 19:8). It is said about Israel: *He has walled me about so that I cannot escape* (Lam 3:7). It is said about Job: *He has set darkness upon my paths* (Job 19:8). It is said about Israel: *He has made me dwell in darkness, like the dead of long ago* (Lam 3:6). It is said about Job: *He has stripped from me my glory* (Job 19:9). It is said about Israel: *They shall also strip you of your clothes* (Ezek 23:26). It is said about Job: *and taken the crown from my head* (Job 19:9). It is said about Israel: *The crown has fallen from our head* (Lam 5:16). It is said about Job: [*He*] *counts me as His adversary* (Job 19:11). It is said about Israel: *He has bent His bow like an enemy, with His right hand set like a foe* (Lam 2:4). It is said about Job: *His troops come on together* (Job 19:12). It is said

[29] In his comment on Ps 38:3/2, Salmon also invokes Job 6:4 and 16:10 and presents a brief comparison between the sufferings of Israel and those of Job. He then refers readers to the more extensive treatment here, in the Lam commentary. Salmon also offers a figurative reading of Ps 38:3/2: "*Your arrows* are an allusion to the many calamities; *and Your hand has come down upon me* is an allusion to the sword that the Mighty and Sublime wields, as He says, '*I myself will fight against you with outstretched hand and strong arm* (Jer 21:5) through which the enemies will triumph'" (Salmon, Pss 11-41).

[30] Salmon makes the image explicit in his brief comment at Ps 22:14/13: "They open their mouths in order to devour me" (Salmon, Pss 11–41).

[31] See Salmon's comment to Lam 5:1 for discussion.

[32] In the Pss commentary, Salmon interprets Ps 44:15/14 entirely through reference to Deut 28:37: *And you shall become a horror, an allegory* [mashal], *and a byword* [*among all the peoples*]. In the verse translation, Hebr. *mashal* is translated as Arab. *mathal* (Salmon, Pss 42–72). For a discussion of these terms, see chapter 4.

about Israel: *And the LORD sent against him* <6b> *bands of the Chaldeans* (2 Kgs 24:2). It is said about Job: *He has put my brethren far from me, and my acquaintances are wholly estranged from me* (Job 19:13). It is said about Israel: *My friends and companions stand aloof from my plague* (Ps 38:12/11).[33] It is said about Job: *He has torn me in His wrath, and hated me* (Job 16:9). It is said about Israel: *I, even I, will rend and go away, I will carry off, and none shall rescue* (Hos 5:14). It is said about Job: *He breaks me with breach upon breach* (Job 16:14). It is said about Israel: *Disaster follows hard on disaster* (Jer 4:20) and *Disaster comes upon disaster, rumor follows rumor* (Ezek 7:26).[34] It is said about the calamities of Job: *I have sewed sackcloth upon my skin* (Job 16:15). It is said about Israel: *They gird themselves with sackcloth, and horror covers them* (Ezek 7:18) and *in Beth-leaphrah, roll yourselves in the dust* (Mic 1:10). It is said about Job: *My lyre is turned to mourning* (Job 30:31). It is said about Israel: *I will turn your feasts into mourning* (Amos 8:10). It is said about Job: [*He*] *fills me with bitterness* (Job 9:18). It is said about the calamities of Israel: *He has sealed me with wormwood* (Lam 3:15). It is said about Job: *He pours out my gall onto the ground* (Job 16:13). It is said about Israel: *My heart is poured out onto the ground* (Lam 2:11). It is said about Job: *But now they make sport of me, men who are younger than I* (Job 30:1). It is said about Israel: *mocking at her downfall* (Lam 1:7) <7a> and *All my enemies have heard of my trouble; they are glad* (Lam 1:21). It is said about Job: *And now I have become their song* (Job 30:9). It is said about the calamities of Israel: *I am the burden of their songs* (Lam 3:63) and *the drunkards make songs about me* (Ps 69:13/12).[35] It is said about Job: *When I rise, they talk against me* (Job 19:18). It is said about the calamities of Israel: *I am the talk of those who sit in the gate* (Ps 69:13/12). It is said about Job: *A senseless, disreputable brood*

[33] Salmon explains in his comment on Ps 38:12/11: "This is also a great complaint of illness: the sick person, when the illness grows long, his friends and companions observe him but a plan [for healing] is not in their power. The way of Israel is likewise: there is no one with a plan to heal them, as it is said, *for vast as the sea is your ruin; who can restore you?* (Lam 2:13), but only the Lord may heal them of their sicknesses, as He says, *I wound and I heal* (Deut 32:39). Likewise, you see that Job said regarding his illness, *He has put my brethren far from me* (Job 19:13); *my kinsmen have gone far from me* [cf. RSV, *my kinsmen have failed me*]. And he said as the communal complaint, *all my allies have become distant from me* [cf. RSV, *my intimate friends abhor me*] (Job 19:19)" (Salmon, Pss 11–41).

[34] Salmon repeats this pair of prooftexts in his discussion of the meaning behind the alphabetic arrangement of Lam 3, below.

[35] In his comment on Ps 69:13/12, Salmon depicts the objects of scorn in terms that resonate with the Karaites' own ascetic practices: "He [David] means, 'When I wore sackcloth in order to humble myself and break away from yearnings of the world through the hardship of haircloth and abandoning the pleasure of soft clothing, I became a parable (*mathal*) for them. When they convened for their parties and their drinking and their depravity, one of them wore a haircloth, and they brought him out on a horse and they said, "Thus was Jabez, and thus was al-Qūmisī!"'" (Salmon, Pss 42–72).

(Job 30:8). It is said about Israel: *I will provoke them with a foolish nation* (Deut 32:21). It is said about Job: *I cry to You [and You do not answer me]* (Job 30:20). It is said about Israel: *Though I call and cry for help [He shuts out my prayer]* (Lam 3:8). It is said about Job: *They do not hesitate to spit at the sight of me* (Job 30:10). It is said about Israel: *I hid not my face from shame and spitting* (Isa 50:6). It is said about Job: *You lift me up on the wind* (Job 30:22). It is said about the calamities of Israel: *For You have taken me up and thrown me away* (Ps 102:11/10).[36] It is said about Job: *But when I looked for good, evil came* (Job 30:26). It is said about Israel: *We look for light and behold, darkness* (Isa 59:9). It is said about Job: *My insides are in turmoil, and are never still* (Job 30:27). It is said about Israel: *My insides, my insides! I writhe in pain!* (Jer 4:19). It is said about Job: *My skin turns black and falls from me* (Job 30:30). It is said about the calamities of Israel: *Now their visage is blacker than soot* (Lam 4:8). It is said about Job: *And when they saw him from afar, they did not recognize him* (Job 2:12). It is said about Israel: *They are not recognized in the streets* (Lam 4:8).

Having established equivalence between the calamities of Israel and the calamities of Job—in <7b> which it is not apparent which one was tested with the greatest trial—we may now state the ways in which the calamities of Israel surpass the calamities of Job and are more distressing and more significant. The transfer of the divine glory away from the midst of Israel: *From the daughter of Zion has departed all her majesty* (Lam 1:6). The absence of prophecy from the prophets: *There is no longer any prophet, and there is none among us who knows how long* (Ps 74:9) and *Her prophets obtain no vision from the LORD* (Lam 2:9). The cessation of sacrificial offerings: *The LORD has scorned His altar* (Lam 2:7) and *Gird on sackcloth and lament, O priests, wail, O ministers of the altar* (Joel 1:13). The destruction of the Temple: *And he* [Nebuzaradan] *burned the house of the LORD, and the king's house* (2 Kgs 25:9). The transfer of Israel's inheritance, *the glorious land*, to the nations: *Our inheritance has been turned over to strangers, our homes to foreigners* (Lam 5:2). The fall of our crown: *The crown has fallen from our head* (Lam 5:16). The dispersion of the entire nation as it is said, *And I will dash them one against the other* (Jer 13:14).[37]

[36] In his comment on Ps 102:11/10, Salmon draws a parallel between the "throwing" in this verse (*va-tashlikheni*) and Deut 29:27/28—*and cast them (va-yashlikhem) into another land*—to indicate that God threw all of Israel "into this exile" (Salmon, Pss 90–106).

[37] Salmon refers back to these comparisons in his comment to Lam 1:12. Saadia Gaon does not make such comparisons in his commentary on the book of Job; see Lenn Goodman, *The Book of Theodicy: Translation and Commentary on the Book of Job by Saadiah ben Joseph al-Fayyūmī*, YJS 25 (New Haven, Conn.: Yale University Press, 1988).

There are some calamities that cannot be enumerated quickly. Therefore it is said, *Look and see if there is any sorrow like my sorrow* (Lam 1:12) and *by bringing upon us a great calamity* (Dan 9:12). For the magnitude of the calamities, we must lament for the things that are no longer and that have passed away, as it is said, *Cut off your hair and cast it away* (Jer 7:29). The *lament* (*qinah*) was established <8a> and ordained over Israel, as it is said, *they made these an ordinance in Israel; behold, they are written in the Laments* (2 Chr 35:25). From the phrase "*in the Laments*," we learn that the *laments* (*qinot*) were made to be used in [actual] lamentation and are not [merely] symbolic, for it is said, *Jeremiah also uttered a lament for Josiah;* [*and all the singing men and singing women have spoken of Josiah in their laments to this day. They made these an ordinance in Israel; behold, they are written in the Laments*] (2 Chr 35:25).

Jeremiah as the Prophet of Lamentations

The phrase *in the Laments* (*'al ha-qinot*; 2 Chr 35:25) makes clear that this book—I mean Lamentations—was prophesied by Jeremiah, and all of the scholars are agreed (*mujmiʿa*) on this, without discrepancy or controversy.[38] Whoever imagines that God's words to Jeremiah, *Take a scroll and write on it all the words* (Jer 36:2), refer to the book of Lamentations is surely mistaken.[39] It was not like that, because God commanded Jeremiah

[38] I.e., the scholars have achieved consensus (*ijmāʿ*). In Islamic jurisprudence, consensus is a legitimate basis for law; this principle carried over into Jewish religious thought in non-legal contexts as well; see Fred Astren, *Karaite Judaism and Historical Understanding* (Columbia: University of South Carolina Press, 2004), 60. Salmon's comment demonstrates that the consensus of the entire Jewish community—unanimous agreement—carried significant weight in establishing the truth of an argument, principle, or interpretation. In his Hebrew polemical poem, *The Wars of the Lord*, Salmon invokes consensus as proof for the sanctity of the Written Torah, over and against the Oral Torah, which is accepted by only part of the Jewish community (*KA*, 73). Salmon's focus on the consensus of the community rather than the consensus of jurisprudents is shared by al-Qirqisānī and the Shāfiʿī school of Islamic law; see Imran Ahsan Niazi, "The Karaites: Influence of Islamic Law on Jewish Law," *Islamic Studies* 32 (1993), esp. 142–45. On the attribution of Lam to Jeremiah, see Jason Kalman, "Authorship, Attribution, and Authority: Jeremiah, Baruch, and the Rabbinic Interpretation of Lamentations," *HUCA* 90 (2019): 27–87. This attribution dates back to the Tannaitic period (first two centuries CE) and appears in *Seder Olam Rabbah*, Targum Lamentations, and the Babylonian Talmud as well as medieval commentaries.

[39] The identification of Lam with the scroll mentioned in Jer 36:2 appears throughout rabbinic literature (e.g., BT Moʿed Qaṭan 26a; *Lam R*, proem 28; *Lam* R on 3:1; and *Leviticus Rabbah* 11:7); in some cases the rabbis discuss which chapter(s) of Lam were recorded on the burned scroll, and which chapters were added only to the replacement scroll (see Kalman, "Authorship," 40–41).

to write all the prophesies that he prophesied from the thirteenth year of King Josiah—since that was the first year that God spoke to Jeremiah, as it is said, *to whom the word of the LORD came in the days of Josiah the son of Amon, king of Judah, in the thirteenth year of his reign* (Jer 1:2)—to the fourth year of King Jehoiakim, as it is said, *In the fourth year of Jehoiakim the son of Josiah, king of Judah, this word came to Jeremiah from the LORD: Take a scroll* (Jer 36:1–2).[40]

<8b> So He commanded him to write all that he prophesied about Israel and Judah and all of the nations, which is set down in the Book of Jeremiah. He read it to the people of Jerusalem and the house of Judah, in order that perhaps they would reflect (*yaʿtabirū*) and be dismayed by some of the threats, and this would motivate their repentance, as it is said, *It may be that the house of Judah will hear all the evil which I intend to do to them, so that everyone may turn from his evil way, and that I may forgive their iniquity and their sin* (Jer 36:3). He wrote it as God commanded him, and he read it to the people in the fifth year of Jehoiakim, but [when] the news reached King Jehoiakim, he burned it up, so God commanded Jeremiah to do it again. So he took up another scroll and wrote upon it what was on the first one, which was burned, and he added other things to it, as it is said, *Take another scroll, and write on it all the former words that were in the first scroll, which Jehoiakim the king of Judah has burned* (Jer 36:28). Then he explained to us and elucidated clearly that this scroll is not Lamentations, but rather, <9a> it was the reports of Nebuchadnezzar [when he was] bound toward this country, and the destruction of the people within it, as it is said, *And concerning Jehoiakim king of Judah you shall say: Thus said the LORD, You have burned this scroll, saying, "Why have you written in it that the king of Babylon will certainly come and destroy this land, and will cut off from it man and beast"* (Jer 36:29). This makes it clear and evident that this scroll [which replaced the one that Jehoiakim had burned] was not Lamentations.[41]

[40] Salmon refutes the identification of Lam and the scroll on historical grounds: Jeremiah was commanded to take the scroll in the fourth year of Jehoiakim's reign, prior to the destruction of Jerusalem recounted in Lam. This refutation would not necessarily satisfy all Jewish thinkers, since Jeremiah's status as a prophet would enable him to prophesy the future destruction of Jerusalem. Salmon mentions Jeremiah's scroll again in his comment to Lam 4:1, where he lists burning the scroll as one of Jehoiakim's grave sins.

[41] I.e., the absence of such a verse in Lam proves that Lam is not the scroll.

Seven Meanings of Lamentations

There are [many] meanings (*maʿānī*) enfolded within these *lamentations* that Jeremiah established, of which I shall mention seven. The first meaning is the nation's regret over what vanished from her—her comfort, her might, her statehood, her nobility—and how she is pained over the lowliness and degradation that she has reached. With respect to this it is said, *How lonely sits the city that was full of people!* (Lam 1:1) and similarly, *Jerusalem remembers in the days of her affliction all the precious things that were hers from days of old* (Lam 1:7).

The second meaning is the enumeration the calamities, as it is said, *The roads to Zion mourn, for none come to the appointed feasts* (Lam 1:4); and *Her foes have become the head* (Lam 1:5); and *From the daughter of Zion has departed all her majesty* (Lam 1:6); and *The enemy has stretched out his hands over all her precious things* (Lam 1:10); and *From on high He sent fire; into my bones He made it descend* (Lam 1:13).

The third meaning is to mention <9b> the reports that are not explained in another prophecy, such as: *Yea, she has seen the nations invade her sanctuary* (Lam 1:10), which are Amon and Moab.[42]

The fourth meaning is to raise a petition[43] to God most high concerning the severity of what the enemies have done, as it is said, *Women are ravished in Zion, virgins in the towns of Judah* (Lam 5:11) and *Princes are hung up by their hands* (Lam 5:12), and there are many similar examples.

The fifth meaning is for the nation to summon[44] one another to repentance, as it is said: *Let us test and examine our ways, and return to the LORD* (Lam 3:40).[45]

The sixth meaning is the confession of offenses, as the nation says: *The LORD is just, for I have rebelled against His word* (Lam 1:18) and *We have transgressed and rebelled* (Lam 3:42).

The seventh meaning is to convey the good news that God announced in this book, such as forgiveness for His nation and its return to statehood, after

42 The full discussion appears in Salmon's comment at Lam 1:10. Note also the historicist element of this third purpose: Salmon aims to corroborate sources and construct a comprehensive historical narrative informed by a range of biblical texts. For discussion, see chapter 6.

43 Arab. *rafaʿa qiṣṣa*. On *qiṣṣa* as petition or complaint, see Blau, *Dictionary*, 546.

44 Arab. *istidʿā*. This theme may allude to the missionary aspect of the Karaite movement, and the parallels between it and the contemporary Shīʿī movement. The word Karaites (Hebr. *qaraʾim*) is the translation of the Arab. *duʿāh* (sg. *dāʿin*), "missionary" or "caller." See Gil, *History*, 784; and my comments in chapter 1.

45 On Salmon's pietistic reading of Lam 3:40, see notes there.

which there will be no more exile, along with an investigation of the enemies' offenses and the exposure of their sins, as it is said, *The punishment of your iniquity, O daughter of Zion, is accomplished, He will keep you in exile no longer* (Lam 4:22).

Many of the prophets had lamented over us, and their lamentation was set down for us so that we would add them to this separate book in order to lament for ourselves, as it is said: *Then those of you who escape* <10a> *will remember Me among the nations where they are carried captive, when I have been broken, their wanton heart has departed from Me* (Ezek 6:9).[46]

He compares *the prophets of the LORD*, in their lamentation over us, to father, mother, and children, describing [the mother's] pain when she sees the children doing what she knows will make the father angry. She curses them and warns them of the father's anger because if the father becomes angry with the children and abandons them, they will perish. Worry and mourning lay claim to the mother on account of [the children]. Israel is compared to the children, as it is said, *You are children of the LORD your God* (Deut 14:1). The Creator is compared to Israel's father, as it is said, *For You are our father* (Isa 63:16) and, as our master Moses said, *Is He not your father, who created you?* (Deut 32:6). The prophets are compared to the mother, as it is said: *But if you will not listen* (Jer 13:17), which means, "If you do not accept this prophecy, then I know that the LORD will be angry and I will cry over you, O my children, O Israel." The prophets' calls for mercy are part of [divine] benevolence. Indeed, every type of prophecy that God imparts to His prophets is [borne] out of compassion and kindliness for Israel, as it is said, *The LORD, the God of their fathers, sent persistently to them by His messengers [because He had compassion on His people and on His dwelling place]* (2 Chr 36:15).

The words <10b> of this book are likewise. He asserted to Israel that whenever they follow [the book] by lamenting for themselves and crying over what happened to them, they will merit His mercy, forgiveness, and pardon, just as the Mighty and Sublime promised in the verse, *You shall weep no more. He will surely be gracious to you* (Isa 30:19).

[46] Thus, Salmon brings verses from other prophets—primarily Isaiah, Jeremiah, Ezekiel, and Hosea—into the Lam commentary; the comment also implies that the laments from these prophetic works may be uttered alongside those from Lam in liturgical contexts.

The Structure of Lamentations and Its Significance

He said that he established this book in five parts, like the five parts of the book of Psalms, so that each part of Lamentations would be said following a part of Psalms.[47] He surely alluded to this in the verses *Arise, cry out in the night, at the beginning of the watches!* (Lam 2:19) and *She weeps bitterly in the night, tears on her cheek* (Lam 1:2). If you consider the divisions of this book in another way, you find seven divisions because the chapter [that begins with the verse] *I am the man* (Lam 3:1) is three sections combined, so that [the sections] become seven altogether. The meaning of this is that when the people transgress clear wisdom, whose foundations are seven—as it is said, *Wisdom has built her house, she has hewn her seven pillars* (Prov 9:1)—they will deserve to lament for themselves by these seven divisions, as I have explained.

As for setting it down alphabetically:[48] that is to make remembering it easier for the educated (*muta'allimīn*).[49] <11a> As for not arranging [the chapter beginning with] *I am the man* (Lam 3:1) into three divisions, indeed this is to magnify the calamities. The first division has three [verses beginning with the letter] *'aleph*, and the second division has three [verses beginning with the letter] *bet*, which doubles the one that came before. Likewise, the next one has three [verses beginning with the letter] *gimmel*, up to verse nine in number, which is more than the second stanza; and so it continues in this fashion to the end of the section, which indicates the multiplicity, magnitude, and succession of the calamities, as it is said, *Disaster follows hard*

[47] According to al-Qirqisānī, prayers should consist only of recitation of the Psalms; see Leon Nemoy, ed., *Ya'qūb al-Qirqisānī's Kitāb al-Anwār wa-l Marāqib—Code of Karaite Law*, 5 vols. (New York: Alexander Kohut Memorial Foundation, 1939–43), VI.7.1). Salmon brings Lam into the Karaite prayer service by correlating its structure to that of Pss. Haggai Ben-Shammai presents Salmon's commentary as the framework for a prayer service that would include verses from the prophets as well as contemporary compositions, and would run parallel to the regular prayer service, which was composed exclusively of verses from Pss; see "Poetic Works and Lamentations of Qaraite 'Mourners of Zion'—Structure and Contents" [Hebrew], in *Kenesset Ezra: Literature and Life in the Synagogue; Studies Presented to Ezra Fleischer*, ed. Shulamit Elitsur et al. (Jerusalem: Ben Zvi, 1994), 225.

[48] I have emended the text, which reads: "as for not setting it down alphabetically . . ."

[49] By explaining the acrostic structure as a mnemonic device for the learned, Salmon approaches Lam as a written text to be studied and memorized. Modern scholars have noted that alphabetic acrostics function as mnemonic aids in literate contexts, rather than predominantly oral/aural ones. Before Salmon, al-Qirqisānī considered the alphabetic arrangement as proof that Hebrew, rather than Aramaic, was the primordial language by which God addressed Adam and the prophets (*KA*, 61–62).

on disaster (Jer 4:20) and *Disaster comes upon disaster, rumor follows rumor* (Ezek 7:26).[50]

Having made a preface with these statements, now I will begin the explication of the language (*alfāẓ*) of this book, then [proceed to] a summation of its meanings (*maʿānī*) and the uncovering of its intentions (*aghrāḍ*). I will mention what I have comprehended from it, based on the words of the scholars (*ʿulamāʾ*),[51] and I will add to that what occurs to me, if there is a benefit for students (*muʿallamīn*) in setting it down.[52] From God I ask succor (*tawfīq*), direction (*rashad*), and guidance (*hidāya*) along the right path with His generous sustenance and His favors.

[50] Cf. rabbinic explanations of the acrostic, e.g., "Why is the Book of Lamentations composed as an alphabetical acrostic? R. Judah, R. Nehemiah, and the Rabbis suggest answers. R. Judah said: Because it is written, *Yea, all Israel have transgressed Thy law* (Dan 9:11), which is written [with all the letters] from *alef* to *taw*; therefore is this Book composed as an alphabetical acrostic, one corresponding to the other. R. Nehemiah said: Although Jeremiah cursed them with the alphabetical acrostic of Lamentations, Isaiah anticipated him and pronounced a healing for them verse by verse down to *Let all their wickedness come before Thee* (Lam 1:22)" (*Lam R* on Lam 1:1).

[51] It is not clear whom Salmon has in mind by *al-ʿulamāʾ*. The word may indicate Karaite scholars whose opinions he knows either from their writings or from personal study. Although Salmon's work on Lam is the earliest extant Karaite commentary on the book, he may have availed himself of oral Karaite learning, or the approaches to Lam and related biblical literature embedded in other Karaite works. Salmon could also have in mind the rabbinic interpretations that he refers to throughout his commentary, both obliquely and explicitly (see chapter 3); thus, Daniel Frank has translated the word as "Sages" in the context of Salmon's similar statement in the introduction to his commentary on Song (*Search Scripture Well*, 147, 293). However, since Salmon refers to rabbinic sages and Rabbanites with other labels throughout the commentary (e.g., *al-awāʾil, al-rabbāniyyūn*), he may use the term *ʿulamāʾ* to indicate a broader category. Salmon may have chosen an ambiguous or inclusive term to refer to the range of scholars whose opinions he deems correct on a case-by-case basis, without regard to their communal affiliation. Salmon uses certain expressions to refer to the whole Jewish community (e.g., *ahl al-jalūt, al-umma*), and he may use *ʿulamāʾ* in a similar spirit of ecumenism. Indeed, the focus of his comment here is that he has included in his commentary the most apt opinions, without regard to the identity of their authors. This project fits with the Karaite rejection of authority for its own sake, by placing total emphasis on the quality of the interpretations themselves.

[52] Yefet ben ʿEli defines his strategy in the same terms in the introduction to his commentary on Genesis. He begins with attention to the language (*lafẓ*)—i.e., the translation—followed by examination of the meanings (*maʿānīhi*)—i.e., the commentary or exegesis. Yefet describes his exegesis as based in the text and the requirements of language or, alternatively, as based in "what we have heard from our teachers and commentators, and what we have read in the books of the past scholars [. . .] and according to what we deem proper." This latter emphasis most closely resembles Salmon's stated method here. See Meira Polliack, "Medieval Karaite Views on Translating the Hebrew Bible into Arabic," *JJS* 47 (1996): 71–72.

Lamentations 1

Lamentations 1:1

אֵיכָה יָשְׁבָה בָדָד הָעִיר רַבָּתִי עָם הָיְתָה כְּאַלְמָנָה רַבָּתִי בַגּוֹיִם שָׂרָתִי בַּמְּדִינוֹת
הָיְתָה לָמַס׃
כיף ג'לסת פראד אלקריה כת'ירה אלקום צארת מת'ל אלארמלה כבירה פי
אלאחזאב רייסה פי אלמדן צארת ללכ'ראג'

How lonely sits the city that once was full of people! How like a widow she has become, she that was great among the nations! She that was a princess among the provinces has become [subject to] the land tax.[1]

<11b> *She that was great among the nations.* In Hebrew usage, when it is necessary to emphasize a feminine form, it is conventional to change the letter [final] *heh* into the letter *tā'*, to which a *yod* is appended—for example, *mele'ati* (*she that was full,* Isa 1:21). It is the same here with *rabbati* (*full*) and *śarati* (*princess*). If the form is masculine, it is emphasized by means of the *yod* alone, as in *shokhni* (Deut 33:16)—which means *the one who dwells* (*shokhen*)—and *ha-magbihi* (Ps 113:5); *ha-mashpili* (Ps 113:6); *ha-yoshvi* (Ps 123:1); *ḥoṣvi* and *ḥoqeqi* (Isa 22:16), and there are many examples like these.[2]

I have translated *'ekhah* as "how," as an expression of amazement. There are five expressions of this type.[3] The first of them is *'ekhakhah* (Song 5:3, Esth 8:6); then *'ekhah*, *'ekh*, *hekh* (1 Chr 13:12), and *'e* [אֵי], as in, *how* [אֵי] *can I pardon you?* (Jer 5:7). For *'ekhah* is a component of *'ekhakhah* and *'ekh* is a component of *'ekhah* and *'e* is a component of *'ekh*. As for *hekh* and *'ekh*: the

[1] Salmon translates Hebr. *mas* (a collective noun representing the labor-force of a conquered population, which the RSV renders "vassal") as Arab. *kharāj* (a tax on lands owned by non-Muslims). The same translation choice is attested in al-Fāsī, who cites three instances of Hebr. *mas* (Gen 49:15, Lam 1:1, and Exod 1:11) and states that "all of them are *kharajāt*" (vol. II, 218), and in Yefet ben ʿEli's commentary on Esther (sc. Esth 10:3; see Wechsler, 313 n. 728, inter alia).

[2] In their biblical contexts, each of these participles describes God; in selecting them to prove his point, Salmon also emphasizes the masculinity of the deity.

[3] See Yūsuf ibn Nūḥ's comments on Song 5:3 and Lam 1:1 in Khan, *The Early Karaite Tradition of Hebrew Grammatical Thought* (Leiden: Brill, 2000), 460–61, 474–75.

Jewish Piety in Islamic Jerusalem. Jessica Andruss, Oxford University Press. © Oxford University Press 2023.
DOI: 10.1093/oso/9780197639559.003.0010

letters *heh* and *'aleph* are among the interchangeable letters (*aḥrūf al-ibdāl*). You will find many instances of the letter *heh* in place of the letter *'aleph* in Scripture. The reason for this is that they [i.e., the letters *heh* and *'aleph*] are among the letters *'aleph, heh, ḥet*, and *'ayin* whose point of articulation is the throat, which Hebrew speakers call "the place of swallowing" (*beit ha-beli'ah*, i.e., pharyngeal consonants). An example of the letter *heh* in place of the letter *'aleph* is: <12a> *ve-'etkhem hoṣi' mitokhah* (*you shall be taken out of it*; Ezek 11:7). Therefore, *hekh* has [the same] meaning as *'ekh*, and there are many similar examples. The subdivision of the word *'ekhah* is like that of *'oyah* (*woe*; Ps 120:5) into *'oy* and *'iy*, as in *Woe* (*'iy*) *to you, O land* (Eccl 10:16).

Now we return to explaining the meaning of *'ekhah*. We say that with this word he [i.e., Jeremiah] intended to convey the awesome humiliation that befell the nation after it had experienced great prosperity. For example, the multitude of her population: the people—ten tribes of them—numbered one million six hundred thousand, as it is said, *In all Israel there were one million one hundred thousand men who drew the sword*[4] (1 Chr 21:5); *and the men of Judah were five hundred thousand* (2 Sam 24:9); *But he did not include Levi and Benjamin in the numbering* (1 Chr 21:6). This figure is only for the soldiers.

As for those under twenty years [of age] and the elderly and others, including children and women: only God knows their number! Even more astonishing than this number is the number of the army of Jehoshaphat, King of Judah, who assembled one million, one hundred and sixty thousand, who were companions of the guard before King Jehoshaphat, <12b> aside from those who were appointed to the fortresses within the city guard and the soldiers, as it is said, *these were in the service of the king, besides those whom the king had placed in the fortified cities throughout all Judah* (2 Chr 17:19). [There were also] these soldiers and those who were not under twenty years [of age] or the elderly, the children, and the women whose number only God knows, and these were among the tribes. The count of the tribe of Levi is not mentioned. And who knows the number of the ten tribes in this age [i.e., at the time of Lamentations], when Jerusalem was emptied of its people!

How lonely sits the city that once was full of people. With the disappearance of the people from the noble site, their enormous wealth vanished as well—wealth unheard of in any of the other empires. This is made clear by

[4] The verse continues: *and in Judah four hundred and seventy thousand who drew the sword* (1 Chr 21:5). Salmon disregards this figure in favor of the larger one from 2 Sam 24:9, which he cites next.

the verse, *with great pains I have provided for the house of the LORD one hundred thousand talents of gold, one million talents of silver, and bronze and iron beyond weighing, for there is so much of it; timber and stone too have I provided* (1 Chr 22:14).

Now since the treasure amounted to four *badras*, the total came to 100,000 talents and <13a> 75,000 talents.[5] Then they reckoned each camel with its harness at ten cubits; this amounted to 1,000 camels for every parasang, since a parasang is 10,000 cubits. This being the case, the full length of the camel train that bore this treasure was 100,000 parasangs and 75 parasangs. They say this is comparable to the distance from Samarqand to Mecca, but in my opinion this calculation is incorrect.

Then he describes to us that David was not satisfied with this treasure and this equipment, so he gathered the heads of the nation and the mighty men and the palace officials of Israel, as it is said, *David assembled at Jerusalem all the officials of Israel, the officials of the tribes, the officers of the divisions that served the king, the commanders of the thousands, the commanders of the hundreds, the stewards of all the property and cattle* (1 Chr 28:1). The king rose to his feet and addressed [them], saying to all who were present, *I have provided for the house of my God, so far as I was able, the gold for the things of gold, the silver for the things of silver* (1 Chr 29:2). Then he bestowed the treasure that he mentioned of his own account. He dedicated it and supplemented it with the first property, as it is said, *Moreover, in addition to all that I have provided for the holy house, I have a treasure of my own gold and silver, and because of my devotion to the house of my God*[6] <13b> *I give it to the house of my God: three thousand talents of gold, of the gold of Ophir, and seven thousand talents of refined silver, for overlaying the walls of the house, and for all the work to be done by artisans, gold for the things of gold and silver for the things of silver. Who then will offer willingly, consecrating themselves today to the LORD?* (1 Chr 29:3–5).

What the chiefs bestowed is also mentioned, as it is said, *Then the leaders of ancestral houses made their freewill offerings, as did also the leaders of the tribes, the commanders of the thousands and of the hundreds, and the officers over the king's work. They gave for the service of the house of God five thousand talents and ten thousand darics of gold, ten thousand talents of silver, eighteen*

[5] Salmon renders Hebr. *kikar* ("round weight, talent") as Arab. *badra*, a large sum of money—equal to 10,000 dirhems, according to Hava (23). For discussion about the value of a *badra* based on its equivalence to different currencies, see Wechsler on Yefet, Esth, 220 n. 287.

[6] Hebr. "the house of my God"; Salmon: "the house of the God of Israel."

thousand talents of bronze, and one hundred thousand talents of iron. Whoever had precious stones gave them to the treasury of the house of the LORD, into the care of Jehiel the Gershonite (1 Chr 29:6–8).

Not content with having bestowed this treasure to the house of the LORD, David commanded Solomon to add to them, as it is said, *You must add more* (1 Chr 22:14). Solomon reigned for three years, and after he was in power, he was emboldened[7] to amass funds and equipment. Then he began to build the house, as it is said, *Then Solomon began to build* [. . .] *on the second day of the second month of the fourth year of his reign* (2 Chr 3:1–2). I have explained this in order to make known that the nation was affluent and that they had a temple built from this treasure, entirely inlaid with red gems, as it is said, *He adorned the house with settings of precious stones* (2 Chr 3:6). [But] their sins became great, and their enemies prevailed over them and [the Temple] was destroyed—*they smashed all its carved work* (Ps 74:6)—and burned down—<14a>*they set Your sanctuary on fire* (Ps 74:7). Then the people of the country were sent into exile, and the prophet indicates astonishment over this by saying, ***How lonely sits the city that once was full of people*** (Lam 1:1).

As for Solomon's wealth, it is said of him that six hundred and sixty-six talents of gold came to him annually, as it is said, *The weight of gold that came to Solomon in one year was six hundred sixty-six talents of gold* (2 Chr 9:13). He was not satisfied with this for it is said, *besides that which the traders and merchants brought;* [*and all the kings of Arabia and the governors of the land brought gold and silver to Solomon*] (2 Chr 9:14).

The next thing to mention is wisdom and the knowledge of the higher realms of the world, as it is said, *All the kings of the earth sought the presence of Solomon to hear his wisdom, which God had put into his mind. Every one of them brought a present, objects of silver and gold, garments, weaponry, spices, horses, and mules, so much year by year* (2 Chr 9:23–24). There was no need to sell off any of this treasure because the provision of Israel's maintenance was sufficient, as it is said, *Those officials supplied provisions for King Solomon* (1 Kgs 5:7/4:27).

The signs—such as [divine] support and victory—became ever greater. What was known from the reports about David, Asa, Jehoshaphat, Ezekiel, and others was beautifully confirmed, and the exposition [of these signs] spread to the extent that no one in the world believed <14b> that anyone could conquer Jerusalem or this nation, as it is said, *The kings of the earth did*

[7] Reading Arab. *jasara* in place of *kasara*. I thank Daniel Frank for suggesting this emendation.

not believe, nor did any inhabitants of the world [that foe or enemy could enter the gates of Jerusalem] (Lam 4:12).

Yet all this overtook them when their sins and offenses became great, as it is said, *and the LORD says: because they have forsaken My law* (Jer 9:12/13). The lamenter was astonished and amazed by this and other examples of the circumstances that befell the nation, so he said, ***How lonely sits the city***.

Some scholars have said that the word *badad* ("lonely") is a reference to *leprosy*, as it is said, *He* [i.e., a leper] *shall live alone* (*badad*)*; his dwelling shall be outside the camp* (Lev 13:46), and that is why the nation was expelled from the chosen place (*al-mauḍiʿ al-khāṣ*), as it is said, *I will drive them out of My house* (Hos 9:15). It was also said about this nation, *I lie awake; I am like a lonely* (*boded*) *bird on the housetop* (Ps 102:8/7). And it is also said, *I have sat lonely* (*badad*) *because of Your hand upon me* (Jer 15:17). Just as *the leper* mourns, so shall [the nation] mourn, as it is said, [*the person who has the leprous disease*] *shall wear torn clothes* (Lev 13:45). Therefore it is said, *In that day the Lord GOD of hosts called to weeping and mourning* (Isa 22:12).

How like a widow she has become. He does not say, "*She has become a widow*, for she has been overtaken by despair," but he says <u>*like*</u> *a widow*, just as it is said, <u>*like*</u> *an enemy* (Lam 2:4,5) or <u>*like*</u> *a foe* (Lam 2:4) in order to inform [us] that <15a> this is an analogy (*ʿalā sabīl al-tamthīl*). It means that she is bereft of the king, the chiefs, statehood, might, Temple, priesthood, prophecy, signs, proofs, and the like. ***Like a widow she has become*** means that when she was cut off from these circumstances, she became like a widow.

She that was great among the nations. This means that she had a prominent position among the nations, as it is said, *Your fame spread among the nations on account of your beauty* (Ezek 16:14). The beauty (*ḥasan*) ascribed [to her] in this verse refers to temporal beauty (*jamāl al-dunya*), victory, [divine] support, and the beauty [bestowed by] the king of heaven. For as we have explained, this nation's means of subsistence were all divine, of heavenly [origin].

He beautified wisdom, so that [foreign] kings came to hear the wisdom of Solomon, carrying presents and momentous offerings, as it is said, *All the kings of the earth sought Solomon [to hear his wisdom]* (2 Chr 9:23) and *Every one of them brought a present* (2 Chr 9:24). So it was with the Queen of Sheba when she called upon Solomon and confirmed what she had heard of his wisdom. So it was with the kings of Babylon, when they dispatched envoys to Hezekiah, to ask him about the news of the falling back of the sun.[8] He

[8] See 2 Kgs 20: the shadow of the sun falls back ten steps, as a sign to Hezekiah that his health will return. When Hezekiah recovers, envoys from Babylon visit, and he shows them the treasures of his house and storerooms.

made this sign great in order to teach them <15b> that signs and miracles were seen exclusively by this favored nation (*al-umma al-makhṣūṣa*). Thus, when all of these elements were withdrawn from the nation, he said, ***How like a widow she has become***—she that was great among all groups and the assembly of nations.

She that was a princess among the provinces means this nation which had been the princess over the people of the world, as it is said about Solomon, *For he had dominion over all the region west of the Euphrates from Tiphsah to Gaza* (1 Kgs 5:4/4:24). This is to say that Solomon made himself master over the people of the world, as a chieftain might gain mastery over Tiphsah and Gaza, which are two neighboring cities with virtually no distance between them—their names being Mīmās and Gaza.[9]

No one from any of the nations dared to attack Israel in the time of Solomon, as it is said, *I will give peace and quiet to Israel in his days* (1 Chr 22:9). And Solomon said in his letter to the king of Tyre, *There is neither adversary nor misfortune* (1 Kgs 5:18/4).[10] After the sins increased, it is said in the report about his descendant Jehoiachim, King of Judah, *The LORD sent against him bands of the Chaldeans, bands of the Arameans* (2 Kgs 24:2). Then Nebuchadnezzar attacked him and triumphed, as it is said, *In the third year of the reign of King Jehoiakim of Judah, King Nebuchadnezzar* <16a> *of Babylon came to Jerusalem and besieged it. The Lord let King Jehoiakim of Judah fall into his power* (Dan 1:1–2). After Jehoiakim there was Jehoiachin, as it is said, *King Jehoiachin gave himself up to the king of Babylon, himself, his mother, his servants, his officers, and his palace officials. The king of Babylon took him prisoner* (2 Kgs 24:12). After that came the *exile* of Zedekiah and the difficult calamities that befell him, as we will explain. All this happened to them because of the magnitude of their offenses and the severity of their rebellions, as it is said, *And the LORD says: Because they have forsaken My law* (Jer 9:12/13).

That is why it is said, ***she that was a princess among the provinces has become a vassal.***[11] She became [subject to] the *kharāj* and the *jizya*,[12] as it is said

[9] Mīmās—later Maiumas Gaza—was the harbor town of inland Gaza; see Itamar Taxel, "The Byzantine-Early Islamic Transition of the Palestinian Coastal Plain: A Re-evaluation of the Archaeological Evidence," *Semitica et Classica* 6 (2013): 75.

[10] Salmon specifies that Solomon communicated with the King of Tyre in writing—*qāla fī kitābihi* ("he said in his writing"), whereas the biblical account states only that he "sent word" (*va-yishlaḥ shelomoh 'el-ḥiram le'mor*).

[11] Salmon glosses Hebr. *mas* (vassal) as one who is subject to the *kharāj* and the *jizya*, which reflects his Arab. translation of the verse, above.

[12] Salmon is not unique in linking the *kharāj* and the *jizya*. Although they were eventually differentiated as a land tax and a poll tax, respectively, during the early Islamic conquests both terms

in the covenant, [*Because you did not serve the LORD your God joyfully and with gladness of heart for the abundance of everything, therefore you shall serve your enemies whom the LORD will send against you, in hunger and thirst, in nakedness and in want of all things.*] *He will put a yoke of iron upon your neck, until He has destroyed you* (Deut 28:47–48).

There are six meanings in this verse; three are noble and three are lowly, base. He begins, first, by saying, ***how lonely sits the city***, to which he adds, ***that once was full of people***. Then he reverses this order by saying ***she that was a princess among the provinces has become a vassal***. The purpose of reversing this third order is to complete the verse in the same way that it began. The word *rabbati* [appears] twice in this verse. The first time [i.e., *that once was full* (*rabbati*) *of people*] means a large quantity, as in *be fruitful and multiply* (Gen 1:22); *the people are* <16b> *still too many* (Judg 7:4); and, *many are saying to me* (Ps 3:3/2), and there are many [other] examples. [The second time,] ***Great*** (*rabbati*) ***among the nations***, it means "great in age," as in *the elder shall serve the lesser* (Gen 25:23) and likewise, *older; and more distinguished* (Num 22:15); *it is not the old that are wise* (Job 32:9); and *senior officers of the king* (Jer 41:1).

How lonely sits the city. [The word *ʾekhah*] governs itself and others (*menaheg ʿaṣmo ve-menaheg aḥerim*). He says, ***<u>How</u>*** (*ʾ**ekhah***) ***lonely sits the city that once was full of people*** **and** ***<u>how</u>*** (*ʾ**ekhah***) ***like a widow she has become, she that was great among the nations! She that was a princess among the provinces has become a vassal***, because the word *ʾekhah* expresses astonishment and amazement. The verse includes some of the noble conditions, and then [it notes] how they are reversed and have become the opposite! This is like the verse *How the faithful city has become a harlot!* (Isa 1:21). He means, "How did the pious city become reckless, with *idolatry* manifest within her, after faith in God and His prophets, offering sacrifices in accordance with her [prophetic] tradition (*sunan*), the service of the house of the Lord, and complete obedience?!"

And how the conditions of obedience were reversed! They had *idols*, as it is said, *As many as the streets of Jerusalem are the altars you have set up*

indicated a general tax on subject populations. These populations paid taxes to Muslim forces in return for their protection, as a component of peace treaties (Gil, *History*, 142 n. 3, 143). The terms represent parallel taxation systems, called *kharāj* in the east and *jizya* in Egypt; see ʿAbdal ʿAziz Duri, "Notes on Taxation in Early Islam," *Journal of the Economic and Social History of the Orient* 17 (1974): 136. Even in the tenth century, Yefet ben ʿEli uses the term *kharāj* sometimes in reference to a poll tax and sometimes to a land tax (Wechsler on Yefet, Esth, 206 n. 234, 313 n. 728, and 315).

to shame, altars to burn incense to Ba'al (Jer 11:13). Thus were the deeds of Ahaz and Menasseh and Amon, which have been described at length. <17a> The prophet expressed amazement over these conditions by saying, *How the faithful city has become a harlot*—moreover, *she that was full of justice! Righteousness lodged in her, but now murderers* (Isa 1:21). [This happened] after David was in this place, as it is said, *David administered justice* (2 Sam 8:15). It is said of Solomon, *All Israel heard of the judgment which the king had rendered* (1 Kgs 3:28), and it is said of Jehoshaphat, *He appointed judges in the land in all the fortified cities of Judah* (2 Chr 19:5) and *Moreover in Jerusalem Jehoshaphat appointed certain Levites and priests* (2 Chr 19:8).

The prophet is amazed by the situation after everything was reversed: after justice came injustice and iniquity, as it is said, *but now murderers* (Isa 1:21). The prophets admonish them for this by saying, *Her officials within her are roaring lions* (Zeph 3:3) and *The prince and the judge ask for a bribe* (Mic 7:3) and *Your princes are rebels and companions of thieves* (Isa 1:23). Amazement such as this is also in the verse, *How He removes it from me! Among our captors He divides our fields* (Mic 2:4). There are similar verses in this book: *How the Lord in His anger has [shut away the community of Zion]* (Lam 2:1), *How the gold has grown dim* (Lam 4:1), and *How they are reckoned as earthen pots* (Lam 4:2).[13]

Lamentations 1:2

בָּכוֹ תִבְכֶּה בַּלַּיְלָה וְדִמְעָתָהּ עַל לֶחֱיָהּ אֵין־לָהּ מְנַחֵם מִכָּל אֹהֲבֶיהָ כָּל רֵעֶיהָ בָּגְדוּ
בָהּ הָיוּ לָהּ לְאֹיְבִים׃
בכא תבכי באלליל ודמעתהא עלי כ'דהא ליס להא מעזי מן כל מחביהא כל
אצחאבהא גדרו בהא צארו להא אעדא

She weeps bitterly in the night, tears on her cheeks; among all her lovers she has none to comfort her; all her friends have dealt treacherously with her, they have become her enemies.

<17b> Since he compares her to a widow at the beginning of the discourse,[14] now he says, ***she weeps bitterly***. This is the way of a widow at night: she ponders what has become of her, when she witnesses all that

[13] Each of these verses begins with the word *'ekhah* ("how!").
[14] Lam 1:1.

women know in the way of comfort and husband and children, and yet she is the opposite of that. She is aggrieved and she weeps for herself.[15] It is the same with Israel: when the people of Zion, the people of Jerusalem, the people of David, the people of Aaron, the priests, and the members of the singers witnessed in this *exile* their enemies' excellent good fortune, they wept for themselves, as it is said: *My tears have been my food day and night* (Ps 42:4/3) and *My eyes are spent with weeping* (Lam 2:11).

Most of the weeping was over the sins and the offenses because they had caused the onset of the afflictions, as it is said, *My eyes shed streams of tears, because men do not keep Your law* (Ps 119:136). Therefore, he sealed this book by saying, <18a> *Woe to us, for we have sinned!* (Lam 5:16).[16] He alludes to this verse when saying, ***she weeps bitterly in the night***. *In the night* alludes to *the darkness of exile*,[17] as it is said, *We grope for the wall like the blind, we grope like those who have no eyes* (Isa 59:10); and *He has made me dwell in darkness like the dead of long ago* (Lam 3:6). This is already mentioned in the covenant since it is said, *You shall grope at noonday* [*as the blind grope in darkness*] (Deut 28:29).[18]

She has none to comfort her means that she has no comforter at all among the people of the world, as it is said, *There is none to guide her among all the sons she has borne; there is none to take her by the hand among all the sons she has brought up* (Isa 51:18). Every nation enacts hostility against Israel, and Israel also enacts hostility against one another even though *baseless hatred* violates what the Lord of the worlds made obligatory for them.[19] It was on

[15] Salmon emphasizes the widow's emotional pain without recognizing her loss of social and legal status, which directly correspond to the historical context of the metaphor. As Mintz notes, "In the ancient Near East *almanah* [widow] designated not so much a woman who has lost her husband as the social status of a woman who has no legal protector and who may thus be abused with impunity. [. . .] The figure of the grieving woman who remains forlornly in place while her sons are taken captive to a far-off land mirrors the simultaneous stasis and dispersion that were Israel's fate" (*Ḥurban*, 24–25).

[16] Salmon uses this verse as the refrain for Lam 5.

[17] Hebr. *ḥoshekh galut*. The trope of the "darkness of exile" recurs throughout Karaite literature. See, e.g., Yefet's interpretation of Ps 90:16–17 (in Frank, *Search Scripture Well*, 197) or the introduction to Yefet's commentary on Exodus, where he also invokes Isa 59:10: "For exile is like darkness and the shadow-of-death and men walk in it like the blind, as it is said (Isaiah 59:10): 'We grope for the wall like the blind' " (qtd. in Polliack, "Rethinking Karaism," 92).

[18] For Salmon, Isa 59:10 fulfills the threat of Deut 28:29.

[19] Hebr. *śin'at ḥinnam* (vain or unjustified hatred). In rabbinic texts, *śin'at ḥinnam*, particularly among Jews, is presented as the reason behind the destruction of the Second Temple. The *locus classicus* is BT Yoma 9b: "However, considering that the people during the Second Temple period were engaged in Torah study, observance of mitzvoth, and acts of kindness, and that they did not perform the sinful acts that were performed in the First Temple, why was the Second Temple destroyed? It was destroyed due to the fact that there was wanton hatred (*śin'at ḥinnam*) during that period. This comes to teach you that the sin of wanton hatred (*śin'at ḥinnam*) is equivalent to the three severe

account of deeds like these that we deserved an extended sojourn in *exile*, as it is said, *Therefore justice is far from us, and righteousness does not overtake us* [. . .] *for our transgressions are multiplied before You* (Isa 59:9, 12).

All her friends have dealt treacherously with her, they have become her enemies means the Assyrians and the Babylonians and all those who were on their side. It is said through Ezekiel, *There were two women, the daughters of one mother* (Ezek 23:2). This means the ten tribes and the kingdom of Judah, which were connected by virtue of being born of one mother, who was Sarah, <18b> as it is said, *and to Sarah who bore you* (Isa 51:2). [Ezekiel] said the meaning of *the daughters of one mother* alludes to the verse *Your father was an Amorite, and your mother a Hittite* (Ezek 16:3) in the sense that they were reared by the Hittites when their deeds imitated [those of the Hittites]. He noted what came before their rebellions, during their youth in Egypt, as it is said, *They played the harlot in Egypt; they played the harlot in their youth* (Ezek 23:3). Then he explained their names by saying, *Oholah was the name of the elder and Oholibah the name of her sister* (Ezek 23:4). With the name Oholah, he eloquently expresses that she is Samaria.[20] With Oholibah, he alludes to Jerusalem, as it is said, *And Oholibah is Jerusalem* (Ezek 23:4).

The reason that the ten tribes are called Oholah is because Shiloh used to be in the *territory of Ephraim*.[21] Then it was destroyed, as it is said, *He forsook His dwelling at Shiloh* (Ps 78:60). Then He favored Jerusalem with His glory, as it is said, *and Oholibah is Jerusalem* (Ezek 23:4)—that is to say, "the one in whom I have settled"—and He called Shiloh "Oholah" because of the verse, *He rejected the tent* (*'ohel*) *of Joseph, He did not choose the tribe of Ephraim* (Ps 78:67).[22] The temple of the Lord is also called a tent (*'ohel*), as in the verse, *Then he brought me to the nave, and measured the jambs; on each side six cubits was the breadth of the tent* (*'ohel*) (Ezek 41:1). <19a> He calls the older one Oholah because they are the ten tribes.[23]

transgressions [on account of which the First Temple was destroyed]: idol worship, forbidden sexual relations, and bloodshed."

[20] Arab. *faṣaḥa*, "to be eloquent." Salmon uses the verb to indicate figurative language. See also Lam 2:1, 2:4, and 5:7.

[21] Ephraim is one of the northern tribes, in the region of Samaria where Shiloh is located.

[22] Whereas the parable of Ezek 23 addresses Samaria and Jerusalem, Salmon's prooftexts focus specifically on Shiloh, an ancient cultic site located in the region of Samaria. Like Jerusalem, Shiloh was a dwelling site of God that was destroyed. See discussion in chapter 6.

[23] Hebr. *gedolah* means both "old" (Oholah being the elder sister) and "large" (the ten tribes being larger, and their territory in the north being more expansive than Judah in the south).

They became mine, and they bore sons and daughters (Ezek 23:4) because all of them were under the protection of the Mighty and Sublime, and were favored by Him, and their numbers were increasing, in the way that I explained in the beginning of this book. He now explains that Israel, after this distinction, grace, and excellence, reverted to unseemly deeds and renounced obedience, as it is said, *Oholah played the harlot while she was Mine* (Ezek 23:5). He describes that the ten tribes passionately embraced the ways (*madhāhib*) of the Assyrians; they loved them and sympathized with them, as it is said, *And she doted on her lovers the Assyrians, warriors clothed in purple, governors and commanders, all of them desirable young men, horsemen riding on horses. She bestowed her harlotries upon them, the choicest men of Assyria all of them* (Ezek 23:5–7). He explained that they would be defiled through their sympathies for them and the worship of their idols, as it is said, *And she defiled herself with all the idols of every one on whom she doted* (Ezek 23:7). That is to say, whenever a way (*madhhab*) or one of their venerated objects arouses their admiration, they [i.e., Oholah and Oholibah] are defiled by it. They did not abandon the deeds that they were introduced to in Egypt, for they were habituated to them, as it is said, *She did not give up her harlotry which she had practiced since her days in Egypt;* <19b> *for in her youth men had laid with her* (Ezek 23:8). When they abandoned obedience to God and chose the deeds of the Assyrians, God strengthened the Assyrians, as it is said, *Therefore I have delivered her into the hand of her lovers, into the hands of the Assyrians, upon whom she doted* (Ezek 23:9).

Sennacherib conquered the country of Samaria in the sixth year of King Hezekiah, as it is said, *In the fourth year of king Hezekiah, which was the seventh year of Hoshea son of Elah, king of Israel, Shalmaneser king of Assyria came up against Samaria* (2 Kgs 18:9). And the king of Assyria exiled them, as it is said, *The king of Assyria carried the Israelites away to Assyria, and put them in Halah, and on the Habor, the river of Gozan, and in the cities of the Medes* (2 Kgs 18:11). Likewise, it is also said in this account, *These uncovered her nakedness; they seized her sons and daughters; and her they slew with the sword; and she became a byword among women* [. . .] *her sister Oholibah saw this* (Ezek 23:10–11). Oholibah was obliged to reflect (*ta'tabir*) upon what happened <20a> to Oholah, and to fear God, may He be elevated. However, she did not do so; rather, she perverted herself even more than Oholah, as it is said, *Yet she was more corrupt than she in her doting and in her harlotry, which was worse than that of her sister* (Ezek 23:11). First, she imitated the act of Oholah, and she passionately embraced the ways (*madhāhib*) of the Assyrians as it is said, *She doted upon the Assyrians, governors and commanders* (Ezek 23:12). Since she was equivalent to the Assyrians, she deserved exile, as it is said: *And I saw that she was defiled; they both took the same way* (Ezek 23:13). By the grace of the Lord of hosts, He did not hasten [to punish] Oholibah, but [instead] granted her respite from the time of Hezekiah to the end of the reign of Zedekiah, and all this was *because He had compassion on His people, and on His dwelling place* (2 Chr 36:15). Then, she increased her rebellions, as it is said, *But she carried her harlotry further; she saw men portrayed upon the wall, the images of the Chaldeans portrayed in vermillion, girded with belts on their loins* (Ezek 23:14–15).

As for the location of their instruction in the hateful ways (*madhāhib*) of the Babylonians[24] it is said, *And the Babylonians came to her into the bed of love, and they defiled her with their lust; and after she was polluted by them, she turned from them in disgust* (Ezek 23:17). When these vile deeds were exposed and her evil activity was uncovered, her Lord renounced her just as He had renounced <20b> her sister, as it is said, *When she carried on her harlotry so openly and flaunted her nakedness, I turned in disgust from her, as I had turned from her sister* (Ezek 23:18). She was not satisfied with these deeds until they increased and became excessive, as it is said, *Yet she increased her harlotry, remembering the days of her youth, when she played the harlot in the land of Egypt and doted upon her paramours there, whose members were like those of asses, and whose issue was like that of horses. Thus you longed for the lewdness of your youth, when the Egyptians handled your bosom for the sake of your young breasts* (Ezek 23:19–21). Because of this, God planted the idea in the minds of the Babylonians and all the Chaldeans that they should unite against Oholibah, as it is said, *Therefore, O Oholibah, thus says the Lord GOD: "Behold, I will rouse against you your lovers from whom you turned in disgust, and I will bring them against you from every side: The Babylonians and the Chaldeans, Pekod and Shoa and Koa, and all the Assyrians with them, desirable young men, governors and commanders all of them, officers and warriors, all of them riding on horses. And they shall come against you from the north with chariots and wagons and a host of peoples; they shall set themselves against you on every side with buckler, shield, and helmet, and I will commit the judgment to them, and they shall judge you according to their judgments* (Ezek 23:22–24).

It is described that he arraigned them for the judgments of the *court*,[25] and [the sentence] was [for them] to be killed—*and dispatch them with their*

[24] A double meaning: the academies of the Rabbanites, based in Iraq, could also be referred to as "the ways" or "the schools" (*madhāhib*) of the Babylonians.

[25] Hebr. *beit din*. Note that the term is post-biblical.

swords; they shall slay their sons and daughters (Ezek 23:47); and to be burned by fire—*and your survivors shall be devoured by fire* (Ezek 23:25); and to be stoned—*and the host shall stone them with stones* (Ezek 23:47); and to be stripped of comfort, exposed—*they shall also strip you of your clothes* (Ezek 23:26); and for the Temple implements to be seized—*and take away your fair jewels* (Ezek 23:26). <21a> He severely punishes harlotry with the spear; therefore the case of Oholibah is described [the same way]: *I will direct my indignation against you, that they may deal with you in fury. They shall cut off your nose and your ears, and your survivors shall fall by the sword. They shall seize your sons and your daughters* (Ezek 23:25). Exhaustion and enfeeblement befell her because her companions betrayed her and their love turned to enmity, as it is said, ***All her friends have dealt treacherously with her, they have become her enemies*** (Lam 1:2).[26]

בָּכוֹ תִּבְכֶּה בַּלַּיְלָה [*bakho tivkeh ba-laylah*; ***She weeps bitterly in the night***]: this [syntax] is customary in Hebrew, and scholars call it the verbal noun (*maṣdar*).[27] For example: *ʾakhol toʾkhlu* (*you certainly ought to have eaten*; Lev 10:18); *ʿaloh naʿaleh* (*let us go up at once*; Num 13:30); *halokh halkhu* (*the trees once went forth*; Judg 9:8); *shamor tishmerun* (*you shall diligently keep;* Deut 6:17), and there are many [others] like these. All these calamities befell us because of the magnitude of our offenses, as it is said, *And the LORD says: "Because they have forsaken My law which I set before them, and have not obeyed My voice, or walked in accord with it"* (Jer 9:12/13).

Lamentations 1:6

וַיֵּצֵא מִבַּת־צִיּוֹן כָּל־הֲדָרָהּ הָיוּ שָׂרֶיהָ כְּאַיָּלִים לֹא־מָצְאוּ מִרְעֶה וַיֵּלְכוּ בְלֹא-כֹחַ לִפְנֵי רוֹדֵף׃
וכ'רג' מן ג'מאעה ציון כל בהג'תהא צארו רוסאהא כאלאיאיל מא וג'דו מרעה
ומצ'ו בלא קווה קדאם אלכ'אלב

[26] Salmon closes the frame on his excursus on Ezek 23 by explicitly tying it to Lam 1:2; elsewhere in the commentary he does not make explicit the connection between the embedded commentary and the main verse. Note that Salmon does not address, on its own terms, the violence against women that is depicted in the passage from Ezekiel. For a contemporary analysis, see Holly Morse, "'Judgment Was Executed upon Her, and She Became a Byword Among Women' (Ezek 23:10): Divine Revenge Porn, Slut-Shaming, Ethnicity, and Exile in Ezekiel 16 and 23," in *Women and Exilic Identity in the Hebrew Bible*, ed. Katherine E. Southwood and Martien A. Halvorson-Taylor, *LHBOT* 631 (New York: T&T Clark, 2018), 129–154.

[27] On the tendency for Karaites (cf. Saadia) to render the Hebr. infinitive construct as the Arab. verbal noun (*maṣdar*), see Meira Polliack, *The Karaite Tradition of Arabic Bible Translation: A Linguistic and Exegetical Study of Karaite Translations of the Pentateuch for the Tenth and Eleventh Centuries CE*, EJM 17 (Leiden: Brill, 1997), 121–26.

From the community of Zion has departed all her majesty. Her princes have become like harts that find no pasture; they fled without strength before the pursuer.[28]

He exiled [the community of Zion] and His majesty, which was the *glory* (*kavod*) of the LORD God of Israel for the people of Zion.[29] This is the most agonizing thing that afflicted the heart of Israel, for God had made [His *glory*] dwell in the midst of Israel so that Israel would be honored over the people of the world because of it. It is said about [His *glory*]: *For how shall it be known that I have found favor in Your sight, I and Your people? Is it not in Your going with us?* (Exod 33:16). It was through the intercession of Moses our master that God made [His *glory*] dwell in the midst of Israel. But when they chose to rebel, <30b> God made four *living creatures* and [four] *wheels* appear to Ezekiel in order to carry the *glory* away, and He exiled them from the fifth year of *the exile of Jehoiachin* to the sixth year.[30] He had compassion for them, so that perhaps they would return and repent. But when they did not repent, it was said, *In the sixth year, in the sixth month, on the fifth day of the month, I sat in my house* (Ezek 8:1).

In this account, the *glory* ascended from upon *the dome*, from between the two *cherubim*, and came to be upon the single *cherub*. Then it ascended from upon the *cherub* to the threshold of the Temple, as it is said, *Now the glory of the God of Israel had gone up from the cherubim on which it rested to the threshold of the house* (Ezek 9:3). Then it ascended from the platform of the house until it came to be upon the firmament which was upon the

[28] Cf. RSV: "From the daughter of Zion has departed all her majesty. Her princes have become like harts that find no pasture; they fled without strength before the pursuer." Salmon and Yefet both translate Hebr. *hadara* ("majesty") as Arab. *bahja* ("splendor"); Saadia renders it with the synonym *bahā'* ("splendor, brilliancy"). Salmon explains that *bahja* indicates the glory (Hebr. *kavod*) or divine presence.

[29] Salmon may be unique among the Arab. translators in making a connection between the Hebr. terms *hadara* ("majesty") and *kavod* ("glory"), and the bulk of his comment hangs on this identification. Al-Fāsī does not present this reading in his entry on h/d/r (vol I, 425). He includes Ps 145:5 (*hadar kevod hodekha*; "the majestic glory of your splendor") among his prooftexts, but without commenting on any relationship between *kavod* and *hadar*. Neither does Yefet b. ʿEli discuss the divine glory in his treatment of this verse; instead, he lists various esteemed persons who departed from Zion. Salmon offers this reading as a secondary interpretation at the end of his comment here: "When the *glory* was transferred, all the majesty was transferred with it, including the majesty of kingship, the majesty of the elders, and the majesty of the name of Israel."

[30] Hebr. *hayyot* (living creatures) and *'ofannim* (wheels); see Ezekiel's vision of the chariot (Ezek 1:4–28).

head of the living creatures. Then it stopped at the eastern gate of the house of the LORD, as it is said, *Then the glory of the LORD went forth from the threshold of the house, and stood over the cherubim. And the cherubim lifted their wings and mounted up from the earth in my sight as they went forth, with the wheels beside them; and they stood at the door of the east gate of the house of the LORD; and the glory of the God of Israel was over them* (Ezek 10:18–19). Then it was transferred away from the eastern gate to the center of the town, as it is said, <31a> *Then the cherubim lifted up their wings, with the wheels beside them; and the glory of the God of Israel was over them* (Ezek 11:22).

We learn that this transfer [of the *glory*] to the center of the town was from two directions. One of them is [learned from] the statement, *and the cherubim lifted their wings*, but it does not say from where or to where [the *cherubim* went]. However, since the last one arrived at the eastern gate, you learn that the transfer was from the eastern gate to *the midst of the city*.[31] The second direction is [learned from] the statement, *and the glory of the LORD went up from the midst of the city, and stood upon the mountain which is on the east side of the city* (Ezek 11:23). This is what indicates that the transfer from the eastern gate was to the center of the city, and from the center of the city it was transferred to the Mount of Olives—which is Jerusalem from the eastern direction[32]—and from the Mount of Olives it was transferred to the gate of the Garden of Eden, as it is said, *I will return again to My place* (Hos 5:15).[33] The dwelling place of the *glory* since ancient times was there, as it is said, *And at the east of the Garden of Eden He placed the cherubim* (Gen 3:24). The verse *And at the east of the Garden of Eden He placed*[34] serves to indicate that the gate of the Garden of Eden faces toward the east. When the *glory* was transferred, all the majesty was transferred with it, including the majesty of kingship, the majesty of the elders, and the majesty of the name of Israel, <31b> about which it is said, *And your renown went forth among the nations because of your*

[31] "The midst of the city": here in Hebr. (*tokh ha-ʿir*) and below in Arab. (*wasṭ al-qarya*).

[32] This parenthetical clause may be Salmon's personal geographic observation, inserted into a set homily about the departure of the divine glory at the time of Israel's exile.

[33] The Mount of Olives was a site of Jewish ritual and liturgical practice from the time of the Arab conquest. See Moshe Gil, "Aliya and Pilgrimage in the Early Arab Period (634–1009)," *The Jerusalem Cathedra* 3 (1983), 169–71.

[34] Salmon leaves open the possibility of a play on words with the Hebr. verb *va-yashken*: not that God placed (transitive) but that God was placed (intransitive), in the sense that God resided there.

beauty, for it was perfect through the splendor which I had bestowed upon you (Ezek 16:14).[35]

Her princes have become like harts. This is because Israel has been likened to harts on the basis of the intensity of their thirst, as it is said, *As a hart longs for flowing streams* [*so longs my soul for You, O God*] (Ps 42:2/1). The reason for likening Israel to harts is that it is in the nature of harts to eat vipers, which are extremely poisonous.[36] When harts consume them, they become hot and urgently seek out water. Yet when they come to streams of water, they do not drink immediately, for God has instilled it in their nature not to drink immediately. When they do drink immediately, they suffer diarrhea and die. So now, seeing water, they remain thirsty for a while, unable to drink; all the same, they cry out and make a clamor.[37] Thus, Israel during this exile is likened to them. The Lord's Torah and the words of the prophets are likened to water, and now they are thirsting for wisdom, when there is much conflict and discord among them, just as it is said, *"Behold, the days are coming," says the Lord GOD, "when I will send a famine on the land; not a famine of bread, nor a thirst for water, but of hearing the words of the LORD"* (Amos 8:11).[38]

Without strength before the pursuer. This means <32a> that when the enemies assailed them, they did not have the strength to flee or to escape, as it

[35] For parallel versions, see *Lam R*, proem 26 and *PdRK*, 13. Note also that this last part returns to the verse at hand (Lam 1:6). When the Glory was transferred, so was "all the majesty." Salmon considers kingship, the elders, and the name of Israel to be majesties. Yefet b. 'Eli advances this reading from the start of his comment on Lam 1:6.

[36] Harts were known as predators of snakes from ancient times, and medieval bestiaries depicted harts' behaviors in finding, drawing out, trampling, and consuming poisonous snakes. See, e.g., the description of Isidore of Seville: "[Deer] are antagonistic to serpents; when they sense themselves burdened with infirmity, they draw the serpents from their caves with the breath from their nostrils, and having overcome the malignancy of the poison, the deer are restored to health by eating the serpents"; see Stephen A. Barney et al., eds., The Etymologies *of Isidore of Seville* (Cambridge: Cambridge University Press, 2006), 248 (= Book XII: 1,18).

[37] Yefet ben 'Eli also reports that harts become desperate for water after eating poisonous snakes. However, Yefet explains that when they find water, they drink it and their thirst abates; see Miriam Goldstein, "The Beginnings of the Transition from *Derash* to *Peshat* as Exemplified in Yefet ben 'Eli's Comment on Psa. 44:24," in *Exegesis and Grammar in Medieval Karaite Texts*, JSSSupp 13, ed. Geoffrey Khan (Oxford: Oxford University Press, 2001), 60–61. Salmon's explanation that God has made it their nature not to drink anticipates his theological application of this simile to Israel later in this comment.

[38] Salmon presents the same explanation in his comment to Ps 42:2/1, with the addition there of a range of explanations for the comparison between God's word and water: "Some of the scholars say that the word of God (*kalām allah*) is compared to water because God made the water free (*mubāḥ*) for the *children of Adam*, as it is said, '*Ho, everyone who thirsts, come to the waters; and he who has no money, come, buy and eat!*' (Isa 55:1) and *But the word is very near you* (Deut 30:14).

Another exegete (*mufassir*) said the meaning of this [verse] is that water comes down from the heavens, just as the word of God comes down from the heavens, as it is said, *Out of heaven He let you hear His voice* (Deut 4:36).

is said, *Flight shall perish from the swift, and the strong shall not retain his strength, nor shall the mighty save his life; he who handles the bow shall not stand, and he who is swift of foot shall not save himself, nor shall he who rides the horse save his life; and he who is stout of heart among the mighty shall flee away naked in that day," says the LORD* (Amos 2:14–16). And all these calamities overtook our fathers because of their many rebellions, as it is said, *And the LORD says: "Because they have forsaken My law which I set before them, and have not obeyed My voice, or walked in accord with it"* (Jer 9:12/13).

Lamentations 1:8

חֵטְא חָטְאָה יְרוּשָׁלַם עַל־כֵּן לְנִידָה הָיָתָה כָּל־מְכַבְּדֶיהָ הִזִּילוּהָ כִּי־רָאוּ עֶרְוָתָהּ
גַּם־הִיא נֶאֶנְחָה וַתָּשָׁב אָחוֹר:
כ'טא אכ'טת ירו עלי ד'לך לשרידה צארת כל מכרמיהא חקרוהא אן נט'רו
עורתהא איצ'א הי תנהדת ורג'עת קהקרי

Jerusalem sinned grievously, therefore she came to wander; all who honored her despise her, for they have seen her nakedness; yea, she herself groans, and turns her face away.[39]

Another said: Since God gave the people of the world some of the commandments through Adam, and some of them through Noah, and some of them through Abraham, and He completed [giving them] all through Moses, so that the entirety became the Torah. In the same way, water falls [from the heavens] a little at a time but [becomes] abundant when it collects. He said: Therefore, the word of God is compared to water.

Another said: When water flows downward a bit at a time it turns into a great river. In the same way, a person studies a thing continuously, so that he becomes knowledgeable. Therefore, the word of God is compared to water.

Another said: Water does not adhere to an elevation. In the same way, only those who humble themselves acquire the word of God.

Another said: Only a thirsty person benefits from drinking water. In the same way, the word of God requires that a person long for it with love and desire.

Another said: Just as with water—the noblest person is not embarrassed to seek it from the lowliest people, so it is with the word of God—the king is obligated to set an example and seek it from the lowliest of people without becoming embarrassed.

Another said: Just as it is with water—one who does not swim well in it enters it without looking and perishes, so it is with the word of God—one who interprets it nonliterally (*min ta'wīlihi*) without knowledge perishes, as it is said: *For the ways of the Lord are right* (Hos 14:10/9).

So he says now, comparing the hart who clamors over streams of waters, seeking to drink: we are likewise in this exile, clamoring and crying out, seeking the truths of Your book, as it is said, *They wander from sea to sea,* [*and from north to west; they shall run to and fro, to seek the word of the LORD, but they shall not find it*]. *In that day the fair virgins and the young men shall faint for thirst* (Amos 8:12–13)."

[39] Cf. RSV: "Jerusalem sinned grievously, therefore she became filthy (*nidah*)." The Hebr. *nidah* (more commonly *niddah*) refers to impurity, often in the context of menstrual impurity. Salmon prefers the broader meaning of the root—to depart, stray, or wander—which he justifies later. On

<36b> In the phrases "Jerusalem sinned grievously" (Lam 1:8) and *Jerusalem remembers* (Lam 1:7), [the word Jerusalem] alludes to the people of Jerusalem.[40] There are many [verses] such as these: *But Zion said, "The LORD has forsaken me"* (Isa 49:14) and, *Saying to Zion, "You are my people"* (Isa 51:16), and many [verses] are likewise. The verse *Jerusalem sinned grievously* alludes to this also, in order to teach that God did not cause whatever befell Israel—in this case, the magnitude of these calamities—to befall them. Rather, it was because their sins increased, as it is said, *Then He said to me, "The guilt of the house of Israel and Judah is exceedingly great; the land is full of blood, and the city full of injustice; for they say, 'The LORD has forsaken the land, and the LORD does not see.' As for Me,* <37a> *My eye will not spare, nor will I have pity, but I will requite their deeds upon their heads"* (Ezek 9:9–10).

Know that God explained in His holy books, through His prophets, the magnitude of the sins of the house of Israel and Judah in order to instruct (*yuʿallim*) *the generations to come* that everything that God did to Israel with respect to this *exile* was proper, equitable, and just, because they had transgressed all the *commandments*. All the sins of Israel and Judah, among other things, are in a single account; he made them the introduction (*ṣadr*) to the *exile* of Hoshea ben Elah and the *ten tribes*:[41]

And this was so, because the people of Israel had sinned against the LORD their God, who had brought them up out of the land of Egypt from under the hand of Pharaoh king of Egypt, and had feared other gods and walked in the customs of the nations whom the LORD drove out before the people of Israel, and in the customs which the kings of Israel had introduced. And the people of Israel did secretly against the LORD their God things that were not right. They built for themselves high places at all their towns, from watchtower to fortified city; they set up for themselves pillars and Asherim on every high hill and under every green tree; and there they burned incense on all the high places, as the nations did whom the LORD carried away before them. And they did wicked things, provoking the LORD to anger, and they served idols, of which the LORD had said to them, "You shall not do this." Yet the LORD warned Israel and Judah by every prophet and

menstrual impurity in ancient context, see Charlotte Elisheva Fonrobert, *Menstrual Purity: Rabbinic and Christian Reconstructions of Biblical Gender* (Stanford, Calif.: Stanford UP, 2000). On intersections between medieval Jewish and Islamic traditions on menstruation, see Haggai Mazuz, "Midrashic Influence on Islamic Folklore: The Case of Menstruation," *Studia Islamica* 108, no. 2 (2013): 189–201.

[40] Salmon cites the incipit from Lam 1:8 in Arab. and the incipit from Lam 1:7 in Hebr.

[41] On the "exile of Hoshea" see the list of the Ten Exiles in Salmon's excursus to Lam 2:4.

every seer, saying, "Turn from your evil ways and keep My commandments and My statutes, in accordance with all the law which I commanded your fathers, <37b> *and which I sent to you by My servants the prophets. But they would not listen, but were stubborn, as their fathers had been, who did not believe in the LORD their God. They despised His statutes, and His covenant that He made with their fathers, and the warnings which He gave them. They went after false idols, and became false, and they followed the nations that were round about them, concerning whom the LORD had commanded them that they should not do like them. And they forsook all the commandments of the LORD their God, and made for themselves molten images of two calves; and they made an Asherah, and worshiped all the host of heaven, and served Baʿal. And they burned their sons and their daughters as offerings, and used divination and sorcery, and sold themselves to do evil in the sight of the LORD, provoking Him to anger. Therefore the LORD was very angry with Israel, and removed them out of his sight; none was left but the tribe of Judah only. Judah also did not keep the commandments of the LORD their God, but walked in the customs which Israel had introduced. And the LORD rejected all the descendants of Israel, and afflicted them, and gave them into the hand of spoilers, until He had cast them out of His sight. When He had torn Israel from the house of David they made Jeroboam the son of Nebat king. And Jeroboam drove Israel from following the LORD and made them commit great sin. The people of Israel walked in all the sins which Jeroboam did;* <38a> *they did not depart from them, until the LORD removed Israel out of His sight, as He had spoken by all His servants the prophets. So Israel was exiled from their own land to Assyria until this day* (2 Kgs 17:7–23).[42]

This is established in the rest of the prophetic books (*al-kutub al-munzala*):

With their backs to the Temple of the LORD, and their faces toward the east, worshiping the sun toward the east (Ezek 8:16);

And He said to me, "Go in, and see the vile abominations that they are committing here." So I went in and saw; and there, portrayed upon the wall round about, were all kinds of creeping things, and loathsome beasts, and all the idols of the house of Israel. And before them stood seventy men of the elders of the house of Israel, with Jaazaniah the son of Saphan standing among them. Each had his censer in his hand, and the smoke of the cloud of incense went up. Then He said to me, "Son of man, have you seen what the elders of the house of Israel are doing in the dark, every man in his rooms of pictures? For they say, 'The

[42] This long citation accords with Salmon's preference for providing historical background through biblical citation rather than his own prose account.

LORD does not see us, the LORD has forsaken the land.'" He said also to me, "You will see still greater abominations which they commit." Then he brought me to the entrance of the north gate of the house of the LORD; and behold, there sat women weeping for <38b> *Tammuz* (Ezek 8:9–14);

Then He said to me, "Have you seen this, O son of man? Is it too slight a thing for the house of Judah to commit the abominations which they commit here, that they should fill the land with violence, and provoke Me further to anger? Lo, they put the branch to their nose (Ezek 8:17);

Even in My house I have found their wickedness (Jer 23:11);

In the entrance, was this image of jealousy (Ezek 8:5);

The sojourner suffers extortion in your midst; the fatherless and the widow are wronged in you. There are men in you who slander to shed blood, and men in you who eat upon the mountains; men commit lewdness in your midst. In you men uncover their fathers' nakedness; in you they humble women who are unclean in their impurity. One commits abomination with his neighbor's wife; another lewdly defiles his daughter-in-law; another in you defiles his sister, his father's daughter (Ezek 22:7; 9–11).

A man and his father go in to the same maiden [. . .] *they lay themselves down beside every altar upon garments taken in pledge* (Amos 2:7–8);

And there were also male cult prostitutes in the land (1 Kgs 14:24);

A conspiracy of her prophets in the midst of her are like a roaring lion tearing the prey; they have devoured human lives; they have taken treasure and precious things; they have made many widows in the midst of her. Her priests have done violence to My law and have profaned My holy things; they have made no distinction between the holy and the common, neither have they taught the difference between the unclean and the clean, and they have disregarded My Sabbaths, so that I am profaned among them. Her princes in the midst of her are like wolves tearing the prey, shedding blood, destroying lives to get dishonest gain. And her prophets have daubed for them with whitewash, seeing false visions and divining lies for them, saying, "Thus says the Lord GOD," when the LORD has not spoken. The people of the land have practiced extortion and committed robbery; they have oppressed the poor and needy, and have extorted from the sojourner without redress. And I sought for a man among them who should build up the wall and stand in the breach before Me for the land, that I should not destroy it, but I found none (Ezek 22:25–30).

Because of these [sins], <39a> [God declared]: *Therefore I have poured out My indignation upon them; I have consumed them with the fire of My wrath* (Ezek 22:31). It is likewise with the verse, ***Jerusalem sinned grievously,***

therefore she came to wander. Therefore she came to wander means requital (*muqābala*).[43]

Likewise, it is known that God said to them on Mount Sinai, ***I am the LORD your God*** (Exod 20:2), but they disavowed His lordship, as it is said, *They have spoken falsely of the LORD and have said, "He will do nothing"* (Jer 5:12). Therefore, He used the nations to put Israel to the test. [The nations] said to [Israel], *"Where is your God?"*[44]

He told them, ***You shall have no other gods besides Me*** (Exod 20:3), but they transgressed that, as it is said, *So the king*[45] *took counsel, and made two calves of gold* (1 Kgs 12:28). And to Judah, it was said, *For your gods have become as many as your cities, O Judah; and as many as the streets of Jerusalem are the altars you have set up to shame* (Jer 11:13). Therefore He established the nations of the world as rulers over us. They summon us to the worship of idols, as is known from the account of Nebuchadnezzar: *Now if you are ready to fall down and worship the image* (Dan 3:15). Ahasuerus commanded prostration and obeisance to Haman in just the same way.[46] Daniel refused to pray to him [i.e., Nebuchadnezzar] just as [Mordechai refused to follow Ahasuerus's command]. Since Hananiah, Mishael, Azariah, Mordechai, and Daniel had faith in the Merciful One, God saved them from their enemies by celestial commands. Likewise, it is known <39b> that Edom demanded that Israel worship the cross, abandon circumcision, and dissolve the Sabbath, just like the *troubles* and the *destructions* that occurred in the kingdom of Greece.[47]

[43] Salmon emphasizes the correlation between cause and effect in matters of sin and punishment. The sin of departing from divine command is requited with the punishment of wandering in exile. What follows this pronouncement is a homily on the Ten Commandments. A similar, though much briefer, discussion appears in *PdRK*, 13. There, the opening words of the book of Jeremiah—*These are the words of Jeremiah*—are read so that *divrei* ("words") is understood to mean *debaray* ("My words," namely, the Ten Commandments). The Midrash then lists a single biblical verse for each commandment to prove that the Israelites had violated it. In six cases, the prooftext there matches the one that Salmon uses in this homily. See my discussion in chapter 3.

[44] Hebr. *'ayeh 'eloheykhem* ("Where is your [pl.] God?"), likely a reference to Ps 42:4/3, *'ayeh 'eloheykha* ("Where is your [sg.] God?").

[45] I.e., Jeroboam.

[46] See Esth 3:2.

[47] These examples relate to each of the four kingdoms: Nebuchadnezzar represents Babylon, Ahasuerus represents Persia and Media, the representation of Edom corresponds to Rome or Christianity (this conflation is present already in rabbinic sources), while Greece is listed at the end. Salmon returns to the image of the four kingdoms in his comment to Lam 3:20, which incorporates Pss 42–43; there he includes the kingdom of Ishmael. On Salmon's treatment of the four kingdoms, see Haggai Ben-Shammai, "The Attitude of Some Early Karaites Towards Islam," in *Studies in Medieval Jewish History and Literature*, vol. 2, ed. Isadore Twersky (Cambridge, Mass.: Harvard University Press, 1984), 8–12. Cf. Salmon's later contemporary, Sahl b. Maṣliaḥ, who arranges the four kingdoms differently in his epistle to Jacob ben Samuel: "They slew my sons, did Babylon's lion, Media, Persia the evildoer, Greece, and Macdeon the malefactor, Ishmael, and Edom the witless" (*KA*, 113).

He said on Mount Sinai, ***You shall not take the name of the LORD your God in vain*** (Exod 20:7). Yet they transgressed that, as it is said, *Though they say, "As the LORD lives," yet they swear falsely* (Jer 5:2). Therefore God most high enclosed us in the hand of the nations. They reproached us and He made their right hand mighty, and they said, "or I will be a Jew (*yahudi*)," just as the psalmist lamented over us when he said, *All the day my enemies taunt me, those who deride me use my name for a curse* (Ps 102:9/8).[48]

The LORD said on Mount Sinai, ***Remember the Sabbath day, to keep it holy*** (Exod 20:8). Our fathers transgressed this *commandment*,[49] as it is said, *You have despised My holy things, and profaned My Sabbaths* (Ezek 22:8); and *In those days I saw in Judah men treading wine presses on the Sabbath day* [. . .] *"What is this evil thing which you are doing, profaning the Sabbath day?"* (Neh 13:15, 17). In Israel today, one defiles[50] the Sabbath by leaving fire in his dwelling place on the Sabbath day; the lamp lit and food cooked for the Sabbath; carrying burdens; reading from foreign books;[51] taking up useless levies;[52] safeguarding their wealth on the Sabbath day; practicing a profession and earning money thereby on the Sabbath day; playing chess and backgammon; <40a> clapping,[53] *zundaba*,[54] singing and crowds; toasting to someone's health;[55] collecting herbs in the walls and the trees; swimming in water; carrying construction tools on the Sabbath day in the concourse, like a candelabra or a lamp and whatever is in that form; *discussing secular matters*;[56] going to a place other than that of prayer and reading; walking around in the marketplaces and congregating on the side streets. All these activities

48 This phrase seems to be the authenticating element of an oath formula, along the lines of "What I swear is true, or I will be a Jew." Salmon's remark here repeats his comment to Ps 102:9/8, where he describes the nations mocking the "vile deeds" of Israel and swearing oaths before witnesses in which being a Jew is the curse that would befall a person who makes a false oath (Salmon, Pss 90–106). The phrase could also indicate a slur in which "Jew" refers to those who break oaths.

49 "Commandment"—Hebr. *miṣvah*; cf. Arab. *farḍ* in the following 6 commandments of Salmon's excursus.

50 Reading *yabdhal* for *yabdal*; see Blau, *Dictionary*, 35.

51 *Al-kutub al-barāniyya*. Salmon's condemnation of foreign books is a prominent theme within his commentary on Ecclesiastes (see esp. his comments to Eccl 3:13 and 12:12 in Robinson, *Asceticism*, 304 and 586–90). The core of Salmon's denunciation seems to be that "any speculation in and occupation with any book other than the books of the prophets is forbidden [*ḥarām*] for Israel, for it leads to the beliefs of the Gentiles" (ibid., 588).

52 *Al-fasā'iq al-mahdūra*; see Blau, *Dictionary*, 503.

53 *Tafsīq*; see Blau, *Dictionary*, 298.

54 Meaning unclear. The term appears only in MSS BL Or. 2516 and BL Or. 2515 (= A and B of Abdul-Karim's edition); but not in BN Hebr. 295 or JTSA Ms. Mic. 3362 (= P and J of Abdul-Karim's edition).

55 On Karaite prohibitions on socializing on the Sabbath, see Hoenig, "An Interdict Against Socializing on the Sabbath," *JQR* 62 (1971): 77–83.

56 Hebr. *śiḥat ḥullin* ("mundane conversation"), a post-biblical moralizing term.

are forbidden (*ḥarām*) on the Sabbath.[57] Therefore, God strengthened the nations over us so that they would vanquish us on account of our Sabbaths and holidays, in our riding on donkeys, being lofty, and they imprisoned us and plundered what was in our homes and did not consider whether it was a Sabbath or a festival.[58]

God said on Mount Sinai: ***Honor your father and your mother*** (Exod 20:12). Israel transgressed this commandment, as it is said, *Father and mother are treated with contempt* (Ezek 22:7); and *For the son treats the father with contempt, the daughter rises up against her mother* (Mic 7:6). Therefore, we deserve to lament for ourselves and say, *We have become orphans, fatherless* (Lam 5:3).

God said on Mount Sinai, ***You shall not kill*** (Exod 20:13). We transgressed this commandment, as it is said, *Also on your skirts is found the lifeblood of the guiltless poor* (Jer 2:34).[59] We killed the prophets and among us today there are those who kill many people by slander.[60] <40b> *Woe to us, for we have sinned!* (Lam 5:16). Therefore we were met with those who spilled our blood: *They have poured out their blood like water* (Ps 79:3).[61] How many of Israel were killed in every age among the nations, and we are in great strife!

God said on Mount Sinai, ***You shall not commit adultery*** (Exod 20:14). They transgressed this commandment, as it is said: *For they are all adulterers* (Jer 9:1/2), and *When I fed them to the full, they committed adultery and trooped to the houses of harlots* [. . .], *each neighing for his neighbor's wife* (Jer 5:7–8), and *One commits abomination with his neighbor's wife* (Ezek 22:11).

57 Salmon's list of Sabbath violations reflects his sectarian perspective; many of the transgressions that he notes were considered permissible in non-Karaite Jewish communities. Salmon's contemporary Sahl b. Maṣliaḥ provides a similar list of Sabbath violations from a Karaite perspective in his epistle to Jacob b. Samuel. There he poses a rhetorical question: "How can I restrain myself when many Jews leave their houses on the Sabbath on their way to their synagogues, carrying various things, such as purses and pieces of apparel, upon their arms, while their wives wear jewelry? And as they do on weekdays, visiting from house to house, so do they also on the Sabbath" (*KA*, 116). Al-Qūmisī's list of Sabbath violations focuses on commercial activities: "They also dispatch cargo letters on the Sabbath, and do similar things that are exceedingly grievous in the sight of the Lord, for they rush around with merchandise, rich and poor, in the manner of the Gentiles, each one in Israel continually pursuing his profit out of his wares, never ceasing, his soul never satiated with running after his merchandise according to the measure of his livelihood, not even when it reaches many thousands (of dinars)" (al-Qūmisī, Sermon, 20).

58 This example also conforms to Salmon's principle of requital in kind, i.e., because the community of Israel failed to observe the Sabbaths and festivals, the nations also fail to respect the Sabbath when attacking the Jews.

59 See also Salmon's comment on Lam 4:1.

60 The referent of this allusion to a slanderer or an informant is unclear. The comment recalls rabbinic discussions about slander as a cause for the destruction of the Temple, but it is not clear who would fit this description in Salmon's own time.

61 See Salmon's commentary to Ps 79 in his excursus at Lam 2:4.

How many in Israel today commit *harlotry and adultery and incest and homosexuality*! Therefore, it happened to the first ones that *Women are ravished in Zion* (Lam 5:11), and there are many today [to whom it applies]: *You shall betroth a wife, and another man shall lie with her* (Deut 28:30).

God said on Mount Sinai, ***You shall not steal*** (Exod 20:15). We transgressed this commandment, as it is said, *Will you steal, murder, commit adultery?* (Jer 7:9). How many in Israel today overpower men for their money and kill them out of poverty, and do not fear the *LORD of hosts*? Therefore we are under the hand of the *nations, by captivity and plunder* (Dan 11:7; Ezra 9:7). *What I did not steal must I now restore?* (Ps 69:5/4); and, *Your ox shall be slain before your eyes, and you shall not eat of it* (Deut 28:31).

God said on Mount Sinai, ***You shall not bear false witness against your neighbor*** (Exod 20:16). We and our fathers transgressed <41a> this commandment, as it is said, *They bend their tongue like a bow; falsehood and not truth* (Jer 9:2/3) and, *Truth has perished, it is cut off from their lips* (Jer 7:28). Therefore the Merciful One handed us over to those who give false testimony against us, as it is said, *For false witnesses have risen against me* (Ps 27:12),[62] and *Malicious witnesses rise up; they ask me of things that I know not* (Ps 35:11).[63] [This outcome] may be witnessed when those who have power over us say to someone whose money they wish to confiscate: "You have killed so-and-so, and you have his money in your possession" [or] "You have purchased stolen goods." But this way [of bearing false witness against us] is not [even] the gravest [example of false witness], for they [also] say: *"You claim that ʿUzayr is the son of the Creator." But this is a false testimony since nothing of the kind was ever heard in Israel. Indeed, they utter a number of words against Israel, [about things] which were not created and do not exist.*[64]

[62] In his comment to Ps 27:12, Salmon renders this verse as a prayer: "See, O Lord, their lies about me, and witness that they are falsehood, untruth and malice" (Salmon, Pss 11–41).

[63] In his comment to Ps 35:11, Salmon reads this verse as a reference to "*the nations*," whom he identifies as those who slander, bear false witness, and dissimulate (Salmon, Pss 11–41).

[64] Salmon refers to Q9:30: "The Jews say that Ezra is the son of God" (*wa-qālati-l-yahūdu ʿuzayrun ibnu-llāhi*). The verse is widely invoked in polemical discourse: Muslim polemicists use it to show that Jews falsely ascribe paternity to God while Jewish polemicists use it to show that the Qurʾān contains factual errors, since Jews do not consider anyone to be the son of God. See Hava Lazarus-Yafeh, *Intertwined Worlds: Medieval Islam and Bible Criticism* (Princeton, N.J., 1992), 50–59. The phrase "Were not created and do not exist" (Hebr. *she-loʾ hayah ve-loʾ nivraʾ*) resembles one recorded in reference to Job in BT Baba Batra 15a: *loʾ hayah ve-loʾ nivraʾ ʾella mashal hayah*, "he did not exist and was not created, but was a parable." Salmon uses the phrase here to indicate that false witnesses testify about events that never occurred and have no connection to reality. The shift from Arab. to Hebr. could be explained as a tendency of Jewish exegetes to use Hebr. when engaging in anti-Islamic discourse. Note, however, that Salmon's similar comments to Lam 3:46 remain in Arab.

God said on Mount Sinai, ***You shall not covet*** (Exod 20:17). We transgressed this commandment, as it is said, *They covet fields, and seize them; and houses, and take them away* (Mic 2:2). Therefore we were dispossessed of our inheritance and our homes, as it is said, *Our inheritance has been turned over to strangers* (Lam 5:2), and *How He removes it from me! Among the rebellious He divides our fields* (Mic 2:4).

Know that there is no sin without its requital. You see [this principle demonstrated] in the report of Hezekiah when he brought the envoys of the king of Babylon into his treasury, <41b> as it is said, *And he showed them his treasure house* (Isa 39:2). God dispatched Isaiah to him, and he told him, *Behold, the days are coming, when all that is in your house, and that which your fathers have stored up till this day, shall be carried to Babylon; nothing shall be left, says the LORD. And some of your own sons, who are born to you, shall be taken away; and they shall be eunuchs in the palace of the king of Babylon* (Isa 39:6–7).

If this judgment was decreed[65] against the likes of Hezekiah the Righteous, on account of his doing this simple thing carelessly, then how many disasters will befall us, who commit how many sins every day?! We mingle with the *nations* and imitate their deeds; we aspire to study their language by means of grammar, and we squander dirhams until we learn it[66]—and we abandon the study of the holy tongue and the examination of the *LORD's commandments*![67] We occupy ourselves with eating and drinking; laughing, amusement, and singing; crowds and entourages;[68] building and trinkets and garments—and we have forgotten the destruction of Jerusalem, and we have neglected the command of God, as it is said, *Remember the LORD from afar, and let Jerusalem come into your mind* (Jer 51:50).

Surely, He clarified for us, through the righteous prophet, that whoever forgets Jerusalem "forsakes the LORD," as it is said, *but you who forsake the LORD, who forget My holy mountain* (Isa 65:11); and *if I forget you, O*

[65] For the Hebraism *jazr* as "decree," see Blau, *Dictionary*, 87.

[66] Salmon may mean that Jews are paying Muslims to instruct them in Arabic grammar and language. Beatrice Gruendler notes the story of the ninth-(?)century grammarian al-Māzinī, who rejected the tuition offer of 100 *dīnārs* by a non-Muslim who wanted to study Sībawayhi's grammatical treatise with him ("Aspects of Craft," 48 n. 62).

[67] Salmon does not criticize the study of Arab. per se, but only insofar as it takes attention away from the study of Torah and the Hebr. language. Yefet provides perspective on the instrumental value of studying Arab. in his introduction to the commentary on Exodus: "It is incumbent upon whoever reads our book that he should not criticize our words in the Arabic language, for it is not our language, but fix his attention on the meanings and objectives" (qtd. in Polliack, "Inversion," 278).

[68] Arab. *da'wāt*; see Blau, *Dictionary*, 215.

Jerusalem (Ps 137:5). This oath <42a> [to] God compelled the nation itself not to forget the destruction of Jerusalem, and therefore He goes so far as to command that the nation itself is compelled to remember the destruction of Jerusalem in every respect, even including diet, and in every prayer and in every Sabbath and festival, so that when one builds a dwelling or dons a garment or rejoices, he does nothing perfectly and completely; rather, he leaves something missing from everything that he produces so that he remembers thereby the destruction of the LORD's house, as it is said, *if I do not set Jerusalem above my highest joy!* (Ps 137:6). Whoever grieves for Jerusalem deserves to see her joy, as it is said, *Rejoice with her in joy, all you who mourn over her* (Isa 66:10). The only one who mourns over her is the one who loves her structures, as it is said, *Be glad for her, all you who love her* (Isa 66:10).[69]

Because there is requital for every sin, [Jeremiah] said, ***Jerusalem sinned grievously, therefore she came to wander*** (*lenidah*). *Lenidah* means that they became *fugitives and wanderers* (*noddim*)[70] among the *nations*, as it is said, *My God will cast them off, because they have not hearkened to Him; they shall be wanderers* (*noddim*) *among the nations* (Hos 9:17). They became *wanderers among the nations* because they wandered away from obedience to God, as it is said, *Woe to them, for they have strayed from Me! Destruction to them, for they have rebelled against Me!* (Hos 7:13).

All who honored her despise her <42b> means that all who used to esteem and revere her above all [other] nations [now] despise her and join forces against her, as it is said, *All who see me mock at me, they make mouths at me,*

[69] This passage is rooted in BT Baba Batra 60b, in which R. Joshua corrects a group of ascetics whose practices of mourning for the Second Temple are too extreme. He tells them: "My sons, come and listen to me. [...] To mourn excessively is impossible, because we do not impose on the community a hardship which the majority cannot endure, as it is written, *Ye are cursed with a curse, yet ye rob me* [*of the tithe*], *even in this whole nation* (Mal 3:9). The Sages therefore have ordained thus. A man may plaster his house, but he should leave a little bare. (How much should this be? R. Joseph says, A cubit square; to which R. Ḥisda adds that it must be by the door.) A man can prepare a full-course banquet, but he should leave out an item or two. (What should this be? R. Papa says: The hors d'oeuvre of salted fish.) A woman can put on all her ornaments, but leave off one or two. (What should this be? Rab said: [Not to remove] the hair on the temple.) For so it says, *If I forget thee, O Jerusalem, let my right hand forget, let my tongue cleave to the roof of my mouth if I remember thee not, if I prepare not Jerusalem above my chief joy*. [. . .] Whoever mourns for Zion will be privileged to see her joy, as it says, *Rejoice ye with Jerusalem etc.*" Salmon's argument seems to be that the Jerusalem Karaites practice appropriate mourning rituals even without the aid of the Talmud, while the Rabbanites fail to follow even their own traditions about mourning. See my discussion in chapter 3.

[70] Hebr., the plural form of the biblical phrase *na' va-nad*, in which God declares that Cain is cursed to be *a fugitive and a wanderer on the earth* (Gen 4:12). Salmon uses this prooftext to support his reading of *lenidah* in the verse. For Salmon, Jerusalem was not punished by becoming "impure," but rather by becoming a "wanderer" among the nations. This reading maintains Salmon's framework of reciprocal punishment: Jerusalem strayed (n/d/d) from divine command and was therefore punished by wandering (n/d/d) in exile.

they wag their heads (Ps 22:8/7), and, *But I am a worm, and no man; scorned by men, and despised by the people* (Ps 22:7/6). The nations used to esteem [Israel] on account of their obedience, as it is said, *And all the peoples of the earth shall see that you are called by the name of the LORD; and they shall be afraid of you* (Deut 28:10). When they observed [Israel's] vile deeds, their affection for them departed from their hearts. This was the case with the Assyrians, who beheld the [golden] calves and carried them off to their land.[71] Likewise, the Babylonians saw the prophet Jeremiah shackled, and they released him and none other, as Nebuzaradan said to Jeremiah, *Now, behold, I release you today from the chains on your hands* (Jer 40:4). With respect to these and similar examples, it is said, ***For they have seen her nakedness.***

Yea, she herself groans, and turns her face away. ["She"] means this nation, and all that overtook her: she was grieved by affliction and she had no comforter, and no one to take her by the hand. Therefore it is said, ***and turn her face away.*** She is requited for her deed, since he described their deeds when he said, *They have forsaken the LORD, they have despised the Holy One of Israel, they are utterly estranged* (Isa 1:4). Now it is said in the lament that she ***turns her face away.*** <43a> By way of description, it is said, *and went backward and not forward* (Jer 7:24). All this happened in Israel according to the multitude of [their] offenses, as it is said, *And the LORD says: "Because they have forsaken My law which I set before them, and have not obeyed My voice, or walked in accord with it"* (Jer 9:12/13).

Lamentations 1:12

לוא אֲלֵיכֶם כָּל־עֹבְרֵי דֶרֶךְ הַבִּיטוּ וּרְאוּ אִם־יֵשׁ מַכְאוֹב כְּמַכְאֹבִי אֲשֶׁר עוֹלַל לִי
אֲשֶׁר הוֹגָה יְהוָה בְּיוֹם חֲרוֹן אַפּוֹ׃
ליס אליכם <u>אנאדי</u> יא כל ג'איזי אלטריק אלתפתו ואנצ'רו ואן איס וג'ע[72] כוג'עי
אלד'י בטש בי אלד'י נחא אללה פי יום שדה גצ'בה

[71] Jeroboam, the first king of the northern kingdom, installed golden calves in Bethel and Dan and urged the people to worship there instead of the Temple in Jerusalem (1 Kgs 12:26–30). This action is condemned as a sin—both for Jeroboam (1 Kgs 12:30) and for the Israelites who perpetuate it (2 Kgs 10:29)—and it is recalled in the context of the deportation of the Israelites to the towns of Assyria following the fall of the northern kingdom (2 Kgs 17:6, 16). The referent of the phrase "and carried them off [*wa-ḥamalūhum*] to their land," is most likely the Israelites, who were deported (2 Kgs 17:6); a rabbinic tradition holds that the Assyrians carried off the golden calves as well (see Louis Ginzberg, *The Legends of the Jews*, vol 4:9 (Trans. Henrietta Szold; Philadelphia: Jewish Publication Society, 1968), 257).

[72] Salmon translates Hebr. *makh'ov* as Arab. *waja'* throughout; this is also the standard translation offered by al-Fāsī (vol. II, 82).

"'It is nothing to you!' I call to all you who pass by. 'Look and see if there is any sorrow like my sorrow which was brought upon me, which the LORD inflicted on the day of His fierce anger.'"

I translated *lo' 'aleykhem* as "Is it nothing to you?"[73] because often for us *lo'* [the negative] has the meaning of *ha-lo'* [the negative interrogative, i.e., "is it not?"] as in *Before their eyes, will they not* [*lo'*] *stone us?* (Exod 8:22/26); and similarly, *For now the slaughter among the Philistines—was it not* [*lo'*] *great?* (1 Sam 14:30).[74] There are many meanings of *ha-lo'*. They have also translated *lo' 'aleykhem* to mean "Heaven forbid that what befell me should befall you!"[75] Yet the first statement is more syntactically correct and more plausible.

He [i.e., Jeremiah] says, "Is it nothing to you? I call to all who pass by the road! Reflect (*i'tabirū*) on my condition and see! Did you witness what happened to me—the sorrow and the magnitude of the calamities that happened to me and to my life?"

There is no nation in the world [to whom] God communicated or for whom He revealed the prophets except for Israel![76] Or for whom He made appear divine glory and celestial fire, and *signs* <46b> and *wonders*, except for Israel! For this reason it is said, ***if there is any sorrow like my sorrow***, just as I explained in the introduction to this book, regarding the calamities that troubled the tried one—namely, Job.[77] The calamities of Israel are far greater, as I have explained. Daniel said, *by bringing upon us a great calamity; for under the whole heaven there has not been done the like of what has been*

[73] Note that Salmon's Arab. verse translation does not match the Arab. paraphrase here in the comment. In other words, Salmon translates according to the language (*lafẓ*) in his verse translation, and according to the sense (*ma'nā*) in his comment. Cf. Yefet b. Eli, who incorporates the sense into the language even within the verse translation, which he renders as *a-laysa* (the negative interrogative). Al-Qirqisānī discusses the criteria for interrogative sentences as one of his exegetical premises: "Some people are of the opinion that interrogative sentences always begin with the interrogative particle *heh* [. . .] and if this particle be missing, there is no interrogation. There are, however, many sentences of this kind without the particle in question." He supports this premise with over twenty biblical prooftexts, including Exod 8:22, as does Salmon (Qirqisāni Studies, 35). On the Arab. rendering of Hebr. rhetorical questions, see Polliack, *Karaite Tradition*, 131. See also Salmon's translation and comment to Lam 3:36, where he translates Hebr. *lo'* as Arab. *a-laysa* within the verse translation itself, probably for theological reasons.

[74] Cf. RSV: "For now the slaughter among the Philistines has not been great."

[75] This reading of Lam 1:12 appears in *Lam R*: "The Community of Israel says to the nations of the world: 'May there not come upon you what has come upon me! May there not occur to you what has occurred to me!'"

[76] Salmon asserts Jewish claims to prophecy over competing Christian and Muslim claims and implies that all prophecy has ceased during the centuries of Jewish exile.

[77] See Salmon's introduction to the commentary.

done against Jerusalem (Dan 9:12). And God said through Ezekiel, *I will do with you what I have never yet done, and the like of which I will never do again* (Ezek 5:9).

Which was brought upon me means "that which was done to me," and this is like the verse, *with whom have You dealt thus?* (Lam 2:20).

Which the LORD inflicted means that He expelled Israel from their country and their Temple, as it is said, *I will drive them out of My house* (Hos 9:15), and likewise as it is said, *He removed them with His fierce blast in the day of the east wind* (Isa 27:8). Its meaning is [expressed] in the beginning of the verse, *Has He smitten them as He smote those who smote them?* (Isa 27:7). This [verse indicates] God's benevolence to this nation, since He spared it and did not destroy it on account of the evilness of its deeds, as I have explained in the introduction to this book.[78] He said, "See My grace: is the smiting of the one who smote him like the smiting of the Lord of the worlds?" The smiter alluded to in this verse is Pharoah and his people; when they exceeded all bounds, God destroyed them completely. <47a>

אִם־כְּהֶרֶג הֲרֻגָיו הֹרָג (Isa 27:7)—"Or have they been killed as their killers were killed?" This means the Canaanites. God commanded that they be killed, and Israel killed them. Was Israel in its entirety killed, like them? That is to say, the way that God destroyed Israel was not like the destruction of Pharoah and his people, and not like [the destruction of] the Canaanites, as it is said, *The whole land shall be a desolation; yet I will not make a full end* (Jer 4:27).[79] In what follows, He also says, *I will make a full end of all the nations* (Jer 30:11).

Then it is said, *By measure* (*besa'sse'ah*), *by expulsion* (*beshalḥah*), *You did contend with them* (Isa 27:8). This means that their destruction only resembled the destruction of their enemies to a certain extent because the expression *besa'sse'ah* means "by the measure," as in *for every measure* (*se'on*; Isa 9:4/5)[80] and *a measure* (*se'ah*) *of fine meal* (2 Kgs 7:18).[81] The meaning of

[78] See the discussion of God's compassion in the first section of Salmon's introduction.

[79] Salmon emphasizes God's restraint also in his comments to Lam 3:22 (where he also invokes Jer 4:27) and Lam 4:1. This theme resurfaces in Salmon's opening remarks to Neḥamot.

[80] Salmon understands Hebr. *se'on* as Arab. *kayl*, "measure," just as it is translated by Saadia in his commentary on Job and by al-Fāsī (vol II, 97). Cf. RSV: "for every boot of the trampling warrior."

[81] Modern scholars distinguish *se'ah* from the *hapax legomenon se'on* (see, e.g., BDB 684). Yet al-Fāsī, like Salmon, lists both words in a single entry (see vol. II, 296–97). Al-Fāsī cites 2 Kgs 7:18, explaining, "This verse, by way of illustration, says that every measure (*se'on*) is measured by the measurer, with shaking, he is paid. Its meaning is, 'By the measure that you measure for your brothers, it is measured for you, with shaking—that is to say, an increase.'"

"by the measure" is, in other words, "to a certain extent." It is not in the root because *by expulsion (beshalḥah)* is like *its shoots (sheluḥoteha) spread about and passed over the sea* (Isa 16:8). *By expulsion You did contend with them* (Isa 27:8) is a statement about its branches; he means to liken Israel to a tree. He says that the destruction that happened to them was in their branches and not in their root, because expulsion (*shalḥah*) is like *its shoots* (*sheluḥoteha*) *spread abroad* (Isa 16:8). He says of its branches that He disputes with them, which is to say, He punishes them.

He removed them with His fierce blast in the day of the east wind (Isa 27:8) means that in His mercy He did not destroy them completely; rather, a large group of them remained. He drove them out into the *exile* by <47b> the hand of the enemy, which is compared to an east wind, as it is said, *The east wind, the wind of the LORD, shall come* (Hos 13:15).

On the day of His fierce anger. Because the exile was the day of the LORD's anger—as He had already established through Moses when He said, *Then My anger will be kindled against them in that day, and I will forsake them* (Deut 31:17)—all of this overtook them when they increased their rebellions, as it is said, *Who is the man so wise that he can understand this? Why is the land ruined and laid waste like a wilderness, so that no one passes through? And the LORD says: "Because they have forsaken My law which I set before them, and have not obeyed My voice, or walked in accord with it"* (Jer 9:11/12–12/13).

Lamentations 1:16

עַל־אֵלֶּה אֲנִי בוֹכִיָּה עֵינִי עֵינִי יֹרְדָה מַּיִם כִּי־רָחַק מִמֶּנִּי מְנַחֵם מֵשִׁיב נַפְשִׁי הָיוּ בָנַי שׁוֹמֵמִים כִּי גָבַר אוֹיֵב׃

עלי האולאי אנא באכיה עיני עיני מחדרה מא אן בעד ענִי מעזי מרד נפשי צארו אולאדי מסתחושין אן תג'בר אלעדו

For these things I weep; my eyes, my eyes cause water to come down;[82] for a comforter is far from me, one to revive my courage; my children are desolate, for the enemy has prevailed.[83]

[82] Salmon's translation follows that of Ibn Nūḥ, who teaches that Hebr. *yordah* ("to come down") must be rendered as Arab. ḥ/d/r II ("to cause to come down") rather than ḥ/d/r VII ("to come down") (*Diqduq*, 476–77).

[83] Cf. RSV: "For these things I weep; my eyes flow with tears."

<54a> [The morphology of] *bokhiyyah* (*weep*) is like *poriyyah* (*fruitful*; e.g., Isa 32:12); *sha'aruriyyah* (*a horrible thing*; Hos 6:10); *homiyyah* (*tumultuous*; Isa 22:2); *remiyyah* (*with slackness*; e.g., Jer 48:10); and *terumiyyah* (*a special portion*; Ezek 48:12).[84] Now he says, ***For these things I weep.*** He enumerates fifty calamities from the beginning of the book to this point.[85] He describes that they happened to the nations, and several meanings are subsumed under each of them. The first is *How lonely sits the city that was full of people! How like a widow she has become, she that was great among the nations! She that was a princess among the cities has become a vassal* (Lam 1:1). And the last of them is, *The Lord has trodden as in a wine press* (Lam 1:15). Since he began with all of these calamities and enumerated them, he now appends the following [calamities] to them, and says, ***For these things I weep.***[86]

My eyes, my eyes (*'eyniy 'eyniy*) ***flow with tears*** means continually, as in the expressions *yom yom* (*day after day*; e.g., Gen 39:10); <54b> *ba-boker ba-boker* (*every morning*; 2 Chr 13:11); and *u-va'erev ba-'erev* (*and every evening*; 2 Chr 13:11). They all [mean] continually. In other words, "I am crying endlessly in this exile; I will have no consolation until the LORD of hosts consoles me." And He will console, as it is said, *When the LORD restores the fortunes of Zion* [. . .] *then our mouths shall be filled with laughter* (Ps 126:1–2).[87] This also indicates with clear evidence that as long as we are in the *exile*—under [the conditions of] *exile*, under [His] wrath—then our mouths will not be full of joy, as it is said, *Rejoice not, O Israel! Exult not like the peoples* (Hos 9:1).

[84] Salmon designates *bokhiyya* as a feminine active participle with an irregular form. Salmon collects other biblical examples of the same phenomenon in order to demonstrate a category of verbs that follow this alternative pattern. Cf. Ibn Nūḥ, who simply states, "The *yod* in it is added. It is (in origin) *bokhah* without the addition of *yod*" (*Diqduq*, 476). Ibn Nūḥ's point hints at historical linguistics (i.e., that morphology may change over time), but his insight must be based, at some level, on a collection of examples like the one that Salmon assembled. Salmon's technique is to provide linguistic evidence without an explicit conclusion; Ibn Nūḥ's technique, in this case, is to present the conclusion without the evidence.

[85] It is not clear how Salmon has reached the number fifty, since he has not kept a running tally. The enumeration of calamities is the second of the seven purposes of Lamentations that Salmon lists in his introduction to the commentary.

[86] Hebr. *'al 'elleh* ("for these things") refers to the calamities mentioned above (an antecedent) rather than something listed afterward (a postcedent). Yefet concurs. These Karaite readings may indirectly refute Midrashic readings, in which the rabbis supplied the referent from beyond the text itself. For example, Tg. Lam identifies "these things" as the slaughter of babies and expectant mothers (see Brady, *The Rabbinic Targum*, 79); *Lam R* explains "these things" as episodes of Jewish martyrdom and persecution at the hands of the Romans (127–28). Alternatively, the Karaites may be drawn to clarify that *'al 'elleh* has an antecedent because this reading contradicts standard Hebr. usage. Such expressions normally introduce new information, as in Lam 3:20, rather than referring back to what proceeds; see Robert B. Salters, *A Critical and Exegetical Commentary on Lamentations*, ICC (London: T&T Clark, 2010), 224.

[87] Cf. RSV: "When the LORD restored the fortunes of Zion [. . .] then our mouth was filled with laughter."

The words *Rejoice not, O Israel!* obliges whoever hears them that rejoicing is not permitted for Israel when they know that God is angry with them. He already clarified the cause [of this punishment] by saying, *For you have played the harlot, forsaking your God* (Hos 9:1).

Since He would rebuke them in the time of statehood for delights and rejoicing when He advised them about what He intended to befall them, including the decree of *exile*—as it is said, *who drink wine in bowls, and anoint themselves with the finest oils, but are not grieved over the ruin of Joseph* (Amos 6:6)—then [this rebuke is] even more [appropriate] during the time of exile when the Temple is destroyed and Israel is in the land of *exile, in trouble, in reproach, in captivity and in disdain; to be mocked, to be derided, to be held in contempt and ignominy;* <55a> *to be plundered and to be despised; to be a desolation, to be crosswise, barren, spurned, forsaken, rejected, contemned, abhorred; sighing, groaning, abandoned, forgotten, slain, consumed, delivered over to the hand of the impudent. It is all the more incumbent upon us to mourn and wail and lament over ourselves, and over the weight of our sins and our offenses and the gravity of our transgressions, and the length of our exile, and the impudence of our faces and the stiffness of our necks*[88] *and the gloom of our darkness, and our iron fetters, until He looks down and sees* (Lam 3:50) *our affliction, so that He looks from the heavens and sees our oppression, so that He looks from the lofty abode of His holiness and turns to us in mercy and grace and compassion; until a spirit from on high strips us bare. Our brothers, Israelites: return and repent! Come together and hold assembly* (Zeph 2:1). *Come, let us return to the LORD; for He has torn, that He may heal us; He has stricken, and He will bind us up* (Hos 6:1). *Come now, let us reason together, says the LORD* (Isa 1:18). *Recall it to mind, you transgressors* (Isa 46:8)! *Remember the LORD from afar, and let Jerusalem come into your mind* (Jer 51:50)! *Rend your hearts, not your garments* (Joel 2:13)! *Return to me with all your heart* [*with fasting, with weeping, and with mourning*] (Joel 2:12)! *Return, O faithless children* (Jer 3:14)! *Return, O Israel, to the LORD your God* (Hos 14:2/1)! *My brother, do not be slow* (Judg 18:9). *How long will you lie there, O sluggard* (Prov 6:9)? <55b> *How long will you waver, O faithless daughter?* (Jer 31:21/22).[89]

For a comforter is far from me. In other words, "How shall I be consoled, when the consoler is far from me? I have no one to console me, to restore my

[88] For this expression, see, e.g., Exod 32:9.

[89] Ben-Shammai considers this Hebrew section to be an embedded *piyyuṭ* ("Poetic Works and Lamentations," 207–208).

soul. Therefore I say openly that this nation cannot be comforted in this *exile*, as it is said, *She refuses to be comforted for her children, because they are not* (Jer 31:14/15); and *In the night my hand is stretched out without wearying; my soul refuses to be comforted* (Ps 77:3/2).[90] *My children are desolate* (Lam 1:13) means they have been deserted by all things that are noble and splendid because the enemy became strong, as it is said, *For the enemy has prevailed.* The strength of the enemy and our [own] weakness are due to the multiplicity of our offenses, as it is said, *And the LORD says: "Because they have forsaken My law which I set before them, and have not obeyed My voice, or walked in accord with it"* (Jer 9:12/13).

Lamentations 1:18

צַדִּיק הוּא יְהוָה כִּי פִיהוּ מָרִיתִי שִׁמְעוּ־נָא כָל־הָעַמִּים וּרְאוּ מַכְאֹבִי בְּתוּלֹתַי וּבַחוּרַי הָלְכוּ בַשֶּׁבִי׃
עאדל <u>מנצף</u> הו אללה אן אמרה כ'אלפת אסמעו <u>אלאן</u> יא כל אלשעוב ואנט'רו וג'עי עואתקי ושבאני סארו פי אלסבי

Just, <u>equitable</u> is God;[91] I have rebelled against His command. Hear, <u>now</u>, all you peoples, and see my pain; my young girls[92] and boys have gone into captivity.[93]

This verse makes it obligatory to acknowledge (*iqrār*) God's justice and His equanimity in every situation. Likewise, the friend (*walīy*) said, *Yet You have been just in all that has come upon us* (Neh 9:33)[94] so that we would know that all of the afflictions that befell us were [caused] by our rebellions. For this reason it is said, ***I have rebelled against His command***; and *But they rebelled and grieved His holy Spirit* (Isa 63:10); and *Because I have been very rebellious* (Lam 1:20). The purpose of his saying ***But hear, all you peoples*** is to inform the nation that this affliction surely happened to them because

[90] Salmon invokes Ps 77:3/2 also in the introduction to the commentary (where he urges reflection [*iʿtibār*] on biblical examples that teach the obligation of mourning) and in his excursus at Lam 3:20.

[91] Arab. *ʿādil munṣif huwa llāh*. Ms. Or. 2516 gives Arab. "God"; other MSS retain Hebr. "LORD."

[92] Arab. *ʿawātiq*, "young girls" (Hava, 444).

[93] Cf. RSV: "The LORD is in the right, for I have rebelled against His word; but hear, all you peoples, and behold my suffering; my maidens and my young men have gone into captivity."

[94] Salmon invokes the same prooftext at Lam 3:42, where he also refers to Nehemiah as *walīy*.

of their contravention [against] God. If it were not for that, this nation would not have experienced the subjugation that they did. <57a>

My maidens and my young men [indicates] the fulfillment of what God set forth in the covenant when He said, *You shall beget sons and daughters, but they shall not be yours; for they shall go into captivity* (Deut 28:41). God decreed upon them four successive retributions,[95] as it is said, *Those who are for pestilence, to pestilence, and those who are for the sword, to the sword; those who are for famine, to famine, and those who are for captivity, to captivity* (Jer 15:2).

Another verse also describes four punishments: *I will appoint over them four kinds of destroyers, says the LORD: the sword to slay, the dogs to tear, and the birds of the air and the beasts of the earth to devour and destroy* (Jer 15:3). The punishments are described another way in another place: *As if a man fled from a lion, and a bear met him; or went into the house and leaned with his hand against the wall, and a serpent bit him* (Amos 5:19). And: *for they proceed from evil to evil* (Jer 9:2/3); and *though they escape from the fire, the fire shall yet consume them* (Ezek 15:7). All these trials overtook us because we abandoned the law (*torah*) of God,[96] as it is said, *And the LORD says: "Because they have forsaken My law which I set before them, and have not obeyed My voice, or walked in accord with it"* (Jer 9:12/13).

[95] Arab. *niqam mutarādifa*. The term *mutarādifa* can mean either successive or synonymous.
[96] This formulation recalls Karaite accusations that the Rabbanites have forsaken Torah in favor of Talmud.

Lamentations 2

Lamentations 2:1

אֵיכָה יָעִיב בְּאַפּוֹ אֲדֹנָי אֶת־בַּת־צִיּוֹן הִשְׁלִיךְ מִשָּׁמַיִם אֶרֶץ תִּפְאֶרֶת יִשְׂרָאֵל וְלֹא־זָכַר
הֲדֹם־רַגְלָיו בְּיוֹם אַפּוֹ׃
כיף יגלט' בגצ'בה יוי עלי ג'מאעה ציון אלקא מן אלסמא אלי אלארץ' פכ'ר
ישראל ולם יד'כר מחל סכינתה פי יום גצ'בה

How the Lord in His anger has shut away the community of Zion! He has thrown down from heaven to earth the splendor of Israel; He has not remembered the site of His presence in the day of His anger.[1]

God said through the faithful prophet: *I spoke to you in your prosperity, but you said, "I will not listen." This has been your way from your youth, that you have not obeyed my voice* (Jer 22:21). This means: I have addressed (*khāṭabtu*) the congregation[2] of Israel about the virtue, treasure, stability, and tranquility that she possesses, as it is said, *Now, therefore, if you will obey My voice and keep My covenant* [. . .] *you shall be to Me a kingdom of priests* [*and a holy nation*] (Exod 19:5–6). <61b>

It is stipulated in the *Book of the Covenant*:[3] *If you walk in My statutes and observe My commandments and do them, then I will give you your rains in their season, and the land shall yield its increase, and the trees of the field shall*

[1] For this meaning of Arab. gh/l/ẓ, see Blau, *Dictionary*, 482. Cf. RSV: "How the Lord in His anger has set the daughter of Zion under a cloud! He has cast down from heaven to earth the splendor of Israel; He has not remembered His footstool in the day of His anger."

[2] Arab. *kanīsa*. Although *kanīsa* may refer to a synagogue or a church, here Salmon refers to a community or congregation. Ms. Or. 2515 attests *jamāʿa* ("community," as in Salmon's Arab. verse translation) instead of *kanīsa*. The Arab. term *kanīsa* may be derived from the Hebr. term *beit ha-kenesset* ("house of assembly"); see Mohammad Gharipour, "Architecture of Synagogues in the Islamic World: History and the Dilemma of Identity," in *Synagogues in the Islamic World* (Edinburgh, University of Edinburgh Press, 2017), 12. The Targum renders the word *kenishta'* (Aram. "congregation"). Alexander interprets it as the Targumist's way of addressing the message of Lamentations to his own community (*Rabbinic Targum*, 7). Note also that Salmon suggests an image of God preaching to a congregation through his use of the verb *khāṭaba*, "to deliver a sermon or oration."

[3] I.e., Torah.

Jewish Piety in Islamic Jerusalem. Jessica Andruss, Oxford University Press. © Oxford University Press 2023.
DOI: 10.1093/oso/9780197639559.003.0011

yield their fruit (Lev 26:3–4)—all the way to the end of the section, and all of it is blessing and beneficence. *If you will obey My commandments which I command you this day [to love the LORD your God, and to serve Him with all your heart and with all your soul], He will give the rain for your land in its season* (Deut 11:13–14).

Then: *And if you will only obey the LORD your God, being careful to do all His commandments [which I command you this day,] the LORD your God will set you high [above all the nations of the earth.] And all these blessings shall come upon you [and overtake you, if you obey the voice of the LORD your God]* (Deut 28:1–2)—to the end of the section. Likewise through Isaiah: *If you are willing and obedient, you shall eat the good of the land* (Isa 1:19); *Hearken diligently unto Me, and eat what is good* (Isa 55:2); *O that you had hearkened to My commandments! [Then your peace would have been like a river]* (Isa 48:18); *I am the LORD your God, who teaches you to profit* (Isa 48:17); *In returning and rest you shall be saved* (Isa 30:15); *To whom He has said, "This is rest; give rest to the weary"* (Isa 28:12). And the meaning of all of these and similar verses is: *I spoke to you in your prosperity* (Jer 22:21).

[Israel] said to the prophets, *I will not listen* (Jer 22:21). The prophets had already described how this nation had received such [a message]. However, when [God] said to them, [*Ask*] *where the good way is; and walk in it* (Jer 6:16), they said, *We will not walk in it* (Jer 6:16). It was said to them, *Give heed to the sound of the trumpet* (Jer 6:17) but they said, *We will not heed* (Jer 6:17). <62a> They said to the seers, *"See not"; and to the prophets, "Prophesy not to us what is right"* (Isa 30:10).[4] *Do not prophesy in the name of the LORD, or you will die by our hand* (Jer 11:21). *The LORD our God did not send you* (Jer 43:2). They repudiated the Creator when they said, *He will do nothing; no evil will come upon us, nor shall we see sword or famine* (Jer 5:12). When it was said to them, *In returning and rest you shall be saved*, they said, *No! We will speed upon horses* (Isa 30:15–16). *We must not mention the name of the LORD* (Amos 6:10). When it was said to them, *For long ago you broke your yoke and burst your bonds*, [they] said, "*I will not serve.*" (Jer 2:20). When You summoned them to repentance, they said, *We are free, we will come no more to You* (Jer 2:31). When it was said, *Keep your feet from going unshod and your throat from thirst*, [they] said, *"It is hopeless, for I have loved strangers [and after them I will go"]* (Jer 2:25). In the same way, it is said now, *I spoke to you in your prosperity, but you said, "I will not listen." This has been your way from*

[4] Lit., "They said to the prophets, '*See not*.' " Eng. translation adjusted to reflect biblical parallelism.

your youth, that you have not obeyed My voice (Jer 22:21), which accords with what is known of [Israel's] ancient deeds.

When God sent Moses to our fathers, He sent him with signs and miracles, to make them visible in their presence, as it is said, *and did the signs in the sight of the people* (Exod 4:30). When they saw the signs, they were obliged to have faith, since they did not encounter the prophet [ordering] anything impermissible.[5] But they did not consider, and [instead] they said, *The LORD look upon you* <62b> *and judge* (Exod 5:21).[6] About this incident, it is said: *Our fathers, when they were in Egypt, did not consider Your wonderful works* (Ps 106:7).

After He revealed the *Ten Plagues* against the Egyptians and He brought [the Israelites] out [of Egypt], after they flourished [even though] the Egyptians pursued them, they should have trusted in the Merciful One (*al-raḥmān*) and not done as they did when they said to Moses, *Is it because there are no graves in Egypt* [*that you have taken us away to die in the wilderness?*] (Exod 14:11). It is said about this sin: [*They*] *rebelled against the Most High at the Red Sea* (Ps 106:7).

The third sin: when they reached Marah[7] and they were not able to drink any of the water there, they were thirsty. They should have known that God has power over whatever He wills, and that He brought them out of Egypt into the *wilderness* only in order to teach [them], through their circumstances, what would happen. Indeed, He conducted them with His mercy. If they had asked Him to be merciful to them and let them drink water as they wanted to do, it would not have befallen them. However, they did not do what was best (*yaṣlaḥ*), [but instead] they quarreled with the messenger (*rasūl*), as it is said, *And the people murmured against Moses, saying, "What shall we drink?"* (Exod 15:24).

The fourth sin: when the people arrived in the *wilderness* of Sinai and their provisions were consumed, they should have requested nourishment from

[5] See Deut 18:20ff on the criteria for evaluating legitimate prophets.

[6] Salmon draws on the prophetological argument that prophets must authenticate their message with visible proofs, and having done so, the people are obligated to recognize them as prophets. Salmon uses Exod 5:21 to show that the Israelites' failure to recognize Moses as a prophet led to their communal suffering. The Israelite supervisors told Moses and Aaron, "*The LORD look upon you and judge*" when the prophets' efforts to intercede with Pharaoh on the Israelites' behalf led Pharaoh to increase the Israelites' workload. Salmon counts the Israelites' failure to recognize Mosaic prophethood as the first of the ten sins that he enumerates below, even though he does not begin numbering them until he reaches the third one. Note that Salmon does not import his list from a single biblical narrative but assembles episodes from the books of Exodus, Numbers, and Deuteronomy.

[7] *Mārātā*. Salmon presents the place name as it appears in Exod 15:23, with a directional *heh* suffix.

God and trusted in Him, for He had the power to provide (*yarzuk*) that for them, no matter where they were. Instead of doing so, they said, *Would that we had died by the hand* <63a> *of the LORD* [*in Egypt, when we sat by the fleshpots and ate bread to the full; for you have brought us out into this wilderness to kill this whole assembly with hunger*] (Exod 16:3). They renounced the beneficence of God, who brought them out of Egypt, when they said, *For you have brought us out into this wilderness* [*to kill this whole assembly with hunger*] (Exod 16:3). When His mercy for them was not exhausted and He sent *manna* down for them from the heavens, they should have been obedient to him out of devotion to Him because of that—specifically, [obedient] to what he said to them through Moses, namely: *Let no man leave any of it till the morning* (Exod 16:19). And this is the fifth sin.[8]

The sixth sin: the Mighty and Sublime commanded them not to go out on the Sabbath day to search for any of the *manna* because He had made that superfluous for them by sending two omers down on Friday.[9] But they did not accept [this], and they went out searching for *manna* in order to gather [it], as it is said, *On the seventh day some of the people went out to gather, and they found none* (Exod 16:27).

The seventh sin: when they reached Refidim and they found no water there, they were thirsty. They should have asked the Merciful One (*al-raḥmān*) to present them with water, just as He presented them with food and a morning meal. Instead of doing that, they quarreled with the messenger (*rasūl*) and they were on the verge of stoning him with rocks, as it is said, *They are almost ready to stone me* (Exod 17:4).

The eighth sin: when He addressed them on *Mount* <63b> *Sinai by signs and wonders*, He made a covenant with them. They accepted the covenant upon themselves and they said, *We will do, and we will obey* (Exod 24:7). Yet even before they moved away from there, they made the *calf* and they worshiped it after forty days. He had already told them, *You shall have no other gods before Me* (Exod 20:3). A short time later they contradicted

[8] Salmon implies that the fifth sin is the Israelites' disobedience to God's command to leave no manna overnight. However, he does not supply the biblical evidence for their disobedience, which appears in the following verse: *But they did not listen to Moses; some left part of it till the morning, and it bred worms and became foul; and Moses was angry with them* (Exod 16:20). The omission of this verse is striking since it reiterates Salmon's focus on the failure to listen to divine instruction as the Israelites' principal sin. The failure to listen is a theme of Salmon's interpretation of Lam 2 in particular, as expressed through his choice of Jer 22:21 as the refrain verse for this chapter.

[9] A daily portion was one omer (Exod 16:16); the double omer on Friday (Exod 16:22) provides an additional portion to consume on the Sabbath.

[themselves], as it is said, *They have turned aside quickly out of the way which I commanded them; they have made for themselves a molten calf [and have worshiped it and sacrificed to it]* (Exod 32:8). They had not moved from the place where they guaranteed the covenant, where they saw the signs and were addressed *face to face* (Deut 5:4)—and yet they made the *calf* and worshiped it. And this is the meaning of the verse, *They made a calf in Horeb and worshiped a molten image* (Ps 106:19).

The ninth sin: *And the people complained in the hearing of the LORD* (Num 11:1), and the whole account.[10]

The tenth sin: the account of the *scouts*, about whom it is said, *and yet have put Me to the proof these ten times* (Num 14:22).[11]

After that, there is the account of Koraḥ and Dathan and Aviram: [*All the congregation of the people of Israel murmured against Moses and Aaron, saying,*] *"You have killed the people of the LORD"* (Num 17:6/16:41). Then: *So Israel yoked himself to Baʿal of Peʿor. And the anger of the LORD was kindled against Israel* (Num 25:3). Then, after Joshua: [*And the people of Israel again did what was evil in the sight of the LORD,*] *and served the Baʿals and the Ashtaroth* (Judg 10:6).

[This pattern of sin continues] in *every generation* from the time of the Judges. They would make <64a> rebellions, as it is said, *And the people of Israel did what was evil in the sight of the LORD and served the Baʿals; and they forsook the LORD, the God of their fathers* (Judg 2:11–12) and *Yet they did not listen to their judges* (Judg 2:17)—these [verses] refer to the era of Joshua. It is said, *But whenever the judge died, they turned back and behaved worse than their fathers* (Judg 2:19).

As for the time of Jeroboam ben Nabat, Baasha, Omri, Ahab, and all the *kings of Israel*, and likewise the *kings of Judah*, including Ahaz, Manasseh, Amon, Jehoahaz, Jehoiakim and Zedekiah, and about every [king] we mentioned, it is said, *This has been your way from your youth* (Jer 22:21). That is why our lord Moses said to them, *You have been rebellious against the LORD [from the day that I knew you]* (Deut 9:24). *From the day that I knew you* alludes to the first day that he knew them, about which it is said, *When Moses had grown up, he went out to his people [and looked on their burdens;*

[10] In this account (Num 11:1–4), God responds to the people's complaints with a fire that burns the outlying areas of the camp and abates through Moses's intercession.

[11] In this account, the scouts (except for Joshua and Caleb) rebel against God by attempting to lead the Israelites back to Egypt instead of going into the land of Canaan.

and he saw an Egyptian beating a Hebrew, one of his people.] *He looked this way and that, and seeing no one* [*he killed the Egyptian and hid him in the sand*] (Ex 2:11–12).

[Moses] went out on the following day and saw two men quarreling. When one struck the other, harming him, he rebuked him by saying to him, *Why do you strike your fellow?* (Exod 2:13). The *evil one* answered, saying, *Who made you a prince and judge over us?* (Exod 2:14). In my opinion, this *evil one* is the [same] one that Moses rescued from <64b> the hand of the Egyptian, and [Moses] killed [the Egyptian] on his account. The proof of this is that no one was present at the time that Moses killed him, [except for this] disgraceful one, as it is said, *seeing no one* (Exod 2:12), [but] this *evil one* said, *as you killed the Egyptian* (Exod 2:14). He put Moses's life at risk by speaking [about that] to him in the presence of informants, as it is said, *When Pharaoh heard of it,* [*he sought to kill Moses*] (Exod 2:15). *From the day that I knew you* (Deut 9:24): Moses said this when he learned of their wicked natures. That is why it is said, *This has been your way from your youth* (Jer 22:21).

Right after that it is said, כָּל־רֹעַיִךְ תִּרְעֶה־רוּחַ (Jer 22:22)—that is to say, "the wind will shepherd all your shepherds"—which means that you will end up in exile, *in the service of the nations*, while your shepherds will not shepherd anything, because leadership will cease, as it is said, [*For the Israelites shall dwell many days*] *without king or prince, without sacrifice* [*or pillar, without ephod or teraphim*] (Hos 3:4) and *Say to the king and the queen mother: "Take a lowly seat, for your beautiful crown has come down from your head"* (Jer 13:18). If a leader were permitted in exile, then a king would be permitted. Likewise, *judges* are not permitted in exile, as it is said, *You shall appoint judges and officers throughout your tribes* (Deut 16:18). This verse eloquently expresses that they were permitted to appoint[12] *judges and officers* only in the Holy Land (*al-arḍ al-muqaddasa*), when there was <65a> sovereignty in Israel. There would be no difference between the days of sovereignty and the days of exile if there had been *judge, prince, and king* in exile. Note that the *king* and the *prince* are put on the same footing in the verse, *without king or prince* (Hos 3:4).

Without sacrifice or pillar, without ephod or teraphim. Absolutely none of this is permissible in exile! It is unlawful (*ḥarām*), just like the cultic use of the *teraphim;* [the verse] says *or teraphim*; it does not say "there are no

[12] Reading *yurattibū*, along with MSS B, J, and P (Abdul-Karim, 67).

teraphim." The only reason that leadership was not withdrawn and the dedication of [*teraphim*] was not prohibited was that the leadership sought, on the contrary, to consume the property of Israel, as it is said, *who eat up my people as they eat bread, and do not call upon the LORD* (Ps 14:4) and *You eat the fat, you clothe yourselves with the wool,* [*you slaughter the fatlings; but you do not feed the sheep*] (Ezek 34:3).[13]

They [i.e., the leaders] had no mercy [for] Israel and their circumstances [under] the *yoke of the nations,* as it is said, *Their own shepherds have no pity on them* (Zech 11:5). God protected Israel, commanded them, and rescued this nation from their control, as He promised them through Ezekiel in the last chapter: *Ho, shepherds of Israel* [*who have been feeding yourselves! Should not shepherds feed the sheep?*] (Ezek 34:2). *Thus says the Lord GOD, Behold, I am against the shepherds; and I will require my sheep at their hand, and put a stop to their feeding the sheep,* [*no longer shall the shepherds feed themselves. I will rescue My sheep from their mouths, that they may not be food for them*] (Ezek 34:10). And now it is said, *The wind shall shepherd all your shepherds* (Jer 22:22).

He affirmed that the shepherds have no <65b> custody [of the people] in exile. God had approached our fathers and spoken to them about the reversal of the beautiful, sublime promises that result from obedience. He informed them that if they abrogated (*fasakhū*) the covenant, they would deserve the opposite of all the benefits that He had promised them, as it is said, *But if you will not hearken to Me, and will not do all these commandments, if you spurn My statutes* (Lev 26:14–15). And likewise, *Take heed lest your heart be deceived* [*and you turn aside and serve other gods and worship them,*] *and the anger of the LORD be kindled against you* [*and He shut up the heavens, so that there be no rain, and the land yield no fruit, and you perish quickly off the good land which the LORD gives you*] (Deut 11:16–17). Likewise: *But if you will not obey the voice of the LORD your God or be careful to do* [*all His commandments and His statutes which I command you this day, then all these curses shall come upon you and overtake you*] (Deut

[13] Salmon accuses Israel's leaders of exploiting sacrificial institutions out of greed for the wealth of donations and the meat of the peoples' offerings. Thus, here Salmon offers a populist theology, in which the Israelite leaders are to blame rather than the general population. This reading also has implications for Karaite anti-Rabbanite polemic, and indeed Karaites often referred to the Rabbanites as "shepherds" or "shepherds of the dispersion" for this reason. See, e.g., Leon Nemoy, "Elijah Ben Abraham and His Tract Against the Rabbanites," *HUCA* 51 (1980), 72–73.

28:15) until the end of the *rebukes* (*tokhaḥōt*).[14] And there are many more [verses] like this.

Since they exceeded all bounds in rebelling, it was said, *The LORD could no longer bear your evil doings [and the abominations which you committed; therefore your land has become a desolation and a waste and a curse, without inhabitant, as it is to this day*] (Jer 44:22). Because of that, they deserved the *exile.*

He [i.e., Jeremiah] established for them a book of lamentation, in order for them to mourn for themselves with it, as I have explained above, and he arranged [the laments] in different chapters. The first chapter is *How lonely sits the city* (Lam 1:1) and this chapter opens with, ***How the LORD in His anger***, which means, "How the Lord in His anger has shut away [the community of Zion]!" [The verse] expresses amazement regarding the people about whom it was said, <66a> *It is because the LORD loves you* (Deut 7:8) and the country about which it was said, *Mount Zion, which He loves* (Ps 78:68). How He shut them away, in His anger over them! He renounced them, as it is said, *The LORD rejected all the descendants of Israel* (2 Kgs 17:20) and *My God will cast them off, because they have not hearkened to Him* (Hos 9:17).

He has thrown down from heaven to earth the splendor of Israel. This means that He threw down from heaven the splendor and might of Israel. The "splendor" of Israel combines several ideas. First: sovereignty, as it is said, *Say to the king and the queen mother: "Take a lowly seat"* (Jer 13:18). Then: the Temple, as it is said, *our holy and beautiful house* (Isa 64:10/11).[15] Then: *glory* and prophecy. There was no splendor more exalted than these qualities, so when she [i.e., Israel] was deprived of them it was said of her: *He has thrown down from heaven to earth the splendor of Israel.*

He has not remembered His footstool in the day of His anger. [Jeremiah] eloquently alludes (*faṣuḥa*) to the Temple and the *ark* and the *glory* that are within it, as it is said, *I had it in my heart to build a house of rest for the ark of the covenant of the LORD, and for the footstool of our God* (1 Chr 28:2). The real sense (*ḥaqīqa*) of ***He has not remembered His footstool*** is, He did not have compassion on this holy place in the time of Nebuchadnezzar, as He did in ancient times, when it was said, *because He had compassion on His people and on His dwelling place* (2 Chr 36:15).

[14] I.e., Deut 28:15–68.

[15] On *al-quds* to indicate the Temple rather than the city of Jerusalem, see Ben-Shammai, "Jerusalem," 450–59.

Lamentations 2:4

דָּרַךְ קַשְׁתּוֹ כְּאוֹיֵב נִצָּב יְמִינוֹ כְּצָר וַיַּהֲרֹג כֹּל מַחֲמַדֵּי־עָיִן בְּאֹהֶל בַּת־צִיּוֹן שָׁפַךְ כָּאֵשׁ חֲמָתוֹ׃
ותר קוסה כאלעדו נצב ימינה כמצ'איק וקתל כל משתהאיי אלעין פי כ'בא
ג'מאעה ציון ספך מת'ל אלנאר חמיתה

He has bent His bow like an enemy, He has raised His right hand like a foe; and He has slain all the pride of our eyes in the tent of the congregation of Zion; He has poured out His fury like fire.[16]

This verse eloquently expresses[17] that after waging war on behalf of Israel and undertaking the destruction of their enemies, God undertook their own destruction, as it is said, <69a> *Therefore He turned to be their enemy, and Himself fought against them* (Isa 63:10). At the time of the siege and their defeat, God said, "*Behold, I will turn back the weapons of war which are in your hands and with which you are fighting against the king of Babylon and against the Chaldeans who are besieging you outside the walls; and I will bring them together into the midst of this city. I Myself will fight against you with outstretched hand and strong arm, in anger, and in fury, and in great wrath. And I will smite the inhabitants of this city*" (Jer 21:4–6).

All of these reversals befell us when we renounced obedience:[18]

The LORD will fight for you (Exod 14:14) was reversed: [*the LORD*] *Himself fought against them* (Isa 63:10).

The peoples have heard, they tremble (Exod 15:14) was reversed: *Night and day you shall be in dread* (Deut 28:66).

Yet the LORD set His heart in love upon your fathers and chose their descendants after them (Deut 10:15) was reversed: *And the LORD rejected all the descendants of Israel* (2 Kgs 17:20).

I will redeem you with an outstretched arm (Exod 6:6) was reversed: *I Myself will fight against you with outstretched hand* (Jer 21:5).

And the people multiplied and grew very strong (Exod 1:20) was reversed: *But I will let a few of them escape* [*from the sword*] (Ezek 12:16).

[16] I am grateful to Daniel Frank for his skillful assistance in the reconstruction and translation of the excursus to Lam 2:4, which is beset with textual difficulties.

[17] F/ṣ/ḥ, "to eloquently express," signals figurative language; see Salmon's comments to Lam 1:2; 2:1; 3:49; 5:7.

[18] This catalogue of reversals anticipates (in reverse!) the section of consolations (*Neḥamot*) with which Salmon concludes the commentary.

Fire came forth from before the LORD and consumed the burnt offering (Lev 9:24) was reversed: *From on high He sent fire* (Lam 1:13).

Therefore when the LORD your God has given you rest [from your enemies round about] (Deut 25:19) was reversed: *And among these nations you shall find no ease* (Deut 28:65).

You shall rejoice in your feast (Deut 16:14) was reversed: *I will turn your feasts into mourning* (Amos 8:10).

Then sang Deborah (Judg 5:1) in victory <69b> was reversed: *Jeremiah also uttered a lament* (2 Chr 35:25).

So Solomon built the house, and finished it (1 Kgs 6:14) was reversed: *And he burned the house of the LORD* (2 Kgs 25:9).

He adorned the house with settings of precious stones (2 Chr 3:6) was reversed: *And then all its carved wood they broke down* (Ps 74:6).

But it is because the LORD loves you (Deut 7:8) was reversed: *I turned in disgust from her* (Ezek 23:18).

[*That the LORD may turn from the fierceness of His anger,*] *and show you mercy* (Deut 13:18/17) was reversed: *For I will show you no favor* (Jer 16:13).

And you shall lend to many nations (Deut 28:12) was reversed: [*The sojourner*] *shall lend to you, and you shall not lend to him* (Deut 28:44).

[*The peoples*] *will say, "Surely this great nation is a wise and understanding people"* (Deut 4:6) was reversed: *For My people are foolish* (Jer 4:22).

And when you eat and are satisfied (Deut 6:11) was reversed: *You shall eat, but not be satisfied* (Mic 6:14).

You grew exceedingly beautiful (Ezek 16:13) was reversed: [*You*] *prostituted your beauty* (Ezek 16:25).

And your renown went forth among the nations because of your beauty (Ezek 16:14) was reversed: *She became a byword among women* (Ezek 23:10) and *You infamous one, full of tumult* (Ezek 22:5).

He has bent His bow like an enemy is an allusion to the acts of divine vengeance, which are likened to arrows, as it is said, *I will spend my arrows upon them* (Deut 32:23)—and [the meaning of "arrows"] is explained by the [next] verse, *They shall be wasted with hunger, and devoured with burning heat* (Deut 32:24). That is the meaning (*maʿnā*) of ***He has bent His bow***, and of *He bent His bow and set me* [*as a mark for His arrow*] (Lam 3:12), as it is said below.

He raised His right hand like a foe means that the acts of divine vengeance will be prodigious and most calamitous, since ***He raised His right hand*** alludes to the work of the lance. [In actuality] there is neither a bow nor a lance, but rather, both of these are used as analogies (*ʿalā sabīl al-tamthīl*) <70a> and approximations. ***Like an enemy*** and ***like a foe*** are like the verse at the beginning of the book—*like a widow she has become* (Lam 1:1)—which inform us that God has not cut off the hope of Israel, as I have explained in what preceded.

He has slain all the pride of our eyes alludes to the verse, *who slew their young men with the sword in the house of their sanctuary* (2 Chr 36:17); and to the verses, *They have poured out their blood like water* (Ps 79:3); *My priests and elders perished in the city* (Lam 1:19); *And the king of Babylon smote them, and put them to death* (Jer 52:27)—and there are many similar verses.

Indeed, the prophets foretold all of these circumstances before they arose. One of [the prophets] was Asaph the Gershonite, peace be upon him,[19] who stated before Jerusalem was built, אֱלֹהִים בָּאוּ גוֹיִם בְּנַחֲלָתֶךָ (Ps 79:1)—"O God, the nations have come into Your inheritance; they have defiled Your holy Temple; they have laid Jerusalem in ruins."[20] God had guaranteed that as long as Israel was obedient, the enemy would not tread on their land, as it is said, *And the sword shall not go through your land* (Lev 26:6).

When [Israel] disobeyed excessively, He first gave the kings of Assyria dominion over the ten tribes, as it is said, *Therefore I delivered her into the hands of her lovers, into the hands of the Assyrians, upon whom she doted. These uncovered her nakedness; they seized her sons and daughters; and her they slew with the sword* (Ezek 23:9–10).[21] [The Assyrians] uprooted them three times, <70b> which means that they exiled them on three occasions. Then, when Judah and Benjamin and the residents of Jerusalem did not reflect (*lam yaʿtabirū*) [and learn their lesson], He gave Nebuchadnezzar dominion over them, and He exiled them four times after Pharaoh Necho had exiled Jehoahaz, making a total of eight exiles. Then, when they returned from Babylon and built the Second Temple and resumed their disobedience,

[19] The pious epithet underscores Salmon's contention that Asaph was a prophet.

[20] Cf. RSV: "the heathen have come into Your inheritance" (Ps 79:1). It is not clear whether Salmon renders Hebr. *naḥalah* ("inheritance") with the false Arab. cognate *niḥla* ("faith, sect") or retains the Hebr. word in his translation since the consonantal text is identical.

[21] Here begins the section on the Ten Exiles, which Salmon also includes in his excursus on Ps 79:1 in the Psalms commentary. The rubric of ten exiles comes from *Midrash ʿEśer Galuyot*; see Adolph (Aharon) Jellinek, *Beit ha-Midrash*, vol. 4 (Jerusalem: Bamberger, 1938), 133–36. Salmon's immediate source was Saadia's commentary on Lam 1:3. See Haggai Ben-Shammai and Bruno Chiesa, "Fragments from the Commentary of Saʿadya Gaon to the Scroll of Lamentations," [Hebr.] *Ginzei Qedem* 3 (2007): 29–87, esp. 72–85, Appendix A. "Saadia's Judeo-Arabic Version of the Midrash on the Ten Exiles in a Karaite Reworking, as preserved in Salmon b. Yerūḥim's commentary on Lam 2:4." Note that a Byzantine Hebr. reworking of Salmon's commentary places this excursus in Salmon's comment to Lam 1:3 (RNL Ms. Evr. IIA.0078). I thank Daniel Frank for directing me to these sources.

they were exiled twice. This makes ten times [in all]—eight of them are scriptural and two have been transmitted orally.[22] This is their explanation:

The first exile [happened] during the time of Pekah ben Remaliah, as it is said, *In the days of Pekah king of Israel Tiglath-pileser king of Assyria came and captured Ijon, Abel-beth-maacah, Janoah, Kedesh, Hazor, Gilead, and Galilee, all the land of Naphtali; and he carried the people captive to Assyria* (2 Kgs 15:29).[23] Isaiah says of this exile: *In the former time He brought into contempt the land of Zebulun and the land of Naphtali* (Isa 8:23/9:1).

The second exile: two of the Assyrian kings made their way to the land of Israel. They defeated the two and a half tribes, and exiled them, as it is said, *So the God of Israel stirred up the spirit of Pul, king of Assyria, and the spirit of Tilgath-pilneser, king of Assyria, and he carried them away, namely, the Reubenites, the Gadites, and* <71a> *the half-tribe of Manasseh, and brought them to Halah, Habor, Hara, and the river Gozan* [*to this day*] (1 Chr 5:26).[24]

The third exile: the rest of the ten tribes—which were five and a half [in number]—as it is said about the siege of Samaria, *And at the end of three years he took it. In the sixth year of Hezekiah, which was the ninth year of Hoshea king of Israel, Samaria was taken. The king of Assyria carried the Israelites away to Assyria* [. . .] *because they did not obey the voice of the LORD their God but transgressed His covenant, even after all that Moses the servant of the LORD commanded; they neither listened nor obeyed* (2 Kgs 18:10–12).[25]

[22] Salmon acknowledges that the last two exiles "have been transmitted orally," following Saadia's comment that the final two exiles occurred during the Second Temple period and "our ancestors transmitted [this history] to us orally" (*mā naqalūhu al-ābā'*; see Ben-Shammai and Chiesa, "Fragments," 70). Salmon's admission of extra-scriptural evidence indicates that he is not wary of oral tradition per se, but only as an instrument of Rabbanite authority.

[23] Tiglath-Pileser III (r. 745–727 BCE), also called Pul, expanded the territory of the Assyrian Empire throughout the ancient Near East, relying heavily on deportation for military, political, and economic purposes. Salmon's "first exile" corresponds to Tiglath-Pileser III's campaigns of 733–732 BCE in Damascus and Israel; see K. Lawson Younger, Jr., "The Deportations of the Israelites, *JBL* 117:2 (1998), 206. Pekah ruled Israel until his assassination in 732 BCE (2 Kgs 15:27–31).

[24] Salmon reads 1 Chr 5:6 as a reference to a second exile, cf. the likelihood that 2 Kgs 15:29 and 1 Chr 5:6 are parallel references to the same event (Younger, "Deportations," 211). Salmon treats Pul and Tiglath Pileser as two separate Assyrian kings. On the Assyrian places where the exiled Israelites were resettled, see Pamela Barmash, "At the Nexus of History and Memory: The Ten Lost Tribes," *AJS Review* 29:2 (2005), 220. Barmash notes that Gozan was an Aramean city under Assyrian rule, which the Bible erroneously presents as a river. Cf. Gozan as another name for the Amu Darya, the major river of central Asia, called the Oxus in Latin sources. On the antiquity of Jewish communities in this region, see Michael Shterenshis, *Tamerlane and the Jews* (Abingdon, U.K.: Routledge, 2002), chapter 2.

[25] Hoshea ascended the throne of Israel after assassinating Pekah in 732 BCE, as a puppet king of the Assyrians under Tiglath-Pileser. When Shalmaneser V ascended the Assyrian throne, Hoshea attempted to secure Egyptian support against Assyria. His attempt failed, and the Assyrians conquered Samaria (the remaining territory of Israel), sent the Israelites into exile, and repopulated the region with exiles from elsewhere (2 Kgs 17). On such "bidirectional" deportations, see Younger,

The fourth exile: the *exile* of Jehoahaz ben Josiah, who is Shallum, as it is said, *For thus says the LORD concerning Shallum the son of Josiah, king of Judah, who reigned instead of Josiah his father, and who went away from this place: "He shall return here no more, but in the place where they have carried him captive, there shall he die"* (Jer 22:11–12).[26]

The fifth exile was at the hand of Nebuchadnezzar.[27] He seized Jehoiakim and 3,023 men with him, as it is said, *This is the number of the people whom Nebuchadrezzar carried away captive: in the seventh year, three thousand and twenty-three Jews* (Jer 52:28). As for Jehoiakim, he died near Jerusalem, while the people were carried off to Babylon, as I described these affairs in my commentary on Daniel.[28]

The sixth exile was the *exile* of Jeconiah, <71b> as it is said, *And he exiled Jehoiachin to Babylon; the king's mother, the king's wives, his officers, and the chief men of the land, he took into captivity from Jerusalem to Babylon* (2 Kgs 24:15).[29]

The seventh exile was the *exile* of Zedekiah, as it is said, *But the army of the Chaldeans pursued the king* (Jer 52:8) and *he put out the eyes of Zedekiah, and bound him in fetters, and the king of Babylon took him to Babylon and put him in prison till the day of his death* (Jer 52:11). In this way, God passed judgment against him, as it is said, *I will bring him to Babylon to the land of the Chaldeans, yet he shall not see it; and he shall die there* (Ezek 12:13). In other words, having been blinded, he will enter Babylon. Eight hundred and thirty-two of the people were exiled along with him, as it is said, *In the eighteenth*

"Deportations," 226–27. Abdul-Karim's ed. concludes with a reference to Exod 24:7, which is not attested in all MSS (see Ben-Shammai and Chiesa, "Fragments," 68).

26 Jehoahaz (r. 609 BCE) was the regnal name of Shallum, the son of Josiah (1 Chr 13:15). He was deposed by Pharaoh Necho II (r. 610–595 BCE) and taken to Egypt, where he died. His older brother, Jehoiakim, was placed on the throne by Pharaoh Necho, thus making Judah into a vassal state (2 Kgs 23:30–36; 2 Chr 36:1–4).

27 Nebuchadnezzar II "the Great" of Babylon (r. 605–562 BCE); also referred to as "Nebuchadrezzar." Salmon divides Nebuchadnezzar's campaigns into waves of exile and destruction, organized according to the figures who were exiled in successive stages.

28 Jehoiakim (r. 609–598 BCE) switched his allegiances between the Egyptians and the Babylonians, depending on which empire was ascendant. In addition to the records of Jehoiakim's reign that are contained in the historical books of the Bible (2 Kgs 23:36–37; 2 Chr 36:5–8), the books of Jeremiah and Daniel also contain references to him. Prophets did not fare well under Jehoiakim: Daniel was sent to Babylon as a high-profile hostage during the siege of Jerusalem (Dan 1:6), while Jeremiah and Uriah risked or lost their lives by prophesying the destruction of Jerusalem (Jer 26).

29 Jeconiah (r. 598–597 BCE), also known as Jehoiachin (2 Kgs 24:8–17; 2 Chr 36:9–10).

year of Nebuchadrezzar he carried away captive from Jerusalem eight hundred and thirty-two persons (Jer 52:29).[30]

The eighth exile was from Egypt, as it is said, *In the twenty-third year of Nebuchadrezzar, Nebuzaradan the captain of the guard carried away captive of the Jews seven hundred and forty-five persons* (Jer 52:30). Since it does not say "*from Jerusalem*," we learn that they were exiled from Egypt and not from Jerusalem.

The ninth exile [took place] at the conclusion of 434 <72a> years [following the completion of] the Second Temple, as it is said, [*Seventy weeks of years are decreed concerning your people and your holy city, to finish the transgression, to put an end to sin, and to atone for iniquity, to bring in everlasting righteousness, to seal both vision and prophet, and to anoint a most holy place. Know therefore and understand that from the going forth of the word to restore and build Jerusalem to the coming of an anointed one, a prince, there shall be*] *seven weeks. Then for sixty-two weeks it shall be built again* (Dan 9:24–25).[31] Vespasian attacked them, as I explained in my comment on [the verse in] Daniel, *Out of one of them came a little horn* (Dan 8:9).[32] He arranged a truce with them for one week—as it is said, *And he shall make a strong covenant with many for one week*. In the middle of the week he broke the truce, destroyed the Temple, and abolished the sacrificial cult, as it is said, *And for half of the week he shall cause sacrifice and offering to cease* (Dan 9:27).

This is what Titus—Vespasian's *killer*—did.[33] Subsequently, some of the survivors settled in a city, which was known as Batīr, near

[30] Zedekiah (r. 597–586 BCE) was the regnal name of Mattaniah, the uncle of Jehoaichin. He was installed by Nebuchanezzar, then blinded and sent into exile during the siege of Jerusalem (2 Kgs 24:17–25:7; 2 Chr 36:11–14). The exile of Zedekiah marks the beginning of the Babylonian exile.

[31] Reading a week as a reference to seven years: seventy weeks is 490 years; seven weeks is 49 years; and sixty-two weeks is 434 years. Saadia refers to Dan 9:24–27 in order to refute arguments that prophecies of redemption do not indicate a future redemption, since they were fulfilled already during the Second Temple period (*The Book of Beliefs and Opinions*, trans. Samuel Rosenblatt, Yale Judaica Series 1 [New Haven, Conn.: Yale University Press, 1948], 319–22). By Saadia's calculation, 70 years elapsed between Daniel's prophecy and the construction of the Second Temple, which stood for 420 years, adding up to the 490 years that Daniel prophesied. For a meticulous consideration of Daniel's chronology in light of ancient and modern scholarship, see Antti Laato, "The Seventy Yearweeks in the Book of Daniel," *Zeitschrift für die alttestamentiche Wissenschaft* 102, no. 2 (1990): 212–25.

[32] Cf. Saadia, who reads Daniel's prophecy in reference to the Greek kings; for him the "little horn" refers to Seleucus (Saadia, Dan, 300–4; 569 n. 60). Vespasian commanded the siege of Jerusalem during the First Jewish-Roman War and ultimately became emperor (r. 69–79 CE).

[33] Hebr. *titus horeg 'asfasyanos*. There is no evidence that Titus killed Vespasian, or that Jews circulated a tradition to this effect. Rather, *horeg* appears to be a scribal misreading of *wa-wazarā'hu* ("and his officers"); see Ben-Shammai and Chiesa, "Fragments," 39; 82–83. Titus was Vespasian's son and successor, first as commander of the Roman forces in Judea during the First Jewish-Roman War (where he captured Jerusalem and destroyed its Temple in 70 CE) and then as emperor (r. 79–81 CE).

Jerusalem.[34] They say that it was like Rome. Because of its greatness, one of the western kings named Hadrian attacked and conquered it, exiling whoever had remained there from Titus's exile to the West.[35] Concerning this tenth exile, it is said in the *covenant*, *And the LORD will bring you back in ships to Egypt* (Deut 28:68).[36]

How many *troubles* came about [through] these two exiles!? The prophet Asaph said about all these circumstances, *The nations have come into Your inheritance* (Ps 79:1). Since he had already described the building of Jerusalem and David's reign in the previous psalm, <72b> when he saw with his prophetic eye the acts of disobedience Israel would commit, he informed [us] that the enemy would triumph over the Temple and destroy it. He juxtaposed [Ps 78 with] *O God, the nations have come into Your inheritance* (Ps 79:1) in order to inform [us] that just as Shiloh had been destroyed because of Israel's acts of rebellion, so would Jerusalem be destroyed. Therefore, he mentioned Shiloh before this psalm, as it is said, *He forsook His dwelling at Shiloh* (Ps 78:60), for it had been in the *territory* (*naḥalah*) *of Ephraim*.[37]

It is said, *They have defiled Your holy Temple* (Ps 79:1). The clause *the nations have come into Your inheritance* (*naḥalah*; Ps 79:1) expresses amazement over what befell [them] and what will [also] befall Israel—the likes of which had not befallen a nation [before], as it is said, *if there be any sorrow like my sorrow* (Lam 1:12), which I have explained above. This is what Ezekiel saw with the prophetic eye: *And he said to them, "Defile the house, and fill the courts with the slain"* (Ezek 9:7).

The *uncircumcised and the impure* were sitting in the *middle gate*, which is the hall, as it is said, *Yea, she has seen the nations invade her sanctuary* (Lam 1:10) and *For strangers have come into the holy places of the LORD's house* (Jer 51:51). They were in the place of Shelemiah, Zechariah, Obed Edom, Shuppim and Hosah and the rest <73a> of the Levites, who were consecrated to the LORD.[38] Worst of all, the people were besieged, the enemy had

[34] Arab. place names: *batīr* (= Betar); *bayt al-maqdis* (= Jerusalem). Betar was the stronghold of Bar Kokhba during the Second Jewish-Roman War. It was the last Judean fortress to fall to the Romans, in 135 CE. See David Ussishkin, "Excavations at Betar, the Last Stronghold of Bar Kokhba" [Hebr.], *Qadmoniot: A Journal for the Antiquities of Eretz-Yisrael and Bible Lands* 41, no. 136 (2008): 108–12.

[35] Hadrian was a Roman emperor (r. 117–35 CE) who came from Hispania.

[36] Lev 26:3–45 and Deut 28 are referred to as "the covenant" in Karaite literature, on the basis of Lev 26:42–45 and Deut 28:69/29:1 (Ben-Shammai and Chiesa, "Fragments," 85 n. 165).

[37] The analogy between Shiloh and Jerusalem is revealed prophetically also to Jeremiah (Jer 26:2–9).

[38] Each gatekeeper guarded one gate: Shelemiah to the east, Zechariah to the north, Obed Edom to the south, and Shuppim and Hosah to the west (1 Chr 26:14–16). Salmon explains that the Temple is no longer administered by those who were consecrated to the task.

conquered their towns and called down the sword upon them, while epidemic, hunger, and catastrophe beset them from every direction. Jeremiah, the prophet of God, was confined [to the court of the guard], shackled in fetters until the infidels unshackled him and freed him from confinement, as it is said, *So Nebuzaradan the captain of the guard and Nebushazban the Rabsaris, Nergalsharezer the Rabmag, and all the chief officers of the king of Babylon sent and took Jeremiah from the court of the guard. They entrusted him to Gedaliah* (Jer 39:13–14).

Afterward his fetters were removed, as it is said, *Now, behold, I release you today from the chains on your hands. If it seems good to you [to come with me to Babylon, come, and I will look after you well]* (Jer 40:4). The *uncircumcised* were in the center of this place, which only the *high priests* should reach! Note that when Uzziah sinned there he was struck with leprosy, yet no evil came upon these infidels![39] All of this is because of the magnitude of our sins, as it is said, *Your iniquities have turned these away* (Jer 5:25) and *The guilt of the house of Israel and Judah is exceedingly great* (Ezek 9:9).

<73b> *They have defiled Your holy Temple* (Ps 79:1) alludes to killing within [the Temple] the priests and Levites who were found there, as punishment for having killed Zechariah ben Jehoiada in Jerusalem. They assaulted him without shame, though he was a priest and a prophet, as it is said, *Should priest and prophet be slain in the sanctuary of the Lord?* (Lam 2:20). *They have laid Jerusalem in ruins* (Ps 79:1) indicates also what Micah the Morasthite prophesied: *Therefore because of you Zion shall be plowed as a field; Jerusalem shall become a heap of ruins* (Mic 3:12).

נָתְנוּ אֶת־נִבְלַת עֲבָדֶיךָ (Ps 79:2)—"They have given the bodies of Your servants to the birds of the air for food, the flesh of Your pious ones to the beasts of the earth." This is just as God decreed over Israel in the *covenant* when He said, *Your dead body shall be food for all birds of the air [and for the beasts of the earth]* (Deut 28:26). And: *I will appoint over them four kinds of destroyers, says the LORD: the sword to slay, the dogs to tear, and the birds of the air and the beasts of the earth to devour and destroy* (Jer 15:3). Your servants are called "*Your pious ones*" because if Israel had done everything [that God asked of them], then they would have been closer to God than everyone [else] in the world. But instead, these trials came upon them as a way of chastisement.[40] As it is said, *As a man* <74a> *disciplines his son, the LORD*

[39] On Uzziah, see 2 Chr 26:19–21; 2 Kgs 15:5.

[40] Arab. *adab*. Salmon recapitulates his statements from the introduction about the purpose of chastisement and the parallels between divine correction of Israel and parental correction of a child.

your God disciplines you (Deut 8:5); *For the LORD reproves him whom He loves* (Prov 3:12); and also *For Israel and Judah have not been forsaken* (Jer 51:5).

שָׁפְכוּ דָמָם (Ps 79:3)—"They have poured out their blood like water round about Jerusalem, and there was none to bury them." Likening the shedding of their blood to water alludes to two things: first, the great volume of water. Similarly, the pouring of blood is also likened to dust, as it is said, *Their blood shall be poured out like dust* (Zeph 1:17). Second, just as water has no measure when someone pours it out, so does the blood of Israel have no measure. They did not see that in killing them [i.e., the people of Israel], they were incurring a sin, as they have been described: *They slay the widow and the sojourner, and murder the fatherless; and they say, "The LORD does not see"* (Ps 94:6–7). *None shall bury her* (Ps 79:3) is in accord with what was decreed against them: *They shall not be lamented, nor shall they be buried* (Jer 16:4). It was said about their king [Jehoiakim], *And his dead body shall be cast out* (Jer 36:30). It was said about the people who had obeyed the false prophets, *And the people to whom they prophesy shall be cast out in the streets of Jerusalem, victims of famine and sword, with none to bury them—them, their wives, their sons, and their daughters. For I will pour out their wickedness upon them* (Jer 14:16).

<74b> Even worse than this is the exhumation of the great ones—the kings, chieftains, priests, prophets, princes, and people of Jerusalem—from their graves. The affliction will befall the living and the dead together, as it is said, *At that time, says the LORD, the bones of the kings of Judah, the bones of its princes, the bones of the priests, the bones of the prophets, and the bones of the inhabitants of Jerusalem shall be brought out of their tombs; and they shall be spread before the sun and the moon and all the host of heaven, which they have loved and served, which they have gone after, and which they have sought and worshiped; and they shall not be gathered or buried; they shall be as dung on the surface of the ground* (Jer 8:1–2). *Kings loved them, princes served them, priests went after them, prophets sought them, the people of Jerusalem bowed down before them.* They were not satisfied to kill without burying, so they also exhumed [the buried] from the grave and did not bury [them] afterward.

Even worse than this was when it was decreed against them that when they were killed they would not be buried, and if they should be exhumed, they would not be buried [again]. He informed [us] that in place of the kings' palaces and the fortifications of Jerusalem there would be graves of *gentiles* so that Jerusalem <75a> in its entirety would become a cemetery, just as the graves of *Christians* and *Muslims* can be seen buried and entombed there today, as it is said, *The houses of Jerusalem and the houses of the kings of Judah—all the houses upon whose roofs incense has been burned to all the host of heaven, and drink offerings have been poured out to other gods—shall be defiled like the place of Topheth* (Jer 19:13).[41]

הָיִינוּ חֶרְפָּה (Ps 79:4) —"We have become a reproach to our neighbors, mocked and derided by those round about us. Thus, we are as it is said, *You shall be a reproach and a taunt, a warning and a horror, to the nations* [*round about you*] (Ezek 5:15). *To our neighbors* (Ps 79:4) alludes to those who are near us, and *round about us* (Ps 79:4) alludes to those who are far off, as it is said, *Those who are near and those who are far from you will mock you* (Ezek 22:5).

עַד־מָה יְהוָה (Ps 79:5)—"How long, O LORD, will you be angry? How long will your jealousy burn like fire?" Regarding *anger*, it is said *that the LORD was very angry with Israel* (2 Kgs 17:18). And regarding *jealousy*, it is said that *they stirred Him to jealousy with strange gods* (Deut 32:16) and *which provokes to jealousy* (Ezek 8:3).

Since Israel is likened to a *wife*, their idol-worship is likened to *idolatry*, as it is said, *Adulterous wife, who received strangers instead of her husband!* (Ezek 16:32). Anything that concerns the Creator's anger is likened to *jealousy* <75b> as it is said, *For I the LORD your God am a jealous God* (Exod 20:5). Just as a woman, when she has wronged her husband and the matter has become clear concerning her, *her belly shall swell and her thigh fall away* (Num 5:27) when she drinks the water of bitterness with the *curses* in it, as it is said, *The priest shall write these curses in a book* [*and wash them off into the water of bitterness*] (Num 5:23)[42]—so it is with Israel: when they transgressed the covenant, worshiped anything other than the LORD, and angered the Creator, they deserved to be overtaken by *acts of retribution*. That is why the anger of the Lord of the worlds is called *jealousy*, as it is said, *Your jealousy burns like fire* (Ps 79:5).

שְׁפֹךְ חֲמָתְךָ אֶל הַגּוֹיִם (Ps 79:6)—"Pour out Your wrath on the nations that do not know You, and on the kingdoms that do not call Your name!" In other

[41] "Gentiles" = Hebr. *goyim* (lit. "nations"); Christians = Hebr. *ʿarelim* (lit. "uncircumcised"); Muslims = Hebr. *benei-qedar* (lit. "Kedarites"). For Karaite reflections on the impurity imparted by Christian and Muslim dead, see also Salmon's comments to Lam 1:7 (Abdul-Karim, 34–38) and Lam 5:18, and Frank's discussion of Yefet's comments to Ps 74:11 (*Search Scripture Well*, 183 [text 5.4] and 205 nn. 4 and 5).

[42] Num 5:11–31. Salmon anticipates readers' familiarity with the laws of the *soṭah* (suspected adulteress). On the structure and significance of this biblical "trial by ordeal," see Adriana Destro, *The Law of Jealousy: Anthropology of Sotah*, Brown Judaic Studies 181 (Providence, R.I.: Brown University Press, 1989).

words, "Pour out Your anger, O LORD, upon them, just as they poured out the blood of Israel like water!" There are [multiple] reasons. First: their wrongdoing and hostilities are numerous, as I explained above.[43] Second: because they are infidels, they do not know Your absolute unity.[44] They do not pray *in the name of the LORD* because truly, *They call on You* [means] professing monotheism and worship, as it is said, *Know the God of your father, and serve Him with a whole heart* (1 Chr 28:9) and *Know that the LORD is God! It is He who made us* (Ps 100:3).

<76a> And as for Israel: first Jacob was confirmed, then You granted approval to his sons; and Israel endured all that was bestowed upon them from the people of Egypt. For had they [i.e., the Israelites] abandoned their religion (*dīn*) completely and joined them, as they [i.e., the Egyptians] wished, they would not have treated them as enemies.[45] Then, *the people believed* (Exod 4:31); *they believed in the LORD and in His servant Moses* (Exod 14:31). Upon Mount Sinai they said, "*We will do and we will obey*"—*All that the LORD has spoken we will do, and we will obey* (Exod 24:7). *On the eighth day* (Lev 9:1) *when all the people saw it, they shouted, and fell on their faces* (Lev 9:24). *Then Israel sang this song: "Spring up, O well!—Sing to it!"* (Num 21:17). *But you who held fast to the LORD your God* [*are all alive this day*] (Deut 4:4). *And the people served the LORD all the days of Joshua* (Judg 2:7). *So Israel put away the Baʿals and the Ashteroth, and they served the LORD only* (1 Sam 7:4).

The days of David and Solomon were eighty years; the time of Asa, the age of Jehosophat, the days of Hezekiah and Isaiah, and how many prophets and seers and Nazirites and righteous ones and pure ones like upright princes were in Israel? They cannot be numbered. For this one and the likes of him, it was said *Pour out Your wrath upon the nations that do not know You,* <76b> *and upon the peoples that do not call on Your name* (Jer 10:25).

This means that in the time of their misfortunes, Israel has no one to call upon for help other than the Lord of the worlds, as it is said, *To You, O LORD, I cried; and to the LORD I made supplication* (Ps 30:9/8); and *I will lift up my hands and call on Your name* (Ps 63:5/4). However, *the nations* call upon *vanities*, as it is said, *For the customs of the peoples are false* (Jer 10:3); and *Do not turn aside after vain things which cannot profit or save, for they are vain* (1 Sam 12:21); and *Those who pay regard to vain idols* [*forsake their true loyalty*]

[43] See comment to Ps 79:3.
[44] Arab. *tawḥīd.*
[45] This passage appears to be corrupt in the MSS. This translation is based on consultation with the parallel in Salmon's comment to Ps 79:6 (Salmon, Pss, 73–89).

(Jonah 2:9). They deserve destruction [from] every side, which is why it is said, *Pour out Your wrath upon the nations* (Jer 10:25). He connected these two ideas elsewhere.[46] Together they represent [Israel's] refusal to obey God, and what [the nations] did to Israel. Concerning them both, he stated, *Pour out Your wrath on the nations* (Ps 79:6).

כִּי אָכַל אֶת־יַעֲקֹב (Ps 79:7)—*They devoured him and they finished him off and they laid waste his habitation.* It is not said "*for he devoured Jacob*," [which would] mean the *ten tribes*; [rather, it is said], *they devoured him*, which means the kingdom of Judah. *They devoured him* in the *Second Temple and they laid waste his habitation*, [which] means the *inheritance of the land and Jerusalem and Zion and the sacred [place] of the LORD*. Thus, it is said here, *For they have devoured Jacob* (Ps 79:7). This means that they consumed Jacob and made his homeland desolate. In this [verse], he [i.e., Asaph] brought together and enumerated some of the various terrible deeds <77a> committed by the enemy against Israel, and he directed his complaint (*shakā*) to God.[47]

Among other things, [he said]: *The nations have come into Your inheritance; they have defiled Your holy Temple; they have laid Jerusalem in ruins. They have given the bodies of Your servants* [. . .] *they have poured out their blood like water* [. . .] *we have become a taunt to our neighbors* (Ps 79:1–4)—and then, *They have devoured Jacob* (Ps 79:7). He said: "See, O LORD, what they have done to us, though they did not know You, or invoke Your name, while they opposed You."[48]

Someone may ask, "Why does [God] say [to Ezekiel]: *You are not sent to a people of foreign speech and a hard language, but to the house of Israel—not to many peoples of foreign speech and a hard language, whose words you cannot understand. Surely, if I sent you to such, they would listen to you. But the house of Israel would not listen to you; for they are not willing to listen to Me; because all the house of Israel are of a hard forehead and of a stubborn heart* (Ezek 3:6–7). Surely this verse proves that if He had sent [prophets] to the *nations*, they would have obeyed, yet Israel did not obey! So how can you say that according to God, Israel is superior to the *nations*?!"

In answer to this, we say: It is known that every end corresponds to its beginning, and the beginning of this narrative is the verse: *Son of man, I send you to the people of Israel, to a nation of rebels* (Ezek 2:3). Then He says, *For you are not sent to a people of foreign speech* <77b> *and a hard language, but*

46 Jer 10.
47 This statement derives from Salmon's translation and comment to Ps 79:7.
48 There appears to be a problem with the text here.

to the house of Israel (Ezek 3:5). Initially He began, *I send you to the people Israel* (Ezek 2:3). Then He told him, "not to a people of foreign language or heavy tongues; but to the house of Israel." In other words, "I did not send you to anyone whose language you would not understand, or who would not understand you, but rather, I sent you to them"—that is to say, to the house of Israel—"whose speech you would understand, and who would understand your speech." *Not to many peoples of foreign speech* (Ezek 3:6): in other words, "Neither did I commission you to journey to many nations, nor to travel to their homelands, though you did not know their languages; but rather, 'I sent you to them'—that is to say, to the house of Israel, who understand you and your speech," as it is said initially, *I send you to the people Israel* (Ezek 2:3). Then He says, *You are sent to the people Israel—surely, if I sent you to such, they would listen to you* (Ezek 3:6).

This [relates] to what was stated previously: "I dispatched you to Israel, who would understand what you say and listen to your speech, not to foreigners[49] who would not understand your speech." Then He informed him that they—I mean this *generation*—would not obey. <78a> Just as He sent Moses to Pharaoh and informed him that he [i.e., Pharaoh] would not choose to obey, so did He inform Ezekiel that these peoples would not choose to obey, as it is said, *But the house of Israel will not listen to you; for they are not willing to listen to Me* (Ezek 3:7). Nevertheless, he went to them with [God's] message, to compel them with the argument (*ḥujja*). Thus, what is said now—*that do not know You* (Ps 79:6)—is correct as we have interpreted it.

אַל־תִּזְכָּר־לָנוּ עֲוֺנֹת רִאשֹׁנִים (Ps 79:8)—"Do not remember against us the offenses of the first ones; let Your compassion come speedily to meet us, for we are very weak." [The psalm] began with complaint over all of the aforementioned calamities that had been conferred upon them because of [their] offenses. [Now] they ask forgiveness and pardon: *Do not remember against us the iniquities of the first ones* (Ps 79:8). *The iniquities of the first ones* alludes to the aforementioned offenses of the fathers and to the offenses of childhood and youth, as it is said, *Remember not the sins of my youth, or my transgressions* (Ps 25:7).

For we are brought very low (Ps 79:8) alludes to the weakness of Israel, when the calamities mentioned above befell them. It is also said, *And in that day* <78b> *the glory of Jacob will be brought low* (Isa 17:4). He means the dynasty

[49] Arab. *ʿajam*. The term generally refers to non-Arabs, and to Persians in particular. In Jewish texts, the term may refer to various non-Hebrew or non-Jewish people (see Blau, *Dictionary*, 424).

(*dawla*) of Jacob. [This verse] alludes to the time of the conquest of the land of *Samaria*, the exile of Hoshea ben Elah, the end of the kingdom (*dawla*) of Israel and their weakness before the enemy, as it is said, *And the fat of his flesh will grow lean* (Isa 17:4).[50] He refers to the destruction of Jerusalem and the *acts of divine vengeance* that befell them. *It shall be as when the reaper gathers standing grain* (Isa 17:5). This means that they were not victims of slaughter—which is likened to the harvest—or harsh persecutions, nor did they reach the point of becoming nomads (*jawālī*) due to their small number, as it is said, *You shall be left few in number* (Deut 28:62). וְנִשְׁאַר־בּוֹ עוֹלֵלֹת (Isa 17:6)—"Gleanings will remain in it." This means that there were righteous ones in Israel. The righteous ones are likened to the *gleanings*: *As when the vintage has been gleaned: there is no cluster to eat* (Mic 7:1). The interpretation [of cluster] is *the righteous and the upright ones*, as it is said, *The godly man has perished from the earth, and there is none upright among men* (Mic 7:2). Then he divides the clusters and the gleanings into two parts. [First]: *as the beating of an olive tree* (Isa 17:6)—just as a scattering (*nathāra*) of olives are scattered in the land, so are the righteous ones (*al-ṣāliḥīn*) dispersed (*mufarraqīn*) throughout the world. [Second]: Others are likened to *two or three berries in the top of the highest bough* (Isa 17:6). That is to say, they are clustered like fruit (*thamr*) <79a> at the top of a tree. In my opinion, they are the people who are clustered together in Jerusalem for worship, who are few in number.[51] Their authority (*amr*) will increase bit by bit, then the *remnant* will appear, as it is said, *four or five on the branches of a fruit tree* (Isa 17:6). At that time, obedience to God will become perfect and deviation within the nation will cease, as it is said, *In that day men will regard their Maker, and their eyes will look to the Holy One of Israel* (Isa 17:7). [The word] *very* is added to *we are brought low* (Ps 79:8). This alludes to the extreme degree of poverty and deprivation from every aspect of knowledge, wisdom, ease, power, statehood, strength, dignity, majesty, and every glorious state.

עָזְרֵנוּ אֱלֹהֵי יִשְׁעֵנוּ (Ps 79:9)—"Help us, O God of our salvation, for the glory of Your name; deliver us, and forgive our sins, for Your name's sake!" *Help us, O God of our salvation* is Israel's confession that they have no other help than Him, the LORD. *God of our salvation*—as it is said, *Our God is a God of salvation* (Ps 68:21/20). *For the glory of Your name, deliver us* (Ps 79:9) means when the *redemption* (*ge'ulah*) becomes manifest, the glory of <79b>

[50] I.e., the "third exile" in Salmon's list, when the remnant of Israel fell to Assyria.
[51] An allusion to the Mourners for Zion.

Your name will become manifest in the world, as it is said, *and I will vindicate the holiness of My great name [which has been profaned among the nations]* (Ezek 36:23) and *the day that I show My glory, says the Lord GOD* (Ezek 39:13). *Deliver us, and forgive our sins, for Your name's sake* (Ps 79:9). That is to say, "Do not regard our sins; do so for the sake of Your name," as it is said, לָמָּה יֹאמְרוּ הַגּוֹיִם (Ps 79:10)—"Why should the nations say, 'Where is your God?' " He informed [us] concerning the nations, that they would look upon us [and behold] the avenging of the outpoured blood of Your servants. Thus, the *evil kingdom of Edom* says, "Where is your God? He has become angry with you, O Jews, and He has chosen us! We are like a new wife; while you and your Torah have become weak and outdated, we and our book are a new people."

[This verse] reverses what they said, so that the avenging of the shed blood of Your servants will be known among the nations before our eyes. We will witness this, as it is said, [*Then my enemy will see, and shame will cover her who said to me, "Where is the LORD your God?"*] *My eyes will gloat over her* (Mic 7:10). The verse, *Let the avenging of the outpoured blood of Your servants* (Ps 79:10) complements the verse above, *They have poured out their blood like water* (Ps 79:3).

תָּבוֹא לְפָנֶיךָ (Ps 79:11)—"Let the groans of the prisoners enter before You; according to Your great power preserve the children of death!"[52] *Let the groans come before You* means, "Our petition to You is sent up from <80a> this prison and You will bring about our release." *Thus would the LORD of hosts do, and save us, for the sake of His great name. According to Your great power preserve the children of death!* The children's parents already have died, and they are left orphans; they are children of death, as it is said, *Abraham does not know us and Israel does not acknowledge us* (Isa 63:16), and *We have become orphans, fatherless* (Lam 5:3).

וְהָשֵׁב לִשְׁכֵנֵינוּ (Ps 79:12)—"Repay our neighbors with complete vengeance in their detention, because of their mockery, with which they mocked You, O Lord." [This verse] must be an allusion to those who inhabited the land of Israel, who inhabited Zion and Jerusalem and the house of *Solomon*. They slandered You and reviled You with that, and they mocked Your religion (*dīn*) and Your book.[53]

[52] Cf. RSV: "those doomed to die" (lit. "children of death").

[53] I.e., those non-Jews who have settled in the land of Israel have flaunted their success as proof of the superiority of their religion over the Torah and the Jewish community.

וַאֲנַחְנוּ עַמְּךָ (Ps 79:13)—"And we Your people, the flock of Your pasture, will thank You forever, from generation to generation will we recount Your praise." [This] means that the situation in which You are our shepherd will resume, as You promised when You said, *I myself will be the shepherd of My sheep, and I will make them lie down* (Ezek 34:15). [You are] the one who carried us.

We have explained this *psalm* here because it joins together with many similar themes in this book. It is said in [the psalm], <80b> *They have poured out their blood like water* (Ps 79:3) and it is said here, *He has slain all the pride of our eyes* (Lam 2:4).

In the tent of the daughter of Zion He has poured out His fury like fire. It means that what befell this nation is amazing, just as Jeremiah lamented over them elsewhere when he said, *My tent is destroyed, and all my cords* [*are broken*] (Jer 10:20). All these calamities overtook us because we did not obey the counsel of God, as it is said, *I spoke to you in your prosperity, but you said, "I will not listen"* (Jer 22:21).

Lamentations 2:6

וַיַּחְמֹס כַּגַּן שֻׂכּוֹ שִׁחֵת מֹעֲדוֹ שִׁכַּח יְהוָה בְּצִיּוֹן מוֹעֵד וְשַׁבָּת וַיִּנְאַץ בְּזַעַם־אַפּוֹ מֶלֶךְ וְכֹהֵן׃
ונת'ר מת'ל אלג'נאן ערישה אפסד קדסה אנסא אללה פי ציון עיד וסבת ורפץ'
בזעם גצ'בה מלך ואמאם

He has scattered his bower like a garden, laid in ruins His Temple; the LORD has brought to an end in Zion festival and Sabbath, and in His fierce anger has spurned king and priest.[54]

I translated *va-yaḥmos* as "He has scattered," as that is closest to its meaning, as in: *He will shake off* (*yaḥmos*) *his unripe grape, like the vine* (Job 15:33). They also say [the clause means] "He uncovered His shelter (*miẓalla*) like the garden," just as a garden has no roof.[55] It is similar to the verse, [*It is for*

[54] Cf. RSV: "He has broken down His booth like that of a garden, laid in ruins the place of His appointed feasts; the LORD has brought to an end in Zion appointed feast and Sabbath, and in His fierce indignation has spurned king and priest."

[55] In the verse translation, Salmon renders Hebr. *sukko* ("His booth") with Arab. *ʿarish* ("bower, hut"); here he paraphrases it with Arab. *miẓalla* ("shaded place, shelter"), which accords with Arab. translations of *sukka* in connection with the festival of Sukkot (see, e.g., Saadia's translation of Lev 23:42 in Joseph Derenbourg, *Saadia Ben Josef Al-Fayyoûmî: Œvres Complètes*, vol. 1

the greatness of your iniquity] *that your skirts are lifted up* (*neḥmesu*), *and you suffer violence* (Jer 13:22), which means the cessation of [divine] support.[56]

They say that *va-yaḥmos* is from [the root] *ḥamas*, as in the verse, *He will shake off* (*yaḥmos*) *his unripe grape, like the vine* (Job 15:33).[57] In other words, He is angry like the grapevine that is angered by its unripe grapes, which do not ripen and become grapes [so] he throws them off [while] they are still unripe. These meanings [i.e., "shaking off" and "uncovering"] are similar to one another. Their purpose is to provide a parable (*mathal*) for the disgrace and the cessation of [divine] support that have overtaken this nation, so that everyone who contemplates them will apprehend their intended meaning. <82b> Its [meaning] is like [that of] the verses, *I will remove its wall, and it shall be devoured; I will break down its wall, and it shall be trampled down* (Isa 5:5) and *Why then have You broken down its walls* (Ps 80:13/12).[58] As for the kingdom itself, it is said, *You have breached all its walls* (Ps 89:41/40).[59]

They say also that the meaning of *va-yaḥmos* is that God became angry with His shelter, in the sense (*maʿnā*) of seizing His Temple and all that was within it, including *the ark and the glory and the altars and the musical instruments and the sacrifices and the temple instruments*, just as every good thing

(Hildesheim: Georg Olms Verlag, 1979), 181). In their own translations of Lam 2:6, Saadia uses Arab. *ẓilāl* ("shade") and Yefet uses Arab. *ʿarīsh*.

56 *Naththara mithl al-jinān ʿarīshahu*, "He has scattered His shelter like a garden." Salmon translates Hebr. *va-yaḥmos* as Arab. *naththara* in order to represent both aspects of its meaning: "to shake off" (as in Job 15:33) and "to uncover" (as in Jer 13:22). Al-Fāsī translates the clause differently—*ghaṣaba ka-l-jinān*, "He seized [His booth] like a garden"—but cites the same proof texts that Salmon offers here. Al-Fāsī explains that the verb *va-yaḥmos* in Lam 2:6 has the same meaning as both Job 15:33 (which "means that the sour grapes were scattered (*yunāthir*) before they had ripened") and Jer 13:22 (which means: "her uncovering and her exposure. At the time when blessing ceased, the woman was exposed, when she was unclothed of garments") (vol. I, 559–60). Saadia's and Yefet's translations of Lam 2:6 reflect the dual meanings of the verb; Saadia opts for *naththara* ("to scatter") while Yefet opts for *kashafa* ("to uncover").

57 Salmon may be thinking of Saadia, who translates *va-yaḥmos* as *wa-yanthur* at Job 15:33 on the basis of Lam 2:6: "*yaḥmos* means 'he scattered,' as in *He scattered His booth like a garden*" (Saadia, Job, 52).

58 Salmon addresses both prooftexts (Isa 5:5 and Ps 80:13/12) in his comment on Ps 80:13/12: "By 'wall' he means the tent of the lord of the worlds, which had been over them. He says now, in the wake of defeat, *Why then have You broken down its walls*, which is like what was said in the song of Isaiah: *I will remove its wall, and it shall be devoured* (Isa 5:5). The meaning of *so that all who pass along the way pluck its fruit* (Ps 80:13/12) is, in other words, 'When providence ceased, everyone coveted [the unprotected bounties of Israel]' " (Salmon, Pss 73–89).

59 In his comment to Ps 89:41/40 Salmon notes that in all the above verses—Isa 5:5, Ps 80:13/12, and Ps 89:41/40 itself—the breached wall means "the cessation of protection and [divine] support." Note that Salmon does not employ technical terminology (e.g., *majāz, istiʿāra*) in the Pss commentary. For discussion of this terminology, see chapter 4.

that was in the garden was taken from it and it was left empty and vacant, as it is said, *And I will make it a waste; it shall not be pruned or hoed* (Isa 5:6).[60]

One who translates *va-yaḥmos* as "He became angry" is justified. However, if someone should say, "How can this relate back to the anger of the Creator?" we would say, "The sterility of the seeds relates back to the Creator and He changes them from one state to [another] state, and the meaning (*maʿnā*) of sterility is [like] the meaning (*maʿnā*) of anger." All these statements conform to the standards of figurative language (*majāz*) and accessibility to human understanding, as it is said, *and despoil of life those who despoil them* (Prov 22:23). The Mighty and Sublime is the agent (*fāʿil*) of good and its opposite, as He says, *I make weal* (*shalom*) *and create woe* (*raʿ*) (Isa 45:7). The meaning of *weal* is well-being and goodness, and the meaning of *woe* <83a> alludes to affliction and punishment and whatever befalls the wicked, as it is said, *The LORD is a jealous God and avenging, the LORD is avenging and wrathful; the LORD takes vengeance on His adversaries and keeps wrath for His enemies* (Nah 1:2).[61]

The LORD has brought to an end in Zion appointed feast and Sabbath means the rejoicing and delights that were theirs on Sabbaths and festivals, as it is said, *And I will put an end to all her mirth, her feasts, her new moons, her Sabbaths, and all her appointed feasts* (Hos 2:13/11).[62] It may be that by his statement, ***the LORD has brought to an end in Zion appointed feast and Sabbath***, he alludes to the fact that when the destruction of Zion is complete and no one remains there after the *exile* for fifty-one years [after] the destruction of the Temple, Sabbath and festival will be forgotten in [Zion]. In other words, there will be no one there to observe the Sabbath, and no one to celebrate the festivals.[63]

[60] This reading—forcible seizure of the Temple—is suggested by al-Fāsī; see note 56.

[61] In this rare dialectical presentation, Salmon enters a philosophical conversation about divine agency in matters of change and causation. The hypothetical objection to Salmon's translation is that emotions and emotional volatility should not be attributed to God. Salmon responds to the objection by observing that just as the growth cycle of seeds does not negate divine agency, neither does divine anger negate the unchanging nature of God, and that both images follow the conventions of biblical figurative language. He argues that God creates everything, from beneficence to punishment. The implication of this last point may be that God creates God's own anger, or its manifestations in the material world.

[62] Salmon continues to advance a Karaite reading of Lamentations: God did not end the obligation of Sabbath and festival observance, but only the elements of joy and celebration that these holy days had previously entailed.

[63] Both interpretations express sectarian views in subtle ways. In the first, Salmon presents the Sabbath as a time of sadness, in contradiction to Rabbanites, who embraced the Sabbath as a time of rejoicing. In the second, Salmon depicts Jerusalem as empty of Jews to observe the Sabbath, reminding readers that the Karaites are engaged in establishing a community in Jerusalem, while the Rabbanites have no large-scale plans to leave the Diaspora and settle in the Holy Land. Yet Salmon's polemical comments are mild in comparison to al-Qūmisī's reading of Lam 2:6, where he

In this verse the word *mo'ed* [is used in] two different senses. [In the context of] *mo'ed ve-shabbat* it alludes to holidays. [In the context of] *shiḥet mo'ado* it alludes to the Temple, because it is called by this word, as in the verse, *Your foes have roared in the midst of Your holy place* (*mo'adekha*) (Ps 74:4), and likewise, *They burned all the meeting places of God* (*mo'adei-'el*) *in the land* (Ps 74:8) alludes to the Temple. Thus, ***laid in ruins His mo'ed*** <83b> means His Temple.

And in His fierce indignation has spurned king and priest alludes to God's rejection of them. He mentions the king and the priest specifically because of the severity of the matter. In other words, since He has rejected the king and the priest, then it is all the more so [that He has rejected] the rest of the nation.

You must learn that all of these verses indicate requital (*muqābala*):

You forsook the Lord, as it is said, *Because you have forsaken the LORD, He has forsaken you* (2 Chr 24:20).

They turned their backs (Isa 1:4); *and went backward and not forward* (Jer 7:24).

And since you have forgotten the law of your God, I also will forget your children (Hos 4:6).

But they kept mocking the messengers of God (2 Chr 36:16); [*The foe gloated over her,*] *mocking at her downfall* (Lam 1:7); *All my enemies have heard of my trouble; they are glad* (Lam 1:21). *Despising His words* (2 Chr 36:16); and we became a reproach for man and despised by people.[64]

[*What will you say when they set as head over you*] *those whom you yourself have taught to be friends to you?* (Jer 13:21); *Her foes have become the head* (Lam 1:5).

They have stirred Me to jealousy with what is no god; they have provoked Me with their idols. So I will stir them to jealousy with those who are no people; I will provoke them with a foolish nation (Deut 32:21).

For they have rejected the law of the LORD of hosts (Isa 5:24); *and the LORD rejected all the descendants of Israel* (2 Kgs 17:20).

accuses the Rabbanites of having corrupted the Sabbaths and overturned the festivals (al-Qūmisī, Sermon, 18 = 46).

[64] The linguistic foundation of this juxtaposition is less solid. In the other sets of biblical verses, Salmon joins biblical verses that share key words or roots in order to represent the religious principle of retribution in kind or reciprocal punishment (*bāb al-muqābala*). Here Salmon presents the connection between the sin and the punishment thematically rather than linguistically, and he summarizes the connection in Arab. rather than with a biblical Hebr. prooftext.

Israel has spurned the good (Hos 8:3); *The Lord has scorned His altar* (Lam 2:7).

And turned aside, refusing <84a> *to obey Your voice* (Dan 9:11); *Woe to them when I turn aside from them!* (Hos 9:12).

Broken the everlasting covenant (Isa 24:5); *Covenants are broken, cities are despised* (Isa 33:8).

As I called, and they would not hear, so they called, and I would not hear (Zech 7:13).

I spread out My hands all the day to a rebellious people (Isa 65:2); *When you spread forth your hands, I will hide My eyes from you* (Isa 1:15).

They have forsaken the LORD, they have despised the Holy One of Israel, they are utterly estranged (Isa 1:4); *The LORD saw it, and despised them* (Deut 32:19).

Everything that overtook us in this *exile* was because our Lord advised us but we did not listen, as it is said, *I spoke to you in your prosperity, but you said, "I will not listen"* (Jer 22:21).

Lamentations 2:18

צָעַק לִבָּם אֶל־אֲדֹנָי חוֹמַת בַּת־צִיּוֹן הוֹרִידִי כַנַּחַל דִּמְעָה יוֹמָם וָלַיְלָה אַל־תִּתְּנִי פוּגַת לָךְ אַל־תִּדֹּם בַּת־עֵינֵךְ׃

צרך' קלבהם אלי אללה יא סור ג'מאעה ציון אחדרי מת'ל אלואד דמעה נהאר וליל לא תג'עלי פתור לך לא תסכת בובו עינך

Their heart cried to God: O wall of the congregation of Zion! Let tears stream down like a wadi day and night! Grant yourself no laxity; let the pupil of your eye not be quiet![65]

I translated *pugat* as "laxity"[66] as in, *So the law is lax* (Hab 1:4). I translated *bat-'eynekh* as pupil, as in, *Keep me as the daughter of the eye* (Ps 17:8) and *the daughter of his eye* (Zech 2:12/8), because the pupil of the eye was

[65] Cf. RSV: "Their heart cried to the Lord! O wall of the daughter of Zion! Let tears stream down like a torrent day and night! Give yourself no rest, your eyes no respite!"

[66] Arab. *futūr*. The same root, in the form *fatra*, appears in the translations of Lam 2:18 by al-Fāsī (vol. II, 446), Saadia (Lam, 99), and Yefet.

called daughter.[67] It was called daughter in the verse, *the daughter of his eye* (Zech 2:12/18).[68]

Their heart cried to the Lord means: after this affliction hit, it was obligatory to cry out to God, as it is said, *O LORD, God of my salvation; by day, I cry out in the night before You* (Ps 88:2/1).[69] ***Their heart*** means the purification of [their] intention (*ikhlāṣ al-niyya*) and innermost thoughts (*bāṭin al-tawīya*).[70]

Let tears stream down like a wadi alludes to the amount of crying over what happened to this nation and her Temple. ***Like a wadi*** is an example of figurative language (*majāz*), just as it is said, ***let the pupil of your eye not rest*** even though rest does not fall upon the pupil. Rather, this is said by way of figurative language (*majāz*) and metaphor (*istiʿāra*). Its meaning (*maʿnā*) is that you will be overwhelmed with crying in these times of prayer and these times of lament over our rebellions and the trial, exile, and abandonment that overtook us <98b> when we did not listen to the counsel of our Creator, as it is said, *I spoke to you in your prosperity, but you said, "I will not listen"* (Jer 22:21).

Lamentations 2:20

רְאֵה יְהוָה וְהַבִּיטָה לְמִי עוֹלַלְתָּ כֹּה אִם־תֹּאכַלְנָה נָשִׁים פִּרְיָם עֹלְלֵי טִפֻּחִים
אִם־יֵהָרֵג בְּמִקְדַּשׁ אֲדֹנָי כֹּהֵן וְנָבִיא׃
אנט'ר יא רב ואלתפת למן בטשת במת'ל הד'א חתי צארת אלנסא תאכלן
ת'מרהם צביאן אלתרביה פהל יקתל פי קדס אללה כהן ונביא

Look, O Lord, and see! Whom have You attacked like this? Should women eat their offspring, children reared? [Should] priest and prophet be slain in God's Temple?

I translated *ṭipuḥim* as "reared" as in, *Those whom I dandled* (*ṭipaḥti*) *and reared* (*ribiti*) *my enemy destroyed* (Lam 2:22). They say *ṭipuḥim* is from *tapaḥ*

[67] Salmon uses two Arab. words for pupil, *ḥadaqa* and *bū'bū'*, in his comment here and at Ps 17:8. He uses the latter term in the verse translation, and both terms throughout the comment.

[68] Cf. RSV: "apple" of the eye in each verse.

[69] In his comment to Ps 88:2/1, Salmon explains, "His words, *O LORD, God of my salvation* mean, 'You are my savior, and I have no savior other than You.' The meaning of *by day I cry out* means the time of exile, which is compared to night."

[70] Salmon returns to these pietistic concepts in his comments to Lam 3:40 and 3:50.

("to spread, extend"), which means that their good heads and intellects become wide when they are reared.

Look, O LORD, and see! [This expression] is calling on God for help during the worst [part] of the situation and magnifying the catastrophe that befell us, as the lamenter says in the beginning of the book: *O LORD, see my affliction!* (Lam 1:9); *See, O LORD, that I am in distress* (Lam 1:20), and just as another prophet said, *Look down from heaven and see* (Isa 63:15). <100a> The meaning [of these verses] is "See our affairs and our grievances and all that has come upon us, just as You saw the affairs of our fathers, as it was said, *I have seen the affliction of My people who are in Egypt* (Exod 3:7)."

The lamenter says, ***Whom have You attacked like this***, which is like the verse, *if there is any sorrow like my sorrow* (Lam 1:12).

Women eat their offspring expresses amazement at what happens in these circumstances: women eat their own children. His intention in mentioning the women is [to show that] they have been stripped of their compassion, as it is said, *The hands of compassionate women have boiled [their own children]* (Lam 4:10). ***Children reared*** is added because the [mother's] heartfelt compassion for the child is greater when he has grown and been reared.[71]

Should priest and prophet be slain in the Temple of the Lord? They say this alludes to what befell the priests and prophets in the Temple when the enemies entered. We have scrutinized this but have not found [any instance in which] the enemies killed a prophet, either within the Temple or outside of it.[72]

One scholar has said that this verse—that is to say, "Are priest and prophet killed before the LORD?"—is a response to the words of the lamenter: ***Should women eat their offspring.***[73] This indicates the severity of what Joash King of Judah perpetrated <100b> by the murder of Zechariah ben Jehoiada.[74]

[71] For an enlightening treatment of maternal lament in connection with this verse in *Lam R*, see Galit Hasan-Rokem, *Web of Life: Folklore and Midrash in Rabbinic Literature* (Stanford, Calif.: Stanford University Press, 2000), chapter 6.

[72] I.e., the prophets were killed by the Israelites, not by foreign enemies. On the motif of propheticide in Jewish literature, see Betsy Halpern Amaru, "The Killing of the Prophets: Unraveling a Midrash," *HUCA* 54 (1983): 153–80.

[73] Salmon seems to uphold this reading, which appears in Tg. Lam, the Talmud, and *Lam R* on 2:20. According to this reading, Jeremiah asks God whether women should eat their own children (thus expressing his horror at the dire situation of the Israelites), and God responds by asking whether priests and prophets should be killed in the Temple (thus insinuating that Israelite suffering is an appropriate punishment for their sin of killing priest and prophet—specifically, Zechariah ben Jehoiada). See Kalman, "Authorship," 67–68; Abdul-Karim, 72.

[74] See 2 Chr 24:20–22 for the death of Zechariah ben Jehoiada, a priest who also functioned as a prophet. He was stoned in the Temple court, by order of King Joash, who had been reared by his (Zecahriah's) father.

How could this matter not be severe, since Jehoiada suffered hardship in order to rescue Joash from the hand of Athalya, and raise him for seven years when the queen had demanded that he be killed? Joash should have remembered Jehoiada, this *pious one*, and [he should have] rewarded his son in gratitude.

He did not do [this, but instead] he did what he [should] not have done: he participated in the killing of Zechariah when he channeled his Lord's message, as it is said: *Then the Spirit of God took possession of Zechariah the son of Jehoiada the priest; and he stood above the people, and said to them, "Thus says God, 'Why do you transgress the commandments of the LORD, so that you cannot prosper? Because you have forsaken the LORD, He has forsaken you.'" But they conspired against him, and by command of the king they stoned him with stones in the court of the house of the LORD. Thus Joash the king did not remember the kindness which Jehoiada, Zechariah's father, had shown him, but killed his son. And when he was dying, he said, "May the LORD see and avenge!"* (2 Chr 24:20–22).

And that Zechariah, peace be upon him, is buried in the noble Jerusalem (*al-quds*), in Samaritikē, which is the *ṣela' ha-'elef ha-yevusi* and today is called the Quarter of the Easterners (*ḥārat al-mashāriqa*), as <101a> Mevōrākh b. Natan, may the mercy of God most high be upon him, mentioned in one of his *wailing songs* (*qinot*): "And I wept facing the tomb of Zechariah, son of Jehoiada, the one whose tomb is known [to be] in *ṣela' ha-'elef*."[75]

[Zechariah ben Jehoiada] was priest and prophet, and that is why [the verse says that] their blood was spilled in the Temple, as it is said, *Therefore He brought up against them the king of the Chaldeans, who slew their young men with the sword in the house of their sanctuary* (2 Chr 36:17) and *He has slain all*

[75] In this rare reference to the urban landscape of his own day, Salmon suggests a location for the Karaite quarter in Jerusalem and indicates that this place is known by three names. Samaritikē derives from the Greek Christian name for a Jerusalem church that memorializes Jesus's encounter with the Samaritan woman at the well (John 4). The place that Salmon designates as *ṣela' ha-'elef ha-yevusi* (Josh 18:28) could be translated literally as "the Jebusite place of the limping cattle." (Note that MT records this place slightly differently—*ṣela' ha-elef ve-ha-yevusi*—which suggests two places [*ṣela' ha-'elef* and *ha-yevusi*], while English translations render the phrase with three proper nouns, suggesting three places.) Salmon explains that both place names refer to what is known in his own time as the Quarter of the Easterners, which Moshe Gil understands as the quarter of the Karaites, who came from the east two centuries after the beginning of Jewish immigration to Jerusalem in the Arab period and settled outside the city walls. See Gil, "The Jewish Quarters of Jerusalem According to Cairo Geniza Documents and Other Sources," *JNES* 41 (1982), 275. On the poet Mevōrākh b. Nathan b. Nīsān, who is also cited by Yefet b. 'Eli, see Gil, "The Jewish Quarters," 275 n. 49 and references there.

the pride of our eyes in the tent of the daughter of Zion (Lam 2:4) and, below, *In the day of Your anger You have slain them, slaughtering without mercy* (Lam 2:21). And all these catastrophes overtook us because we did not accept the guidance of our Creator, as it is said, *I spoke to you in your prosperity, but you said, "I will not listen"* (Jer 22:21).

Lamentations 3

Lamentations 3:1

אֲנִי הַגֶּבֶר רָאָה עֳנִי בְּשֵׁבֶט עֶבְרָתוֹ׃
אנא אלרג'ל נט'ר אלצ'עף בקצ'יב חלטתה

I am the man who has seen affliction under the rod of His wrath.

ʿŎnî is "afflicted" (ḍaʿīf), as in "affliction" (ḍuʿf).[1] Thus ʿōnî is "affliction" (ḍuʿf), as in, *in the furnace of affliction* (ʿōnî; Isa 48:10). ʿŎnî is the form in the *construct state* (*samukh*), as in the phrase *on Your servant's misery* (ʿŏnî; 1 Sam 1:11). ʿŎnyî (Lam 3:19) is "my affliction" (ḍuʿfī). I have already made it clear in the introduction to the Book of Psalms that it was entirely revealed by the prophets [who are] mentioned <103a> there.[2] Indeed, they said this [as] instruction for Israel (*taʿlīm le-yiśraʾel*) so that [Israel] would use it to plead with God. The surest proof of this comes from the speech of Asaph the Gershonite:[3] *O God, the nations have invaded Your inheritance* (Ps 79:1). This prophecy was

[1] "Affliction" based on biblical prooftexts; Arabic lexicons do not list it as a meaning of the root ḍ/ʿ/f. In his Psalms commentary, Salmon translates ʿ*oni* with one of two Arab. roots: sh/q/w (which relates to misery and complaint) and ḍ/ʿ/f (which relates to weakness and affliction). For the former, which is more prevalent, see, e.g., Salmon's translation of Pss 10:2, 18:28/27, 22:25/26, 37:14, 40:18/17, 69:30, 70:6/5, 74:21, 82:3, 86:1, 88:10, 107:10, 109:16, 109:22, 119:92. For the latter, see, e.g., Salmon's translation of Pss 14:6, 34:7/6, 35:10, 140:13/12. Note that Salmon uses both Arabic words to translate certain Hebrew pairs such as ʿ*oni ve-khoʾev* ("afflicted and in pain," Ps 69:30/29) or ʿ*oni va-rash* ("afflicted and destitute," Ps 82:3). For Lam 3:1, Saadia renders ʿ*oni* as ʿ*adhāb* ("agonies"; Saadia, Lam, 100) and Yefet renders it *shaqāʾ* ("misery").

[2] Here Salmon applies to Lamentations a Karaite view of prayer, which he also presents in the introduction to his commentary on the Psalms. There, Salmon argues *contra* Saadia that the psalms were revealed by the prophets whose names appear in the superscriptions, and that the psalms were recorded in the Bible so that future generations would utter them as prayers. See Jonathan Shunary, "Salmon b. Yeruham's Commentary on the Book of Psalms," *JQR* 73 (1982): 159; Uriel Simon, *Four Approaches to the Book of Psalms from Saadia Gaon to Abraham Ibn Ezra*, SUNY Series in Judaica, trans. Lenn J. Schramm (Albany: State University of New York Press, 1991), 59–71.

[3] Salmon considers Asaph to be a prophet, along with all the figures whose names are mentioned in the headings of psalms (Shunary, "Salmon ben Yeruham's Commentary," 161, and Simon, *Four Approaches*, 70).

Jewish Piety in Islamic Jerusalem. Jessica Andruss, Oxford University Press. © Oxford University Press 2023.
DOI: 10.1093/oso/9780197639559.003.0012

not about the people of Jerusalem[4] during the time in which Asaph spoke when, to the contrary, they were in [a time of] might and dominion, majesty, statehood, and copious grace. And yet, he said *they have invaded* [. . .] *they have defiled* [. . .] *they have reduced* [. . .] *they have left* [. . .] *they have poured out* (Ps 79:1–3). All this is in the past tense[5] so that when this matter came to pass, we would speak [appropriately] for what had happened. There are many such examples in the words of the prophets. Likewise, David said, *My God, my God, why have You forsaken me?* (Ps 22:2/1) and *Dogs surround me, a pack of villains encircles me* [. . .] *they divide my clothes among them* (Ps 22:17/16, 19/18). Not a single one of these situations that are described befell David. Rather, he said them by means of the Holy Spirit, [as] instruction for Israel (*taʿlīm le-yiśraʾel*) so that they would use them to plead during this *exile*.[6] The sons of Koraḥ, Assir and Elkanah, and the father of Asaph did likewise: when they were in the wilderness, in the tabernacle of the Lord, with the glory and fire from heaven and signs and wonders and marvelous sights, <103b> they said, *As with a deadly wound in my body, my adversaries taunt me, while they say to me continually, "Where is your God?"* (Ps 42:11/10).

It is the same with Jeremiah's words, ***I am the man***.[7] He spoke these [words] by means of the Holy Spirit, [as] instruction for Israel (*taʿlīm le-yiśraʾel*) so that they would lament over themselves with these *lamentations*. We know that Jeremiah spoke this book through the Holy Spirit because of the verse *Jeremiah composed laments for Josiah, and to this day all the male and female singers commemorate Josiah in the laments* (2 Chr 35:25), which alludes to the verse *The breath of our nostrils, the LORD's anointed, was taken in their pits* (Lam 4:20).[8]

The reason that he put his lamentation over Josiah into this book—which is in fact the *laments* over the nation—is because the calamity was sent down

[4] Arab. *al-quds*. One of the rare instances when the term signifies Jerusalem (usually *yerushalayim*) rather than the Temple.

[5] Hebr. *lashon ʿavar*. Ibn Nūḥ uses the same Hebr. terminology (Khan, *The Early Tradition*, 146). See discussion in chapter 2, in the section on "The Translation of Lamentations."

[6] Salmon does not make this point in his explanations of Ps 22:2/1, 17/16–19/18 in his Psalms commentary. However, he does gesture toward an exilic application of the psalm when he remarks, in his comment to Ps 22:1, that the superscription—*the Hind of the Dawn*—compares the hind, who seeks out the male deer in the dawn, to Israel, who seeks out their Lord at the end of the exile.

[7] On the many traditional and scholarly attempts to identify "the man" of Lamentations 3, see Kim Lan Nguyen, *Chorus in the Dark: The Voices of the Book of Lamentations* (Sheffield, U.K.: Sheffield Phoenix, 2013), esp. chapter 5.

[8] Salmon reads Lam 4:20 as an allusion to King Josiah, following a tradition that dates back at least as far the Targum and is accepted also by Yefet ben ʿEli. See Salmon on Lam 4:20 and notes there.

when Josiah passed away.[9] At that point, Jehoahaz was carried to Egypt, shackled, and then he died, as it is said, *But he took Jehoahaz away; and he came to Egypt, and died there* (2 Kgs 23:34). Then Nebuchadnezzar was victorious over Jehoiakim, as it is said, *And the Lord delivered Jehoiakim king of Judah into his hand* (Dan 1:2), and Nebuchadnezzar carried Jehoiachin to Babylon, shackled and blinded, and confined him to prison for thirty-seven years. Afterward Nebuchadnezzar also carried Zedekiah to Babylon, <104a> shackled and blinded, and confined him to prison until he died, as it is said, *where he put him in prison till the day of his death* (Jer 52:11). Therefore, [Jeremiah] set down in writing the lamentation over Josiah in this book, and no one in this nation will contradict that the book of Lamentations was authored by Jeremiah of Anathoth.[10]

I am the man who has seen affliction (Lam 3:1). He indicates in this verse that "Verily, I have seen the misery and the affliction (*al-ḍuʿf*) that was foretold by the prophets. It was said to the ancients: *and the LORD will scatter you among the peoples* (Deut 4:27); *and I will scatter you among the nations* (Lev 26:33); *and I will lay your cities waste* (Lev 26:31); *the LORD will bring you, and your king whom you set over you* [*to a nation that neither you nor your fathers have known*] (Deut 28:36); and *the LORD will bring a nation against you from afar* (Deut 28:49).They heard these threats. They heard, but they did not see it as witnesses, whereas I [Jeremiah] witnessed it and I observed it."

Likewise, they also heard from Isaiah everything that would befall them on the day that the enemy triumphed over them in Jerusalem, and how each condition would come to pass. The ancients heard but the *generation of* [*His*] *wrath* witnessed, as it is said:[11]

מַשָּׂא גֵּיא חִזָּיוֹן מַה־לָּךְ אֵפוֹא כִּי־עָלִית כֻּלָּךְ לַגַּגּוֹת (Isa 22:1)—"This is the prophecy concerning this vision. What remains for you, that you have gone up, in your entirety, to the rooftops?" Jerusalem is called <104b> the *valley of*

[9] Salmon asserts that Lam 3 fits the genre and purpose of a communal lament, even though it is written in the first-person singular voice of the prophet Jeremiah. This assertion may suggest that Salmon is arguing against others who thought that Lam 3 was an individual lament, or perhaps even a historical poem without liturgical significance. Such an argument recalls the debate between Saadia and the Karaites over whether or not the psalms constituted mandatory prayers, received by prophetic inspiration (Simon, *Four Approaches*, 59–71). Given the central role of Lamentations in Karaite liturgy, Salmon's comment here may reflect a similar debate about the role of Lamentations in Jewish liturgy more broadly.

[10] *Le-yermiyahu*. In his Psalms commentary, Salmon argues (*contra* Saadia) that the preposition *le* found in the superscriptions of specific psalms indicates authorship (Simon, *Four Approaches*, 69–70). Salmon uses the same construction here to designate Jeremiah as the prophetic author of the book of Lamentations.

[11] Here begins Salmon's excursus on Isa 22:1–14.

vision because all the prophets prophesied over it frequently, and they would gather and meet together there during the three pilgrimage festivals.[12]

Then he said: מַה־לָּךְ אֵפוֹא (Isa 22:1)—"What remains now for you," [that is, for you] who used to say, *The days grow long, and every vision comes to nought* (Ezek 12:22) and [for you who] used to say, *Let Him make haste, let Him speed His work, that we may see it* (Isa 5:19)?[13] Now Nebuchadnezzar, the one you were threatened with, has indeed arrived, and he has besieged you. Indeed, now you have gone up, all of you, to the rooftops, following the known custom. When the enemy triumphed over the country, drawing the sword, the people of the country had no escape other than fleeing to the rooftops and appealing to God for salvation. It is also possible that the statement *that you have gone up, all of you, to the housetops* (Isa 22:1) indicates that people climbed up to the rooftops so that they would see the enemy blockading Jerusalem.

תְּשֻׁאוֹת מְלֵאָה עִיר הוֹמִיָּה (Isa 22:2)—"Full of clamor, jumbled-up city, exultant town! Now your slain are not slain with the sword or dead in battle." תְּשֻׁאוֹת מְלֵאָה means, "O, you who were full with the clamor <105a> of people"—as it is said, *the city that was full of people* (Lam 1:1)—"now you have become a jumbled-up, confused, mixed-up city," as it is said, *she is jumbled and wayward* (Prov 7:11), and there are those who are *confused*, as it is said, *like doves of the valleys, they are all confused* (Ezek 7:16). *Exultant town*: now the mourning is great for the city that used to be exultant with many pleasures, because her slain ones are not slain by the sword or dead in battle, but rather, in the gravest way of all, which is that the people were besieged, with *pestilence* and *famine*, at home.

כָּל־קְצִינַיִךְ (Isa 22:3)—"All your princes have fled together, without the bow they were captured. All of you who were found were captured, though they had fled from far away." *All your princes have fled together, without the bow they were captured* refers to when Zedekiah the king and the rest of the princes fled to Jericho, toward Jordan. The company of Nebuchadnezzar overtook them, as it is said, *But the army of the Chaldeans pursued the king, and overtook him*

[12] Al-Fāsī also identifies *the valley of vision* (*ge' ḥizzayon*) with Jerusalem (vol. II, 52), although without the explanation that Salmon provides here. Saadia translates the locale as *bayt al-maqdis*, also meaning Jerusalem, in his Isaiah commentary; see Haggai Ben-Shammai, "Jerusalem in Early Medieval Jewish Bible Exegesis," in *Jerusalem: Its Sanctity and Centrality to Judaism, Christianity, and Islam*, ed. Lee I. Levine (New York: Continuum, 1999), 450.

[13] In the biblical context, both statements are invoked as authentic sayings. The first is uttered by those who ridicule the prophet and his predictions of punishment (Ezek 12:22), while the second depicts the cavalier mentality of the Jerusalemites before their punishment (Isa 5:19).

in the plains of Jericho (2 Kgs 25:5), so that we would know that when he fled, there was an army and leaders with him in a group, as it is said, *all* <105b> *of you who were found were captured, though they had fled far away*. This means that they seized him and all who were with him, and shackled them, as it is said, *Then they captured the king* (2 Kgs 25:6). The reason that they seized him in Jericho was because the first of their victories over the country was there, as is known about the war of Jericho. [Nebuchadnezzar] conquered it, and then they surrendered [to] the king, as it is said, *In that day their strong cities will be like the deserted places of the wood* (Isa 17:9). By this he means that the fortified villages of Israel would be [deserted] because of what was commanded to befall them from their enemies, like what happened in Jericho concerning Israel. He fixed a time when they would abandon the tillable land and the trees of the estate and they would forfeit the country to them from before Israel, as it is said, *Now Jericho was shut up from within and without* (Josh 6:1). Then the enemies took Zedekiah, the king of Judah.

They were captured [means] that they were taken by means of terror, fear, and dismay of the enemy; even though they had strength, they did not inspire the people to draw weapons. *Having fled while the enemy was still far away* means that when they saw the enemy from afar, they fled out of fear, as it is said, *When Zedekiah king of Judah and all the soldiers saw them, they fled* (Jer 39:4). <106a>

עַל־כֵּן אָמַרְתִּי שְׁעוּ מִנִּי אֲמָרֵר בַּבֶּכִי אַל־תָּאִיצוּ לְנַחֲמֵנִי עַל־שֹׁד בַּת־עַמִּי (Isa 22:4)—"Therefore I said: 'Withdraw from me, leave me to weeping; do not try to comfort me for the plundering of all my people." When Isaiah saw the calamities that would befall Jerusalem, he lamented over Israel just as Jeremiah lamented, and he set it down in writing so that they would lament over themselves in exile, occupying themselves with neither joy nor gladness, as it is said at the end of this passage: *Therefore I said: "Withdraw from me, leave me to weeping"* (Isa 22:4). The word *she'u* is [as in] *Withdraw from him* (*she'eh me'alav*; Job 14:6). Whenever *mem* follows [the verb], it should be translated as "to withdraw," but whenever *'aleph* follows, by contrast, it has the sense of seeing, [as in] *And the LORD saw Abel* (*va-yisha' yhwh 'el-hevel*) *and his offering* (Gen 4:4); and *Men will see their Maker* (*yish'eh ha-'adam 'al-'ośehu*) [. . .] *they will not see their altars* (*ve-lo' yish'eh 'el-ha-mizbeḥot*; Isa 17:7–8). When I investigated what I explained to you about this meaning, I found it [to be] just as I described it to you.[14]

[14] The preposition that follows the verb sh/'/h changes its meaning: when followed by *min* it means "to withdraw from" and when followed by *'el* it means "to see." Al-Fāsī enumerates the many

Do not labor to comfort me—that is to say, there is no one to console us over these sorrowful calamities. And how could a person be consoled, when the one who was master became a servant of the kingdom; the one who was <106b> free became imprisoned; the one who shackled kings became shackled; the one who was a blessing became a curse; the one who demanded taxes from kings, his hands became taxed and his head humiliated; the one who governed became governed; the one who was content became subject to anger; the one who was followed became a follower; the one who was pleasantly remembered became shamefully remembered; the one who was beloved became odious; the one who was master became contemptible, lowly;[15] the one who was strong became weak; the one who was wealthy became poor; the one who was knowledgeable became ignorant; the one who was sated became hungry; the one who was not thirsty became thirsty; the one who was healthy became sickly; the one who commanded became commanded; the one who was king over kings became the servant of the kings over him; the one who had an inheritance would have that inheritance taken from him and possessed by his enemies; the one whose father was affectionate became an orphan—contemptible, vile, lowly, and disdained, as it is said, *All who see me mock me; they hurl insults, shaking their heads* (Ps 22:8/7).[16]

How could a person be consoled about the destruction of His Temple and the lack of prophecy and the lack of kingship, <107a> priesthood, glory,[17] sacrificial offerings and the rest? *Only [apart] from all goodness is there no joy.*[18] *All joy turns to gloom* (Isa 24:11); *For the Israelites will live many days without king or prince* (Hos 3:4)—*no inner sanctuary, no Temple, no porch, no courts, no gate, no gatekeeper, no judge, no officer, no Temple singer, no musicians, no one making atonement, no one sounding the clarion call,*[19] *no burnt*

facets of this word without explaining the role of prepositions in determining meaning. He uses Gen 4:4 and Isa 17:7 to illustrate the first meaning, *qabūl* ("to receive" as well as "to perceive" by sight or hearing) and Isa 22:4 and Job 14:6 to illustrate the third meaning, *kaff* ("renunciation") (vol. II, 691–92).

15 The doubling of synonyms here—which is not a feature of the rest of the passage—suggests that *dhalīl* ("lowly") is a gloss for the less familiar term *mahān* ("contemptible").

16 This passage is structured around the repetition of the phrase "the one who was X became Y" (*wa-man kāna* X *ṣāra* Y). Occasional rhyme seems to occur by coincidence rather than by design. Ben Shammai identifies this passage as one of the *piyyuṭim* that could be inserted into the Karaite mourning liturgy ("Poetic Works and Lamentations," 212–13).

17 Arab. *waqār*, i.e., the divine presence; Hebr. *kavod*. See Salmon's excursus at Lam 1:6 and discussion in chapter 3.

18 Hebr. *raq mikkol ṭovah 'ayn śimḥah*. This phrase is not biblical.

19 As in 1 Chr 15:24; the instrument was likely a "long, straight, slender metal tube, with flaring end," not the ram's horn (*BDB*, 348).

offering and no grain offering, no mixing,[20] *no pouring out, no pure frankincense, no sweet spices, no sin offering and no guilt offerings, no peace offering of fed beasts, no offering of the firstborn, no Passover sacrifices, no holiness offerings, no tithe, no contributions, no illness offering, no offering of the first fruits, no freewill offering, no thanksgiving offering, no kingship, and no priesthood.*[21]

Do not labor to comfort me for the destruction of the daughter of my people (Isa 22:4). Oh Israel, how can you be in good spirits and joyous in exile? In another passage from *the oracle concerning the valley of vision* (Isa 22:1), it is said about someone who rejoices, *Surely this iniquity will not be forgiven you till you die* (Isa 22:14).

כִּי יוֹם מְהוּמָה וּמְבוּסָה וּמְבוּכָה (Isa 22:5)—"For the LORD God of hosts has a day of tumult and trampling and confusion in the valley of revelation (*waḥy*), quaking of the walls and turning to the mountains." <107b> *A day of tumult* alludes to the tremendous tumult that will happen on a day of the enemies' victory. *Trampling* alludes to all of Israel in the siege, and their being trampled in punishment, as it is said, *The LORD has trodden as in a wine press* (Lam 1:15). *Confusion* alludes to the degree of stratagem and bewilderment, as it is said, *In that day, says the LORD, courage shall fail both king and princes* (Jer 4:9). *The Lord God of hosts* means that all of these conditions are from the LORD, as it is said, *According to their way I will do to them* (Ezek 7:27). *The valley of vision* means that a time is appointed in Jerusalem [when] the walls will tremble and people will turn to flee to the mountains, and they will hope for the mountains to fall down upon them and for the cliffs to conceal them from the enemy, as it is said, *And they shall say to the mountains, Cover us, and to the hills, Fall upon us* (Hos 10:8).

וְעֵילָם נָשָׂא אַשְׁפָּה (Isa 22:6)—"And Elam carried the quiver with a retinue of people and horsemen, and the people of Kir uncovered the shield."[22] Know also that Nebuchadnezzar rallied many nations to him, to battle against Israel and Jerusalem. The people of Elam came from afar, while from nearby

[20] He refers to mixing (*belulah*), e.g.; grain with oil in the Temple offering (see, e.g., Lev 2:5).

[21] Note that this Hebrew dirge focuses on the Temple and the loss of cultic rituals, personnel, and institutions. Cf. two similar lists, in both Hebr. and Arab., from Salmon's introduction, where he notes the loss of prophetic, legal, political, cultural, and educational institutions alongside those of the Temple and Temple service. Ben Shammai considers this passage as another example of how Salmon models the insertion of liturgical poetry into the Karaite mourning liturgy ("Poetic Works and Lamentations," 214–15). The same dirge appears, in a less developed form, in Salmon's comment to Song 1:13. See Frank, *Search Scripture Well*, 153–54 and esp. n. 44, where he notes a similar rabbinic *piyyuṭ* from the Yom Kippur service, which has been dated to before the eighth century.

[22] Salmon renders Hebr. "Kir" as "the people of Kir." Note that this construction also requires explanation in his comment to Lam 1:8, i.e., "Jerusalem" refers to "the people of Jerusalem."

Jerusalem there were the people of Kir, who are Aram and Damascus, as it is said, *"And the people of Syria shall go into exile to Kir," says the LORD* (Amos 1:5); *and the Samarians* <108a> *from Kir* (Amos 9:7). *And Kir uncovered the shield* means that the enemy used the shield to tear down the wall of Jerusalem. The first statement is more likely.[23]

וַיְהִי מִבְחַר־עֲמָקַיִךְ (Isa 22:7)—"Your best valleys were full of retinues, and the horsemen set their faces toward the gate of Jerusalem."[24] This means that the best place was full of people for the enemies' horses. *And the horsemen took their stand at the gate* alludes to conquest and victory, for indeed they were headed to Jerusalem[25] when they entered.

וַיְגַל אֵת מָסַךְ יְהוּדָה (Isa 22:8)—"He has removed the covering of Judah, and turned[26] in that day, to the weapons of the House of the Forest of Lebanon."[27] This means: "O, you people of Judah! When you saw that God had torn away your covering and ended His support for you, you did not love [Him] and you did not return, but instead you took refuge in your own strength and your direction. You gathered water and you prepared the necessary supplies for the siege, and you decreed that you would tie down the enemy until Pharaoh's army came for you, so that he would drive this calamity away from you. But [God] unleashed Nebuchadnezzar against you, and as for Pharaoh's army: *Behold, Pharaoh's army which came to help you is about to return to* <108b> *Egypt, to its own land* (Jer 37:7).[28]

וְאֵת בְּקִיעֵי עִיר־דָּוִד רְאִיתֶם (Isa 22:9): "And you saw the breaches of the city of David, and the waters within it were many, so you collected these waters of the lower pool" so that it would be a water source[29] for you in the days of the siege, because you presumed that the days of the siege would be easy.

וְאֶת־בָּתֵּי יְרוּשָׁלַם סְפַרְתֶּם (Isa 22:10)—"You counted the dwellings of Jerusalem, and you razed the dwellings in order to fortify the wall." This means that they would count how many houses each man had, and they would leave him some while razing some [others], in order to repair the wall with the stones [that were culled from the razed houses].

[23] Since the text attests only one interpretation of *and Kir uncovered the shield*, it is not clear which explanation Salmon refers to as "the first."

[24] Salmon renders Hebr. *ha-sha'rah* ("the gate") as "the gate of Jerusalem" (*bāb al-quds*).

[25] Arab. *al-quds*.

[26] Arab. *'iltafata*. Al-Fāsī also translates Hebr. n/b/ṭ with Arab. l/f/t IV ("to turn, to face"), (vol. I, 213–14).

[27] Salmon renders Hebr. *ya'ar* ("the forest") as Hebr. *ya'ar ha-levanon* ("the Forest of Lebanon").

[28] The parallel is clearer in Arab.: God "removed (*kashafa*) the covering of Judah" and "unleashed (*kashafa*) Nebuchadnezzar."

[29] Arab. *'auda*. This translation is contextual.

וּמִקְוָה עֲשִׂיתֶם בֵּין הַחֹמֹתַיִם (Isa 22:11)—"You made a junction between the two walls to the water of the old pool. But you did not turn to the One who crafted it; you did not look to the One who created it long ago."[30] This means that you built a trench between the walls so that the enemy would not be able to intrude upon you. "You did not look to the One who created it" means the Lord of the worlds, who had governed over the people of this town and who had saved it from the hand of the enemy—such as Zerah the Ethiopian or Sennacherib and all those who had intended [to capture] it.[31] You did not trust in Him, but you trusted <109a> in Pharaoh and his people, and in your own self-governance. But Pharaoh did not benefit you, as it is said, *For Egypt's help is worthless and empty* (Isa 30:7), and *The helper will stumble, and he who is helped will fall* (Isa 31:3). What you built of the wall, and the trench and the tools, will not benefit you; rather, the enemy will be victorious, and God will call you to lamentation and weeping, as it is said:

וַיִּקְרָא אֲדֹנָי יְהוִה צְבָאוֹת בַּיּוֹם הַהוּא לִבְכִי וּלְמִסְפֵּד (Isa 22:12)—"God, the everlasting God, called on that day to weeping and mourning and tearing out hair and wrapping up in haircloth." The meaning of *In that day the Lord God of hosts will call* is that God imposes on the people of the *exile* the obligation of weeping and lamenting over Zion and Jerusalem, and over the calamities of the people of the *exile*, as I have explained above.[32] Then he reports that the people of the *exile* violated what God had imposed upon them, as it is said, *and behold, joy and gladness* (Isa 22:13). They did the opposite of [what God obliged them to do]! There was no mourning or distress for them, but only "delights and joy, killing oxen and slaughtering sheep, eating meat and drinking wine: 'drink and eat, for tomorrow we will die!'" (Is 22:13).[33] This means <109b> that not only do they not mourn over the calamities that will befall [them]; they say "Let's eat and let's drink because we will surely die, and

[30] Cf. RSV: "You made a reservoir between the two walls for the water of the old pool. But you did not look to him who did it, or have regard for him who planned it long ago."

[31] Zerah the Ethiopian: the king who attacked Judah during the reign of King Asa; he and his armies were annihilated by God (2 Chr 14). Sennacherib: the Assyrian king who conquered Israel in 722 BCE and besieged Jerusalem but was prevented by God from capturing it (2 Kgs 18).

[32] See, e.g., the section on "Mourning as a Religious Obligation" in the introduction to the commentary.

[33] The Karaites abstained from both meat and wine in Jerusalem, and perhaps elsewhere also, as a pious response to the cessation of Temple sacrifice. For Salmon, Isa 22:13 indicts the Rabbanites, who continued to indulge in the consumption of meat and wine during the exile. On the dietary asceticism of the Karaites, see, e.g., Sahl b. Maṣliaḥ's Epistle to Jacob ben Samuel (*KA* 113); Jacob Mann, *Texts and Studies in Jewish History and Literature*, vol. 2 (Cincinnati, Ohio: Hebrew Union College Press, 1931–35), 108–110; and Yoram Erder, "The Mourners of Zion: Karaites in Jerusalem in the Tenth and Eleventh Centuries," in *Karaite Judaism*, 216.

after death there is nothing."[34] This [verse] describes the Dahrīyya.[35] Their words contradict the words of the believers because it is the custom of the pious ones to say to one another, "We are obliged to put our affairs in order, for tomorrow we will die." The pious ones among us hope for reward after death, as it is said, *But the righteous finds refuge in his death* (Prov 14:32).[36] As for the wicked, they say, "There is nothing for us other than what we enjoy in this world."

וְנִגְלָה בְאָזְנָי יְהוָה צְבָאוֹת (Isa 22:14)—"The speech of God is revealed before me"—in other words, "it is known to me"—that "this offense will not be

[34] Salmon cites this verse also in his comment on Eccl 8:11. There he explains the false reasoning of those who believe that wicked deeds are acceptable to God because they have not witnessed the punishment of their predecessors, who also committed wicked deeds: "The wicked pass away while doing their [wicked] deeds, and yet he that comes after does not reflect on them; on the contrary, he is led to do as they had done or even worse. They grow bold and excessive, for they say: if this deed were offensive to Allah, they would already have received retribution, and since we witness no retribution coming down swiftly upon them, let us exploit the same opportunity to eat and drink and commit sin in every way, for our joy will not be complete in any other way. Thus they become even bolder in their doing of evil, as the people who said: 'Where is the God of judgment?' (Mal 2:17); and as they that said: 'Yea, they that work wickedness are set up' (Mal 3:15); and as he that said: 'Let us eat and drink; for tomorrow we shall die' (Isa 22:13). Had they considered that this world is not the Abode of Recompense and had they known that the Hereafter is the Abode of Claim, they would have been restrained and fearful and frightened of Allah the all-powerful who gives respite" (Robinson, *Asceticism*, 462–63).

[35] The Dahrīyya are depicted in medieval Arab. texts as a sect organized around heretical beliefs, yet their precise identity is unclear. In philosophical texts, incl. Saadia's *Book of Beliefs and Opinions*, the Dahrīyya are those who advance certain false philosophies about the eternity of the world. The fact that Salmon invokes the Dahrīyya here suggests that he connects them to more general impiety based on false beliefs about death and the impossibility of punishment in the Hereafter. In this sense, his use of the term aligns with its Qur'ānic origins. There the Prophet commands belief in God, revelation, punishment for sins, the creation of the world, reward, and resurrection. Those who refute those truths by saying, "There is nothing except our life in the world; we die and we live, and we are destroyed only by time (*dahr*)" are speaking from conjecture rather than knowledge (Q45:24). Following the contrast presented in this verse, Muslims likely coined the term *Dahrīyya* to refer loosely to a range of people whose theological beliefs contradicted those that are commanded in Q45. Salmon's invocation of the Dahrīyya here seems to follow this usage. For an overview of Dahrīyya, see the entry on this topic by Goldziher and Goichon in *EI2*; for discussion as well as copious references to the term in Jewish and Muslim texts, see Harry Austryn Wolfson, *Repercussions of the Kalam in Jewish Philosophy* (Cambridge, Mass.: Harvard University Press, 1979), 153–59. Ilana Sasson surveys polemics against the Dahrīyya in the writings of Yefet, Saadia, and Muslim thinkers such as al-Jāḥiẓ, al-Ghazālī, and the Ikhwān al-Ṣafā', which align with Salmon's discussion here. Note that Jewish writers count some irreligious Jews among the Dahrīyya (Yefet, Prov, 113–15).

[36] The text reads, "The pious ones among us do *not* hope for reward after death," ומנא אלצאלחין מא ירג'וה מן אלת'ואב בעד אלמות. Yet this reading would seem to be a mistake, for the prooftext of Prov 14:32 teaches that the righteous *do* hope for such reward. Although Salmon only invokes this prooftext once in his commentary on Lamentations, it appears five times in his commentary on Ecclesiastes, and he affirms this meaning in all cases. He notes that the righteous one has hope in his death because he has performed the commandments (Eccl 1:3), his righteousness is affirmed at the time of his death (Eccl 3:2), he will not suffer pain in the Hereafter (Eccl 5:15), he is joyful about what awaits him (Eccl 7:1), and he knows that God has forgiven the sins that he has come to regret (Eccl 7:3) (Robinson, *Asceticism*, 188, 280, 374, 402, 406).

forgiven you until you die, says the LORD."[37] In other words, you will die, and your offenses will be upon you because you did not repent. You will attempt to take them back, but you will be punished because of them.[38] You will know that the decree is not as you said or as you supposed, but rather it is as He said: *For behold, the day comes, burning like an oven, when all the arrogant and all evildoers will be stubble* (Mal 3:19/4:1).[39] Thus, all that the prophets have said from the reports of Israel, and whatever God informed them about, <110a> has come to pass through you, because you renounced obedience to Him and abrogated His covenant.[40] [Jeremiah] recorded it[41] in its entirety in his book so that they would know that everything that God did was truly necessary for Him to do, as it is said, *The Rock, His word is perfect* (Deut 32:4). Know that the reason He exiled Israel is *because they did not obey the voice of the LORD their God but transgressed His covenant, even all that Moses the servant of the LORD commanded; they neither listened nor obeyed* (2 Kgs 18:12). Since they renounced obedience, they deserved for the prophet to lament over them with every kind of lamentation. Having completed the first two chapters—and having enumerated many of our calamities in them—he now begins the third chapter, in which he sets down three verses [for each letter] in order to augment the calamity and enumerate in [the verses] descriptions that pain the heart, as it is said, ***I am the man who has seen affliction*** (Lam 3:1). We have explained ***I am the man*** in what preceded.

Under the rod of His wrath alludes to the likening of the enemy to the rod, as it is said first regarding the king of Assyria, *Ah, Assyria, the rod of My anger, the staff of My fury* (Isa 10:5) and as it is said of Nebuchadnezzar, *The rod has blossomed, pride has budded* (Ezek 7:10). The "four kingdoms" are likened to "two staffs," as we have explained in the commentary on the Song of Songs.[42]

[37] Cf. RSV: "The LORD of hosts has revealed Himself in my ears: 'Surely this iniquity will not be forgiven you till you die,' says the Lord GOD of hosts." Salmon recasts the mythic imagery of the biblical verse in two stages. First, he translates "the LORD" to "the speech of God"; second, he interprets this expression as a euphemism to indicate that the speaker knows certain information.

[38] For ʿ/q/b VI as punishment, see Blau, *Dictionary*, 445.

[39] Salmon returns to Mal 3:17–19 throughout his corpus. Here the verses teach that once a wicked person dies, he can no longer pretend to escape punishment because the punishment will already be upon him. In his comment to Eccl 12:14, Salmon uses Mal 3:19 to show that punishment will befall the wicked on a "specific designated day" (Robinson, *Asceticism*, 598–601).

[40] Abrogation (*faskh*) is familiar from Christian and Muslim polemics that God has supplanted earlier revelations with more recent ones. Here Salmon suggests that the transhistorical Jewish community has abrogated their covenant with God.

[41] Arab. *dawwanahu*.

[42] Salmon may be referring to his overall approach to reading figurative imagery in the Song of Songs, as well as to his discussion there of these particular examples. The image of the "four kingdoms" comes from Dan 8:22 and the "two staffs" from Zech 11:7. On Salmon's Songs commentary, see Daniel Frank, "Karaite Commentaries on the Song of Songs from Tenth-Century Jerusalem,"

Indeed, they were *the generation* <110b> *of His wrath*, as it is said, [*for the LORD has rejected and*] *forsaken the generation of His wrath* (Jer 7:29).

It is the custom that when a criminal commits a crime, the sultan chastises him first with a beating. It is likewise with Israel: when they commit a crime and rebel, retribution befalls them, and He beats them with everything that He threatened them with, including blows, as it is said, [*I will punish you according to your ways, while your abominations are in your midst.*] *Then you will know that I am the LORD, who smite* (Ezek 7:9).[43] Since they did not obey the word of God and they transgressed His covenant, they deserved that His beating should befall them, as it is said, *Because they did not obey the voice of the LORD their God but transgressed His covenant, even all that Moses the servant of the LORD commanded; they neither listened nor obeyed* (2 Kgs 18:12).

אוֹתִי נָהַג וַיֹּלַךְ חֹשֶׁךְ וְלֹא־אוֹר׃
איאיי סאק וסייר פי ט'למה ולא נור

3:2 He has driven [me] and brought me into darkness without any light.[44]

in *With Reverence for the Word: Medieval Scriptural Exegesis in Judaism, Christianity, and Islam*, ed. Jane Dammen McAuliffe et al. (Oxford: Oxford University Press, 2003), 51–69.

[43] Thus begins the parable of the sultan who punishes a criminal, which Salmon develops as an extended parable through his comments to Lam 3:1–8. The parable at once recalls the "king mashal" of Midrashic literature—in which God is likened to an emperor of the Greco-Roman type (see David Stern, *Parables in Midrash* [Cambridge, Mass.: Harvard University Press, 1991], 19–23; 93–97)—and suggests mimetic possibilities with actual systems of criminal justice in the Islamic world. While the Arab. word "sultan" means 'authority' or 'government' in Salmon's era, here the analogy to God suggests that Salmon intends a human ruler. Few crimes have fixed penalties in Islamic law, leaving rulers and local administrators to determine exact sentencing. For the range of penalties, including imprisonment and banishment, see Rudolph Peters, *Crime and Punishment in Islamic Law* (Cambridge, Cambridge UP 2005), 30–38; for a discussion of jurists' reluctance to authorize severe punishments, see Intisar Rabb, *Doubt in Islamic Law* (Cambridge: Cambridge UP 2015), chapter 1. Although the details of the sultan's punishments in Salmon's parable are inspired by the biblical verses, medieval Islamic sources provide evidence for most of the punishments that Salmon identifies, as well as the prison environment itself. In *Justice, Punishment, and the Medieval Muslim Imagination* (Cambridge: Cambridge University Press, 2008), Christian Lange shows that prisons consisted of cells for holding prisoners (30); prisons were run by—and in some sense belonged to—the sultan, governor, or police prefect (27, 51, 93); punishments included fettering (with shackles, chains, or iron collars), flogging, rough clothing, and exposure (85, 92). Public humiliation figured prominently in penal situations; sources describe criminals paraded around the city on a camel, spat upon by onlookers (85) or forced to beg in public and turn over their alms to the prison guards (92–93). I am unaware of evidence for Jewish experiences with these penal practices; S. D. Goitein does not address criminal justice in *A Mediterranean Society: The Jewish Communities of the Arab World as Portrayed in the Documents of the Cairo Geniza*, 5 vols. (Berkeley: University of California Press, 1967–88). Nevertheless, Salmon's parable indicates his familiarity with real penal practices, perhaps because he had witnessed such punishment on public display.

[44] Salmon translates Hebr. *ḥoshekh* "darkness" as Arab. *ẓulma*; Saadia (Lam, 100) and Yefet also use the root ẓ/l/m but in the form *ẓalām*.

By this he means driving and sending me out into the exile,[45] as it is said in the covenant, *The LORD will bring you, and your king* [*whom you set over you, to a nation that neither you nor your fathers have known*] (Deut 28:36). This is what happened to Hoshea ben Elah, king of Israel (the king of Assyria exiled him along with the people of Samaria and the rest of the ten tribes), and with Jehoahaz (Pharaoh Necho exiled him to Egypt), and with Jehoiachin and Zedekiah (Nebuchadnezzar exiled both of them with the *exile* of Judah), <111a> as I have explained above.[46]

Likewise, it is known that when the sultan punishes a criminal, he announces him and summons him, so that the people will know the magnitude of his crime. The Lord of the worlds, mighty and sublime, did likewise to His nation, when the punishments of pestilence, the sword, and famine befell it: *The sword to slay, the dogs to tear, and the birds of the sky and the beasts of the earth to devour and destroy*[47] and [other] punishments that he does not enumerate. He sent them into exile in order to call them out among the nations of the world, as it is said, *In that men said of them, 'These are the people of the LORD, and yet they had to go out of His land'* (Ezek 36:20). He made these conditions for them because they exceeded all bounds in rebellions and they transgressed His covenant, which He had spoken when the master, the prophet, recited God's commandments to their fathers and they said, *We will do and we will obey* (Exod 24:7). But they did not obey and they did not do,[48] as it is said, *Because they did not obey the voice of the LORD their God but transgressed His covenant, even all that Moses the servant of the LORD commanded; they neither listened nor obeyed* (2 Kgs 18:12).[49]

45 As Salmon explains in his comment to Lam 1:2, "night" and "darkness" typically allude to exile. Cf. the anonymous explanation recorded in *Lam R* that darkness refers to this world, as opposed to the world to come (*Lam R* on Lam 3:2).

46 On the sins of Hoshea ben Elah, see Salmon's excursus at Lam 1:8; on the historical circumstances of his exile, see Salmon's excursus at Lam 2:4.

47 This litany of punishments is a reworking of Jer 15:2–3.

48 *Fa-lam yaqbalū wa-lam yafʿalū*. Salmon asserts that the Israelites did not fulfill the promise they made in Deut 24:7 to do (*naʿaśeh*) and to hear/obey (*nishmaʿ*) the commandments. His translation of these terms partially matches that of Saadia, who translates Deut 24:7 rather loosely: "Then he took up the book of the covenant and read it to the people, and they said, 'All that God has commanded in it, we will obey it (*naqbalahu*) and we will do it (*naṣnaʿahu*).'" These translations represent two different solutions to a long-standing conundrum: Why do the Israelites promise to "do" the commandments before they promise to "hear" them? Saadia's solution is to reverse the verbs, so that the Israelites promise to hear, and then do. Salmon's translation respects the word order but translates the Hebr. root sh/m/ʿ with the Arab. root q/b/l, lending it the sense of "to obey" (see Blau, *Dictionary*, 524). Al-Fāsī does not list Arab. q/b/l as a translation of Hebr. sh/m/ʿ, but he notes that in some instances (e.g., 1 Sam 22:14 and 1 Chr 11:25) the Hebr. verb connotes obedience (vol. II, 683).

49 The final clause of the verse *they neither listened nor obeyed* connects Salmon's excursus at Lam 3:1 with the refrain verse of this chapter of the commentary.

אַךְ בִּי יָשֻׁב יַהֲפֹךְ יָדוֹ כָּל־הַיּוֹם׃
כ'אץ פייה ירג'ע יקלב צ'רבתה טול אלזמאן

3:3 Surely against me He turns His blow again and again all the time.[50]

"His blow" alludes to the decrees and troubles that befell them <111b> in the time of exile so that they had neither stability nor tranquility, as it is said, *And among these nations you shall find no ease* (Deut 28:65), and *For I will show you no favor* (Jer 16:13). Just as it is the custom of the sultan, when he punishes a criminal, to announce him and repeat his punishment continuously, so is it with Israel: since He struck them with great punishments, then He announced them and called them out into the world among the nations of the world. In every generation, He places it in the hearts of the nations to repeat chastisement and affliction upon them, and all this is because of the magnitude of our crimes, as it is said, *Because they did not obey the voice of the LORD their God but transgressed His covenant, even all that Moses the servant of the LORD commanded; they neither listened nor obeyed* (2 Kgs 18:12).

בִּלָּה בְשָׂרִי וְעוֹרִי שִׁבַּר עַצְמוֹתָי׃
אכ'לק בשרי וג'לדי כסר עט'אמי

3:4 He has worn out my flesh and my skin, and broken my bones.[51]

All of these descriptions are attributed to God's action, for before this chapter it is said, *You did invite as to the day of an appointed feast* (Lam 2:22). [Jeremiah] alludes to the LORD with the verses, *the rod of His wrath* (Lam 3:1), *He has driven me* (Lam 3:2), and *Surely against me He turns* (Lam 3:3).[52] As for the meaning of ***He has worn out my flesh***, it is to say, "He has worn out my flesh <112a> and my skin with many blows." ***He has worn out*** means we have been afflicted by the nations of the world, and weakened. The matter has exhausted us

[50] Cf. RSV: "Surely against me He turns His hand again and again the whole day long." Salmon makes two significant adjustments in his Arab. translation. First, he avoids divine anthropomorphism by translating *yad* [God's] "hand" as *ḍarba* ([God's] "blow," or "strike"). Second, he translates Hebr. *yom* ("day") as Arab. *zamān* ("time"), which enables him to apply the verse more directly to the time of the exile. Saadia and Yefet likewise render *yom* as *zamān*. Yefet follows Salmon in translating *yad* as *ḍarba*, but Saadia leaves it as *yad*.

[51] Cf. RSV: "He has made my flesh and my skin waste away and broken my bones." Salmon renders Hebr. *baśar* ("flesh") with the Arab. cognate *bashar*.

[52] In other words: even though God is not explicitly identified within these verses, readers understand these verses with respect to God because Lam 3 is a continuation of Lam 2, where God is addressed unequivocally (vv. 20–22).

to the most extreme condition, and no strength remains, just as it is said, *Israel is worn out; already they are among the nations* [*as a useless vessel*] (Hos 8:8).[53]

Just as it is the custom of the sultan who punishes a criminal to announce him and repeat the punishment upon him continuously until his body is worn out and afflicted, so does God do to Israel. He inflicts His blows upon them, then He repeats chastisements upon them in every generation until they are worn out; then He exiles them and calls them out. All this is because of our crimes, as it is said, *Because they did not obey the voice of the LORD their God but transgressed His covenant, even all that Moses the servant of the LORD commanded; they neither listened nor obeyed* (2 Kgs 18:12).

בָּנָה עָלַי וַיַּקַּף רֹאשׁ וּתְלָאָה:
בנא עליי ואחדק ואסקאני סם ועלקם

3:5 He has besieged and enveloped me; my settlement is poison and bitterness.[54]

He has besieged and enveloped me alludes to the imprisonment of exile. In other words, "He imprisoned me among the nations, so that I would not achieve deliverance and escape from among them," as it is said, *I am shut in so that I cannot escape* (Ps 88:9/8). That is to say, "I am imprisoned; I am not capable of getting out of this prison."

The word *ro'sh* means the greatest of calamities, as it is said, *Behold, I will feed* <112b> *this people with wormwood and give them poisonous water* (*mei-ro'sh*) *to drink* (Jer 9:14/15).[55] It may be that with the word *poison* he alludes to the sciences that invent (*'ulūm al-mubdi'īn*) for God [things] that He did not say, as it is said, *They gave me poison for food* (Ps 69:22/21).[56] The translation

[53] Salmon reads the verse literally: the people of Israel are physically debilitated by their many sufferings. Cf. a rabbinic explanation that flesh, skin, and bones refer to the community, the Sanhedrin, and the mightiest men (*Lam R* on Lam 3:4).

[54] Cf. RSV: "He has besieged and enveloped me with bitterness and tribulation." In the verse translation, Salmon renders Hebr. *tela'ah* as Arab. *'alqam* ("bitterness"); in his explanation, however, he seems to understand the word to mean "weakness."

[55] Cf. unattributed Midrashim in which *ro'sh* and *tela'ah* refer to Nebuchadnezzar and Nebuzaradan, or to Vespasian and Trajan (*Lam R* on Lam 3:5; and similar on Lam 3:10).

[56] In his comment to Ps 69:22/21, Salmon interprets poison as heresy. For him, the verse "means that they made schools of apostasy (*madhāhib riddiyya*) and altered the commandments and expanded the conflict (*khilāf*). They did not do what is obligatory, but they did its opposite, as it is said, *For My people have committed two evils: they have forsaken Me, the fountain of living waters, and hewed out cisterns for themselves, broken cisterns, that can hold no water* (Jer 2:13). His word *be-varuti* ("in my food") is from [the verse] *nor did he eat food with them* (*ve-lo' vara' 'itam laḥem*; 2 Sam 12:17). He combined the two conditions to which wisdom, nourishment, and drink are compared, as it is said,

of the word *tela'ah* is "weakness," as in *all the weakness* (Exod 18:8). The intended meaning is that [God] weakens this nation and enfeebles it.

Just as the sultan punishes a criminal, then announces him and repeats chastisements upon him, then exhausts his body, then imprisons him and weakens his strength, so does the Creator of the world do when Israel sins. He punishes them and announces them and repeats blows upon them, and exhausts them and imprisons them as it is said, *Because they did not obey the voice of the LORD their God but transgressed His covenant, even all that Moses the servant of the LORD commanded; they neither listened nor obeyed* (2 Kgs 18:12).

בְּמַחֲשַׁכִּים הוֹשִׁיבַנִי כְּמֵתֵי עוֹלָם:
פי מואצ'ע מט'למה אג'לסני כמותי מן אלדהר

3:6 He has made me dwell in darkness like the dead of long ago.[57]

He has made me dwell in darkness. He compares Israel, and [their conditions] during the exile and the absence of prophecies, to correspond with darkness <113a> because, when the criminal was imprisoned within it, he became like one who despaired of the life of the world.[58] He says this person is ***like the dead of long ago***, which is similar to *like one forsaken among the dead* (Ps 88:6/5). Therefore, it is said, *We stumble at noon as in the twilight, among those in full vigor we are like dead men* (Isa 59:10). He alludes to the duration that the people of the exile would linger—which is many years. As is known, we have completed 1,385 years from the exile of Jeconiah to now, and we have completed 888 years from the destruction of the Second Temple to now.[59]

Come, eat of my bread and drink of the wine I have mixed (Prov 9:5). He means, 'When I was hungry or thirsty for knowledge, [for] something from the book of God, and I looked at something from their books, I found them like murderous poison'" (Salmon, Pss 42–72).

[57] Hebr. *be-maḥashakim*; Arab. *fī mawāḍiʿ muẓlima* (cf. Saadia: *fī ẓulmāt* [Lam, 100], and Yefet: *fī l-ẓulmāt*). All three translators render Hebr. *ʿolam* as Arab. *al-dahr*.

[58] On darkness as an allusion to exile for Salmon and Yefet, see comment to Lam 1:2 and notes there.

[59] Salmon composed the Lamentations commentary between 951 and 956 CE, most likely in 954. There is some confusion about this date in the manuscripts. The following dates are attested, all referring to the years that have passed since the destruction of the Second Temple: 885 years (ת'מאן מאה כ'מסה ות'מאנין in BN Heb. 295 [Egyptian, dated 5378 (1618 CE)] and JTSA Ms. Mic 3362 [dated 5429 (1669 CE)]; abbreviated as תתפה in Paris MS 295); 888 years (תתפ"ח in BL Or. 2516); and the certainly incorrect 865 years (תתס"ה in BL Or. 2513). See Abdul-Karim, 114 n. 19 and Samuel Poznanski, "Karaite Miscellanies," *JQR* 8 (1896): 688 n. 3. The latter date—888 years after the destruction—seems most likely, since throughout his commentary on Lamentations, Salmon refers to his commentary on Psalms as though it had already been written (see Lam 2:19, 3:1, 5:20), and Salmon dates that commentary to "887 years (תתפז) after the destruction of the Second Temple," i.e., to 953 (see Salmon's comment to Ps 85:6/5; Poznanski, "Karaite Miscellanies," 688 n. 2; and Robinson, *Asceticism*, 18). In

Just as the sultan punishes a criminal, and announces him and repeats chastisement upon him, and exhausts his body, and weakens him and imprisons him and makes his nourishment as harmful as can be,[60] then transfers him from prison to an underground cell so that he will remain there forever—so does the LORD God of hosts do to Israel, because of the magnitude of their crimes, as it is said, *Because they did not obey the voice of the LORD their God but transgressed His covenant, even all that Moses the servant of the LORD commanded; they neither listened nor obeyed* (2 Kgs 18:12).

גָּדַר בַּעֲדִי וְלֹא אֵצֵא הִכְבִּיד נְחָשְׁתִּי׃
ג'דר בסבבי ולא אכ'רג' ת'קל קידי

3:7 He has walled me about so that I cannot escape; He has put heavy chains on me.

He has walled me about refers to the confusion[61] of this exile.[62] <113b> I said [that this was] a device [to prevent] entering or escaping, as it is said, *And I will build a wall against her* (Hos 2:8/6). ***He has put heavy chains on me*** alludes to the fetters that overtook the kings of the nation, as it is said of Jehoiakim, *Against him King Nebuchadnezzar of Babylon came up, and bound him with fetters* (2 Chr 36:6). And it is said about Zedekiah, *He put out the eyes of Zedekiah, and bound him in fetters* (Jer 39:7; 52:11) and also, *when he took him bound in fetters* (Jer 40:1). It also means that they were all bound in fetters. It is to this that he alludes in the verse, *Make a chain!* (Ezek 7:23). [The conditions that] we are under today are more severe than fetters, as it is said, *He will put a yoke of iron on your neck* (Deut 28:48).

order to convert this year into the Western calendar, we must know the date that Salmon reckoned for the destruction of the Second Temple. Karaites reckoned this date to be 66; cf. the generally accepted Jewish view of 68 as the year of the destruction (Gil, *History*, 798–99). Therefore, Salmon composed the commentary as early as 951 CE (following Gil's calculation of 885 years after the destruction in 66 CE) and as late as 956 (following Poznanski's calculation of 888 years after the destruction in 68 CE); in either case the Psalms commentary would have been written beforehand. Note also that basing dates on the years since the exile of Jehoiachin was a distinctively Karaite practice (Gil, *History*, 798).

60 The reference to harmful food is better suited to Salmon's reading of the previous verse (Lam 3:5).

61 Arab. *taḥayyur*. Salmon's interpretation is based in a pun: a garden that is enclosed or walled off (*ḥayr*) comes from the same root as *taḥayyur* ("confusion," "helplessness," "bewilderment").

62 A series of rabbinic comments anticipate Salmon's extended parable of the sultan punishing a criminal: "Rabbi Aibu said: this alludes to the Arab jail. Rabbi Berekiah said: It alludes to the stronghold of the Persians. The Rabbis say: It refers to the mines of the Samaritans" (*Lam R* on Lam 3:7, 191).

Just as a sultan punishes the criminal and announces him and repeats chastisement upon him and exhausts his body, then transfers him to an underground cell so he will remain there forever, then he fetters him with heavy fetters, so too does the LORD of hosts do to Israel because of the greatness of their crimes, as it is said, *Because they did not obey the voice of the LORD their God but transgressed His covenant, even all that Moses the servant of the LORD commanded; they neither listened nor obeyed* (2 Kgs 18:12).

גַּם כִּי אֶזְעַק וַאֲשַׁוֵּעַ שָׂתַם תְּפִלָּתִי׃
איצ'א אד'א אצרך' ואגות' סד ען צלאתי

3:8 Though I call out and cry for salvation, He shuts out my prayer.[63]

<114a> He means, "Throughout the time of exile, I have been crying out and calling for help, and He has not had mercy on me, and He has not heard my prayer. He threatened me with this, as it is said, *See, I am setting a plumb line in the midst of My people Israel; I will never again pass them by* (Amos 7:8); and *You have wrapped yourself with a cloud so that no prayer can pass through* (Lam 3:44)." The reason for this is that God summoned them to obedience (*ṭāʿa*) to Him, but they did not obey (*lam yaqbalū*).[64] So now, when they call out for salvation, they deserve that He not answer them, as it is said, *Just as, when I called, they would not hear, so, when they called, I would not hear* (Zech 7:13) and *Then they will cry to the LORD, but He will not answer them; He will hide His face from them* (Mic 3:4).[65]

And cry for salvation means continuously.[66] It may be that when he says *though I call out* he is alluding to the time of [the enemy's] triumph, while *and cry for help* [alludes] to the time of exile.[67]

[63] Note that Salmon offers no linguistic comment but skips directly to an interpretation of the verse's meaning. This omission stands out against others who note the unusual spelling of *śatam* (cf. *satam*), e.g., Ibn Nūḥ (*Diqduq*, 480) and the anonymous Judeo-Persian Bible commentary published by Khan: *Early Karaite Grammatical Texts* (Atlanta: Society of Biblical Literatures, 2000), 292. The rabbis offered a Midrashic reading: "the word is written so that it can be read as *she-tam*, i.e., 'because' the congregation 'has finished' (*she-tammu*) their prayer" (*Lam R* on Lam 3:8).

[64] Salmon presents Arab. q/b/l as a translation for Arab. ṭ/w/ʿ, thus underscoring the possibility of reading q/b/l as "to obey," as in his comment at Lam 3:2 and his invocation there of Exod 24:7.

[65] Salmon employs the hermeneutic of *middah ke-neged middah*, which he formulates in Arab. as "the principle of requital" (*bāb al-muqābala*) throughout the commentary. See discussion in chapter 3.

[66] Arab. *ḥāl baʿd ḥāl*, "in situation after situation," i.e., continuously.

[67] Salmon reconciles an apparent redundancy by applying the verbs "call out" and "cry for salvation" to two distinct historical situations.

Just as the sultan punishes the criminal, then he announces him, then he repeats chastisement upon him and exhausts his body and imprisons him, then he transfers him to an underground cell where he remains forever, then he makes his fetters heavy, and if he [i.e., the criminal] raises a petition[68] or he calls and cries out for salvation, [the sultan] does not answer, so the LORD of hosts does to Israel, as it is said, *When you stretch out your hands, I will hide My eyes from you* (Isa 1:15). All this <114b> is because of the magnitude of the crimes, as it is said, *Because they did not obey the voice of the LORD their God but transgressed His covenant, even all that Moses the servant of the LORD commanded; they neither listened nor obeyed* (2 Kgs 18:12).

גָּדַר דְּרָכַי בְּגָזִית נְתִיבֹתַי עִוָּה:
ג'דר טרקי בחג'ארה מהנדמה וג'מיע סבלי עוג':

3:9 He has blocked my ways with hewn stones, He has made my paths crooked.

ʿAvvâ, heʿĕvū, mĕʿūvvāt, and whatever [words] are like these, all have to do with crookedness.[69] It means that they are ways of confusion, and not rightly guided. That is to say, he traveled the road that he deserved.[70] It was a straight course and not otherwise, as it is said, *You shall grope about at noon*, and then, *the blind grope in darkness* (Deut 28:29).[71] And what is the meaning of *in darkness*? Consider that the blind person sees when he walks in the light, for we say that when the blind person walks in the light, someone who sees observes him and guides him along the straight path. If another person sees him [about to] fall into a pit, he grabs his hand so that he will not fall. But if a blind person walks in darkness, then he does not see, for he will not be

[68] Arab. *rafaʿa qiṣṣa*. On *qiṣṣa* as a petition or complaint, see Blau, *Dictionary*, 546.

[69] Arab. *taʿwīj*. Sc. Ezek 21:32/ 27, *a ruin, a ruin, a ruin* [עַוָּה עַוָּה עַוָּה]; Jer 3:21, *because they have perverted their way* [כִּי הֶעֱווּ אֶת־דַּרְכָּם]; Eccl 1:15, *what is crooked cannot be made straight* [מְעֻוָּת לֹא־יוּכַל לִתְקֹן]. Al-Fāsī states, "All have to do with crookedness (*iʿwijāj*)" (vol. II, 377).

[70] Arab. *ʾaslaka fī mā ʾistaḥaqqa*. The near-rhyme and the pious content of this line suggest that it may have been a maxim familiar to Salmon's readers. Salmon often introduces paraphrases of his own devising with the term *ay* ("in other words," or "that is to say"), but that would not preclude him from occasionally using the formula to introduce a pertinent Arab. proverb. C. M. H. Versteegh notes that *ay* was used alongside *yaʿnī* ("he/it means") and *qāla* ("he said") for anaphoric references in the early Islamic tradition of Qurʾān exegesis; see *Arabic Grammar and Qurʾānic Exegesis in Early Islam*, SSLL 191 (Leiden: Brill, 1993), 69.

[71] The theological purpose of this explanation is to exonerate God. God does not make paths crooked; rather, a sinful person finds it impossible to follow the straight path that God has provided.

rescued, and no one will see him to rescue him. The situation of Israel in this exile is like this. They are in darkness, and there is no prophet, no teacher, and no knowledge among them, as it is said, *Some were fools through their sinful ways, and because of their iniquities suffered affliction* (Ps 107:17).[72] <115a> And all this happened to us because of the magnitude of the crimes, as it is said, *Because they did not obey the voice of the LORD their God but transgressed His covenant, even all that Moses the servant of the LORD commanded; they neither listened nor obeyed* (2 Kgs 18:12).

דֹּב אֹרֵב הוּא לִי אֲרִיה בְּמִסְתָּרִים:
<u>מת'ל</u> דב מכמן הוא לי <u>מת'ל</u> אלאסד פי אלמסאתר

3:10 He is to me <u>like</u> a bear lying in wait, <u>like</u> a lion in hiding.[73]

He means that He gives the predatory beasts power over us in order to destroy us, as it is said, *And I will let loose the wild beasts among you, which shall rob you of your children* (Lev 26:22), and also, *So I will be to them like a lion, like a leopard beside the way. I will fall upon them like a bear robbed of her cubs, I will tear open their breast* (Hos 13:7–8). His intention may be to compare enemies to lions and bears.[74] Likewise, it is said, *The first was like a lion . . . And behold, another beast, a second one, like a bear* (Dan 7:4–5). And they lie in hiding like wild animals, just as it is said about them, *He lurks in secret like a lion in his covert* (Ps 10:9). All this is because of the magnitude of the crimes, as it is said, *Because they did not obey the voice of the LORD their God but transgressed His covenant, even all that Moses the servant of the LORD commanded; they neither listened nor obeyed* (2 Kgs 18:12).

דְּרָכַי סוֹרֵר וַיְפַשְּׁחֵנִי שָׂמַנִי שֹׁמֵם:
טרקי אזאל ופסכ'ני ג'עלני מסתוחש

3:11 He led me off my way and tore me to pieces; He has made me desolate.

[72] Salmon connects the "ways" of Lam 3:9 to the "sinful ways" of Ps 107:17. The latter verse clarifies that it is the sinner who makes the ways treacherous, not God.

[73] Salmon has added the comparative word *mithl* ("like") to emphasize the figurative element of the verse.

[74] Perhaps Salmon has in mind an interpretation like that proposed in *Lam R*, in which the lion and the bear refer, respectively, to Nebuchadnezzar and Nebuzaradan, or to Vespasian and Trajan (see *Lam R* on Lam 3:10; and similar on Lam 3:5).

I translated *va-yefashḥeni* as "he tore me to pieces" [in accord with] the language of the Targum, <115b> for the Targum of *And Samuel hewed (va-yeshassef) Agag in pieces before the LORD in Gilgal* (1 Sam 15:33) is, in the Targum, *u-fashaḥ yat 'agag.*[75]

He has led me off my way means that the welfare and excellence of [my way] were reversed and [divine] support ceased. Being torn to pieces (*tafsīkh*) alludes to ripping apart and scattering, as it is said, *And I will dash them one against another* (Jer 13:14). All this befell us because of the magnitude of crimes, as it is said, *Because they did not obey the voice of the LORD their God but transgressed His covenant, even all that Moses the servant of the LORD commanded; they neither listened nor obeyed* (2 Kgs 18:12).

דָּרַךְ קַשְׁתּוֹ וַיַּצִּיבֵנִי כַּמַּטָּרָא לַחֵץ:
אותר קוסה ואנצבני מת'ל אלהדף ללנשאב

3:12 He bent his bow and set me as a mark for his arrow.

By this he means the aim and the target. In other words, "He made me His target, and He aimed the affliction at me," as it is said, *You only have I known of all the families of the earth; [therefore I will punish you for all your iniquities]* (Amos 3:2) and as it was said above, *He has bent His bow like an enemy* (Lam 2:4). And all this befell us because of the magnitude of crimes, as it is said, *Because they did not obey the voice of the LORD their God but transgressed His covenant, even all that Moses the servant of the LORD commanded; they neither listened nor obeyed* (2 Kgs 18:12).

הֵבִיא בְּכִלְיוֹתָי בְּנֵי אַשְׁפָּתוֹ:
אדכ'ל פי כלאיי נשאשיב ג'עבתה

3:13 He drove into my heart the arrows of His quiver.

Since he just said, *He bent his bow and set me* (Lam 3:12), he now says, ***He drove into my heart.*** In other words, "He accomplished everything that He intended

[75] I.e., The Targum presents the root f/sh/ḥ as a translation of sh/s/f ("to hew in pieces" in 1 Sam 15:33), suggesting that both roots, which are both biblical hapaxes, have the same meaning. Note Salmon's use of comparative Semitics: he draws attention to the Aram. translation at the same time that he relies on the Arab. cognate root f/s/kh in both his verse translation and his Arab. comment. Ibn Nūḥ provides the same explanation, and also cites the Targum on 1 Sam 15:33, as the basis for his Arab. translation as f/s/kh (*Diqduq*, 480–81).

to do to me," as in the verse, *The LORD has done what He purposed* (Lam 2:17). The meaning of ***He drove into my heart*** <116a> alludes to pains reaching [the level at which] one is killed. The meaning of ***the arrows of His quiver*** means the blows are compared to the arrows, as it is said, *They shall be wasted with hunger, and devoured with burning heat* (Deut 32:24), and it is said, *For Your arrows have sunk into me* (Ps 38:3/2), and likewise, *When I loose against them My deadly arrows of famine* (Ezek 5:16). And all these calamities befell us because of the magnitude of crimes, as it is said, *Because they did not obey the voice of the LORD their God but transgressed His covenant, even all that Moses the servant of the LORD commanded; they neither listened nor obeyed* (2 Kgs 18:12).

הָיִיתִי שְּׂחֹק לְכָל־עַמִּי נְגִינָתָם כָּל־הַיּוֹם׃
צרת צ'חך לכל שעבי נגמאתהם טול אלזמאן

3:14 I have become the laughingstock of all my people, their tunes throughout time.[76]

I have become the laughingstock of all my people. It is probable that the speaker of this verse is the righteous one of the nation.[77] He describes that someone had made him a laughingstock[78] in the nation by mocking him when he saw him lamenting and crying and tearing his hair and dressing in haircloth, mourning over what had become of him [and] the nation.[79] They mocked him and made him a laughingstock and a mockery, just as he described some of the nations' practices that concern the wickedness of the nation, since it is said, *I am the talk of those who sit in the gate, and the drunkards make songs about me* (Ps 69:13/12).[80] Some of the scholars say that the

[76] Cf. RSV: "I have become the laughingstock of all peoples, the burden of their songs all day long." Salmon and Yefet both translate Hebr. *neginah* as Arab. *naghma* (see Blau, *Dictionary*, 706); cf. Saadia, *lahn* (Lam, 101). All three terms mean "tune" or "melody," but the Karaite translators selected an Arab. cognate. All three translators render Hebr. *yom* ("day") as Arab. *zamān* ("time").

[77] I.e., the prophet Jeremiah.

[78] Reading *huz'a* for *hazza*: the *hamza* is missing, as is common in Judeo-Arabic orthography.

[79] These behaviors may also apply to the Karaite rituals of mourning: lamentation, crying, tearing hair, dressing in haircloth, and mourning over the state of the Jewish community.

[80] Salmon also cites this verse in his introduction to the commentary. His comment to Ps 69:13/12 suggests that Karaites experience the same scorn and derision that righteous Israelites experienced in biblical times: "He [i.e., David?] means, 'When I wore sackcloth in order to humble myself and break away from yearnings of the world through the hardship of haircloth and abandoning the pleasure of the softness of clothing, I became an example (*mathal*) for them. When they convened for their parties and their drinking and their depravity, one of them wore a haircloth, and they brought him out on a horse and they said, 'Thus was Jabez, and thus was al-Qūmisī!' "

meaning of ***I have become the laughingstock of all my people*** alludes to the nation that <116b> we are enslaved to, that governs us, while another says instead that ***of all my people*** alludes to all the nations, that is to say, it means "of all peoples."[81] The first statement is more likely.[82] All these afflictions have befallen us because of the magnitude of crimes, as it is said, *Because they did not obey the voice of the LORD their God but transgressed His covenant, even all that Moses the servant of the LORD commanded; they neither listened nor obeyed* (2 Kgs 18:12).

הִשְׂבִּיעַנִי בַמְּרוֹרִים הִרְוַנִי לַעֲנָה׃
אשבעני מן אלזעאראת ארואני מן אלעלקם

3:15 He has filled me with bitternesses,[83] He has sated me with wormwood.

This means instead of the good things that had sated me, He turned them to bitter ones, as it is said, *Ephraim has given bitter provocation* (Hos 12:14). After Ephraim rebelled, bitterness overtook them, and He traded what He had given me to drink—*the cup of salvation* (Ps 116:13)—and instead He gave me bitterness to drink, as it is said, *You who have drunk at the hand of the LORD the cup of His wrath* (Isa 51:17) and *You shall drink your sister's cup which is large and deep* (Ezek 23:32) and *You shall drink it and drain it out, and pluck out your hair* (Ezek 23:34).[84] Everything that has happened has befallen us because of the magnitude of calamities[85] and crimes, as it is said, *Because they*

[81] In other words: this second reading would be appropriate only if the biblical verse read "of all the peoples" (*ʿamim*), whereas the verse actually says "of all my people" (*ʿami*). Salmon may be pointing to a rabbinic interpretation of Lam 3:14 (also in connection with Ps 69:13/12): "This refers to the nations of the world who sit in theatres and circuses" (*Lam R* on Lam 3:14).

[82] I.e., Salmon thinks it more likely that the people who mock the righteous are members of "the nation that we are enslaved to" rather than all the gentile nations. "The nation that we are enslaved to" most obviously indicates Islamic rule over Jews, yet Salmon may also imply Rabbanite ascendancy over Karaites.

[83] Cf. RSV: "He has filled me with bitterness." The Arab translators maintain the plural form of Hebr. *merorim*. Salmon and Yefet translate it as *zaʿārāt* ("bitternesses;" see Blau, *Dictionary*, 272) while Saadia opts for the cognate *marārāt* (not *marāʾir*) (Lam, 101). The plural form is exegetically meaningful; for Salmon, the verse refers to multiple "bitternesses," which he enumerates in the following comments.

[84] Salmon also invokes these prooftexts in his comment to Ps 116:13. For Salmon, the range of cup imagery—from a cup of salvation to a cup of wrath—indicates the necessity of thanking God for His provision of good as well as its opposite, even when the latter is difficult. He interprets *the cup of salvation* as a symbol of the joy of salvation, while in Ezek 23:33 and Jer 51:17 the cup is a symbol of the exile.

[85] The insertion of "calamities" (*maṣāʾib*) in this formulation would seem to be an early scribal slip since Salmon consistently mentions calamities as a punishment rather than a cause for punishment. The word appears in all MSS of Abdul-Karim's ed., excepting BL Or. 2515.

did not obey the voice of the LORD their God but transgressed His covenant, even all that Moses the servant of the LORD commanded; they neither listened nor obeyed (2 Kgs 18:12).

וַיַּגְרֵס בֶּחָצָץ שִׁנָּי הִכְפִּישַׁנִי בָּאֵפֶר׃
וג'רש והשם באלחצא אסנאני מרגני פי אלרמאד

3:16 He has made my teeth grind on gravel, and made me cower in ashes.

<117a> *Va-yagres* is derived from *garaś*, as in *crushed* (*gereś*) *new grains* (Lev 2:14). *Hikhpishani* is a hapax legomenon.[86] They say that [it means] "He made me tremble." The letters *bā*ʾ and *fā*ʾ are the same, so the meaning *hikhpishani* is as if to say "he buried me in ashes," and [it is] likewise with the words *barzel* and *farzel*. *He blows* (*nashaf*) *upon them* (Isa 40:24) and *blows* (*nashavah*) *upon it* (Isa 40:7) and *from the highest places* (*ʿal-gappei*) (Prov 9:3),[87] and there are many more like these, which are called interchangeable letters (*aḥruf al-ibdāl*).[88]

He has made my teeth grind on gravel. After having said above, *He has filled me with bitternesses* (Lam 3:15), now he describes some of the many bitternesses [including] the affliction of shattered teeth.

"I was buried in ashes" alludes, for example, to the verse *Roll in ashes* (Jer 6:26) and similarly, the verse *Roll yourselves in the dust* (Mic 1:10). All these calamities have befallen us because of the magnitude of crimes, as it is said, *Because they did not obey the voice of the LORD their God but transgressed His covenant, even all that Moses the servant of the LORD commanded; they neither listened nor obeyed* (2 Kgs 18:12).

וַתִּזְנַח מִשָּׁלוֹם נַפְשִׁי נָשִׁיתִי טוֹבָה׃
וכ'לית מן אלסלאמה נפשי יא יוי נסית אלכ'יר

3:17 My soul is bereft of peace, O LORD, I have forgotten what goodness is.[89]

86 Arab. *kalima fardīya*.

87 This final example of interchangeable letters is unclear. Salmon seems to compare *gabbei* and *gappei*, although he gives no biblical citation for the first term.

88 Salmon notes that he has written a separate book (*kitāb mufrad*) on the interchangeable letters (see comment to Lam 1:14). He gives the letters in their Arab. form here, although the treatise examined cases from biblical Hebr. See also Salmon's comment on Lam 3:26, where he treats *hā*ʾ and *mem* as interchangeable letters.

89 Cf. RSV: "My soul is bereft of peace, I have forgotten what happiness is." Salmon translates Hebr. *ṭovah* ("goodness") as Arab. *khayr* ("goodness") throughout.

He means "You, O LORD, deprived my soul of peace, just as You forsook me and granted the enemies victory over me," as it is said, *We looked for peace, but no good came* (Jer 8:14/15).[90] They say also that ***my soul is bereft*** (*va-tiznaḥ*) ***of peace*** means "my soul forfeited peace and is distant from it" because *va-tiznaḥ* is probably <117b> "opposition" (*muwājaha*), and it probably refers back to the soul.[91]

I have forgotten what goodness is alludes to the duration of tarrying in this *exile*: it endures to the extent that we have forgotten everything good and gracious that [we do not experience] during [it]. We count misfortune and misery and we even collect the tax (*jizya*) that we hand over to our leaders.[92] And all this happened to us because of the magnitude of our crimes, as it is said, *Because they did not obey the voice of the LORD their God but transgressed His covenant, even all that Moses the servant of the LORD commanded; they neither listened nor obeyed* (2 Kgs 18:12).

וָאֹמַר אָבַד נִצְחִי וְתוֹחַלְתִּי מֵיְהוָה:
וקלת קד באד ט'פרי ורג'איי מן יוי <u>קד בעד</u>

3:18 So I say, "My victory has gone, and my hope from the LORD <u>has gone</u>."[93]

They say *niṣḥi* is "my victory"—*niṣaḥon* in the language of the Targum.[94] They say that *niṣḥi* is from *neṣaḥ* and means "my extent,"[95] which is to say, "my perseverance." *Ve-toḥalti* means everything that they hoped for, as it is said, *We looked for peace, but no good came* (Jer 8:14/15).[96] And all these calamities overtook us because of the magnitude of our crimes, as it is said, *Because they did not obey the*

[90] Salmon repeats this prooftext in his comment to Lam 3:18.

[91] I.e., the soul may be the subject or the direct object of the verb.

[92] *Jizya*: the tax on non-Muslims living under Islamic rule. For background, see Ziauddin Ahmed, "The Concept of Jizya in Early Islam," *Islamic Studies* 14 (1975): 293–305; Moshe Gil, "Religion and Realities in Islamic Taxation," *IOS* 10 (1980): 21–33; and A. D. Muztar, "Dhimmīs in an Islamic State," *Islamic Studies* 18 (1979): 65–75. Countless documents from the medieval Jewish community depict the *jizya* as an onerous burden. See, e.g., Marina Rustow, *Heresy and the Politics of Community: The Jews of the Fatimid Caliphate* (Ithaca, N.Y.: Cornell University Press, 2008), 190–91 and Mark R. Cohen, *Poverty and Charity in the Jewish Community of Medieval Egypt* (Princeton, N.J.: Princeton University Press, 2006). See also Salmon's comment on Lam 1:1 and notes there.

[93] Cf. RSV: "So I say, 'Gone is my glory, and my expectation from the LORD.'" Salmon adds—or more accurately, repeats—a clause in order to fill a perceived ellipsis in the biblical text (on this practice, see Polliack, *The Karaite Tradition*, 222–24). Note that Salmon applies the logic of *menaheg ʿaṣmo u-menaheg aḥerim* (see chaper 2, section on "Linguistic Principles to Justify a Translation Choice") without identifying it as such.

[94] "Language of the Targum" may simply mean Aram.; the Tg. translates *niṣḥi* in Lam 3:19 as *tuqfi*.

[95] So also in Saadia's translation.

[96] See also the comment to Lam 3:17.

voice of the LORD their God but transgressed His covenant, even all that Moses the servant of the LORD commanded; they neither listened nor obeyed (2 Kgs 18:12).

זְכָר־עָנְיִי וּמְרוּדִי לַעֲנָה וָרֹאשׁ:
אד'כר שקאיי ואנחדארי אלעלקם ואלסם

3:19 Remember my misery and my decline, the bitterness and the poison![97]

This is his appeal to God for salvation. In other words: Just as You saw <118a> the misery of our fathers in Egypt—as it is said, *I have seen the affliction of My people* (Exod 3:7)—so now it is said, "O LORD, remember the misery that I was in." He alludes to the difficulty of the exile with the word *ʿōnyīy* ("my affliction"). Likewise, Joseph referred to his banishment with this word when he said, *For God has made me fruitful in the land of my affliction* (*ʿōnyīy*) (Gen 41:52). ***My decline*** alludes to the decline of dominion, statehood, and grace, as in *And bring the declining poor into your house* (Is 58:7), just as I have translated *her decline* (Lam 1:7).

The bitterness and the poison mean the poison of exile, as it is said, *Behold! I will feed this people with bitterness* [*and give them poisonous water to drink*] (Jer 9:14/15)[98] and everything that overtook us because of our crimes, as it is said, *Because they did not obey the voice of the LORD their God but transgressed His covenant, even all that Moses the servant of the LORD commanded; they neither listened nor obeyed* (2 Kgs 18:12).

זָכוֹר תִּזְכּוֹר וְתָשׁוֹחַ עָלַי נַפְשִׁי:
אד'כאר תד'כר ותנחני עליי נפסי

3:20 My soul continually calls it to mind, and is bowed down within me.

O my brother, know that I have translated *zākhôr* as "call to mind" (*idhkār*). It has a long vowel (*thaqīl*)[99] in Arabic and it is not conjugated[100] because it

[97] Cf. RSV: "Remember my affliction and my wandering, the wormwood and the gall!"

[98] Yefet also renders Hebr. *laʿanah* and *roʾsh* as Arab. *ʿalqam wa-samm* in his translation of Lam 3:19; cf. the translation of Jer 9:14/15, where he offers instead *zaqqūm* and *samm* (Yefet, *Jer*, 187). Al-Fāsī states that *ʿalqam* is said to be *zaqqum* (vol. II, 172). *ʿAlqam* may refer to a certain plant (Hava suggests colocynth or wild cucumber, 487) as well as bitterness more generally, while *zaqqūm* is a tree with bitter fruits mentioned in the Qurʾān (see, e.g., Q44:43).

[99] Khan, *Early Karaite Tradition*, 61. Salmon refers to the long *alif* in *idhkār*.

[100] Arab. *lā iḥtashama*. Meaning inferred from context.

is a *maṣdar* [verbal noun] akin to *ʾakhol* ("eat"), *shamor* ("keep"), and *ʾamor* ("say"), and many similar ones. I did not say *dhakara tadhakara*[101] because *dhakara* is *zĕkhōr* in Hebrew, and in fact *zĕkhōr* [has the sense of] the imperative, as in *Remember* [*zĕkhōr*] *Your servants* (Deut 9:27). It is in the disjoined state (*mukhrat*), whereas *Remember* [*zĕkhār*] *my affliction* (Lam 3:19) <118b> is conjoined (*samukh*),[102] and it would be [translated into Arabic as] *udhkur*, the imperative. Its nominal form may be in most of the translation. I do not proceed according to what these and other verbal nouns (*maṣādir*) require because I regret that whoever reads my book is interested in the syntax (*naẓm*) of meanings (*maʿānī*), but he will not search for the meanings (*maʿānī*) unless he masters these morphological bases (*uṣūl*).[103] On the contrary, *udhkur* proceeds from it in the way of a hint (*tanbīḥ*) and provocation (*taḥrīk*). Because *zākhôr tizkōr* refers to the soul, it is said "My soul surely calls to mind, and is bowed down within me."

In other words, "She remembers what has passed and departed from her, and she is bowed down and broken since she has no consolation and no comforter." Likewise, the [sage of the] Koraḥites[104] said, *My God, my soul is cast down within me, [therefore I remember You from the land of Jordan and of Hermon, from Mount Mizar]* (Ps 42:7/6), [which] he said before this: *Why are you cast down, O my soul, and why are you disquieted within me?* (Ps 42:12/11). He means, "In this exile there is no one to hold my hand and no one to comfort me," as it is said, *There is none to guide her among all the sons she has borne* (Is 51:18). Rather, I console my soul, and I tell her, "Be patient (*ʾiṣbirī*), wait until the time comes when God, for His part, will redeem us," as it is said, *Until the LORD from heaven looks down and sees* (Lam 3:50), and *Until the Spirit is poured upon us from on high* (Isa 32:15). Indeed, He promised <119a> relief (*faraj*), and I will surely increase my gratitude to Him *with glad shouts and songs of thanksgiving* (Ps 42:5/4), as it is said, *Again I will build you, and you shall be built* (Jer 31:4); *yet will say in your ears* (Is 49:20); *ever singing*

[101] As in Yefet's rendering: *dhakara tadhakara nafsī*.

[102] Ibn Nūḥ also uses the grammatical term *mukhrat* (Hebr. "disjoined"), although he is more inclined to contrast it with the Arab. term *muḍāf* ("conjoined") than the Hebr. term *samukh*, which Salmon uses here. For Ibn Nūḥ, words may be conjoined or disjoined in terms of their form or their meaning. See Khan, *The Early Karaite Tradition of Hebrew Grammatical Thought: Including a Critical Edition, Translation, and An Analysis of the* Diqduq *of ʿAbū Yaʿqūb Yūsuf ibn Nūḥ on the Hagiographa*, SSLL 32 (Leiden: Brill, 2000), 112–15.

[103] On *uṣūl* as a technical linguistic term, see Khan, *The Early Karaite Tradition*, 147. For medieval discussions of syntax (*naẓm*), see Key, *Language*, 228–31.

[104] This psalm is ascribed to a *maśkīl* (sage) of the Koraḥites (Ps 42:1), and Salmon refers to a masculine singular author throughout his remarks.

Your praise! Selah (Ps 84:5/4); *they still bring forth fruit in old age* [. . .] *to show that the LORD is upright* (Ps 92:15–16/14–15).[105]

Now he says: אֱלֹהַי עָלַי נַפְשִׁי תִשְׁתּוֹחָח (Ps 42:7/6)—"It is bowed down within me because of this." He says, "O God, my soul is confused, and bowed down within me; that is why I call you to mind from the land of Jordan, from the Hermons, and from the mount of Zoar."[106] When he said, *Why are you bowed down, O my soul, and why are you disquieted within me? Hope in God* (Ps 42:12/11), he felt compassion for his soul, for it did not bear patiently and it did not console itself, as it is said in another place, *My soul refuses to be comforted* (Ps 77:3/2).[107] He adds to [his] complaint to God by saying, "O my God, my soul will not accept consolation and will not wait patiently, because I am in the depth of the Jordan, drowning, and here I am calling out to You for salvation, and *therefore I remember You from the land of Jordan* (Ps 42:7/6).[108] I also cry out to You for salvation against the enemies who are against us like the beast of Hermon." He compares the enemies that are against us to the animals of the mountain of Zoar. Solomon alludes to this by saying, *From the peak of Senir and Hermon, [from the dens of lions, from the mountains of leopards]* (Song 4:8).[109]

Some of the scholars—may God have mercy on them—<119b> said that in this verse (i.e., Ps 42:7/6) he means the four kingdoms: by Jordan he alludes to the kingdom of Babylon; by Hermon to Media and Persia; Mount Mizhar is an allusion to his life—he means Greece—and the fourth kingdom he mentions separately in the first [verse] of the chapter that follows this one, according to what he explained of this in the verse, *From deceitful and unjust men deliver me!* (Ps 43:1).[110]

[105] In his comment to Ps 92:16/15, Salmon brings together the themes of praising God and remembering God's justice: "He means that they praise, and in their praise they remember that God is upright in all His deeds, and He recompenses everyone according to his deed, with equity and justice, as it is said, *The Rock, [His work is perfect; for all His ways are justice]* (Deut 32:4). In this psalm there is much language indicating the language of Moses as it is said, *to declare Your steadfast love in the morning* (Ps 92:3/2). He seals the psalm by saying, *to show that the LORD is upright; He is my rock, and there is no unrighteousness in Him*" (Salmon, Pss 90–106).

[106] Arab. *zaghar*. On the translation of biblical place names into Arab., see Polliack, *The Karaite Tradition*, 203–7.

[107] Salmon finds in Ps 77:3/2 a reference to the obligation for perpetual mourning in the time of exile. His comment on this verse also includes his mandate for reflection (*iʿtibār*) on the biblical stories of Jacob and David, which offer instruction in the necessity of mourning during this time of loss. He invokes this verse also in his comment to Lam 1:16. See discussion in chapter 6.

[108] Karaites recognized the complaint (Arab. *shakwa*) as a form of prayer, represented primarily in the Psalms. On Yefet's use of the term, see Frank, *Search Scripture Well*, 179, 202. In complaint, as in lamentation, the worshiper recounts to God instances of suffering and oppression.

[109] In his comment to Song 4:8, Salmon reads the den of lions as an allusion to Nebuchadnezzar, who took Judah into exile, and the mountains of leopards as an allusion to Persia and Media, whose kingdom is like a leopard (Evr.-Arab. I 1406; 108b).

[110] This statement matches Salmon's comment to Ps 42:7/6, although there he presents this reading as his own opinion rather than attributing it to anonymous scholars. Salmon's agreement with

תְּהוֹם־אֶל־תְּהוֹם קוֹרֵא (Ps 42:8/7)—"Deep calls to deep at the sound of Your watercourses; all Your currents and Your waves have passed over me." The meaning of *deep* [*calls to*] *deep* means "king after king." How many kings are in four kingdoms? [So many that] their number increases over you when you count them, and every one that comes has the meaning (*ma'nā*) of slaughter and horror.[111] Therefore, it is said, *at the sound of Your watercourses*—which is to say that he calls to them during difficult matters, like a watercourse in which waters stream without tranquility or stability. In the same way, we have no tranquility or stability among us, as it is said, *And among these nations you shall find no ease* (Deut 28:65). The meaning of *all Your currents and Your waves have passed over me* is "You are the one, O LORD, who gave them power over me <120a> as [I] deserved."

יוֹמָם יְצַוֶּה יְהוָה חַסְדּוֹ (Ps 42:9/8)—"By day God commands His grace and by night His song is with me: a prayer to the Omnipotent One of my life."[112] After he described the severity of the matter of the kingdoms, and how we are drowning among them, he said, "And when I, O Lord, appeared among them in the day, [it was] for [my] livelihood or to spend money. But now I am in personal peril. If it were not for the grace of the LORD I would have been destroyed," as it is said, *Yet for all that, when they are in the land of their enemies* [*I will not spurn them, neither will I abhor them so as to destroy them utterly*] (Lev 26:44). He said, "So when I turned away from my way of life I was amazed by how I became free on that day. The night grows long with thanksgiving and glorification" as it is said, *and at night His song is with me, a prayer to the God of my life* (Ps 42:9). "A prayer" is my prayer to the All-Powerful, the Living, on account of my deliverance and the preservation of my soul from destruction.[113]

אוֹמְרָה לְאֵל סַלְעִי (Ps 42:10/9)—"I say to the Omnipotent One, my rock: 'Why is it as though You have forgotten me? Why do I walk in the

this interpretation, as well as his pious blessing on the scholars who proposed it, suggest that the "scholars" that he has in mind are not Rabbanites. Typically, Salmon uses the expression *ba'ḍ al-'ulamā'* in reference to a single scholar (i.e., "one of the scholars"); I have translated it in the plural here (i.e., "some of the scholars") because Salmon uses a plural verb and plural object pronoun in reference to them. The fourth kingdom is that of Ishmael, as Salmon briefly states in his comment at Ps 43:1: "I have already explained this in what precedes, and you know that by his words, *a deceitful person* (Ps 43:1), he suggests the son of Hagar, just as he says, *by his cunning he shall make deceit prosper under his hand* (Dan 8:25). We will explain this accordingly in the commentary on Daniel, with the help of God" (Salmon, Pss 42–72).

[111] Reading *haul*, as in MSS B, J and P.

[112] Salmon translates Hebr. *shir* ("song") as Arab. *nashīd*, following the Arab. title of the biblical Song of Songs as *nashīd al-anāshīd*.

[113] Salmon makes liberal use of the divine names: the Omnipotent One (*al-ṭā'iq*); the All-Powerful (*al-qādir*); the Living (*al-ḥayy*).

darkness of the enemy's oppression?'"[114] He asks: "Why has the one who gives us grace decreed that we should live among the nations by His mercy? My heart is not at peace. He does not guide the one who seeks and asks for salvation forever. I ask, *Why have You forgotten me?* not, 'Extend my life forever, O LORD' and not, 'O Lord, I am black of face because of the oppression of the enemies.'" <120b>

בְּרֶצַח בְּעַצְמוֹתַי (Ps 42:11/10)—"With murder in my bones, my enemies taunt me while they say to me continually, 'Where is your God?'" He said, "O Lord, their words to me, 'Where is your God?' seem like murder in my bones." He becomes jealous for [the sake of] Your name, and therefore the Mighty and Sublime promises Israel that when they ask for salvation and cry and say, *Why should they say among the peoples, 'Where is their God?,'* then *the LORD will become jealous for His land, and have pity on His people* (Joel 2:17, 18).

מַה־תִּשְׁתּוֹחֲחִי (Ps 42:12/11)—"Why are you cast down, O my soul, and why are you frantic within me? Wait patiently for the Lord; for I will increase my gratitude to Him, and He will be a help for me before Him, and He will be my God." As it is said, *You shall be My own possession among all peoples* (Exod 19:5); and *So you shall be My people* (Jer 11:4). And the meaning of *Why are you cast down* is the same as what I explained the first time.[115]

שָׁפְטֵנִי אֱלֹהִים וְרִיבָה (Ps 43:1)—"Vindicate me, O God, and vindicate my cause against a nation not uncultivated; from a person of deception and deviation, let me escape!"[116] I have explained above that he mentions the fourth kingdom separately in the beginning of this chapter. *A deceitful person* <121a> alludes to the kingdom of the son of Hagar.[117] Along the same lines, it is said about him, *By his cunning he shall make deceit prosper under his hand* (Dan 8:25), as we have explained in the commentary on Daniel with a clear and evident explanation.[118]

כִּי־אַתָּה אֱלֹהֵי מָעוּזִּי (Ps 43:2)—"For You are the God who fortifies me; why have You forsaken me? Why do I walk about in darkness because of

[114] Salmon modifies the biblical question, "Why have You forgotten me?" to read "Why is it as though You have forgotten me?"

[115] Ps 42:12/11 = Ps 42:6/5.

[116] Cf. RSV: "Vindicate me, O God, and defend my cause against an ungodly people; from deceitful and unjust men deliver me!"

[117] I.e., the Islamic empire.

[118] Salmon's commentary on Daniel is no longer extant. Salmon's remarks here and in the following paragraph suggest that he offers a highly messianic interpretation.

the oppression of the enemy?" (Ps 43:2). Earlier he said, *I walk* (*'ēlēkh*) [*in darkness*] (Ps 42:10/9) but here he says, *I walk about* (*'ethallēkh*) [*in darkness*] because the kingdom of the maidservant's son is greater and more difficult [than the earlier kingdoms under which Israel was oppressed], as it is said, *terrible and dreadful and exceedingly strong* (Dan 7:7).[119] It is said about this, *Deliver me, O LORD, from lying lips* (Ps 120:2). And he seeks salvation from [the oppressions of the kingdom], as in the verse, *Woe is me, that I sojourn in Meshech* (Ps 120:5), continuing until the end of that chapter. There are many descriptions like these, as I have explained at the end of Daniel.

שְׁלַח־אוֹרְךָ וַאֲמִתְּךָ (Ps 43:3)—"Send out Your light and the truth of Your promises; they will safeguard me and bring me in to Your holy mountain and to Your dwelling places." He says *Send out Your light* because he began by mentioning darkness.[120] "Your truth" means the confirmation and fulfillment of the promises. He [places this verse] after he mentioned the kingdom of the son of Hagar because the only king after that will be the king of Israel, as it is said, <121b> *But the saints of the Most High shall receive the kingdom, and possess the kingdom forever, for ever and ever* (Dan 7:18). *Your holy mountain* means the house of the Lord, the holy Mount, and *Your dwelling places* means the courts and the chambers and everything like that.

וְאָבוֹאָה אֶל־מִזְבַּח אֱלֹהִים (Ps 43:4)—"I will enter the altar of the Omnipotent Lord, my exceeding joy, and I will thank You with the lyre, O Lord, O God." Just as he said, *For I shall again praise* [*Him*] (Ps 42:11/12), he says here, *I will enter the altar of God*. He mentions four things: [he indicates] pilgrimage (*ḥajj*) by saying, *I will enter*; sacrifice (*qurban*) by mentioning the altar; gratitude (*shukr*) by saying, *the lyre*; and he concludes this with patience (*ṣabr*) and hope (*rajāh*), as he also says, *Why are you cast down* [. . .] *and why are you disquieted within me?* (Ps 42:12/11 and Ps 43:5). Therefore, the verse [***My soul***] ***continually calls it to mind*** means what the congregation (*kanīsa*) of Israel remembers [while] her soul is bowed down within her, as it is said, *These things I remember, as I pour out my soul* (Ps 42:5/4). This bowing down has overtaken us because of our enemies, as it is said, *They have said to you,*

[119] Salmon follows the principle that a difference in morphology reflects a difference in meaning. Ps 43:2 repeats the question from Ps 42:10/9, except that the Hebr. verb has shifted from the *qal* form (*'ēlēkh*) to the *hitpa'el* form, *'ethallēkh*. In his Arab. translation Salmon uses *'amḍīy* (a standard translation for *'ēlēkh*) in the first instance and *'atasallak* in the second. Presumably *'atasallak* is s/l/k form V, although this form is rare even in Judeo-Arabic (see the single reference, to Ibn Aqnīn, who uses it to mean "to behave, to comport o.s.," in Blau, *Dictionary*, 306). Salmon may have opted for this unusual form of s/l/k because it mirrors the t-infix pattern of the Hebr. *'ethallēkh* (Salmon, Pss 42–72).

[120] See Ps 43:2 and 42:10/9.

"Bow down, that we may pass over" (Isa 51:23) and as it is said, *For our soul is bowed down to the dust* (Ps 44:26/25). And all this has overtaken us because of the crimes, as it is said, *Because they did not obey the voice of the LORD their God but transgressed His covenant, even all that Moses the servant of the LORD commanded; they neither listened nor obeyed* (2 Kgs 18:12).

זֹאת אָשִׁיב אֶל־לִבִּי עַל־כֵּן אוֹחִיל:
הד'א ארד אלי קלבי עלי ד'לך אצבר

3:21 This I call to mind, and therefore I wait patiently.

<122a> That is to say, I call this trait[121] to mind and I honor it, and therefore I patiently bear everything that overtakes me and every calamity that befalls me, because the calamities of the people—the people of the exile—are many, commensurate with the magnitude of the crimes, as it is said, *Because they did not obey the voice of the LORD their God but transgressed His covenant, even all that Moses the servant of the LORD commanded; they neither listened nor obeyed* (2 Kgs 18:12).

חַסְדֵי יְהוָה כִּי לֹא־תָמְנוּ כִּי לֹא־כָלוּ רַחֲמָיו:
פצ'איל יוי אן מא פניו אן מא פניו רחמאתה <u>לנא</u>

3:22 The graces of the LORD are not consumed; His mercies <u>for us</u> are not consumed.[122]

After having said *But this I call to mind, and therefore I have hope* (Lam 3:21), he now makes known which traits are the ones that "I pondered and honored, and for the sake of which I patiently bear every calamity." He says, *The graces of the LORD are not consumed*, which is to say that we deserved destruction, but the grace of the LORD of hosts and His mercy for us were not consumed, as it is said, *Yet I will not make a full end* (Jer 4:27), and *I will not spurn them, neither will I abhor them so as to destroy them utterly* (Lev 26:44).[123] He turned to the duty of our destruction because the magnitude of our sins

[121] Arab. *khaṣla*. Salmon anticipates the "traits" referred to in the following verse, Lam 3:22.

[122] Cf. RSV: "The steadfast love of the LORD never ceases, His mercies never come to an end." Salmon and Yefet translate Hebr. *ḥesed* ("lovingkindness") with Arab. *faḍl*, as is common in Judeo-Arabic translation (see al-Fāsī, vol. I, 567). Cf. Saadia, who translates the term as *iḥsān* ("excellence") in this verse (Lam, 101).

[123] Salmon emphasizes God's restraint also in his comments to Lam 1:12 (where he also invokes Jer 4:27 and Lam 4:1). He returns to this theme in his opening remarks to Neḥamot.

was greater than the deeds of Sodom and Gomorrah, as it is said, *For the offense of the community of my people has been greater than the sin of Sodom* (Lam 4:6). *Because they did not obey the voice of the LORD their God but transgressed His covenant, even all that Moses the servant of the LORD commanded;* <122b> *they neither listened nor obeyed* (2 Kgs 18:12).

חֲדָשִׁים לַבְּקָרִים רַבָּה אֱמוּנָתֶךָ:
ג'דד ללבכור כת'ירה חקיקתך

3:23 They are new every morning; great is Your truth.[124]

That is to say, "Every day Your grace and Your beneficence are renewed."[125] The meaning is: "Your truth and Your mercy are great in each and every *generation*." If not for that, we would have been destroyed, because the crimes are great, as it is said, *Because they did not obey the voice of the LORD their God but transgressed His covenant, even all that Moses the servant of the LORD commanded; they neither listened nor obeyed* (2 Kgs 18:12).

חֶלְקִי יְהוָה אָמְרָה נַפְשִׁי עַל־כֵּן אוֹחִיל לוֹ:
קסמי אללה קאלת נפסי עלי ד'לך אצבר לה

3:24 "The LORD is my portion," says my soul, "therefore I will wait patiently on Him."[126]

That is to say: the nations' portion is the grace of this world, as it is said, *Men whose portion in life is of the world: may their belly be filled with what You have stored up for them* (Ps 17:14).[127] Israel's portion is the Lord of the worlds, as it is said, *The LORD is my chosen portion and my cup* (Ps 16:5),[128] and it

[124] Cf. RSV: "Great is Your faithfulness."

[125] Salmon supplies the subject: it is God's grace and excellence that are renewed (building on the previous verse); not God's angels (as in Midrash; see, e.g., *Lam R* on Lam 3:22).

[126] Cf. RSV: "'The LORD is my portion,' says my soul, 'therefore I will hope in Him.'"

[127] Note that in his comment to Ps 17:14 Salmon does not apply this verse to the non-Israelite nations, but rather to those whose love is limited to "the affairs of the world and its delights." His comment to Lam 3:24 accords with Midrashic interpretations that contrast the monotheistic faith of Israel with that of the nations, who worship sun, moon, wood, and stones (*Lam R* on Lam 3:24).

[128] In his comment to Ps 16:5, Salmon explains: "The pious one (i.e., David) says, 'You, O Lord, are my portion. I have no object of worship other than You,' as it is said, *The LORD is my portion; I promise to keep Your words* (Ps 119:57) and '*The LORD is my portion,' says my soul* (Lam 3:24). By 'You hold my lot,' he refers to the recompense of the Hereafter (*thawāb al-ākhira*)" (Pss 11–41).

is said also, *I say, You are my refuge, my portion* [*in the land of the living*] (Ps 142:6/5).[129] God is my portion and my share and the one that I worship; that is why I will wait and patiently bear everything that befalls me until [God] sees my affairs, as it is said, *I will bear the indignation of the LORD because I have sinned against Him, until He pleads my cause and executes judgment for me* (Mic 7:9).[130]

טוֹב יְהוָה לְקֹוָו לְנֶפֶשׁ תִּדְרְשֶׁנּוּ:
אללה ג'ואד לראג'יה לנפס תלתמסה

3:25 God is good to those who wait for Him, to the soul that seeks Him.[131]

<123a> This means that the Mighty and Sublime is gracious to those who wait for Him, as it is said, *Those who wait for Me shall not be put to shame* (Isa 49:23); and *But they who wait for the LORD shall renew their strength* (Isa 40:31); and *But those who wait for the LORD shall possess the land* (Ps 37:9). Blessed is the one who waits patiently and hopes for relief from the Lord of the worlds, and patiently bears the calamities of this exile, and induces his soul to toil and complaint and worship.[132] [God] will remember all that he does, and He will recompense him, as it is said:

טוֹב וְיָחִיל וְדוּמָם לִתְשׁוּעַת יְהוָה:
כ'יר ללד'י יתמכ'ץ' <u>ותכון נפסה</u> סאכתה <u>צאברה</u> למגות'ת יוי

3:26 It is good for the one who bears [it] <u>with his soul</u> silent, <u>waiting patiently</u> for salvation from the LORD.[133]

This means that it is not good for a person to cry out like a woman in labor, as it is said, *Like a woman with child, who writhes and cries out in her pangs, when she is near her time, so were we because of You, O LORD; we were with child, we writhed, we have as it were brought forth wind* (Isa 26:17–18). The meaning of *dumam* is a silent soul, patiently awaiting the birth pangs

[129] In his comment to Ps 142:6/5, Salmon glosses *the land of the living* as a reference to the "abode of recompense" (*dār al-thawāb*) (Pss 107–150).
[130] Note the suspension of the refrain verses at this point of the commentary.
[131] Cf. RSV: "The LORD is good to those who wait for Him, to the soul that seeks Him."
[132] Karaites considered complaint (*shakwa*) to be a form of prayer.
[133] Cf. RSV: "It is good that one should wait quietly for the salvation of the LORD."

of exile, as it is said, *Be still before the LORD, and wait patiently for Him* (Ps 37:7).[134]

I have translated *dumam* as "silent," as in *to a silent stone* (Hab 2:19) because *'even* (Hebr., "stone") is feminine, as it is said, *the top stone* (*ha-'even ha-rishonah*; Zech 4:7), and *Behold, this stone* (*ha-'even ha-zo't*) *shall be a witness against us* (Josh 24:27), and similarly in the Aramaic language it is said, *And a stone was brought* (*ve-heytayit 'even ḥadah*) *and laid* <123b> *upon the mouth of the den* (Dan 6:18).[135] It is also said in the account of Tyre, *Who was ever destroyed like silence in the midst of the sea?* (Ezek 27:32). The meaning is: like *a silent stone*, which has no hope when it falls into the depth of the sea. And now *dumah* and *dumam* are the same in this sense because the *hā'* and the *mem* are included in the interchangeable letters (*aḥruf al-ibdāl*).[136] Likewise, all of these [forms] have the same meaning: *Truly* (*'amnam*) *I have sinned* (Josh 7:20)—its translation is "truly"—and *Truly* (*'amnam*) *you are the people* (Job 12:2); *Besides, she is truly* (*'amnah*) *my sister, the daughter of my father* (Gen 20:12); and *Truly* (*'amnam*) *I know that it is so* (Job 9:2).[137] As for *the oracle concerning Dumah* (Isa 21:11), this alludes to Dumah the son of Ishmael, as in the verse, *Mishma, Dumah, Massa* (Gen 25:14). In [the verse], [*The dead do not praise the LORD, nor do*] *any that go down into dumah* (Ps 115:17); it is a name for the grave.[138] *My soul would soon have dwelt in dumah* (Ps 94:17)[139] likewise [refers to the grave]. Therefore, someone who seeks God in this *exile*, and whose soul patiently bears its torment and waits for the relief of the LORD, will be blessed, as it is said, ***It is good for the one who bears it*** (Lam 3:26).[140]

טוֹב לַגֶּבֶר כִּי־יִשָּׂא עֹל בִּנְעוּרָיו׃
מא אג'וד ללרג'ל אן יחמל אלניר מן חדאת'תה

3:27 What is good for a man is to bear the yoke in his youth.

[134] Salmon glosses *dom lyhwh* as "be silent and forbear" (*'uskut wa-'iṣbir*) in his comment to Ps 37:7 (Salmon, Pss 11–41).

[135] In each example the Hebr. word *'even* ("stone") is treated as grammatically feminine.

[136] Note that Salmon gives the Hebr. for the letter *mem* and the Arab. for the letter *hā'*. See also Salmon's comment on Lam 3:16, where he treats *bā'* and *fā'* as interchangeable letters.

[137] I.e., the same word may be spelled with the letter *mem* or the letter *heh*.

[138] Accordingly, in his translation of Ps 115:17, Salmon renders Hebr. *kol yordei dumah* ("all who go down into silence") as Arab. *kull munḥadiray al-qabr* ("all who go down to the grave"), (Salmon, Pss 107–150).

[139] Salmon notes this meaning in his comment to Ps 94:17 and refers readers also to Ps 115:17.

[140] Salmon does not specify whether the relief will come in this world or in the Hereafter.

With this [dictum] he alludes to a person's desire and impulse to be obedient from the days of his youth, when <124a> a person has the strength to accomplish what he is unable to do in the time of old age and senility, when a person is at the point of becoming [too] weak to do what he needs to do, and also, he does not learn anything new.[141] Will he remain in the world [long enough] to become old or not? A person is obliged to hasten to greater readiness in his youth, as it is said, *Remember also your Creator in the days of your youth* (Eccl 12:1)[142] and *In the morning sow your seed* (Eccl 11:6),[143] and here it is said, ***What is good for a man is to bear the yoke in his youth.***

Indeed, Israel is likened to a calf in the context of command and prohibition, as it is said, *Ephraim was a trained heifer that loved to thresh* (Hos 10:11).[144] The command is likened to the yoke, the deed is likened to sowing, and recompense for action is likened to the person's harvest, as it is said, *Sow for yourselves righteousness, reap according to grace* (Hos 10:12).[145] ***What is good for a man is to bear the yoke in his youth***—it alludes to the yoke of Torah—is [based upon] this sound principle.[146]

יֵשֵׁב בָּדָד וְיִדֹּם כִּי נָטַל עָלָיו׃
יג'לס פראד ויסכת אן חמל עליה

3:28 Let him sit alone and be silent, for he carries it upon him.

Know that *badad* is "alone," [as in] *A bird alone on the housetop* (Ps 102:8/7) <124b> and solitary. ***Let him sit alone and be silent*** means "How good it is for a person to bear the yoke of the Torah and to withdraw from the people for worship, and to be silent about what does not concern him. One of the

141 Cf. Salmon's comment at Eccl 11:6, where he notes that a person who grows physically weak in his old age may continue to be mentally astute and possess great scientific learning (Robinson, *Asceticism*, 550).

142 Salmon outlines the problem in similar terms in his comment to Eccl 12:1, emphasizing the physical strength necessary to accomplish good deeds as well as the fact that one cannot predict how long his life may continue (Robinson, *Asceticism*, 558).

143 Salmon interprets the "seeds" of Eccl 11:6 as "good works," noting that God may accept the good deeds that a person performs during his youth as well as his old age (Robinson, *Asceticism*, 549–50).

144 An extended parable (*tamthīl*); see chapter 4.

145 Reading Hebr. *ḥesed* as Arab. *faḍl* (following Salmon's translation of Lam 3:22 above); cf. RSV: "reap according to steadfast love." Salmon invokes Hos 10:12 in his comment to Eccl 11:6, but there it appears without this interpretation.

146 The concept of Torah as a "yoke" dates back to antiquity. In *Lam R* the rabbis understand this verse as referring to the yokes of Torah, marriage, and profession, as each of these obligations should be embraced as early as appropriate (*Lam R* on 3:27).

conditions for worship is diminishing [one's] eagerness for anything that is not in the category of the affairs of the Hereafter, as Jeremiah said in another place, *I sat alone, because Your hand was upon me* (Jer 15:17).[147]

For he carries (*naṭal*) ***it upon him***: what he means is that he carries the yoke of the Torah upon his neck; he sits alone and keeps silent and waits patiently for relief from God. Likewise, he says, *I lie awake, I am like a bird alone on the housetop* (Ps 102:8/7). Know that the word *naṭal*, when the *nun* is in it, is from the language of Targum, as it is said, *And it was lifted* (*u-neṭilat*) *up from the ground* (Dan 7:4). Similarly, *He lifted them up* (*va-yenaṭṭelem*) *and carried them all the days of old* (Isa 63:9) and *And sand is weighty* (*neṭel*) (Prov 27:3)—in all [these cases] it [means] to lift up and carry. And when the *nun* is not in it, it means to throw, as in *Take me up and throw me* (*haṭiluni*) *into the sea* (Jonah 1:12) and *And Saul cast* (*yaṭel*) *the spear* (1 Sam 18:11; 20:33).[148]

יִתֵּן בֶּעָפָר פִּיהוּ אוּלַי יֵשׁ תִּקְוָה:
יג'על פי אלתראב פמה לעל איס רג'א

3:29 Let him put his mouth in the dust—there may yet be hope.

By this he means, let him not set out to raise himself up or deem himself superior. <125a> He should scorn himself and humble himself until his soul reaches the dust. Perhaps when he does this, his Lord will have mercy on him and forgive his sins, as it is said, *It may be that the LORD, the God of hosts, will be gracious to the remnant of Joseph* (Amos 5:15); and similarly, *Perhaps you may be hidden on the day of the wrath of the LORD* (Zep 2:3). Because the sins of a person are many, perhaps when his soul exerts itself, He [i.e., God] will forgive him, and he will have hope of recompense.

יִתֵּן לְמַכֵּהוּ לֶחִי יִשְׂבַּע בְּחֶרְפָּה:
יעטי לצ'ארבה כ'דה ישבע במעירה

3:30 Let him give his cheek to the smiter, and be filled with insults.

147 So also Yefet's translation of Jer 15:17: "I did not sit with the community" (Yefet, Jer, 203).

148 Al-Fāsī likewise lists these verses under the same entry (ṭ/l) but distinguishes between these meanings. He agrees with Salmon that in the case of Jonah 1:12 and 1 Sam 18:11 the word means to raise (r/f/ʿ) and to carry (ḥ/m/l), and he provides comparative linguistic evidence from the "Syrian" language (vol. II, 12–13).

This verse obliges a person in this *exile* not to be scornful when he is overtaken by abasement and contempt. He may say to himself, "How long will I patiently bear hatred? I would [rather] renounce my obligation in order to be honored (*ʿazīz*)."[149] Perhaps he would become more lowly than he had been, and perhaps he would endure for only a small amount of time, and then he would die and his portion in the world to come would be taken from him. Even if he were to achieve some strength, there is no escape from death, and he will be led to a *burning fire*, as it is said, *For their worm shall not die, their fire shall not be quenched* (Isa 66:24); *When all the arrogant and all the evildoers will be stubble* (Mal 3:19/4:1). <125b>

But better and more excellent than this is patience in the religion of truth and sufferance, as it is said, ***Let him give his cheek to the smiter, and be filled with insults.*** What he mentions is more difficult than [taking] a blow, and that is being struck on the cheek, as it is also said, *I gave my back to the smiters, and my cheeks to those who pulled out the beard* (Isa 50:6). In this verse he includes the most severe of the various types of abasement that happen, and he makes known that the result of patient forbearance is beautiful, as it is said, *And I know that I shall not be put to shame* (Isa 50:7); and *He who vindicates me is near* [. . .] *behold, the Lord GOD helps me* (Isa 50:8–9). ***And be filled with insults***: he mentions kinds of slander, impudence, and abuse. [God] will not abandon the one who patiently bears everything that his Lord brings upon him, as it is said:

כִּי לֹא יִזְנַח לְעוֹלָם אֲדֹנָי׃
אן לא יתרך ללאבד אללה

3:31 For God will not cast off forever.[150]

This means that when God saw these deeds of Israel and the excellence of their patience and their sufferance, He did not abandon them, as it is said, *I have seen his ways, and I will heal him* (Isa 57:18). ***Forever*** means that he will not remain in this condition for eternity [as long as he] repents, as it is said, *For I will not contend forever, nor will I always be angry* (Isa 57:16).

[149] Salmon seems to allude to Jewish apostates; see the following paragraph, where he contrasts this person against those who persevere "in the religion of truth and sufferance."
[150] Cf. RSV: "For the Lord will not cast off forever."

כִּי אִם־הוֹגָה וְרִחַם כְּרֹב חֲסָדָיו:
אן ואן כאן קד נחא ישראל מן הד'א אלבלד והד'א אלקדס וירחם בכת'רה פצ'לה

3:32 Even though He drove Israel out of this country and this Temple, He will be merciful according to the abundance of His grace.[151]

<126a> I have made clear in what preceded that the word *hogah* means "he drove out"[152] as it is said, *When he was driven out* (*hogah*) *of the highway, all the people went on* (2 Sam 20:13). Now when he says, ***even though He drove out***, he alludes to the expulsion of Israel from this holy land (*al-balad al-muqaddas*), as it is said, *He drove them out with His fierce blast in the day of the east wind* (Isa 27:8). [In the verse] *I will drive them out of My house. I will love them no more* (Hos 9:15), it is said that even though the Lord expelled Israel, He promised that He would have mercy on them and bring them back, as it is said, *The LORD will have compassion on Jacob* (Isa 14:1).

כִּי לֹא עִנָּה מִלִּבּוֹ וַיַּגֶּה בְּנֵי־אִישׁ:
אן מא אשקא מן ראיה וצ'רב בני אלרג'ל

3:33 For He does not of His own accord afflict or strike the sons of a man.[153]

[I interpret the verse as follows] because the first [term] governs itself and governs others (*menaheg ʿaṣmo ve-menaheg aḥerim*). In other words, He does not afflict Israel of His own accord, and He does not harm them of His own accord. I have translated *va-yaggeh* as [though it were] *va-yakkeh* because [*gimmel* and *kaf*] are among the interchangeable letters (*ḥurūf al-ibdāl*).[154] Similarly, in the verse *For the mouths of liars will be stopped* (*yissaker*) (Ps 63:12/11), the meaning [of *yissaker*] is [the same as] *yisgor* (Gen 2:21)—*yissaker*

[151] Cf. RSV: "But, though He cause grief, He will have compassion according to the abundance of His steadfast love." In this Arabic translation, Salmon presents the contextual meaning (*maʿnā*) of the verse as though it were its direct translation (*tafsīr*).

[152] See Salmon's comments to Lam 1:5 and 1:12. Salmon and Yefet render Hebr. h/g/h as Arab. n/ḥ/w in all three verses. Saadia uses the root n/ḥ/w in Lam 1:15 and 3:32 but renders the Hebr. h/g/h more loosely in Lam 1:12, as *ḥassaranī* ("He grieved me."). Al-Fāsī lists Arab. n/ḥ/w as one meaning of this Hebr. word, which he illustrates with 2 Sam 20:13, without including Lam 3:32 among his prooftexts (vol. I, 421–22).

[153] Cf. RSV: "For He does not willingly afflict or grieve the sons of men."

[154] On the interchangeable letters, see Salmon's comments to Lam 3:16 and 26, and notes there.

and *yisgor* mean the same thing.[155] ***The sons of a man*** alludes to the children of Jacob, as it is said, <126b> *Jacob was a quiet man* (Gen 25:27). They say it is like the phrases *the sons of Adam* or *the sons of Seth.*[156]

This verse is one of the descriptions of the Creator, for He does not want to punish the criminal. Rather, His desire is for the sons of man to obey Him so that He [may] reward them, as it is said, *Have I any pleasure in the death of the wicked, says the Lord GOD, and not rather that he should turn from his way and live?* (Ezek 18:23); and it is also said, *For I have no pleasure in the death of any one* (Ezek 18:32). He singles out Israel, as it is said, *Precious in the sight of the LORD* [*is the death of His saints*] (Ps 116:15).[157] Therefore it is said here, ***for He does not of His own accord afflict.*** They have translated *va-yaggeh* as "he caused distress and he caused grief" in [the verse *How long will*] *You torment me* (Job 19:2).[158]

לְדַכֵּא תַּחַת רַגְלָיו כֹּל אֲסִירֵי אָרֶץ:
ולא מן מראדה שא לידכדך תחת רג'ליה כל סג'ניי אלארץ'

3:34 And it is not at all His desire to crush under foot all the prisoners of the earth.[159]

For He does not of His own accord afflict (Lam 3:33) governs itself and governs others (*menaheg ʿaṣmo ve-menaheg aḥerim*).[160] This means that

155 Salmon provides the same explanation, also invoking the principle of interchangeable letters, in his comment to Ps 63:12/11 (Salmon, Pss 42–72).

156 Salmon reads Hebr. *benei ʾish* ("sons of a man") in reference to the descendants of Jacob, namely, the biblical Israelites and the Jews after them.

157 Salmon explains further in his comment to Ps 116:15: "Know that by 'His saints' he means Israel, as it is said, [*They have given the bodies of Your servants to the birds of the air for food,*] *the flesh of Your saints to the beasts of the earth* (Ps 79:2). Now he says, 'The exile is precious to the Lord of the worlds.' In other words, it is not His desire, but rather He does this to them because of the magnitude of their sins, as it is said, *for He does not of His own accord afflict* (Lam 3:33). That is to say that it is not His desire that this affliction overtake Israel, but rather He did this because of their many rebellions, just as it is also said, *for I have no pleasure in the death of any one* (Ezek 18:32). Thus it is said, *Precious in the sight of the Lord* [*is the death of His saints*] (Ps 116:15)" (Salmon, Pss 107–150).

158 This description partly matches Saadia's translation of Job 19:2: *ʾilā kam taḥsirūn nafsī wa-tawajʿūnī bi-l-kalām* (Saadia, Job, 60).

159 Cf. RSV: "To crush under foot all the prisoners of the earth." Note the Midrashic reading in which the verse alludes to Nebuchadnezzar (*Lam R* on Lam 3:34).

160 Salmon extends the force of the Hebr. phrase *loʾ . . . millibo* (Arab. *mā . . . min rāʾyihi*—"it is not of His own accord" in Lam 3:33) to the following verse. This extension is a stretch, especially because Lam 3:34 is in a different poetic unit from vv. 31–33 (its verses begin with the Hebr. letter *lamed* rather than *kaf*). Salmon asserts that God does not wish to enact the punishments reported in Lam 3:34. He offers no reason for the extension of this application, aside from the rhetorical principle of *menaheg ʿaṣmo ve-menaheg aḥerim*. By embedding this point in the Arab. verse translation, Salmon suggests that it is the contextual meaning of the verse and not his interpretation.

crushing Israel beneath His blows and making them prisoners in the earth, among the *nations*, is not the Lord's desire, but rather because of their offenses and their crimes, as it is said, *Because they did not obey the voice of the LORD their God but transgressed His covenant, even all that Moses the servant of the LORD commanded; they neither listened nor obeyed* (2 Kgs 18:12).[161]

לְהַטּוֹת מִשְׁפַּט־גָּבֶר נֶגֶד פְּנֵי עֶלְיוֹן:
לאמיאל חכם אלרג'ל קדאם וג'ה אלעאלי

3:35 To turn aside the right of a man in the presence of the Most High.

<127a> This means that the LORD struck Israel and afflicted them, crushed them, and imprisoned them because they turned aside a person's rights in His presence, and therefore He sent down these [punishments] upon them, as it is said, *Because they did not obey the voice of the LORD their God but transgressed His covenant, even all that Moses the servant of the LORD commanded; they neither listened nor obeyed* (2 Kgs 18:12).

לְעַוֵּת אָדָם בְּרִיבוֹ אֲדֹנָי לֹא רָאָה:
לאעואג' אלאדמי פי כ'צומתה יוי אַליס ינט'ר

3:36 To subvert a man in his cause; does the LORD not see?[162]

I have translated *lo' ra'ah* (*He does not see*) as [though it were] *ha-lo' ra'ah* [*Does He not see?*]. There are many similar [instances] in the book.[163] They say, rather, these conditions befell them because they executed their judgments crookedly, as it is said, *They judge not with justice* (Jer 5:28). Their deeds are not concealed from the LORD because *He knows all the deeds of the sons of man*, so He requites them according to their deeds, as it is said, *Because they did not obey the voice of the LORD their God but transgressed His covenant, even all that Moses the servant of the LORD commanded; they neither listened nor obeyed* (2 Kgs 18:12).

[161] Note the return of 2 Kgs 18:12, the refrain that has been suspended since Lam 3:24.
[162] Cf. RSV: "To subvert a man in his cause; the LORD does not approve."
[163] See, e.g., Salmon's remarks at Lam 1:12 and the footnotes there. There he adds the interrogative *heh* (= Arab. *a-laysa*) in his comment but not in his verse translation, as he does here.

מִי זֶה אָמַר וַתֶּהִי אֲדֹנָי לֹא צִוָּה:
מן הד'א קאל וכאנת יוי <u>מא וצא</u> ולא אמר

3:37 Who has spoken and it was? The Lord <u>did not order</u> and did not command.[164]

This means that when God spoke <127b> every one of them did something that God had not commanded, as it is said, *Which I did not command or decree, nor did it come into My mind* (Jer 19:5). And because they did these vile deeds, they deserved *exile*, as it is said, *Because they did not obey the voice of the LORD their God but transgressed His covenant, even all that Moses the servant of the LORD commanded; they neither listened nor obeyed* (2 Kgs 18:12).

מִפִּי עֶלְיוֹן לֹא תֵצֵא הָרָעוֹת וְהַטּוֹב:
מן אמר אלעאלי ליס תכ'רג' אלבלאיא ואלכ'יר

3:38 From the command of the Most High, do not affliction and good come?[165]

He means, "Has it not (*a-laysa*) already happened to you, O Israel? You know that when you obeyed, you had the best of things, as it is said, *If you walk in My statutes and observe My commandments and do them, then I will give you your rains in their season, and the land shall yield its increase, and the trees of the field shall yield their fruit* (Lev 26:3–4), [continuing] until the end of this passage. And when you rebelled, you were destroyed, as it is said, *But if you will not hearken to Me* (Lev 26:14), and the entire account [that follows]. If it had been His will to destroy the people, then He would not have guided you on the path that one is saved by walking upon. Therefore, it is said, *For He does not of His own accord afflict* (Lam 3:33) and this interpretation is syntactically correct. One who says that *to turn aside the right of a man* (Lam 3:35) [means the same thing as]

[164] Cf. RSV: "Who has commanded and it came to pass, unless the Lord has ordained it?" Salmon translates one Hebr. verb (*ṣivvah*, "he commanded") into two Arab. verbs (the cognate *waṣṣā*, "he ordered," and its more familiar synonym, *amar*). For the double translation of a single Hebr. term, see Khan, *The Early Karaite Tradition*, 133, and Polliack, *The Karaite Tradition*, 181–99.

[165] Cf. RSV: "Is it not from the mouth of the Most High that good and evil come?" The translators circumvent the image of God's mouth in different ways. Salmon: "from the command of" (*min amr*); Saadia: "from the speech of" (*min qawl*); Yefet: "from within" (*min fī*; although this may be a direct representation of Hebr. *mippi*). The Karaite translators render Hebr. *ha-ra'ot* ("evils") as Arab. *balāyā* ("afflictions") while Saadia gives Arab. *shurūr* ("evils").

to subvert a man in his cause (Lam 3:36) has erred according to God, may God forgive us and them. Likewise, one who interprets ***affliction and good*** as obedience and rebellion is not on target, because afterward it is said:[166] <128a>

מַה־יִּתְאוֹנֵן אָדָם חָי גֶּבֶר עַל־חֲטָאָו:
קאל איש יקדר יענת אלאנסאן אלחי רג'ל עלי כ'טאיאה

3:39 He says, how is a living person foreordained to sin?[167]

This means that God had already made known what would overtake the person if he abandoned obedience: *But if you will not obey the voice of the LORD your God* [*or be careful to do all His commandments and His statutes which I command you this day, then all these curses shall come upon you and overtake you*] (Deut 28:15). A man is not foreordained to commit a sin. He says, "I did not know, but if it had been told to me, then I would not have sinned," and therefore it is said, ***How is a living man foreordained to sin?***

One of the interpreters has said that the meaning (*maʿnā*) of ***a living man*** is that a man is foreordained to transgress for the remainder of [his] life. According to this interpretation, we have committed a crime by saying, *From the command of the Most High, do not affliction and good come?* (Lam 3:38). However, when we corrected the syntax of this translation as we have explained, then its meaning is apparent: anyone who experiences human hardship has protested against his Lord. He has clarified [this] for him and made him understand and guided him. We are obliged [to translate it in this way], since this is how the matter is.

נַחְפְּשָׂה דְרָכֵינוּ וְנַחְקֹרָה וְנָשׁוּבָה עַד־יְהוָה:
נתפש טרקנא ונפחץ ונרג'ע אלי אללה

3:40 Let us test and examine our ways, and return to the LORD!

ʿAd and *ʾel* are the same, and so is *ʿal* <128b> as in the verse, [*She*] *prayed to* (*ʿal*) *the LORD, and wept bitterly* (1 Sam 1:10).[168] ***Let us test and examine our ways*** means: since God has made His argument obligatory upon us, and we

166 Salmon creates continuity between the verses by suppressing the refrain again.
167 Cf. RSV: "Why should a living man complain, a man, about the punishment of his sins?"
168 All these prepositions mean "to" in the phrase "to the LORD."

have no argument against Him,[169] and we are not foreordained to transgress, *nor have we any recourse while we are oppressed and suppressed under His feet, beaten and shackled, is it not incumbent upon us to repent of our offenses so that He will see our oppression, and hear our cries, and contend in our disputes, and be gracious to our remnant, and collect our dispersed, and gather our scattered ones, and wall up the breach, and establish the ruined ones, and build back what was destroyed, and make the branch sprout, and make the bud blossom, and open the fount for the sake of His name*, as it is written, *For My own sake, for My own sake, I do it, for how should it be profaned?* (Isa 48:11).[170]

Let us test and examine our ways: we are obliged to tell one another during this *exile* that we must examine our affairs and abandon whatever we are engaged in that God does not approve of, because He will know everyone's secret.[171] ***Examine*** alludes to the purification of [one's] intention (*ikhlāṣ al-niyya*) and the improvement of [one's] innermost thoughts (*aṣlāḥ al-ṭawīya*), because [one's] external (*ẓāhir*) deeds are accepted only insofar as [one's] belief (*iʿtiqād*) is good. When a person improves <129a> his internal quality (*bāṭin*) and his external quality (*ẓāhir*), [then] God accepts his repentance.[172] Therefore it is said, ***Let us test and examine our ways, and return.***

נִשָּׂא לְבָבֵנוּ אֶל־כַּפָּיִם אֶל־אֵל בַּשָּׁמָיִם׃
נרפע קלובנא מע כפופנא אלי אלטאיק פי אלסמא

3:41 Let us lift up our hearts and hands to the Omnipotent One in heaven:[173]

[169] Arab. *ḥujja* ("argument"). On its range of meanings, see the entry in EI2 by L. Gardet and M. G. S. Hodgson. While the term has technical applications in Kalām and philosophical texts, Salmon employs it here in the sense in which it appears in the Qur'ān, i.e., that humans should have no *ḥujja* ("argument") against God (Q4:165).

[170] This non-biblical Hebr. passage may be an embedded liturgical composition.

[171] Arab. *kull wāḥid yuʿallam bi-sarīratihi.*

[172] Salmon brings a pietistic notion to the fore: the object of one's examination is one's self. Cf. al-Qūmisī, where God's Torah is the object of examination (Qūmisī, Sermon, 21 = 69). Salmon may be drawing on a Sufi ethical context here and in his comments to Lam 2:18 and 3:50. The Muslim pietist Muḥāsibī (d. 243/857) was also concerned with the *ikhlāṣ* ("purification" or "sincerity") of the worshiper's *niyya* ("intention"). See "Muhasibi: Moral Psychology," in Michael Sells, *Early Islamic Mysticism* (New York: Paulist, 1996), 171–96. For a superb analysis of Muḥāsibī and points of connection to the later Jewish pietist Baḥya ibn Paqūda (ca. 1050–1120), see chapter 7 in Diana Lobel, *A Sufi-Jewish Dialogue: Philosophy and Mysticism in Baḥya Ibn Paqūda's* Duties of the Heart (Philadelphia: University of Pennsylvania Press, 2007), esp.152–54. In his *Treatise on Asceticism* (*Risālat al-zuhd*), Muḥāsibī provides instruction on how to examine one's intention without succumbing to the distortions of one's ego. Note that *niyya*—a term not found in the Qur'ān—may have been influenced by Jewish notions of *kavvanah* (A. J. Wensinck, "*Niyya*," in *EI2*). I thank Jane Mikkelson for directing my attention to Muḥāsibī.

[173] Cf. RSV: "Let us lift up our hearts and hands to God in heaven." Salmon translates the Hebr. word *ʾel* ("God") as *al-ṭāʾiq* ("The Omnipotent One.")

Just as He made it obligatory for deeds to correspond with belief, so He made it obligatory that during the time of prayer whatever is visible when a person rises and bends and prostrates himself and speaks and cries and raises his hands must correspond with his belief. Everything that he does [outwardly] and believes [inwardly] points to God, as it is said, ***Let us lift up our hearts and hands.***[174] Then, with this, we confess our offenses by saying:

נַחְנוּ פָשַׁעְנוּ וּמָרִינוּ אַתָּה לֹא סָלָחְתָּ:
נחן אג'רמנא וכ'אלפנא אנת מא צפחת

3:42 We have committed crimes and rebelled, and You have not forgiven.[175]

We have committed crimes alludes to the confession of offenses, as it is said, [*He who conceals his transgressions will not prosper,*] *but he who confesses*—because confession [comes] before repentance—*and forsakes them will obtain mercy* (Prov 28:13). He mentions *crime* specifically because that is more severe than *sin.*[176] He knows now that when the sinner confesses his offense, it is as though [the offense] does not exist. He repents to God <129b> and deserves pardon. Likewise, it is said, *Let the wicked forsake his way* (Isa 55:7).

And You have not forgiven means that the penitent is also obliged to recognize that God certainly made to befall the people whatever He made to befall them because [they] deserved [it], as the friend (*walīy*) said, *Yet You have been just in all that has come upon us* (Neh 9:33).[177] And God said, *Because of the iniquity of his covetousness I was angry, I smote him* (Isa 57:17). Because of their crimes God exiled them from their homeland, as it is said, *Because they did not obey the voice of the LORD their God but transgressed His covenant, even all that Moses the servant of the LORD commanded; they neither listened nor obeyed* (2 Kgs 18:12).[178]

[174] This comment explains the process of *ikhlāṣ al-niyya* and *aṣlāḥ al-tawīya* (see Lam 3:40) in the context of prayer.

[175] Cf. RSV: "We have transgressed and rebelled, and You have not forgiven." Salmon and Yefet render Hebr. p/sh/ʿ as Arab. j/r/m ("to commit crime") while Saadia uses dh/n/b ("to commit offense") (Lam, 102).

[176] "Crime" (Hebr. *peshaʿ*; corresponding to Arab. *dhanb*, "offense") is more severe than "sin" (Hebr. *ḥaṭṭaʾt*): implying a taxonomy of sin.

[177] Salmon refers to Nehemiah as *walīy* ("friend") also in his comment to Lam 1:18, using the same prooftext.

[178] Here the refrain returns, perhaps concluding an internal unit in the commentary of Lam 3:38–42.

סַכֹּתָה בָאַף וַתִּרְדְּפֵנוּ הָרַגְתָּ לֹא חָמָלְתָּ׃
ט'ללת באלגצ'ב וכלבתנא קתלת ומא שפקת

3:43 You have shaded Yourself in anger and seized us, slaying without pity.[179]

This means: after the shadow of Your mercy had been upon us, it became the reverse: the shadow of wrath and anger. And after You had seized our enemies, You seized us, as it is said, *For the LORD will rise up as on Mount Perazim* (Isa 28:21).[180] [The verse from Lamentations] says that just as the *LORD of hosts* did to Baʿal Perazim by killing the Philistines, the enemies of Israel—as it is said: *The LORD has broken through my enemies before me, like a bursting flood* (2 Sam 5:20)—so now the Lord rises in retribution against Israel. And He did the same in the time of Joshua—as it is said, *Sun stand you still at Gibeon, and you Moon* <130a> *in the valley of Aijalon* (Josh 10:12), so that Israel could take vengeance on their enemies. Along with this great sign, God helped them by also waging war against their enemies, as it is said, *While they were going down the ascent of Beth-horon, the LORD threw down great stones from heaven upon them as far as Azekah, and they died* (Josh 10:11). In the same way, [God later] supported the enemies against Israel, and He waged war against [Israel], as it is said, *Therefore He turned to be their enemy* (Isa 63:10); and as it is said, *He will be wroth as in the valley of Gibeon; to do His deed—strange is His deed!* (Isa 28:21). Thus, it is said here, ***You have shaded Yourself with anger and pursued us.***

Slaying without pity means that God also reversed the part of His mercy that had been theirs, as it is said, *In His love and in His pity He redeemed them* (Isa 63:9). But now it is said, **slaying without pity**, and also, *The Lord has destroyed without mercy all the habitations of Jacob* (Lam 2:2). And all these calamities befell us because of the magnitude of crimes, as it is said, *Because they did not obey the voice of the LORD their God but transgressed His covenant, even all that Moses the servant of the LORD commanded; they neither listened nor obeyed* (2 Kgs 18:12).

[179] Cf. RSV: "You have wrapped Yourself with anger and pursued us, slaying without pity." Salmon renders Hebr. s/k/h ("to cover") as Arab. ẓ/l/l ("to shade") in both this verse and the following one. Al-Fāsī notes that the Hebr. verb s/k/h has ten categories of meaning, the first of which is *ẓalāl* (vol. II, 320). Saadia also uses this rendering in his translation of Lam 3:43–44, but Yefet opts instead for s/y/j II ("to fence in").

[180] So also in Salmon's excursus to Lam 2:4.

סַכּוֹתָה בֶעָנָן לָךְ מֵעֲבוֹר תְּפִלָּה:
ט'ללת באלגמאם לך מן ג'ואז אלצלאה

3:44 You have shaded Yourself with a cloud so that no prayer can pass through.[181]

This, too, is a reversal of their previous circumstances. <130b> It was said concerning the acceptance [of prayer], *He has spread a cloud for a covering* (Ps 105:39).[182] He used to govern them with His mercy but since they rebelled, it is said, ***You have shaded Yourself with a cloud.*** This means that when we pray to Him, a cloud appears in the atmosphere so that we know that our prayers are not accepted, as it is said, *Even though you make many prayers, I will not listen* (Isa 1:15).[183] And all these calamities overtook us because of the magnitude of crimes, as it is said, *Because they did not obey the voice of the LORD their God but transgressed His covenant, even all that Moses the servant of the LORD commanded; they neither listened nor obeyed* (2 Kgs 18:12).

סְחִי וּמָאוֹס תְּשִׂימֵנוּ בְּקֶרֶב הָעַמִּים:
קלע ואזהאד תג'עלנא פי וסט אלשעוב

3:45 You have made us torn and scattered in the midst of the peoples.[184]

I translated *seḥi* as "torn," as in *The LORD tears down* (*yissaḥ*) *the house of the proud* (Prov 15:25), and likewise, *He will snatch and tear you* (*ve-yissaḥakha*) *from your tent* (Ps 52:7/5).[185] By the word *seḥi* he alludes to our exile and to our being torn from His Temple and from the Holy Land, as it is said, [*And the LORD uprooted them from their land in anger and fury and great wrath,*] *and cast them into another land, as at this day* (Deut 29:27/28); and *But the vine was picked up in fury, cast down to the ground* (Ezek 19:12).

[181] Cf. RSV: "You have wrapped Yourself with a cloud so that no prayer can pass through." See note to Salmon's translation of Lam 3:43.

[182] Ps 105:39, which Salmon interprets straightforwardly in his comment there, describes the condition of the Israelites when God led them from Egypt and into the wilderness (Salmon, Pss 90–106).

[183] Salmon's interpretation replaces the mythological image, in which God is wrapped in a cloud, with a reading in which God controls the natural world and make signs for human beings through it.

[184] Cf. RSV: "You have made us offscouring and refuse among the peoples."

[185] Curiously, Salmon does not translate *ve-yissaḥakha* with the Arab. root q/l/ʿ in his Psalms commentary (see Pss 42–72). There as well, Salmon reads Ps 52:7/5 in reference to exile and the destruction of the Temple.

Scattered means that whenever we are scattered among the peoples, then no one among us desires [God], and all who know us renounce us and hate us unjustly, as it is said, *And with what violent hatred they hate me* (Ps 25:19).[186] And all these calamities befell us because of the magnitude of crimes, as it is said, *Because they did not obey the voice of the LORD their God but transgressed His covenant, even all that Moses the servant of the LORD commanded; they neither listened nor obeyed* (2 Kgs 18:12).

פָּצוּ עָלֵינוּ פִּיהֶם כָּל־אֹיְבֵינוּ:
פתחו עלינא אפמאמהם כל אעדאנא

3:46 All our enemies open their mouths against us.[187]

<131a> This also is an addition to the calamities; that is, as long as we are under their hand and they hate us, they are not ashamed to spread falsehood and deceit against us, as it is said, *For false witnesses have risen against me, and they breathe out violence* (Ps 27:12).[188] Some give false evidence against the nation, and some give evidence against an individual from [the nation], in order to work strategically against the nation, whether for the ruin of a soul, or the seizure of money, or the seizure of female relatives,[189] or the extortion of a child, just as [it is] in the pact.[190] And all this is because of the magnitude of crimes, as it is said, *Because they did not obey the voice of the LORD their God but transgressed His covenant, even all that Moses the servant of the LORD commanded; they neither listened nor obeyed* (2 Kgs 18:12).

פַּחַד וָפַחַת הָיָה לָנוּ הַשֵּׁאת וְהַשָּׁבֶר:
אלפזע ואלפכ'תה צאר לנא ואלתשויש ואלכסר

3:47 Panic and snare have come upon us, confusion and rupture.[191]

186 This prooftext supports Salmon's point because in his translation of Ps 25:19, Salmon renders *violent hatred* (*śin'at ḥamas*) as "unjust hatred" (*bighḍa al-ẓulm*) (Salmon, Pss 11–41).

187 Salmon, Saadia, and Yefet all render the verse literally, suggesting that an "open mouth" is a familiar Arab. idiom, meaning "to spread lies."

188 Salmon cites this verse in his excursus on the Ten Commandments (Lam 1:8). There it serves as evidence that the Israelites have been punished for their transgression of the commandment against bearing false witness. In his comment to Ps 27:12, Salmon renders the verse as a prayer: "See, O Lord, their lies about me, and witness that they are falsehood, untruth and malice" (Pss 11–41).

189 Arab. *ḥarim*; referring either to a sacred place or to female family members (i.e., Eng. "harem"). I have opted for the latter, since the term appears between money and children, which suggests a personal business or domestic framework rather than a communal religious one.

190 Arab. *'ahd*.

191 Cf. RSV: "Panic and pitfall have come upon us, devastation and destruction." Salmon translates Hebr. *she't* ("destruction") as Arab. *tashwīsh* ("tumult, confusion"), thus connecting this verse to his

Ha-she't ("confusion") derives from the same root as *ruin* (*sho'ah*) *and devastation* (Zeph 1:15). ***Panic and snare have come upon us*** alludes to the uninterrupted succession (*tawātur*) of calamities, as it is said, *He who flees from terror shall fall into the pit* (Jer 48:44). In other words, when the afflictions began, whenever people escaped <131b> from one affliction, they fell into a worse one, as it is also said, *As if a man fled from a lion, and a bear met him* (Amos 5:19).

Panic alludes to dread and alarm, as in the verse *Day and night you shall be in dread* (Deut 28:66). ***Snare*** alludes to falling into something like a pit, as it is said, *You have put me in the depths of the pit* (Ps 88:7/6). ***Confusion*** alludes to the confusion that overtook the nation and [their] helplessness because [their] strength was slight, as it is said, *In that day, says the LORD, courage shall fail both king and princes* (Jer 4:9). ***Rupture*** alludes to the rupture of the nation, as it is said, *Rupture upon rupture is called* (Jer 4:20); and *Woe is me because of my rupture!* (Jer 10:19); and *For the rupture of the daughter of my people is my heart ruptured* (Jer 8:21).[192] ***Panic and snare*** and ***confusion and rupture*** are paired because they are designated as equivalents in the lament, as it is said, *These two things have befallen you* (Is 51:19). And all this happened to us because of the magnitude of crimes, as it is said, *Because they did not obey the voice of the LORD their God but transgressed His covenant, even all that Moses the servant of the LORD commanded; they neither listened nor obeyed* (2 Kgs 18:12).

פַּלְגֵי־מַיִם תֵּרַד עֵינִי עַל־שֶׁבֶר בַּת־עַמִּי׃
אקסאם אלמא תחדר עיני עלי כסר ג'מאעה שעבי

3:48 My eyes flow with channels of water because of the rupture of the congregation of my people.[193]

description of Jerusalem as a confused city (see Salmon's comment to Lam 3:1, following the description of Isa 22:2), and his description of the distressed soul as confused (see Salmon's comment to Lam 3:20, following the description of Ps 42:7/6). Note also that Salmon has represented the alliteration of Hebr. *paḥad va-faḥat* with Arab. *al-faza' wa-l-fakhta*. On *fakhta* as a snare or trap, see Blau, *Dictionary*, 492.

[192] I have translated these verses to match Salmon's reading of the key word *shaver* (which he translates to Arab. as *kasr*, "breaking, fracturing, fragmentation, rupture"). Cf. the RSV translations, respectively: "Disaster follows hard on disaster" (Jer 4:9); "Woe is me because of my hurt!" (Jer 10:19); and "For the wound of the daughter of my people is my heart wounded" (Jer 8:21). For Salmon's interpretation of the latter verse, see his excursus on Jer 8 at Lam 4:1.

[193] Cf. RSV: "My eyes flow with rivers of tears because of the destruction of the daughter of my people." Salmon, Saadia, and Yefet all translate Hebr. *palgei-mayim* ("channels of water") as Arab.

<132a> By this he means the abundant crying and mourning over what has befallen us during this long, lingering, difficult, afflicted exile.[194] The first thing a person is obliged to do is cry over his sins because they are the cause of our tarrying in this exile, as it is said, *My eyes shed streams of tears* (Ps 119:136). Next [he is obliged to cry over] the weakness and rupture, decline, humiliation, and disgrace that we experience in [exile], as it is said, *My eyes flow with rivers of tears over the rupture of the daughter of my people* (Lam 3:48); and Jeremiah also says in another place, *For the rupture of the daughter of my heart is my heart ruptured* (Jer 8:21).[195] And all this befell us because of the magnitude of our crimes, as it is said, *Because they did not obey the voice of the LORD their God but transgressed His covenant, even all that Moses the servant of the LORD commanded; they neither listened nor obeyed* (2 Kgs 18:12).

עֵינִי נִגְּרָה וְלֹא תִדְמֶה מֵאֵין הֲפֻגוֹת׃
עיני אנצבת ולא תסכת מן גיר סכות

3:49 My eyes are poured out; they are not quiet, [they are] without silence.[196]

I translated *niggerah* as "poured out," which derives from, *We are like water spilt (ha-niggarim) on the ground* (2 Sam 14:14) and *Like waters poured down (mugarim) a steep place* (Mic 1:4).[197] I translated *tidmeh* as "to be quiet" as in, *Let the pupil of your eye not be quiet* (Lam 2:18), which is a metaphor (*istiʿāra*).[198] This verse also means <132b> abundant weeping and

aqsām al-māʾ ("divisions of water"). Al-Fāsī supports this reading by glossing the root p/l/g as "division" (vol. II, 463).

194 This verse serves as a refrain in the liturgical poem (*piyyuṭ*) "I Shall Go Forth Weeping," beautifully translated by Laura Suzanne Lieber in *Jewish Aramaic Poetry from Late Antiquity: Translations and Commentaries*, EJM 75; Cambridge Genizah Studies 8 (Leiden: Brill, 2018), 73–74. The various reasons for weeping that are listed in that poem relate to the siege and fall of Jerusalem and culminate with the exile; cf. Salmon's focus on the exile as the exclusive reason for weeping.

195 For discussion of this verse, see Salmon's comments to Lam 3:47 and 4:1 and notes there.

196 Cf. RSV: "My eyes will flow without ceasing, without respite."

197 Al-Fāsī includes both prooftexts—although he does not include Lam 3:49—in his long entry on g/r (vol. I, 342–45). He does not explain g/r Niphal in terms of exhaustion, as Salmon does, but rather as the downward flow of water along watercourses. His explanation moves beyond lexicography into the realm of hydrology as he discusses the gushing of water when a breach is made in a wadi.

198 See Salmon's comment to Lam 2:18.

lamentation over [the situation that] we are in. Just as the Koraḥites said, *My tears have been my food day and night* (Ps 42:4/3), so is it said through Joel, *Awake, you drunkards* (Joel 1:5).

When one is commanded to weep, how could he allow himself to rejoice or to cheer himself with pleasures and amusement? The *LORD of hosts* particularly forbade us from pleasures and joy, as it is said, *Rejoice not, O Israel! Exult not like the peoples* (Hos 9:1). Since this was said in the time of statehood, how [could it be otherwise] in the time of exile? [Rather,] it is all the more so [commanded] that we are not to rejoice! Among the things that give clear evidence of what we have said is the verse *Who drink wine in bowls* (Amos 6:6). That is how he rebuked our fathers for joy and pleasures and amusements, and drinking wine from shallow drinking vessels without mourning over the rupture of Israel, as it is said, *but are not grieved over the ruin of Joseph* (Amos 6:6). [The "ruin of Joseph"] means what the kings of Assyria did to them, and what the prophet informed them of: that He wanted to exile them. So mourning and distress became obligatory for them; they were not to rejoice. Since they did not obey this [command], *exile* was decreed for them, as it is said afterward, *Therefore they shall now be the first of those to go into exile, and the revelry of those who stretch themselves shall pass away* (Amos 6:7).

If this [failure to mourn] was the reason that part of <133a> the nation was exiled—for mourning and severe distress were obligatory for them even while the Temple was thriving and the state existed and *the glory of the Lord was among them, and* [*there were*] *high priests, kings, chiefs, heads, princes, heads of fathers, judges, administrative officials, seers, teachers, Levitical singers, melody-carriers, superintendents, sacrifices, servants of the service of the house of the Lord, and gatekeepers*—then how [would it be] once all of Israel had been exiled, and everything that we have mentioned had vanished from them? It is all the more obligatory for us [now] to mourn and not to rejoice![199]

[199] Similar passages appear in Salmon's comment to Lam 4:15 and in the introduction, where he states that one of the main purposes of his Lamentations commentary is to show that mourning was obligatory in the time of Israel's grandeur, and that it is all the more so obligatory in the time of exile. Note here the historical specificity: the remarks of Amos pertain to the time of the Assyrian capture of Israel, which then serves as a warning and a lesson to others. For discussion of this hermeneutic of reflection on history, see chapter 6.

Woe and wailing for those whose nights and days are nothing but amusement, drinking, toasting, delights, crowds, and singing with mandolins and tambourines and the other things for entertainment, intoxication,[200] buffoonery, breaking contracts,[201] perpetrating rebellions with impertinence, and impudence of face, because this is severe according to God. Our tarrying in this exile is lengthened because of this, as it is said, *Salvation is far from the wicked* (Ps 119:155).

One of the eloquent statements of Jeremiah is *O daughter of my people, gird on sackcloth* [*and roll in ashes; make mourning as for an only son, most bitter lamentation*] (Jer 6:26). He made it known that it was obligatory for Israel to put on sackcloth and wallow in the dust and mourn completely, just as a man mourns over his only son, of whom he has no other.[202] <133b> This was before the affliction happened, as it is said, *For suddenly the destroyer will come upon us* (Jer 6:26). After the onset of the affliction and the magnitude of the calamities, it was also said, *For this I will lament and wail* (Mic 1:8) and *For this gird you with sackcloth, lament and wail* (Jer 4:8). This is the height of eloquence (*faṣāḥa*). As long as the wrath of the Lord and His anger are not turned back from us, we are obliged to [comport ourselves] in the manner described: we should not rejoice, and our mouths should not be full of delights, so that the Lord of the worlds will turn back, reunify Israel, rebuild Zion, and His anger will vanish. Thus it is said, *A Song of Ascents. When the LORD restored the fortunes of Zion* [. . .] *Then our mouth was filled with laughter* (Ps 126:1–2). The verse *Then our mouth was filled with laughter* (Ps 126:2) means "At that time when our mouths are filled with joy," since we are obliged to be filled with crying while in exile, as it is said, ***My eyes are poured out; they are not quiet***—that is to say, [my eyes] will not rest [from crying].

The meaning of ***without silence*** is to say "Do not doubt that the magnitude of [our] affliction is [the cause of my crying]." And all this befell us due to the magnitude of crimes, as it is said, *Because they did not obey the voice of the LORD their God but transgressed His covenant, even all that Moses the servant of the LORD commanded; they neither listened nor obeyed* (2 Kgs 18:12).

200 Arab. *zarjana*, "deception" or "intoxication" (Lane, 1224–25).

201 Arab. *takhāli*ʿ, "to annul, dissolve, or break confederacy, league, compact, or covenant" (Lane, 790).

202 For an analogue, see the rabbinic parables in the second proem of *Lam R*, which compare God to a king who mourns when the last of his sons has died.

עַד־יַשְׁקִיף וְיֵרֶא יְהוָה מִשָּׁמָיִם׃
אלי אן ישרף וינט'ר יוי מן אלסמא

3:50 Until the LORD from heaven looks down and sees.

This [verse] <134a> makes known that if Israel corrected (*aṣlaḥū*) their deeds, purified their intentions (*ikhlāṣ al-niyya*),[203] mourned over [the conditions] that they were in, and wept for themselves, they would deserve that the *LORD of hosts* would look down upon them in His mercy, just as He had mercy on our fathers in Egypt when they cried out to Him, as it is said, *In the course of those many days the king of Egypt died. And the people of Israel groaned under their bondage, and cried out for help, and their cry under bondage came up to God. And God heard their groaning, and God remembered His covenant with Abraham, with Isaac, and with Jacob. And God saw the people of Israel, and God knew their condition* (Exod 2:23–25). Likewise, it is also said here *My eyes flow with channels of tears* (Lam 3:48) and *My eyes are poured out* (Lam 3:49) ***until the LORD from heaven looks down and sees.***

עֵינִי עוֹלְלָה לְנַפְשִׁי מִכֹּל בְּנוֹת עִירִי׃
עיני פאעלה לנפסי אכת'ר מן כל בנאת קריתי

3:51 My eye is the agent for my soul, more than all the daughters of my city.[204]

This means that "My eye pours out tears and crying, more than all who cry and lament." And this is because of the magnitude of sin, as it is said, *Because they did not obey the voice of the LORD their God but transgressed His covenant, even all that Moses the servant of the LORD commanded; they neither listened nor obeyed* (2 Kgs 18:12).

צוֹד צָדוּנִי כַּצִּפּוֹר אֹיְבַי חִנָּם׃
ציד צאדוני כאלטיר אעדאיי מג'אן

3:52 I have been hunted like a bird by those who were my enemies without cause.

[203] See also Salmon's comments to Lam 2:18 and 3:40.

[204] Cf. RSV: "My eyes cause me grief at the fate of all the maidens of my city." Arab. translators vary in their translation of Hebr. *ʿolela* here: Salmon gives *fāʿila*; Yefet *faʿalat*; Saadia *tabaqqat* ("remain"). The verse is not treated in al-Fāsī's dictionary.

With this verse he alludes to the verse *Behold, I am sending for many fishers, says the LORD, and they shall catch them* (Jer 16:16), because it likens us, in the hand of the enemy, to the fish <134b> of the sea, as it is said, *For You make men like the fish of the sea, like crawling things that have no ruler* (Hab 1:14). During this exile, we are in the hand of our enemies like the bird in the snare. Therefore, he likens us in the same way [i.e., to birds] upon our deliverance by saying, *We have escaped as a bird from the snare of the fowlers* (Ps 124:7).

My enemies without cause means without any offense of mine against them, as it is said, *For no fault of mine, they run and make ready* (Ps 59:5/4), as it is said, *Because they did not obey the voice of the LORD their God but transgressed His covenant, even all that Moses the servant of the LORD commanded; they neither listened nor obeyed* (2 Kgs 18:12).

צָמְתוּ בַבּוֹר חַיָּי וַיַּדּוּ־אֶבֶן בִּי׃
אקמעו פי אלביר חיאתי <u>וזיג'ו</u> ואלקו חגר עליי

3:53 They smothered my life in the pit <u>and turned</u> [from me] and cast stones upon me.[205]

Ṣamtu is derived from *leṣmitut* (Lev 25:23; 30),[206] which means uprooting[207] and cutting off. *Va-yadu* [means] "they cast" as in *and have cast lots (yadu) for my people* (Joel 4:3/3:3). Its meaning in [the context of] this confinement is *You have put me in the depths of the pit* (Ps 88:7/6). ***And cast stones upon me*** (Lam 3:53) alludes to the constant *troubles* that overtook the people of the exile. All this overtook us because of the magnitude of our crimes, as it is said, *Because they did not obey the voice of the LORD their God but transgressed His covenant, even all that Moses the servant of the LORD commanded; they neither listened nor obeyed* (2 Kgs 18:12).

[205] Cf. RSV: "They flung me alive into the pit and cast stones upon me."

[206] Cf. al-Fāsī, who translates ṣ/m/t differently in Lam 3:53 and Lev 25. Like Salmon, he uses the root q/m/ʿ in Lam 3:53 ("to suppress," form I; cf. form IV in Salmon's translation) and glosses the phrase *ṣamtu ba-bor* as "the imprisonment of exile." In Lev 25, he interprets the word as *battāt* (vol. II, 516), which Blau glosses as "irrevocable" (*Dictionary*, 30).

[207] Reading *isti'ṣāl* for *istiṣāl*, as Judeo-Arabic often drops the hamza. Note, however, that the word *tasta'ṣil* appears, with hamza intact, in Salmon's translation to Lam 3:66.

צָפוּ־מַיִם עַל־רֹאשִׁי אָמַרְתִּי נִגְזָרְתִּי׃
טפת אלמיא עלי ראשי קלת אנקטעת

3:54 Water flowed over my head; I said, "I am cut off."[208]

<135a> *Ṣafu* is [from the same root] as *heṣif* (Deut 11:4)—it overflowed—and *va-yaṣef ha-barzel* (2 Kgs 6:6), "He made the iron float," [which] means, "I had become like a drowned man who had despaired of life," as it is said, *Therefore I remember You from the land of Jordan* (Ps 42:7/6).[209] He means "from the pit of water," as it is also said, *I sink deep in mire, where there is no foothold; I have come into deep waters* (Ps 69:3/2), and *in the regions dark and deep* (Ps 88:7/6). ***I said, "I am cut off"*** means that He does not afflict many from this nation with despair.[210] It is said about [this experience], *I said in my alarm, "I am driven far [from Your sight]"* (Ps 31:23/22). Therefore, it is similar to *But I said, "I have labored in vain"* (Isa 49:4), and likewise, Asaph describes that many of the nation say *All in vain have I kept my heart clean* (Ps 73:13). The words here are similar: [by] ***I am cut off*** he means the pit of despair. That is because of the magnitude of crimes, as it is said, *Because they did not obey the voice of the LORD their God but transgressed His covenant, even all that Moses the servant of the LORD commanded; they neither listened nor obeyed* (2 Kgs 18:12).

קָרָאתִי שִׁמְךָ יְהוָה מִבּוֹר תַּחְתִּיּוֹת׃
דעית אסמך יא רב מן אלביר אלספלי

3:55 I called on Your name, O Lord, from the depths of the pit.

He means that they call upon You, O *LORD*, from this *exile*, which resembles *the depths of the pit*, as it is said, *You have put me in the depths of the pit* (Ps 88:7/6).[211] <135b> One of those who does not understand has supposed that the verse *They smothered my life in the pit* (Lam 3:53) and the rest of what is

[208] Cf. RSV: "Water closed over my head; I said, 'I am lost.'" Salmon, Saadia, and Yefet all translate Hebr. *ṣafu* with the Arab. root ṭ/f/f (although in different forms), and Hebr. *nigzarti* as Arab. *inqaṭaʿtu*, "I am cut off."

[209] Salmon provides the interpretive meaning of the imagery. Cf. al-Fāsī, who lists all three biblical verses, as well as the literal meaning (*ḥaqīqa*; see chapter 4) of 2 Kgs 6:6: "The literal meaning of the verse *He made the iron float* is that the branch made the iron float, that is to say, it made it rise upon the water" (vol. II, 522). On the root ṭ/f/f as "to overflow; to float," see Blau, *Dictionary*, 402.

[210] Perhaps drawing attention to the individual voice of despair rather than the communal one.

[211] Salmon's comment to Ps 88:7/6 also presents an actualizing interpretation (Salmon, Pss 73–89).

mentioned were Jeremiah's words to himself when he was thrown into the pit,[212] but this errs in [several] respects. The first of them is the statement *and cast stones upon me* (Lam 3:53), for neither stones nor anything else was thrown at him. The second is that he said, *water flowed over my head* (Lam 3:54), but the pit into which Jeremiah was thrown had no water in it, as he said, *and there was no water in the cistern, but only mire* (Jer 38:6). Indeed, it is correct in all respects that this [passage] is not said about Jeremiah, but it must be that all of these verses were said about Israel, as instruction (*taʿlīm*) for them, as we have explained above.[213]

I called on Your name, O LORD. "I called on Your name, O LORD, from the depths of the pit." He means that when he compared this *exile* to the *depths of the pit*, he said, *I called on Your name, O LORD*. In other words, "Nothing was left for me other than calling upon You for salvation," as it is said, *Out of the depths I cry to You, O LORD!* (Ps 130:1). The Mighty and Sublime had promised that whenever we cried out to Him and returned to Him, He would accept us and transfer us out of this *exile*, as Nehemiah ben Hacaliah said in his prayer, *Remember the word which You did command* <136a> *Your servant Moses, saying, "If you are unfaithful, I will scatter you among the peoples; but if you return to Me and keep My commandments and do them, though your dispersed be under the farthest skies, I will gather them thence and bring them to the place which I have chosen, to make My name dwell there"* (Neh 1:8–9). It is said *Then they cried to the LORD in their trouble, and He delivered them from their distress; He brought them out of darkness and gloom, and broke their bonds asunder* (Ps 107:13–14).

קוֹלִי שָׁמָעְתָּ אַל־תַּעְלֵם אָזְנְךָ לְרַוְחָתִי לְשַׁוְעָתִי׃
צותי סמעת לא תכ'פי אד'נך לפרג'תי לתצ'רעי

3:56 You heard my voice: "Do not cover Your ear to my relief, to my supplication!"[214]

Know that the articulation (*makhraj*) of all of these words (*alfāẓ*) is an articulation (*makhraj*) of the *past* (*ʿavar*)—*I called* (Lam 3:55); *You heard* (Lam 3:56); *You came near* [. . .] *You said* (Lam 3:57); *You have taken up* [. . .] *You have redeemed* (Lam 3:58); *You have seen* (Lam 3:59–60)—but their meaning

212 Jer 38:1–13.

213 See Salmon's opening comments at Lam 3:1, where he frames the entire discourse as "instruction for Israel" (*taʿlīm le-yiśraʾel*). Likewise, in the case of Lam 3:55, the words of the prophet Jeremiah do not refer to his own experience; they are prophetically revealed utterances intended to provide religious instruction for the people of the exile.

214 Cf. RSV: "You did hear my plea, 'Do not close Your ear to my cry for help.'"

(*maʿnā*) is the *future* (*ʿatid*).[215] In the Hebrew language, there are many [instances] like these, as it is said, *O God, the nations have come into Your inheritance; they have defiled Your holy Temple; they have laid Jerusalem in ruins. They have given* (Ps 79:1–2).[216] All of this language (*lafẓ*) [is expressed] in the *past* (*ʿavar*), but at the time when it was said, nothing of the sort had happened.[217] The meaning (*maʿnā*) of all of them is *future* (*ʿatid*). Therefore, with his words *You did hear my plea* he means, "Hear my voice, O LORD! Do not hide Your hearing from my prayer and my relief and my supplication."

קָרַבְתָּ בְּיוֹם אֶקְרָאֶךָּ אָמַרְתָּ אַל־תִּירָא:
קרבת אי תתקרב פי יום אדעוך קלת אי תקול לא תכ'שא

3:57 You came near—that is to say, "You will come near"—when I will call on You. You said—that is to say, "You will say"—'Do not fear!'[218]

<136b> Just as You promised when You said, *Fear not, for I am with you* (Gen 26:24) and *Fear not, you worm Jacob* (Isa 14:14) and *Fear not, O Jacob my servant* (Isa 44:2).

רַבְתָּ אֲדֹנָי רִיבֵי נַפְשִׁי גָּאַלְתָּ חַיָּי:
כ'אצמת יא יוי מכ'אצמי נפסי פככת אי תפך חיאתי

3:58 You have taken up my cause, O Lord, You have redeemed—that is to say, "You will redeem"—my life.

[215] Salmon uses Hebr. terms in both cases: *ʿavar* ("past") and *ʿatīd* ("future"). Karaites of the tenth century employed a mix of Hebr. and Arab. grammatical terminology. The principle that verbs formed in the past may imply the future is known also from al-Qirqisānī's principles of biblical exegesis (Qirqisāni Studies, 36; premise nineteen); from al-Fāsī, who notes that a translator must "be conversant with [. . .] the perfect, the imperfect, and what is apparently a perfect, but used as an imperfect, and an apparent imperfect which stands for a perfect" (see Polliack, "Karaite Views," 77); and from Ibn Nūḥ, who distinguishes between past form on the level of language (*lafẓ*) and future sense at the level of meaning (*maʿnā*) in the same terms that Salmon employs here (see Khan, *The Early Karaite Tradition*, 91–93; 135). Salmon aggressively applies these syntactical principles to his translation of Lam 3:57–60 by rendering the verbs in both past and future tenses, side by side (see discussion in chapter 2, section on "Linguistic Principles"). Modern biblical scholars have debated the verbal tense of these verses as well, with several arguing that they should be understood as precatives or imperatives. See Iain W. Provan, "Past, Present and Future in Lamentations 3:52–66: The Case for a Precative Perfect Re-Examined," *VT* 41 (1991): 164–75. Alan Cooper suggests reading them as emphatic assertions; see "The Message of Lamentations," *JANES* 28 (2001): 18. On *makhraj* as an articulation, utterance, pronunciation, or sound, see Blau, *Dictionary*, 174. With this choice of words Salmon demotes tense to the status of pronunciation, a superficial aspect of language in contrast to the meaning (*maʿnā*) or intention (*murād*) of language.

[216] See Salmon's excursus at Lam 2:4 for full treatment.

[217] On this principle of prophetic speech (also in connection with Ps 79:1–3), see comments to Lam 2:4 and 3:1.

[218] Cf. RSV: "You did come near when I called on You; You did say, 'Do not fear.'"

[This is] just as David also asked, *Contend, O LORD, with those who contend with me* (Ps 35:1), and the Mighty and Sublime promised this when He said, *For I will contend with those who contend with you* (Isa 49:25).

רָאִיתָה יְהוָה עַוָּתָתִי שָׁפְטָה מִשְׁפָּטִי׃
נט'רת אי אנט'ר יא יוי עוג'י אחכם חכמי

3:59 You have seen—that is to say, "See"—O Lord, that he has perverted me; judge my cause.[219]

Just as he said above, *He has made my paths crooked* (Lam 3:9); [here] he says, "Look: he has perverted my causes and my circumstances. Hear my rights and decide my case!" just as the Koraḥites say, *Vindicate me, O God, and defend my cause* (Ps 43:1).

רָאִיתָה כָּל־נִקְמָתָם כָּל־מַחְשְׁבֹתָם לִי׃
נט'רת אי אנט'ר כל נקמתהם אלד'י פעלו בי אנט'ר כל אפכארהם לי

3:60 You have seen—that is to say, "See"—all their vengeance, that they did to me; "See" all their plots against me.

<137a> He means, "Requite them according to the vengeance that they inflicted on me, and what they did in Your Temple. For they will not be satisfied with what they have done to me unless they plot and discuss our destruction," as it is said, *They said to themselves, "We will utterly subdue them"* (Ps 78:4), and it is said, *They conceive words of deceit* (Ps 35:20).

שָׁמַעְתָּ חֶרְפָּתָם יְהוָה כָּל־מַחְשְׁבֹתָם עָלָי׃
סמעת מעירתהם יא יוי כל אפכארהם עליי

3:61 You have heard their taunts, O Lord, all their plots against me.

That is to say: "They have united against me continually with vengeance, as it is said, *You have seen all their vengeance* (Lam 3:60) and *Let the avenging of the outpoured blood of Your servants* [*be known among the nations before our*

219 Cf. RSV: "You have seen the wrong done to me, O LORD; judge You my case."

eyes!] (Ps 79:10). ***All their plots against me*** means what they planned for my destruction, their taunts of falsehood and futility, and their plots against me. Also, how they plan to drive me away from the authority of my religion, as it is said, *Nay, for Your sake we are slain all the day long, and accounted as sheep for the slaughter* (Ps 44:23/22).

שִׂפְתֵי קָמַי וְהֶגְיוֹנָם עָלַי כָּל־הַיּוֹם׃
שפתי מקאומי והדירהם עליי טול אלזמאן

3:62 The lips and grumblings[220] of those who oppose me are against me throughout time.[221]

<137b> By this he means false testimony against Israel and futilely taking sides against them. So he says, "O *LORD*, requite them for this." ***And their grumblings are against me throughout time*** means that they never called [upon God] and they never feared God when [speaking falsely against] me.

שִׁבְתָּם וְקִימָתָם הַבִּיטָה אֲנִי מַנְגִּינָתָם׃
ג'לוסהם וקיאמהם אלתפת אנא נגמאתהם

3:63 Behold their sitting and their rising; I am their songs.

He means, "When they rise and when they sit, I am not absent from their thoughts." Just as it is said about Sennacherib, *I know your sitting down and your going out and your coming in, and your raging against Me* (Isa 37:28), so is it said here, "O Lord, look and consider these circumstances." ***I am their songs*** mean that these enemies were not satisfied with all of their aforementioned deeds, so they made me into a ditty for themselves, as it is said, *I have become the laughingstock of all my people, their tunes throughout time* (Lam 3:14). The circumstances [resulting from] the action of the nations are summarized at the end of this chapter: *All our enemies open their mouths against us* (Lam 3:46); *I have been hunted like a bird* (Lam 3:52); *Water flowed over my head* (Lam 3:54); *All their vengeance* (Lam 3:60); *You have heard* <138a> *their taunts* (Lam 3:61); *The lips of those who oppose me* (Lam 3:62); and ***Behold their sitting and their rising.***

220 Arab. *hadīr* (see Hava, 812).
221 Cf. RSV: "The lips and thoughts of my assailants are against me all the day long."

תָּשִׁיב לָהֶם גְּמוּל יְהוָה כְּמַעֲשֵׂה יְדֵיהֶם׃
תרד להם מכאפאה יא יוי כפעל ידיהם

3:64 You will return to them a recompense, O Lord, according to the work of their hands.

This means, "You will recompense them with the likes of what they have done, including shedding the blood of Israel, just as You promised through Your prophets, O Lord, when You said, *If you are paying Me back, I will requite your deed upon your own head* (Joel 4:4/3:4), and as Isaiah says also, *The voice of the LORD, rendering recompense to His enemies!*" (Isa 66:6). As for requiting them for killing, it is said, *Every man's sword will be against his brother* (Ezek 38:21). It is said about Edom, *So that every man from Mount Esau will be cut off by slaughter* (Obad 1:9), and *For my sword has drunk its fill in the heavens; behold, it descends for judgment upon Edom* (Isa 34:5). It is said about the rest of the nations, *For the LORD is enraged against all the nations* (Isa 34:2). As for what they did: *And have given a boy for a harlot, and have sold a girl for wine, and have drunk it* (Joel 4:3/3:3), and their requital for this [deed] is, *If you are paying Me back, I will requite your deed upon your own head* (Joel 4:4/3:4). As for the verse, *You have sold the people of Judah and Jerusalem to the Greeks* (Joel 4:6/3:6), their requital for this <138b> deed is, *I will sell your sons and your daughters into the hand of the sons of Judah* (Joel 4:8/3:8). *May the Lord do thus, so that His name may be magnified.*[222]

תִּתֵּן לָהֶם מְגִנַּת־לֵב תַּאֲלָתְךָ לָהֶם׃
תעטי להם כסר אלקלב לענתך <u>תעטי</u> להם

3:65 You will give them a broken heart; <u>You will give</u> them Your curse.[223]

They translated *meginnat-lev* ("a broken heart") from *Who has delivered (miggen) your enemies into your hand!* (Gen 14:20).[224] I have translated

[222] Note the elements of requital in this passage. The final line (in Hebr.) may have liturgical significance: *ken ya'aśeh adonai lema'an shemo ha-gadol*, "May the LORD do thus, so that His name may be magnified."

[223] Cf. RSV: "You will give them dullness of heart; Your curse will be upon them." Salmon applies the principle of *menaheg 'aṣmo ve-menaheg aḥerim* without stating it explicitly by repeating the first verb in the second clause.

[224] Salmon's translation of *meginnat lev* follows the Targum (Abdul-Karim, 79; see Alexander, *Targum*, 162 n. 92). The translation of Lam 3:65 on the basis of Gen 14:20 does not come from al-Fāsī or Saadia. Al- Fāsī specifically glosses the Hebr. word *miggen* as "the one who made strong and

*ta'alatkha lahem—****You will give them your curse****—*from [the letters] *'aleph*, *lamed*, and *heh*. With this [verse] he alludes to the verse *And the LORD your God will put all these curses (ha'alot) upon your foes* (Deut 30:7).

תִּרְדֹּף בְּאַף וְתַשְׁמִידֵם מִתַּחַת שְׁמֵי יְהוָה:
תכלב בגצ'ב ותסתאצלהם מן תחת סמאואת יוי

3:66 You will pursue them in anger and uproot them from under the LORD's heavens.[225]

That is to say, "You will pursue them in Your anger, so they will have no stability and no standing in the world, as it is said, *from under the LORD's heavens*. The wicked are described the same way when it is said, *but are like chaff which the wind drives away* (Ps 1:4); *and became like the chaff of the summer threshing floors; and the wind carried them away* (Dan 2:35); and *You shall winnow them and the wind shall carry them away, and the tempest shall scatter them* (Is 41:16). ***From under the LORD's heavens*** means "from beneath Your heavens, O LORD," as when it is said, *in order for the LORD* and *in order for You, LORD*.

delivered up" (*aladhī makkana wa-aslama*) in the context of Gen 14:20, and he distinguishes this meaning from that of Lam 3:65, which he connects with Hebr. *yagon* ("sorrow") as in Isa 35:10 (vol. II, 187). Along the same lines, Saadia translates *miggen* as Arab. *ḥasra* ("grief"). By contrast, Salmon's translation of *miggen* as Arab. *kasr* ("breaking") accords literally with the Aram. translation of the Tg.: *tevirut-libba'*.

[225] Cf. RSV: "You will pursue them in anger and destroy them from under Your heavens, O LORD."

Lamentations 4

Lamentations 4:1

אֵיכָה יוּעַם זָהָב יִשְׁנֶא הַכֶּתֶם הַטּוֹב תִּשְׁתַּפֵּכְנָה אַבְנֵי־קֹדֶשׁ בְּרֹאשׁ כָּל־חוּצוֹת:
כיף יצדא אלד'הב ויתגייר אלג'והר אלג'יד תנספכן חג'ארה אלקדס פי
ג'מלה אלאזקה

How the gold has become rusty, how the fine jewel is changed! The holy stones lie scattered at the head of every street.[1]

<139a> The lamenter opens this fourth chapter with a speech that pains the heart. With this verse he expresses amazement over the afflictions that befell this nation and her Temple due to the anger of the Lord of the worlds, because they used to presume that God would not destroy this Temple. It is said that they used to say, "*This is the Temple of the LORD, the Temple of the LORD, the Temple of the LORD*" (Jer 7:4). He did not leave them to their presumption, but rather He informed them that if they persisted in their rebellions, He would destroy the Temple just as He had destroyed Shiloh, and that this presumption of theirs was a false presumption,[2] as it is said, *Do not trust in these deceptive words* (Jer 7:4) and *Therefore will I do to the house which is called by My name, and in which you trust,* [*and to the place which I gave to you and to your fathers, as I did to Shiloh*] (Jer 7:14).

Indeed, the Mighty and Sublime made Shiloh an object of reflection (*iʿtibār*) for Israel. In other words: whenever they disobeyed, He would destroy the Temple, just as <139b> He had destroyed Shiloh, as He said: *Go now to My place that was in Shiloh, where I made My name dwell at first, and see what I did to it for the wickedness of My people Israel* (Jer 7:12).

[1] Cf. RSV: "How the gold has grown dim, how the pure gold is changed! The holy stones lie scattered at the head of every street." Salmon explains his translation after the excursus, at the end of the comment.

[2] Arab. *ẓann kādhib*.

Jewish Piety in Islamic Jerusalem. Jessica Andruss, Oxford University Press. © Oxford University Press 2023.
DOI: 10.1093/oso/9780197639559.003.0013

Likewise, He made King Saul an object of reflection (*iʿtibār*) for the kings of the house of David. Since they chose rebellions and sins, they deserved the destruction of this Temple, as it is said in the *covenant*: *And I will lay your cities waste, and will make your sanctuaries desolate* (Lev 26:31).

[Jeremiah] described some of the gravest (*kabāʾir*) of their rebellions in the time of Jehoiakim and Zedekiah. One of the vile deeds is Jehoiakim's burning of the book of the Lord of the worlds, as it is said, *It was the ninth month, and the king was sitting in the winter house and there was a fire burning in the brazier before him. As Jehudi read three or four columns, the king would cut them off with a penknife and throw them into the fire in the brazier, until the entire scroll was consumed in the fire that was in the brazier* (Jer 36:22–23).

Another [vile deed] is the killing of Uriah the son of Shemaiah when he conveyed the words of God to them, as it is said, *There was another man who prophesied in the name of the LORD, Uriah the son of Shemaiah from Kiriath Jearim. He prophesied against this city and against this land in words like those of Jeremiah. And when King Jehoiakim, with all his warriors and all the princes, heard* <140a> *his words, the king sought to put him to death; but when Uriah heard of it, he was afraid and fled and escaped to Egypt* (Jer 26:20–21). At that point, Jehoiakim sent a leader along with an army to Egypt in order to bring Uriah back to him, as it is said, *Then King Jehoiakim sent to Egypt certain men, Elnathan the son of Achbor and others with him, and they fetched Uriah from Egypt and brought him to King Jehoiakim, who slew him with the sword and cast his dead body into the burial place of the common people* (Jer 26:22–23).

Next they demanded that he kill Jeremiah, as they are described as saying, *Let this man be put to death* (Jer 38:4), and also, *Then the priests and the prophets said to the princes and to all the people, "This man deserves the sentence of death, because he has prophesied against this city, as you have heard with your own ears"* (Jer 26:11). The gravest aspect of this account is that they intended to kill him only because he prophesied and communicated the word of God (*kalām allah*) to them. Another one of the grave offenses is that they prohibited him from prophesying and told him, "*Do not prophesy in the name of the LORD, or you will die by our hand*" (Jer 11:21).

Another [vile deed] is that they beat him, as it is said, *And the princes were enraged* <140b> *at Jeremiah, and they beat him* (Jer 37:15). Another [vile deed] is that they threw him into the cistern, as it is said, *So they took Jeremiah and cast him into the cistern of Malchiah, the king's son, which was in the court of the guard* (Jer 38:6). How many times, moreover, did they attack him? They imprisoned him, as it is said, *and imprisoned him* (Jer 37:15); and it is said, *when Jeremiah had come to the dungeon cells* (Jer 37:16). But they were not satisfied with imprisoning him, so they shackled him in exile.

All of them used to say, "*The time is not near! Build houses! This city is the caldron, and we are the flesh*" (Ezek 11:3).[3] In other words, "We don't see anything [like] what the prophet says about *exile* coming soon. Build houses, and make a livelihood, for Jerusalem is the pot and we are the meat!"—that is to say, we are safe within it. [Ezekiel] brought an answer to them from God most high: *This city shall not be your caldron* (Ezek 11:11)—that is to say, it will not be a pot for you, as in your parable (*mathal*). You will <u>not</u> be the meat inside it, because the first [term] governs itself and others.[4]

I will judge you at the border of Israel (Ezek 11:11) indicates *Riblah, in the land of Hamath* because Riblah is at the borders of the land of Israel, as it is said, *And the boundary shall go down from Shepham to Riblah on the east side of Ain* (Num 34:11).[5] When he described <141a> the magnitude of their offenses—to which they said, *This city is the caldron, and we are the flesh* (Ezek 11:3)—God commanded Ezekiel to coin a parable (*mathal*) of the [same] kind that they were saying, as it is said, *And utter a parable* (mashal) *to the rebellious house and say to them, Thus says the Lord GOD: Set on the pot, set it on, pour in water also* (Ezek 24:3).[6] "Preparing the pot" is the announcement (*taʿrīfa*) that Nebuchadnezzar, who is likened to the fire, had reached Jerusalem, and would gather into it the limbs of every member. *All the good pieces, the thigh and the shoulder* (Ezek 24:4) means that he intends for king, chief, noble, and priest to come together in Jerusalem at the time of the siege. The enemy's sword would work from the outside, while plague and hunger would work from the inside, and the people would be consumed by

[3] Cf. RSV: "'The time is not near to build houses.'" Modern interpreters read the verse to mean that new construction is unwarranted because the population of Jerusalem had decreased after the initial exiles. Salmon's interpretation—that the people urge new construction because they imagine that the prophets' predictions of destruction are still far off—aligns with that of later medieval exegetes such as Rashi and David Kimḥi. See Moshe Greenberg, *Ezekiel 1–20*, ABC 22 (New York: Doubleday, 1983), 187.

[4] I.e., *This city shall <u>not</u> be your caldron* and *you shall <u>not</u> be flesh in the midst of it*. On the exegetical principle *menaheg ʿaṣmo u-menaheg aḥerim*, see chapter 2, "Linguistic Principles to Justify a Translation Choice."

[5] It was at Riblah that Nebuchadnezzar executed the sons of King Zedekiah and the nobles of Judah, and blinded King Zedekiah before shackling him and carrying him off to Babylon. Salmon considers Ezek 11:11 as a prophecy foretelling these events at Riblah.

[6] In presenting Ezek 24:1–14 as God's response to the remnant in Jerusalem, Salmon skips over the more immediate response found in Ezek 11:5–12. There, God adapts the peoples' parable of the pot so that it communicates the destruction yet to come. The parable of the pot in Ezek 24 relates to the destruction of Jerusalem specifically and includes additional elements—notably the fire, the bones, and the foul odor—which Salmon interprets next. See chapter 4 for discussion.

fire. When the enemy conquered the town, the best of those who were there would be killed, as it is said, *Who slew their best men with the sword in the house of their sanctuary* (2 Chr 36:17).[7] He alludes to these conditions with the verse, *Take the choicest one of the flock, pile the logs under it* (Ezek 24:5). Then it is said, *Therefore thus says the Lord GOD: Woe to the bloody city* (Ezek 24:6). He knows that this city constantly spilled the blood of the guiltless, as it is said, *now murderers* (Isa 1:21) and *also on your skirts is found the lifeblood* <141b> *of the guiltless poor* (Jer 2:34).[8] That is why [God] calls it *the bloody city* (Ezek 24:6). *To the pot whose odor*[9] *is in it* (Ezek 24:6) means the one whose fetid odor is in it—in other words, the offenses that they did not give up, as it is said, *Their deeds do not permit them to return to their God* (Hos 5:4).

Take it out piece after piece (Ezek 24:6) means the departure of the king, princes, mighty ones, and *the chief priest and Zephaniah the second priest, and the three keepers of the threshold* (Jer 52:24), and the eunuch *who had been in command of the men of war* (Jer 52:25), *and seven men of the king's council* [. . .] *and the secretary of the commander of the army who mustered the people of the land; and sixty men of the people of the land* (Jer 52:25). Some were exiled in the seventh year, and in the eighth year, and in the twenty-third year. All of the exiles together are combined in the verse, *Take it out piece after piece*, as it was said earlier, *But you shall be brought forth out of the midst of it. You have feared the sword;* [. . .] *And I will bring you forth out of the midst of it, and give you into the hands of foreigners* (Ezek 11:7–9).

No lot will fall upon it (Ezek 24:6)[10] means that the enemy will not have to cast lots for everything that they plunder from it, as it is said regarding the plunder of Midian, *The men of war had taken* <142a> *booty, every man for himself* (Num 31:35). A better [interpretation] of *let no lot fall upon it* is that up to this point, the blow of destruction had not fallen upon her.[11]

[7] Salmon reads Hebr. *baḥurīm* (2 Chr 36:17) not as "young men" but as "choice men" or "best men," indicating the elites.

[8] Salmon also cites this verse in his excursus at Lam 1:8, as evidence for the violation of the commandment against killing.

[9] Salmon understands Hebr. *ḥel'ah* as a fetid odor, as does al-Fāsī (see vol. I, 550, where he glosses the term as *zuhūka* (or more likely, *zuhūma*, "offensive smell") and *sanākha*, "rankness"); cf. RSV, "to the pot whose rust is in it." For an overview of the term in the Jewish exegetical tradition, see Moshe Greenberg, *Ezekiel 21–37*, ABC 22A (New York: Doubleday, 1997), 499. Greenberg favors the translation "filth," following the view that it refers to "the encrusted residue of cooked matter stuck to the inside of a pot that fouls it disgustingly."

[10] Cf. RSV: "without making any choice."

[11] Salmon's preferred interpretation—that the "lot" (Hebr. *goral*) signifies that "the blow of destruction" has not fallen on Jerusalem—is echoed by Leslie C. Allen, who argues that "lot" has a secondary meaning of "retribution"; see "Ezekiel 24:3–14: A Rhetorical Perspective," *CBQ* 49 (1987), 409. Cf. Greenberg, who refutes "retribution" as a possible meaning for "lot" (*Ezekiel 21–37*, 500).

This time is the time of destruction, *for the blood she has shed is still in the midst of her* (Ezek 24:7). That is to say, the blood that she had shed was visible and revealed without shame, rather than being concealed, as it is said, *She did not pour it upon the ground to cover it with dust* (Ezek 24:7).

Requital befalls [them] in this parable, as it is said, *To rouse My wrath, to take vengeance, I have set on the bare rock the blood she has shed, that it may not be covered* (Ezek 24:8). Then it is said, *Therefore thus says the Lord GOD: Woe to the bloody city! I also will make the pile great* (Ezek 24:9). That is to say, "Because of what they have done, I have also increased the furnace for them," which means that [He has stoked] the heat of the fire. *Heap on the logs, kindle the fire* (Ezek 24:10) means that the retributions will multiply, as we have explained in the verse, *From on high He sent fire; into my bones He made it descend* (Lam 1:13).

Boil well the flesh (Ezek 24:10) means, "Annihilate the meat by increasing the kindling." This means the expulsion and annihilation of everyone who is within Jerusalem. *Mix the spices* (*ve-harqaḥ ha-merqaḥah*) (Ezek 24:10) means to perfect the calamity, just as <142b> [whatever is] cooking in the pot is perfected by means of seasoning and aroma. The derivation is related to *blended as by the perfumer* (*roqaḥ mirqaḥat*; Exod 30:25) and *He makes the sea like a pot of ointment* (*ka-merqaḥah*; Job 41:23/21).[12] *And let the bones be burned up* (Ezek 24:10) means the burning of the bones. *Let [them] be burned up* (*yeḥaru*) is from *The bellows blow fiercely* (*naḥar*) (Jer 6:29). As it is said, *From on high He sent fire into my bones* (Lam 1:13).

Then set it empty upon the coals (Ezek 24:11) means that they emptied Jerusalem of all the good things, as it is said in reference to Nebuchadnezzar, *He has made me an empty vessel* (Jer 51:34). *That it may become hot, and its copper burn, that its filthiness may be melted in it, its odor consumed* (Ezek 24:11) means that whoever committed evil and wickedness will not remain in it [i.e., Jerusalem], and it [i.e., Jerusalem] will remain empty.

In vain have I wearied myself; [its thick odor does not go out by fire] (Ezek 24:12). This pot has been worn out by the stubborn ones. Most of its offensive smell had not left it [previously], but now its offensive smell leaves by means of the fire. This means that many kings intended to destroy this city and cleanse it of its filth,[13] but they did not achieve that. Now, by means of this fire—which means "by this retribution"—it will become clean.[14]

[12] Al-Fāsī likewise connects the two verses. He glosses Ezek 24:10 as "cook the cooked food" (*'uṭbukh al-ṭabīkh*) and notes that *merqaḥah* is *'iṭr* ("perfume") in Arab. (vol. II, 627).

[13] Arab. *falādha*; see Blau, *Dictionary*, 514.

[14] Reading *tatanaẓẓaf* for *tatanaḍḍaf*.

Next he interpreted the meaning (*fassara al-maʿnā*) [of the parable][15] by saying, *Its odor is your filthy lewdness. Because I would have cleansed you and you were not cleansed from your filthiness, you shall not be cleansed any more till I have satisfied* <143a> *My fury upon you* (Ezek 24:13). With the appearance of the *wrath of the Lord*, the people would have no healing, as it is said, *till the wrath of the LORD rose against his people, till there was no remedy* (2 Chr 36:16).

It is because of these conditions that the prophets lament over us, as Jeremiah says, מַבְלִיגִיתִי עֲלֵי יָגוֹן עָלַי לִבִּי דַוָּי (Jer 8:18)—*My distress is eased, my heart ails me.*[16] This, too, is instruction for Israel (*taʿlīm le-yiśraʾel*) in how to lament for themselves. [Jeremiah] says, "This distress will be eased for me, and the grief that is upon me ails my heart."[17] I have translated *davvay* as "to ail," as in, *our heart ailed* (*daveh*; Lam 5:17).[18]

The meaning (*maʿnā*) of *mabligiti* ("is eased") is that this fragmentation wounds me continually. There were three expulsions in the time of the ten tribes, five expulsions in the time of Jeremiah, and two expulsions in the time of the Second Temple, as I have explained above.[19] [Exile] did not happen with a single expulsion. Thus, the meaning of *ha-mablig shod ʿal-ʿaz* is "He who eases the destruction of the strong" (Amos 5:9). This means [that] when the Creator wishes to destroy the strong, He unleashes affliction upon him little by little, in one circumstance after another, in order to make visible the power of the All-Powerful. If the Mighty and Sublime wished, He would lay him waste in a single attack, as it is said about Nineveh, *He will not take vengeance twice on His foes* (Nah 1:9), which means that *He will make a full end* (Nah 1:9) in a single attack <143b> and not in several attacks. He will bring hardship and vengeance upon you, and that is the meaning of *my distress is eased* (Jer 8:18).[20]

[15] This construction makes clear that for Salmon, *maʿnā* refers to the parable's interpretation.

[16] Thus begins an excursus on Jer 8:18–22. The opening verse is notoriously difficult. I have translated it in light of Salmon's interpretation, which he crafts over the next several pages. The rabbis also included Jer 8:18 in their discourses on Lamentations (see, e.g., *Lam R*, Proem 32). There the verse is glossed in Midrashic terms: "What means '*mablighiti*'? Because there are none (*mibli*) who meditate (*hogim*) in the Torah to perform Divine precepts and meritorious acts, I have made My house into My wine-press (*gitti*). For all that, *'My heart is faint within Me'* over the destroyed Temple."

[17] Salmon manipulates the syntax of the verse and disrupts its chiastic structure by translating the single Hebr. word *yagon* with a double construction in Arab.: *hādhā l-ghamm wa-l-ḥasra* ("this distress . . . and the grief"). Cf. al-Fāsī, who uses *ḥasra* (vol. I, 230–31), and Yefet, who uses *ghamm* (Yefet, Jer, 185).

[18] I have chosen the English word "ail" since Salmon includes physical and emotional pain.

[19] See Salmon's excursus on the Ten Exiles in Lam 2:4. For discussion, see chapter 6.

[20] Jeremiah 8:18 has long troubled commentators. The Hebr. noun *mabligit* is a hapax, although Salmon and al-Fāsī discuss it alongside the root b/l/g (e.g., Amos 5:9; Job 10:20; Ps 39:4). Both

When he says, "*my heart ails*," he means that the hearts of Israel will be pained in this exile until they cry out for redemption, as it is said, הִנֵּה־קוֹל שַׁוְעַת בַּת־עַמִּי (Jer 8:19)—"This is the voice of the congregation of my people, calling for redemption from the distant land. 'Is the LORD not in Zion? Is her king, the LORD, not within her? The LORD, is He not there? Surely He has not deprived [Zion] of His mercy; He did not transfer the *glory* from within Israel."[21] The answer comes from the LORD, who says: "*Why have they provoked Me to anger with their graven images, and with their foreign idols?*" (Jer 8:19)[22] and *By setting their threshold by My threshold and their doorposts beside My doorposts, with only a wall between Me and them, they have defiled My holy name by their abominations* (Ezek 43:8).

Israel answers by saying, עָבַר קָצִיר כָּלָה קָיִץ (Jer 8:20)—"The harvest, the summer has vanished, and we have not been saved."[23] He likens the killing that befell us during the siege—as it is said, *The dead bodies of men shall fall like dung upon the open field, like sheaves after the reaper, and none shall gather them* (Jer 9:21/22)—to the picking of grapes and all the summer fruits, as it is said, <144a> *Glean thoroughly as a vine the remnant of Israel; like a grape-gatherer pass your hand again over its branches* (Jer 6:9). Now he says, "O LORD, the reaping and picking have come upon us together. Our tarrying has been long, and we have not yet been aided." The lamenter returns to his lament and says, עַל־שֶׁבֶר בַּת־עַמִּי (Jer 8:21)—"For the rupture of all my people has ruptured me; I have become dark[24] and loneliness has taken hold of me." This is because the rupture is tremendous, as it is said, *For vast as the sea is your ruin* (Lam 2:13).

Salmon and al-Fāsī translate Hebr. b/l/g with Arab. r/f/h ("to ease"). Yet this meaning does not fit the context of Jer 8:18 as well as it fits the other prooftexts; thus, it requires additional maneuverings. Al-Fāsī renders the verse as a rhetorical question by adding *a-lam* (the negative interrogative): "Will the distress that is upon me not be eased?" (vol. I, 230–31). Salmon instead offers a theological-historical framework through which to understand the difficult verse: God eases distress in order to prolong punishment. Yefet takes a third tack in his translation of Jer 8:18, where he renders *mabligiti* as Arab. *ṣabrī* ("my patience, my forbearance"), i.e., "My patience will be eased."

21 The final sentence is a pious addition, not based in the biblical verse.

22 Salmon does not translate this part of the verse into Arab.

23 Salmon omits a verb in his translation; the omission does not appear to be a scribal error. MT: *ʿavar qaṣir kalah qayiṣ* (*the harvest is passed, the summer is ended*); cf. Salmon: *the harvest, the summer is vanished*; cf. Yefet: *the time of the harvest is passed, the time of summer is vanished* (Yefet, Jer, 185).

24 Salmon translates Hebr. *qadarti* as Arab. *taṭalkhamtu*, as do al-Fāsī (vol. II, 539) and Yefet (Yefet, Jer, 185). Blau lists *hitqader* as the primary Hebr. meaning (*Dictionary*, 404).

הַצֳּרִי אֵין בְּגִלְעָד (Jer 8:22)— "Is there no theriac[25] in the mountains of Jerash,[26] or no physician there? Why, then, have all my people not recovered?" These words [follow] the way of lament, torment, bitterness,[27] burning, and pain. That is to say, there is no theriac, and no healer, in the world. Gilead is mentioned because in ancient times, theriac was customarily made in Gilead and exported from Gilead, as it is said, *Then they sat down to eat; and looking up they saw a caravan of Ishmaelites coming from Gilead,* [*with their camels bearing gum, balm, and myrrh*] (Gen 37:25). That is why [Jeremiah] also says, in a narrative about Egypt, *Go up to Gilead, and take balm* (Jer 46:11). One of the scholars says that the meaning (*maʿnā*) of *balm* alludes to Torah. <144b> In other words, they do not apply what is in the Torah, though their healing is within it, and [God] is the most sublime physician.

Then he says, *O that my head were waters, and my eyes a fountain of tears* (Jer 8:23/9:1), [which is] like the statement here, *My eyes, my eyes cause water to come down* (Lam 1:16) and *My eyes flow with channels of water* (Lam 3:48).

Thus he also laments in this chapter[28] by saying, אֵיכָה יוּעַם זָהָב—"How the gold has become rusty,[29] how the good, fine jewel has changed."[30] This is the lamenter's [way of] speaking about the most extreme pain that there is. He [means] that it is known that gold does not rust, just as it was known that the enemy would not triumph over this nation, as it is said, *The kings of the earth did not believe, or any inhabitants of the world* [*that foe or enemy could enter the gates of Jerusalem*] (Lam 4:12). So when the enemy did in fact triumph over this nation and destroy her Temple, [Jeremiah] said, ***How the gold has become rusty, how the fine jewel is changed!***

Next, and more astonishing: ***the holy stones lie scattered***—which means, "How the stones of the Temple were strewn in the alleyways at the time of destruction!" The stones that he described were stones of *ten cubits* and

25 Salmon and Yefet translate Hebr. *ḥaṣari* ("balm") as Arab. *tiryāq* ("theriac, remedy").

26 Salmon and Yefet identify the biblical "Gilead" with the mountains of Jerash; al-Fāsī notes that Gilead is the settled place of the tribe of Manasseh (vol. I, 328).

27 For *zaʿr* as bitterness, see Blau, *Dictionary*, 272; see also Salmon's translation of Lam 3:15.

28 I.e., Lam 4; Lam 1, 2, and 4 begin as laments, with the Hebr. word *ʾekhah*.

29 For Hebr. *yuʿam* in Arab. translation: Salmon uses ṣ/d/ʾ ("to become rusty"); Yefet uses gh/t/w ("to be concealed"); and al-Fāsī (vol. II, 403–4) uses both kh/b/ʾ ("to be concealed") and kh/m/d ("to become dim," which is the standard translation of Hebr. k/k/h, as in, e.g., Lev 13:6). There is a rabbinic precedent for reading *yuʿam* in the sense of being covered over (see, e.g., *Lam R* on Lam 4:1).

30 Salmon translates Hebr. *ketem* as Arab. *jawhar* ("jewel"); cf. al-Fāsī, "gold, akin to what is called 'pure gold' (Hebr. *paz*; Ps 21:4/3)" (vol. I, 153). In his own translation of Ps 21:4/3, Salmon resorts to a false cognate, *fāʾiz*, understanding not a "crown of pure gold" (Hebr. *ʿaṭeret paz*) but rather a "turban of the victor" (Arab. *ʿiṣābat al-fāʾiz*), which he then glosses as a "king's crown" (*tāj al-melekh*).

stones of <145a> *eight cubits.*[31] As for [the stones] above the foundation, they are better—like these stones. [The stones] above the foundations are better. He compares these stones according to their orderliness, except that the vaults of stone and the vault of cut cedars were toppled,[32] as it is said, *And above were costly stones, hewn according to measurement, and cedar* (1 Kgs 7:11). The reason for the cedar is that it holds back the leaves of gold since the house bears them. Then jewels were inlaid in the gold, as it is said, *and stones for setting, antimony, colored stones, all sorts of precious stones* (1 Chr 29:2), and *He adorned the house with settings of precious stones* (2 Chr 3:6). It is known that the enemy seized all of these jewels, as it is said, *they broke down* (Ps 74:6). And everything that befell us was because of the magnitude of our offenses, as it is said, *Your iniquities have turned these away, and your sins have kept good from you* (Jer 5:25).

Lamentations 4:6

וַיִּגְדַּל עֲוֺן בַּת־עַמִּי מֵחַטַּאת סְדֹם הַהֲפוּכָה כְמוֹ־רָגַע וְלֹא־חָלוּ בָהּ יָדָיִם׃
ועט'ם ד'נוב ג'מאעה שעבי אכת'ר מן כ'טיה סדום אלמקלובה מת'ל טרפה עין
ומא צברו פיהא אלאיאדי

For the offense of the congregation of my people was greater than the sin of Sodom, which was overthrown as in the blink of an eye and no hands struck her.

For the offense of the congregation of my people was greater indicates the sins of Israel, which were greater than the offenses of Sodom.[33] Since the matter was described in this way, how can [God] equate Israel with the people of Sodom, as He says in another place, *All of them have become like Sodom to Me* (Jer 23:14)? We say that God described their conditions in every time as they were at that time. When they were equal in sin to Sodom, He said, *All of them have become like Sodom unto Me* (Jer 23:14), and when they surpassed the deeds of Sodom, it is said, *As I live, says the Lord God, your sister Sodom and her daughters* <150b> *have not done as you and your daughters have done* (Ezek 16:48).[34] Now he describes the

[31] See 1 Kgs 7:10.

[32] Meaning unclear.

[33] The verse pairs the offenses (Hebr. *'avon*; Arab. *dhunūb*) of "my people" and the sins (Hebr. *ḥaṭṭa't*; Arab. *khāṭāyā*) of Sodom; here Salmon pairs the sins (*khāṭāyā*) of Israel and the offenses (*dhunūb*) of Sodom. This shuffling complicates the taxonomy of sin suggested by Salmon's comment to Lam 3:42.

[34] For a similar comparison, see *Lam R* on this verse. There the rabbis note that Scripture ascribes greater sin to the tribes of Judah and Benjamin (acc. Gen 28:20) than it does to the people of Sodom

gravest of the deeds of Sodom. As for the deeds of Israel, I have already explained the majority of them above.[35] Therefore it is said, ***For the offense of the congregation of my people was greater.***

Which was overthrown as in a moment.[36] Three interpretations were proposed. One scholar said that Sodom was overthrown as in the blink of an eye; the LORD of hosts overthrew it quickly, as it is said, *And He overthrew those cities* (Gen 19:25), so they were not burdened or pained by being overthrown by human hands. Another one said, He did not delay in overthrowing them, but rather He overthrew them quickly. And another one said that Sodom was destroyed quickly and its buildings were not attacked by human hands, since no one could achieve this except for the Lord of hosts, just as He promised when He said, *I will restore your fortunes* (Jer 29:14).[37] The first statement is the most correct one made about this.[38] What befell us was like what befell Sodom in the way of *an overthrow like that of Sodom and Gomorrah, Admah and Zeboim, which the LORD overthrew in His anger* (Deut 29:22/23). All these calamities befell us because of the magnitude of our offenses, <151a> as it is said, *Your iniquities have turned these away, and your sins have kept good from you* (Jer 5:25).

Lamentations 4:11

כִּלָּה יְהוָה אֶת־חֲמָתוֹ שָׁפַךְ חֲרוֹן אַפּוֹ וַיַּצֶּת־אֵשׁ בְּצִיּוֹן וַתֹּאכַל יְסוֹדֹתֶיהָ׃
אתם אללה חמיתה ספך שדה גצ'בה ואג'ג' אלנאר פי ציון ואכלת אסאסאתהא

God gave full vent to His wrath, He poured out His hot anger; and He kindled a fire in Zion, which consumed its foundations.

(acc. Ezek 9:9). In *Genesis Rabbah* this observation occasions the question, "Why, then, was a remnant of Judah and Benjamin spared and not of Sodom?" The proposed answer is that the people of Judah and Benjamin attempted to perform the precepts, while the people of Sodom did not (ctd. in *Lam R* on Lam 4:6, 221 n. 2).

[35] See the excursus at Lam 1:8.

[36] Eng. follows the Hebr. wording, not Salmon's Arab. gloss.

[37] The application of this prooftext is unclear. It seems to be part of the incorrect interpretation that Salmon reports, and thus he does not trouble himself to explain it. In the biblical context of Jer 29:14, God promises to restore Israelite fortunes and return them to their land. Perhaps, in the interpretation presented here, a city destroyed by God, rather than by human hands, would be primed for divine restoration. Salmon does not cite Jer 29:14 elsewhere in the commentary, and the verse is missing from Sabih's edition of Yefet's Jeremiah commentary.

[38] And in fact, Salmon has woven this interpretation into his own translation of Lam 4:6 by rendering Hebr. *kemo rega'* ("as in a moment") as Arab. *mithl ṭarfat al-'ayn* ("as in the blink of an eye").

This is just as He threatened when He said, *And I will heap evils upon them;* [*I will spend My arrows upon them; they shall be devoured with burning heat and poisonous pestilence*] (Deut 32:23–24). Therefore He made all of the curses that He mentioned befall Israel, as it is said, *He has confirmed His words, which He spoke against us* (Dan 9:12); *and the curse and oath* [*which are written in the law of Moses the servant of God*] *have been poured out upon us* (Dan 9:11). God did to us just what He threatened would happen to us, as it is said, *Therefore thus says the Lord God: Behold, My anger and My wrath* [*will be poured out*] (Jer 7:20). Since the Mighty and Sublime had not [previously] completed [what] He had threatened, [now] it is said, ***The LORD gave full vent to His wrath.***[39]

And He kindled a fire in Zion because God had already communicated to them through Jeremiah that if they did not remember the Sabbath as He had commanded them, and sanctify it, then they would deserve that their country be burned and that they be exiled from it, as it is said, *But if you do not listen to Me, to keep the Sabbath day holy,* [*and not to bear a burden and enter by the gates of Jerusalem on the Sabbath day, then I will kindle a fire in its gates, and it shall devour the palaces of Jerusalem and shall not be quenched*] (Jer 17:27). The reason for this great anger is that their transgression burned and blazed like a fire, as it is said, *For* <155a> *wickedness burns like a fire* (Isa 9:17/18) and *Through the wrath of the LORD of hosts* [*the land is burned*] (Isa 9:18/19).[40] And all these calamities overtook us because of the magnitude of our offenses, as it is said, *Your iniquities have turned these away, and your sins have kept good from you* (Jer 5:25).

Lamentations 4:15

סוּרוּ טָמֵא קָרְאוּ לָמוֹ סוּרוּ סוּרוּ אַל־תִּגָּעוּ כִּי נָצוּ גַּם־נָעוּ אָמְרוּ בַּגּוֹיִם לֹא יוֹסִפוּ לָגוּר׃
זולו יא נג'ס נאדו אליהם אלגוים זולו זולו לא תדנו אן כ'אצמו איצ'א אצ'טרבו
קאלו פי אלאמם לא יזידו ללמג'אורה

[39] Cf. *Lam R* on Lam 4:11; the rabbis emphasize that God directed His wrath against *Zion* and *its foundations* rather than the people. For them, Asaph's song (Ps 79:1) expresses gratitude that God "poured out His wrath upon wood and stone and not upon Israel." Stern explains that the rabbis were motivated by apologetic reasons to interpret Lam 4:11 against the plain sense, and this Midrash shows how the rabbis used interpretation as a tool for overcoming historical trauma (*Parables in Midrash*, 24–42). This reasoning does not inform Salmon's treatment of Lam 4:11, but it does color his comment on Lam 1:12.

[40] Requital in kind (*muqābala*): the Israelites violated the laws of kindling; therefore, divine anger is kindled against them. As in his excursus at Lam 1:8, Salmon suggests that the entire Jewish community is guilty of violating precepts that only Karaites accept (sc. the Karaite prohibition against Sabbath fires).

"Away, you polluted one!" *the nations*[41] cried at them; "Away! Away! Do not come near!" So they quarreled and also wandered, and in the nations[42] they said, "They shall sojourn with us no longer."[43]

I translated *naṣu* in [the way of] *when men quarrel* (*yinnaṣu*; Deut 25:11).[44] ***Away, you polluted one*** is what we witness the *nations* saying <159a> to us: "You are polluted and filthy." Yet they are *uncircumcised, eating swine's flesh and the abomination and mice* (Isa 66:17), and thricefold [stricken] with *gonorrhea, menstrual blood, and genital emission, and those stricken with every kind of skin disease.* They say to Israel—to the *seed of Abraham, Isaac, and Jacob, who are called holy, treasured, chosen, sons of prophets, the stock of kings, seed of princes, bearers of the Lord's arms, girt with testimony, and knowing justice*—they say to them, ***"Away, you polluted one!"*** Then, they withdraw from them and they say, ***"Away! Away! Do not come near!"***

We learn that the reason for this is our quarrel with the prophets and our going against their words. This verse says ***and also wandered*** after the verse *They wandered, blind* (Lam 4:14). The first phrase alludes to the First Temple and the second phrase alludes to the Second Temple. It is also said that they deserve to wander a second time: *And this again you will do: Cover the LORD's altar with tears* (Mal 2:13). Just as He made it obligatory to weep over the destruction of the First Temple—as it is said, *In that day the Lord GOD of hosts called to weeping and mourning* (Isa 22:12)—He likewise made it obligatory to weep over the destruction of the Second Temple, as it is said, *And this again you will do: Cover* <159b> *the LORD's altar with tears, with weeping* (Mal 2:13).[45]

How could he not weep for himself—for the dispossession of His grace, and being handed over to his enemies? *From this inheritance of the beautiful*

[41] Hebr. *al-goyim*.

[42] Arab. *umam*. Typically Salmon translates Hebr. *goyim* as Arab. *aḥzāb* in the verses, while using *umam* in his comments. Al-Fāsī likewise prefers the latter translation (vol. I, 310–11).

[43] Cf. RSV: "Away! Unclean!" men cried at them; "Away! Away! Touch not!" So they became fugitives and wanderers; men said among the nations, "They shall stay with us no longer." Salmon's translation reads *nadu* instead of *naṣu*, i.e., reading Lam 4:15 (*naṣu gam naʿu*) on analogy to Gen 4:12 (*naʿ va-nad*).

[44] The Qal form is attested only at Lam 4:15; for Salmon the verb has the same meaning as the Niphal form as found at Deut 25:11. This reading of the verse is among those presented in *Lam R*: "The Israelites were not exiled until they became quarrelsome (*maṣṣot*) towards the Holy One, blessed be He" (on Lam 4:16). The root n/ṣ/h is not in al-Fāsī's dictionary.

[45] Salmon reads this verse as a command rather than a historical description of Israelite despair.

[*land*], *then Zion, the royal city, then Jerusalem, the holy city, then our holy Temple and our splendor,* as it is said, *And I will give it into the hands of foreigners for a prey* (Ezek 7:21)?[46]

And how could he not weep over the transfer of the LORD's glory from among Israel, as it is said, *And the Spirit lifted me up and brought me in the vision* (Ezek 11:24), and it is said, *From the daughter of Zion has departed all her majesty* (Lam 1:6)?[47]

And how could he not weep over the lack of prophecy and prophets, as it is said, *I will also command the clouds* [*that they rain no rain upon it*] (Isa 5:6)?

And how could we not weep[48] over the cessation of kingship, as it is said, *Without king or prince* (Hos 3:4)?

And how could we not weep over the cancellation of offerings, as it is said, *Because cereal offering and drink offering are withheld from the house of your God* (Joel 1:13)?

And how could we not weep over the idleness of the *priests* from their steps, as it is said, *Gird on sackcloth and lament, O priests* (Joel 1:13)?

And how could we not weep over the idleness of the Levites from their melodies, and the elders from sitting in wisdom, as it is said, *The elders have ceased from the gate* (Lam 5:14)?

And how could we not weep over the falling of our crown and our glory, as it is said, *The crown has fallen from our head* (Lam 5:16)?

And how could we not weep over the magnitude of our sins, as it is said, *Woe to us, that* <160a> *we have sinned!* (Lam 5:16)?

And how could we not weep over the blackening of our faces, as it is said, *Now their visage is blacker than soot* (Lam 4:8)?

And how could we not weep over our lowliness, as it is said, *You foolish and senseless people* (Deut 32:6)?

And how could we not weep over the blindness of our vision, as it is said, *We grope for the wall like the blind* (Isa 59:10)?

And how could we not weep over our ignorance, as it is said, *Some were fools through their sinful ways* (Ps 107:17)?[49]

[46] Thus begins Salmon's homiletical litany: rhetorical questions impressing upon his audience the depth of their suffering and the absolute necessity of mourning.

[47] As in his comment to Lam 1:6, Salmon reads Ezek 8–11 as a description of the transfer of the divine glory in stages, ever farther away from the Temple and the Holy Land. See chapter 3.

[48] At this point the refrain shifts from "and how could *he* not weep" to "and how could *we* not weep."

[49] In his remarks at Ps 107:17, Salmon translates Hebr. *ʾevilim* ("fools") as Arab. *juhhāl* ("ignorant ones"): "*Some were fools through their sinful ways* means that they were ignorant, by dint of

And how could we not weep over the impudence of our faces, as it is said, *Yet you have a harlot's brow,* [*you refuse to be ashamed*] (Jer 3:3), and over descriptions like these? It is said, *Awake, you drunkards, and weep* (Joel 1:5) and *My tears have been my food* (Ps 42:4/3); *O that my head were waters* (Jer 8:23/9:1).[50]

When he says ***in the nations they said***, he means that when the nations seized them and exiled them, they [i.e., the nations] said that God was angry at these people and drove them out of their country, forever, never to return to the proximity of their Temple. And all these conditions befell us because of the magnitude of our offenses, as it is said, *Your iniquities have turned these away, and your sins have kept good from you* (Jer 5:25).

Lamentations 4:17

עוֹדֵינוּ תִּכְלֶינָה עֵינֵינוּ אֶל־עֶזְרָתֵנוּ הָבֶל בְּצִפִּיָּתֵנוּ צִפִּינוּ אֶל־גּוֹי לֹא יוֹשִׁעַ׃
בעד הוד'א נחן תפנא אעיננא אלי מעונתנא באלהבא בדידבתנא אלד"י
תדידבנא אלי חזב לא יגית' ולא יפרג'

Our eyes failed, ever watching vainly for help; in our watching we watched for a nation which could not save and could not liberate.[51]

their crimes. This dictum should be approached with discernment (*tamyīz*) so that you learn its truth, which is that every excellent thing should be requited according to its excellence, in beauty. This is an analogy (*qiyās*) based on reason. The creator of the world set His excellences—worldly excellence and celestial excellence—upon Israel, so they were obliged to obey the creator of the world in every respect. But since they requited their creator with rebellions, He said to them, *Do you thus requite the LORD, you foolish and senseless people?* (Deut 32:6). Thus we learn that their rebellious actions are an indication of their ignorance, as it is said, *some were fools*. In other words, *through their sinful ways* teaches that they were *fools*, and this interpretation is correct" (Salmon, Pss 107–150).

[50] For the same litany with minor variations, see Salmon's excursus at Ps 42:4/3. Some prooftexts are different (e.g, Ezek 3:7 there vs. Jer 3:3 here to demonstrate impudent countenances), and the refrain there reads, "how could he not weep" throughout (without switching from "he" to "we"). Salmon begins that version by invoking Ps 42:4/3 as proof of the daily obligation to mourn: "Just as he compares the *offering* (*qurban*) to bread because that [was offered] morning and evening, and because it was a *daily offering* (*tamid*), so he compares weeping in *exile* to food because it is his continual obligation" (Pss 42–72). On liturgical elements within the commentary, see Ben-Shammai, "Poetic Works and Lamentations."

[51] Cf. RSV: "Our eyes failed, ever watching vainly for help; in our watching we watched for a nation which could not save." Salmon translates Hebr. *lo yoshea*ʿ ("which could not save") with two Arab. verbs: *lā yughīth wa-lā yafraj* ("which could not save and could not liberate"), perhaps because neither Arab. root has the full semantic range of the Hebr. Yet al-Fāsī (vol. II, 692) and Yefet use only the

Jeremiah lamented over this nation, which had abandoned calling upon God, and [instead] called upon the nations. First [they called upon] the kings of Assyria, as it is said, *For Ahaz took from the house of the LORD and the house of the king and of the princes, and gave tribute to the king of Assyria; but it did not help him* (2 Chr 28:21). In this [same vein], Hosea said, *When Ephraim saw his sickness, and Judah his wound* (Hos 5:13). They were obliged <161b> to return to God and seek healing from Him when the calamity happened to them, but they did not do so. Rather, they sent [dispatches] to the king of Assyria and to the king of Yareb—the name of a city[52]—but he was unable to bring you healing: *But he is not able to cure you or heal your wound* (Hos 5:13). This means that when a boil comes suddenly upon someone [and] he falls ill, it is in the nature of the skillful physician (*al-ṭabīb al-ḥādhiq*) to cleanse the place [of the boil] and wash it. When illness falls upon someone, he [i.e., the physician] brings well-being. But now [God] says: "The one you sent for, the one you called upon for support, *is not able to cure you or heal your wound* (Hos 5:13). How was he capable of healing you, when I am the one who [heals you] in this way? *For I will be like a lion to Ephraim* (Hos 5:14)."

Then, [God] threatened to transfer the *glory* from among the people, as He says, *I will return again to My place, until they acknowledge their guilt and seek My face, and in their distress they seek Me* (Hos 5:15).[53] He means, "I will abandon them until they abandon seeking support from the *nations*[54] and say, *Assyria shall not save us* (Hos 14:4/3); and [until] they seek healing from Me"—as it is said next, *In their distress they seek Me* (Hos 5:15)—"and [until] they say, *Come, let us return to the LORD; [for He has torn, that He may heal us; He has stricken, and He will bind us up.] After two days He will revive us* (Hos 6:1–2)."

Next, and worse than this: the time Nebuchadnezzar made Zedekiah swear an oath and make a covenant that he would not rebel against him, [which would] violate the oath.[55] <162a> But [Zedekiah] sent dispatches seeking help from the people of Egypt, as it is said, *But he rebelled against him by sending ambassadors to Egypt, that they might give him horses and a large army* (Ezek 17:15). This brought nothing but trouble to him, as it is said, *Behold, Pharaoh's*

Arab. root gh/w/th. For the Karaite practice of rendering one Hebr. word with multiple Arab. words, see Polliack, *The Karaite Tradition*, 181–99, and Khan, *The Early Karaite Tradition*, 133.

[52] Salmon seems to understand *melekh yareb* (Hos 5:13) as a place reference (i.e., the king of Yareb) rather than an epithet for the Assyrian king (i.e., "the king that will contend").

[53] See Salmon's excursus to Lam 1:6; chapter 3.

[54] Retribution in kind (*bāb al-muqābala*).

[55] See 2 Chr 36:13 for a possible reference to an oath.

army, which came to help you [is about to return to Egypt] (Jer 37:7).[56] That was Isaiah's meaning when he said, *Woe to those who go down to Egypt for help* (Isa 31:1). In this prophecy he announced that the result [will be] the destruction of everyone, as it is said, *When the LORD stretches out His hand, the helper will stumble, and he who is helped will fall, and they will all perish together* (Isa 31:3). He alludes to Israel and also makes it known that when they took their gifts to Egypt, it did not benefit them and it did not save them from the enemies' hand, as it is said: *They carry their riches on the backs of asses* [. . .] *and their treasures on the humps of camels, to a people that cannot profit them. For Egypt's help is worthless and empty* (Isa 30:6–7) and *Therefore shall the protection of Pharaoh turn to your shame* (Isa 30:3). He also rebuked them through Hosea, as it is said, *They make a covenant with Assyria* (Hos 12:1), and as it is said afterward, *The LORD has an indictment against Judah* (Hos 12:2).

When they went on to Egypt after the destruction of the Temple, God dispatched Nebuchadnezzar against them in the thirty-second year of his reign. He destroyed Egypt, killed the Israelites who were there, and exiled the remainder, just as Jeremiah and Ezekiel had prophesied. For Jeremiah, it was said, *I will take* <162b> *the remnant of Judah who have set their faces to come to the land of Egypt to live* (Jer 44:12) and *so that none of the remnant of Judah* [. . .] *shall escape* (Jer 44:14). For Ezekiel, it was said, *Ethiopia, and Put, and Lud, and all Arabia, [and Libya, and the people of the land that is in league, shall fall with them by the sword]* (Ezek 30:5). *The people of the land that is in league* alludes to Israel. This [prophecy] announced the destruction of Egypt so that Israel would not hold out hope of being saved by them [i.e., the Egyptians], as it is said, *And it shall never again be the reliance of the house of Israel, recalling their iniquity, when they turn to them for aid* (Ezek 29:16).

Our eyes failed indicates that everyone who trains his eye on human aid surely trains his eye on *vanity* and *emptiness*, as it is said, *For vain is the help of man* (Ps 60:13/11; 108:13/12)[57] and as it is said, *Cursed is the man who trusts in man* (Jer 17:5).

Also, ***In our watching we watched***: we abandoned our reliance on God and we depended on the aid of the *nations*, and we learned their ways. All these

[56] Cf. *Lam R* on Lam 4:20, in which divine intervention—not Zedekiah's treaty violation—leads Pharaoh Necho's army to turn back (Jer 37:7). In that Midrash, God brings the skeletons of the Egyptians who were drowned during the Exodus to the surface of the sea. Once the Egyptians are reminded that the Israelites' ancestors drowned their own ancestors, they refuse to provide military support.

[57] In his comment to Ps 60:13/11, Salmon explains: "He means that a human being does not have [the capacity to] help: *for of what account is he?* (Isa 2:22)," (Pss 42–72).

calamities, which the prophet has enumerated in this book, were brought upon us, as it is said, *Your iniquities have turned these away, and your sins have kept good from you* (Jer 5:25).

Lamentations 4:20

רוּחַ אַפֵּינוּ מְשִׁיחַ יְהוָה נִלְכַּד בִּשְׁחִיתוֹתָם אֲשֶׁר אָמַרְנוּ בְּצִלּוֹ נִחְיֶה בַגּוֹיִם:
ריח אנפנא מסיח יוי עלק בסבב פסאדאתהם אלד'י קלנא אן פי ט'לה נעיש בין אלאחזאב

The breath of our nostrils, the LORD's anointed, was ensnared by their corruption, of whom we said, "Under his shadow we shall live among the nations."[58]

The breath of our nostrils, the LORD's anointed alludes to Josiah.[59] Know that the kingdom of Judah was able to live by means of Josiah's standing *vis-à-vis* the Creator, because He extended his life. [Josiah] was completely obedient, as it is said: *He did what was right in the eyes of the LORD, and walked in the ways of David his father; and he did not turn aside to the right or the left. For in the eighth year of his reign, while he was yet* <164b> *a boy, he began to seek the God of David his father; and in the twelfth year he began to purge Judah and Jerusalem of the high places, the Asherim, and the graven and molten images* (2 Chr 34:2–3). The entire account explicates his virtues and his seemly deeds. It is said in the other copy,[60] *Before him there was no king like him, who turned to the LORD with all his heart* (2 Kgs 23:25).

[58] Cf. RSV: "The breath of our nostrils, the LORD's anointed, was taken in their pits."

[59] The tradition of relating this verse to Josiah is at least as old as Tg. Lam, which renders the verse expansively: "*King Josiah, who was as dear to us as the breath of* the spirit *of life in* our nostrils *and was anointed with* the anointing *oil* of the LORD, was locked *up in Egypt's* snare *of corruption.* It was he of whom we said, 'In the shadow *of his merit* we will live among the nations'" (Brady, *Rabbinic Targum*, 39–44, 153, 165). There is rabbinic precedent for also reading Lam 4:1—*how the gold has grown dim*—as an allusion to the death of King Josiah, who was "like a golden ornament" (*Lam R* on 4:1).

[60] Arab., *nuskha*; a copy, such as a scribe would make in order to disseminate a manuscript. Salmon's use of the term suggests that he understands the biblical books of Kings and Chronicles as copies, that he recognizes that copies of manuscripts do not match one another in every detail, and, further, that one text may offer something that the other text has left out or expressed less eloquently. He uses the term *nuskha* once in the Lam commentary, and also in his commentaries on Pss (2:5, 105:14, 105:16, 106:48, and 107:43) and Song (1:17). He variously refers to Kgs or Chr as the "other" copy. This flexibility suggests that Salmon considers both books to be copies of a common source, or that their chronological relationship is not especially important to his discussion. In general,

Yet even with this [i.e., the righteousness of Josiah], the wrath of God was great against the deeds of Ahaz and Manasseh and Amon, who preceded [him], as it is said, *Still the LORD did not turn from the fierceness of His great wrath, by which His anger was kindled against Judah, because of all the provocations with which Manasseh had provoked Him. And the LORD said, "I will remove Judah also out of my sight"* (2 Kgs 23:26–27).

For this reason, they [i.e., the Judahites] did not deserve for someone like Josiah to remain among them, as it is said, ***he was ensnared by their corruption.*** Since God willed that Josiah would not see the exile, He made him pass away as a trial (*mumtaḥin*) in order to compensate him (*li-yaʿūḍahu*) in the Abode of the Hereafter (*dār al-ākhira*), as it is said, *For the righteous man is taken away from calamity* (Isa 57:1).[61] This was elucidated by the prophecy of Hulda the prophetess, when she said, *Because your heart was penitent and you humbled yourself before God when you heard His words* (2 Kgs 22:19 = 2 Chr 34:27); but, *Behold, I will gather you to your fathers, and you shall be gathered to your grave in peace* [*and your eyes shall not see all the evil which I will bring upon this place and its inhabitants*] (2 Kgs 22:20 = 2 Chr 34:28). *In peace* means that he would not see the *exile*, <165a> just as it was said to Abraham, *As for yourself, you shall go to your fathers in peace* (Gen 15:15)[62]—in other words, "you will not see servitude and affliction." [God's] words to Zedekiah, *You shall die in peace. And as spices were burned for your fathers* [*the former kings who were before you, so men shall burn spices for you and lament for you*] (Jer 34:5), mean "You will surely die a natural death and not be killed by the sword, as it is said, *You shall not die by the sword* (Jer 34:4)."

Then, after Josiah passed away, Jeremiah taught the [meaning] of the matter. The people had had turned away, so he lamented over them with a lament of torment, as it is said, *Jeremiah also uttered a lament for Josiah; and all the singing men and singing women have spoken of Josiah in their laments* (2 Chr 35:25). Since the people felt compassion for the one who was loftier

Salmon's experience with medieval manuscript culture provides a model for his concept of how biblical texts may have been drafted, organized, and disseminated. Note that Blau, citing Goitein, occasionally reads *nuskha* as a synonym for Hebr. *sefer*, "book" (*Dictionary*, 692).

[61] Yefet explains the same theological principle in his comment on Isa 57:1–2, also drawing heavily on 2 Kgs 22. For discussion, see chapter 2, in the section on "Biblical Citations from Outside Lamentations."

[62] Yefet follows this line of reasoning in his commentary on Genesis: "*You shall go to your fathers in peace* (Gen 15:15). By this he means peace from witnessing these conditions of your children" (Yefet, Gen, 79*).

than they, their hearts pained them and they mourned deeply, as it is said, *All Judah and Jerusalem mourned for Josiah* (2 Chr 35:24).

The breath of our nostrils. Jeremiah said this, along with the calamities of Israel that he enumerated in this passage and in others—namely, the entire book of Lamentations—on the day that Jeremiah mourned over Josiah. He lamented over all of it, and Israel knew everything that would befall them from the magnitude of the affliction because of their many offenses, as it is said, *Your iniquities have turned these away, and your sins have kept good from you* (Jer 5:25).

Lamentations 4:22

תַּם־עֲוֹנֵךְ בַּת־צִיּוֹן לֹא יוֹסִיף לְהַגְלוֹתֵךְ פָּקַד עֲוֹנֵךְ בַּת־אֱדוֹם גִּלָּה עַל־חַטֹּאתָיִךְ׃
כמל פני ד'נבך יא ג'מאעה ציון לא יעאוד ליג'ליך אפתקד ד'נבך יא ג'מאעה
אדום כשף ען כ'טאיאך

The punishment of your offense, O congregation of Zion, is completed; He will keep you in exile no longer. But your iniquity, O congregation of Edom, He will punish; He will uncover your sins.

<166a> He set this good news[63] down in writing in this *book*, so that anyone who read about these calamities, and heard about what happened to this nation—that nothing remained to it—would have hope. He placed this good news in this *book* in order to fortify whoever numbered these calamities while lamenting over himself in this *exile*.[64]

With this good news, he intended two lofty meanings that are the root of all good news. The first is forgiveness and pardon, which are the root of ending every calamity, as it is said, *Your iniquities have turned these away* (Jer 5:25).[65] Forgiveness and pardon will become complete with the redemption, as it is said, *For in My wrath I smote you,* [*but in My favor I have had mercy on*

[63] Arab. *bishāra*; Salmon uses the term (incl. pl., *bishārāt*) four times in this passage.

[64] Salmon twice notes that the good news was set down in writing (Arab. *athbata*; *ja'ala*), presumably by the prophet Jeremiah or by the *mudawwin* (biblical editor, redactor). Muslim scholars use similar wording to note the transition from oral to written textual forms (see Gruendler, *Book Culture*, 26). This construction also recalls Karaite theories of biblical composition, in which biblical materials were oral before being edited and recorded in writing (see Polliack, "Inversion," 286–95).

[65] Abdul-Karim: "The phrase does not really give the sense meant by the author. What Salmon no doubt meant was that the absence of God's pardon and forgiveness was the reason for all the calamities" (84).

you] (Isa 60:10). Second, he mentions the acts of retribution from the enemy. It had been said, *But to you also the cup shall pass* (Lam 4:21), [but] now it is said, ***The punishment of your offense, O congregation of Zion, is completed.*** This means that Israel will no longer be in possession of any offense, as [Jeremiah] mentions, *In those days and in that time, says the LORD, offense shall be sought in Israel, and there shall be none;* [*and sin in Judah, and none shall be found; for I will pardon those whom I leave as a remnant*] (Jer 50:20).

He will keep you in exile no longer. <166b> This is God's assurance of safety (*amān*) to the Israelites.[66] After He gathers them from the regions of the world, He will not send them into exile again, as it is said, *I will plant them upon their land, and they shall never again be plucked up out of the land* [*which I have given them*] (Amos 9:15). It is said, *They shall no more be a prey to the nations, nor shall the beasts of the land devour them; they shall dwell securely, and none shall make them afraid* (Ezek 34:28). He made this assurance of safety (*amān*) as clear as possible for us by saying, *And I will provide for them plantations of renown* [*so that they shall no more be consumed with hunger in the land, and no longer suffer the reproach of the nations*] (Ezek 34:29). He also makes known that He will raise up shepherds for this nation, to tend it with truth and fairness. There will be neither fear nor terror for them from any circumstance whatsoever, as it is said through Jeremiah, *I will set shepherds over them* [*who will care for them, and they shall fear no more, nor be dismayed, neither shall any be missing*] (Jer 23:4).

But your iniquity, O congregation of Edom alludes to what the Assyrians did in the First Temple, when they took up their position along the roads and seized anyone who escaped the sword of Nebuchadnezzar and made him surrender to the enemy, as it is said, *You should not have stood at the parting of the ways to cut off his fugitives* (Obad 1:14).

He will uncover your sins alludes to what they did in the Second Temple. They destroyed it at the time that Vespasian attacked them, as it is said in the book of Daniel, *And out of one of them came forth a little horn,* <167a> *which grew exceedingly great* (Dan 8:9), and I have explained this narrative clearly in the commentary on Daniel.[67]

Notice how the *psalmist* combines his appeal [to God] for help from what [both] Edom and Babylon did during the destruction of the First and Second Temples [respectively]. He says, *Remember, O LORD, against the Edomites*

[66] Arab. *li-banī isrā'īl* in Ms. Or. 2516; Hebr. in other MSS.
[67] See Salmon's discussion of the "ninth exile" in his comment to Lam 2:4.

the day of Jerusalem (Ps 137:7), and then he says, *O daughter of Babylon, you devastator!* (Ps 137:8). Edom is mentioned first because it is closer to us than Babylon and it is a convention in Hebrew to mention the closest one first, as we have explained elsewhere. Know that the land of Uz, which is mentioned in this narrative, alludes to Mount Seʿir because this is the country that the descendants of Esau conquered from the Horites, as it is said, *The Horites also lived in Seʿir formerly* (Deut 2:12), so the Horites are among the descendants of Seʿir. Uz was from Dishon, and this country was known by his name, as it is said, *in the land of Uz* (Job 1:1).

Lamentations 5

Lamentations 5:1

זְכֹר יְהוָה מֶה־הָיָה לָנוּ הַבִּיטָה וּרְאֵה אֶת־חֶרְפָּתֵנוּ׃
אד'כר יא רב איש כאן לנא אלתפת ואנט'ר איא מעירתנא

Remember, O Lord, what has befallen us; behold, and see our disgrace![1]

<167b> ***Remember, O Lord, what has befallen us*** alludes to the enumerable totality of calamities [that befell] ancient Israel. He [i.e., Jeremiah] mentioned them from the beginning of the book until the point where we complete it. Thus he says in summary, ***Remember, O Lord, what has befallen us.***

Remember, O Lord, against the Edomites the day of Jerusalem (Ps 137:7) and also, *Remember, O Lord, how Your servant is disgraced* (*ḥerpat*) (Ps 89:51/50). [These verses] mean: "Oh, how the nations disgrace Your servants and Your friends, and anyone You have honored, such as *the priests, the sons of Aaron* and *the singers, the sons of Levi* and *the sons of David*," as it is said, *with which Your enemies disgrace* (*ḥerfu*), *O LORD, with which they disgrace* (*ḥerfu*) *the footsteps* [*of Your anointed*] (Ps 89:52/51).

We have no measure for the abundance of our sins, for the sake of Your great name, as it is said, *Arise, O God, plead Your cause; remember how the impious disgrace You* (*ḥerpatkha*) *all day!* (Ps 74:22)—[which] means that in invoking the [divine] name, the nations are truly *impious*. This is because God did not honor them, choose them, favor them, or address them, as it is also said, *Remember this, O LORD, how the enemy disgraces* (*ḥeref*), *and an impious people reviles Your name* (Ps 74:18).

In this, the fifth chapter—I mean [the part that begins] ***Remember, O Lord, what has befallen us***—he intends to complete the enumeration of the

[1] Salmon translates Hebr. ḥ/r/f as Arab. ʿ/y/r throughout this passage. It is a challenge to translate these roots consistently; here I have opted for "disgrace." In the biblical verses that Salmon cites, the Hebr. is variously translated (in RSV) as to "defy," "taunt," "mock," "reproach," "rebuke," and "disgrace." See Salmon's comments on Lam 3:30, 3:61.

Jewish Piety in Islamic Jerusalem. Jessica Andruss, Oxford University Press. © Oxford University Press 2023.
DOI: 10.1093/oso/9780197639559.003.0014

hostilities that <168a> the enemies committed against the nation, which they committed against her in ancient times as well as recent times. Just as the ancestors said, *Let not all the hardship seem little to You that has come upon us* (Neh 9:32), so they also appealed to God for help during the affliction that we experience in this exile. [Jeremiah] prefaces this appeal for help [by saying], "Remember *the nations' disgrace* (*ḥerpah*) *against Israel*" because when we searched in our books, we found that whenever one of the *nations* disgraced Israel, God empowered him [i.e., the Israelite] [against the one who disgraced him], as is known from the matter of Goliath the Philistine, who said: *I disgrace* (*ḥerafti*) *the ranks of Israel this day* (1 Sam 17:10). It is also said there, *Surely he has come up to disgrace* (*leḥaref*) *Israel* (1 Sam 17:25), and *He has disgraced* (*ḥeref*) *the armies* [*of the living God*] (1 Sam 17:36). [Goliath] disgraced Israel from time to time. Yet how many [more times] will Israel be disgraced, during over thirteen hundred years of being in *exile* to whenever [the exile] will end for us?! As it is said, *All the day my enemies disgrace me* (*ḥerfuni*), *those who deride me use my name for a curse* (Ps 102:9/8).[2] Similarly, [I am] *a man of contention* [. . .] *all of them curse me* (Jer 15:10).

When Israel is disgraced, God empowers him to destroy [the one who is disgracing], as it is said, *And when he* [i.e., a Philistine giant] *disgraced* (*va-yeḥaref*) *Israel, Jonathan the son of Shim'e-i, David's brother, slew him* (2 Sam 21:21).[3] [Since that is the case for one who disgraces Israel], then how much the more so[4] would God <168b> destroy one who disgraces God and His friends, just as He destroyed Sennacherib when He said, *By your servants you have disgraced* (*ḥerafta*) *the Lord, and you have said, "With my many chariots"* (Isa 37:24).[5] Thereupon God brought retribution upon him, as it is explained in his [i.e., Isaiah's] account. Indeed, disgrace breaks the heart and aggrieves it, as it is said, *Disgrace* (*ḥerfati*) *has broken my heart* (Ps 69:21/20). The Mighty and Sublime informed us that He is merciful to us and helps us, as it is said, *He has sent me to bind up the brokenhearted* (Isa 61:1). The Mighty and Sublime has left us in this *exile* under *the hand of the nations*, as a *disgrace* (*leḥerpah*) *and derision* (Jer 20:8), because of the magnitude of

[2] Salmon clarifies in his comment to Ps 102:9/8: "What the nations rebuke Israel for is their vile deeds of the past and present (*mutaqqadima wa-muta'akhkhira*)" (Pss 90–106).

[3] Wars between Philistines and Israel continued until David and the soldiers slew the four giants, effectively ending the Philistine military threat (2 Sam 21:15–22).

[4] On *'aḥrā wa-'awkad* as "all the more so," see Blau, *Dictionary*, 122, 781.

[5] From Isaiah's message to Hezekiah, in which God promises to defend Jerusalem against Assyrian attack and invasion (Isa 37:21–35).

our sins, as it is said, *You have become guilty by the blood which you have shed* (Ezek 22:4). *Woe to us* (Lam 5:16).

Lamentations 5:2

נַחֲלָתֵנוּ נֶהֶפְכָה לְזָרִים בָּתֵּינוּ לְנָכְרִים:
נחלתנא אנקלבת ללגרבא ביותנא ללאג'נביין

Our inheritance has been turned over to strangers, our homes to foreigners.

Our inheritance is a term that governs itself and others (*menaheg ʿaṣmo ve-menaheg aḥerim*). It is as though [Jeremiah] said: "***Our homes*** *have been turned over* ***to foreigners***." This alludes to the transfer of our inheritance, and returning it to the *nations*, as Micah says in his lament: *In that day they shall take up a taunt song against you, and wail with bitter lamentation,* [*and say, "We are utterly ruined; He changes the portion of my people; how He removes it from me!"*] (Mic 2:4).

As for Israel, [God] will pass judgment upon them. First, there will be no one to divide the land among them by lot until *the time of the end* (Dan 11:35, 12:4; 12:9), as it is said, *Therefore you will have none to cast the line by lot in the assembly of the LORD* (Mic 2:5). And the reason <169a> for this, as he explains, is because of their deeds and [specifically] their seizure of people's estates, as it is said, *Woe to those who devise wickedness and work evil upon their beds!* [. . .] *They covet fields, and seize them* (Mic 2:1–2). Consider this requital: it is said, *Woe to those who devise wickedness*, and the counterpart of this is, *Therefore thus says the LORD: Behold, against this family I am devising evil* (Mic 2:3) and *They covet fields, and seize them* (Mic 2:2). This means that He intends to parcel out this land to our enemies. This requital is also like what is said through Isaiah when he describes their evil deeds, such as: *Woe to those who join house to house, who add field to field* (Isa 5:8). Now, the requital for this deed is: *The LORD of hosts has sworn in my hearing: "Surely many houses shall be desolate"* (Isa 5:9). This means: you had many of these houses because you seized [them]; [now] they will become deserted—these large, good, excellent houses will be destroyed and divided, without a single resident within them. *For ten acres of vineyard shall yield but one bath* (Isa 5:10). Then he describes the scarcity of blessings from the seized estates: from a single tenth of a vineyard of any measure, not one dry measure will come, and the seeds of the land that are produced from it will be the tenth, as it is said, <169b> *and the ephah one tenth of a homer* (Ezek 45:11).

The same [outcome] is known from [the account of] what Ahab did with Naboth the Jezreelite.[6] On account of [Ahab's] deeds—and any that are akin to them or resemble them—they [i.e., the Israelites] deserved to have this holy land seized from them, and [to have] possession given to their enemies, as it is said, *Your country lies desolate, your cities are burned with fire; in your very presence foreigners devour your land; it is desolate, as overthrown by foreigners* (Isa 1:7). That is why our ancestors cried out to God in this circumstance, as it is said, *In the land that You gave to our fathers to enjoy its fruit and its good gifts* [*behold, we are slaves*] (Neh 9:36).

It is even worse that the Lord's house, which they had made, was in the hand of the *nations* [than it is that] the country itself [was conquered]. The *uncircumcised* took possession of *the house of Solomon* and *Zion*, and it was likewise with every place in it that had belonged to Israel. It is mentioned that [the foreigners] triumphed over it and Israel did not have *an open mouth* (Ezek 29:21).[7] And all this was on account of the magnitude of our sins: *Woe to us, for we have sinned!* (Lam 5:16).

Lamentations 5:7

אֲבֹתֵינוּ חָטְאוּ וְאֵינָם וַאֲנַחְנוּ עֲוֹנֹתֵיהֶם סָבָלְנוּ׃
אבאנא אכ'טו וליסהם ונחן ד'נובהם אזדמלנא

Our fathers have sinned, and are no more; and we bear their offenses.[8]

[6] When King Ahab coveted the vineyard of Naboth the Jezreelite, Ahab's wife Jezebel arranged for Naboth to be murdered under false pretenses, in order to remove his claim upon the land that Ahab desired (1 Kgs 21).

[7] I.e., Israel no longer experienced prophecy after the loss of the Temple. On *pithon peh* ("an open mouth"), see James M. Kennedy, "Hebrew *Pitḥôn Peh* in the Book of Ezekiel," *VT* 41, no. 2 (1991): 233–35.

[8] Salmon and Yefet translate this verse almost identically, while Saadia's translation is much looser. In each case, Hebr. *avonot* ("iniquities") is rendered as Arab. *dhunūb* ("offenses"). Al-Fāsī lists Hebr. *avon* with the root ʿ/w/h ("to pervert") because it constitutes a perversion of the truth (vol. II, 377; see also my notes to Salmon's comment to Lam 3:9).

Our fathers have sinned, and are no more means that our fathers sinned and were punished for their deeds by <173a> violent death, plague, hunger, captivity, exile, and all of the calamities that befell them. It was obligatory for their children, the people of the exile, to reflect (*yaʿtabirū*) and to return (*yarjiʿū*) to God, great is His memory, and to repent (*yatūbū*) and not to do as it is said, *we bear their offenses*, which means that we persist in the offenses of our fathers and thereby extend our tarrying in this *exile*.[9]

In this sense, Jeremiah said in another place, *Let us lie down in our shame, and let our dishonor cover us* (Jer 3:25). This dictum is obligatory for us in our prayer, as it is said, *But if they confess their iniquity and the iniquity of their fathers* [. . .] *then I will remember My covenant with Jacob, and I will remember My covenant with Isaac and My covenant with Abraham, and I will remember the land*] (Lev 26:40).[10] We are obliged to recite the psalm, *Who can utter* (Ps 106:2)[11] in our prayers because the *confession of sins*[12] is within it—as it is said, *Both we and our fathers have sinned* (Ps 106:6)[13]—and to prostrate ourselves with our faces on the ground.[14] It is obligatory for anyone who prays these prayers not to revert after the confession of his sins, so that his sins do not become more severe [as they would if he were to] confess his offenses in the morning and then revert to them in the evening. It is said of [such

[9] For a Karaite explanation of this teaching, see Sahl b. Maṣliaḥ: "Know that he who justifies himself by saying, 'I have walked in the way of my fathers' will gain nothing by it, for did not our God say: *Be not like your fathers* (Zech 1:4), and again: *And that they should not be like their fathers, a stubborn and rebellious generation* (Ps 78:8)? This shows that there is no duty resting upon us to follow our fathers unconditionally; rather it is our obligation to scrutinize their ways and to set up their deeds and judgments over against the words of the Law" (*KA*, 118). Sahl's epistle explicitly sets out to correct the Rabbanites. The appearance of a parallel homily here in Salmon's commentary suggests that Salmon is also polemicizing against Rabbanite models of religious behavior. The "fathers" that Salmon has in mind, then, may include the sages from whom the Rabbanites inherited their religious outlook and customs, as well as the Rabbanites themselves.

[10] Salmon reads this conditional language as a command (i.e., "they must confess their iniquity and the iniquity of their fathers," etc.). See his comment to Ps 106:6, in note below.

[11] I.e., all of Ps 106, not this verse alone.

[12] Hebr. *vidduy avonot*.

[13] See Salmon's comment to Ps 106:6: "Then we learn how we are obliged to confess offenses, because [God] made this obligatory for us when He said in the *Torah*, *But if they confess their offense* (Lev 26:40). Thus: 'You must state, and then annihilate, [all] kinds of sins, including sin, *offense*, and *evil*.' Thus he mentions [them] all" (Pss 90–106).

[14] Here Salmon links prostration with confession; elsewhere he links prostration with prayer (e.g., Lam 3:41; Ps 5:4/3). The specification "with our faces on the ground" may be a form of prostration used during confession, or a general description of prostration. Medieval Jewish practices of prostration are not well known. Roberto Tottoli mentions prostration among Jews and Christians in pre-Islamic and early Islamic periods, but he focuses on Christian examples; see "Muslim Attitudes Toward Prostration (*sujūd*): I. Arabs and Prostration at the Beginning of Islam and in the Qurʾān," *Studia Islamica* 88 (1998), 6–15. Marion Holmes Katz cites Muslim legal scholars who represent prostration as a universal practice: *Prayer in Islamic Thought and Practice* (Cambridge: Cambridge University Press, 2013), 85–87.

people], *And the Lord said: "Because this people draw near with their mouth and burden Me with their lips, [while their hearts are far from Me, and their fear of Me is a commandment of men learned by rote"*] (Isa 29:13).[15]

According to God, this is blameworthy. And so it is obligatory for us, O my brothers, to counsel ourselves, and not to make contract with what does not remain—with what perishes—<173b> and not to forfeit eternal bliss for fleeting bliss. O Israel, repent (*tūbū*) and return (*irjiʿū*) to the Merciful One! Pity your souls for the Day of Judgment,[16] for *a day of rebuke* (Hos 5:9),[17] for *a day of vengeance* (Jer 46:10), for a day of *burning like an oven*, as it is said, *"For behold, the day comes, burning like an oven"* (Mal 3:19/4:1).

One scholar has said that the meaning of ***and we bear their offenses*** is that we are imprisoned in this *exile* because of the deeds of our fathers who came before, and that this is like what happened to the *generation of the wilderness*, since it is said, *And your children shall be shepherds in the wilderness forty years, and shall suffer for your faithlessness* (Num 14:33). This statement errs in two respects. The first respect is that God does not requite the children for the offenses of their fathers and He does not requite the fathers for the offenses of their children, just as He does not reward the children for the obedience of their fathers and He does not reward the fathers for the obedience of their sons. Indeed, this holy book stipulates[18] that *the soul that sins shall die. The son shall not suffer for the iniquity of the father, nor the father suffer for the iniquity of the son; the righteousness of the righteous shall be upon himself, and the wickedness of the wicked shall be upon himself* (Ezek 18:20).[19]

[15] Karaite polemicists routinely invoke Isa 29:13 to attack Rabbanites for following a law of human, rather than divine, origin (for an early attestation, see al-Qūmisī, Sermon, 77). Thus, the prooftext here implies that Rabbanites confess their sins and then revert to them, and it underscores Salmon's argument that Rabbanite sins impede the movement toward piety and redemption. I have modified the RSV translation of Isa 29:13 to better reflect Salmon's Karaite reading: rather than "[they] honor me with their lips," I have rendered k/b/d (Piel) as "[they] burden."

[16] Hebr. *yom ha-din*. Although the Arab. phrase *yawm al-dīn* is common in the Qur'ān and later Islamic discourse, the expression is not biblical, unlike the other expressions that Salmon chains together here.

[17] Cf. RSV: "day of punishment."

[18] *Naṣṣ hādhā l-kitāb al-muqaddas*. Salmon may understand the following statement—that only the sinner will die—as a general principle recorded in Scripture.

[19] I have not been able to identify the exact source of the interpretation that Salmon recounts here. However, some Midrashic passages attempt to reconcile Ezek 18:20 with contradictory biblical statements about the communicability of sin between generations. E.g.: "One verse says, 'visiting the guilt of the parents upon the children' (Exod 20:5), and one verse says, 'A parent shall not share the burden of a child's guilt, nor shall a child share the burden of the parent's guilt' (Ezek 18:20). [This means] if the parents were guiltless, [God] will suspend [retribution] for them [i.e., the children]. But if not, He will not suspend [retribution] for them. They told a parable: To what is the matter alike?

The other respect [in which the scholar errs] concerns the forty-year delay for the *generation of the wilderness*. Rather, it was to destroy the fathers—the judgment of destruction was upon them—as it is said, *In this wilderness they shall come to a full end, and there they shall die* (Num 14:35). <174a> Thus, [God] said, *shall suffer for your faithlessness* (Num 14:33), so that the children would grow up and enter into the land with knowledge and they would be strong and they would fight. The meaning of *shall suffer for your faithlessness* alludes to them [i.e., the children] being detained because you [i.e., the fathers] exceeded all bounds of iniquity. In other words, "So that you will perish just as they perished," as it is said, *after all the men of war had perished* (Deut 2:16). At that point [i.e., after the older generation had perished], [the children] were commanded to enter the land.

There is also a distinction between the people of the *exile* and the children of the people of the wilderness, which is that the children of the *generation of the wilderness* were *righteous*, as it is said, *But you who held fast to the LORD your God are all alive this day* (Deut 4:4). Regarding the people of the exile, however, it is said, *their iniquities and their fathers' iniquities together, says the LORD* (Isa 65:7). It is said about [the people of the exile], *They have all gone astray, they are all alike corrupt; there is none that does good* (Ps 14:3).[20] He eloquently expressed [this] in the *covenant*, with the meaning that we mentioned: *And those of you that are left shall pine away in your enemies' lands because of their iniquity, and also because of the iniquities of their fathers they shall pine away like them* (Lev 26:39). *Those of you that are left shall pine away in your enemies' lands because of their iniquity* indicates that the people of the exile will be requited for their [own] offenses. *And also because of the iniquities of their fathers they shall pine away like them* (Lev 26:39) means from what is in their hand as well as the offense of their fathers, as it is said, ***and we bear their offenses***. Therefore we say, *Woe to us, for we have sinned!* (Lam 5:16).

It is like one who borrowed 100 *maneh* and he forgave him of the debt. His son came and borrowed 100 *maneh* from the king, and he forgave him of the debt. Then the son's son came and borrowed 100 *maneh* from the king, and he forgave him of the debt. He didn't lend the fourth [son], because of his forefathers, because they had to be forgiven [of their deeds]. And thus Scripture states, 'Our fathers have sinned and are no more, and we must bear their guilt' (Lam 5:7)"; see David W. Nelson, trans., *Mekhilta de-Rabbi Shimon bar Yoḥai*, Tractate Baḥodesh (Philadelphia: JPS, 2006), 153.

[20] Salmon's comment to Ps 14:3 also considers this verse to be a depiction of the people of the exile: "Indeed, this description describes our era, and it is said about us, *They have all gone astray*" (Pss 11–41).

Lamentations 5:15

שָׁבַת מְשׂוֹשׂ לִבֵּנוּ נֶהְפַּךְ לְאֵבֶל מְחֹלֵנוּ׃
עטל סרור קלבנא אנקלב ללחזן טבלנא

The joy of our heart has ceased; our drumming has been turned to mourning.[21]

Since he mentioned above the cessation of the beauty and excellence of this nation, he follows that by saying, שָׁבַת מְשׂוֹשׂ — "all our joys have come to an end," as it is said, *And I will make to cease from the cities of Judah and from the streets of Jerusalem the voice of mirth and the voice of gladness* (Jer 7:34) and *I will put an end to all her mirth* (Hos 2:13/11). ***Our dancing has been turned to mourning*** means that whatever was joyous (*ṭarab*) was reversed, as it is said, *The mirth of the timbrels is stilled* (Isa 24:8) and *I will turn your feasts into mourning, and all your songs into lamentation* (Amos 8:10). *Woe to us, for we have sinned!* (Lam 5:16).

Lamentations 5:16

נָפְלָה עֲטֶרֶת רֹאשֵׁנוּ אוֹי־נָא לָנוּ כִּי חָטָאנוּ׃
וקעת עצאבה רווסנא אלויל לנא אן אכ'טינא

The crown has fallen from our head; woe to us, for we have sinned!

<177b> ***The crown has fallen from our head*** alludes first to *the house of the LORD*, as it is said, *Our holy Temple, our pride* (*tif'artenu*) (Isa 64:10/11),[22] and then to the power of the state, as it is said, *Say to the king and queen mother, "Take a lowly seat"* (Jer 13:18) and as it is said in the second chapter of this book, *He has thrown down from heaven to earth the splendor* (*tif'eret*) (Lam 2:1). He spoke of the kingdom of Ephraim just as he

[21] Salmon translates Hebr. *meḥolenu* ("our dancing") as Arab. *ṭablnā* ("our drumming") in MSS except Or. 2515, which reads *faraḥnā* ("our joy"). *Ṭablnā* may be a textual corruption of *ṭarabnā* ("our joy"), since Salmon uses *ṭarab* in the comment. However, connections between dancing and drumming are well attested, even in the Bible (e.g., Jer 31:4). See Abdul-Karim, 85.

[22] Cf. RSV: "our holy and beautiful house."

describes the end of state power in the kingdom of Judah: *Behold, the Lord has one who is mighty and strong; like a storm of hail* [*a destroying tempest, like a storm of mighty, overflowing waters, he will cast down to the earth with violence.*] *The proud crown* (*ʿateret*) *of the drunkards of Ephraim will be trodden under foot; and the fading flower of its glorious beauty* (*tifʾarto*) (Isa 28:2–4).

Woe to us, for we have sinned informs us of the reason that He made this nobility end—namely, because our sins were vast and our offenses were many—in order to direct our attention to repentance and returning to God, as it is said, *Return, O Israel, to the LORD your God, for you have stumbled because of your iniquity. Take words with you and return to the LORD* (Hos 14:1/2–2/3). Yet Israel persisted in all of that with obstinacy and sin; they backslid in [their] repentance, as it is said, *You have rejected me, says the LORD, you keep going backward* (Jer 15:6).

Lamentations 5:17

עַל־זֶה הָיָה דָוֶה לִבֵּנוּ עַל־אֵלֶּה חָשְׁכוּ עֵינֵינוּ׃
עלי הד'א צאר וג'ע קלבנא עלי הד'א אט'למת אעיננא

For this our heart ails, for these things our eyes have grown dim,

<178a> Since [Jeremiah] mentions the falling of the crown from [our] head, and he ends that [verse] by mentioning sin, [here] he says: ***For this our heart ails.*** He means that just as our hearts are pained by the falling of our crown, so is it obligatory for our hearts to be pained over our sins and offenses. Who is able to count the quantity of our grief and sorrows? For it is said about all of this, *For my groans are many and my heart ails* (Lam 1:22) and *My grief is beyond healing, my heart ails within me* (Jer 8:18).

For these things our eyes have grown dim means the darkening of our faces and the dimming of our eyes due to the calamities that he has enumerated. That is why he said, ***For these things our eyes have grown dim.*** Just as he enumerated the calamities from the first book, then he said about all of them, *For these things I weep* (Lam 1:16), so does he describe here the grave catastrophes and says that it is on their account [that we suffer]: ***For these things our eyes have grown dim.***

Lamentations 5:18

עַל הַר־צִיּוֹן שֶׁשָּׁמֵם שׁוּעָלִים הִלְּכוּ בוֹ:
עלי ג'בל ציון תוחש אלת'עאלב סלבו פיה

For Mount Zion which lies desolate; jackals plunder it.[23]

After saying, *for this our heart ails* (Lam 5:17) he now describes two terrible circumstances. First: the destruction of Zion, as it is said, *Zion shall be plowed as a field; Jerusalem shall become a heap of ruins* (Mic 3:12; Jer 26:18), and *Zion has become a wilderness, Jerusalem a desolation. Our holy* <178b> *and beautiful house* (Isa 64:9/10–10/11).

[Second]: after the destruction, ***jackals plunder it***. Even worse than *the jackals* are *the impure, the uncircumcised, adulterers, nocturnal emitters, prostitutes, menstruants, lepers, porters of funeral biers, and those who make the eastern gate a house of filth, just as they are rebuked and reviled within it. Five times every day they proclaim*[24] *the name of the idol and the statue and the image,* [*they make*] *the house of slaughter a resting-place, the house of their worship, and they also proclaim the name of the false prophet. They stand and throw stones at the Israelites—the chosen ones, and the sons of Aaron who serve the Lord—when they approach the holy gate. We are in great strife— Woe to us, for we have sinned!* (Lam 5:16).[25]

Lamentations 5:19

אַתָּה יְהוָה לְעוֹלָם תֵּשֵׁב כִּסְאֲךָ לְדֹר וָדוֹר:
אנת יא רב ללאבד תת'בת כרסיך לג'יל וג'יל

But you, O LORD, reign forever; Your throne endures to all generations.

[23] Cf. RSV: "Jackals prowl over it."

[24] Arab. *mukhrizim* (see Blau, *Dictionary*, 592). The Hebr. cognate, *makhrizim*, is post-biblical (Jastrow, *Dictionary*, 664). The verb is repeated in the next line.

[25] Salmon's transition to Hebrew may signal reticence to insult Islam and Christianity in the lingua franca, or perhaps he considers biblical language more fitting for his message. Salmon uses similar polemical language to describe the presence of non-Jews on the Temple Mount in his comments at Lam 1:7, 2:7; Ps 38:10; and Eccl 9:6. For the latter passage and bibliography on Karaite anti-Christian and anti-Muslim polemics, see Robinson, *Asceticism*, 496–97 and notes there.

Since he began this chapter with the verse *Remember, O LORD, what has befallen us* (Lam 5:1) as a way of prompting sympathy, now he ends it in the same way by saying, "O Lord, You remain steadfast forever. Our lifespan is short; bring us out of this *exile*." It is a convention of the prophets to mention the brevity of the [human] lifespan and to ask about the proximity of *redemption* (*ge'ulah*). I have explained <179a> these tendencies in *a prayer of Moses* (i.e., Ps 90).[26] ***Your throne endures to all generations*** alludes to [God's] judgment over the enemies, as it is said, *He has established His throne for judgment* (Ps 9:8/7).[27]

Lamentations 5:20

לָמָּה לָנֶצַח תִּשְׁכָּחֵנוּ תַּעַזְבֵנוּ לְאֹרֶךְ יָמִים:
לא ללגאיה תנסאנא תתרכנא לטול אלאיאם

You will not forget us forever, [or] forsake us for so long.[28]

This means: how long will we be abandoned in this *exile*? This is like the words of David: *How long, O Lord? Will You forget me forever?* (Ps 13:2/1), and all of the psalms, as we have explained elsewhere.[29]

[26] In his comment to Ps 90:1 (*Lord, You have been our refuge in all generations*), Salmon identifies biblical verses that contrast the brevity of the human lifespan with the eternity of God (e.g., Ps 89:48/47 and Ps 90:10). In the case of Ps 90:1, Salmon explains that Moses "begins first by announcing the excellence of the Creator who is pre-existent (*qadīm*), the world which is new (*muḥdath*), and the human who perishes" (Salmon, Pss 90–106).

[27] The enemies are mentioned in the previous verse (Ps 9:7/6). Salmon gives a perfunctory reading of Ps 9:8/7 in his Psalms commentary: "It means that He is mighty and sublime, enduring forever" (Salmon, Pss 1–10).

[28] Cf. RSV: "Why do You forget us forever, why do You so long forsake us?" Salmon renders Hebr. *lāmmā* ("why?") as the Arab. particle of negation (*lā'* or *lam*), thus transforming a plaintive question into the confident assertion that God will not forget forever. This substitution appears throughout Salmon's commentary on the Psalms, as a technique for transforming accusations of divine neglect into the denial of such abandonment. See, e.g., Salmon's translations of Pss 10:1, 43:2, and 43:24. Saadia uses the same technique, for Lam 5:1 and elsewhere (see Ratzaby, *Targum*, 106, and Abdul-Karim, 85); Yefet does not.

[29] In his comment on Ps 13:1, Salmon includes this psalm in the category of those that "complain about the matter of exile." He explains that Israelite sins have led to the concealment of God's face through long years of exile, and he enumerates the periods of exile from the time of Isaac and Jacob through the Babylonian exile and the current period of exile following the destruction of the Second Temple (Pss 11–41).

Lamentations 5:21

הֲשִׁיבֵנוּ יְהוָה אֵלֶיךָ וְנָשׁוּבָה חַדֵּשׁ יָמֵינוּ כְּקֶדֶם׃
רדנא יא רב אליך ונרג'ע ג'דד איאמנא מת'ל אלזמאן אלקדים

Bring us back to you, O LORD, that we may return! Renew our days as of old!

This means: "Smooth the way, so that the paths of obedience are clear for us." As Jeremiah said in another place, *Bring me back, let me come back, for You are the LORD my God* (Jer 31:17/18) and likewise, *Restore us again, O God of our salvation* (Ps 85:5/4).[30] He is also striving for the reunification of Israel, as the Mighty and Sublime promised. ***Renew our days as of old***—He had announced this good news through Jeremiah in the verses *Their children shall be as of old* (Jer 30:20) and *Then the offering of Judah and Jerusalem will be pleasing to the LORD as in the days of old* (Mal 3:4).

Lamentations 5:22

כִּי אִם־מָאֹס מְאַסְתָּנוּ קָצַפְתָּ עָלֵינוּ עַד־מְאֹד׃
אן ואן זהאדה זהדת בנא סכ'טת עלינא ג'דא

Even though You had rejected us [and] You were <179b> exceedingly angry with us.[31]

Have mercy upon us, with Your excellence, and bring us back to You, just as You promised us when You said, *I will give them one heart and one way, that they may fear Me for all time,* [*for their own good and the good of their children after them*] (Jer 32:39). And [You] also said through Ezekiel, *A new heart I will give you, and a new spirit I will put within you; and I will remove from your body the heart of stone and give you a heart of flesh* (Ezek 36:26).[32]

[30] Salmon identifies this verse as a call of petition to God (Salmon, Pss 73–89).

[31] This verse poses interpretive challenges, both grammatically (i.e., how to understand *ki 'im*) and theologically (i.e., it is problematic for a lament psalm, in which lamentation is intended to inspire divine aid, to conclude with assertions of divine abandonment). The theological difficulty has led to the Jewish liturgical convention—unremarked upon here by Salmon—of repeating the more appropriate penultimate verse after reciting Lam 5:22. Salmon renders Hebr. *ki 'im* with Arab. *an wa-in* ("even though"), both here and in Lam 3:32. For discussion, see Robert Gordis, "Critical Notes: The Conclusion of the Book of Lamentations (5:22)," *JBL* 93, no. 2 (1974): 289–93, and note that Gordis resolves the conundrum in the same way that Salmon does in his translation.

[32] Salmon's final verse comment is strongly homiletical.

Glossary of Salmon's Arabic Terms

ACHE—*alam*

AFFLICTION—*balā'*

ALLEGORY—*mathal*

ALLUDE—*yushīr*

AMUSEMENT; JOY—*ṭarab*

ARGUMENT—*ḥujja*

ASSEMBLY; COMMUNITY; CONGREAGTION—*jamā'a*

BENEFICENCE; EXCELLENCE—*iḥsān*

BENEVOLENCE—*luṭf*

BLESSING; GRACE—*ni'ma*

BLISS—*ladhdha*

CALAMITIES—*maṣā'ib* (sing. *muṣiba*)

CHASTISEMENTS—*'adāb*

CHEER—*ṭīb*

COMFORTER—*mu'azzin*

COMPASSION—*shafaqa*

COMPLAINT; GRIEVANCE—*shakwa*

CONFESSION—*iqrār*

CONSOLATION—*'azā'*

CRIMES—*jarā'im* (sing. *jarīma*)

DAMAGE—*adhan*

DEGRADATION—*hawān*

DELIGHT—*surūr*

DISDAIN—*istiḥfāf*

DISPERSAL—*tabdīd*

DISTRESS—*ghamm*

DIVINE GLORY—*waqar*

DUTY; OBLIGATION—*wujūb*

EQUITY; FAIRNESS—*naṣafa*

EXCELLENCE—*ḥusn*

GRACE—*faḍl*

GRAVE OFFENSES—*kabāʾir* (sing. *kabīra*)

GRIEF—*ḥasra*

HARDSHIP—*shadīda*

HARDSHIP; ADVERSITY—*ʿanat*

INSTRUCTION—*taʿlīm*

JOY—*faraḥ*

KINDLINESS—*raʾfa*

KINDNESS—*faḍl*

LAMENT—*nawḥ*

LAMENTER—*nāʾiḥ*

TO LIKEN; TO COMPARE—*maththala*

LIKENING; ANALOGY—*tamthīl*

LOWLY—*dhull*

MISERY—*shaqāʾ*

MOURNING—*ḥuzn; taḥazzun*

NATION—*umma*

OFFENSES—*dhunūb* (sing. *dhanb*)

PAIN—*wajaʿ*

PAINS—*āfāt*

PARABLE—*mathal*

PARDON—*safḥ*

PATIENCE; FORBEARANCE—*ṣabr*

PENITENT—*tāʾib*

PRIEST—*imām*

PRIESTHOOD—*imāma*

PROSTRATION—*sujūd*

REBELLIONS; DISOBEDIENCE—*maʿāṣī*

RECOMPENSE—*mukāfāh*

REGRET—*taʾassuf*

RENOUNCE—*zahida*

REPENTANCE—*tawba*

REQUITAL—*muqābala*

RETRIBUTION; VENGEANCE—*niqma*

REVERENCE—*hayba*

REVERSAL—*ʿaks*

RIGHTEOUS ONES—*ṣāliḥīn*

RUIN—*talaf*

SCATTERING—*tashtīt*

SEEMLY—*jamīl*

SIGN—*āya*

SINS—*khaṭāyā* (sing. *khaṭāʾ*)

SPLENDOR—*fakhr*

STATEHOOD—*dawla*

SUCCOR—*ghiyāth*

SUFFERANCE—*iḥtimāl*

SUPPORT—*nuṣr*; *nuṣra*

SYMPATHY—*taḥannun*

TEMPLE—*quds*

TORMENT—*maḍḍ*

TRIALS—*miḥan*

TUMULT; CONFUSION—*tashwīsh*

UNSEEMLY—*ghayr jamīl*

VILE; REPREHENSIBLE—*qabīh*

WAYS—*madhāhib* (sing. *madhhab*)

WORRY; SEVERE DISTRESS—*ightimām*

WRONGDOING—*ẓulm*

Bibliography

Manuscripts

Salmon b. Yerūḥīm, Invocation to the Commentary on Lamentations
Collated by Daniel Frank:
JTSA Ms. Mic. 3362 (Adler 14)
RNL Evr. I 561

Salmon b. Yerūḥīm, Commentary on Psalms
RNL Evr. Arab. I 1345 (IMHM 55207); transcribed by James T. Robinson
RNL Evr. I 556 (IMHM 52708); transcribed by Daniel Frank
RNL Evr. I 557 (IMHM 50970); transcribed by James T. Robinson
RNL Evr. I 558 (IMHM 53303); transcribed by James T. Robinson

Yefet ben ʿEli, Commentary on Isaiah
BL Or. 2502 (Marg. 281) (F6275); transcribed by James T. Robinson

Yefet ben ʿEli, Commentary on Lamentations
Preliminary edition by Daniel Frank on the basis of:
RNL Evr. Arab. I 213
RNL Evr. Arab. I 3806

Printed Sources

Abdul-Karim, Mohammed Abdul-Latif. *Commentary of Salmon Ben Yeruham on Lamentations*. Ph.D. diss., University of St Andrews, 1976.

Abdul-Raof, Hussein. *Arabic Rhetoric: A Pragmatic Analysis*. Culture and Civilization in the Middle East. New York: Routledge, 2006.

Ahmed, Ziauddin. "The Concept of Jizya in Early Islam." *Islamic Studies* 14 (1975): 293–305.

Albrektson, Bertil. *Studies in the Text and Theology of the Book of Lamentations with a Critical Edition of the Peshitta Text*. Studia Theologica Lundensia 21. Lund, Sweden: Gleerup, 1963.

Alexander, Philip S. *The Targum of Lamentations*. The Aramaic Bible 17b. Collegeville, Minn.: Liturgical Press, 2007.

Alexander, Philip S. "The Mourners for Zion and the Suffering Messiah: *Pesikta rabbati* 34—Structure, Theology, and Context." In *Midrash Unbound: Transformations and Innovations*, edited by Michael Fishbane and Joanna Weinberg, 137–57. Oxford: Littman Library of Jewish Civilization, 2013.

Ali, Samer M. *Arabic Literary Salons in the Islamic Middle Ages: Poetry, Public Performance, and the Presentation of the Past*. Poetics of Orality and Literacy. Notre Dame, Ind.: University of Notre Dame Press, 2010.

Allen, Leslie C. "Ezekiel 24:3–14: A Rhetorical Perspective." *Catholic Biblical Quarterly* 49 (1987): 404–14.

Alobaidi, Joseph. *Le Commentaire des Psaumes par le Qaraïte Salmon ben Yeruham (Psaumes 1–10): Introduction, Édition, Traduction*. Berlin: Peter Lang, 1996.

Alobaidi, Joseph. *The Book of Daniel: The Commentary of R. Saadia Gaon: Edition and Translation*. Berlin: Peter Lang, 2006.

Alter, Robert. *The Art of Biblical Poetry*. New York: Basic Books, 1985.

Amaru, Betsy Halpern. "The Killing of the Prophets: Unraveling a Midrash." *Hebrew Union College Annual* 54 (1983): 153–80.

Anderson, Gary. *A Time to Mourn, A Time to Dance: The Expression of Grief and Joy in Israelite Religion*. University Park: Pennsylvania State University Press, 1991.

Assaf, Simḥah. "Prayer by Salman ben Yerūḥam [?] the Karaite" [Hebrew]. *Zion* 3 (1928–29): 88–94.

Astren, Fred. *Karaite Judaism and Historical Understanding*. Columbia: University of South Carolina Press, 2004.

Astren, Fred. "The Dead Sea Scrolls and Medieval Jewish Studies: Methods and Problems." *Dead Sea Discoveries* 8, no. 2 (2001): 105–23.

Barmash, Pamela. "At the Nexus of History and Memory: The Ten Lost Tribes." *Association for Jewish Studies Review* 29, no. 2 (2005): 207–36.

Barney, Stephen A., W. J. Lewis, J. A. Beach, Oliver Barney, and Muriel Hall. *The* Etymologies *of Isidore of Seville*. Cambridge: Cambridge University Press, 2006.

Barth, Lewis M. "The 'Three of Rebuke and Seven of Consolation': Sermons in the 'Pesikta de Rav Kahana.'" *Journal of Jewish Studies* 33 (1982): 503–16.

Ben-Shammai, Haggai. "Rabbanite and Karaite Attitudes Toward Aliya." *The Jerusalem Cathedra* 3 (1983): 190–91.

Ben-Shammai, Haggai. "The Attitude of Some Early Karaites Towards Islam." In *Studies in Medieval Jewish History and Literature*, vol. 2, edited by Isadore Twersky, 3–40. Cambridge, Mass.: Harvard University Press, 1984.

Ben-Shammai, Haggai. "Fragments of Daniel al-Qūmisī's Commentary on the Book of Daniel as a Historical Source." *Henoch* 13 (1991): 259–81.

Ben-Shammai, Haggai. "Return to the Scriptures in Ancient and Medieval Judaism and Early Islam." In *Les retours aux écritures: fondalmentalismes présents et passés*, edited by Évelyne Patlagean and Alain Le Bouilluec, 319–39. Louvain-Paris: Peeters, 1993.

Ben-Shammai, Haggai. "Poetic Works and Lamentations of Qaraite 'Mourners of Zion'—Structure and Contents" [Hebrew]. In *Kenesset Ezra: Literature and Life in the Synagogue; Studies Presented to Ezra Fleischer*, edited by Shulamit Elitsur, Mosheh David Her, Avigdor Shinan, and Gershon Shaked, 191–234. Jerusalem: Ben Zvi, 1994.

Ben-Shammai, Haggai. "A Unique Lamentation on Jerusalem by the Karaite Author Yeshuʿa ben Judah" [Hebrew]. In *Masʿat Moshe: Studies in Jewish and Islamic Culture Presented to Moshe Gil*, edited by Ezra Fleischer, Mordechai Akiva Friedman, and Joel Kraemer, 93–102. Jerusalem: Bialik Institute, 1998.

Ben-Shammai, Haggai. "Jerusalem in Early Medieval Jewish Bible Exegesis." In *Jerusalem: Its Sanctity and Centrality to Judaism, Christianity, and Islam*, edited by Lee I. Levine, 447–66. New York: Continuum, 1999.

Ben-Shammai, Haggai. "Kalām in Medieval Jewish Philosophy." In *History of Jewish Philosophy*, Routledge History of World Philosophies 2, edited by Daniel H. Frank and Oliver Leaman, 115–48. New York: Routledge, 2003.

Ben-Shammai, Haggai. "Major Trends in Karaite Philosophy and Polemics in the Tenth and Eleventh Centuries." In *Karaite Judaism: A Guide to Its History and Literary Sources*, Handbuch der Orientalistik 73, edited by Meira Polliack, 339–61. Leiden: Brill, 2003.

Ben-Shammai, Haggai. "The Tension Between Literal Interpretation and Exegetical Freedom: Comparative Observations on Saadia's Method." In *With Reverence for the Word: Medieval Scriptural Exegesis in Judaism, Christianity, and Islam*, edited by Jane Dammen McAuliffe, Barry D. Walfish, and Joseph W. Goering, 33–50. Oxford: Oxford University Press, 2003.

Ben-Shammai, Haggai, and Bruno Chiesa. "Fragments from the Commentary of Saadia Gaon to the Scroll of Lamentations" [Hebrew]. *Ginzei Qedem* 3 (2007): 29–87.

Berkey, Jonathan P. *Popular Preaching and Religious Authority in the Medieval Islamic Near East*. Seattle: University of Washington Press, 2001.

Berlin, Adele. *The Dynamics of Biblical Parallelism*. Bloomington, Ind.: Indiana University Press, 1985.

Berlin, Adele. *Lamentations: A Commentary*. Old Testament Library. Louisville, Ky.: Westminster John Knox, 2002.

Berlin, Adele. "Psalms and the Literature of Exile: Psalms 137, 44, 69, and 78." In *The Book of Psalms: Composition and Reception*, Supplements to the *Vetus Testamentum* 99, Formation and Interpretation of Old Testament Literature 4, edited by Peter W. Flint and Patrick D. Miller, 65–86. Leiden: Brill, 2005.

Berlin, Adele. "On Writing a Commentary on Lamentations." In *Lamentations in Ancient and Contemporary Cultural Contexts*, Society of Biblical Literature Symposium Series 43, edited by Nancy C. Lee and Carleen Mandofolo, 3–12. Atlanta, Ga.: Society of Biblical Literature, 2008.

Blau, Joshua. *A Dictionary of Medieval Judaeo-Arabic Texts*. Jerusalem: Israel Academy of Sciences and Humanities, 2006.

Bosworth, David A. "Daughter Zion and Weeping in Lamentations 1–2." *Journal for the Study of the Old Testament* 38, no. 2 (2013): 217–37.

Brady, Christian M. M. *The Rabbinic Targum Lamentations: Vindicating God*. Studies in Aramaic Interpretation of Scripture 3. Leiden: Brill, 2003.

Brady, Christian M. M. "Targum Lamentations." In *Great Is Thy Faithfulness? Reading Lamentations as Sacred Scripture*, edited by Robin A. Parry and Heath A. Thomas, 70–76. Eugene, Ore.: Pickwick, 2011.

Braude, William G., and Israel J. Kapstein, trans. *Pesikta de Ṙab Kahana: R. Kahana's Compilation of Discourses for Sabbaths and Festal Days*. 1975. Reprint, Philadelphia: Jewish Publication Society, 2002.

Brody, Robert. *The Geonim of Babylonia and the Shaping of Medieval Jewish Culture*. New Haven, Conn.: Yale University Press, 1998.

Brown, Francis, S. R. Driver, and Charles A. Briggs. *Hebrew and English Lexicon of the Old Testament*. Cambridge: Riverside Press, 1906.

Buber, Salomon, ed. *Midrasch Echa Rabbati*. 1899. Reprint, Hildesheim: Georg Olms, 1967.

Chiesa, Bruno, and Wilfrid Lockwood, eds. *Yaʿqūb al-Qirqisānī on Jewish Sects and Christianity: A Translation of "Kitāb al-anwār," Book I, with Two Introductory Essays*. Frankfurt am Main: Lang, 1984.

Cohen, A., trans. *Midrash Rabbah Lamentations*. 1939. Reprint, London: Soncino, 1983.

Cohen, Mark R. *Poverty and Charity in the Jewish Community of Medieval Egypt* Princeton, N.J.: Princeton University Press, 2006.

Cohen, Mordechai Z. *Three Approaches to Biblical Metaphor: From Abraham Ibn Ezra and Maimonides to David Kimhi*. Études sur le Judaïsme Médiéval 26. Leiden: Brill, 2003.

Cohen, Norman J. "Structure and Editing in the Homiletic Midrashim." *Association for Jewish Studies Review* 6 (1981): 1–20.

Cooper, Alan. "The Message of Lamentations." *Journal of Ancient Near Eastern Studies* 28 (2001): 1–18.

Davidson, Israel. *The Wars of the Lord: The Complete Arguments of the Karaite Salmon ben Yeruḥim Against Rav Saʿadyah Ga'on*. New York: Bet Midrash ha-Rabanim de-'Amerikah, 1934.

de Hoop, Raymond. "Lamentations: The Qinah-Metre Questioned." In *Delimitation Criticism: A New Tool in Biblical Scholarship*, edited by Marjo Korpel and Josef Oesch, 80–104. Assen, the Netherlands: Van Gorcum, 2000.

Derenbourg, Joseph, Hartwig Derenbourg, Mayer Lambert, and Wilhelm Bacher. *Version Arabe du Livre de Job de R. Saadia ben Iosef al-Fayyoûmî*. Paris, 1899. Reprinted as *Saadia Ben Josef Al-Fayyoûmî: Œvres Complètes*. 2 vols. Hildesheim: Georg Olms Verlag, 1979.

Destro, Adriana. *The Law of Jealousy: Anthropology of Sotah*. Brown Judaic Studies 181. Providence, R.I.: Brown University Press, 1989.

Dobbs-Allsopp, F. W. *Weep, O Daughter of Zion: A Study of the City-Lament Genre in the Hebrew Bible*. Rome: Pontifico Biblico, 1993.

Dobbs-Allsopp, F. W. "Tragedy, Tradition, and Theology in the Book of Lamentations." *Biblical Interpretation* 7 (1999): 235–71.

Dobbs-Allsopp, F. W. *Lamentations: A Bible Commentary for Teaching and Preaching*. Louisville, Ky.: John Knox, 2002.

Drory, Rina. *Models and Contacts: Arabic Literature and Its Impact on Medieval Jewish Culture*. Leiden: Brill, 2000.

Duri, ʿAbdul ʿAziz. "Notes on Taxation in Early Islam." *Journal of the Economic and Social History of the Orient* 17 (1974): 136–44.

Epstein, I., ed. *The Babylonian Talmud*. 35 vol. London: Soncino, 1935–52.

Erder, Yoram. "The Negation of Exile in the Messianic Doctrine of the Karaite Mourners of Zion." *Hebrew Union College Annual* 68 (1997): 109–40.

Erder, Yoram. "The Mourners of Zion: Karaites in Jerusalem in the Tenth and Eleventh Centuries." In *Karaite Judaism: A Guide to Its History and Literary Sources*, Handbuch der Orientalistik 73, edited by Meira Polliack, 213–35. Leiden: Brill, 2003.

Erder, Yoram. *The Karaite Mourners of Zion and the Qumran Scrolls: On the History of an Alternative to Rabbinic Judaism*. Turnhout, Belgium: Brepols, 2017.

Ferris, Paul Wayne, Jr. *The Genre of Communal Lament in the Bible and the Ancient Near East*. Atlanta, Ga.: Scholars Press, 1992.

Feuerstein, Salomon. *Der Commentar des Karaërs Salmon ben Jerucham zu den Klaglierdern*. Krakau: 1898.

Fokkelman, J. P. *Reading Biblical Poetry: An Introductory Guide*. Translated by Ineke Smit. Louisville, Ky.: Westminster John Knox, 2001.

Frank, Daniel. "The *Shoshanim* of Tenth-Century Jerusalem: Karaite Exegesis, Prayer, and Communal Identity." In *The Jews of Medieval Islam: Community, Society, and*

Identity. Études sur le Judaïsme Médiéval 16, edited by Daniel Frank, 199–245. Leiden: Brill, 1995.

Frank, Daniel. "Karaite Exegesis." In *Hebrew Bible/Old Testament: The History of Its Interpretation*, vol. 1, bk. 2, edited by Magne Saebø, 110–28. Gottingen, Germany: Vandenhoeck & Ruprecht, 2000.

Frank, Daniel. "Karaite Commentaries on the Song of Songs from Tenth-Century Jerusalem." In *With Reverence for the Word: Medieval Scriptural Exegesis in Judaism, Christianity, and Islam*, edited by Jane Dammen McAuliffe, Barry D. Walfish, and Joseph W. Goering, 51–69. Oxford: Oxford University Press, 2003.

Frank, Daniel. "Karaite Prayer and Liturgy." In *Karaite Judaism: A Guide to Its History and Literary Sources*, Handbuch der Orientalistik 73, edited by Meira Polliack, 559–89. Leiden: Brill, 2003.

Frank, Daniel. *Search Scripture Well: Karaite Exegesis and the Origins of the Jewish Bible Commentary in the Islamic East.* Études sur le Judaïsme Médiéval 29. Leiden: Brill, 2004.

Frank, Daniel. "The Limits of Karaite Scripturalism: Problems in Narrative Exegesis." In *"A Word Fitly Spoken:" Studies in Qur'an and Bible Exegesis, Presented to Haggai Ben-Shammai*, edited by Meir M. Bar-Asher, Simon Hopkins, Sarah Stroumsa, and Bruno Chiesa, 41–82. Jerusalem: Ben Zvi Institute, 2007.

Frank, Daniel. "Recovering Japheth Ben Eli's 'Lost' Commentary on Lamentations." The 17th Annual Conference of the Society for Judaeo-Arabic Studies, Vanderbilt University, August 15–18, 2016.

Frank, Daniel. "Mourners of Zion." In vol. 19 of *The Encyclopedia of the Bible and Its Reception*, edited by Constance Furey, et al., 1303–7. Boston/Berlin: DeGruyter, 2021.

Freedman, David Noel. "Acrostic Poems in the Hebrew Bible: Alphabetic and Otherwise." *Catholic Biblical Quarterly* 48 (1986): 408–31.

Friedlander, Israel. "The Arabic Original of the Report of R. Nathan Habablí." *Jewish Quarterly Review* o.s. 17 (1905): 747–61.

Garr, W. Randall. "The Qinah: A Study of Poetic Meter, Syntax and Style." *Zeitschrift für die alttestamentiche Wissenschaft* 95 (1983): 54–75.

Gharipour, Mohammad. "Architecture of Synagogues in the Islamic World: History and the Dilemma of Identity." In *Synagogues in the Islamic World*, 6–18. Edinburgh, University of Edinburgh Press, 2017.

Gil, Moshe. "Religion and Realities in Islamic Taxation." *Israel Oriental Studies* 10 (1980): 21–33.

Gil, Moshe. "The Jewish Quarters of Jerusalem (A.D. 638–1099) According to Cairo Geniza Documents and Other Sources." *Journal of Near Eastern Studies* 41 (1982): 261–78.

Gil, Moshe. "Aliya and Pilgrimage in the Early Arab Period (634–1009)." *The Jerusalem Cathedra* 3 (1983): 163–73.

Gil, Moshe. *A History of Palestine, 634–1099.* Translated by Ethel Broido. Cambridge: Cambridge University Press, 1992.

Gil, Moshe. "The Jewish Community." In *The History of Jerusalem: The Early Muslim Period (638–1099)*, edited by Joshua Prawer and Haggai Ben-Shammai, 163–200. Jerusalem: Ben Zvi, 1996.

Gil, Moshe. "The Origins of the Karaites." In *Karaite Judaism: A Guide to Its History and Literary Sources*, Handbuch der Orientalistik 73, edited by Meira Polliack, 73–118. Leiden: Brill, 2003.

Ginzberg, Louis. *The Legends of the Jews*, vol 4:9. Translated by Henrietta Szold. Philadelphia: Jewish Publication Society, 1968.

Goitein, Shelomo Dov. *A Mediterranean Society: The Jewish Communities of the Arab World as Portrayed in the Documents of the Cairo Geniza.* 5 vols. Berkeley: University of California Press, 1967–88.

Goldstein, Miriam. "The Beginnings of the Transition from *Derash* to *Peshaṭ* as Exemplified in Yefet ben 'Eli's Comment on Psa. 44:24." In *Exegesis and Grammar in Medieval Karaite Texts*, Journal of Semitic Studies Supplement 13, edited by Geoffrey Khan, 41–64. Oxford: Oxford University Press, 2001.

Goldstein, Miriam. "'Arabic Composition 101' and the Early Development of Judaeo-Arabic Bible Exegesis." *Journal of Semitic Studies* 55 (2010): 451–78.

Goldstein, Miriam. "Sahl (Abū'l Sarrī) ben Maṣliaḥ." In vol. 4 of *Encyclopedia of Jews in the Islamic World*, 5 vols., edited by Norman A. Stillman, 211–12. Leiden: Brill, 2010.

Goldstein, Miriam. *Karaite Exegesis in Medieval Jerusalem: The Judeo-Arabic Pentateuch Commentary of Yūsuf ibn Nūḥ and Abū al-Faraj Hārūn*. Tübingen: Mohr Siebeck, 2011.

Goodman, Lenn E. *The Book of Theodicy: Translation and Commentary on the Book of Job by Saadiah ben Joseph al-Fayyūmī; Translated from the Arabic with a Philosophic Commentary*. Yale Judaica Series 25. New Haven, Conn.: Yale University Press, 1988.

Gordis, Robert. "Critical Notes: The Conclusion of the Book of Lamentations (5:22)." *Journal of Biblical Literature* 93, no. 2 (1974): 289–93.

Gottwald, Norman K. *Studies in the Book of Lamentations*. Studies in Biblical Theology 14. Chicago: Allenson, 1954.

Greenberg, Moshe. *Ezekiel 1–20: A New Translation with Introduction and Commentary*. Anchor Bible 22. New York: Doubleday, 1983.

Greenberg, Moshe. *Ezekiel 21–37: A New Translation with Introduction and Commentary*. Anchor Bible 22A. New York: Doubleday, 1997.

Greenstein, Edward L. "The Book of Lamentations: Responses to Destruction or Ritual of Rebuilding?" In *Religious Responses to Political Crisis*, Library of Hebrew Bible/Old Testament Studies 444, edited by Henning Graf Reventlow and Yair Hoffman, 52–71. London: T&T Clark, 2008.

Greenstein, Edward L. "Lamentations and Lament in the Hebrew Bible." In *The Oxford Handbook of the Elegy*, edited by Karen A. Weisman, 67–85. Oxford: Oxford University Press, 2010.

Grossman, Avraham. "Aliya in the Seventh and Eighth Centuries." *The Jerusalem Cathedra* 3 (1983): 174–87.

Gruendler, Beatrice. *Book Culture Before Print: The Early History of Arabic Media*. Beirut: American University of Beirut, 2011.

Gruendler, Beatrice. "Aspects of Craft in the Arabic Book Revolution." In *Globalization of Knowledge in the Post-Antique Mediterranean, 700–1500*, edited by Sonja Brentjes and Jürgen Renn, 31–66. London: Routledge, 2016.

Gwaltney, W. C. "The Biblical Book of Lamentations in the Context of Near Eastern Literature." In *Scripture in Context II: More Essays on the Comparative Method*, edited by William W. Hallo, James C. Moyer, and Leo G. Purdue, 191–211. Winona Lake, Ind.: Eisenbrauns, 1983.

Hamori, A. "Ascetic Poetry (*zuhdiyyāt*)." In *Abbasid Belles Lettres*, edited by Julia Ashtiany, T. M. Johnstone, J. D. Latham, and R. B. Serjeant, 265–74. Cambridge: Cambridge University Press, 1990.

Hasan-Rokem, Galit. *Web of Life: Folklore and Midrash in Rabbinic Literature*. Translated by Batya Stein. Stanford, Calif.: Stanford University Press, 2002.

Hava, J. G. *Al-Farāʾid al-Durriyya: Arabic-English Dictionary*. 1899. Reprint, New Delhi: Goodword Books, 2001.

Heath, Peter. "Metaphor." In vol. 3 of *Encyclopedia of the Qurʾān*, 5 vols., edited by Jane Dammen McAuliffe, 384–88. Leiden: Brill, 2001–2006.

Heemskerk, Margaretha T. *Suffering in the Muʿtazilite Theology: ʿAbd al-Jabbār's Teaching on Pain and Divine Justice*. Islamic Philosophy, Theology, and Science 41. Leiden: Brill, 2000.

Heemskerk, Margaretha T. "ʿAbd al-Jabbār b. Aḥmad al-Hamadhānī." In vol. 3 of *The Encyclopedia of Islam*, 3rd ed., edited by Kate Fleet, Gudrun Krämer, Denis Matringe, John Nawas, and Everett Rowson, 9–18. Leiden: Brill, 2007.

Heim, Knut M. "The Personification of Jerusalem and the Drama of her Bereavement in Lamentations." In *Zion, City of Our God*, edited by Richard S. Hess and Gordon J. Wenham, 129–69. Grand Rapids, Mich.: Eerdmans, 1999.

Heinemann, Joseph. "The Proem in the Aggadic Midrashim: A Form-Critical Study." *Scripta Hierosolymitana* 22 (1971): 100–122.

Heinrichs, Wolfhart. *The Hand of the Northwind: Opinions on Metaphor and the Early Meaning of Istiʿāra in Arabic Poetics*. Wiesbaden: Deutsche Morgenländische Gesellschaft, 1977.

Heinrichs, Wolfhart. "On the Genesis of the Ḥaqîqa-Majâz Dichotomy." *Studia Islamica* 59 (1984): 111–40.

Heinrichs, Wolfhart. "Contacts Between Scriptural Hermeneutics and Literary Theory in Islam: The Case of Majāz." *Zeitschrift für Geschichte der Arabisch-islamischen Wissenschaften* 7 (1991): 253–84.

Heinrichs, Wolfhart. "On the Figurative Language (*majāz*) in Muslim Interpretation and Legal Hermeneutics." In *Interpreting Scriptures in Judaism, Christianity, and Islam: Overlapping Inquiries*, ed. Mordechai Z. Cohen and Adele Berlin, 260–65. Cambridge: Cambridge University Press, 2016.

Hillers, Delbert. "Observations on Syntax and Meter in Lamentations." In *A Light unto My Path: Old Testament Studies in Honor of Jacob M. Myers*, Gettysburg Theological Studies 4, edited by Howard N. Bream, Ralph D. Heim, and Carey A. Moore, 265–70. Philadelphia: Temple University Press, 1974.

Hillers, Delbert. *Lamentations: A New Translation with Introduction and Commentary*. 2nd ed. Anchor Bible 7A. Garden City, N.Y.: Doubleday, 1992.

Hirschfeld, Hartwig. *Qirqisāni Studies*. Jews College 6. London: Jews College, 1918.

Hoenig, Sidney B. "An Interdict Against Socializing on the Sabbath." *Jewish Quarterly Review* 62 (1971): 77–83.

Ivry, Alfred L. "The Utilization of Allegory in Islamic Philosophy." In *Interpretation and Allegory: Antiquity to the Modern Period*, Studies in Intellectual History 101, edited by Jon Whitman, 153–80. Leiden: Brill, 2000.

Jastrow, Marcus. *A Dictionary of the Targumim, Talmud Babli, Talmud Yerushalmi, and Midrashic Literature*. 1886–1903. Reprint, New York: Judaica Treasury, 2004.

Jellinek, Adolph (Aharon). *Bet ha-Midrash*. 5 vols. Jerusalem: Bamberger, 1938.

Johnstone, Barbara. *Repetition in Arabic Discourse: Paradigms, Syntagms, and the Ecology of Language*. Philadelphia: J. Benjamins, 1991.

Jones, Linda G. "'He Cried and Made Others Cry': Crying as a Sign of Pietistic Authenticity or Deception in Medieval Islamic Preaching." In *Crying in the Middle Ages: Tears of History*, edited by Elina Gertsman, 102–35. New York: Routledge, 2012.

Jones, Linda G. *The Power of Oratory in the Medieval Muslim World*. Cambridge: Cambridge University Press, 2012.

Kalman, Jason. "Authorship, Attribution, and Authority: Jeremiah, Baruch, and the Rabbinic Interpretation of Lamentations." *Hebrew Union College Annual* 90 (2019): 27–87.

Kassis, Riyad Aziz. *The Book of Proverbs and Arabic Proverbial Works*. Supplements to the *Vetus Testamentum* 74. Leiden: Brill, 1999.

Katz, Marion Holmes. *Prayer in Islamic Thought and Practice*. Themes in Islamic History 6. Cambridge: Cambridge University Press, 2013.

Kennedy, James M. "Hebrew *Pitḥôn Peh* in the Book of Ezekiel." *Vetus Testamentum* 41, no. 2 (1991): 233–35.

Khan, Geoffrey. "The Opinions of al-Qirqisānī Concerning the Text of the Bible and Parallel Attitudes Towards the Text of the Qur'ān." *Jewish Quarterly Review* 81 (1990): 59–73.

Khan, Geoffrey. *Early Karaite Grammatical Texts*. Atlanta, Ga.: Society of Biblical Literatures, 2000.

Khan, Geoffrey. *The Early Karaite Tradition of Hebrew Grammatical Thought: Including a Critical Edition, Translation and Analysis of the* Diqduq *of 'Abū Ya'qūb Yūsuf ibn Nūḥ on the Hagiographa*. Studies in Semitic Languages and Linguistics 32. Leiden: Brill, 2000.

Khan, Geoffrey. "Biblical Exegesis and Grammatical Theory in the Karaite Tradition." In *Exegesis and Grammar in Medieval Karaite Texts*, Journal of Semitic Studies Supplement 13, edited by Geoffrey Khan, 41–64. Oxford: Oxford University Press, 2001.

Khan, Geoffrey. "The Contributions of the Karaites to the Study of the Hebrew Language." In *Karaite Judaism: A Guide to Its History and Literary Sources*, Handbuch der Orientalistik 73, edited by Meira Polliack, 291–318. Leiden: Brill, 2003.

Khan, Geoffrey. "Ibn Nūḥ, Joseph (Abū Ya'qūb Yūsuf)." In vol. 2 of *Encyclopedia of Jews in the Islamic World*, 5 vols., edited by Norman A. Stillman, 528–29. Leiden: Brill, 2010.

Kobler, Franz, ed. *Letters of Jews Through the Ages*, 2 vols. East and West Library. Philadelphia: Jewish Publication Society, 1978.

Kraemer, Joel. "The Islamic Context of Medieval Jewish Philosophy." In *The Cambridge Companion to Medieval Jewish Philosophy*, edited by Daniel H. Frank and Oliver Leaman, 38–68. Cambridge: Cambridge University Press, 2003.

Krakowski, Eve. "Nathan ha-Bavlī." In vol. 3 of *The Encyclopedia of Jews in the Islamic World*, 5 vols., edited by Norman A. Stillman, 560. Leiden: Brill, 2010.

Kugel, James. *The Idea of Biblical Poetry: Parallelism and Its History*. New Haven, Conn.: Yale University Press, 1981.

Laato, Antti. "The Seventy Yearweeks in the Book of Daniel." *Zeitschrift für die alttestamentiche Wissenschaft* 102, no. 2 (1990): 212–25.

Labahn, Antje. "Fire from Above: Metaphors and Images of God's Actions in Lamentations 2:1–9." *Journal for the Study of the Old Testament* 31, no. 2 (2006): 239–56.

Lambert, David A. *How Repentance Became Biblical: Judaism, Christianity, and the Interpretation of Scripture*. Oxford: Oxford University Press, 2016.

Lane, Edward William. *An Arabic-English Lexicon*. 1863–93. Reprint, Beirut: Librairie du Liban, 1968.

Lange, Christian. *Justice, Punishment and the Medieval Muslim Imagination*. Cambridge Studies in Islamic Civilization. Cambridge: Cambridge University Press, 2008.

Laoust, H. "Ibn al-Djawzī, ʿAbd al-Raḥmān b. ʿAlī b. Muḥammad Abu'l-Farash b. Al-Djawzī." In vol. 3 of *The Encyclopedia of Islam*, 2nd ed., edited by B. Lewis, V. L. Ménage, C. Pellat, and J. Schacht, 751–52. Leiden: Brill, 1971.

Lasker, Daniel J. "Islamic Influences on Karaite Origins." In *Studies in Islamic and Jewish Traditions II*, Brown Judaic Studies 110, edited by William M. Brinner and Stephen D. Ricks, 23–47. Atlanta, Ga.: Scholars Press, 1989.

Lasker, Daniel J. "The Dead Sea Scrolls in the Historiography and Self-Image of Contemporary Karaites." *Dead Sea Discoveries* 9, no. 3 (2002): 281–94.

Lasker, Daniel J. Review of Yoram Erder, *The Karaite Mourners of Zion and the Qumran Scrolls* (2017); Ilana Sasson, *The Arabic Translation and Commentary of Yefet ben ʿEli on the Book of Proverbs, vol. 1* (2016); and Golda Akhiezer, *Historical Conscriousness, Haskalah, and Nationalism Among the Karaites of Eastern Europe* (2018). *European Journal of Jewish Studies* 15 (2020): 1–8.

Lauterbach, Jacob Z. *Mekhilta de-Rabbi Ishmael: A Critical Edition on the Basis of the Manuscripts and Early Editions with an English Translation, Introduction, and Notes*. 3 vols. 1933. Reprint, Philadelphia: Jewish Publication Society, 1976.

Lazarus-Yafeh, Hava. *Intertwined Worlds: Medieval Islam and Bible Criticism*. Princeton, N.J.: Princeton University Press, 1992.

Lieber, Laura Suzanne. *Jewish Aramaic Poetry from Late Antiquity: Translations and Commentaries*. Études sur le Judaïsme Médiéval 75; Cambridge Genizah Studies 8. Leiden: Brill, 2018.

Lobel, Diana. *A Sufi-Jewish Dialogue: Philosophy and Mysticism in Bahya ibn Paquda's* Duties of the Heart. Philadelphia: University of Pennsylvania Press, 2007.

Maman, Aharon. "Karaites and Mishnaic Hebrew: Quotations and Usage." *Scripta Hierosolymitana* 37 (1998): 264–83.

Maman, Aharon. *Comparative Semitic Philology in the Middle Ages*. Translated by David Lyons. Studies in Semitic Languages and Linguistics 40. Leiden: Brill, 2004.

Mann, Jacob. *The Jews in Egypt and Palestine Under the Fāṭimid Caliphs*. 2 vols. Oxford: Oxford University Press, 1920–22.

Mann, Jacob. "A Tract of an Early Karaite Settler in Jerusalem." *Jewish Quarterly Review* 12 (1921–22): 257–98.

Mann, Jacob. *Texts and Studies in Jewish History and Literature*. 2 vols. Cincinnati, Ohio: Hebrew Union College Press, 1931–35.

Mansoor, Menahem. *The Book of Direction to the Duties of the Heart*. From the Original Arabic Version of Baḥya ben Joseph Ibn Paquda's *al-Hidāya ilā Farāʾiḍ al-Qulūb*. 1973. Reprinted by Littman Library of Jewish Civilization. London: Routledge & Kegan Paul, 2004.

Markon, I. D. "The Commentary on the Scroll of Ruth by the Karaite Salomon ben Yerōḥam." In *Livre d'Hommage à la mémoire du Dr Samuel Poznański (1864–1921) offert par les amis et les compagnons du travail scientifique* (Hebrew), 78–96. Leipzig: Warsaw Committee of the Great Synagogue, 1927.

Marwick, Lawrence. "The Order of the Books in Yefet's Bible Codex." *Jewish Quarterly Review* 33 (1942–43): 445–60.

Marwick, Lawrence. "Studies in Salmon ben Yeruham." *Jewish Quarterly Review* 34 (1944): 475–80.

Marwick, Lawrence. *The Arabic Commentary of Salmon ben Yeruham the Karaite on the Book of Psalms, Chapters 42–72, Edited from the Unique Manuscript in the State Public Library in Leningrad.* Philadelphia: Dropsie College, 1956.

Mazuz, Haggai. "Midrashic Influence on Islamic Folklore: The Case of Menstruation." *Studia Islamica* 108, no. 2 (2013): 189–201.

McAuliffe, Jane Dammen. "Ibn al-Jawzī's Exegetical Propaedeutic: Introduction and Translation." *Alif: Journal of Comparative Poetics* 8 (1988): 101–13.

Miller, Charles William. "Reading Voices: Personification, Dialogism, and the Reader of Lamentations 1." *Biblical Interpretation* 9 (2001): 393–408.

Miller, Patrick D. *They Cried to the Lord: The Form and Theology of Biblical Prayer.* Minneapolis, Minn.: Fortress, 1994.

Mintz, Alan. *Ḥurban: Responses to Catastrophe in Hebrew Literature.* New York: Columbia University Press, 1984.

Mitchell, Mary Louise. "Reflecting on Catastrophe: Lamentations 4 as Historiography." In *The Function of Ancient Historiography in Biblical and Cognate Studies*, Library of Hebrew Bible/Old Testament Studies 489, edited by Patricia G. Kirkpatrick and Timothy D. Goltz, 78–90. London: T&T Clark, 2008.

Morse, Holly. "'Judgment Was Executed upon Her, and She Became a Byword Among Women' (Ezek 23:10): Divine Revenge Porn, Slut-Shaming, Ethnicity, and Exile in Ezekiel 16 and 23." In *Women and Exilic Identity in the Hebrew Bible, Library of Hebrew Bible/Old Testament Studies* 631, 129–154, edited by Katherine E. Southwood and Martien A. Halvorson-Taylor. New York: T&T Clark, 2018.

Muztar, A. D. "Dhimmīs in an Islamic State." *Islamic Studies* 18 (1979): 65–75.

Nelson, W. David. *Mekhilta de-Rabbi Shimon bar Yoḥai: Translated into English, with Critical Introduction and Annotation.* Philadelphia: Jewish Publication Society, 2006.

Nemoy, Leon. *Yaʿqub al-Qirqisani's Kitāb al-Anwār wa-l Marāqib—Code of Karaite Law.* 5 vols. New York: Alexander Kohut Memorial Foundation, 1939–43.

Nemoy, Leon. "Did Salmon ben Jeroham Compose a Commentary on Ruth?" *Jewish Quarterly Review* 39 (1948): 215–16.

Nemoy, Leon. *Karaite Anthology: Excerpts from the Early Literature.* Yale Judaica Series 7. New Haven, Conn.: Yale University Press, 1952.

Nemoy, Leon. "The Epistle of Sahl ben Maṣliaḥ." *Proceedings of the American Academy for Jewish Research* 38/39 (1970–71): 145–77.

Nemoy, Leon. "The Pseudo-Qūmisīan Sermon to the Karaites." *Proceedings of the American Academy for Jewish Research* 43 (1976): 49–106.

Nemoy, Leon. "Elijah ben Abraham and His Tract Against the Rabbanites." *Hebrew Union College Annual* 51 (1980): 63–87.

Neubauer, Adolf. *Medieval Jewish Chronicles and Chronological Notes.* 2 vols. Oxford: Clarendon Press, 1887–95.

Nguyen, Kim Lan. *Chorus in the Dark: The Voices of the Book of Lamentations.* Sheffield, U.K.: Sheffield Phoenix, 2013.

Niazi, Imran Ahsan. "The Karaites: Influence of Islamic Law on Jewish Law." *Islamic Studies* 32 (1993): 137–47.

Nir, Sivan, and Meira Polliack. "'Many Beautiful Meanings Can Be Drawn from Such a Comparison': On the Medieval Interaction View of Biblical Metaphor." In *Exegesis and Poetry in Medieval Karaite and Rabbanite Texts*, 40–79, edited by Joachim Yeshaya and Elisabeth Hollender. Études sur le Judaïsme Médiéval 68; Karaite Texts and Studies 9. Leiden: Brill, 2016.

Olyan, Saul M. *Biblical Mourning: Ritual and Social Dimensions*. Oxford: Oxford University Press, 2004.

Ong, Walter. *Orality and Literacy: The Technologizing of the Word*. 1982. Reprint, New York: Routledge, 1991.

Orton, David E. (comp.). *Poetry in the Hebrew Bible: Selected Studies from* Vetus Testamentum. Leiden: Brill, 2000.

Peters, J. R. T. M. *God's Created Speech: A Study in the Speculative Theology of the Muʿtazilî Qâdî l-quḍāt Abûl-Ḥasan ʿAbd al-Jabbâr bn Aḥmad al-Hamadânî*. Leiden: Brill, 1976.

Peters, Rudolph. *Crime and Punishment in Islamic Law: Theory and Practice from the Sixteenth to the Twenty-First Century*. Themes in Islamic Law 2. Cambridge: Cambridge University Press, 2005.

Pinsker, Simḥa. *Liqqute qadmoniyyot: le-qorot dat bene miqra*. 2 vols. Vienna: Adalbert della Torre, 1860.

Polliack, Meira. "Medieval Karaite Views on Translating the Hebrew Bible into Arabic." *Journal of Jewish Studies* 47 (1996): 64–84.

Polliack, Meira. *The Karaite Tradition of Arabic Bible Translation: A Linguistic and Exegetical Study of Karaite Translations of the Pentateuch for the Tenth and Eleventh Centuries CE*. Études sur le Judaïsme Médiéval 17. Leiden: Brill, 1997.

Polliack, Meira. "Major Trends in Karaite Biblical Exegesis in the Tenth and Eleventh Centuries." In *Karaite Judaism: A Guide to Its History and Literary Sources*, Handbuch der Orientalistik 73, edited by Meira Polliack, 63–413. Leiden: Brill, 2003.

Polliack, Meira. "Rethinking Karaism: Between Judaism and Islam." *AJS Review* 30 (2006): 67–93.

Polliack, Meira. "David ben Abraham al-Fāsī." In vol. 2 of *The Encyclopedia of Jews in the Islamic World*, 5 vols., edited by Norman A. Stillman, 34–36. Leiden: Brill, 2010.

Polliack, Meira. "Historicizing Prophetic Literature: Yefet ben ʿEli's Commentary on Hosea and Its Relationship to al-Qūmisī's *Pitron*." In *Pesher Naḥum: Texts and Studies in Jewish History and Literature from Antiquity Through the Middle Ages Presented to Norman (Naḥum) Golb*, edited by Joel L. Kraemer and Michael G. Wechsler, 149–86. Chicago: Oriental Institute of the University of Chicago, 2012.

Polliack, Meira. "The Karaite Inversion of 'Written' and 'Oral' Torah in Relation to the Islamic Arch-Models of Qurʾan and Hadith." *Jewish Studies Quarterly* 22 no. 3 (2015): 243–302.

Polliack, Meira, and Eliezer Schlossberg. "Historical-Literary, Rhetorical and Redactional Methods of Interpretation in Yefet ben ʿEli's Introduction to the Minor Prophets." In *Exegesis and Grammar in Medieval Karaite Texts*, Journal of Semitic Studies Supplement 13, edited by Geoffrey Khan, 1–40. Oxford: Oxford University Press, 2001.

Poznanski, Samuel. "Karaite Miscellanies." *Jewish Quarterly Review* 8 no. 4 (1896): 681–704.

Poznanski, Samuel. "The Anti-Karaite Writings of Saadiah Gaon." *Jewish Quarterly Review* 10 (1897–98): 238–76.

Poznanski, Samuel. "The Karaite Literary Opponents of Saadiah Gaon in the Tenth Century." *Jewish Quarterly Review* 18 (1906): 209–50.

Provan, Iain W. *Lamentations*. New Century Bible Commentary. Grand Rapids, Mich.: Eerdmans, 1991.

Provan, Iain W. "Past, Present, and Future in Lamentations 3:52–66: The Case for a Precative Perfect Re-Examined." *Vetus Testamentum* 41 (1991): 164–75.

Qutbuddin, Tahera. "*Khuṭba*: The Evolution of Early Arabic Oration." In *Classical Arabic Humanities in Their Own Terms: Festschrift for Wolfhart Heinrichs*, edited by Beatrice Gruendler and Michael Cooperson, 176–273. Leiden: Brill, 2008.

Qutbuddin, Tahera. *Arabic Oration: Art and Function*. Handbook of Oriental Studies 131. Leiden: Brill, 2019.

Rabb, Intisar. *Doubt in Islamic Law: A History of Legal Maxims, Interpretation, and Islamic Criminal Law*. Cambridge Studies in Islamic Civilization. Cambridge: Cambridge University Press, 2015.

Ratzaby, Yehudah. "Targum of Rabbenu Saadia Gaon on Lamentations." *Tarbiz* 13 (1942): 92–106.

Ratzaby, Yehudah. "Selections from Rav Sa'adia's Commentary on Lamentations." *Bar Ilan Annual* 20–21 (1983): 349–80.

Ratzaby, Yehudah. *A Dictionary of Judaeo-Arabic in Rav Saadia's Tafsīr*. Ramat Gan, Israel: Bar Ilan University Press, 1985.

Ratzaby, Yehudah. "New Passages from R. Saadia's Commentary on Lamentations." *Sinai* 95 (1985): 1–23.

Reinert, B. "Ma<u>dj</u>āz in Arabic Literature." In vol. 5 of *The Encyclopedia of Islam*, 2nd ed., edited by C. E. Bosworth, E. Van Donzel, B. Lewis, and C. Pellat, 1025–26. Leiden: Brill, 1985.

Robinson, Chase F. *Islamic Historiography*. Themes in Islamic History 1. Cambridge: Cambridge University Press, 2003.

Robinson, James T. *Asceticism, Eschatology, Opposition to Philosophy: The Arabic Translation and Commentary of Salmon ben Yeroham on Qohelet (Ecclesiastes)*. Études sur le Judaïsme Médiéval 45; Karaite Texts and Studies 5. Leiden: Brill, 2012.

Rubin, Uri. "Morning and Evening Prayers in Early Islam." *Jerusalem Studies in Arabic and Islam* 10 (1987): 40–53.

Rustow, Marina. *Heresy and the Politics of Community: The Jews of the Fatimid Caliphate*. Conjunctions of Religion and Power in the Medieval Past. Ithaca, N.Y.: Cornell University Press, 2008.

Saadia Gaon. *The Book of Beliefs and Opinions*. Translated by Samuel Rosenblatt. Yale Judaica Series 1. New Haven, Conn.: Yale University Press, 1948.

Sabih, Joshua A. *Japheth ben Ali's Book of Jeremiah: A Critical Edition and Linguistic Analysis of the Judaeo-Arabic Translation*. Copenhagen International Seminar. London: Equinox, 2009.

Salters, Robert B. *A Critical and Exegetical Commentary on Lamentations*. International Critical Commentary. London: T&T Clark, 2010.

Sasson, Ilana. *The Arabic Translation and Commentary of Yefet ben 'Eli on the Book of Proverbs*, vol. 1. Études sur le Judaïsme Médiéval 67; Karaite Texts and Studies 8. Leiden: Brill, 2016.

Schley, Donald G. *Shiloh: A Biblical City in Tradition and History*. Journal for the Study of the Old Testament Supplement 63. Sheffield, U.K.: JSOT Press, 1989.

Schofer, Jonathan Wyn. "Protest or Pedagogy: Trivial Sin and Divine Justice in Rabbinic Narrative." *Hebrew Union College Annual* 74 (2003): 243–78.

Schökel, Alonso. *A Manual of Hebrew Poetics*. Studia Biblica 11. Rome: Editrice Pontifico Instituto Biblico, 1988.

Sells, Michael. "Muhasibi: Moral Psychology." In *Early Islamic Mysticism*, 171–96. New York: Paulist, 1996.

Shunary, Jonathan. "Salmon b. Yeruham's Commentary on the Book of Psalms." *Jewish Quarterly Review* 73 (1982): 155–75.

Shterenshis, Michael. *Tamerlane and the Jews*. Abingdon, U.K.: Routledge, 2002.

Simon, Udo. "Majāz." In vol. 3 of *Encyclopedia of Arabic Language and Linguistics*, edited by Kees Versteegh, 116–23. Leiden: Brill, 2008.

Simon, Uriel. *Four Approaches to the Book of Psalms from Saadia Gaon to Abraham Ibn Ezra*. Translated by Lenn J. Schramm. SUNY Series in Judaica. Albany: State University of New York Press, 1991.

Sirat, Colette. "The Mutakallimūn and Other Jewish Thinkers Inspired by Muslim Theological Movements." In *A History of Jewish Philosophy in the Middle Ages*, 15–56. Cambridge: Cambridge University Press, 1996.

Skoss, Solomon L. *The Hebrew-Arabic Dictionary of the Bible, Known as Kitāb Jāmiʿ al-Alfāẓ (Agron), of David ben Abraham al-Fāsī, the Karaite*. Yale Oriental Series, 20–21. New Haven, Conn.: Yale University Press, 1936–45.

Steiner, Richard. *A Biblical Translation in the Making: The Evolution and Impact of Saadia Gaon's* Tafsīr. Cambridge, Mass.: Harvard University Press, 2010.

Stemberger, Günther. "The Derashah in Rabbinic Times." In *Preaching in Judaism and Christianity: Encounters and Developments from Biblical Times to Modernity*, Studia Judaica 41, edited by Alexander Deeg, Walter Homolka, and Heinz-Günther Schöttler, 7–21. Berlin: Walter de Gruyter, 2008.

Stern, David. *Parables in Midrash: Narrative and Exegesis in Rabbinic Literature*. Cambridge, Mass.: Harvard University Press, 1991.

Stern, Elsie R. *From Rebuke to Consolation: Exegesis and Theology in the Liturgical Anthology of the Ninth of Av Season*. Brown Judaic Studies 338. Providence, R.I.: Brown University, 2020.

Stillman, Norman A. *The Jews of Arab Lands: A History and Sourcebook*. Philadelphia: Jewish Publication Society, 1979.

Stroumsa, Sarah. "Saadya and Jewish Kalām." In *The Cambridge Companion to Medieval Jewish Philosophy*, edited by Daniel H. Frank and Oliver Leaman, 71–90. Cambridge: Cambridge University Press, 2003.

Swartz, Merlin. *Ibn al-Jawzī's* Kitāb al-Quṣṣāṣ wa'l-Mudhakkirīn. Pensée Arabe et Musulman 47. Beirut: Dar el-Machreq Éditeurs, 1971.

Swartz, Merlin. "Arabic Rhetoric and the Art of the Homily in Medieval Islam." In *Religion and Culture in Medieval Islam*, edited by Richard G. Hovannisian and Georges Sabagh, 36–65. Cambridge: Cambridge University Press, 1999.

Swartz, Merlin. *A Medieval Critique of Anthropomorphism. Ibn al-Jawzī's* Kitāb Akhbār Aṣ-Ṣifāt. *A Critical Edition of the Arabic Text with Translation, Introduction, and Notes*. Islamic Philosophy, Theology and Science, Texts and Studies 46. Leiden: Brill, 2002.

Taxel, Itamar. "The Byzantine-Early Islamic Transition of the Palestinian Coastal Plain: A Re-evaluation of the Archaeological Evidence." *Semitica et Classica* 6 (2013): 73–106.

Thomas, Heath A. *Poetry and Theology in the Book of Lamentations: The Aesthetics of an Open Text*. Sheffield, U.K.: Sheffield Phoenix, 2013.

Tirosh-Becker, Ofra. "Linguistic Study of a Rabbinic Quotation Embedded in a Karaite Commentary on Exodus." *Scripta Hierosolymitana* 37 (1998): 380–407.

Tirosh-Becker, Ofra. "The Use of Rabbinic Sources in Karaite Writings." In *Karaite Judaism: A Guide to Its History and Literary Sources*, Handbuch der Orientalistik 73, edited by Meira Polliack, 317–37. Leiden: Brill, 2003.

Tirosh-Becker, Ofra. *Rabbinic Excerpts in Medieval Karaite Literature*. 2 vols. [Hebrew]. Jerusalem: Bialik Institute, 2011.

Toorawa, Shawkat M. *Ibn Abī Ṭāhir Ṭayfur and Arabic Writerly Culture: A Ninth-Century Bookman in Baghdad*. RoutledgeCurzon Studies in Arabic and Middle Eastern Literatures 7. New York: RoutledgeCurzon, 2005.

Tottoli, Roberto. "Muslim Attitudes Toward Prostration (*sujūd*): I. Arabs and Prostration at the Beginning of Islam and in the Qur'ān." *Studia Islamica* 88 (1998): 5–34.

Urbach, Ephraim Elimelech. *The Sages: Their Concepts and Beliefs*. 2 vols. Translated by Abraham Israels. Jerusalem: Magnes, 1975.

Ussishkin, David. "Excavations at Betar, the Last Stronghold of Bar Kokhba [Hebrew]. *Qadmoniot: A Journal for the Antiquities of Eretz-Yisrael and Bible Lands* 41, no. 136 (2008): 108–112.

Versteegh, C. H. M. *Arabic Grammar and Qur'ānic Exegesis in Early Islam*. Studies in Semitic Languages and Linguistics 19. Leiden: Brill, 1993.

Visotzky, Burton. "The Misnomers '*Petihah*' and 'Homiletic Midrash' as Descriptions for Leviticus Rabbah and Pesikta de Rav Kahana." *Jewish Studies Quarterly* 18 (2011): 19–31.

Walfish, Barry Dov. "The Mourners of Zion ('Avelei Siyyon): A Karaite '*Aliya* Movement of the Early Arab Period." In *Eretz Israel, Israel, and the Jewish Diaspora: Mutual Relations*, edited by Menachem Mor, 42–52. Lanham, Md.: University Press of America, 1991.

Walfish, Barry Dov, and Mikhail Kizilov. *Bibliographica Karaitica: An Annotated Bibliography of Karaites and Karaism*. Études sur le Judaïsme Médiéval 43; Karaite Texts and Studies 2. Leiden: Brill, 2011.

Wansbrough, John. "*Majāz al-Qur'ān*: Periphrastic Exegesis." *Bulletin of the School of Oriental and African Studies, University of London* 33 (1970): 247–66.

Wechsler, Michael G. *The Arabic Translation and Commentary of Yefet ben 'Eli the Karaite on the Book of Esther: Edition, Translation, and Introduction*. Études sur le Judaïsme Médiéval 36; Karaite Texts and Studies 1. Leiden: Brill, 2006.

Wechsler, Michael G. "Japheth (Abū 'Alī Ḥasan) ben 'Eli." In vol. 3 of *Encyclopedia of Jews in the Islamic World*, 5 vols., edited by Norman A. Stillman, 11–13. Leiden: Brill, 2010.

Wechsler, Michael G. "Salmon ben Jeroham (Sulaym ibn Ruḥaym)." In vol. 4 of *The Encyclopedia of Jews in the Islamic World*, 5 vols., edited by Norman A. Stillman, 216–18. Leiden: Brill, 2010.

Wechsler, Michael G. *The Book of Conviviality in Exile (*Kitāb al-īnās bi'-l-jalwa*): The Judaeo-Arabic Translation and Commentary of Saadia Gaon on the Book of Esther*. Biblia Arabica. Leiden: Brill, 2015.

Westermann, Claus. *Praise and Lament in the Psalms*. Translated by Keith R. Crim and Richard N. Soulen. Atlanta, Ga.: Knox, 1981.

Westermann, Claus. *Lamentations: Issues and Interpretation*. Translated by Charles Muenchow. Minneapolis, Minn.: Fortress, 1994.

Wieder, Naphtali. *The Judean Scrolls and Karaism*. Jerusalem: Ben Zvi, 2005.

Wolfson, Harry Austryn. *Repercussions of the Kalam in Jewish Philosophy*. Cambridge, Mass.: Harvard University Press, 1979.

Younger, K. Lawson, Jr. "The Deportations of the Israelites." *Journal of Biblical Literature* 117, no. 2 (1998): 201–27.

Zawanowska, Marzena. *The Arabic Translation and Commentary of Yefet ben 'Eli the Karaite on the Abraham Narratives (Genesis 11:10–25:18): Edition and Introduction*. Études sur le Judaïsme Médiéval 46; Karaite Texts and Studies 4. Leiden: Brill, 2012.

Zawanowska, Marzena. "Islamic Exegetical Terms in Yefet ben ʿEli's Commentaries on the Holy Scriptures." *Journal of Jewish Studies* 64 (2013): 306–25.

Zawanowska, Marzena. "Review of Scholarly Research on Yefet ben ʿEli and His Works." *Revue des études juives* 173 (2014): 97–138.

Zawanowska, Marzena. "The Bible Read Through the Prism of Theology: The Medieval Karaite Tradition of Translating Explicit Anthropomorphisms into Arabic." *Journal of Jewish Thought and Philosophy* 24 (2016): 163–223.

Zawanowska, Marzena. "'Where the Plain Meaning is Obscure or Unacceptable . . .': The Treatment of Implicit Anthropomorphisms in the Medieval Karaite Tradition of Arabic Bible Translation." *European Journal of Jewish Studies* 10 (2016): 1–49.

Biblical Verses

For the benefit of digital users, indexed terms that span two pages (e.g., 52–53) may, on occasion, appear on only one of those pages.

Genesis
1:22, 193
2:21, 291–92
3:24, 64–65, 66, 201–2
4:4, 257, 257–58n.14
4:12, 212n.70, 325n.43
11:30, 54n.80
14:20, 312–13, 312–13n.224
15:15, 38–39, 331, 331n.62
19:25, 323
20:12, 287
21:7, 54n.80
21:33, 169n.1
25:14, 287
25:23, 193
25:27, 291–92
26:24, 309
28:20, 322–23n.34
37:25, 321
37:34–35, 158, 175
39:10, 217–18
41:52, 173n.10, 278
49:15, 187n.1
Exodus
1:11–12, 187n.1
1:20, 229
2:11–12, 225–26
2:12, 226
2:13, 226
2:14, 226
2:15, 226
2:23–25, 305
3:7, 250, 278
4:30, 223
4:31, 239
5:21, 223, 223n.6
6:6, 229
8:22, 214n.73
8:22/26, 214
14:11, 223
14:14, 229
14:31, 239
15:14, 229
15:23, 223n.7
15:24, 223
16:3, 223–24
16:16, 224n.9
16:19, 223–24
16:20, 224n.8
16:22, 224n.9
16:27, 224
17:4, 224
18:8, 267–68
19:5, 282
19:5–6, 221
20:2, 207
20:3, 207, 224–25
20:5, 238, 340–41n.19
20:7, 68n.25, 208
20:8, 67n.23, 68n.25, 208–9
20:12, 67, 68, 68n.25, 140–41, 209
20:13, 67n.23, 140–41, 209
20:14, 67n.23, 209–10
20:15, 67n.23, 68n.25, 210
20:16, 68n.25, 210
20:17, 211
23:14–17, 175n.24
24:7, 232–33n.25, 239, 265, 270n.64
27:4, 224–25
30:25, 318
32:8, 224–25
32:9, 218n.88
33:16, 200
34:23, 175n.24

Leviticus
2:5, 259n.20
2:14, 276
9:1, 239
9:24, 230, 239
10:18, 199
13:6, 321n.29
13:45, 191
13:46, 191
23:42, 244–45n.55
25, 306n.206
25:23, 306
25:30, 306
26:3–4, 221–22, 294–95
26:3–45, 235n.36
26:6, 231
26:14, 294–95
26:14–15, 227–28
26:22, 272
26:31, 148–49, 255, 315
26:33, 255
26:39, 153–54, 341
26:40, 339–40, 339n.12
26:42–45, 235n.36
26:44, 171–72, 173n.12, 281, 284–85
Numbers
5:11–31, 238n.42
5:23, 238
5:27, 238
11:1, 225
11:1–4, 225n.10
13:30, 199
14:22, 225, 225n.11
14:33, 43–44, 153–54, 340–41
14:35, 153–54, 341
17:6/16:41, 225
21:17, 239
22:15, 193
25:3, 225
31:35, 317–18
34:11, 316–17
Deuteronomy
2:12, 333–34
2:16, 153–54, 341
4:4, 153–54, 239, 341
4:6, 230
4:27, 255
4:30–31, 173
4:36, 202–3n.38
5:4, 224–25
6:11, 230
6:17, 199
7:8, 228, 230
8:5, 172–73, 172n.8, 236–37
9:24, 225–26
9:27, 278–79
10:15, 229
11:4, 307
11:13–14, 221–22
11:16–17, 227–28
13:18/17, 230
14:1, 184
16:14, 230
16:16, 175n.24
16:18, 226
18:20, 223n.5
24:7, 265n.48
25:11, 325, 325n.44
25:19, 230
28, 235n.36
28:1–2, 222
28:10, 212–13
28:12, 230
28:15, 227–28, 295
28:15–68, 228n.14
28:26, 236–37
28:29, 195, 195n.18, 271–72
28:30, 209–10
28:31, 210
28:35, 177
28:36, 255, 265
28:37, 178n.32
28:41, 220
28:44, 230
28:47–48, 192–93
28:48, 269
28:49, 255
28:61, 177
28:62, 241–42
28:65, 230, 266, 281
28:66, 229, 301
28:68, 234–35
28:69/29:1, 235n.36
29:22/23, 323
29:27/28, 180n.36, 299
30:7, 312–13

30:14, 202–3n.38
31:17, 216
32:4, 169n.2, 170, 262–63, 280n.105
32:6, 119–20, 184, 326, 326–27n.49
32:7, 143
32:16, 238
32:19, 248
32:21, 178–80, 247
32:23, 230
32:23–24, 324
32:24, 230, 273–74
32:39, 179n.33
33:16, 187
Joshua
4, 251n.75
6:1, 256–57
7:20, 287
10:11, 298
10:12, 298
18:28, 251n.75
24:27, 287
Judges
2:7, 239
2:11–12, 225
2:17, 225
2:19, 225
5:1, 230
7:4, 193
9:8, 199
10:6, 225
18:9, 218
1 Samuel
1:10, 295–96
1:11, 253–54
7:4, 239
12:21, 239–40
14:30, 214
15:33, 62, 273, 273n.75
17:10, 335–36
17:25, 335–36
17:36, 335–36
18:11, 289, 289n.148
20:33, 289
22:14, 265n.48
2 Samuel
1:11–12, 176
1:17, 158, 176
5:20, 298
8:15, 193–94
12:17, 267–68n.56
14:14, 302–3
20:13, 291, 291n.152
21:21, 336–37
24:9, 188, 188n.4
1 Kings
3:28, 193–94
5:4/4:24, 192
5:7/4:27, 190
5:18/4, 192
6:14, 230
7:10, 322n.31
7:11, 321–22
12:26–30, 213n.71
12:28, 207
14:24, 206
21, 338n.6
2 Kings
6:6, 307, 307n.209
7:17–23, 141–42
7:18, 95, 215–16, 215n.81
10:29, 213n.71
15:5, 236n.39
15:27–31, 232n.23
15:29, 232, 232n.24
17, 232–33n.25
17:6, 213n.71
17:7–23, 37, 67, 204–5
17:16, 213n.71
17:18, 238
17:20, 228, 229, 247
18, 261n.31
18:9, 197–98
18:10–12, 232
18:11, 197–98
18:12, 48, 262–63, 264, 265, 266, 267, 268, 269, 270, 271–72, 273–76, 277–78, 283–85, 292–93, 294, 297, 298, 299, 300, 301, 302, 304, 305, 306, 307
20, 191n.8
22, 331n.61
22:19, 38–39, 331
22:20, 38–39, 331
23:25, 38, 330
23:26–27, 331
23:30–36, 233n.26
23:34, 254–55

2 Kings (*cont.*)
23:36–37, 233n.28
24:2, 178–80, 192
24:8–17, 233n.29
24:12, 192
24:15, 233
24:17–25:7, 234n.30
25, 136–37
25:5, 256–57
25:6, 256–57
25:9, 180, 230
Isaiah
1:2, 169
1:4, 213, 247, 248
1:6, 177
1:7, 338
1:9, 171–72
1:15, 248, 271, 299
1:18, 218
1:19, 222
1:21, 187, 193–94, 316–17
1:23, 194
2:22, 329n.57
5:5, 245, 245nn.58–59
5:6, 81, 119–20, 245–46, 326
5:8, 337–38
5:9, 337–38
5:10, 337–38
5:19, 98n.45, 256, 256n.13
5:24, 247
5:25, 178–80
8:23/9:1, 232
9:4/5, 95, 215–16
9:17/18, 324
9:18/19, 324
10:5, 96, 263–64
14:1, 291
14:14, 309
16:8, 95, 215–16
17:4, 241–42
17:5, 241–42
17:6, 241–42
17:7, 241–42, 257–58n.14
17:7–8, 257
17:9, 256–57
21:11, 287
22, 40n.54
22:1, 255–56, 259
22:2, 217, 256, 300–1n.191
22:3, 256–57
22:4, 257–59, 257–58n.14
22:5, 258
22:6, 259–60
22:7, 260
22:8, 260
22:9, 260
22:10, 260
22:11, 261
22:12, 191, 261–62, 325
22:13, 261–62, 261–62nn.33–34
22:14, 259, 262–63
22:16, 187
24:5, 248
24:8, 342
24:11, 258–59
25:8, 54
26:17–18, 286–87
27:7, 215
27:8, 95–96, 215–16, 291
28:2–4, 342–43
28:12, 222
28:21, 298
29:13, 339–40, 340n.15
30:3, 328–29
30:6–7, 328–29
30:7, 261
30:10, 222–23
30:15, 222
30:15–16, 222–23
30:19, 54, 184
31:1, 328–29
31:3, 261, 328–29
32:12, 217
32:15, 279–80
33:8, 248
34:2, 312
34:5, 312
35:3–4, 127
35:10, 312–13n.224
37:21–35, 336n.5
37:24, 336–37
37:28, 311
39:2, 211
39:6–7, 211
40:1, 54
40:1–26, 177n.27

40:7, 276
40:24, 276
40:31, 286
41:16, 313
44:2, 309
45:7, 246
46:8, 218
48:9, 53
48:10, 253–54
48:11, 295–96
48:17, 222
48:18, 222
49:4, 307
49:14, 204
49:20, 279–80
49:23, 286
49:25, 310
50:6, 178–80, 290
50:7, 290
50:8–9, 290
51:2, 196
51:16, 204
51:17, 275–76
51:18, 195–96, 279–80
51:19, 301
51:23, 283–84
51:50, 218
54:5, 174
55:1, 202–3n.38
55:2, 222
55:7, 297
57:1, 38–39, 331
57:1–2, 39, 331n.61
57:16, 290
57:17, 297
57:18, 290
58:7, 278
59:9, 178–80, 195–96
59:10, 119–20, 195, 195nn.17–18, 268, 326
59:12, 195–96
60:10, 332–33
60:14, 54
61:1, 336–37
61:3, 155–56
62:5, 174
63:9, 289, 298
63:10, 219–20, 229, 298
63:15, 250
63:16, 184, 243
64:9/10–10/11, 344
64:10/11, 228, 342–43
65:2, 248
65:7, 153–54, 341
65:11, 70–71, 211–12
66:1, 88n.33
66:6, 312
66:10, 70–71, 72–73, 211–12
66:17, 325
66:24, 290

Jeremiah
1:1, 51, 67
1:1–2:3, 51
1:2, 181–82
2:4, 169
2:13, 267–68n.56
2:20, 222–23
2:25, 222–23
2:31, 222–23
2:34, 140–41, 209, 316–17, 317n.8
3:3, 119–20, 327, 327n.50
3:12, 171
3:14, 218
3:21, 271n.69
3:25, 339–40
4:8, 156, 175–76, 304
4:9, 259, 301, 301n.192
4:19, 178–80
4:20, 178–80, 185–86, 301
4:22, 230
4:27, 53n.79, 215, 215n.79, 284–85, 284n.123
5:2, 68n.25, 208
5:7, 187–88
5:7–8, 209–10
5:12, 207, 222–23
5:25, 48, 236, 321–22, 323, 324, 327, 329–30, 332–33
5:28, 293
6:9, 320
6:16, 222–23
6:17, 222–23
6:26, 175, 276, 304
6:29, 318
7:4, 148–49, 314
7:9, 68n.25, 210

Jeremiah (*cont.*)
7:12, 148–49, 314
7:14, 148–49, 314
7:20, 324
7:24, 213, 247
7:28, 210
7:29, 96, 177, 181, 263–64
7:34, 342
8, 40n.54, 301n.192
8:1–2, 237
8:15, 277–78
8:18, 319, 319nn.16–17, 319–20n.20, 343
8:19, 320, 320n.21
8:20, 320
8:21, 301, 301n.192, 302, 320
8:22, 321
8:23/9:1, 119–20, 321, 327
9:1/2, 209–10
9:2/3, 68n.25, 210, 220
9:11/12–12/13, 216
9:12/13, 48, 191, 192, 199, 202–3, 213, 218–19, 220
9:14/15, 267–68, 278, 278n.98
9:16/17, 176
9:21/22, 320
10, 240n.46
10:3, 239–40
10:19, 301, 301n.192
10:20, 244
10:25, 239–40
11:4, 282
11:13, 193–94, 207
11:21, 222–23, 315
13:14, 180, 273
13:17, 184
13:18, 226, 228, 342–43
13:21, 247
13:22, 244–45, 245n.56
14:16, 237
15:2, 220
15:2–3, 265n.47
15:3, 220
15:6, 343
15:10, 335–36
15:17, 191, 288–89, 289n.147
15:33, 236–37
16:4, 237
16:13, 230, 266
16:16, 306
17:5, 329
17:27, 324
19:5, 294
19:13, 237–38
20:8, 336–37
21:4–6, 229
21:5, 178n.29, 229
22:11–12, 233
22:21, 48, 221, 222–23, 224n.8, 225–26, 244, 248, 249, 251–52
22:22, 226, 227
23:4, 333
23:11, 206
23:14, 137, 322–23
26, 233n.28
26:2–9, 235n.37
26:11, 315
26:18, 344
29:14, 323, 323n.37
30:11, 95–96, 215
30:20, 346
31:4, 279–80, 342n.21
31:14/15, 218–19
31: 17/18, 346
31: 21/22, 218
32:29, 346
34:4, 331–32
34:5, 331–32
36:1–2, 181–82
36:2, 181–82, 181n.39
36:3, 182
36:22–23, 315
36:28, 182
36:30, 237
37:7, 259n.21, 260, 328–29, 329n.56
37:15, 315–16
37:16, 315–16
38:1–13, 308n.212
38:4, 315
38:6, 45–46, 307–8, 315–16
39:4, 257
39:7, 269
39:13–14, 235–36
40:1, 269
40:4, 212–13, 236

41:1, 193
43:2, 222–23
44:12, 329
44:14, 329
44:22, 228
46:10, 102, 104, 117, 340
46:11, 321
48:44, 301
50:20, 332–33
51:5, 24–25, 174, 236–37
51:17, 275n.84
51:34, 318
51:50, 211
51:51, 235–36
52, 136–37
52:8, 233–34
52:11, 233–34, 254–55, 269
52:24, 317
52:25, 317
52:27, 231
52:28, 233
52:29, 233–34
52:30, 234
Ezekiel
1:4–28, 200n.29
2:3, 240–41
3:5, 240–41
3:6, 240–41
3:6–7, 240
3:7, 241, 327n.50
5:9, 214–15
5:15, 178–80, 238
5:16, 273–74
6:9, 184
7:9, 264
7:10, 96, 263–64
7:16, 256
7:18, 178–80
7:21, 119–20, 325–26
7:23, 269
7:26, 178–80, 185–86
7:27, 259
8–11, 65–66, 326n.47
8:1, 200
8:3, 238
8:5, 206
8:9–14, 205–6
8:16, 205
8:17, 206
9:3, 64–65, 200–1
9:7, 235
9:9, 236, 322–23n.34
9:9–10, 204
10:18–19, 64–65, 200–1
11, 40n.54, 97, 99–100
11:3, 99–100, 316–17, 316n.3
11:5–12, 316n.6
11:7, 187–88
11:7–9, 317
11:11, 97–98, 316–17, 316n.5
11:22, 64–65, 200–1
11:23, 64–65, 201–2
11:24, 119–20, 326
11:30, 97–98
12:13, 178–80, 233–34
12:16, 229
12:22, 98n.45, 256, 256n.13
15:7, 220
16:3, 196
16:13, 230
16:14, 64–65, 191, 201–2, 230
16:25, 230
16:32, 238
16:48, 137, 171–72, 322–23
17:15, 328–29
17:20, 178–80
18:20, 153–54, 340, 340–41n.19
18:23, 292
18:32, 292, 292n.157
19:12, 299
21:32/27, 271n.69
22:4, 336–37
22:5, 230, 238
22:7, 67, 68, 68n.25, 140–41, 206, 209
22:8, 68n.25, 69–70, 208–9
22:9–11, 206
22:11, 209–10
22:25–30, 206
22:31, 206–7
23, 40n.54, 145, 199n.26
23:2, 196
23:3, 196
23:4, 196–97
23:5, 197
23:5–7, 197

Ezekiel (*cont.*)
23:7, 197
23:8, 197
23:9, 197
23:9–10, 146–47, 231–32
23:10, 230
23:10–11, 197–98
23:11, 145, 197–98
23:12, 197–98
23:14–15, 197–98
23:17, 198
23:18, 198, 230
23:19–21, 198
23:22–24, 198
23:25, 198–99
23:26, 178–80, 198–99
23:32, 275–76
23:33, 275n.84
23:34, 275–76
23:47, 198–99
24, 40n.54
24:1–14, 316n.6
24:3, 98, 99–100, 316–17
24:3–5, 98
24:4, 316–17
24:5, 316–17
24:6, 98, 316–18, 317n.11
24:6–14, 98
24:7, 317–18
24:8, 318
24:9, 318
24:10, 318, 318n.12
24:11, 318
24:12, 318
24:13, 319
24:14, 98
27:32, 287
29:16, 329
29:21, 338
30:5, 329
34:2, 227
34:3, 226–27
34:10, 227
34:15, 244
34:28, 333
34:29, 333
36:20, 265
36:23, 242–43
36:26, 346
38:21, 312
39:13, 242–43
41:1, 196
43:8, 320
45:11, 337–38
48:12, 217
Hosea
2:8/6, 269
2:13/11, 246, 342
2:16/18, 174
3:2/3, 173
3:4, 226, 258–59, 326
3:40, 119–20
4:6, 247
5:4, 316–17
5:9, 102, 104, 117, 340
5:13, 328, 328n.52
5:14, 178–80, 328
5:15, 63–65, 66, 201–2, 328
6:1, 218
6:1–2, 328
6:10, 217
7:12, 172, 178–80
7:13, 212
8:3, 248
8:8, 266–67
9:1, 105n.5, 217–18, 303
9:12, 248
9:15, 191, 215, 291
9:16, 177
9:17, 212, 228
10:8, 259
10:11, 288
10:12, 288, 288n.145
11:8, 105n.5, 171–72
12:1, 328–29
12:2, 328–29
12:14, 275–76
13:7–8, 272
13:15, 216
14:1/2–2/3, 343
14:2/1, 105n.5, 218
14:4/3, 328
14:10/9, 202–3n.38
Joel
1:5, 119–20, 302–3, 327
1:8, 175–76

1:13, 119–20, 180, 326
2:12, 218
2:17, 282
2:18, 282
4:3/3:3, 306, 312
4:4/3:4, 312
4:6/3:6, 312
4:8/3:8, 312
Amos
1:5, 259–60
2:7–8, 206
2:14–16, 202–3
3:2, 273
5:9, 319, 319–20n.20
5:15, 289
5:19, 220, 301
6:6, 156–57, 175, 218, 303
6:7, 303
6:10, 222–23
7:8, 270
8:9–10, 156
8:10, 176, 178–80, 230, 342
8:11, 92, 93–94, 202
8:12–13, 202–3n.38
9:7, 259–60
9:11, 175–76
9:15, 333
Obadiah
1:9, 312
1:14, 333
Jonah
1:12, 289, 289n.148
2:9, 239–40
Micah
1:4, 302–3
1:8, 156, 175–76, 304
1:10, 178–80, 276
2:1–2, 337–38
2:2, 68n.25, 337–38
2:3, 337–38
2:4, 194, 211, 337
2:5, 337–38
2:20, 211
3:4, 270
3:12, 236, 344
6:2, 169
6:14, 230
7:1, 241–42
7:2, 241–42
7:3, 194
7:6, 68, 140–41, 209
7:9, 285–86
7:10, 243
Nahum
1:2, 246
1:9, 319
Habakkuk
1:4, 248–49
1:14, 306
2:19, 287
Zephaniah
1:15, 301
1:17, 237
2:1, 218
2:3, 289
3:3, 194
3:5, 169
Zechariah
1:4, 339n.9
2:12/18, 248–49
4:7, 287
7:13, 248, 270
11:5, 227
11:7, 263–64n.42
Malachi
2:13, 325
2:17, 262n.34
3:4, 346
3:9, 71–72, 212n.69
3:15, 262n.34
3:17–19, 263n.39
3:19/4:1, 102, 104, 117, 262–63, 263n.39, 290, 340
Psalms
1:4, 313
2:5, 330–31n.60
3:3/2, 193
5:4/3, 339n.14
9:7/6, 345n.27
9:8/7, 345, 345n.27
10:1, 345n.28
10:9, 272
11:4, 80n.13
13:1, 345n.29
13:2/1, 345
14:3, 153–54, 341, 341n.20

Psalms (*cont.*)
14:4, 226–27
16:5, 285–86, 285n.128
17:8, 248–49, 249n.67
17:14, 285–86, 285n.127
19:2/1, 142n.19
21:4/3, 321n.30
22:1, 254n.6
22:2/1, 253–54, 254n.6
22:7/6, 212–13
22:8/7, 212–13, 258
22:14/13, 178–80, 178n.30
22:17/16, 253–54
22:17/16–19/20, 253–54, 254n.6
25:7, 241
25:19, 300, 300n.186
27:12, 210, 210n.62, 300, 300n.188
30:9/8, 239–40
31:23/22, 307
35:1, 310
35:11, 210, 210n.62
35:20, 310
37:7, 286–87, 287n.134
37:9, 286
38:3/2, 178–80, 178n.29, 273–74
38:10, 344n.25
38:12/11, 178–80, 179n.33
39:4, 319–20n.20
42, 40–41, 40n.54
42:1, 279n.104
42:2/1, 92–94, 202, 202–3n.38
42:4/3, 106n.7, 119–20, 119n.45, 194–95, 207n.44, 302–3, 327, 327n.50
42:5/4, 279–80, 283–84
42:6/5, 282n.115
42:7/6, 41–42, 42n.61, 43, 172n.5, 279–80, 280–81n.110, 300–1n.191, 307
42:8/7, 281
42:9/8, 172–73, 173n.12, 281
42:10/9, 282–83, 283n.119, 281–82, 283n.120
42:11/10, 253–54, 282
42:12/11, 279–80, 282, 283–84
42–43, 207n.47
43:1, 172n.5, 280, 280–81n.110, 282, 310
43:2, 282–83, 283n.119, 283n.120, 345n.28
43:3, 283
43:4, 283–84
43:5, 283–84
43:24, 345n.28
44:15/14, 178–80, 178n.32
44:23/22, 310–11
44:26/25, 283–84
52:7/5, 299, 299n.185
59:5/4, 306
60:13/11, 329, 329n.57
63:5/4, 239–40
63:12/11, 291–92, 292n.155
68:21/20, 242–43
68:31/30, 173n.11
69:3/2, 307
69:5/4, 210
69:13/12, 178-80, 179n.35, 274-75, 274n.80, 275n.81
69:21/20, 336–37
69:22/21, 267–68, 267–68n.56
73:13, 307
74:4, 247
74:6, 190, 230, 321–22
74:7, 190
74:8, 247
74:9, 180
74:11, 238n.41
74:18, 335
74:22, 335
77:3/2, 106n.7, 116n.37, 159–60, 175n.21, 218–19, 219n.90, 280, 280n.107
78, 150, 151, 235
78:4, 310
78:8, 151n.35, 339n.9
78:60, 150, 196, 235
78:67, 196
78:68, 228
79, 40–41, 40n.54, 46, 209n.61
79:1, 146, 150, 231, 231n.20, 231n.21, 235, 236, 253–54, 324n.39
79:1–2, 34n.47, 308–9
79:1–3, 253–54, 309n.217
79:1–4, 240
79:2, 236–37, 292n.157
79:3, 140–41, 209, 231, 237–38, 239n.43, 243, 244
79:4, 238
79:5, 238

79:6, 238–40, 239n.45, 241
79:7, 240–41, 240n.47
79:8, 241–42
79:9, 242–43
79:10, 242–43, 310–11
79:11, 243
79:12, 243
79:13, 244
80:13/12, 245, 245nn.58–59
84:5/4, 279–80
85:5/4, 346
85:6/5, 268–69n.59
88:2/1, 249, 249n.69
88:6/5, 268
88:7/6, 45, 301, 306, 307–8, 307n.211
88:9/8, 267
89:41/40, 245, 245n.59
89:48/47, 345n.26
89:51/50, 335
89:52/51, 335
90, 345
90:1, 345n.26
90:10, 345n.26
90:16–17, 195n.17
91:4, 80n.13
92:3/2, 280n.105
92:6/5, 170
92:15–16/14–15, 279–80
92:16/15, 280n.105
94:6–7, 237
94:17, 287, 287n.139
99:5, 88n.33
100:3, 238–39
102:8/7, 191, 288–89
102:9/8, 208, 208n.48, 335–36, 336n.2
102:11/10, 178–80, 180n.36
104:24, 170
105:14, 330–31n.60
105:16, 330–31n.60
105:39, 299, 299n.182
106, 339n.11
106:2, 339–40
106:6, 339–40, 339n.10, 339n.12
106:7, 223
106:19, 224–25
106:48, 330–31n.60
107:13–14, 308
107:17, 119–20, 271–72, 272n.72, 326, 326–27n.49
107:43, 330–31n.60
108:13/12, 329
110:1, 88n.33
113:5, 187
113:6, 187
114:3, 80n.13
115:17, 287, 287nn.138–39
116:13, 275–76, 275n.84
116:15, 292, 292n.157
119:43, 169
119:57, 285n.128
119:78, 80n.13
119:89–90, 173n.10
119:91, 170
119:92, 172–73, 173n.10, 253n.1
119:136, 47, 195, 302
119:137, 24, 138–39, 169, 169n.2
119:155, 304
120:2, 282–83
120:5, 187–88, 282–83
123:1, 187
124:2–3, 172–73, 173n.11
124:7, 306
126:1–2, 217–18, 304
126:2, 304
130:1, 308
132:7, 88n.33
137:5, 70–71, 72, 211–12
137:5–6, 72
137:6, 70–71, 211–12
137:7, 333–34, 335
137:8, 333–34
142:6/5, 285–86, 286n.129
145:5, 200n.29
145:17, 24, 138–39, 169, 169n.2, 171
Proverbs
3:12, 236–37
3:19, 170
6:9, 218
7:11, 256
9:1, 185
9:3, 276
9:5, 267–68n.56
14:32, 261–62, 262n.36
15:25, 299

Proverbs (*cont.*)
22:23, 246
27:3, 289
28:13, 297
28:23, 108
Job
1:1, 333–34
1:16, 177
1:17, 177
1:19, 177
1:20, 177
2:7, 177
2:12, 178–80
6:4, 178–80, 178n.29
9:2, 287
9:18, 178–80
10:20, 319–20n.20
12:2, 287
14:6, 257–58n.14
15:33, 81, 244–45, 245n.56, 245n.57
16:9, 178–80
16:10, 178–80, 178n.29
16:12, 178–80
16:13, 178–80
16:14, 178–80
16:15, 178–80
17:6, 178–80
19:2, 292, 292n.158
19:6, 178–80
19:8, 178–80
19:9, 178–80
19:11, 178–80
19:12, 178–80
19:13, 178–80, 179n.33
19:18, 178–80
19:19, 179n.33
30:1, 178–80
30:8, 178–80
30:9, 178–80
30:10, 178–80
30:20, 178–80
30:22, 178–80
30:26, 178–80
30:27, 178–80
30:30, 178–80
30:31, 178–80
32:9, 193
41:23/21, 318
Song of Songs
1:13, 106n.7, 259n.21
1:17, 330–31n.60
4:8, 280, 280n.109
5:3, 187–88, 187n.3
Lamentations
1, 48, 140n.16, 321n.28
1–2, 131–32
1–4, 26–27
1:1, 26n.24, 62n.17, 183, 187–94, 217, 228, 230–31, 256, 277n.92
1:2, 40n.54, 54, 77, 77n.8, 136, 144, 145, 174n.14, 185, 194–99, 229n.17, 265n.45, 268n.58
1:3, 231n.21
1:4, 26n.24, 156, 183
1:5, 26n.24, 183, 247, 291n.152
1:6, 26n.24, 63–66, 77, 92–94, 119–20, 180, 183, 199–203, 258n.17, 326, 326n.47, 328n.53
1:7, 26n.24, 136n.10, 178–80, 183, 204, 238–39, 247, 278, 344n.25
1:8, 37, 42n.58, 61n.13, 66–73, 134n.5, 139, 140, 203–13, 259n.22, 265n.46, 317n.8, 323n.35, 324n.40
1:9, 250
1:10, 26n.24, 61n.13, 183, 183n.42, 235–36
1:12, 36, 53n.79, 91, 94–96, 177, 180n.37, 181, 213–16, 235, 250, 284n.123, 291n.152, 293n.163, 324n.39
1:13, 26n.24, 177, 183, 218–19, 230, 318
1:14, 31–32, 276n.88
1:15, 217, 259, 291n.152
1:16, 36, 156, 216–19, 321, 343
1:18, 24, 26n.24, 138–39, 169, 169n.2, 183, 219–20, 297n.176
1:19, 231
1:20, 219–20, 250
1:21, 178–80, 247
1:22, 35n.50, 54n.80, 80, 83–84, 186n.50, 343
2, 26–27, 48, 80, 266n.52, 321n.28
2:1, 77n.8, 88–89, 90, 194, 196n.20, 221–28, 229n.17, 342–43
2:2, 298
2:4, 40–41, 40n.54, 53n.78, 61n.13, 77n.8, 135n.9, 146, 150, 178–80, 191, 196n.20, 204n.41, 209n.61, 229–44,

251–52, 265n.46, 273, 298n.180, 309nn.216–17, 319n.19, 333n.67
2:4–5, 80
2:5, 191
2:6, 35n.50, 80–82, 84, 191, 244–48
2:7, 180, 248, 344n.25
2:9, 180
2:11, 79n.11, 178–80, 194–95
2:13, 91, 177, 179n.33, 320
2:17, 273–74
2:18, 80, 84–87, 248–49, 296n.172, 302–3, 302n.198, 305n.203
2:19, 79n.11, 185, 268–69n.59
2:20, 215, 236, 249–52
2:21, 83n.20, 251–52
2:22, 266–67
3, 26–27, 34n.49, 46, 48, 49, 131–32, 166, 179n.34, 266n.52
3:1, 34n.47, 40n.54, 42n.58, 61n.13, 96–97, 98n.45, 106n.7, 172n.5, 185–86, 253–64, 266–67, 268–69n.59, 300–1n.191, 308n.213, 309n.217
3:2, 264–65, 266–67, 270n.64
3:3, 30–31, 266–67
3:4, 43, 266–67, 267n.53
3:5, 267–68, 267n.55, 269n.60, 272n.74
3:6, 178–80, 195, 268–69
3:7, 178–80, 269–70
3:8, 178–80, 270–71
3:9, 271–72, 272n.72, 310, 338n.8
3:10, 267n.55, 272
3:11, 62, 272–73
3:12, 178–80, 230, 273–74
3:13, 273–74
3:14, 274–75, 275n.81, 311
3:15, 178–80, 275–76, 321n.27
3:16, 31–32, 276, 287n.135, 291n.154
3:17, 276–77, 277n.96
3:18, 62, 277–78, 277n.90
3:19, 253–54, 277n.94, 278–79, 278n.98
3:20, 40–43, 40n.54, 61n.13, 172n.5, 207n.47, 217n.86, 219n.90, 278–84, 300–1n.191
3:21, 284–85
3:22, 53n.79, 215n.79, 284–85, 284n.121, 285n.125, 288n.145
3:23, 285
3:24, 285–86, 285nn.127–28
3:25, 286
3:25–33, 48n.68
3:26, 31–32, 276n.88, 286–87, 291n.154
3:27, 287–88
3:28, 62, 288–89
3:29, 289
3:30, 289–90, 335n.1
3:31, 290
3:32, 31, 291, 346n.31
3:33, 31–34, 291–93, 292n.157, 292n.160, 294–95
3:33–34, 32, 149n.33
3:34, 292–93, 292n.160
3:35, 293, 294–95
3:36, 214n.73, 293, 294–95
3:37, 294
3:38, 294–95
3:38–41, 48n.68
3:39, 295
3:40, 26n.24, 103–4, 104n.3, 183, 183n.45, 249n.70, 295–96, 297n.174, 305n.203
3:40–41, 122n.54
3:41, 296–97, 339n.14
3:42, 26n.24, 139, 183, 219n.94, 297, 322n.33
3:43, 298, 299n.181
3:44, 270, 299, 299n.183
3:45, 299–300
3:46, 210n.64, 300, 311
3:47, 76, 300–1, 302n.195
3:48, 47, 301–2, 305, 321
3:49, 87n.31, 229n.17, 302–4, 302n.197, 305
3:50, 48n.68, 218, 249n.70, 279–80, 296n.172, 305
3:51, 305
3:52, 305–6, 311
3:52–55, 45–46
3:53, 42n.59, 306, 306n.206, 307–8
3:54, 307–8, 311
3:55, 34n.48, 43–44, 46–47, 307–9, 308n.213
3:55–66, 48n.68
3:56, 308–9
3:56–60, 33
3:57, 308–9

Lamentations (*cont.*)
3:57–60, 33–34, 309n.215
3:58, 308–10
3:59, 310
3:59–60, 308–9
3:60, 310–11
3:61, 310–11, 335n.1
3:62, 311
3:63, 178–80, 311
3:64, 312, 312n.222
3:65, 34n.47, 312–13, 312–13n.224
3:66, 306n.207, 313
4, 26–27, 48, 136n.11, 321n.28
4–5, 131–32
4:1, 18, 37, 40n.54, 97–98, 144, 149n.30, 149n.32, 182n.40, 194, 209n.59, 215n.79, 284n.123, 301n.192, 302n.195, 314–22, 321n.29, 330n.59
4:2, 61n.13, 61n.16, 194
4:4, 136–37
4:6, 43, 137, 171–72, 284–85, 322–23, 322–23n.34, 323n.38
4:8, 119–20, 178–80, 326
4:10, 250
4:11, 323–24, 324n.39
4:12, 190–91, 321
4:14, 325
4:15, 53n.78, 106n.7, 118–21, 119n.45, 157, 303n.199, 324–27, 325n.43, 325n.44
4:16, 325n.44
4:17, 327–30
4:19, 61n.13, 96n.43
4:20, 38, 39, 62–63, 96n.43, 149n.31, 254, 254n.8, 329n.56, 330–32
4:21, 332–33
4:22, 26n.24, 183–84, 332–34
5, 26–27, 27n.26, 48, 61n.13, 140n.16
5:1, 178n.31, 335–37, 345, 345n.28
5:2, 180, 211, 337–38
5:3, 68, 140–41, 209, 243
5:7, 44n.64, 69n.28, 77n.8, 102, 104–6, 144, 151–53, 154–55, 196n.20, 229n.17, 338–41, 340–41n.19
5:11, 26n.24, 183, 209–10
5:12, 26n.24, 183
5:14, 119–20, 326
5:15, 342
5:16, 48, 119–20, 140–41, 178–80, 195, 195n.16, 209, 326, 336–37, 338, 341, 342–43, 344
5:17, 319, 343, 344
5:18, 238n.41, 344
5:19, 344–45
5:20, 268–69n.59, 345
5:21, 346
5:22, 52–53, 346, 346n.31
Ecclesiastes
1:3, 262n.36
1:15, 271n.69
3:2, 262n.36
3:13, 208n.51
5:15, 262n.36
7:1, 262n.36
7:3, 262n.36
8:11, 262n.34
9:1, 143n.21
9:6, 344n.25
10:16, 187–88
11:6, 288, 288n.141, 288n.143, 288n.145
12:1, 288, 288n.142
12:12, 208n.51
12:14, 263n.39
Esther
3:2, 207n.46
8:6, 187–88
10:3, 187n.1
Daniel
1:1–2, 192
1:2, 254–55
1:6, 233n.28
2:35, 313
3:15, 207
6:18, 287
7:3, 173n.11
7:4, 62, 289
7:4–5, 272
7:7, 282–83
7:18, 283
8:9, 234, 333
8:22, 172n.5, 263–64n.42
8:25, 280–81n.110, 282
9:11, 186n.50, 248, 324
9:12, 181, 214–15, 324
9:14, 169
9:24–25, 234

9:24–27, 234n.31
9:27, 234
11:7, 210
11:16, 176n.25
11:35, 337–38
12:4, 337–38
12:9, 337–38
Ezra
9:7, 210
Nehemiah
1:8–9, 308
9:32, 335–36
9:33, 169, 169n.2, 219–20, 219n.94, 297
9:36, 338
13:15, 208–9
13:17, 208–9
1 Chronicles
5:6, 232n.24
5:26, 232
11:25, 265n.48
13:12, 187–88
13:15, 233n.26
15:24, 258n.19
21:5, 188, 188n.4
21:6, 188
22:9, 192
22:14, 188–89, 190
26:14–16, 235n.38
28:1, 189
28:2, 88n.33, 89, 228
28:9, 238–39
29:2, 189, 321–22
29:3–5, 189
29:6–8, 189–90
2 Chronicles
3:1–2, 190
3:6, 190, 230, 321–22
9:13, 190
9:14, 190
9:23, 191–92
9:23–24, 190
9:24, 191–92
13:11, 217–18
14, 261n.31
17:19, 188
19:5, 193–94
19:8, 193–94
24:20, 247
24:20–22, 250n.74, 251
26:15, 89
26:19–21, 236n.39
28:21, 328
34:2–3, 38, 330
34:27, 38–39, 331
34:28, 38–39, 331
35:3, 175n.23
35:24, 331–32
35:25, 176, 181–82, 230, 254, 331–32
36:1–4, 233n.26
36:5–8, 233n.28
36:6, 269
36:9–10, 233n.29
36:11–14, 234n.30
36:13, 328n.55
36:15, 184, 197–98, 228
36:16, 247, 319
36:17, 177, 231, 251–52, 316–17, 317n.7

Rabbinic Sources

For the benefit of digital users, indexed terms that span two pages (e.g., 52–53) may, on occasion, appear on only one of those pages.

Mekhilta de Rabbi Ishmael, 57–58, 68
II:35, 68n.26
Mekhilta de Rabbi Shimon bar Yoḥai, 340–41n.19
Midrash Lamentations Rabbah
on Lam 1:1, 186n.50
on Lam 1:12, 214n.75
on Lam 1:16, 217n.86
on Lam 1:22, 54n.80
on Lam 2:20, 250n.71, 250n.73
on Lam 3:1, 181n.39
on Lam 3:2, 265n.45
on Lam 3:4, 267n.53, 267n.55
on Lam 3:5, 272n.74
on Lam 3:7, 269n.62
on Lam 3:8, 270n.63
on Lam 3:10, 267n.55, 272n.74
on Lam 3:14, 275n.81
on Lam 3:22, 285n.125
on Lam 3:24, 285n.127
on Lam 3:27, 288n.146
on Lam 3:34, 292n.159
on Lam 4:1, 321n.29, 330n.59
on Lam 4:6, 322–23n.34
on Lam 4:11, 324n.39
on Lam 4:16, 325n.44
on Lam 4:20, 329n.56
proem 2, 304n.202
proem 12, 177n.28
proem 25, 63–64
proem 26, 202n.35
proem 28, 181n.39
proem 32, 319n.16
Mishnah, 58, 59–60
m. Soṭah 1:7–9, 68–69n.27
Pesikta de Rav Kahana
13, 51, 202n.35, 207n.43
13:8, 67
13:11, 63–64
16.6, 177n.27
18:3, 54n.80
20:3, 54n.80
Pesikta Rabbati, 110n.18, 122n.55
Seder Olam Rabbah, 181n.38
Talmud (Babylonian)
Baba Batra 15a, 210n.64
Baba Batra 60b, 71–72, 212n.69
Berakhot 31b, 35n.50, 82n.17
Mo'ed Qatan 26a, 181n.39
Yoma 9b, 195–96n.19
Targum Lamentations
on Lam 1:16, 217n.86
on Lam 2:1, 221n.2
on Lam 2:20, 250n.73
on Lam 3:11, 273, 273n.75
on Lam 3:19, 277n.94
on Lam 3:28, 289
on Lam 3:65, 312–13n.224
on Lam 4:20, 254n.8, 330n.59

Qurʾānic Verses

For the benefit of digital users, indexed terms that span two pages (e.g., 52–53) may, on occasion, appear on only one of those pages.

Qurʾān
3:14, 144n.23
4:165, 296n.169
9:30, 210n.64
12:111, 144nn.23–24
44:43, 278n.98
45:24, 262n.35
59:2–3, 144n.23

General Index

For the benefit of digital users, indexed terms that span two pages (e.g., 52–53) may, on occasion, appear on only one of those pages.

Aaron b. Elijah, 177n.27
Abbasid government, 7–8
Abbasid poetry, 86–87
Abd al-Jabbār, 173n.9
Abdul-Karim, Mohammed Abdul-Latif, xxiii–xxv, xxvi–xxvii, 19n.3, 170n.8, 174n.13, 232–33n.25, 268–69n.59, 275n.85, 332n.65, 342n.21
abrogation (*faskh*), 227–28, 262–63, 263n.40
Abū al-Faraj Hārūn, 16
Abū ʿUbayda, 80n.12
accuracy, 59, 90, 104, 142
actualizing interpretations. *See* interpretation
admonition. *See* exhortation
affectation, 121–22, 121n.50. *See also* mourning
affective techniques, 104–6, 117–22, 124, 131–32, 157–58
agency, divine, 172n.7, 246n.61
Ahab, 338, 338n.6
Aḥmed ibn Ṭulūn, 7–8
ʿ*ajam* (foreigners), 241n.49
Akhbār Baghdād (Chronicle of Baghdad), 111–12, 111–12n.24
Alexander, Liz, 68–69n.27
Alexander, Philip S., 151n.34, 221n.2
Allen, Leslie C., 317n.11
alliteration, 74, 76, 300–1n.191
allusion (*ishāra*), 87. *See also* meaning (*maʿnā*)
alphabet, Judeo-Arabic, xxviii
alphabetic acrostics, 26–27, 27n.26, 131–32, 179n.34, 185–86, 185–86nn.49–50
ambiguity, 16, 27–28, 79–80, 84, 99, 133–34
Amos, book of, 63–64, 141–42, 157
anger, divine
  abatement of, 290
  exile and destruction of Temple and, 216, 228, 245–46, 299, 314
  father's anger compared to, 184
  as figurative language, 80–82, 84, 88–89, 246, 246n.61
  idolatry and, 204–5, 238–39, 320, 331
  against Israel, 178–80, 225, 227–28, 244, 319
  in Lamentations, 132, 194, 221, 228, 244, 298, 323–24, 324n.39, 324n.40, 346
  penitence as a salve to, 175–76, 176n.26, 304
  against Sodom and Gomorrah, 323
annals, 132, 141–42
anthropomorphism, divine, 80–81, 80n.13, 82–84, 82n.17, 266n.50, 294n.165
apocalypse. *See* eschatology
apostasy, 267–68n.56, 290n.149
Arabic-Islamic scholarship
  historiography, 131, 161
  Jewish engagement with, xvii, 5, 6–7, 163–65
  literary theory, 75, 78, 82n.16, 86, 89–90, 100
Arabic language, xxv–xxvi
  Lam Commentary and, 13–14, 22–23, 30–34, 35–36, 40, 45–46, 48–49, 76, 164, 165
  in medieval Judaism, xvii, 16–17, 30n.34, 60–61, 107n.11, 111–12, 163–64
  Salmon's attitude toward, 164–65, 211, 211n.67
  See also terminology, Arabic

Aramaic, 61, 62, 164, 185n.49, 277n.94, 287, 289n.148
argument (*ḥujja*), 241, 295–96, 296n.169
argumentation, 49–50
Ark of the Covenant, 89, 148, 228
Asaph, 150, 231, 231n.19, 235, 240, 253–54, 253n.3, 307
asceticism, 8–9, 71, 72, 156n.41, 159–60, 175n.19, 179n.35, 261n.33
ascetic poetry (*zuhdiyyāt*), 117, 120
aṣlaḥ, 39–40, 223. *See also* Muʿtazilism
assonance, 76
Assyria and Assyrians
  conquest and, 204–5, 232, 232n.23, 232n.24, 232–33n.25, 242n.50, 265, 303
  deportation to, 213n.71, 232n.23, 232–33n.25
  divine punishment and, 96–97, 231–32, 263–64, 328–29
  golden calves and, 212–13, 213n.71
  Jerusalem and, 3–4, 261n.31, 303n.199, 333, 336n.5
Astren, Fred, 159–60, 181n.38
authority
  interpretation and, 42, 61, 186n.51
  Karaite rejection of Rabbanite, xx–xxi, 5, 7–8, 56–57, 125–26, 147n.28, 163, 165–66, 232n.22, 339, 339n.9
  of Scripture, 97, 105, 135–36
baʿalei miqraʾ or *benei miqraʾ*, 10–12. *See also* Karaism
Babylon and Babylonians
  and divine punishment, instrument of, 96–97, 229
  four kingdoms and, 42–43, 172n.5, 207n.47, 280
  Hezekiah and, 191–92, 191n.8, 211
  and Jerusalem, destruction of, xi–xii, 3–4, 131–32, 147, 182
  and Judah, conquest of, 133–34, 138–39, 233nn.27–28, 235–36, 254–55, 269
  medieval Jewish, 7n.6, 56n.1
  in Oholah and Oholibah, 145, 146–47, 196, 198
  prophecies concerning, 98–99, 182, 316n.5
  in Psalms, 333–34
Babylonian exile, 3–4, 173n.11, 192, 233–34, 234n.30, 345n.29
badras (currency), 189, 189n.5
Baḥya ibn Paqūda, 142n.19, 296n.172
Bar-Asher, Moshe, 63n.20
Barmash, Pamela, 232n.24
Barney, Stephen A., 202n.36
Barth, Lewis, 110n.18
basmala, 169n.1
bāṭin (internal), 79n.11, 99n.47, 104, 249, 296, 297
Batīr/Betar, 234–35, 235n.34
belief (*iʿtiqād*), 104, 296, 297. See also *bāṭin* (internal)
Ben Bag-Bag, 27n.27
benevolence or kindness (*luṭf*), 24–25, 173n.9
Ben-Shammai, Haggai, 8n.8, 9–10, 9n.13, 22–23, 49, 55, 106n.7, 110n.17, 116–17, 185n.47, 207n.47, 218n.89, 258n.16, 259n.21, 327n.50
Berkey, Jonathan P., 121, 121n.50, 123–24
Berlin, Adele, 74n.1, 74n.2, 75
biblical poetry, 74–75, 74n.1, 76
biblical scholarship
  and Bible, composition of, 332n.64
  grammar and, 309n.215
  Karaite program of, 6–8, 9–17
  Karaite vs. Rabbanite, 46–47, 56–57
  piety and, 166
  of Salmon, 13–14, 18–22, 35–42, 164–65, 205n.42
Bibliographica Karaitica (Walfish and Kizilov), xxiv–xxv
bitterness (*ʿalqam*), 267, 267n.54, 278n.98
book culture (10th century), 110–11
Book of Admonition (*Sefer Tokaḥah*), 107n.11, 108. *See also* Sahl b. Maṣliaḥ
Book of Beliefs and Opinions, 94, 138n.13, 234n.31, 262n.35. *See also* Saadia Gaon
Book of Direction to the Duties of the Heart, 142n.19. *See also* Baḥya ibn Paqūda
books, holy, 24, 135–36, 139, 172–73, 173n.9, 204
Brady, Christian M. M., 62n.17, 88n.32
Brody, Robert, 14–15n.30, 111–12n.24
calamities (*maṣāʾib*), 94–95, 275n.85
  complaint about, 241, 258

enumeration of, 217, 335, 343
Israel and, 94–95, 214–15, 241–42, 244, 267–68, 273–74
Job and, 94–95, 177–81
Josiah and, 254–55, 331, 332
Lamentations and, 25–26, 103, 183, 185–86, 217n.85
pious interpretation of, 139, 204, 284–85, 286, 304, 332–33, 332n.65, 339
prophecies about, 257, 260, 261–63, 318
reflection (*iʿtibār*) and, 105, 152
refrain and confession of, 48, 140
righteousness and, 38–39
Zedekiah and, 192
chastisements (*ʾadāb*), 103, 134, 137, 138, 171–73, 172n.8, 236–37, 236n.40. *See also* punishment, divine; sultan and criminal (parable)
chiastic structures, 319n.17
Christianity and Christians
anti-Christian polemic and, 214n.76, 344n.25
anti-Jewish polemic and, 165–66, 242–43, 263n.40
ʿarelim (uncircumcised), 238n.41
churches of, 221n.2, 251n.75
as Edom, 207, 207n.47
graves of, 237–38
homiletical literature of, 116–17n.38
Muʿtazilites and, 138
prostration and, 339n.14
Chronicles, books of, 37, 38, 40, 132, 141–42, 330–31n.60
cities, Islamic, 124–25
commandments
alteration of, 267–68n.56
covenant and, 221–22, 227–28, 265, 265n.48, 294–95, 308
Karaite piety and, 4, 70
miṣvah vs. *farḍ*, 208n.49
neglect vs. vigilance of, 110–11, 211
piety and, 262n.36
reflection (*iʿtibār*) and, 147, 162
revealed, 82–83
transgression of, 131, 134, 204–5
See also Ten Commandments
commentary genre, xvii–xix, 5, 21–24, 25–26, 28, 131, 165, 166
comparative Semitics, 14, 57–58, 61, 273n.75
compensation (*ʿiwaḍ*), 38–39, 40, 149, 149n.31, 152–53, 331
complaint (*shakwa*), 132, 179n.33, 240, 241, 250, 280, 280n.108, 286, 286n.132
confession (*iqrār*)
Karaite vs. Rabbanite, 335n.1
Lamentations and, 25–26, 139, 183
refrains and, 48
as religious obligation, 49, 297, 339–40, 339n.12, 339n.14
confusion, 259, 269, 300–1, 300–1n.191
consensus (*ijmāʿ*), 26, 181n.38
consolation, 217–19, 258–59. See also *neḥamot*
consonance, 76
constructive theology, 6–7. *See also* theology
Cooper, Alan, 132n.2, 309n.215
corporeality, divine, 80–81, 80n.13, 82–84, 82n.17, 266n.50, 294n.165
covenant, 173n.12, 221, 224–25, 339–40
abrogation of, 227–28, 262–63, 263n.40
Book of the, 173, 195, 221–22, 221n.3, 234–35, 235n.36, 236–37, 265, 341
chastisement and, 172, 172n.7
in Jewish history, 151, 164, 166
transgression of, 48, 134, 171–72, 204–5, 232, 238, 248, 265
creation, works of, 142–43, 142n.19
crimes (*jarāʾim*), 32–33, 69, 83, 140, 141, 141n.18, 295, 297, 297n.176, 326–27n.49. *See also* sultan and criminal (parable)
criminal justice, 264n.43

Dahrīyya, 261–62, 262n.35
dāʿī, 11–12
Damascus Covenant, 11–12
dancing, 342n.21
Daniel, book of, 18–19, 20, 43, 233n.28
David
asceticism and, 179n.35, 274n.80
leadership and, 189–91, 193–94, 239, 336n.3
mourning and, 115–17, 121, 144, 158–59, 176, 254–55, 280n.107
piety and, 285n.128, 330
as psalmist, 169n.1, 310, 345

David, house of, 88–89, 111–12, 148–49, 151, 194–95, 204–5, 315, 335
Day of Judgment. *See* eschatology
dead bodies, 236–38, 238n.41, 315, 320
Dead Sea Scrolls, 12n.24
death
  Dahrīyya and, 261–62, 262n.35
  homiletics and fear of, 105–6, 113–14, 118, 118n.44, 121
  of Josiah as divine mercy, 38–39, 254–55, 331–32
  metaphors of, 85–86
  mourning and, 158–60, 159n.46, 175
  pious approach to, 243, 262–63, 262n.36, 290, 292
derashah, 109. *See also* homiletics; Midrashic traditions
Derenbourg, Joseph, 244–45n.55
despair, 174, 191, 268, 307, 307n.210
Diaspora, 5–6, 7–8, 72–73, 112–13, 128–29, 156n.41, 246–47n.63. *See also* exile
Diqduq (Grammar of Ibn Nūḥ), 16. *See also* Ibn Nūḥ
direct address, 105–6, 105n.5, 107–8, 109–11, 113–14
disgrace (*ḥerpah*), 47, 81, 245, 302, 335–37
disobedience. *See* obedience and disobedience
Drory, Rina, 111n.23
drumming, 342, 342n.21
Dumah, 287

Ecclesiastes, book of, 20
Edom, 172n.5, 207, 207n.47, 242–43, 312, 332, 333–34, 335
eisegesis, 104
ellipsis, 84, 99, 277n.93
emotional response, 117–22, 131–32. *See also* affective techniques
Ephraim, 171–72, 178–80, 196, 196n.21, 235, 275–76, 288, 328, 342–43
Erder, Yoram, 11–12, 12n.23
eschatology
  homiletics and, 102, 104–6, 113–14, 117–18, 340
  Karaites and, 5–6, 7–8, 12–13, 43, 47
  Lam Commentary and, 6–7, 43–44
  reflection (*iʿtibār*) and, 131, 154
  terminology, 340n.16
Esther, book of, 21n.16, 30n.34, 187n.1
ethical instruction, xix, 20, 47, 76, 104, 106, 112, 117, 141–42, 143–44, 145–46, 149–50, 154–55, 162, 164
exhortation
  Arabic-Islamic, 112–14, 123–24
  emotional response and, 117–18
  homiletics and, xx, 102, 104–5, 109–10
  Karaites and, 8, 107, 108, 125–26
  Lam Commentary and, 22–23, 34–35, 49, 68, 104
  oral vs. textual, 109–10, 125–26
  Rabbanites and, 109, 110–12, 111n.23
  as religious obligation, 126–29
  as reminder, 127, 128
Exilarch, 111–12
exile
  allusions to, 265n.45, 270, 271–72, 275n.84, 277, 278, 291, 299, 306
  in biblical history, 173n.11, 192, 197–98, 213n.71, 232n.23, 232n.24, 232–33n.25, 265, 329
  causes of, 37, 48, 203–5, 206–7, 262–63, 294, 297, 340
  as chastisement, 172–3
  conditions of, 120, 190, 194–96, 217–19, 226–28, 241–42, 327, 327n.50, 335–36
  consolations during, 53–54, 332–33
  darkness of, 195, 195n.17, 218, 268, 268n.58, 271–72
  as divine abandonment, 200, 345
  as divine restraint, 94–96, 215, 216
  God's provisions during, 3, 24–25, 172–73, 174
  hart analogy and, 202, 202–3n.38
  interpretation and, 28–29, 43–44
  Josiah's protection from, 38–39, 331
  Karaites and, 5–6, 166, 261n.33
  Lam Commentary and, 25–26, 183–84
  Lamentations and, 3–5
  mourning and, xx–xxi, 156–57, 158, 159n.46, 175, 280n.107, 303–4, 303n.199
  people of (*ahl al-jāliya*), 105, 174n.15, 284, 341

pious instruction for, xvii–xviii, 6–7, 34, 41–42, 47, 261–63, 279–80, 286, 287, 296, 302
prayer during, 46–47, 302n.194, 345, 345n.29
prophecies about, 45–46, 253–55, 257, 259, 307–8, 318, 324
Rabbanites responsible for, 57–58, 69–70, 93, 131, 150–54, 339
as reciprocal punishment, 207n.43, 212, 212n.70
reflection (*iʿtibār*) and, 133, 135–36, 140, 141–42, 145, 146–47, 161, 162
sultan and criminal (parable) and, 265, 266, 266n.50, 267, 268, 269
ten exiles, 146–47, 231–35, 232n.22, 242n.50, 319
extended metaphor. See *tamthīl*
Ezekiel, book of
divine glory, transfer of (Ezek 8–11), 63–66, 200–2
as historical source, 37, 133–34, 141–42
Oholah and Oholibah (Ezek 23), 144–46, 147, 148, 196–99, 199n.26
parable of the pot (Ezek 11 and 24), 97–100, 316–19
Salmon and, 40–41
al-Fāsī, David b. Abraham, 14–16
Kitāb Jāmiʿ al-Alfāẓ, 187n.1, 200n.29, 213n.72, 215nn.80–81, 245n.56, 246n.60, 248n.66, 256n.12, 257–58n.14, 260n.26, 265n.48, 271n.69, 278n.98, 284n.122, 289n.148, 291n.152, 298n.179, 302n.197, 305n.204, 306n.206, 307n.209, 309n.215, 312–13n.224, 317n.9, 318n.12, 319n.17, 319–20n.20, 320n.24, 321n.26, 321nn.29–30, 325n.42, 327–28n.51, 338n.8
fear, 117–22, 127, 145–46, 197–98, 309, 333. *See also* homiletics
figurative language (*majāz*), 37, 46, 99, 136, 263–64n.42
ḥaqīqa and, 88–90
istiʿāra and, 79–87
in Lam Commentary, 80–82, 83–87, 246, 246n.61, 249, 272n.73
mathal, 91–92, 97–100
Qurʾān and, 77, 78n.9, 82n.16, 86–87, 100
Salmon's approach to, xix–xx, 28–29, 30–31, 73, 74–80, 84, 86–87, 87n.30, 99n.47, 100–1, 196n.20, 229n.17
Scripture and, 82–83, 82n.16
tamthīl, 91–97
florilegia, 27–28
Fonrobert, Charlotte Elisheva, 203–4n.39
footstool of God, 88–89, 88n.32, 90, 228
forbearance. *See* patience or forbearance
four kingdoms, 42–43, 96, 172, 172n.5, 207n.47, 263–64, 263–64n.42, 280, 280–81n.110, 281, 282
Frank, Daniel, 10–11, 10n.18, 20–21, 21n.18, 30n.37, 35n.50, 106n.7, 170n.8, 172n.5, 177n.27, 186n.51, 190n.7, 229n.16, 231n.21, 238n.41, 259n.21, 280n.108
Freedman, David Noel, 27n.26
Friedlander, Israel, 111–12n.24
future (*ʿatid*), 33, 308–9, 309n.215

Garden of Eden, 64–65, 66, 201–2
Gardet, L., 296n.169
Garr, W. Randall, 74n.2
Gaza, 192, 192n.9
Genesis, book of, 18–19, 28n.31, 143, 186n.52, 331n.62
Geniza, 3, 111–12n.24, 251n.75
Geʾonim, 56, 57–58, 111–12
Gharipour, Mohammad, 221n.2
al-Ghazālī, 262n.35
Gil, Moshe, 11, 59n.8, 107n.10, 201n.33, 251n.75, 268–69n.59
Gilead, 232, 321, 321n.26
glory (*kavod*), 64–66, 200–2, 200n.28, 200n.29, 202n.35, 228, 258–59, 258n.17, 326n.47, 328
God. *See* agency, divine; anger, divine; anthropomorphism, divine; corporeality, divine; justice, divine; mercy, divine; presence, divine; punishment, divine; restraint, divine; speech, divine
golden calves, 204–5, 207, 212–13, 213n.71
Goldstein, Miriam, 169n.1, 202n.36

Gordis, Robert, 346n.31
Gozan, 232, 232n.24
grammar
  figurative language and, 18, 75, 77, 84, 88
  Karaites and, 9–10, 13–14, 16, 20–21
  Lam Commentary and, xxiii, 22–23, 28–29, 32, 34, 36, 44, 142, 164, 165, 199, 199n.27, 279n.102, 287n.135, 309n.215, 346n.31
Greenberg, Moshe, 317n.9, 317n.11
grief, 31, 291n.151, 292, 305n.204, 312–13n.224, 319, 319n.17, 343
  homilies and, 117–22, 157
  Lamentations and, 4, 131–32
  liturgical poetry and, 119n.46
  See also mourning
Grossman, Avraham, 7n.6
Gruendler, Beatrice, 211n.66, 125n.62

Hadrian, 234–35, 235n.35
ḥalqa, 124–25
hapax legomena, 31–32, 276, 319–20n.20
ḥaqīqa, 87–90, 89n.34, 100–1, 228, 307n.209. *See also* figurative language (*majāz*)
harts, 92–94, 200, 202, 202–3nn.36–38
Harūn al-Rashīd, 117–18
Ḥasan al-Baṣrī, 121–22
hatred, unjust (*śin'at ḥinnam*), 195–96, 195–96n.19, 300, 300n.186
healing, 22–23, 52–53, 54, 127, 290, 319, 321, 328
Hebrew Bible, xxv, 9–10, 20–21, 133–34, 133–34n.4, 135–36, 137, 147n.28, 166
Hebrew language
  Karaites and, 9–14, 18, 35–36, 57–58, 185n.49
  Lam Commentary and, 24, 210n.64, 344n.25
  linguistic scholarship of, 31–33, 83–84, 187, 199, 217n.86, 333–34
  Salmon's contemporaries and, 16–17
  translation of, 29–30, 30n.34, 76, 253n.1, 294n.164
Hebrew lemmata, 40, 165
Hebrew poetry, 74, 74n.1, 106n.7, 258–59, 259n.21. *See also* liturgical poetry
Heinemann, Joseph, 109–10
Heinrichs, Wolfhart, 80n.12, 85–87, 87n.30, 96
hermeneutics, xvii–xviii, xx, 25–26, 28, 34–35, 57–58, 75–76, 91, 102, 133, 134–36, 158, 161–62, 164, 165, 175n.19
Hezekiah, 191–92, 191n.8, 197–98, 211, 232, 239, 336n.5
historical reflection. *See* reflection (*iʿtibār*)
historical thought, 131–36, 160–61
  historical-contextual, 37, 136–37, 142, 183n.42
  historical-homiletical, 133, 133n.3, 134–36, 142–44
  historical-theological, 134, 134n.5, 138–42, 160–61, 319–20n.20
historiography, 136n.11, 143–44, 160, 161
Hodgson, M. G. S., 296n.169
homiletics, 104
  Arabic-Islamic, 101, 113–16, 117
  as exegetical practice, xvii–xxi, 18, 26–27, 35–36, 37, 43, 46, 47, 90, 100–1, 102–6, 124, 141–44, 160–61, 162
  of grief vs. fear, 117–22
  in Judaism, 103n.1, 109–12, 164
  Karaites and, 12–14, 15, 16–17, 106–8, 156–58
  Lam Commentary and, 22–23, 34–35, 49, 106n.7, 151, 152–54, 165, 166, 326n.46, 346n.32
  orality and, 50, 123–26, 128–29
  rabbinic, 50–51, 51n.74, 52, 62–63, 66–68, 70, 71, 72, 109–12
  reflection (*iʿtibār*) and, 130–31, 133, 133n.3, 134–35
Horites, 333–34
Hoshea ben Elah, 37, 141–42, 197–98, 204, 204n.41, 232, 232–33n.25, 241–42, 265, 265n.46
Hulda, 38–39, 331
human lifespan, 345, 345n.26
hypomnēma, 116–17, 116–17n.38

Ibn Aqnīn, 283n.119
Ibn al-Jawzī, 114–15, 114n.29, 115nn.32–33, 117, 118, 121, 121n.50, 123–24

Ibn Nūḥ, Yūsuf, 14–15, 16, 28–29, 33, 36, 187n.3, 216n.82, 217n.84, 254n.5, 270n.63, 273n.75, 279n.102, 309n.215
Ibn Qutayba, 80n.12
ʿibrāt (admonitions/lessons), 134–35. *See also* reflection (*iʿtibār*)
idols and idolatry, 131–32, 145, 152, 193–94, 195–96n.19, 204–6, 207, 224, 238, 239–40, 320, 344. *See also* Oholah and Oholibah
Ikhwān al-Ṣafāʾ, 262n.35
imaginary ascription, 85–86, 96. *See also* metaphor
immigration, 7n.6
  debates on, 8n.11, 14–15n.29
  Karaites and, 5–6, 7–8, 8n.8, 107n.10, 251n.75
  al-Qumisī and, 8–9, 9n.13, 107, 128–29, 155–56
  See also return to Jerusalem
incipits, xxvi, 22–23, 34–35, 48–49, 204n.40
instruction for Israel (*taʿlīm le-yiśraʾel*)
  actualizing interpretations and, 47
  Bible as, 131, 133, 204
  Jeremiah and, 254, 307–8, 319
  Lam Commentary and, 130, 166
  Lamentations as, xvii–xviii, 6–7, 18, 24–26, 34, 43, 45, 46, 102, 253–54, 308n.213
intellectual history, 56n.1
intention (*murād*) of language, 309n.215. *See also* meaning (*maʿnā*)
interchangeable letters (*ḥurūf al-ibdāl*), 31–32, 32n.40, 187–88, 276, 276nn.87–88, 287, 287n.135, 291–92, 291n.154, 292n.155
interpretation, 42–44
  actualizing, 41–42, 43–47, 98–99, 307n.211
  historical-contextual, 37, 43–44, 45–46, 98–99, 99n.46, 106, 124, 133–34, 136–37, 142, 159–61
  Karaites and, 5–6, 7–8, 10–11, 10n.18, 20, 94, 161–62
  language vs., 28–29, 36
  "scripture interprets itself," 27–28, 27n.27, 54, 65–66
  sin and, 43–44, 152, 154
  translation and, xxv, xxvii, 29–30, 31, 171n.1
interrogatives, 36, 214, 214n.73, 293, 293n.163, 319, 319–20n.20
introduction (*muqaddima*, *ṣadr*), 22–29, 138–39, 165, 171–86
invocation (*khuṭba*, *dībāja*), 169–70, 169n.1, 170n.8
Iraq, 7–8, 11–12, 155–56
Isaiah (prophet), 51, 186n.50, 239, 255
Isaiah, book of, 16n.36, 38, 40–41, 184n.46, 256n.12
Ishmael (kingdom of), 172n.5, 207n.47, 280–81n.110
Islam, medieval, 101, 106, 161, 344n.25
Islamic East, 101, 121, 123
Islamic expansion, 5
Islamic scholarship. *See* Arabic-Islamic scholarship
Islamic West, 123
Ismaʿīlī missionizing, xixn.1, 11–13
istiʿāra (borrowing), 85–86. *See also* metaphor
iʿtibār. *See* reflection (*iʿtibār*)
iʿtibārāt, 134–35. *See also* reflection (*iʿtibār*)
Ivry, Alfred L., 97n.44

jackals, 344
Jacob, 239, 291–92, 305, 339–40
  mourning and, 115–17, 144, 158–60, 175, 280n.107
Jacob ben Samuel, 16–17, 58–59, 107–8, 207n.47, 209n.57
al-Jāḥiẓ, 80n.12, 262n.35
jealousy, 206, 238, 238n.42, 246, 247, 282
Jehoahaz ben Josiah (Shallum), 146–47, 225–26, 231–32, 233, 233n.26, 254–55, 265
Jehoiachin (Jeconiah), 192, 200, 233, 233n.29, 254–55, 265, 268, 268–69n.59
Jehoiakim, 37, 181–82, 182n.40, 192, 225–26, 233, 233n.26, 233n.28, 237, 254–55, 269, 315
Jehoshaphat, 188, 190–91, 193–94

Jeremiah (prophet), 45–46, 51, 97–98, 105n.5, 233n.28, 254–55, 307–8, 315–16, 324, 331–32
as author of Lamentations, xvii–xviii, 3, 6–7, 18, 26, 26n.25, 34, 102, 130, 181–82, 181n.38, 182n.40, 332n.64
consolations and, 22–23, 127, 186n.50
as prophet for exile, 24–25, 174
as righteous one of the nation, 274–75, 275n.82
Jeremiah, book of, 37, 40–41, 97–98, 133–34, 141–42
Jericho, 256–57
Jeroboam, 204–5, 207, 207n.45, 213n.71, 225–26
Jerusalem
divine presence and, 63–65, 66, 200–2
Karaites and, 5–9, 12–13, 14–15, 107, 107n.10, 108, 128–29, 166, 251, 251n.75
in Lam Commentary, 37, 67, 76, 190–91, 193–94, 255–56, 256n.12, 260
mourning and, 70–73, 156
Salmon and, 135–36, 246–47n.63
See also return to Jerusalem
Jerusalem, destruction of, 62n.17, 82, 324
Asaph prophesies, 231, 235, 236, 237–38, 240, 241–42, 308–9
Ezekiel prophesies, 98–99, 196, 316–17, 316n.3, 316n.6, 318
history and, 3–4, 130, 131–32, 133, 134, 136n.11, 192, 234n.32, 234n.33, 261n.31, 321
Isaiah prophesies, 255, 256, 257, 258–60, 261–62, 336n.5
Jeremiah prophesies, 182, 182n.40, 233n.28, 235n.37
literary responses to, 5n.3, 51, 62n.17, 74, 103
liturgy of, 22–23, 119–20, 259n.21, 302n.194, 325–26
mourning and, 70–71, 159–60, 211–12
prophecy and, 97–98, 344
reflection (*iʿtibār*) and, 140, 144–51, 161
Jewish-Roman Wars, 234–35nn.33–34
Jewish scholarship, xvii, 5, 18, 164–65
jizya, 192–93, 192–93nn.11–12, 277, 277n.92
Joash, 250–51, 250n.74
Job, book of, 18–19, 172n.8, 180n.37, 215n.80
Job, sufferings of, 94–95, 177–81, 177n.27, 178n.29, 179n.33, 214–15
Johnstone, Barbara, 49–50, 120n.48
Jones, Linda G., 115–16, 123
Joseph, 156–57, 173n.10, 175, 196, 218, 278, 289, 303
Josiah, 181–82, 233
allusions to, 96n.43, 254n.8
death of, 38–39, 149n.31, 330–32
laments for, 176, 181, 254–55, 332
in Targum, 62–63, 330n.59
Judah
historical context, 3–4, 131–32, 133–34, 181–82, 188–5, 193–94, 196, 196n.23, 204–5, 207, 208–9, 225–26, 231–32, 233n.26, 236–38, 240, 260, 261n.31, 265, 280n.109, 312, 322–23n.34, 328–29, 330–33, 342–43, 346
reflection (*iʿtibār*) on, 139, 141–42, 145–47, 150–51
Judea, 131–32, 176n.25, 234–35nn.33–34
Judges, era of, 148, 225
jurisprudence, 77, 181n.38
justice, divine, 204
acknowledgment of, 24, 169, 169n.2, 171–72, 172n.7, 219–20, 280n.105
Lam Commentary and, 54, 128, 183
Muʿtazilism and, 39–40, 138–41
reflection (*iʿtibār*) and, 134, 135–36, 149, 160–61
in Targum, 62n.17

Kalām, 296n.169
Kalman, Jason, 26n.25, 181nn.38–39, 250n.73
kal va-ḥomer, 175n.19
kanīsa, 221n.2, 283–84
Karaism, 10–11, 12–13, 35–36, 56, 125–26, 161–62
Karaite liturgy
biblical lament and communal mourning, 27, 156, 157, 159–60, 255n.9
communal recitation and, 49–50, 125
neḥamot and, 55, 55n.82

preaching assemblies and, 112
refrains and, 49, 166
Karaites of Jerusalem
biblical authority and, 5, 125–27, 133–34n.4, 135–36, 147n.28
biblical scholarship and, 9–17, 28–29, 199n.27
commentary tradition of, xviii, 6–7, 20
eschatology of, 5–6, 7–8, 12–13, 43
Hebrew and, 35–36
hermeneutics of, 44, 82n.17
homiletics and, 107–12, 123–29
and Lamentations, significance for, xxiii–xxiv, 5–6, 15, 16–17, 21–22, 25, 165–66
liturgy of, 27–28, 49, 50, 55, 255n.9
missionizing and, 11–14, 112–13, 183n.44
mourning and, 70–73, 116–17, 122, 155–60, 274n.79
name of, 10–12, 12n.23, 59n.8, 155–56
piety and, 47, 176n.26
prayer and, 46–47, 253n.2, 280n.108, 286n.132
Rabbanites and, 56–57, 58–61, 70–73, 122, 147, 150–51, 154–55, 161–62, 163, 165–66, 212n.69, 220n.96, 227n.13, 339n.9, 340n.15
redemption and, 8n.11, 151n.34
return, mandate of, 7–10
Sabbath and, 208n.55, 246–47nn.62–63, 324n.40
scholars of, 14–17
settlement in Jerusalem, 5–6, 7–9, 8n.8, 14, 107n.10, 251, 251n.75
Katz, Marion Holmes, 339n.14
kavvanah, 296n.172. *See also* purification of intention
Key, Alexander, 90
Khan, Geoffrey, 12–13, 278n.99, 279nn.102–3
kharāj, 187, 187n.1, 192–93, 192–93nn.11–12
khuṭba, 112–15, 170n.8, 221, 221n.2
Kimḥi, David, 316n.3
king mashal, 264n.43. *See also* Midrashic traditions
Kings, books of, 37, 38, 40–41, 132, 133–34, 141–42, 330–31n.60
Kitāb Jāmiʿ al-Alfāẓ (al-Fāsī), 16. *See also* al-Fāsī
Kizilov, Mikhail, xxiv–xxv
Krakowski, Eve, 111–12n.24

Lamentations, 3–5
authorship, traditional notions of, 26, 181–82, 181–82nn.38–40, 254–55
composition of, 132n.1
figurative language in, 74–76
historical context of, 130, 131–32, 133–34n.4
Karaites and, 5–7
Karaite scholarship on, 14–17
in Targum, 62–63, 62n.17
Lane, Edward W., 161, 304nn.200–1
Lange, Christian, 264n.43
language (*lafẓ*), 28–29, 33–34, 90, 186, 186n.52, 214n.73, 308–9, 309n.215. *See also* meaning (*maʿnā*)
Lasker, Daniel J., 11n.19, 12n.24, 138n.13, 147n.28
law
gratitude for, 172–73, 173n.10
Islamic, 117, 123–24, 181n.38, 264n.43
Karaite vs. Rabbanite, xx–xxi, 5, 56–57, 58, 147n.28, 152, 154, 324n.40, 339n.9, 340n.15
mourning and, 115–16
reflection (*iʿtibār*) and, 144, 160
transgression of, 48, 103, 186n.50, 191, 192, 195, 204–5, 206, 247
leprosy and lepers, 62n.17, 156, 191, 236, 344
lexicology
al-Fāsī and, 16
figurative language and, 77, 84, 88, 90
Salmon's techniques of, 13–14, 22–23, 28–29, 34–35, 62–63, 77, 105–6
Lieber, Laura, xxvii, 5n.3, 119n.46, 302n.194
likening. See *tamthīl*
linguistics, 18, 28–29, 88
Hebrew, 187–88, 193, 199, 199n.27, 217, 308–9, 309n.215
Targum and, 62–63
translation methods and, 31–34

literacy, 124–26
literary homily, 109–10. *See also* homiletics
literary production, 124–25
literary theory, Arabic
  figurative language and, 78–79
  ḥaqīqa, 88–90
  Lamentations and, 75
  majāz and *istiʿāra*, 79–87
  mathal, 91–92, 100
  Salmon and, 75, 77–78, 100–1
  tamthīl, 91–92
liturgical poetry (*piyyuṭim*), xixn.1, 52, 119n.46, 302n.194
  Karaite mourning and, 13–14, 22–23, 27–28, 34–35, 43, 49, 106n.7, 218n.89, 258n.16, 259n.21
liturgy
  exegesis and, 27–28
  Karaite, 5–6, 9, 20, 116–17, 155–56, 255n.9
  Lam Commentary and, xxiii–xxiv, 14–15, 49, 50, 55, 165, 166
  Lamentations as, 5–6, 18, 26–27, 74, 124
  rabbinic, 4–5, 5n.3, 122
Lobel, Diana, 296n.172

madhhab, 56n.1, 197–98, 198n.24, 267–68n.56
majesty, 64, 65–66, 200–2, 200n.28, 200n.29, 202n.35
majlis, 124–25
makhraj, 308–9, 309n.215
Markon, I. D., 19n.10
Marwick, Lawrence, 19n.11, 40–41
masāʾil (linguistic issues), 15, 16
maṣdar (verbal noun), 199, 199n.27, 278–79
mashal. *See* parable (*mathal*/*mashal*)
Masoretes (*baʿalei masorah*), xxv, 10n.17, 33n.43
Masoretic text, xxv, 251n.75, 320n.23
mawʿiẓa. *See* homiletics
al-Māzinī, 211n.66
Mazuz, Haggai, 203–4n.39
meaning (*maʿnā*)
  of figurative language, 230, 246, 249, 281, 319, 319n.15, 321
  ḥaqīqa vs., 89, 89n.34, 90, 100–1
  of Lamentations, 183
  language (*lafẓ*) vs., 28–29, 31, 33–34, 77, 81, 83, 87, 186, 186n.52, 214n.73, 278–79, 291n.151, 295, 308–9, 309n.215
Media, 172n.5, 207n.47, 280, 280n.109
memorization, 110–11, 113–14, 124–25, 185n.49
menaheg ʿaṣmo u-menaheg aḥerim, 32–33, 34, 277n.93, 291–93, 292n.160, 312n.223, 316, 316n.4, 337
menstruation, 156, 203–4n.39, 325, 344
mercy, divine, 53–54, 171–74, 173n.12, 184, 223–24, 227, 285, 305
  consolations and, 54, 127, 128, 215n.79, 289, 291, 346
  exile and, 24–25, 31, 95–96, 140, 215, 270, 284–85, 284n.123, 320, 332–33, 336–37
  Josiah and, 38, 39, 331
  reversal of, 298, 299
messianism, 5, 7–8, 11–12, 46, 107, 145, 150–51, 154–55, 282n.118
metaphor (*istiʿāra*), 75, 77, 78–80, 83–84, 83n.20, 100–1, 133–34
  in Lam Commentary, 80, 84–87, 249, 302–3
  "old" vs. "new," 86–87, 87n.30
  See also *tamthīl*
meter, 74, 74n.2. *See also* syntax
methodology of book, xxiii–xxvii
Mevōrākh b. Nathan b. Nīsān, 251, 251n.75
mīʿād (appointment), 123–24
Micah, book of, 63–64
middah keneged middah (measure for measure), 68–69, 141n.18, 215–16, 270n.65. *See also* reciprocal punishment
Midrashic traditions, 95–96, 264n.43, 340–41n.19
  on divine glory, transfer of, 63–66
  homiletical, 51, 51n.74, 109–10, 110n.17, 112
  Karaite knowledge of, 56–58, 217n.86
  Lam Commentary and, xx–xxi, 63, 70, 164
  on Lamentations, 4–5, 177n.28, 267n.55, 270n.63, 285n.125, 285n.127, 292n.159, 319n.16, 324n.39

Mikkelson, Jane, 296n.172
Mīmās (Maiumas Gaza), 192, 192n.9
Mintz, Alan, 134n.5, 195n.15
Mishnah, 58, 59–60
missionizing, xixn.1, 11–14, 16–17, 108, 112–13, 183n.44
Mitchell, Mary Louise, 136n.11
mnemonic devices, 185n.49. *See also* memorization
monotheism, 238–39, 285n.127
moral instruction, 109, 110–11, 117, 208n.56
  in Lam Commentary, 102, 103, 134–35, 136, 161–62
morphology, xxv–xxvi, 28–29, 36, 217, 217n.84, 278–79, 283n.119
Morse, Holly, 199n.26
Moses, 48, 58–59, 184, 200, 216, 241
  rebellions of Israelites against, 223–26
  revelation at Sinai, 202–3n.38, 239
Mount of Olives, 63–65, 66, 201–2, 201n.33
Mount Seʿir, 333–34
Mourners for Zion (ancient), 151n.34. *See also* Karaites of Jerusalem
mourning, 164, 342
  biblical exemplars of, 159, 159n.46, 175–76, 280n.107
  homily and, xx, 55, 117–22, 124, 157–58, 325–27, 327n.50
  Karaism and, 7–9, 155–60, 161–62, 274n.79
  of Karaites vs. Rabbanites, xx–xxi, 5–6, 70–73, 122, 211–12, 212n.69
  Lamentations and, 6–7, 228
  liturgy and, 4–5, 27–28
  as religious obligation, 25–26, 47, 49, 115–17, 219n.90, 261–62, 280n.107, 302–4, 305, 325
mudawwin, 133–34n.4, 332n.64
mufassir, 171n.1, 202–3n.38
Muḥāsibī, 296n.172
muḥkam, 79n.11, 99n.47
mukhrat (disjoined), 278–79, 279n.102
Muslim scholarship. *See* Arabic-Islamic scholarship
mutashābih, 79n.11, 99n.47
Muʿtazilism, xixn.1, 39, 40, 138, 138n.13, 149n.31, 164, 170n.7, 173n.9
Naboth the Jezreelite, 338, 338n.6
name transfer, 96, 96n.43. *See also* metaphor
Nathan ha-Bavlī, 111–12, 111–12n.24
Near East, 11, 88–89, 121, 195n.15, 232n.23
Nebuchadnezzar, 3–4, 89, 96–97, 96n.43, 98–99, 146–47, 182, 192, 207, 207n.47, 231–32, 233, 233n.27, 234n.30, 254–55, 256–57, 259–60, 263–64, 265, 267n.55, 269, 272n.74, 280n.108, 292n.159, 316–17, 316n.5, 318, 328–29, 333
Nebuzaradan, 180, 212–13, 234, 235–36, 267n.55, 272n.74
Necho II, 146–47, 231–32, 233n.26, 265, 329n.56
neḥamot, 22–23, 28, 28n.29, 52–55, 54n.81, 127–28, 186n.50, 215n.79, 229n.18, 284n.123
Nehemiah, 219n.94, 297n.177, 308
Nelson, David W., 340–41n.19
Nemoy, Leon, 11, 107n.11, 108n.12
Neubauer, Adolf, 111–12n.24
Niazi, Imran Ahsan, 181n.38
Ninth of Av, 4–5, 5n.3, 51, 67, 67n.24, 110, 119n.46, 122, 177n.27
nuskha (copy), 37, 330, 330–31n.60
oaths, 70–71, 208n.48, 211–12, 324, 328–29, 328n.55
Obed Edom, 235–36, 235n.38
obedience and disobedience, 143, 146–47, 150, 153–55, 171–72, 173, 193–94, 197, 212–13, 222, 223–25, 224n.8, 227–28, 229, 231–32, 235, 240–42, 262–63, 265, 265n.48, 266, 269, 270, 288, 294–95, 340, 346
Oholah and Oholibah, 144, 145–47, 148, 196–99
old age, 288, 288n.141, 288n.143
Ong, Walter, 120n.48
orality
  biblical composition and, 332n.64
  homiletics and, 104–5, 106, 107–12, 110n.17, 116–17, 123–24, 125, 126–27, 128–29
  Lamentations and, 74

orality (*cont.*)
  oral transmission and, 63, 135–36, 146–47, 232n.22
  oratory and, 112–13
  textuality and, 49–51, 63n.20, 110n.17, 120n.48, 124–26
oratory. See *khuṭba*
Oral Law or Oral Torah, xx–xxi, 56–57, 58, 125–26, 154, 181n.38

Palestine, 7–8, 9–10, 10n.17, 14–15, 50–51, 56n.1, 61, 107, 110n.18, 174n.15
paper, introduction of, 124–25
parable (*mathal/mashal*), 77, 78–79, 79n.10, 91–92, 91n.37, 96–97, 178n.32
  al-Qūmisī and, 155–56
  rabbinic, 63–64, 304n.202
  of the unripe grape, 81, 244–45, 245n.56
  See also Oholah and Oholibah; pot, foul-smelling (parable); sultan and criminal (parable)
parallelism, 31, 74, 88, 222n.4
paraphrase
  of Arabic, 271n.70
  in Lam commentary, xxv, 22–23, 34–35, 36, 45–46, 83, 105n.5, 214n.73, 244–45n.55
  of rabbinic literature, 35n.50, 60–61, 66
  Targum and, 62–63
paronomasia, 95–96
past (*ʿavar*), 33, 308–9, 309n.215
patience or forbearance (*ṣabr*), 41–42, 127, 279–80, 282, 283–87, 287n.134, 289, 290
Pekah, 232, 232n.23, 232–33n.25
penitence. *See* repentance
Pentateuch, 16n.36, 19n.2, 82–83
Persia, 4, 7–8, 11–12, 42–43, 155–56, 172n.5, 207n.47, 241n.49, 269n.62, 280, 280n.109
personification, 74, 74n.3
Pesikta de Rav Kahana, 5n.3
  editorial history of, 52, 110n.18
  as homiletical, 51n.74, 110n.16
  Lam Commentary and, 50–51, 57–58, 63–64, 66, 67, 68, 69–70
  Ninth of Av and, 110, 122n.55
  See also *Rabbinic Sources index*
Philistines, 214, 214n.74, 335–37, 336n.3
pious counsel. See *waʿẓ*
poetry
  Abbasid, 86–87
  Arabic-Islamic scholarship of, 85–87, 88
  ascetic (*zuhdiyyāt*), 117, 120
  Hebrew, 106n.7, 258–59, 259n.21
  Lamentations as, 30–31, 37, 74–75, 74n.1, 76, 79n.11, 131–32, 136, 136n.11
  oratory and, 113–15
  Wars of the Lord and, 60–61
  See also figurative language (*majāz*); liturgical poetry (*piyyuṭim*)
polemics
  contra Dahrīyya, 262n.35
  Jewish-Christian, 242–43, 263n.40, 344n.25
  Jewish-Muslim, 210n.64, 263n.40, 344n.25
  Karaite identity and, 9–10
  Karaite-Rabbanite, 14–15, 56, 59, 108, 147, 154–55, 156n.41, 160, 175n.19, 227n.13, 246–47n.63, 340n.15
  in Lam Commentary, xvii, 34–35, 120, 165–66
  reflection (*iʿtibār*) and, 131, 135–36, 147, 154–55, 160
  Salmon and, xviii, 13–14, 34–35, 57–58, 72–73, 93, 339n.9
Polliack, Meira, 30n.35, 44, 46, 56n.1, 122n.56, 125–26, 199n.27, 214n.73, 277n.93, 309n.215
population, 188, 188n.4
populism, 227n.13
pot, foul-smelling (parable), 97–100, 316–19, 316n.6, 317n.9
Poznanski, Samuel, 268–69n.59
practical piety, 6–8, 12–13, 47
praise, 3–4, 23–24, 114–15, 138–39, 169n.1, 279–80, 280n.105, 283–84, 287
prayer
  as complaint, 280n.108, 286n.132
  exile and, 249, 308, 345
  God does not hear, 178–80, 270, 299, 308–9
  instruction for, 70–71, 104, 211–12, 297, 297n.174, 339–40, 339n.14

Karaites and, 5, 49, 72–73, 165–66
Lam Commentary and, xxiii, 124, 165, 166
psalms as, 24n.20, 46–47, 173n.12, 185n.47, 210n.62, 253n.2, 255n.9, 281, 300n.188
preaching
in Arabic-Islamic contexts, 112–13, 114–16, 117–18, 123–24
Karaites and, 11, 107–8, 126–27
Rabbanites and, 111–12
rabbinic, 50–51, 51n.74, 109–10, 110n.17
as textual practice, 116–17, 128–29
weeping and, 121–22, 121n.50, 121n.52
presence, divine, 63–66, 70, 148, 200–2, 200n.28, 258–59, 258n.17
prison, 155–56, 233–34, 254–55, 264n.43, 269
proems (*petiḥta'ot*), 51–52, 109–10
prophets and prophecy
actualizing interpretations and, 44, 45–47
books of, 19n.11, 40–41, 58–59, 67, 133–34, 135–36, 141–42, 208n.51
consolations and, 22–23, 52–54, 54n.81, 127, 128
defiance of, 97–98, 98n.45, 134, 222–23, 240–41, 325
on destruction, 3–4, 231, 235, 255–56, 262–63, 316n.3, 328–29
false, 206, 237, 344
figurative language and, 75, 99
homiletics and, 103n.1, 105, 117–18, 121, 164
instructions of, 103, 139, 150, 156, 174, 184, 204–5
Lam Commentary and, 24–25, 27, 34–35, 37, 92, 184n.46, 185n.47, 202
language of, 105n.5, 309n.217, 345
legitimacy of, 223n.5, 223n.6
loss of, 151, 175–76, 180, 191, 193, 214–15, 214n.76, 228, 239, 258–59, 259n.21, 268, 271–72, 326, 338n.7
mourning and, 121, 157, 158
propheticide, 140–41, 209, 233n.28, 236, 249, 250–51, 250n.72, 250nn.73–74, 315
psalms and, 24n.20, 46–47, 253–54, 253n.2, 255n.9
prostration, 339–40, 339n.14
Proverbs, book of, 18–20, 63–64
Psalms
in exile, purpose of, 34, 46–47, 255n.9, 280n.108
Karaites and, 20, 41n.56
Lam Commentary and, 19n.11, 24, 26, 34–35, 40–43, 185
Pumbeditha (rabbinic academy), 111–12
punishment, divine, 214–16, 219–20, 272, 293, 319
covenant and, 227–28
Israel's enemies as source of, 96–97, 192–93, 254–55, 260–61, 328–29, 335–37
justice and, 24, 32–33, 138–41, 172–73, 172n.7, 262–63, 292–93, 297, 337–38
Lam Commentary and, 30–31, 88, 98–99, 104–6, 152–54, 221, 229–30, 231–39, 242–43, 244, 332
pious interpretation of, 284–85
in rabbinic literature, 51, 55, 68
reflection (*i'tibār*) and, 131, 134–35
and sultan and criminal, parable of, 264, 265, 266, 267, 268, 269
See also reciprocal punishment
purification of intention (*ikhlāṣ al-niyya*), 249, 296, 296n.172, 297, 297n.174, 305

qara' or *qara'im*, 10–13, 183n.44. *See also* Karaism; Karaites of Jerusalem
qeri'ei ha-shem, 11–12
qinah (lament), 74n.2, 170n.8, 181–82, 229, 254
neḥamot and *qinot*, 54n.81, 127
al-Qirqisānī, Ya'qūb, 14–15, 14–15n.29, 19n.2, 33, 35n.50, 36, 60–61, 82–83, 94, 169n.1, 181n.38, 185n.47, 185n.49, 214n.73, 309n.215
qiṣṣa, 114–17, 115n.31, 183n.43, 271n.68. *See also* homiletics
Quarter of the Easterners, 251, 251n.75
al-Qūmisī, Daniel, 9n.13, 14–15, 19n.2, 107n.10, 274n.80, 296n.172
Sermon of, 8–9, 107–8, 110–11, 112–13, 125–26, 128–29, 155–56, 157, 159–60, 176n.26, 209n.57, 246–47n.63, 340n.15

Qumran, 11–12, 12n.23
Qur'ān, 27n.27, 113–14, 117–18, 262n.35
  argument and, 50, 296n.169
  exegesis of, 78–79, 123–24, 131, 164
  figurative language and, 75, 77, 78n.9, 82n.16, 86–87, 100
  meaning (*ma'nā*) and, 89n.34
  reflection (*i'tibār*) and, 143–44, 160
Qutbuddin, Tahera, 113n.26, 115n.31, 118n.44, 169n.1

Rabbanites
  Karaite polemics against, 156n.41, 175n.19, 220n.96, 227n.13, 246–47n.63, 340n.15
  Karaites and, 8n.11, 56–58, 60–61, 60n.9, 122, 122n.56, 125–26, 151n.34, 163–64, 261n.33, 339n.9
  Salmon's polemics against, 59–60, 70, 72–73, 93, 131, 147, 150–51, 152, 154–56, 160, 161, 212n.69, 275n.82
  sermon culture of, 109, 111–12
rabbinic sages, 4–5, 71–72, 212n.69
  Karaites and, 154
  Salmon and, 42, 50–51, 57–58, 59–60, 61, 63, 339n.9
rabbinic traditions
  academies and, 14–15, 57–58, 111–12
  on exile and redemption, 4–6, 8n.11, 154
  hermeneutics and, 54n.80, 68, 82–83, 100, 141n.18, 175n.19, 324n.39
  homiletics and, 66–70, 109–10, 123
  Karaites and, 56–63, 135–36
  Lam Commentary and, 42, 172n.8, 186n.51, 269n.62, 322–23n.34
  on Lamentations, 181n.39, 186n.50
  law and, 147n.28, 152
  mourning and, 70–73, 122, 212n.69, 304n.202
  refrains and, 50–52
Rashi, 316n.3
reciprocal punishment (*bāb al-muqābala*), 247–48
  Lam Commentary and, 67, 206–7, 209n.58, 211, 212, 212n.70, 213, 247n.64, 270, 312, 312n.222, 318, 324, 324n.40, 328n.54, 337–38
  rabbinic literature and, 68–70, 141n.18, 270n.65
  Ten Commandments and, 140–41, 206–13
  See also punishment, divine
redemption
  cries for, 45–46, 320
  Karaites and, 5–9, 43, 166
  Karaites vs. Rabbanites and, 28–29, 70, 72–73, 151n.34, 152–55, 163, 340n.15
  Lam Commentary and, xvii–xviii, 142, 164
  mourning and, 25, 47, 122, 155–56
  neḥamot and, 52–54, 128
  prophecy and, 234n.31, 332–33, 345
  reflection (*i'tibār*) and, 131, 140, 144, 162
reflection (*i'tibār*)
  definitions of, xx–xxi, 131, 143, 164
  hermeneutics of, 34–35, 133, 145, 161–62, 166
  history and, 130, 161, 182
  methods of, 133n.3, 142–44, 160–61
  mourning and, 155–60, 219n.90, 280n.107, 303n.199
  on Oholah and Oholibah, 144–47, 196–99
  as religious obligation, 25, 105, 144, 147, 160, 175, 175n.20, 339
  Salmon and, 130–31, 133–36, 142nn.19–20
  on Shiloh, 148–51, 196, 235, 314–15
  on sins of the fathers, 151–55
  on ten exiles, 146–47, 150, 231–32
refrains
  in homilies, 118–20, 119n.46, 325–27, 326n.48
  in Lam Commentary, 22–23, 28, 34–35, 48–52, 109–10, 114–15
  suspension of, 293n.161, 295n.166, 297n.178
relief (*faraj*), 279–80, 286, 287, 287n.140, 289, 308–9
repentance
  biblical, 10n.14, 163, 182, 222–23
  confession and, 112–13, 297
  in exile, 173, 218, 339
  failure to repent, 105–6, 175–76, 262–63, 343

Karaites and, 5–10, 11, 49, 108, 150–51, 155–56, 176n.26
Lamentations and, 103, 290, 296
mourning and, 25, 72, 155–56
as obligation, 131, 340
redemption and, 8n.11, 45–46, 140, 151–52
summon to, 25–26, 103, 183
repetition, 49–50, 52, 74, 109–10, 120n.48, 258n.16
requital in kind (*muqābala*). *See* reciprocal punishment
restraint, divine, 53–54, 215n.79, 284n.123
retribution. *See* punishment, divine
return to Jerusalem, 5–6, 7–14, 14–15n.29, 155–56, 175n.19. *See also* immigration
reversals
catalogue of, 229–30
of exile, 154, 162
of good conditions, 193–94, 273, 298, 299, 342
neḥamot and, 22–23, 52–54, 55n.82, 127, 128
Revised Standard Version (RSV), xxv, xxvn.6
rhetoric
Arabic, xx, 78, 93n.38, 100–1, 110, 112–13
homiletics and, 104–6
of al-Qūmisī, 8, 9, 107
of Salmon, xx, 37, 58, 59–60, 102–3, 104, 141–42, 151
rhetorical questions, 107, 113–14, 118–20, 157, 209n.57, 214n.73, 319–20n.20, 325–27
rhyme, 60–61, 113–14, 115n.33, 138–39, 258n.16, 271n.70
rhythm, 120. *See also* repetition
Riblah, 316–17, 316n.5
righteous, the, 11–12, 131, 134–35, 142–44, 152–54, 241–42, 262n.36, 340, 341
Robinson, James T., 16, 21n.16, 29–30, 30n.34, 133n.3, 170n.7, 262n.34, 262n.36, 263n.39, 268–69n.59
Rosen-Zvi, Ishay, 68–69n.27
rupture, 47, 300, 301–2, 303, 320
Rustow, Marina, 56n.1, 60n.9
Ruth, book of, xviii, 18–19, 19n.10
Saadia Gaon, 15n.30
Book of Beliefs and Opinions, 94, 138n.13, 234n.31, 262n.35
Commentary on Daniel, 234n.32
Commentary on Job, 177n.27, 180n.37
Commentary on Lamentations, 14–15, 15n.31
exhortation and, 110–11, 111n.23
grammatical thought of, 199n.27
hermeneutics of, 94
Midrash and, 231n.21, 232n.22
on psalms, 24n.20, 46–47, 253n.2, 255n.9, 255n.10
Salmon and, 13–15, 58, 164
on suffering, 172n.8
translation choices, 31, 31n.38, 200n.28, 215n.80, 244–45nn.55–56, 245n.57, 248n.66, 253n.1, 256n.12, 265n.48, 266n.50, 268n.57, 274n.76, 275n.83, 277n.95, 284n.122, 291n.152, 292n.158, 294n.165, 297n.175, 298n.179, 300n.187, 301–2n.193, 305n.204, 307n.208, 312–13n.224, 338n.8, 345n.28
translation style, 30n.34
Sabbath
cessation of (Lam 2:6), 81, 244, 246
Christian persecution and, 207
destruction of Jerusalem and, 70–71, 211–12
homilies and, 68n.25, 69–70, 109, 110, 111–12
Karaite concept of, 69–70, 208–9, 208n.55, 209n.57, 246–47nn.62–63
of rebuke and consolation (Ninth of Av), 51, 67, 122, 177n.27
reciprocal punishment and, 209n.58, 324, 324n.40
transgression of, 206, 208–9, 224, 224n.9
ṣaddiq (just), 169, 169n.2. *See also* justice, divine
Sahl b. Maṣliaḥ, 14–15, 16–17, 261n.33, 339n.9
exhortation and, 107–9, 112–13, 128–29, 209n.57
on four kingdoms, 172n.5, 207n.47
rabbinic traditions and, 58–60

Salmon ben Yerūḥīm
biblical scholarship of, 13–14, 18–22, 31–32
Commentary on Daniel, 19n.9, 233, 280–81n.110, 282, 282n.118, 333
Commentary on Ecclesiastes, xviii, 16, 18–20, 21n.16, 29–30, 79n.10, 91n.36, 133n.3, 142–43, 142n.20, 208n.51, 262n.36
Commentary on Esther, xviii, 18–19, 19n.7
Commentary on Lamentations, xvii–xviii, 6–7, 18–23, 19n.8, 34–35, 185–86, 268–69n.59
Commentary on Psalms, xviii, 18–20, 19n.4, 24n.20, 40–41, 43, 80n.14, 91n.36, 116–17, 118–19, 142–43, 146, 169n.2, 172n.5, 173n.10, 178n.32, 231n.21, 245nn.58–59, 253–54, 253nn.1–2, 254n.6, 255n.10, 268–69n.59, 299n.185, 330–31n.60, 345n.28
Commentary on Song of Songs, xviii, 18–19, 30n.37, 35n.50, 40–41, 96, 263–64, 263–64n.42
contemporaries of, 14–17
dates of, 17n.38, 19n.8, 268–69n.59
Lamentations, approaches to, xvii–xviii, 6–7, 25
translation and, xxv, 29–30, 30nn.34–35
Wars of the Lord, 13–14, 58, 60–61, 163, 181n.38
salvation history, 10n.18, 43, 44, 130–31
samar, 124–25
Samaria, 145–46, 150–51, 196, 196nn.21–22, 197–98, 232, 232–33n.25, 241–42, 259–60, 265
samukh (construct state), 253–54, 278–79, 279n.102
Saperstein, Marc, 103n.1
Sasson, Ilana, 170n.7, 262n.35
Saul (king), 116, 148–49, 158, 176, 289, 315
Schoeler, Gregor, 108n.13, 116–17, 116–17n.38
scribes, xxv–xxvi, 10n.17, 48–49, 330–31n.60
scripturalism, 11–12, 42, 66, 124, 156
Scripture
figurative language and, 77, 94
history and, 137
human comprehension of, 82, 83–84, 99
"interprets itself," 27–28, 27n.27, 54, 65–66
Karaites and, 5, 9–11, 49, 99n.47
Muslim and Jewish approaches to, 75, 79n.11, 99n.47, 131
reflection (*iʿtibār*) on, 134–36, 142–43, 149
"speaks in human language," 35–36, 35n.50, 73, 82–83, 82nn.16–17, 100
sectarianism, 9–10, 11–12, 56–58, 69–70, 161, 209n.57, 246–47n.63
self-purification, 104. See also *bātin* (internal); purification of intention
Sennacherib, 197–98, 261, 261n.31, 311, 336–37
Sermon of al-Qūmisī. *See* al-Qūmisī
sermons
Arabic-Islamic, 112–16, 117–18
mourning and, 121–22
oral and textual, 116–17, 123, 124–27, 128–29
of pious counsel (*waʿẓ*), 113–15, 117, 118
al-Qūmisī and, 8–9, 155–56
Rabbanite, 111–12
Sahl and, 16–17, 107–10
socio-historical context, 123–26
Shāfiʿī school, 181n.38
Shalmaneser V, 197–98, 232–33n.25
shalosh ḥaggim (three festivals), 158, 175–76, 175n.24
Shekhina, 63–64
Shelemiah, 235–36, 235n.38
Shīʿī movement, 183n.44
Shiloh, 148–51, 196, 196nn.21–22, 235, 235n.37, 314
Shuppim and Hosah, 235–36, 235n.38
simile or similarity (*tashbīh*), 84n.23, 86–87, 91n.36, 202n.37
sin
biblical history and, 38–39, 192, 213n.71, 223–26, 223n.6, 236–37, 238–39, 250–52, 250n.73, 314–16, 333
confession of, 25–26, 48, 219–20, 242–43, 297

and covenant, transgression of, 67, 203–13, 264
as crooked path, 271–72, 271n.71
divine justice and, 24, 138–42, 292–93
exile and, 43–44, 190, 231–32, 294, 342, 345n.29
of the fathers, 104–5, 338–41, 340–41n.19
as foreordained, 295
forgiveness for, 332–33
identification of, 37, 134n.5
mourning and, 47, 195–96, 302, 343
Rabbanites and, 57–58, 69–70, 227–28, 340n.15
rabbinic treatments of, 51, 195–96n.19
reciprocal punishment for, 69, 207n.43, 247–48
reflection (*iʿtibār*) on, 131, 134, 135–36, 142–47, 148–55, 174, 182, 262n.34, 314–15
repentance and, 49, 102, 103, 289, 343
of Sodom and Gomorrah, compared to Israel, 137, 171–72, 284–85, 322–23, 322–23n.34
taxonomy of, 297n.176, 322n.33
slander, 140–41, 206, 209, 209n.60, 210n.63, 243, 290
social history, 56n.1
sociology, 77
Sodom, 137, 322–23, 322–23nn.33–34
Gomorrah and, 171–72, 284–85, 323
Solomon, 76, 190, 191–92, 192n.10, 193–94, 230, 239, 280
Song of Songs, 20, 43, 76, 281n.112
sources, xxiii–xxvii
speech, divine, 75, 82–83, 93–94, 93n.39. *See also* figurative language
Stern, David, 110n.17, 264n.43, 324n.39
suffering
collective, 4
compensation for, 40, 149, 149n.31, 152–53
as divine justice, 138
instructive value of, 69, 172, 172n.8, 290
of Israel vs. Job, 94–95, 177–81, 177n.27, 178n.29
redemptive, 151n.34
sin and, 103, 152–54, 340–41
Sufi piety, xixn.1, 104, 296n.172
sultan and criminal (parable), 264, 264n.43, 265, 266, 267, 268, 269, 269n.62, 270, 271
sūq al-warrāqīn, 124–25
Sura (rabbinic academy), 14–15, 111–12
Swartz, Merlin, 114–16, 114n.29, 115n.32
syntax (*naẓm*)
Lam Commentary and, 34n.49, 102, 199, 214, 278–79, 294–95, 309n.215, 319n.17
Lamentations and, 74
Salmon and, 18, 28–30, 32, 36

al-Ṭabarī, 116–17n.38
taḥmīd, 23–24, 114–15, 138–39, 169, 169n.1
Talmud (Babylonian), 4–5, 57–58, 70–73, 181n.38, 211–12, 212n.69, 220n.96, 250n.73. See also *Rabbinic Sources index*
tamthīl, 77, 78–79, 91–92, 91n.36, 100–1
in Lam Commentary, 92–97, 191–92, 202, 215–16, 230–31, 288, 288n.144
taqrīb ʾilā ifhām banī ādam (accessibility to human understanding), 81–84, 99, 246
taqwā, 118n.44
taxation, 187, 187n.1, 192–93, 192–93nn.11–12, 277, 277n.92
Temple
divine presence and, 63–66, 70, 200–1, 326n.47
God's footstool and, 88–89, 88n.32, 228
terminology, xxvin.7, 174n.16, 196, 254n.4
Temple, destruction of
aftermath of, 174, 175–76, 191, 218, 258–59, 259n.21
causes of, 195–96n.19, 209n.60
divine anger and, 81, 244, 245–47, 246n.60, 299, 314–15, 321–22
expulsion and, 215, 291
first and second, 325, 333–34
historical context, 3–4, 131–32, 190
as historical marker, 268, 268–69n.59
Karaite response to, 72–73, 261n.33
mourning over, 3, 118–20, 122, 156

Temple, destruction of (*cont.*)
Ninth of Av and, 51, 67n.24, 110, 177n.27
prophecy and, 173n.11, 198–99, 231, 235, 236, 240, 308–9, 333, 342–43
reflection (*iʿtibār*) and, 146, 148–49, 150, 180
Ten Commandments, 67–70, 140–42, 207n.43, 208–11, 300n.188
ten exiles, 204n.41, 242n.50, 319n.19, 333n.67
Salmon's catalogue of, 135–36, 146–47, 230–35, 319
Ten Plagues, 223
ten tribes, 240
population of, 188
sins and exile of, 37, 141–42, 146–47, 196–97, 196n.23, 204, 231–32, 265, 319
terminology, Arabic, 164, 309n.215
Salmon's use of, xx, 73, 75, 77–80, 79n.10, 79n.11, 84–92, 100–1, 245n.59
textuality
admonition and, 108–9, 110–11
Bible and, 332, 332n.64
orality and, 49–50, 63n.20, 110n.17, 116–17, 120n.48, 123, 124–27
oratory and, 112–14
Thaʿlab, 86
theology
figurative language and, 82, 84, 88, 90
and Josiah, death of, 38–40, 330–32
Karaite, 8, 47
of Lam Commentary, 6–7, 25, 164
of Lamentations, 132, 132n.2
rabbinic, 5, 5n.3
reflection (*iʿtibār*) and, 133, 134, 134n.5, 135–36, 138–42, 149, 151, 152–53, 154, 160–61
of sin and punishment, 32, 37, 149n.33
See also Muʿtazilism
theriac (*tiryāq*), 321. *See also* healing
thirst, 92–94, 93n.38, 192–93, 202, 202–3nn.37–38, 222–23, 224, 258, 267–68n.56
Tiglath-Pileser III (Pul), 232, 232n.23, 232n.24, 232–33n.25
Tiphsah, 192
Tirosh-Becker, Ofra, 60–61
Titus, 234–35, 234n.33
Toorawa, Shawkat M., 124–25
Torah
as balm, 321
Book of the Covenant and, 173, 195, 221–22, 221n.3, 234–35, 235n.36, 236–37, 265, 341
Christian polemic and, 242–43
oral vs. written, 58, 70, 125–26, 147, 147n.28, 154, 181n.38, 220n.96, 296n.172
return to, 4, 38
"speaks in human language," 82–83, 100
as water, 92, 93–94, 202, 202–3n.38
as yoke, 288–89, 288n.146
Tottoli, Roberto, 339n.14
Trajan, 267n.55, 272n.74
translation, xxv, 9–10, 14, 28–34, 30nn.34–35, 171n.1
translation notes, xxiii–xxvii
trope. *See* metaphor
Ṭulunids, 7–8
two staffs, 96, 263–64, 263–64n.42
Tyre, king of, 192, 192n.10, 287

ʿ*ulamā*ʾ, 28–29, 186, 186n.51
Uriah (prophet), 97–98, 233n.28, 315
Uz, 333–34

Vespasian, 234–35, 234n.32, 234n.33, 267n.55, 272n.74, 333
Visotzky, Burton, 51n.74, 110n.16

Walfish, Barry Dov, xxiv–xxv
wālīy. *See* Nehemiah
waʿẓ (pious counsel), 102–3, 112–15, 115n.31, 117, 118, 120–22
Wars of the Lord, 13–14, 58, 60–61, 181n.38. *See also* Salmon ben Yerūḥīm
water
blood spilled like, 140–41, 209, 231, 237, 238–39, 240, 243, 244
"flowed over my head" (Lam 3:54), 45–46, 307–8, 307n.209, 311
harts thirsting for, 92–94, 202, 202–3n.38
overflowing, 342–43
poisonous, 267–68, 267–68n.56, 278
and siege, preparation for, 260, 261
sins in Mosaic period and, 223, 224
in Soṭah ritual, 238
Temple and, 71

weeping as, 216, 301–3, 302n.197, 321, 327
word of God and, 92, 93n.39
watercourses, 281, 302n.197
wealth, 116, 158, 175, 188–90, 208–9, 227n.13, 258
Wechsler, Michael, 17n.38, 19n.2, 19n.10, 21n.16, 30n.34, 170n.7
weeping
in exile, obligation of, 8–9, 47, 261–62, 301–2, 304
homily of, 118–20, 157, 325–27, 327n.50
Karaite piety and, xx, 121–22
Lam Commentary and, 54, 136, 156, 194–95, 216–18, 248, 249, 305
in liturgical poetry (*piyyuṭim*), 302n.194
in Muslim contexts, 118, 121, 121n.50, 121n.52
widows
figurative language and, 76–77, 136, 174n.14, 187, 191–92, 193, 194–95, 217, 230–31
social and legal status of, 195n.15
in Targum, 62n.17
Wieder, Naphtali, 12n.24
wilderness narratives, 144, 152–54, 223–24, 299n.182, 340–41
writerly culture, Arabic, 124–25. *See also* textuality
Written Torah, 125–26, 181n.38

Yefet b. ʿEli, 20n.15
Arabic, attitude toward, 211n.67
Commentary on Daniel, 172n.5
Commentary on Esther, 187n.1, 192–93n.12
Commentary on Exodus, 195n.17, 211n.67
Commentary on Genesis, 28n.31, 186n.52, 331n.62
Commentary on Isaiah, 331n.61
Commentary on Jeremiah, 289n.147, 319–20n.20, 320nn.23–24, 321nn.25–26, 323n.37
Commentary on Lamentations, 17, 20–21, 21n.16, 26–27, 28, 34n.49, 55n.82, 172n.6, 254n.8
Commentary on Psalms, 202n.37, 238n.41
darkness of exile and, 195n.17
grammar and, 214n.73, 217n.86
hermeneutics of, 99n.46, 99n.47
among Karaite scholars, 14–15, 16, 19n.7, 19n.10, 280n.108
Muʿtazilite thought and, 39–40, 170n.7, 262n.35
Salmon, compared, xviii, 17n.38, 20–21, 21n.16, 26–27, 28, 34n.49
translation choices, 31, 31n.38, 200n.28, 200n.29, 202n.35, 244–45nn.55–56, 248n.66, 253n.1, 266n.50, 268n.57, 274n.76, 275n.83, 278n.98, 279n.101, 284n.122, 291n.152, 294n.165, 297n.175, 298n.179, 300n.187, 301–2n.193, 305n.204, 307n.208, 319n.17, 321n.29, 327–28n.51, 338n.8, 345n.28
translation style, 30n.34
Younger, K. Lawson, Jr., 232n.23, 232n.24, 232–33n.25
youth, 288, 288n.143
Yūsuf al-Baṣīr, 16

ẓāhir (external), 30n.37, 79n.11, 99n.47, 104, 296, 297
Zawanowska, Marzena, 82n.17, 99n.47
Zechariah, 51
Zechariah (gatekeeper), 235–36, 235n.38
Zechariah ben Jehoiada, 236, 250–52, 250nn.73–74
Zedekiah (Mattaniah), 234n.30
exile of, 3–4, 192, 233–34, 254–55, 256–57, 265, 269, 316n.5
rebellions of, 37, 225–26, 315, 328–29, 329n.56
Salmon on, 37, 136–37
Zerah the Ethiopian, 261, 261n.31
Zion
daughter of, 62–63, 63n.19
historical context of, 3–4, 131–32
lament over, 71–72, 156, 212n.69, 261–62, 325–26
Mourners for (Karaites), 5, 155–56
people of, 194–95, 200, 204, 228
restoration of, 217–18, 304
zoology, 77
Zunz, Leopold, 110n.18